Policing America: An Introduction

Policing America: An Introduction

Second Edition

Willard M. Oliver
Professor of Criminal Justice
Sam Houston State University

Wolters Kluwer

Published by Wolters Kluwer in New York.

Wolters Kluwer Legal & Regulatory U.S. serves customers worldwide with CCH, Aspen Publishers, and Kluwer Law International products. (www.WKLegaledu.com)

Cover image: iStock.com/brazzo

To contact Customer Service, e-mail customer.service@wolterskluwer.com, call 1-800-234-1660, fax 1-800-901-9075, or mail correspondence to:

Wolters Kluwer
Attn: Order Department
PO Box 990
Frederick, MD 21705

Printed in the United States of America.

1 2 3 4 5 6 7 8 9 0

ISBN 978-1-5438-1087-5

Library of Congress Cataloging-in-Publication Data application is in process.

About Wolters Kluwer Legal & Regulatory U.S.

Wolters Kluwer Legal & Regulatory US delivers expert content and solutions in the areas of law, corporate compliance, health compliance, reimbursement, and legal education. Its practical solutions help customers successfully navigate the demands of a changing environment to drive their daily activities, enhance decision quality and inspire confident outcomes.

Serving customers worldwide, its legal and regulatory portfolio includes products under the Aspen Publishers, CCH Incorporated, Kluwer Law International, ftwilliam.com and MediRegs names. They are regarded as exceptional and trusted resources for general legal and practice-specific knowledge, compliance and risk management, dynamic workflow solutions, and expert commentary.

The wicked flee when no man pursueth,
but the righteous are bold as a lion.

— Proverbs 28:1

Inscribed on the National Law Enforcement Officers
Memorial wall
Washington, D.C.

This book is dedicated to the men and women of law enforcement who have given the ultimate sacrifice of devotion: their lives in the line of duty.

A special dedication goes to the most recent officers killed in the line of duty as of the completion of this book:

Trooper Brooke Jones-Story
Illinois State Police
34 years old with 12 years of service
Struck and killed while conducting a traffc stop
End of Watch: March 28, 2019
&
Trooper Gerald Wayne Ellis
Illinois State Police
36 years old with 11 years of service
Killed by wrong way driver
End of Watch: March 30, 2019

A portion of the proceeds from this book will be sent to the National Law Enforcement Officer's Memorial Fund to honor these men and women.

SUMMARY OF CONTENTS

Chapter 10: Patrol   271

Chapter 11: Investigations   297

Chapter 12: Force   321

Chapter 13: Accountability   351

Chapter 14: Stress   381

This book was written with the benefit of having taught and conducted research on policing for the past 25 years, and having served as a summer police officer, a large metropolitan police officer, and retiring as a military police officer. It is that combination of education and practical experience that I hope to be able to communicate in this textbook *Policing America: An Introduction 2nd edition*.

The variety of perspectives, however, made for somewhat a challenge in trying to determine how to approach this book. Having served as a police officer, I understand that the police officer is a street-level bureaucrat and is instrumental in shaping what is American policing. This is because police officers still retain the fairly wide amount of discretion, and what happens on the street, what police officers do, has a powerful impact on the police department, and it drives the organization. Therefore, the police officer's perspective, even when it differs with either police management or research, should never be overlooked.

Research also serves a purpose in helping us to gain an insight into American policing by giving a bird's-eye view into commonalities between and amongst the more than 18,000 police agencies and approximately 800,000 law enforcement officers. It also, sometimes, gives us new insights into the actions of individual police officers and their departments. It cannot, however, always provide a contextual understanding of American policing because of the many limitations inherent in research methods.

Another perspective into American policing comes from police administration and management, because they are the people who run the police organizations, and what they do and how they see things is critical to understanding what police departments and police officers do. However, while their perspective is important, when they steer the police organization it is often equated to steering a big ship with a very small rudder.

That last notion also makes an assumption that is not always true in American policing, and that is we are dealing with large bureaucratic organizations. Most of the police departments in America are small-town and rural agencies employing under 20 police officers. Still further, not all police agencies are police departments, but many are composed of offices of the sheriff, marshal, and constable. What may prove true for the large metropolitan police department may not hold true for the small-town police chief with a force of three officers, or the sheriff's office with five deputies.

Still another perspective on American policing is the fact that when we talk about these agencies, they are mostly local and municipal, yet sheriffs' offices serve at the county level, and there are also state and federal agencies as well. We assume these police agencies are all the same. Sometimes those assumptions are wrong.

One other perspective that must be pointed out, one not represented in this book, is that policing in America is very different from policing in the rest of the world. Most other countries have one police department that operates geographically throughout the country but reports to a higher executive authority. American policing is far more decentralized. Therefore, this book is very American-centric out of necessity. Rather than detailing an international or comparative perspective, the book focuses on American policing in the cities, town, and counties, as well as local, state, and federal levels.

In order to achieve an understanding of American policing, all of these perspectives are incorporated into the book. The focus of the book is on a contextual understanding of concepts in American policing. It is supported by the academic research, balanced with the voice of the American police officer. Additionally, when addressing matters that pertain largely to police administration, the book attempts to balance the research with the voice of the administrator as well. The ultimate goal of this textbook is to provide a balanced understanding of policing from an academic perspective without losing sight of the realities of policing as performed by the men and women of law enforcement who do this job every day. It is the reader who will judge if I have achieved this goal.

Willard M. Oliver
Huntsville, Texas

ACNOWLEDGMENTS

The author would like to thank all of the people at Wolters Kluwer who have been so supportive of this book, including David Herzig, associate publisher; Terry Johnson, senior field representative; Kaesmene Banks, development editor; Elizabeth "Betsy" Kenny, development editor; and Christine Becker, project manager. All of you have been a joy to work with in the production of this book. Finally, I would like to thank the reviewers (listed below) of both the first edition and the drafts of the second edition. Your feedback was immensely helpful in shaping the final publication.

Roy E. Allen, Piedmont Community College

Michael Costelloe, Northern Arizona University

Gordon A. Crews, Marshall University

Mengyan Dai, Old Dominion University

Robert J. Durán, University of Tennessee—Knoxville

William Harmening, Washington University

John David Reitzel, California State University—San Bernadino

Philip W. Rhoades, Texas A&M

Jodi Rowlands, Lehigh Carbon Community College

Angela Wartel, Lewis Clark State College

Willard M. Oliver is a professor of criminal justice at Sam Houston State University in Huntsville, Texas. He holds a Ph.D. and M.A. from West Virginia University in political science, with an emphasis on crime policy, and a M.S. and B.S. from Radford University in criminal justice, with an emphasis on policing. He has taught and conducted research in criminal justice for over 25 years with his focal areas being all things policing, to include community policing, stress in policing, small-town and rural policing, homeland security policing, the history of policing, and more recently, depolicing. He served as a summer police officer in New Jersey, as a county police officer in the Washington, D.C. metropolitan area, and is a retired officer from the United States Army Military Police Corps. He is a voracious reader, enjoys writing, and is an avid runner, having completed over a dozen marathons to date.

■ *"The policeman's job is the highest calling in the world."*[1] —*August Vollmer*

Dallas Police Department automobile bearing the inscription: Serving since 1881.

CHAPTER 1

Policing

After reading this chapter, you will be able to:

1. Describe what is meant when the police are referred to as the "thin blue line" and "sheepdogs" of our American society.
2. Define the term *police*.
3. Explain why it has been said that "democracy is always hard on the police" by way of the policing paradox.
4. Identify the importance of the U.S. Constitution and the American form of government as it relates to the police.
5. Explain the role of the police in the criminal justice system.
6. Describe the two models of the criminal justice system.
7. Identify the many purposes and functions of the police in our society.
8. Discuss how the many goals of policing often create unrealistic expectations, ambiguity, and role conflict in policing.
9. Differentiate the three styles of policing in America according to James Q. Wilson.

Policing in the United States is one of the most important professions in our democratic society for the safety, security, and stability it provides the American people. Highlighting their importance, the police have often been called the **"thin blue line"** (see Box 1.1).[2] The blue represents the police, while the line is that which stands between citizens and perpetrators, order and chaos, good and evil. Perhaps one of the most popular quotes to this effect is attributed to George Orwell, the author of the books *1984* and *Animal Farm*,[3] who said, "People sleep peaceably in their beds at night only because rough men stand ready to do violence on their behalf."[4] The police, both men and women today, stand ready, 24/7/365, to respond to emergency calls, use their authority and powers of arrest to defuse dangerous situations, and to use deadly force if they must.

Box 1.1 History in Practice: *The Thin Blue Line*

The poem *Tommy,* by English Poet Rudyard Kipling, is based on the commonly used slang name for a British soldier – Tommy. The poem deals with how the military is often despised and ridiculed in peace time, but well loved when war breaks out. In the poem, Kipling calls the military the "thin red line," suggesting that all that stands between peace and anarchy is the military.

Many refer to the modern police as something very similar, although in this case, because of the traditional blue uniform of the police they are seen as the "**thin blue line**." The phrase suggests that all that stands between peace and anarchy on the streets of America is the police.

The origin of the term "thin blue line" is not altogether clear. One of the first definitive uses of the phrase was in an ABC documentary by David L. Wolper Productions titled "The Thin

Blue Line" in 1965. In 1988, Errol Morris wrote and directed a documentary film by that title, *The Thin Blue Line.* The movie recounts the shooting death of Dallas Police Officer Robert W. Wood when he stopped a stolen car. Through a series of interviews and reenactments, it documents the tragedy surrounding the officer's death. When the prosecutor in the film reaches his closing argument, he invokes the police as being "the thin blue line."

Lt. Col. Dave Grossman once interviewed a veteran who presented him with an image that visually depicts the role of the police in our society.[5] The veteran thought that most people in the world were sheep; "gentle, decent, kindly creatures who are essentially incapable of true aggression."[6] And, he noted, there is nothing wrong with being a sheep, for they make the world a better and pleasant place.[7] But the veteran also explained, however unfortunate it is, there are wolves in this world, and it is the wolves who "feed on the sheep without mercy."[8] As Grossman elaborates, "there are evil men in this world and they are capable of evil deeds. The moment you forget that or pretend it is not so, you become a sheep. There is no safety in denial."[9] By denial, Grossman meant that many people do not want to believe that there is evil in the world, and so they remain in denial up until they are confronted by the wolf.

Fortunately, as the veteran saw it, there is another kind of "human subspecies," which he called the "**sheepdog**."[10] Sheepdogs are "faithful vigilant creatures who are very much capable of aggression when circumstances require."[11] "I am a sheepdog," the veteran explained, "I live to protect the flock and confront the wolf."[12] As he saw it, "there are wolves (sociopaths) and packs of wild dogs (gangs and aggressive armies) abroad in the land, and

the sheepdogs (the soldiers and policemen of the world) are environmentally
and biologically predisposed to be the
ones who confront these predators."[13]
It is his belief that it is a very natural thing for sheepdogs to gravitate to
policing.

Sheepdog watching over sheep, upon which the analogy is based.

The father of American policing,
August Vollmer, would most likely
agree, for as he explained in the quote
at the beginning of Chapter 1, policing
is a vocation, a call to one of the most
honorable professions there is (see Box
1.2).[14] It is the sheepdog that answers
the call. While the profession may be a
calling, this is not to say that the job is

Box 1.2 History in Practice: August Vollmer and the Professionalization of American Policing

August Vollmer is considered by many to be the **Father of American Policing**. He earned this appellation because of how significantly he transformed American policing in the early twentieth century.

In the nineteenth century, policing was created to largely serve the political elites and was often corrupt and brutal. When August Vollmer was elected as the town marshal in Berkeley, California, in 1905, it was the same there as well. The previous town marshals had taken advantage of their position to control the underworld and become rich through corrupt and brutal ways. Vollmer, a Veteran of the Spanish-American War and a postal carrier, vowed to clean up the town if elected. He not only cleaned up the town, he worked to clean up all of policing.

Serving as town marshal for two terms, from 1905-1909, and then appointed as Police Chief of Berkeley from 1909 until his retirement in 1932, Vollmer advocated for changes in polic-ing. He was one of the first to adopt bicycle patrols, motor vehicle patrols, police academy

training, and in-service training of his police offi-cers. He was the first Police Chief to adopt the polygraph and one-way radios to policing, the first to create a crime lab, and the first to cre-ate a policing program in higher education that ultimately became the Criminology and Criminal Justice degrees so common in American col-leges and universities today. He also was the first police professor ever, teaching first at the University of Chicago and later at the University of California. His entire career was focused on improving police education and he worked toward establishing policing as a professional career, akin to being a doctor, dentist, or law-yer. He is primarily responsible for what became known as the reform movement and profession-alization movement in American Policing. For all of this, he is rightly known as the Father of American Policing.

Source: Oliver, W.M. (*2017*). *August Vollmer: The Father of American Policing.* Durham, NC: Carolina Academic Press.

without its difficulties. It can be boring, frustrating, and dangerous.[15] It has been called both "dirty work"[16] and an "impossible job."[17] Police officers must often deal with death, handle dead bodies, and attend autopsies.[18] On a near-daily basis, they must see and face the darker side of humanity. And through-out their career, they will face higher levels of stress and burnout than most other occupations, they will most assuredly sustain repeated injuries on the job, and, although rare, they face daily the threat of being killed in the line of duty.[19] Despite all of this, policing is one of the greatest jobs in the world.

A police chaplain for the New York Police Department tries to relay this to each new academy recruit class when he explains, "This is the most excit-ing and magnificent career anyone could ever enter upon. There's nothing in the world as meaningful as what you are doing."[20] Most police officers will agree and will voice that it is a good and exciting profession, despite all the hardships and aggravations they face. One police officer explained it like this:

> You know how good it feels when you can help someone just find an address, or locate a service they need? Just a small thing like that? Well, magnify that a thousand times, we get to do that every day, and there isn't anything that feels that good. You really can make a difference in just the day-to-day stuff to the really important life-changing stuff. Every day. It's a great job.[21]

Talk to those who have retired from policing and while the adjective *excit-ing* will be gone, replaced with ones like *honorable*, most will still tell you it is a worthy profession. Understanding policing and the role the sheep-dogs perform in our society is the purpose of Chapter 1. Toward that end, it first defines terms used throughout the book, and then explores the complex nature of policing in our American democracy. Next, it looks at how policing fits in both our system of government, as well as the criminal justice system. And finally, it explores the purpose and function of the police in America.

Police

The term *police* has its origins in the word used by the ancient Greeks, **poli-teuein**, which means a citizen engaged in politics.[22] The root of *politeuein* is *polis*, which means a city or state, or more specifically, what the ancient Greeks saw as the ideal form of government, the city-state (a city that is also its own country like Monaco or Singapore today).[23] The concept of policing was conceived of as citizens of the city-state who were engaged in politics, which was governance for the greater good of the people.[24] At the time, this was not a special office or organization of government, but rather something for which all citizens were responsible.

The modern term *police* defined as a civil force under government control tasked with enforcing the law, did not develop until the sixteenth century and was derived from the medieval Latin word for policy.[25] The word appeared in both France and England about this time, and came into common usage through the establishment in 1829 of what is referred to as the first police department in the world—the London Metropolitan Police (see Chapter 2). The police in London were a civil force, under government control, granted special authority and powers of arrest to prevent crime and disorder.[26] It was specifically this use of the word in London, England, that brought the term into common usage in the United States, beginning in the 1830s with the establishment of the first police department in America, the Boston Police Department, in 1838.

In more recent times, scholars have wrestled over the proper definition of the term **police**.[27] Some scholars have focused on the goods that the police provide to society, and thus they define policing by the outcomes such as public safety, order maintenance, and law enforcement.[28] Others felt that the police should be defined by what they do in general, the various functions they perform in our society, including such things as crime reduction, crime prevention, and the processing of criminal information.[29] Others disagreed and felt that what the police really do is to focus on compliance with the rule of law, hence the police were defined more definitively as law enforcement.[30] Still others believed it made more sense to define the police by the key method they employed to accomplish their job and they concluded that was by way of coercive force, ranging from the simple presence of the police to deter crime to the extreme circumstances of using deadly force.[31] It is from this last reasoning that one of the most commonly used definitions of the police you will come across is Carl Klockars's, "Police are institutions or individuals given the general right to use force by the state within the state's domestic territory."[32] Yet, many felt this was too narrowly focused and argued that policing should be defined by the respect and authority inferred upon them by the public, in a sense the consent of the governed, which they defined as police legitimacy.[33]

In many ways, all of these definitions are correct to an extent. From the old definitions, we see that the police are citizens given special authority, including the power of arrest, and are under the control of civil government for the greater good of the people, to prevent crime and disorder. From the more modern definitions, it is equally true that the police obtain their legitimacy from the consent of the governed to process certain information and use coercive force, to enforce the law, to achieve public safety, order maintenance, and law enforcement.

Sometimes the easiest way to define something is to explain what something is not. For instance, the police are not a military force, but rather a civil force. A military force is controlled by the government for the purpose of going to war to win that war through the use of deadly force. A police force is a civil force, controlled by the people, for the purpose of protecting society through the enforcement of the law with the use of deadly force as a last resort. The police are not a military or occupying force. Nor are they a private security agency.[34] Private security works for private interests, individuals who pay for personal protection. The police are a public entity, one that works for the people through the local government. In light of both of these, despite the fact that there are military police and private police (of which the

New recruits for the BART police in San Francisco being sworn in.

author has been both), they will not be included in this book because neither are civil, or public, police.

Often overlooked in many of these definitions are the so-called trappings of the police profession itself. When talking about the police, we often talk about *sworn officers*, those who take a civil oath of office that bestows on them the special authority and powers of the police through the local government they serve. This is a legal concept that gives the police special powers to enforce the laws, and it sets them apart from the average citizens. The badge is usually a symbolic representation of this authority. Another part of being a police officer is the right and duty to carry a firearm. While this may still fall under the concept of coercive powers, fully sworn officers are authorized to carry a firearm, typically on or off duty, as part of their responsibilities under the law. This is why we often define the police as those who carry a badge and a gun.

The complexities of defining the term *police* have much to do with the nature of policing in a democracy, the subject of the next section. Suffice to say, there is a need for a more solid definition of the police, especially if an entire book is going to address that very subject. While it may be easiest to convey the definition as the formal organization of sheepdogs in our society, something more detailed is probably necessary. So, for the purposes of this book, the police are defined as a civil force that is a constituted body of people under the control of government, who are given special authority (sworn) to enforce the rules, regulations, and laws of the jurisdiction they serve, being subject to those same laws, and are authorized the use of coercive force to maintain public safety and prevent crime and disorder for the benefit of the people, while being held publicly accountable to those same people. What should become quickly clear from this definition is the fact that the police are authorized to use force for the benefit of the people, yet most people do not want force used against them. It is this which sets up the difficulties of policing in a democracy.

Policing in a Democracy

In the late 1960s, police scholar George Berkley visited the police in West Germany at a time in which that country was still divided into East and West and recovering from World War II.[35] Berkley went on a ride-along with a police officer by the name of Altifuchs down the famous Autobahn. Altifuchs was a former Nazi, a police officer under Hitler's so-called Third Reich, a totalitarian government that came to power by playing on people's fears, and then, in the name of security, stripped the people of all their civil rights. "During the Nazi period," Altifuchs explained to Berkley, "a policeman knew where he stood and what he was expected to do."[36] The policeman knew this because he merely followed the orders of those in charge, and if they told him to arrest someone, beat someone, or kill someone, he did so without question. The police officer had no authority to disobey and the citizen had no recourse against the actions of the police. After the war, West Germany moved to establish a democracy and Altifuchs lamented, "Now, we have such complicated laws regarding the firing of guns that we never know whether to use them or not."[37] He then bemoaned, "Democracy is always hard on the police."[38]

Democracy is always hard on the police because in a democracy, people have rights. In America, people are granted liberties, something we often call **civil rights**, which provide us with, among others, the individual freedoms to assemble, to speak, to publish our opinions, and to worship as we see fit (First Amendment). In addition, the police cannot arbitrarily or on the whims of those in power appear at our doorstep in the middle of the night, batter it down, search our homes, and drag us off to jail as prisoners of the state. We have rights against unreasonable searches and seizures, afforded to us in the U.S. Constitution (Fourth Amendment). These rights, however, make the profession of the police officer very difficult because the police officer is faced with a great dilemma. On one hand, they must enforce the law, while, on the other hand, they must protect our rights.

Many police scholars have wrestled with this apparent **policing paradox**.[39] Herman Goldstein noted, "The police, by the very nature of their function, are an anomaly in a free society."[40] If people are free, it would seem that an organization that can take away people's freedoms should not exist, thus the anomaly Goldstein speaks of. Another author, Gary Marx, saw the irony in the situation when he said, "It is ironic that police are both a major support and a major threat to a democratic society."[41] The reason the police are a major support to a democratic society is because they provide security. In order for a democratic society to flourish there must be stability in our communities. If criminals are free to terrorize us on the streets and in our homes and we have to fear our every action, such as going to the store, going out to dinner, or sleeping in our own bed, then we have no freedom. Yet the reason the police are a major threat to a democratic society is because they are the very people who are authorized legally to take away our freedoms through the power to stop us, detain us, search us, and arrest us. The very people who protect our rights and civil liberties are the very same people authorized to take them away from us.

This then leads us to another paradox. As one policing scholar explained, "There is a paradox in the fact that a democratic society needs protection by police and from police."[42] Even the police recognize this reality, for as Atlanta Police Commissioner George Napper explained from his perspective, "I've always felt that a democracy had to be not only protected by the police, but also protected from the police in terms of the awesome power and authority they have."[43] To achieve stability and security, we need police protection, while, at the same time, we must ensure that there are safeguards in place to protect citizens against too much power on the part of the police.[44] The Father of the Constitution, James Madison, explained this to the American people when he wrote in Federalist Papers, No. 51:

> If men were angels, no government would be necessary. If angels were to govern men, neither external nor internal controls on government would be necessary. In framing a government which is to be administered by men over men, the great difficulty lies in this: You must first enable the government to control the governed; and in the next place oblige it to control itself. A dependence on the people is, no doubt, the primary control on the government; but experience has taught mankind the necessity of auxiliary precautions.[45]

As Madison points out, since there is the potential for abuse, it is imperative that the people have various means of controlling the police, both internally and externally. Much of what will be discussed throughout this book are various means of controlling the police, including such topics as police management and internal affairs units which focus on internal controls; Supreme Court decisions and citizen review boards that focus on external controls; while things like cameras focus on both (dashboard cameras versus citizens filming the police with cell phones). Yet, while controlling the police is a necessity in our society, we must be cautious for it can create problems as well.

The problem with controlling the police is that control can also be taken to extremes.[46] If the police are controlled too much, then society ties their hands and they become ineffective. This means that the security we so strongly desire in our lives then disappears because the police are no longer authorized to act in the face of threats to our security, naturally resulting in anarchy. If we choose to go in the other direction, allowing police unfettered authority, then we may end up losing the freedoms we so desire, naturally resulting in repression—a police state.[47] This creates tension, for as one policing scholar explained, "Democratic societies experience a continual tension between the desire for order and the desire for liberty"; however, "both are essential."[48] This tension creates a balancing act for the police, as East Palo Alto Police Chief Ron Davis explains:

> Police officers at the lowest level of the organization have enormous power to make arrests, take freedom from individuals, and use coercive force. The police chief has to be able to manage this awesome responsibility so that the officers are part of the democracy and not opposing it. At the same time, the chiefs must balance the needs of the community and the political needs along with the issues of civil rights.[49]

Los Angeles police officers balancing between the peoples' right to peaceably assemble versus the peoples' safely.

It is this struggle for balance that makes democracy so hard on the police.

This struggle also creates an enduring problem for the police.[50] As one scholar, Roberts, explained when addressing the police, "The ultimate paradox is that the law enforcement agencies are themselves caught in the vortex of forces they cannot control and yet, are criticized when these forces rage out of control."[51] Those factors that cause crime and disorder are typically well beyond the control of the police, yet the police are the ones to whom society looks to deal with these problems. If, however, the police are too heavy-handed in dealing with crime, "they will be accused of gestapo-like tactics."[52] The police then have to figure out "how to battle crime effectively in a society in which nothing is being done about the causes of crime while, at the same time, the society, by and large, is suspicious of the police."[53] And because people have their freedoms in America, they have the right to challenge the police, to speak out against them, to pit themselves in opposition. Police scholar Bruce Smith realized this 75 years ago when he wrote of what he called the police problem:

> No matter how efficient a police force may be, and no matter how careful it is to observe civil liberties of long standing, it will always have to fight its way against an undercurrent of opposition and criticism from some of the very elements which it is paid to serve and protect, and to which it is in the last analysis responsible. This is the enduring problem of a police force in a democracy.[54]

Policing in a free American society requires that we find some means of balancing the use of police power with the rights and freedom of its citizens. This is not just a dilemma for the police, but one for any democratic society.[55] Abraham Lincoln recognized this fact when he delivered his first message to the U.S. Congress, speaking shortly after the Civil War had begun. In that speech he pondered this very same dilemma when he asked, "Is there, in all republics, this inherent, and fatal weakness? Must a government, of necessity, be too strong for the liberties of its own people, or too weak to maintain its own existence?"[56] It truly is a struggle and a dilemma to try and balance both freedoms and security (see Box 1.3). But just because it is hard does not mean it is not worth doing; in fact, it is imperative to our very survival as a free nation. Police Chief Charles Ramsey of the Philadelphia Police Department drives this point home when he explains:

> The ultimate goal of the police is to create a society that is free of crime and where everyone's rights are safe and secure. That is the ideal, something to reach for, but something that we will probably never fully achieve. There will always be challenges and obstacles that get in the way.[57]

The means by which we continually engage in this struggle to achieve the ideal is through our republican form of government, which is the subject of the next section.

Box 1.3 Ethics in Practice: The Police Paradox

The **policing paradox** at the most basic level is that *in a free democracy, there should be no police, for the police can take away our freedoms*. The irony of having the police in a democratic society is that while they are protectors of democracy, they are also its biggest threat. As a result, not only do we need the protection *of* the police, we need protection *from* the police. Order and liberty, then, are both necessary components of democracy and the police often struggle trying to balance these two, which is why it has been said that democracy is hard on the police.

Ask Yourself:

Does preservation of a democratic society depend on strong reliance on the police? Why or why not?

If you do not agree, then what is democracy's strongest reliance?

Source: Vollmer, A. (1936). *The Police and Modern Society.* Berkeley: University of California Press, p. 237.

Police and Government

In the winter of 1787, after the Constitution had been drafted, John Jay, James Madison, and Alexander Hamilton took to writing under the name *Publius* in the hopes that their words would influence the people of the states to ratify the United States Constitution. The people were naturally suspicious of government, having only recently thrown off the oppressive English government after a long-protracted war. Hamilton, writing in what came to be known as the Seventeenth Federalist Paper, tried to convince the people that one reason to support ratification is because the U.S. Constitution left the administration of criminal justice in the hands of the state and local governments. It did not create a national police force, and by having the police controlled by state and local governments, as Hamilton saw it, served as a means of protecting the people against tyranny when he wrote:

> There is one transcendent advantage belonging to the province of the state governments, which alone suffices to place the matter in a clear and satisfactory light, I mean the ordinary administration of criminal and civil justice. This, of all others, is the most powerful, most universal, and most attractive source of popular obedience and attachment. It is that which, being the immediate and visible guardian of life and property, having its benefits and its terrors in constant activity before the public eye, regulating all those personal interests and familiar concerns to which the sensibility of individuals is more immediately awake, contributes, more than any other circumstance, to impressing upon the minds of the people, affection, esteem, and reverence towards the government. This great cement of society, which will diffuse itself almost wholly through the channels of the particular governments, independent of all other causes of influence, would

insure them so decided an empire over their respective citizens as to render them at all times a complete counterpoise, and, not unfrequently, dangerous rivals to the power of the Union.

While Hamilton argued that the criminal justice system being in the hands of state and local government gave the people power over the national government, he also notes indirectly that in the minds of most people, the police are often the sole representation of government. Police Chief August Vollmer said the same thing, but in more practical language, when he asked, "The President of the United States—you don't really know him, do you? What do your fellow citizens know of your mayor—or even your governor? But you know and they know the policeman on the beat. He represents the government. To most people he *is* the government."[58] And more recently, scholar Jeremy Travis articulated, "Of all governmental functions, the policing function is arguably the most visible, the most immediate, the most intimately involved with the well-being of individuals and the health of communities."[59]

What all three of these quotes highlight is that the police are a part of government and that the most visible of all government agencies is the police. The uniform, the marked car, and the ease of contacting them (911) all make the police officer the most omnipresent of government employees. It is their placement in our system of government that is important to our understanding of the relationship between the power and authority of the police officer with that of the citizenry.

We often use the word **democracy** to describe our system of government, but that is inherently wrong. The term *democracy* has come to have many meanings, but what a pure democracy would entail is that all of the people have a vote on all of the issues. As that would be impractical, for most of us have neither the time nor the inclination, the founding fathers created a Republican form of government. In a **Republic**, the people vote for individuals who represent their interests in and before government. The document that created this system is the **U.S. Constitution**, created in 1787, ratified in 1788, and put into action in 1789, and it is the supreme law of the land. That law serves as the ultimate law for the police. As former Police Chief Lee Brown explained, "The Constitution is the overarching document that guides how police officers, and certainly the police chief, govern themselves."[60] In addition, to how the police are governed, Brown saw the relationship of the police to the Constitution as being "one of the most important elements of government because their role is to protect the Constitution. If they do that, then in my estimation," he explained, "they become the most important employees in city government."[61] Police Chief Ramsey echoes this sentiment when he tells his officers, "We must never compromise our staunch defense of the Constitution and the bedrock foundation it guarantees. We must never buy into the notion—as the police in Nazi Germany did—that taking away individual rights is somehow the way to solve our crime problems and create safer communities."[62]

The Constitution creates a republican form of government known as **federalism**, which allows for both a central national government and more localized state governments to share power (note that missing from the definition are local governments, which are granted the right to exist by their respective state governments). In some policy areas the national government is granted sole power and authority, such as maintaining the military or the right to enter into treaties with other countries. In some cases, it is the state governments that are granted total authority over certain areas of government such as education and the police (which they can delegate to local jurisdictions). Then there are those areas where the federal and state governments both share powers, such as transportation and health policy.

In addition to the federalist form of government, the Constitution establishes a **separation of powers** by creating three branches of government: the legislative (U.S. Congress), the executive (the president), and the judiciary (the U.S. Supreme Court) (see Figure 1.1). This separation of power is to prevent any one person or group of persons from having total power of government, otherwise known as a *totalitarian government*. By providing a system of **checks and balances**, where no one entity is in total control and the other entities can override decisions by the other branches of government, it prevents the concentration (and abuse) of power. Most states follow this same framework with the state legislatures, governors, and state supreme courts, while local governments also organize in a similar fashion with city councils, mayors, and local courts. The manner in which this is important for policing is the fact that the police are operated by the executive branch, enforce the laws made by the legislative branch, and are checked by the judiciary branch to ensure their actions are constitutional.

It is important to understand that the police are controlled by the government. To oversee the police and to grant them the necessary power and authority to perform their job, it is necessary that they be controlled by government. As there are many forms of government, such as cities and counties, the form which the police assumes is reflected by the type of government overseeing them, such as police departments in cities and sheriff's offices in counties. This helps to narrow the power and authority of the police by defining the **police jurisdiction**, the specific area where the police are legally authorized to enforce the law, within the town limits or within the county limits. Still further, the legal jurisdiction of the police will also define the function of the police, specifically describing the extent of their legal authority. For instance, some agencies' legal jurisdiction is to enforce the law within a small town, while others may police the entire state, but only for violations of game laws, such as state game wardens (see Chapter 3 for more on the wide array of police agencies).

Now, recognizing that the police are under the power and authority of the government, it is equally important to recognize that the government that controls the police is granted their power and authority by the people.

Figure 1.1 Three Branches of Government/Separation of Powers

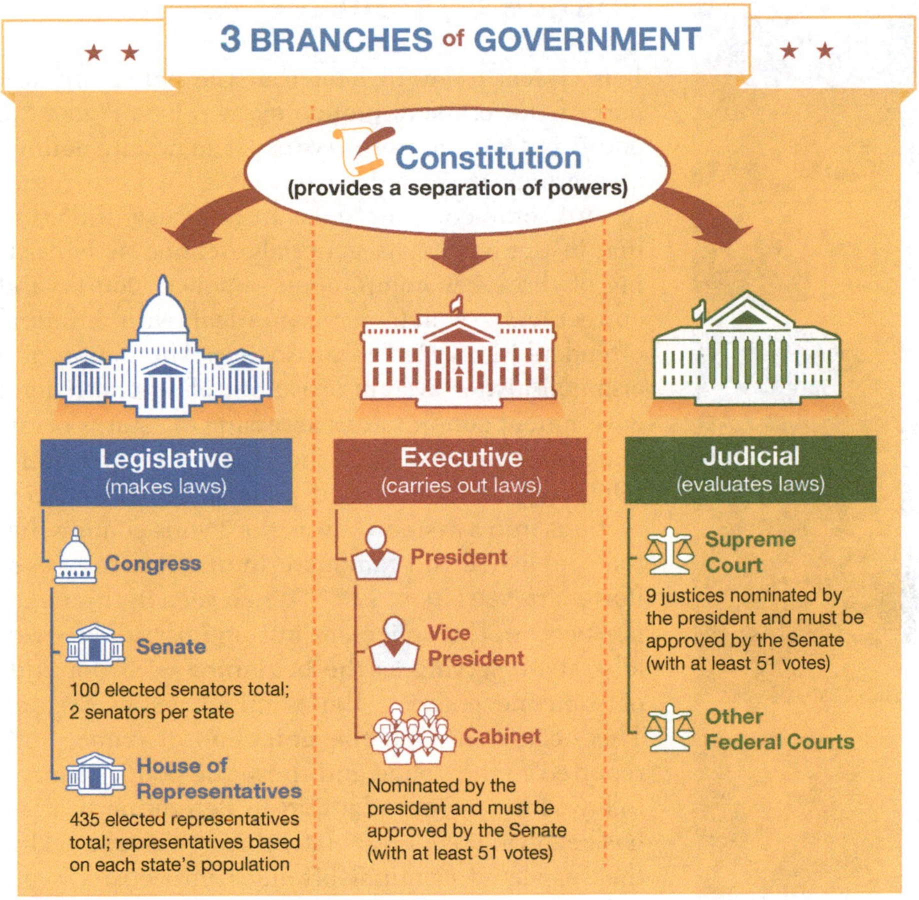

3 BRANCHES of GOVERNMENT

★ ★   ★ ★

Constitution
(provides a separation of powers)

Legislative
(makes laws)

Executive
(carries out laws)

Judicial
(evaluates laws)

Congress

Senate

100 elected senators total;
2 senators per state

House of Representatives

435 elected representatives
total; representatives based
on each state's population

President

Vice President

Cabinet

Nominated by the
president and must be
approved by the Senate
(with at least 51 votes)

Supreme Court

9 justices nominated by
the president and must be
approved by the Senate
(with at least 51 votes)

Other Federal Courts

Source: By 111Alleskönner - Own work, CC BY-SA 3.0 de, https://commons.wikimedia.org/w/index.php?curid=22851075.

The people vote into office their representatives who will either control the police (for example, the mayor); who will make the laws that the police enforce (for example, members of the state legislature); and in many cases, those who will oversee the police to ensure that their behavior is constitutional (for example, members of the state supreme courts—where elected). In the end, it is the people that oversee government, and since the police are part of government, it is the people who oversee the police. Former Attorney General Robert F. Kennedy once wrote, "In the words of the old saying, every society gets the kind of criminal it deserves. What is equally true is that every community gets the kind of law enforcement it insists on."[63] What Kennedy meant was that in our form of government, the people oversee the police, and that they have it in their power to control the police and establish the proper balance between security and individual freedoms.

The three branches of government: the legislative, executive, and judicial.

Police and the Criminal Justice System

It is typical today to hear that the police are also part of the **criminal justice system** (see Figure 1.2 and Box 1.4). The term *system* is generally defined as a group of related parts that all work together toward some common goal. In this case, the criminal justice system is generally defined as consisting of three key components—police, courts, and corrections—which serve to deal with criminal offenders in our American society. The notion of a criminal justice system arose out of several federal government commissions assessing the status of law and justice in America in the 1930s, and later in the 1960s, which then linked police, courts, and corrections into a system. It was the 1960s commission that published the famous criminal justice system flowchart (see Figure 1.2).[64] When seen in this larger perspective, the police are but one part of an overall system, serving as the beginning or "front end" of someone entering the criminal justice system. This occurs through the **detection** of crime, both reported to the police and those the police observe, followed by an **investigation** to determine if a law has been violated, and finally through **arrest**, taking the suspected criminal offender into custody and then turning the charges over to the courts. The person entering will then be afforded a fair hearing by the second component, the courts, and if found guilty, will be sentenced in some manner to be supervised by the third component, corrections.

There are many different perspectives on the criminal justice system, and some even argue whether or not it is a system at all. Some have argued that it is really three separate institutions that work independent of each other.[65] Policing is assuredly its own institution, having its own history, culture, purpose, and goals, and it does not report to any form of criminal justice super organization. Others have argued that it is not really a system, but a network, where the various components come into contact and communicate with one another only when circumstances necessitate.[66] There is some truth to all of this, for the three components do not always work together and, in fact, sometimes they seemingly work against each other. The reasons for this are many, but one professor of law, Herbert Packer, tried to explain it this way: There

Figure 1.2 The Criminal Justice System

What is the sequence of events in the criminal justice system?

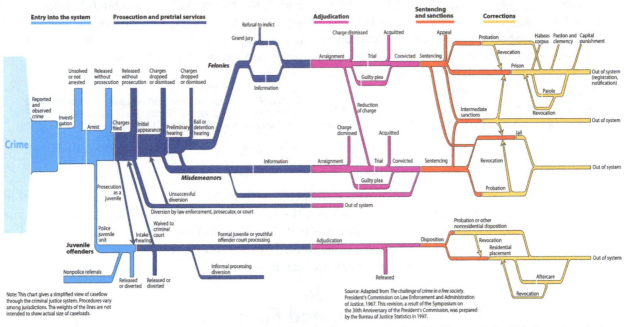

Note: This chart gives a simplified view of caseflow through the criminal justice system. Procedures vary among jurisdictions. The weights of the lines are not intended to show actual size of caseloads.

Source: Adapted from *The challenge of crime in a free society*. President's Commission on Law Enforcement and Administration of Justice, 1967. This revision, a result of the Symposium on the 30th Anniversary of the President's Commission, was prepared by the Bureau of Justice Statistics in 1997.

Source: Bureau of Justice Statistics. (1988). *Report to the Nation on Crime and Justice.* Washington, D.C.: U.S. Department of Justice, pp. 56–57.

are really two different models of the criminal process.[67] On one hand, there is the **crime control model** which is focused on ensuring that criminals are removed from society and placed in jail or prison, where they can no longer commit crime. If this model is accurate, then the police should be about enforcing the laws, making arrests, and going after those that harm society, whatever the costs.

On the other hand, there is also the **due process model** which states that the criminal justice system is about protecting the rights of all citizens and that the entire process should ensure that no right is violated at every step of the process. In this case, the police would be more concerned with civil liberties, and making arrests would only be done as a means for protecting everyone's rights, including both the victim and the perpetrator. Which model is being used will determine how the police perform their job. In the crime control model, security trumps civil liberties, while in the due process model, civil liberties trump security. Once again, we return to the dilemma of policing in a democratic society.

This also highlights another important facet of policing: trying to understand the goal of not just the criminal justice system, but policing itself. Earlier, Chief Ramsey was quoted as saying that "the ultimate goal of the police is to create a society that is free of crime," yet the police perform all manner

---

Box 1.4 Policing in Practice: America's Criminal Justice System

Just as our government is organized into three branches, our criminal justice system has **three distinct parts: police, courts, and corrections**. Each part has a direct effect on the function of the others. The courts define who the police can arrest and other police activities, corrections adapts to who is convicted by the courts, and sentencing is influenced by how successful the corrections system is in reforming criminals. Changing any part of the criminal justice system affects the other parts, so the process must be viewed as a whole.

Source: President's Commission on Law Enforcement and Administration of Justice. (1967). *The Challenge of Crime in a Free Society*. Washington, D.C.: U.S. GPO, p. 7.

---

of service and traffic enforcement that does not inherently focus on that ultimate goal.[68] In this case, the key word is "ultimate," for Ramsey sees the ultimate goal as crime control, but that means that there are other goals the police are trying to achieve. Understanding the purpose and function of the police in our American society is the focus of the next section.

Police Purpose and Function

The purpose and function of the police is a topic that has many answers, both philosophical and practical. From the philosophical perspective, because policing is part of government, the police help to achieve the ultimate goal of government. Philosophers as far back as Aristotle have argued that the chief purpose of government is justice when he wrote, "Justice is the bond of men in states, for the administration of justice, which is the determination of what is just, is the principle of order in political society."[69] James Madison, in Federalist Papers No. 51, reflected this sentiment when he wrote, "Justice is the end of government. It is the end of civil society. It ever has been and ever will be pursued until it be obtained, or until liberty be lost in the pursuit."[70] Therefore, the ultimate goal, the entire purpose and function of the police, is to pursue **justice (see Box 1.5)**.

Although justice may be the ultimate goal philosophically, there are so many roles that the police play in our society that it is easy to lose track of the ultimate goal. As one author explained it, "A simple answer to the question as to what the urban policeman does is that he does everything. . . . In broad general terms, it can be said that police deal with virtually every kind of emergency human problem."[71] The **police roles** include the enforcement of criminal law, but they also perform many other roles in our society, including traffic enforcement, investigations, patrol, emergency response, first responder care, vice enforcement, search and rescue, citizen education, business and well-visit checks, crowd control, recovering property, testifying

---

Box 1.5 Policing in Practice: The National Law Enforcement Officer's Memorial (NLEOM)

"It is not how these officers died that made them heroes, it is how they lived."
— Vivian Eney Cross, Survivor
A quote featured at the NLEOM

The ultimate goal of law enforcement is to pursue justice, and some pay the ultimate price for this pursuit. The **National Law Enforcement Officers Memorial (NLEOM)** was dedicated on October 15, 1991, and is located in Washington, D.C., in the 400 block of E. Street, N.W. It is the nation's memorial dedicated to honoring all police officers in the United States who were killed in the line of duty. The memorial features a small pool and two curving, 304-foot-long marble walls upon which are etched the names of the more than 20,000 police officers who have lost their lives.

The landscape features many flowers and trees, and overseeing the two marble walls are several statutes of lions, which serve as a symbol of strength, courage, and valor. Every May, the memorial celebrates Police Week, where, at a candlelight vigil, the names of the fallen officers over the previous year are read aloud and honored for their sacrifice. In honor of these police officers, a portion of all sales of this book will be gifted to the National Law Enforcement Officers Memorial Fund.

For more information about the NLEOM, go to http ://www.nleomf.org/.

---

in court, community relations programs, kid camps, and crime prevention, among so many others. All of this can be further divided into the many **police tasks** that an officer performs in the course of performing one of these roles. For instance, traffic enforcement may entail running radar, watching for red light violations, stop sign violations, responding to accidents, directing traffic, and roadside assistance of disabled vehicles. Each of these may also entail the police officer performing several roles.[72] In the response to a traffic accident, for example, the officer has to respond to the call, secure the scene, check for injuries, keep traffic flowing, conduct an investigation, and, let's say it is a driving while intoxicated suspect, make an arrest.

Police officers perform many roles and conduct many functions or tasks in the performance of their job, but there are two complications in this. The first is **role expectation**. Many people perceive the police in a certain way and they expect the police to act in a certain manner. A simple example of this is when a person's car breaks down, they expect the police to assist them road side. Some believe the police will fix their car, or have it towed and give them a ride somewhere. If people lock their keys in the car, they expect the police to break into their car for them. More complex is how many people believe the role of the police is to protect individuals, when in reality, the role of the police is to protect the community. People have many expectations of the police, but these expectations are also complicated by the many roles the police perform. If you go to a fast-food restaurant, you expect the cashier to take your order, take your money, and deliver your food. It is simple because that is all they do. Now, what do you expect of the police? The answer is far more complicated because it depends upon your needs at the moment. The more complex the job, the more ambiguous it is to perform, thus creating more conflicts.[73] This **role ambiguity** of the police, it was once said, "is built into the very structure of law enforcement by the variety of duties imposed upon police practitioners by the law, custom, and ethical requirements of the society they live in."[74] This complication of roles can also lead to **role conflict** where the police have to perform certain roles in our society that come into conflict.[75] One merely has to go back to the policing in a democratic society to recognize the conflicts that can arise: the police are charged with protecting our civil liberties, but they can also take them away.

As a result of the ultimate goal of justice being so broad and because the role of the police can be so complicated, many look to the set of police goals or functions that they perform as a means of categorizing what the police do.[76] For instance, again, Chief Ramsey spoke of creating a society free of crime as the ultimate goal. While that may be the ultimate goal, even Chief Ramsey recognizes that this is impossible in reality and therefore most speak of **crime control/reduction** as a key function of the police, to enforce the laws so that crime, everything from burglary to homicide, is reduced.[77] Another function is **disorder control/reduction**, and that is to reduce those things that disrupt a civil society, such as people being drunk in public, disturbing the peace, as well as nuisances such as litter, graffiti, and noise. More recently, the concept of **fear reduction** has been seen as a function of the police, to implement measures that reduce the public's fear of crime, and not necessarily as a part of either crime or disorder reduction.[78] In addition, many have focused on **crime prevention**, those measures taken in advance to prevent crime from occurring, as a proper role for the police. Still another goal of the police has been to enhance the **quality of life** by improving neighborhoods and communities through an application of both formal and informal measures to increase citizen satisfaction. **Order maintenance** has also been considered a goal or function of the police.[79] Different from disorder reduction, which is merely working to reduce the number of violations, here it is the more informal measures to maintain social control in communities with arrest being a last resort. Still others see **service delivery**, those functions the police perform that provide a service to the public (for example, well visits, educational programs, home security surveys) as a goal/function, and others talk of a key police goal being **community organization**.[80] Each of these goals and functions of the police, again, entail that the police must perform many different roles and tasks in the performance of their duties and each requires a very different approach to the way the police carry out their duties, what is often referred to as the *styles of policing*.

James Q. Wilson, a political scientist who spent much of his career looking at the issue of crime, conducted a study wherein he looked at eight different communities to see how the police performed their duties.[81] What he found was that different communities wanted different things from their police, similar to the previous quote from Robert Kennedy, which said that people get the kind of policing they insist upon. What Wilson concluded was that there were three **styles of policing** that different communities insisted upon: the watchman style, the legalistic style, and the service style. In the **watchman style**, police departments and their officers serve as a force that works to maintain order and control crime by its presence. When issues arise, the police intervene to restore order through their use of discretion and coercion, employing such things as verbal warnings, presence, or forcing people to leave the area. Police departments operating under this style typically reserve arrest only for the more serious felonious crimes, the major crimes, while dealing more informally with minor crimes.

The **legalistic style** of policing is generally found in police departments where authority is highly centralized and officers are required to show evidence of their work. Police are focused on authority and control through the uniform enforcement of laws and arrest is seen as the primary means for dealing with problems. Police departments operating under this style actively enforce the law against both major and minor crimes, as well as traffic violations.

Finally, there is the **service style**, which sees the police as performing a set of services to the public to solve community problems, where presence is only to provide service and arrest is also a last resort. The focus of the department is on community relations, public satisfaction, and treating citizens (customers) with respect. Police departments operating under this style typically only make arrests for both major and minor crimes as a last resort.

Wilson's central argument is that the public influences the government and the type of government then influences the style of policing. So, it is important to understand that because the police are decentralized and local, they can be controlled by the people. However, a word of caution is perhaps necessary today regarding Wilson's three styles of policing.[82] Wilson published his study in 1968, and since then, many researchers have tried to verify his findings with their own studies. None of them have found much support for Wilson's three styles of policing.[83] That may be because of problems with the studies or, more likely, because policing has changed since the 1960s, becoming more similar in style. While this may be the case, Wilson's typology is important at least for purposes of police history, but more fundamentally, for understanding the nature and relationship between the police, government, and the people.

Conclusion

While August Vollmer stated, "The policeman's job is the highest calling in the world," it is also one of the most complicated.[84] In the United States, it could be said that the police are the paid sheepdogs of our society. They are a civil force that is a constituted body of citizens who are given special authority and are under the control of the government. They are administered by the executive branch to enforce the laws of the legislative branch, and are overseen by the judiciary branch. While they are part of the criminal justice system, the component that is charged with the first introduction to the system through detection, investigation, and arrest, they are also their own institution with their own history, customs, and manners for performing their institutional duties. They are assuredly a unique force because while they are not the military, they are authorized the use of coercive force, to maintain public safety and prevent crime and disorder for the benefit of the people, while being held publicly accountable to those same people. This is part of what makes policing such a difficult job because in policing a democratic society, the same organization tasked with protecting the liberties of its citizens is charged with the authority to take away those liberties. The other part that makes policing difficult is that while the ultimate goal of policing may be justice, the police take on so many roles in our society that it can lead to ambiguity over their proper role in society, which can further lead to expectations that are too difficult to meet and to conflicts between these varied roles. These are simply many of the reasons that policing has been called an "impossible job."[85]

To understand our system of policing in America, it is important to understand American policing development, its origins, and its roots. While the term *policing* may have come out of the Greek word *politeuein*, our system of policing is largely based on the English system. Once the United States became independent of England, policing then underwent a slow development, from policing being a part of the political machine, to reforms aimed at the professionalization of the police, to the community policing movement, and, today, a growing emphasis on homeland security.

Just the Facts

1. The police have been called the "thin blue line" and the "sheepdogs" of our American society, suggesting they are all that stands between peace and anarchy.

2. The roots of the word *police* come from the Greek word *politeuein* meaning politics, or citizens engaged in politics. The police are a civil force that is a constituted body of people under the control of government, who are given special authority (sworn) to enforce the rules, regulations, and laws of the jurisdiction they serve, being subject

to those same laws, and are authorized the use of coercive force, to maintain public safety and to prevent crime and disorder for the benefit of the people, while being held publicly accountable to those same people.

3. Policing in a democracy is often considered counterintuitive and establishes the police paradox, that while the people are free, a government force exists that can take away their freedom to achieve greater security.

4. The United States Constitution creates the American form of government, a Federalist Republic, adhering to a separation of powers for purposes of checks and balances, and is the supreme law of the land.

5. The police are part of the criminal justice system, a system which consists of three parts, police, courts, and corrections, and its role in this system is detection, investigation, and arrest.

6. There are two models of criminal justice operating in America, the crime control model, which is concerned about enforcing the law to make America safe, and the due process model, which is more concerned about protecting the civil liberties of American citizens.

7. The purpose of the police has been said to be crime control/reduction, disorder control/reduction, fear reduction, crime prevention, improving quality of life, order maintenance, service delivery, and community organization.

8. While the police pursue justice, they perform numerous roles and tasks to achieve this, and often the expectations of the police do not match with the realities of policing, thus creating both role ambiguity and role conflict.

9. James Q. Wilson noted that community demands shape the style of policing, which typically fall into three categories: watchman, legalistic, and service.

Ask Yourself

1. Are the analogies of the "thin blue line" and the "sheepdog" of our American society accurate reflections of who the police are, or do they cause citizens to abdicate their responsibility to the government for protection?

2. Recognizing the policing paradox of trying to balance the concepts of freedom with security, what are the best methods for the police to achieve this delicate balance?

3. Detail the importance of the United States Constitution to policing, considering this from both the police point of view (security and the rule of law) and the citizen point of view (freedom and civil liberties).

4. The police are said to be a part of the criminal justice system, but what relationship do they have with the other two components (courts and corrections), and how do the responsibilities of the police impact the system itself?

5. There are numerous purposes and functions of the police, but what should be the proper role of the police in our society? And if there is more than only one, do these roles create ambiguity and conflict?

Keywords

Arrest

Checks and balances

Civil rights

Community organization

Crime control model

Crime control/reduction

Crime prevention

Criminal justice system

Democracy

Detection

Disorder control/reduction

Due process model

Fear reduction

Federalism

Investigation

Justice

Order maintenance

Police

Police jurisdiction

Police roles

Police tasks

Policing paradox

Politeuein

Quality of life

Republic

Role ambiguity

Role conflict

Role expectation

Separation of powers

Service delivery

Sheepdog

Styles of policing

Watchman

Legalistic

Service

Sworn officers

Thin blue line

United States Constitution

Endnotes

1. Collins, F.L. (1924). A professor who cleaned up a city. *Collier's*, November 8, 12, & 37, at p. 12.
2. The origin of the term "thin blue line" is not altogether clear. One of the first definitive uses of the phrase was in an ABC documentary by David L. Wolper Productions titled "The Thin Blue Line" in 1965. See http://www.davidlwolper.com/shows/details.cfm?showID=209.
3. Orwell, G. (1950). *1984*. New York, NY: Signet Classics; Orwell, G. (1996). *Animal farm*. New York, NY: Signet Classics.
4. There is some debate over the origin of the quote. See O'Toole, G. (2014). People sleep peacefully in their beds at night only because rough men stand ready to do violence on their behalf. Quote Investigator. Retrieved online at http://quoteinvestigator.com/2011/11/07/rough-men/.
5. Grossman, D. (2009). *On killing: The psychological cost of learning to kill in war and society*. New York, NY: Back Bay Books; see also Grossman, D. (2012). On combat: *The psychology and physiology of deadly conflict in war and peace*. 3rd ed. Millstadt, IL: Human Factor Research Group.
6. Grossman, D. (2009). *On killing: The psychological cost of learning to kill in war and society*. New York, NY: Back Bay Books, p. 183.
7. Grossman, D. (2000). On sheep, wolves, and sheepdogs. Retrieved online at https://www.killology.com/sheep-wolves-and-sheepdogs.
8. Grossman, D. (2000). On sheep, wolves, and sheepdogs. Retrieved online at https://www.killology.com/sheep-wolves-and-sheepdogs.
9. Grossman, D. (2000). On sheep, wolves, and sheepdogs. Retrieved online at https://www.killology.com/sheep-wolves-and-sheepdogs.
10. Grossman, D. (2009). *On killing: The psychological cost of learning to kill in war and society*. New York, NY: Back Bay Books, p. 183.
11. Grossman, D. (2009). *On killing: The psychological cost of learning to kill in war and society*. New York, NY: Back Bay Books, p. 183.
12. Grossman, D. (2000). On sheep, wolves, and sheepdogs. Retrieved online at https://www.killology.com/sheep-wolves-and-sheepdogs.
13. Grossman, D. (2009). *On killing: The psychological cost of learning to kill in war and society*. New York, NY: Back Bay Books, p. 183.
14. Collins, F.L. (1924). A professor who cleaned up a city. *Collier's*, November 8, 12, & 37.
15. Barker, M. (1985). *Cops: Their lives in their own words*. New York, NY: Pocket Books.

16. Drew, S.K., Milles, M.B., & Gassaway, B.M. (2007). *Dirty work*. Waco, TX: Baylor University Press.

17. Hargrove, E.C. & Glidewell, J.C. (1990). *Impossible jobs in public management*. Lawrence, KS: University Press of Kansas.

18. Preib, M. (2010). *The wagon and other stories from the city*. Chicago: The University of Chicago Press.

19. For stress, see, for instance, Kensing, K. (2014). The 10 most stressful jobs of 2013. Retrieved online at http://www.careercast.com/jobs-rated/10-most-stressful-jobs-2013; for injuries, assaults, and line of duty deaths, see National Law Enforcement Memorial Fund. (2014). Deaths, assaults & injuries. Retrieved online at http://www.nleomf.org/facts/officer-fatalities-data/daifacts.html.

20. Rachlin, H. (1991). *The making of a cop*. New York, NY: Pocket Books, p. 12.

21. Barker, J.C. (1999). *Danger, duty, and disillusion: The worldview of Los Angeles police officers*. Long Grove, IL: Waveland Press, Inc., p. 212.

22. Carter, D. (2014). Translating Thucydides. University of Reading. Retrieved online at http://www.reading.ac.uk/web/FILES/classics/Translating_Thucydides.pdf.

23. See *Oxford English Dictionary* entry for "police." Retrieved online at http://www.oed.com/view/Entry/146823?rskey=x0ACr2&result=1&isAdvanced=false#eid.

24. Held, D. (1987). *Models of democracy*. London, England: Polity Press.

25. See *Oxford English Dictionary* entry for "police." Retrieved online at http://www.oed.com/view/Entry/146823?rskey=x0ACr2&result=1&isAdvanced=false#eid.

26. Metropolitan Police Act 1829, 1829 Chapter 44, Geo 4. Retrieved online at http://www.legislation.gov.uk/ukpga/Geo4/10/44/contents.

27. Bittner, E. (1976). Community relations. In *Police community relations: Images, roles, and realities*. A.W. Cohn & E.C. Viano (Eds.). Philadelphia, PA: J.B. Lippincott; Goldstein, H. (1977). *Policing in a free society*. Cambridge, MA: Ballinger; Klockars, C.B. (1985). *The idea of police*. Beverly Hills, CA: Sage; Manning, P.K. & Van Maanen, J. (1978). *Policing: A view from the street*. Santa Monica, CA: Goodyear; Reiss, A.J., Jr. (1967). *The police and the public*. New Haven, CT: Yale University Press; Sherman, L. (2001). Consent of the governed: Police, democracy, and diversity. In *Policing, security, and democracy: Theory and practice*. M. Amir & S. Einstein (Eds.). Huntsville, TX: OICJ; Sklansky, D.A. (2005). Police and democracy. *Michigan Law Review*, 103, 1699-1830; Skolnick, J. (1966). Justice without trial. New York, NY: John Wiley & Sons; Wilson, J.Q. (1968). *Varieties of police behavior*. Cambridge, MA: Harvard University Press.

28. See Klockars, C.B. (1985). *The idea of police*. Beverly Hills, CA: Sage.

29. Reiss, A.J. Jr. (1992). Police organization in the twentieth century. In *Modern policing, crime, and justice: A review of research*. Vol. 15. M. Tonry & N. Morris (Eds.). Chicago: University of Chicago Press; Shearing, C. (1992). The relation between public and private policing. In *Modern policing, crime, and justice: A review of research*. Vol. 15. M. Tonry & N. Morris (Eds.). Chicago: University of Chicago Press; Wilson, J.Q. (1968). *Varieties of police behavior*. Cambridge, MA: Harvard University Press.

30. Sklansky, D.A. (2005). Police and democracy. *Michigan Law Review*, 103, 1699-1830; Wilson, J.Q. (1968). *Varieties of police behavior*. Cambridge, MA: Harvard University Press.

31. Bittner, E. (1979). The functions of the police in modern society. Bethesda, MD: National Institute of Mental Health; Klockars, C.B. (1985). *The idea of police*. Beverly Hills, CA: Sage

32. Klockars, C.B. (1985). *The idea of police*. Beverly Hills, CA: Sage, p. 12.

33. Jones, T., Newburn, T., & Smith, D.J. (1996). Policing and the idea of democracy. *British Journal of Criminology*, 36, 182-198; Sherman, L. (2001). Consent of the governed: Police, democracy, and diversity. In *Policing, security, and democracy: Theory and practice*. M. Amir & S. Einstein (Eds.). Huntsville, TX: OICJ; Wilson, J.Q. (1968). Varieties of police behavior. Cambridge, MA: Harvard University Press.

34. Shearing, C. (1992). The relation between public and private policing. In *Modern policing, crime, and justice: A review of research*. Vol. 15. M. Tonry & N. Morris (Eds.). Chicago: University of Chicago Press.

35. Berkley, G. (1969). *The democratic policeman*. Boston, MA: Beacon Press.

36. Berkley, G. (1969). *The democratic policeman*. Boston, MA: Beacon Press, p. 1.

37. Berkley, G. (1969). *The democratic policeman*. Boston, MA: Beacon Press, p. 1.

38. Berkley, G. (1969). *The democratic policeman*. Boston, MA: Beacon Press, p. 1.

39. See especially Roberts, E.F. (1961). Paradoxes in law enforcement. *Journal of Criminal Law and Criminology*, 52, 224-228.

40. Goldstein, H. (1977). *Policing in a free society*. Cambridge, MA: Ballinger, p. 1.

41. Marx, G.T. (2001). Police and democracy. In *Policing, security, and democracy: Theory and practice*. M. Amir & S. Einstein (Eds.). Huntsville, TX: OICJ, p. 36.

42. Marx, G.T. (2001). Police and democracy. In *Policing, security, and democracy: Theory and practice*. M. Amir & S. Einstein (Eds.). Huntsville, TX: OICJ, p. 35.

43. Isenberg, J. (2010). *Police leadership in a democracy: Conversations with America's police chiefs*. Boca Raton, FL: CRC Press, p. 29.

44. Jones, T., Newburn, T., & Smith, D.J. (1996). Policing and the idea of democracy. *British Journal of Criminology*, 36, 182-198.

45. Madison J. (1788/1961). No, 51, Madison. In *The federalist papers*. C. Rossiter (Ed.). New York, NY: New American Library, pp. 321-322.

46. See Skolnick, J. (1966). *Justice without trial*. New York, NY: John Wiley & Sons.

47. Bayley, D.H. (2002). Law enforcement and the rule of law: Is there a tradeoff? *Criminology & Public Policy*,

2, 133-154; Chevigny, P.G. (2002). Conflict or rights and keeping order. *Criminology & Public Policy*, 2, 155-160.

48. Marx, G.T. (2001). Police and democracy. In *Policing, security, and democracy: Theory and practice*. M. Amir & S. Einstein (Eds.). Huntsville, TX: OICJ, p. 42.

49. Isenberg, J. (2010). *Police leadership in a democracy: Conversations with America's police chiefs*. Boca Raton, FL: CRC Press, pp. 27-28.

50. Manning, P.K. & Van Maanen, J. (1978). *Policing: A view from the street*. Santa Monica, CA: Goodyear.

51. Roberts, E.F. (1961). Paradoxes in law enforcement. *Journal of Criminal Law and Criminology*, 52, 224-228, p. 226.

52. Roberts, E.F. (1961). Paradoxes in law enforcement. *Journal of Criminal Law and Criminology*, 52, 224-228, p. 226.

53. Roberts, E.F. (1961). Paradoxes in law enforcement. *Journal of Criminal Law and Criminology*, 52, 224-228, p. 226.

54. Smith, B. (1940). *Police systems in the United States*. New York, NY: Harper & Brothers Publishers, p. 77; See also Roberts, E.F. (1961). Paradoxes in law enforcement. *Journal of Criminal Law and Criminology*, 52, 224-228, p. 226.

55. Kappeler, V.E., Sluder, R., & Alpert, G. (1998). *Forces of deviance: Understanding the dark side of policing*. 2nd ed. Prospect Heights, IL: Waveland Press.

56. Lincoln, A. (1861). First message to Congress, July 4, 1861. Retrieved online at http://teachingamericanhistory.org/library/document/message-to-congress-in-special-session/

57. Ramsey, C.H. (2014). The challenge of policing in a democratic society: A personal journey toward understanding. New Perspectives in Policing.Retrieved online at https://www.ncjrs.gov/pdffiles1/nij/245992.pdf, p. 12.

58. Collins, Frederick L. (1924). A Professor Who Cleaned up a City. *Collier's*, November 8, 12, & 37, at p. 12.

59. Skolnick, J.H. (1999). Ideas in American policing. Police Foundation. Retrieved online at http://www.police-foundation.org/sites/g/files/g798246/f/Skolnick%20%281999%29%20-%20On%20Democratic%20Policing.pdf

60. Isenberg, J. (2010). *Police leadership in a democracy: Conversations with America's police chiefs*. Boca Raton, FL: CRC Press, p. 30.

61. Isenberg, J. (2010). *Police leadership in a democracy: Conversations with America's police chiefs*. Boca Raton, FL: CRC Press, p. 30.

62. Ramsey, C.H. (2014). The challenge of policing in a democratic society: A personal journey toward understanding. New Perspectives in Policing. Retrieved online at https://www.ncjrs.gov/pdffiles1/nij/245992.pdf, p. 12.

63. Kennedy, R.F. (1964). *The pursuit of justice*. New York, NY: Harper & Row, Publishers, p. 42.

64. President's Commission on Law Enforcement and Administration of Justice. (1967). *The challenge of crime in a free society*. Washington, DC: U.S. GPO.

65. Marion, N.E. & Oliver, W.M. (2006). *The public policy of crime and criminal justice*. Upper Saddle River, NJ: Prentice Hall.

66. Cox, S.M. & Wade, J.E. (1998). *The criminal justice network: An introduction*. 3rd ed. Boston, MA: McGraw-Hill Inc.

67. Packer, H.L. (1964). Two models of the criminal process. *University of Pennsylvania Law Review*, 113, 113-125.

68. Ramsey, C.H. (2014). The challenge of policing in a democratic society: A personal journey toward understanding. *New Perspectives in Policing*. Retrieved online at https://www.ncjrs.gov/pdffiles1/nij/245992.pdf, p. 12.

69. Aristotle. (2000). Politics. Trans. by Jowett, B. New York, NY: Dover Publications, p. 29.

70. Madison J. (1788/1961). No, 51, Madison. *In The federalist papers*. C. Rossiter (Ed.). New York, NY: New American Library, p. 324.

71. Currant, J. (1972). *Police and law enforcement*, 1973-1974. Vol. II. New York, NY: AIMS Press, Inc., p. 112.

72. Goldstein, H. (1977). *Policing in a free society*. Cambridge, MA: Ballinger.

73. Niederhoffer, A. & Blumberg, A. (1976). *The ambivalent force: Perspectives on the police*. 2nd ed. Hinsdale, IL: Dryden Press, p. 64.

74. Rhodes, T.N. (2015). Officers and school settings: Examining the influence of the school environment on officer roles and job satisfaction. *Police Quarterly*, 18, 134-162.

75. Bittner, E. (1974). Florence Nightingale in search of Willie Sutton: A theory of police. In H. Jacob (Ed.), *The Potential for Reform in Criminal Justice*, pp. 17-44. Beverly Hills, CA: Sage Publications; Klockars, C.B. (1980). The Dirty Harry problem. *Annals of the American Academy of Political and Social Scences*, 452, 33-47.

76. Bittner, E. (1970). *The functions of the police in modern society*. Chevy Chase, MD: National Institute of Mental Health; Goldstein, H. (1977). *Policing in a free society*. Cambridge, MA: Ballinger.

77. Karn, J. (2013). *Policing and crime reduction: The evidence and its implications for practice*. Washington, DC: Police Foundation; Manning, P.K. (1978). The police: Mandate, strategies and appearance. In P.K. Manning & J. Van Maanen (Eds.), *Policing: A view from the streets* (pp. 7-31). Santa Monica, CA: Goodyear.

78. Cordner, G. (2010). *Reducing fear of crime: Strategies for police*. Washington, DC: Office of Community Oriented Policing, U.S. Department of Justice.

79. Wilson, J.Q. (1968). *Varieties of police behavior*. Cambridge, MA: Harvard University Press.

80. Goldstein, H. (1977). *Policing in a free society*. Cambridge, MA: Ballinger; Wilson, J.Q. (1968). *Varieties of police behavior*. Cambridge, MA: Harvard University Press.

81. Wilson, J.Q. (1968). *Varieties of police behavior*. Cambridge, MA: Harvard University Press.

82. Wilson, J.Q. (1968). *Varieties of police behavior*. Cambridge, MA: Harvard University Press.

83. Hassell, K., Zhao, J., & Maguire, E. (2003). Structural arrangements in large municipal police organizations: Revisiting Wilson's theory of local political culture. *Policing: An International Journal of Police Strategy & Management*, 26, 231-250; Liederback, J. &

Travis, L.F. (2008). Wilson redux: Another look at varieties of police behavior. *Police Quarterly, 11,* 447-467; Zhao, J., He, N., & Lovrich, N. (2006). Effect of local political culture on policing behaviors in the 1990s: A retest of Wilson's theory in more contemporary times. *Journal of Criminal Justice, 34,* 569-578; Zhao, J., Ren, L., & Lovrich, N. (2010). Wilson's theory of local political culture revisited in today's police organizations: Findings from longitudinal panel study. *Policing: An International Journal of Police Strategies & Management, 33,* 287-304.

84. Collins, F.L. (1924). A professor who cleaned up a city. *Collier's,* November 8, 12, & 37, at p. 12.

85. Hargrove, E.C. &Glidewell, J.C. (1990). *Impossible jobs in public management.* Lawrence, KS: University Press of Kansas.

■ *"From one end of the country to the other we have notice[d] that the old-time policeman is doomed and a new type is being developed."*[1] —*August Vollmer*

Police Chief August Vollmer of the Berkeley (CA) Police Department, "The Father of American Policing."

CHAPTER 2

History

After reading this chapter, you will be able to:

1. Describe the development of societies and the associated changes in the development of the police.
2. Explain the influence of English policing on American policing.
3. Summarize the development of the police in the English system of policing.
4. Identify the four eras of policing in America.
5. Discuss the political era of policing as it relates to the spoils and patronage systems.
6. Explain the motivation for change in policing during the reform era.
7. Detail the importance of police-community relations as it relates to the development of community policing in the community era.
8. Examine the significant impact that the terrorist attacks of September 11, 2001 had on American policing and the changes it has made in policing during the security era.

The father of American policing, August Vollmer, wrote the opening quote of this chapter in 1931 as he was reflecting on the changes he had witnessed in policing throughout his 27-year career as police chief of the Berkeley, California, Police Department. Vollmer was highlighting the fact that policing in the early twentieth century was vastly different from that of the nineteenth century, for policing had undergone some serious changes. One could easily say that this sentiment equally holds true for policing today, considering that policing in the twenty-first century is very different from policing in the twentieth century.[2] Political, economic, social, and technological factors all come to bear on societal changes, and as a result, the police change along with the rest of society. In the twentieth century, even as late as 1999, it was uncommon to see a citizen, let alone a police officer, with a cell phone.[3] Today, however, the cell phone is a ubiquitous communication device and police officers, like most citizens, depend upon them to do their job.[4]

While policing has undergone numerous changes in the twenty-first century, policing is rooted in long-held traditions that still influence the police officers and police departments of today. As Brian MacDonald, who came from a family of three generations of New York City police officers, wrote in his book *My Father's Gun*, "Some sixty years after my grandfather's death, over thirty years since my father retired, and not some twelve years since my brother left the job, we are still a family delineated by the badge and gun of the NYPD."[5] Just as the history of policing in McDonald's family shapes them today, policing of the past helps define American policing today. This is why noted police historian Samuel Walker said the police are "to a great extent, the prisoners of the past. Day-to-day practices are influenced by deeply ingrained traditions."[6] It is important, then, to understand how these deeply ingrained traditions have shaped and changed the mission, duties, and structure of policing across time which gave us the system of policing we know today.

The development of policing in America is wholly rooted in the English tradition of policing, but before we start there, it is important to understand how policing developed in the modern world, across time. Early societies had no need for a formal police force, but as they grew and developed the police became necessary for societies to survive. Because America was an English colony, during the 169 years of British rule the American style of policing closely followed the English style of policing. Once America began adopting its own police departments, it developed a system that was very unique and American-centric, and one that has passed through many changes over time. To convey this heritage of policing, Chapter 2 first details how societies develop and, in particular, how they develop the need for police. Then, because of the influence of English policing on American policing, it uses the evolution of policing in England as its prime example. Finally, it focuses on specific development of policing in America by framing the history in what have been called the four eras of American policing: political, reform, community, and security.[7]

Societies and the Development of the Police

In 1997, a professor of geography by the name of Jared Diamond published what has to be one of the best titles for an academic book ever written: *Guns, Germs, and Steel*, which was subtitled *The Fates of Human Societies*.[8] Not only was the title well received, but so was the book, for it won the Pulitzer Prize, one of the most coveted of publishing awards. The book's title is actually a reference to why some societies flourish and grow, while others remain stagnant or limited in scope. Diamond argues that those societies that manage to build superior weapons and militaries (guns), have natural immunities to diseases or develop them through medicine/science (germs), and build strong centralized governments that promote national industries (steel) are the societies that thrive. Conversely, those societies with weak militaries, no immunity to diseases, and the inability to build centralized governments remain limited. This explains why there are some dominant countries in the world like the United States and China, while there are still small bands and tribes such as those living in South America's Amazon and the primitive Fayu Band, which still exists today in New Guinea, just north of Australia.

Diamond further explains that all of these societies once existed as **bands**, but some continued to develop into **tribes**, then **chiefdoms**, and finally **states**, the last being another way of saying a centralized form of government—a country. One of the things he mentions as a distinguishing factor for knowing the difference is whether there exists in these societies a professional police force. He says that "Modern American society and the Fayu differ in the presence or absence of a *professional police force*, cities, money, distinctions between rich and poor, and many other political, economic, and social institutions."[9] Therefore, understanding the four types of societies that Diamond talks about in *Guns, Germs, and Steel* helps us to understand how and why police departments came into existence.

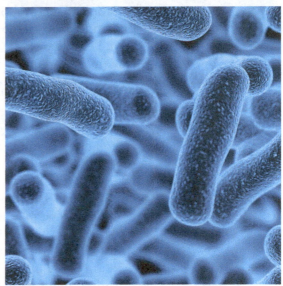

Bands

The population of bands only number in the dozens, they are family based, and tend to be nomadic. They are often referred to as "hunters and gatherers" by anthropologists. Most humans lived this way dating back 40,000 years ago, and even as recently as 11,000 years ago, this was still the primary way most people lived in the world. Leadership tended to be, what Diamond calls, *egalitarian*, meaning "there is no formalized social stratification into upper and lower classes, no formalized or hereditary leadership, and no formalized monopolies of information and decision making."[10] Yet, he also points out that this does not mean that everyone is equal in this type of society, it is just that there is no formalization of leadership and power. The key for us to understand is how these societies' leadership resolved conflicts, something our modern laws and police are most often tasked to do for us today. In the bands, there were "no formal institutions, such as laws, *police*, and treaties to resolve conflicts within and between bands."[11] This meant that conflict resolution was informal and handled by the members of the bands themselves, generally on the spot, and by whatever means necessary.

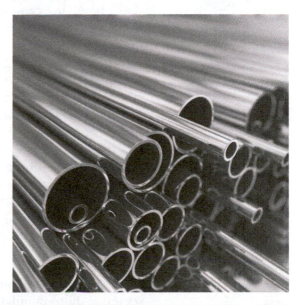

According to Jared Diamond, the three building blocks for successful nations are guns, germs, and steel.

Tribes

Tribes are a development beyond the bands, in that they tend to number in the hundreds, have more fixed settlements (villages), and are kin based, meaning they are generally based on extended family associations being "related to everyone else, by blood, marriage, or both."[12] They remain egalitarian as Diamond discussed, but they often have a tribal leader—a chief or "big-man." In regard to conflict resolution, Diamond points to the relationships among the tribe as being the key: "Those ties of relationship binding all tribal members make *police*, laws, and other conflict-resolving institutions of larger societies unnecessary, since any two villagers getting into an argument will share many kin, who apply pressure on them to keep it from becoming violent."[13] The English historian Charles Reith called this type of policing **kin policing** which he described as a "force exercised indirectly by the people, from below, upwards."[14] Despite the name *kin policing*, however, as Diamond explains, "like bands, tribes lack a...*police force*."[15]

Chiefdom

Chiefdoms grow larger than tribes and tend to number in the thousands, although they still remain fixed in villages. They also tend to develop class relationships between the rich and the poor, thus they are no longer egalitarian. They also create a more centralized hierarchy of government and leadership which is often hereditary (for example, kings and queens). Because chiefdoms tend to grow larger and the bonds of the people are no longer based on kinship, other institutions have to step in to control people and deal with conflict resolution, such as religion, for "religion helps solve the problem of how unrelated individuals are to live together without killing each other—by providing them with a bond not based on kinship."[16] The other mechanism that chiefdoms can employ are the formalization of the informal means of social control. The best example of this can be found in England, which put into place after the Norman conquest of 1066 the **frankpledge system.**[17]

In the frankpledge system, small groups (bands) were placed into a *tithing*—a collection of ten men and their families—who would be responsible for each other, and a leader, the *tithingman*, would be responsible for conflict resolution within the group. The tithings were then collected into groups of ten called the *hundred*, a sort of tribe; and the head of the hundred was the *hundredman*, who was responsible for dealing with conflicts between tithings. The multiple hundreds then collectively served as a chiefdom. The frankpledge system is really a great example of a chiefdom taking the informal means of control that had existed in the bands and tribes and formalizing them for purpose of social control.

State

The development of a society into a state is the final movement into modern society, where populations grow into the multiple thousands, all living in towns and cities, which tend to become more *non*-egalitarian all the time. The government becomes highly formalized through a centralized hierarchy, with leaders that are generally elected, and bureaucracies that specialize in a particular service (such as the police). In the case of conflict resolution, laws are created, judges are appointed, and a police force is established. This is the modern government that surrounds all of us, all of the time, at all levels: local (the approximately 20,000 cities and just over 3,000 counties in the United States), state (all 50), and national (the federal government).

These police forces do not, however, develop overnight as societies transition from chiefdoms to states, but rather, they take time to develop and grow. Our very own police system in the United States was brought over with the English when America was nothing but an English colony beginning in 1607 with the settling of Jamestown in Virginia. Which means that to understand our system of policing in America, we must first begin with the English system of policing the modern state.

The English System of Policing

The antecedents of policing in the English system began with the previously mentioned Norman Conquest of 1066. In the aftermath of the invasion, as the Normans increased the power of the State, they added to the frankpledge system over the next two hundred years and formalized the changes with the Statute of Winchester in 1285.[18] They first established a **night watch** to protect the interests of the cities. At first, the position was mandatory service for all adult males, but this was an inconvenience, so many did not show or they paid for a substitute. Needless to say, the quality of substitutes was so poor it left one newspaper to state that "Since substitutes have been allowed, the patrol is composed principally of the most worthless part of the community, not to use a more appropriate term. It is like setting wolves to guard the sheep."[19] In time, the position was changed to a lowly paid position.

The night watchman was tasked with watching for enemy attacks, fires which threatened the towns and cities made entirely of wood, and alerted the populace to crimes by raising the **hue and cry**.[20] This amounted to shouting for help when trouble was at hand, and calling upon the people to assist in dealing with the problem. The night watch also performed mundane tasks, such as lighting the lamps at night. Soon after, a day watch was added, known

Charlie Rouse was one of the last of the old watchmen, armed with a rattle, truncheon, and cutlass in London, England. Photo courtesy of the Library of Congress.

as the **ward**, and it was responsible for similar activities during the daytime, but also picked up the duties of clearing refuse so as to protect against diseases.

The members of the watch-and-ward were typically of very low quality, due in part to their low pay and the nature of the work. They were often ridiculed and held in contempt, "due to the unfortunate reputation they had acquired of being old, decrepit, lazy, drunk, corrupt, and ineffectual."[21] One contemporary author, Smollett, had one of his literary characters explain, "I start every hour from my sleep, at the horrid noise of the watchmen bawling the hour through every street, and thundering at every door; a set of useless fellows, who serve no other purpose but that of disturbing the repose of the inhabitants."[22] There was, however, much truth in the complaints.

To supervise those in the watch and ward, the most capable of them was appointed to the role of **constable**, but they were only paid slightly better than their peers. The constable was generally assigned to a very large district, and it was not unheard of for a constable to supervise upward of a 100 watchmen, meaning they too were ineffective in their job. So, it is not surprising that they too were equally derided in the literature of the time, for even William Shakespeare ridiculed the constable through his character Constable Dogberry in the play *Much Ado About Nothing*. Shakespeare's description of the bumbling constable was so accurate that "the name Dogberry has itself come to mean any foolish, blundering, or stupid official"[23] (see Box 2.1).

Box 2.1 History of Policing: *Much Ado About Nothing* and the English Constable

The ineptitude of the English **constables** was well documented in the literature of the time. In the Shakespeare play *Much Ado About Nothing,* written in 1598, one of the most memorable characters is Constable Dogberry. Dogberry is the constable over a district in Messina, Sicily, and his intelligence is little better than his men, but Dogberry tries to sound intelligent. As a result, he often uses words in the wrong manner. Although they sound right, they are incorrect, which is known in English literature as a *malapropism*, but to many, because of Shakespeare, it has come to be known as a **Dogberryism**. In one case he speaks of his sidekick, Verges, "Goodman Verges, sir, speaks a little off the matter—an old man, sir, and his wits are not so *blunt.*" What he meant to say was sharp. In another exchange, he explains, "Our watch, sir, have indeed *comprehended* two *auspicious* persons, and we would have them this morning examined before your worship." Dogberry was trying to say that they had apprehended two suspicious persons, not that they understood two successful persons. And in another line, Dogberry states "O Villain! Thou wilt be condemned into everlasting *redemption* for this." He meant to say "damnation."

The Sheriff

While the constable and watch-and-ward system provided some means of protection within the towns and cities, and the frankpledge system provided a mechanism for handling disputes among the people, one position was added to protect the King's interests throughout England and that was the appointment of the **shire-reeve**, more commonly known as the **sheriff.** Since the early 1200s, the story of Robin Hood robbing from the rich and giving to the poor made famous the Sheriff of Nottingham, who relentlessly pursued Robin Hood. The sheriff, in many ways, is portrayed quite accurately, for the shire-reeve was appointed by the King and responsible for protecting the King's interest in their assigned county. The sheriff collected taxes, held court for minor crimes, and was responsible for investigating cases, including those brought to him by the constable. The sheriff, however, did not typically become involved in crimes unless they affected the crown in some manner, such as dereliction of paying taxes or poaching on the King's property. The latter problem would also motivate the king to create another law enforcement position known as the **royal forester,** later becoming the **royal gameskeeper**, the precursor to modern-day game wardens.[24]

The Thief-Takers

The sheriff, constable, and watch-and-ward system were fully implemented by the late 1200s and would remain the primary method for dealing with crime and disorder in England from the fourteenth through the eighteenth centuries. Little changed over this 500-year period, but come the late 1700s, England had industrialized, the population of the cities increased rapidly, and the problems of crime and disorder rose dramatically. Despite all of these problems, only a few changes emerged as possible solutions.

One attempt at dealing with crime was implemented in 1693 and was formally known as the **parliamentary reward system**, or more popularly as the **thief-taker** system.[25] The system drew on the old adage that "it takes a thief to catch a thief," thus if any thief was willing to "rat out" another thief, the government would pay them for the information. One thief-taker became infamous and was featured in numerous plays and novels, and that was Jonathan Wild. The mid-eighteenth-century author Henry Fielding, author of *Tom Jones*, also penned his own novel on Wild titled *The Life of Mr. Jonathan Wild the Great*.[26] While the system worked well to some degree (although not so much for Wild, as he was himself ratted out and eventually hanged for his crimes), it did not alleviate the problems of crime and quickly fell into disuse.[27]

Bow Street Runners

The author of the book on Wild, Henry Fielding, was not altogether successful as a writer, and so he studied law and became a lawyer. He was appointed in 1748, as the Magistrate for the Bow Street District in London, England.

Henry Fielding (1707–1754) was the magistrate of the Bow Street District in London and created the "Bow Street Runners." He is perhaps more famous for the novel *Tom Jones.*

Fielding then did something unusual. Rather than wait for cases to be brought before him, Fielding hired six constables to act as a quasi-police force and investigation unit, which were formerly known as Principal Officers and were initially nicknamed "Mr. Fielding's People," but rather quickly they became known by the more popular appellation of the **Bow Street Runners** (in actuality, a bow street runner was a rank of the Principal Officers).[28] Although Henry Fielding died in 1754, his half-brother John succeeded him as magistrate and continued the practice of paying informants, conducting investigations, carrying out criminal raids, posting wanted flyers, registering criminals, having his runners carry firearms and handcuffs, and patrolling Bow Street on horse and foot—all practices of a modern police force. When the new London Metropolitan Police were created in 1829, the days of the Bow Street Runners were numbered.

The London Metropolitan Police

In 1797, another magistrate, Patrick Colquhoun, was inspired by the work of Henry and John Fielding and attempted to resolve a serious crime problem in London's East End. Merchants were losing money from thieves located along the wharfs of the River Thames, so Colquhoun received permission to create his own police force, with 50 officers policing over 30,000 men working the river trade. The police were not well received and numerous skirmishes resulted, including the loss of one officer, but in the end, Colquhoun's police drove down the level of theft and from a cost-benefit standpoint, he was successful—the amount of merchandise recovered far outweighed the cost of the police.

Colquhoun's Marine Police Force (also known as the Thames River Police) was even more successful in the long term for it gave Colquhoun the ability to think about crime, crime prevention, and how best to organize a police force to address the problem of crime. He wrote several books, including a *Treatise on the Police of the Metropolis*, in which he advocated that "police in this country may be considered as a new science…in the prevention and detection of crimes, and in those other functions which related to internal regulations for the well ordering and comfort of civil society."[29] Two decades later, this treatise was read by a member of the British Parliament and would be put into action to create what is generally considered the first modern police department in history.[30]

In 1822, England's Home Secretary, **Robert Peel** was also faced with the problem of rising crime, particularly in London (see Box 2.2). Drawing upon the works of Fielding and Colquhoun, Peel created a proposal for a

Box 2.2 **History in Practice: Robert Peel and the Modern Police Force**

Robert Peel was born on February 5, 1788, in Bury, Lancashire, England. His father was a member of the British Parliament and was officially Sir Robert Peel, 1st Baronet. Highly educated, Peel entered politics like his father at a young age (21) and was eventually appointed as the Chief Secretary in Dublin. There, drawing upon Patrick Colquhoun's writings, he established the Royal Irish Constabulary, men who were later called "**Peelers**." He served through a series of other positions before being name the Home Secretary in 1822. It was in this position, in 1829, that Peel helped to establish the **London Metropolitan Police Force** whose officers became known as "**Bobbies**." Although the police were not well received at first, they did help to reduce crime and, in time, earned a positive reputation. In 1834, Peel became the Prime Minister of England, and then served a second term from 1841-1846. He continued in politics and was knighted with the title of "Sir" for his service to the Crown, which is why he is generally referred to as Sir Robert Peel—although officially Sir Robert Peel, Second Baronet (and his son was dubbed Sir Robert Peel, Third Baronet). On June 29, 1850, Peel was thrown from his horse and died from his injuries three days later.

Watch the modern London Metropolitan Police Commissioner tell the history of Sir Robert Peel at https://www.gov.uk/government/history/past-prime-ministers/robert-peel- 2nd-baronet.

Home Secretary Robert Peel, who created the London Metropolitan Police in 1829.

One of the earliest known photographs of a London Metropolitan Police Officer, known as a "Peeler" and later a "Bobby" after Sir Robert Peel. The photo was taken in the 1850s.

professional police force. Although not well received initially, Peel continued to refine his proposal, which ultimately resulted in the passage of the **Metropolitan Police Act of 1829.**[31] While many previous entities, like the Bow Street Runners, had engaged in police practices, the London Metropolitan Police is generally considered to be the first modern police department in the world.[32] The creation of the police department was narrowly passed, for many people feared that it was yet another military force that would be used against them. In fact, when the organization was not yet a month old, it was being described as a "military body employed in civil duties."[33]

Once the act was passed, Peel was charged with supervising the creation of the new police department, and he made the unusual move of hiring two men to lead the newly formed organization: **Charles Rowan** and **Richard Mayne.** Although it was atypical to place two people in charge of such an organization, it worked, for Rowan brought in his military experience to discipline the new police force (an officer once noted of Rowan, "there never was a stricter disciplinarian"),[34] and Mayne had served as a barrister (lawyer) and understood the complexities of both organization and management. They hired over 1,000 new officers from outside of the city, farm boys mostly, because they made "the best Police men," for they had "not so much to *unlearn*," and they had no political ties, thus avoiding political corruption from the start. These new police officers walking a beat in their new uniforms and shiny badges soon became affectionately known as "Bobbies," named for the first police department's founder, Robert Peel, later *Sir* Robert Peel (see Box 2.3).

The impact of England's form of policing on America was profound. For all intents and purposes, at least until July 4, 1776, America was England and, as a result, emulated the style of policing found in England. Among the 13 original colonies could be found the sheriff, constables, and the watch-and-ward system in various towns and cities. After America declared itself independent of England, not much changed, at least not in the new 13 states. At the national level, through the Judiciary Act of 1789, the office of the United States Federal Marshal was created, but their primary function was to serve the courts in the territorial possessions, land owned by the United States of America but not yet formed into states. Then, in the 1830s, facing increasing problems of crime and three major riots in four years, Boston (Massachusetts) decided to follow the London model and began to create, in 1838, what was to become the first modern police department in America (see Box 2.4.).[35]

The American System of Policing

Two leading police scholars, Kelling and Moore, in 1988, published a paper that divided American policing into three eras: political, reform, and community.[36] Since then, most police scholars have come to accept these three eras as defining and categorizing the development of American policing across time. More recently, because of the terrorist attacks on September 11, 2001,

Box 2.3 History in Practice: Peel's Principles?

A common feature of any discussion about Sir Robert Peel and the London Metropolitan Police Department is what has come to be known as *Peel's Principles*. This was a list of 9 (sometimes as many as 12) key principles that form the foundation of not only the London Metropolitan Police, but all police departments. Some examples of Peel's Principles include:

- The police must be stable, efficient, and organized along military lines.
- The police must be under government control.
- The distribution of crime news is essential.
- Good appearance commands respect.

The concepts of Peel's Principles surely still apply today, but there is only one problem with calling them Peel's Principles—he didn't write them. Scholars, finding no evidence in Peel's writings that he had crafted this list in advance of the creation of the London Metropolitan Police, have often assumed that Charles Rowan and Richard Mayne wrote them, not Peel. Yet, more recently, in searching for the source of Peel's Principles, several scholars traced the list back to an early twentieth-century author who simply laid out a list of what Peel, Rowan, and Mayne believed a police department should be. Hence, while the list of Peel's Principles is a nice foundational list of what makes a police department a police department, it was the invention of policing textbook authors—a tradition this author chose not to carry on.

Source: Lentz, S.A. & Chaires, R.H. (2007). Invention of Peel's principles: A study of policing textbook history. *Journal of Criminal Justice, 35,* 69-79.

Box 2.4 Policing in Practice: The Patron Saint of the Police and the Blue Mass

It is common among police officers, and not just those of the Catholic faith, to share the imagery of a winged soldier, poised to thrust a sword through a devilish-looking creature, who is pinned to the ground by his foot. The depiction is of **St. Michael the archangel,** who is **the patron saint and protector of police officers**. The image appears on medals, pins, pendants, and prayer cards that police officers share with one another as a sign of respect, honor, and to pray for their protection as they perform their duties.

In the Catholic Church's calendar of Saints, the Church honors St. Michael on September 29, and historically, dating back to the middle ages, the day was referred to as *Michaelmas*. In more recent times, many Catholic Church's throughout America offer what is referred to as a Blue Mass, a special service to honor those who wear they blue of policing, which is commonly held on the feast day of the patron saint of policing. It was started by the Reverend Thomas Dade and was first held on September 29, 1934, at St. Patrick's Catholic Church in Washington, D.C.

In addition to the imagery of St. Michael as the patron saint of the police, very often the famous prayer to St. Michael created by Pope Leo XIII is included:

St. Michael the Archangel, defend us in battle. Be our defense against the wickedness and snares of the Devil. May God rebuke him, we humbly pray, and do thou, O Prince of the heavenly hosts, by the power of God, thrust into hell Satan, and all the evil spirits, who prowl about the world, seeking the ruin of souls. Amen.

Table 2.1	The Four Eras of Policing			
Elements	**Political Era**	**Reform Era**	**Community Era**	**Homeland Security Era**
Authorization	Politics and law	Law and professionalism	Community support (political), law, professionalism	National/International threats (politics), law (intergovernmental), professionalism
Function	Broad social services	Crime control	Broad, provision of service	Crime control, antiterrorism / counterterrorism, intelligence gathering
Organizational design	Decentralized	Centralized, classical	Decentralized, task forces, matrices	Centralized decision-making, decentralized execution
Relationship to environment	Intimate	Professionally remote	Intimate	Professional
Demand	Decentralized, to patrol and politicians	Centralized	Decentralized	Centralized
Tactics and technology	Foot patrol	Preventive patrol and rapid response to calls for service	Foot patrol, problem solving, etc.	Risk assessment, police operations centers, information systems
Outcome	Citizen political satisfaction	Crime control	Quality of life and citizen satisfaction	Citizen safety, crime control, antiterrorism

Sources: Kelling, G.L. & Moore, M.H. (1988). The evolving strategy of policing. *Perspectives on Policing no. 4.* Washington, DC: National Institute of Justice; Oliver, W.M. (2005). The era of homeland security: September 11, 2001 to...*Crime & Justice International, 21,* 9-17.

and the development of the concepts and structure of homeland security, some scholars have argued we have moved beyond the community era and are now in an era of security.[37] Understanding these four eras and what each entails is the subject matter for the rest of this chapter (see Table 2.1).

The Political Era (1830–1930)

The political era of American policing is considered to range from the 1830s through the 1920s. While this is nearly one hundred years of history, little changed in the political orientation of policing during this time period. Kelling and Moore commence the era by specifically focusing on the creation of the first modern police force in America, the Boston Police Department (1838).[38] Only a handful of police departments followed, such as New York and Cincinnati, and as police historian E. H. Monkkonen explained, "The complete transition from the constable-watch system to the uniformed police took two decades in Boston, 1838–1859; a decade in New York, 1843–1853; and 11 years in Cincinnati, 1848–1859."[39] Very few police departments were

Box 2.5 Samuel Battle: The NYPD's First Black Police Officer

Samuel "Big Sam" Battle was born on January 16, 1883, in New Bern (NC), and he weighed sixteen-and-a-half pounds, simply a precursor to the imposing stature he reached as a man—6 feet, 3 inches tall, and weighing 280 pounds. He was his father's 22nd child and his mother's 11th, and "as a member of his family's first postslavery generation," his biographer explains, "Battle was freer to be a boy, not a *boy*." That did not mean, however, that he would not face his own trials and tribulations for being the first black police officer on an all-white police force in New York city when he joined in 1911. Again, as his author explained, "When Samuel Battle broke the color line as New York City's first African American cop in the second decade of the twentieth century, he had to fear his racist colleagues as much as criminals." Despite everything being against him, he stayed the course and did his job and navigated the overt and covert racism of the time period. Gradually, he began to win over his fellow officers and was eventually given the vote to attend the Sergeant's Academy (1926). As if he had not already broken enough barriers, he was later promoted to become NYPD's first black lieutenant on the force (1935). He then had one more barrier to break when he was elevated to become the parole commissioner in 1941.

Battle, over the course of his career, had come to know the American poet, novelist, and playwright Langston Hughes, who was himself breaking barriers in his own field. Battle convinced Langston to write his biography. Despite making a good start at it, unable to find a publisher, the project languished. Samuel Battle died on August 7, 1966, and the following year, Langston Hughes died. The man who was so deserving of a biography, did not see one published in his lifetime, but 50 years later, Arthur Browne, using portions of the Langston Hughes biography, published *One Righteous Man: Samuel Battle and the Shattering of the Color Line in New York*.

Source: Browne, A. (2015). *One righteous man: Samuel Battle and the shattering of the color line in New York.* Boston, MA: Beacon Press.

established during this antebellum period and then the Civil War practically ground their establishment to a halt. However, after the war, and as the country moved out of reconstruction, the establishment of uniformed police departments, according to Monkkonen "happened virtually overnight."[40] The emphasis, however, is on how and why police departments were established in the post–Civil War era and their close ties to politics (see Box 2.5).

It should be noted that the police during the political era did many of the things that are common for police to do today, such as patrolling a beat, responding to crimes, and making arrests. In addition, the police performed functions that would be rather alien to modern-day police departments, such as dealing with stray animals, providing a crude form of counseling, and running soup kitchens, and many agencies such as Boston housed the homeless in their police barracks on cold winter nights when the temperatures dropped below freezing. The primary reason for the police performing these functions is that they were the only service organization operating around the clock that could perform these duties. Eventually, animal control, social workers, and charitable organizations (for example, the Red Cross) came into existence and took over many of the responsibilities the police performed during this era. Despite all of this, however, the police were not truly organized to protect and serve the public, but they were created to protect and serve the political machine.[41]

American politics in the late 1800s was run largely by **political machines**. It was a very corrupt system that did anything and everything to gain power, and once in power, to keep that power. Elections were far more vicious than they are today, with politicians bribing voters with money, liquor, and other forms of vice, and using strongmen and gangs to prevent certain groups from voting—all depending on which party was then in power. There was also a strong relationship between the politicians and businesses, as well as the vice lords. The politicians accepted money from the businessmen to get elected, and once elected, they continued to accept money to prevent any laws from being passed that might hurt those businesses. For instance, if workers wanted to organize into labor unions, businesses would pay the politicians to prevent laws from being passed that would allow such organizations to exist, thus remaining in power by pleasing the businesses. The vice lords, which were running such illegal operations as gambling casinos, brothels, and keeping saloons open on the Sabbath, also had to pay off the politicians to keep their corrupt businesses running so that they could remain open and profitable. At the center of all of this, as an extension of the political machine, were the police.

The police during the political era were simply doing the bidding of the political machine. For instance, if workers wanted to organize a strike or protest against some business, the business owners merely had to notify the politicians who would then dispatch the police to either arrest the strikers, beat them into submission, or both, thus protecting the businessmen's interests and keeping the political machine in power. The political machine also needed a means by which to receive payoffs from the vice lords for them to continue operating. The police became the extortionists for the political machines by telling brothels, gambling halls, and saloons that they had to pay the police weekly for protection, because if they did not, the police would close them down. This money was then funneled up to the political machine, with each layer taking a cut. This form of bribery was known as the **spoils system** ("to the victor goes the spoils").[42] For instance, in Chicago, it was learned that there was a price list for paying off the police. A massage parlor had to pay the police $25 weekly, a brothel between $50 and $100, a gambling hall had to pay $25 per week per gaming table, and for a saloon to open on Sunday it cost $50 per month.[43]

Another system, closely related to the spoils system, was the **patronage system**. In 1894, the Lexow Committee was formed in New York City to probe into the problems of police corruption. The testimony collected exceeded 10,000 pages and the level of extortion by the police was extensive, including bribery, counterfeiting, voter intimidation, scams, election fraud, and brutality. One important discovery by the committee was the realization that not only was there a price list for keeping vice establishments open in New York City, but there was a price list for becoming a police officer and later being promoted within the department. The political patronage system allowed for the mayor to appoint all government officials, including every police officer, but there was a price to pay to the political machine before that could happen. If someone wanted to be a police officer, he had to first pay a $300–$500 bribe. If a police officer wanted to be promoted, "men paid as much as $4,000 to become sergeants and a captaincy routinely costs $12,000—sums that no man could afford himself," much less on a police officer's salary.[44] This is how the famous New York Police Department (NYPD) Detective Thomas Byrnes managed to accumulate a total savings of $600,000 ($16 million in modern dollars) by the time of his forced retirement, all on a $5,000 annual salary.[45]

In addition to both the patronage and spoils system, **police brutality** was a common and related practice. Police often used force on people rather than making an arrest, or they applied force to make some demand on behalf of the political machine, such as busting up a strike or beating up a vice lord who failed to comply with the weekly or monthly

A picture of President Theodore Roosevelt in 1904, eight years after he had served as the chair of the New York City Police Commission.

pay-offs. One rather famous police officer on the NYPD was Inspector Alexander "Clubber" Williams, who on his first day as a police officer sent the two biggest toughs to the hospital to gain control of his new beat. "There is more law in a policeman's nightstick," Clubber, who was aptly named, liked to say, "than in a decision of the Supreme Court."[46]

One other means by which the police employed brutality was through what was known as the **third degree**, a process by which suspects were tortured and beaten to gain a confession.[47] As one retired police captain from the NYPD explained it, "The 'third degree,' too, means rough stuff when required . . . against a hardened criminal. I never hesitated. I've forced confessions—with fist, blackjack, and hose—from men who would have continued to rob and kill if I had not made them talk."[48] The third degree was commonplace, and the police were quite effective at obtaining confessions, whether the person was actually guilty of the crime or not.[49]

The Reform Era (1930–1980)

In light of the control over the police by politicians in the political era, and the corruption and brutality that went with that arrangement, there were many calls for reforming the police in the early twentieth century.[50] It was, however, America's move to Prohibition that would ultimately be the catalyst for reform. As America engaged in the "great experiment" of making the import/export and manufacture/sales of intoxicating liquors illegal, a black market quickly sprang up and the American Mafia rose to power. Instead of curtailing the consumption of illegal alcohol, it appeared to aggravate it, and the police became ever more corrupt and brutal. A national crime commission known as the **Wickersham Commission** was formed in 1928 by President Herbert Hoover and named for its chair—former U.S. Attorney General George Wickersham.[51] The commission's reports confirmed what most Americans already knew—the police in the United States were corrupt and brutal and reforms were badly needed.

The first of the successful reformers and who has since become known as the "father of American policing," was **August Vollmer**, the police chief from Berkeley, California.[52] There was nothing in Vollmer's past to suggest he would make a reform-oriented police chief. He had operated a feed store, served in the Philippines during the Spanish-American War, and was a postal carrier from 1900–1905. After stopping a runaway rail-cart from crashing into a passenger train, Vollmer was asked to run for the position of town marshal in 1905, an election he won by a landslide. Vollmer's predecessor was typical of the political era of policing in that he was corrupt and on the take from the illegal gambling establishments. Everyone wanted Vollmer to clean up the town and close the gambling establishments, and once elected he did something very strange for policing at the time—he actually closed down those establishments.

Vollmer believed that police should enforce the law, but he was also kind and compassionate and believed that the police existed to help the citizens of the community (he once babysat a young boy for a month so his mother could take a job and get on her feet). He was against the political corruption common during that time period and he was vehemently against police use of the third degree. Vollmer said in a 1913 newspaper interview, "I don't believe a police officer should be a brute; nor do I believe in the 'third degree.' I believe a police officer should help those who need help, that the department should help find jobs for the needy, and that wherever there is the slightest doubt in the minds of the officers that a man is guilty, they should give the accused the benefit of that doubt."[53] He was truly a progressive police chief for his time and perhaps even by today's standards.

In his tenure as marshal (1905–1909) and police chief (1909–1932), Vollmer adopted all manner of reforms for his department, including fielding bicycles to all of his officers and creating in-service training and a police academy. He developed preservice screening of officers by using a variety of tests including the Army alpha intelligence test. He was one of the earliest police chiefs to hire women and minority officers (see Box 2.6). He created the first crime lab in the United States when he served as the Los Angeles police chief for one year (1923–1924). It was there that he also created a rapid-response tactical unit and the process of analyzing crimes by locations, today known as "hot spot" policing. Several of his most significant

Box 2.6 History in Practice: The First Female Police Officer — Wells, Baldwin, or Owens?

During the reform era, many Progressive police chiefs, such as August Vollmer, began hiring **female police officers**. Up until the early 20th Century, policing was solely a male profession with some departments hiring what were called, "Police Matrons"—women who did not have full police powers but assisted with female offenders and juveniles. While Vollmer hired the first female police officer in 1925, others had hired female officers earlier.

For many years, **Alice Stebbins Wells**, who was hired by the Los Angeles Police Department in 1910, was considered the first female police officer in American history. Eventually, it was learned that the City of Portland (OR) had sworn-in **Lola Greene Baldwin** as a police officer in 1908, and many thought she was the first female police officer. That was, at least, until a retired DEA agent by the name of Rick Barrett was researching his family's history with the Chicago PD and discovered that Marie Owen had been hired by the Chicago Police Department as a police officer in the 1890s!

Marie Owens was the daughter of an Irish-famine immigrant who moved to Ottawa, Canada. After marrying, her husband Thomas moved the family to Chicago, but he contracted typhoid fever and died in 1888. Marie was left alone to raise their five children. Needing a job, she found one in 1889 with the City of Chicago's health department. At that time, the enforcement of child-labor laws became a chief concern of the city and Owens was transferred to the police department in 1891. She was sworn in as a detective sergeant and was given a police star. She retired in 1923, after 32 years with the police department, and died in 1927 at the age of 74.

The debate over Owens being the first police officer centers on her role and title. She worked with juveniles and women, but was a detective sergeant. Was she a police officer or a police matron? Although more evidence is needed, we should at least now ask who was first, Wells, Baldwin, or Owens?

Source: Mastony, C. (2010, Sept. 1). Was Chicago home to the country's 1st female cop? *Chicago Tribune*.

---

impacts on American policing were his role in developing the lie detector (polygraph) and his creation of the first program for police higher education at the University of California at Berkeley.[54] In fact, the reason that you are probably reading this book and majoring in criminal justice is because of Police Chief August Vollmer.

Vollmer was also instrumental in educating many of America's future police chiefs and he influenced them to develop policing as a profession—what has become known as the **professional model** of policing.[55] Vollmer believed that just like doctors, dentists, and lawyers, police officers should be educated first to do their job and that they should have professional standards and a code of ethics. He advocated police education and hoped that one day all police officers would be required to have a bachelor's degree in what was then called "criminology" (which explores theories of why people commit crime), but is today is more commonly called

J. Edgar Hoover, Federal Bureau of Investigation Director from 1924 to 1972.

"criminal justice" (which explores how best to organize to deal with the problems of crime). Many of his police officers went on to advocate the same type of professionalization and reforms as police chiefs, with his most important disciple being **O.W. Wilson.** Wilson held several positions as police chief before becoming the Dean of the School of Criminology at the University of California at Berkeley, and eventually he served eight years as the Superintendent of the Chicago Police Department (1960–1967). He authored *Police Administration*, which became the definitive textbook on the subject for most of the twentieth century, and after conducting a study on police deployment, he realized that single officer patrol cars were a better use of police resources and actually promoted officer safety.[56]

The other individual responsible for the professionalization of the police was August Vollmer's contemporary, **J. Edgar Hoover**, who served as the director of the Federal Bureau of Investigation (FBI) from 1924 until his death in 1972.[57] Hoover also believed that his agents should be professional, well-trained, disciplined, and neither corrupt nor brutal. Hoover was instrumental in the creation of the *Uniform Crime Reports*, an annual publication detailing the amount of crime in the United States, the FBI's "ten most wanted list," and for emphasizing crime fighting over all other duties.[58]

The changes that took place during the reform era caused the police to become more focused through the application of the law, and to prevent corruption and brutality, police organizations became more centralized. As the emphasis was on crime fighting, using the police for **preventive patrol** became common and there was a strong emphasis on applying technology to ensure a **rapid response** by the police.[59] Police communications moved from street-corner call-boxes, to one-way radios, then two-way radios, and eventually the 911 system. Police also began purchasing "police package" vehicles such as the Ford Crown Victoria, the Dodge Dart, and the Chevrolet Caprice with enhanced features that allowed them to drive fast and run continuously. Still further, the use of technology for police detection became common place as crime labs became the norm, fingerprinting technology was applied to police work, and criminal investigation became more specialized (for example, homicide, robbery, burglary, motor vehicle theft). The police, thus, became the experts, and all of this was well represented in the old black-and-white television show, *Dragnet,* when Sergeant Joe Friday would say in an interview, "Just the facts, ma'am." The notion was that the police were the experts and all they needed were the facts of the case to be able to solve it. It turns out that the professionalization of the police had some serious drawbacks—one of them being that it alienated the police from the community.

The Community Era (1980-2001)

Police and community relations began to fall apart in the 1960s, fueled by the baby boom—the largest birth cohort the nation has ever known—and such issues as the Vietnam War, women's rights, civil rights, and campus unrest (the baby boom college students who did not like the traditional ways of college administrators). The police resorted to old tactics to deal with the new problems, and the use of police clubs on college students, spraying protestors with water cannons, and using police dogs to attack civil rights marchers created more animosity between the police and the public. In addition, the police who were now focused primarily on crime fighting found that crime was rising uncontrollably, riots were breaking out all over the country, and the protests continued. The fact that crime was rising and police-community relations were at an all-time low caused many to realize that something had to change, and the answer was to find some way to reestablish police and community relations.[60]

The earliest attempt came out of a conference held at Michigan State University that focused on **police-community relations**.[61] The idea behind the police-community relations movement implemented in the 1960s was to educate police officers on the various populations they police. The belief was that not all people perceive the police the same and that each population had different needs. So, police were educated on various race and ethnic groups, the elderly, youth, and the mentally ill. By better understanding these various populations, the police could improve relations, and some of the programs that resulted were elderly welfare checks and police youth camps.

Another idea was to develop small community teams that would work specific neighborhoods so that all of the officers became long-term members of the community coming to understand the day-in and day-out problems of the specific neighborhood to which they were assigned. This was known as **team policing**.[62] Although team policing was found to decrease fear and improve community relations, it was not highly successful in reducing crime or disorder partly because it did not fit within the model of policing that existed at the time: rapid response and crime fighting. In addition, because it was not traditional police work the officers assigned to team policing units tended to be those close to retirement or who had difficulties operating under traditional patrol methods.[63]

By the late 1970s, there was a realization that much of what police did under the professional model was not successful (see Chapter 9). As a result, people began asking what the police could do to be more successful. This resulted in several ideas. The first was law professor Herman Goldstein's idea about problem-solving policing which has come to be known as **problem-oriented policing** or "POP" in policing circles.[64] Goldstein believed that police responded to calls-for-service and treated them as isolated incidents, with no past and no future. The goal was simply to deal with the problem and move on to the next one. What the police were dealing with were the symptoms of the problem, not the problem itself. It is like taking nighttime medicine for a cold. You are dealing with the symptoms (for example, runny nose, sore throat, coughing, etc.), not the underlying problem which is the virus or bacterial infection. If police applied a problem-solving method to calls-for-service that they receive all the time, such as a domestic dispute at the same house every Friday night, not only would they solve the problem, but once solved, they would not have to return to the same house for the same call every week.

The other idea actually came in an article in *The Atlantic Monthly* by two scholars, James Q. Wilson and George L. Kelling. They proposed the **broken windows theory** which posited that when a neighborhood is not well kept (people don't fix their broken windows) it sends a signal to people that no one cares about the neighborhood.[65] This invites additional problems, such as more broken windows, abandoned cars, graffiti, etc., which eventually leads to more serious crime. The best way to prevent crime is for people to take ownership in their neighborhood and call the police for abandoned cars, call public works to fill the potholes in their streets, and to get rid of graffiti as fast as it goes up. If the neighborhood is already crime ridden, then the goal is to clean up the neighborhood, drive out the criminal element, and get people to take a renewed interest in their neighborhood. One program known as **weed and seed** is a good example of this concept because it is based on the idea that one has to weed the garden before one plants the seeds, so the police and community must drive out the criminal element and clean up the neighborhood to get people to take an interest in reclaiming their neighborhood.[66]

The overall result of both of these ideas developed into the concept of community-oriented policing or **community policing**.[67] Under community policing, the police and community work together in partnership to identify and solve problems that involve crime (for example, drug dealing, prostitution) and public disorder (for example, graffiti, abandoned cars, potholes). Programs that bring the police and community closer together include such things as foot patrols and bicycle patrols, permanent assignment of police officers to specific neighborhoods, and informational meetings between the police and community members. Community policing, like team policing before it, has been successful in reducing fear of crime and increasing public satisfaction with the police, but there is scant evidence that it has in fact reduced crime.[68]

The community policing era is said to have progressed through three generations: innovation, diffusion, and institutionalization.[69] The first generation, innovation, took place in the early 1980s, as a few police departments tried adopting community policing and problem-oriented policing, usually in one or two neighborhoods to see what the results were. By the late 1980s and early 1990s, community policing moved into the diffusion stage as police departments across the country began to adopt various aspects of community policing ranging from foot patrols to permanent beat assignments and neighborhood substations to problem-oriented policing. In 1994, the federal government signed into law the Violent Crime Control and Law Enforcement Act of 1994, known as the **COPS Bill,** which created funding for police departments nationwide to hire new police officers and deploy new technology for creating or enhancing their community policing programs.[70] As a result of the over $8.8 billion in funding, community policing became common—or institutionalized—throughout the United States. There is a good chance that your local police department or your university police were recipients of a COPS grant.

The Security Era (2001-present)

On September 11, 2001, when 19 members of Al-Qaeda hijacked four airplanes and crashed two into the twin towers of the World Trade Center in New York City, one into the Pentagon in Arlington, Virginia (where the Arlington County Police were the first to respond), and one into a field near Shanksville, Pennsylvania, because of the bravery of those onboard (the plane was believed to have been heading for the U.S. Capitol or the White House), America and its police entered the era of homeland security. Ever since those tragic events, which for many of you may only be vague memories, America has been ever vigilant against further terrorist attacks and it has created a large mechanism called **homeland security.**[71] While many do think of homeland security as being primarily focused on the Department of Homeland Security created in 2002, homeland security also means the entire network and infrastructure of federal, state, and local assets that are focused on protecting America's homeland. That includes the police.

Ever since September 11, 2001, the police have experienced many changes in adapting to their role in homeland security, and as a result, while the concepts of community policing have not been entirely abandoned, policing has moved into an era of homeland security. Police departments across the country have developed homeland security bureaus or units, and states have created offices of homeland security with roles assigned usually to the state police. All police agencies are moving toward learning how better to respond to both terrorist attacks and natural disasters through what is known as the **National Response Framework**—a set of guiding principles for coordinating the response of all agencies—and through the **National Incident Management System**—a structured framework for all federal, state, and local government agencies that will respond to such attacks/disasters.[72] The most important aspect of this last system is learning the **Incident Command System,** which is how police and other emergency response agencies such as fire departments and emergency medical

U.S. Department of Homeland Security, Customs, and Border Protection federal law enforcement officers.

teams organize their response.[73] The system consists of a management staff to handle large scale incidents and includes such positions as the incident commander and his or her staff—someone in charge of personnel, operations, logistics, and finances.

In addition to being prepared for terrorist attacks and natural disasters, the police have also been involved in developing new ways for sharing information and turning that information into actionable intelligence through analysis. This method has come to be known as **intelligence-led policing**. One way in which the police share information regarding potential threats is through **fusion centers**.[74] Located throughout the United States, these fusion centers are a way for agencies to share and obtain information related to various terroristic threats. *A Congressional Investigation of the Fusion Centers*, published in 2012, however, found that there was no evidence of any fusion center uncovering a terroristic threat or plot and most of the reports they issued were focused on criminal activity, mostly pertaining to drugs and human smuggling.[75]

The police have also been involved in **joint terrorism task forces**.[76] These task forces generally consist of federal, state, and local police agencies, conducting investigations into potential terror threats. They are almost always comprised of the FBI, which is the lead agency in the United States for investigating terror threats and the local police agency where the investigation is being conducted. The benefit of the joint terrorism task force is to enhance communications between the agencies and to overcome the problems of jurisdiction. Finally, while many police departments have created **counterterrorism units** in their police departments, many of these tend to be minimally staffed and often serve as a point of contact for receiving threat information and coordinating with the fusion centers.[77] In very few cases do the counterterrorism units consist of a tactical unit that could respond to terror threats and attacks, such as the NYPD's counterterrorism unit.

Conclusion

Primitive societies do not need a formal police force, for they have other mechanisms for social control. Once a society becomes a state, however, these mechanisms no longer suffice and a new institution, the police, must be developed to preserve the peace and deal with criminal matters. The American system of policing is almost entirely based on the English system, both early and modern. The early forms of policing that England instituted, such as the watch, the ward, the constable, the sheriff, and the game warden, were all emulated in America when it was part of England, and even after it declared itself independent. Then, beginning in the late 1830s, with America facing its own crime problems, cities began creating police departments modeled loosely on the London model.

American policing then moved through a political era, where the police served as an extension of the political machines, and graft, corruption, and brutality were endemic. Then, under the example of Police Chief August Vollmer, American policing underwent a series of reforms, attempting to eliminate politics from policing, to educate police officers, and to focus on crime control. In the 1960s, when the focus on professionalism and technology created a divide between the police and the community, the community era became the focus of the police in the late twentieth century, where police focused on its relationship with the community by becoming problem solvers and working alongside the community. Then came September 11, 2001, and America turned toward focusing on security against terrorism, and the police became more security-minded.

Just the Facts

1. The development of societies progresses through four stages: bands, tribes, chiefdoms, and states. Formal police forces were only developed in the last stage, states.

2. America was originally established as 13 colonies of Great Britain, so America was England. By virtue of that fact, transported to the new world were the police practices common at the time in England: the watch, the ward, the constable, and the sheriff. America had a crime problem in the 1830s. Particularly in Boston, there were three major riots between 1834 and 1838. A solution to this problem was found across the Atlantic with the relatively new civilian police force created in London, England, by Robert Peel, the London Metropolitan Police.

3. The four eras of police in America have been identified as the political, reform, community, and (homeland) security.

4. When policing developed in America in the 1800s, predominately in the late 1800s, local political machine politics were at their height. Whichever party sat in elected office wielded enormous money from corporate powers attempting to protect their enterprises and from corrupt activities that paid graft money to remain in business. As police departments were created, they became the natural extension of the political machine by funneling graft money to the political machine and punishing those who failed to pay.

5. The political machines became too powerful and corrupt in America by the early twentieth century, and there were calls for removing politics from government services like the police. This launched the era of reform in American policing.

6. By the mid-twentieth century, America's diversity began placing strains on the police, and the police-community relations movement was designed to educate the police about the needs of the various populations it policed. This eventually developed into the community era when the varying needs of each community, down to the neighborhood level, were taken into consideration for improved policing by having the police and community work in partnership to solve the problems of crime and social disorder.

7. The terrorist attacks of September 11, 2001, severely challenged American's sense of security, and governments moved quickly to try to enhance American security post-attacks to include authorizing the police more powers to investigate terrorist activity and crime.

Ask Yourself

1. Is it possible that after the creation of a state, for the old ways of the band, tribe, or chiefdoms, to still work so as to avoid the development of formal police departments, or are modern police departments absolutely necessary in our society?

2. Considering the early English methods of policing, what are the relationships between government protecting the people and the people protecting themselves? Who is ultimately responsible for the protection of individuals? Who is ultimately responsible for the protection of society?

3. Think of the critical role that police reformers such as Police Chief August Vollmer had in fundamentally changing American policing. Compare and contrast American policing before and after Chief Vollmer.

4. The community era was based on the concept that the police and community should work in partnership to solve the problems of crime and disorder. What are the problems associated with the police and who are agents of government working so closely with the people? What are the problems associated with getting the people to work with the police?

5. Since September 11, 2001, the emphasis in American policing has been on improving security, ranging from the police use of databases, license plate readers, drones, SWAT teams, etc. Does the increase of police (government) power make us more secure? Does it make us more free?

Keywords

Band
Bow Street Runners
Broken windows
Chiefdom
Community policing
Constable
COPS Bill
Counterterrorism units
Frankpledge system
Fusion centers
Homeland Security
Hoover, J. Edgar
Hue and cry
Incident Command System (ICS)
Intelligence-led policing
Joint Terrorism Task Force (JTTF)

Kin policing
Metropolitan Police Act of 1829
National Incident Management System (NIMS)
National Response Framework (NRF)
Night watch
Patronage system
Peel, Robert
Police brutality
Police-community relations
Political machine
Preventive patrol
Problem-oriented policing
Professional model of policing
Rapid response

Rowan, Charles and Richard Mayne
Royal forester/gameskeeper
Sheriff
Shire-reeve
Spoils system
State
Team policing
Third degree
Three generations
Tribe
Vollmer, August
Ward
Weed and seed
Wickersham Commission
Wilson, O.W.

Endnotes

1. Vollmer, A. (1931). Police education. *Journal of Criminal Law and Criminology, 22,* 7-8.

2. Stone, C. & Travis, J. (2011). Toward a new professionalism in policing. *New Perspectives on Policing.* Washington, DC: Harvard Kennedy School of Government/National Institute of Justice.

3. Tuckel, P. & O'Neill, H. (2005). Ownership and usage patterns of cell phones: 200-2005. *AAPOR—SAS Section on Survey Research Methods.* Retrieved from www.amstat.org/sections/srms/proceedings/y2005/Files/JSM2005-000345.pdf.

4. Raines, L. (2013). Cell phone ownership hits 91% of adults. *Pew Research Center.* Retrieved from www.pewresearch.org/fact-tank/2013/06/06/cell-phone-ownership-hits-91-of-adults/.

5. McDonald, B. (1999). *My father's gun: One family, three badges, one hundred years in the NYPD.* New York, NY: Plume Books, p. 308.

6. Walker, S. (1983). *The police in America: An introduction.* New York, NY: McGraw-Hill, p. 2.

7. Kelling, G.L. & Moore, M.H. (1988). The evolving strategy of policing. *Perspectives on Policing, No. 4.* Washington, DC: National Institute of Justice; Oliver, W.M. (2006). The fourth era of policing: Homeland security. *International Review of Law, Computers, and Technology, 20,* 49-62; Oliver, W.M. (2009). Policing for homeland security: Policy and research. *Criminal Justice Policy Review, 20,* 253-260.

8. Diamond, J. (1997). *Guns, germs, and steel: The fates of human societies.* New York, NY: W.W. Norton.

9. Diamond, J. (1997). *Guns, germs, and steel: The fates of human societies.* New York, NY: W.W. Norton, p. 267.

10. Diamond, J. (1997). *Guns, germs, and steel: The fates of human societies.* New York, NY: W.W. Norton, p. 269.

11. Diamond, J. (1997). *Guns, germs, and steel: The fates of human societies.* New York, NY: W.W. Norton, p. 268.

12. Diamond, J. (1997). *Guns, germs, and steel: The fates of human societies.* New York, NY: W.W. Norton, p. 271.

13. Diamond, J. (1997). *Guns, germs, and steel: The fates of human societies.* New York, NY: W.W. Norton, p. 271.

14. Reith, C. (1952). *The blind eye of history.* London, England: Faber, p. 20; See also Reith, C. (1938). *The police idea.* Oxford, England: Oxford University Press; Reith, C. (1940). *Police principles and the problem of war.* Oxford, England: Oxford University Press; Reith, C. (1943). *British police and the democratic ideal.* Oxford, England: Oxford University Press; Reith, C. (1948). *A short history of police.* Oxford, England: Oxford University Press.

15. Diamond, J. (1997). *Guns, germs, and steel: The fates of human societies.* New York, NY: W.W. Norton, p. 272.

16. Diamond, J. (1997). *Guns, germs, and steel: The fates of human societies.* New York, NY: W.W. Norton, p. 278.

17. Morris, W.A. (1910). *The frankpledge system.* New York, NY: Longmans, Green, and Co.

18. Oliver, W.M. & Hilgenberg, J.F. (2010). *A history of crime and criminal justice in America.* 2nd ed. Durham, NC: Carolina Academic Press.

19. As cited in Monkkonen, E.H. (1981). *Police in urban America, 1860-1920.* New York, NY: Cambridge University Press, p. 42.

20. Oliver, W.M. & Hilgenberg, J.F. (2010). *A history of crime and criminal justice in America.* 2nd ed. Durham, NC: Carolina Academic Press.

21. McCouat, P. (2014). Watchman, goldfinders, and the plague bearers of the night. *Journal of Art in Society.* Retrieved from www.artinsociety.com/watchmen-goldfinders-and-the-plague-bearers-of-the-night.html

22. McCouat, P. (2014). Watchman, goldfinders, and the plague bearers of the night. *Journal of Art in Society.* Retrieved from www.artinsociety.com/watchmen-goldfinders-and-the-plague-bearers-of-the-night.html

23. McCouat, P. (2014). Watchman, goldfinders, and the plague bearers of the night. *Journal of Art in Society.* Retrieved from www.artinsociety.com/watchmen-goldfinders-and-the-plague-bearers-of-the-night.html

24. Bazeley, M.L. (1921). The extent of the English forest in the thirteenth century. *Transactions of the Royal Historical Society, 4,* 140-172; Kirby, C. (1933). The English game law system. *The American Historical Review, 38,* 240-262; Kirby, C. & Kirby, E. (1931). The Stuart game prerogative. *The English Historical Review, 46,* 239-254; Manning, R.B. (1994). Unlawful hunting in England, 1500-1640. *Forest and Conservation History, 38,* 16-33.

25. Oliver, W.M. & Hilgenberg, J.F. (2010). *A history of crime and criminal justice in America.* 2nd ed. Durham, NC: Carolina Academic Press.

26. Fielding, Henry. (2004). *Jonathan Wild.* New York, NY: Oxford University Press; Fielding, Henry. (2008). *Tom Jones.* New York, NY: Oxford University Press.

27. Howson, G. (1970). *Thief-taker general: Jonathan Wild and the emergence of crime and corruption as a way of life in eighteenth-century England.* New Brunswick, NJ: Transactions, Inc.

28. Beattie, J.M. (2012). *The first English detective: The bow street runners and the policing of London, 1750-1840.* New York, NY: Oxford University Press; Cox, D.J. (2006). *'A certain share of low cunning': An analysis of the work of bow street principal officers 1792-1839 with particular emphasis on their provincial duties.* Unpublished dissertation. Retrieved from http://lib.haifa.ac.il/electronictexts/1409055/1409055.pdf.

29. Colquhoun, P. (1800). *A treatise on the police of the metropolis.* Retrieved online at www.gutenberg.org/files/35650/35650-h/35650-h.htm, p. 8.

30. Colquhoun, P. (1800). *A treatise on the police of the metropolis.* Retrieved online at www.gutenberg.org/files/35650/35650-h/35650-h.htm.

31. Emsley, C. (2009). *The great British bobby: A history of British policing from the 18th century to the present.* London, England: Quercus; Miller, W.R. (1999). *Cops and bobbies: Police authority in New York and London, 1830-1870.* 2nd ed. Columbus, OH: Ohio State University Press.

32. Emsley, C. (2009). *The great British bobby: A history of British policing from the 18th century to the present.* London, England: Quercus; Miller, W.R. (1999). *Cops and bobbies: Police authority in New York and London, 1830-1870.* 2nd ed. Columbus, OH: Ohio State University Press; Walker, S. (1983). *The police in America: An introduction.* New York, NY: McGraw-Hill.

33. Emsley, C. (2009). *The great British bobby: A history of British policing from the 18th century to the present.* London, England: Quercus, p. 46.

34. Miller, W.R. (1999). *Cops and bobbies: Police authority in New York and London, 1830-1870.* 2nd ed. Columbus, OH: Ohio State University Press, *p. 40*

35. Lane, R. (1967). *Policing the city: Boston, 1822-1885.* New York, NY: Atheneum.

36. Kelling, G.L. & Moore, M.H. (1988). The evolving strategy of policing. *Perspectives on Policing, No. 4.* Washington, DC: National Institute of Justice.

37. Oliver, W.M. (2006). The fourth era of policing: Homeland security. *International Review of Law, Computers, and Technology, 20,* 49-62; Oliver, W.M. (2009). Policing for homeland security: Policy and research. *Criminal Justice Policy Review, 20,* 253-260; Schafer, J.A., Burruss, G.W., & Giblin, M.J. (2009). Measuring homeland security innovation in small municipal agencies: Policing in a post-9/11 world. *Police Quarterly, 12,* 263-288.

38. Kelling, G.L. & Moore, M.H. (1988). The evolving strategy of policing. *Perspectives on Policing, No. 4.* Washington, DC: National Institute of Justice.

39. Monkkonen, E.H. (1981). *Police in urban America, 1860-1920.* New York, NY: Cambridge University Press, p. 42.

40. Monkkonen, E.H. (1981). *Police in urban America, 1860-1920.* New York, NY: Cambridge University Press, p. 42.

41. Monkkonen, E.H. (1981). *Police in urban America, 1860-1920.* New York, NY: Cambridge University Press, p. 42.

42. Walker, S. (1997). *Popular justice: A history of American criminal justice.* New York, NY: Oxford University Press.

43. Abbott, K. (2007). *Sin in the second city: Madams, ministers, playboys and the battle for America's soul.* New York, NY: Random House.

44. Dash, M. (2007). *Satan's circus: Murder, vice, police corruption, and New York's trial of the century.* New York, NY: Three Rivers Press, p. 49.

45. Conway, J.N. (2010). *The big policeman: The rise and fall of America's first, most ruthless, and greatest detective.* Guildford, CT: Lyons Press; Dash, M. (2007). *Satan's circus: Murder, vice, police corruption, and New York's trial of the century.* New York, NY: Three Rivers Press.

46. Dash, M. (2007). *Satan's circus: Murder, vice, police corruption, and New York's trial of the century.* New York, NY: Three Rivers Press, p. 50; Monkkonen, E.H. (1981). *Police in urban America, 1860-1920.* New York, NY: Cambridge University Press, p. 39.

47. Skolnick, J.H. & Fyfe, J.J. (1993). *Above the law: Police and the excessive use of force.* New York, NY: Free Press.

48. Willemse, C.W. with G.J. Lemmer & J. Kofoed. (1931). *Behind the green lights.* New York, NY: A.A. Knopf, p. 246.

49. Skolnick, Jerome H. & Fyfe, James J. (1993). *Above the law: Police and the excessive use of force.* New York, NY: The Free Press.

50. Kelling, G.L. & Moore, M.H. (1988). The evolving strategy of policing. *Perspectives on Policing, No. 4.* Washington, DC: National Institute of Justice.

51. National Commission on Law Observance and Enforcement. (1931). *Report on the enforcement of the prohibition laws of the United States.* Washington, DC: U.S. G.P.O.

52. Carte, Gene E. & Elaine H. Carte. (1975). *Police reform in the United States: The era of August Vollmer, 1905-1932.* Berkeley: University of California Press.

53. *The Fort Wayne Sentinel,* October 10, 1913.

54. Alder, K. (2007). *The history of an American obsession: The lie detector.* New York, NY: The Free Press; Oliver, W.M. (2013). *The history of the academy of criminal justice sciences (acjs): Celebrating 50 years, 1963-2013.* Greenbelt, MD: ACJS.

55. Carte, Gene E. & Elaine H. Carte. (1975). *Police reform in the United States: The era of August Vollmer, 1905-1932.* Berkeley: University of California Press.

56. Wilson, O.W. (1972). *Police administration.* New York, NY: McGraw-Hill.

57. Gentry, C. (2001). *J. Edgar Hoover: The man and the secrets.* New York, NY: W.W. Norton & Company.

58. Federal Bureau of Investigation. (2014). A brief history of the FBI. Retrieved from www.fbi.gov/about-us/history/brief-history

59. Hoover, L.T. (2014). *Police crime control strategies.* Clifton Park, NY: Delmar Cengage.

60. Kelling, G.L. & Moore, M.H. (1988). The evolving strategy of policing. *Perspectives on Policing, No. 4.* Washington, D.C.: National Institute of Justice.

61. Myer, R.W. (2013). Police-community relations. In K.J. Peak (Ed.), *Encyclopedia of community policing and problem solving* (pp.284-288). Thousand Oaks, CA: Sage.

62. Braga, A.A. (2013). Team policing. In K.J. Peak (Ed.), *Encyclopedia of community policing and problem solving* (pp.401-403). Thousand Oaks, CA: Sage.

63. Greene. J.R. (1987). Foot patrol and community policing: Past practices and future prospects. *American Journal of Police, 6,* 1-15; Sherman, L., et al. (1973). *Team policing: Seven case studies.* Washington, DC: Police Foundation.

64. Goldstein, H. (1979). Improving policing: A problem-oriented approach. *Crime & Delinquency, 25,* 236-258; Goldstein, H. (1990). *Problem-oriented policing.* New York, NY: McGraw-Hill.

65. Wilson, J.Q. & Kelling, G.L. (1982, March). Broken windows: The police and neighborhood safety. *Atlantic Monthly, 249,* 29-38.

66. Dunworth, T., Mills, G., Cordner, G., & Greene, J. (1999). *National evaluation of weed and seed: Cross-site analysis.* Washington, DC: National Institute of Justice.

67. Oliver, W.M. (2007). *Community-oriented policing: A systemic approach to policing.* 4th ed. Upper Saddle River, NJ: Prentice Hall.

68. Blumstein, A. & Wallman, J. (2000). *The crime drop in America.* New York, NY: Cambridge University Press; Zimring, F.E. (2007). *The great American crime decline.* New York, NY: Oxford University Press.

69. Oliver, W.M. (2000). The third generation of community policing: Moving through innovation, diffusion, and institutionalization. *Police Quarterly,* 3, 367-388.

70. Oliver, W.M. (2007). *Community-oriented policing: A systemic approach to policing.* 4th ed. Upper Saddle River, NJ: Prentice Hall.

71. Oliver, W.M., Marion, N.E., & Hill, J.B. (2014). *Introduction to homeland security: Policy, organization, and Administration.* Boston, MA: Jones & Bartlett Learning.

72. Oliver, W.M., Marion, N.E., & Hill, J.B. (2014). *Introduction to homeland security: Policy, organization, and Administration.* Boston, MA: Jones & Bartlett Learning.

73. Oliver, W.M. (2007). *Homeland security for policing.* Upper Saddle River, NJ: Prentice Hall; Oliver, W.M., Marion, N.E., & Hill, J.B. (2014). *Introduction to homeland security: Policy, organization, and Administration.* Boston, MA: Jones & Bartlett Learning.

74. United States Senate. (2012). *Federal support for an involvement in state and local fusion centers.* Washington, DC: U.S. Senate. Also available online at www.hsgac.senate.gov/subcommittees/investigations/media/investigative-report-criticizes-counterterrorism-reporting-waste-at-state-and-local-intelligence-fusion-centers

75. United States Senate. (2012). *Federal support for an involvement in state and local fusion centers.* Washington, DC: U.S. Senate. Also available online at www.hsgac.senate.gov/subcommittees/investigations/media/investigative-report-criticizes-counterterrorism-reporting-waste-at-state-and-local-intelligence-fusion-centers

76. Oliver, W.M. (2007). *Homeland security for policing.* Upper Saddle River, NJ: Prentice Hall; Oliver, W.M., Marion, N.E. & Hill, J.B. (2014). *Introduction to homeland security: Policy, organization, and Administration.* Boston, MA: Jones & Bartlett Learning.

77. Oliver, W.M., Marion, N.E., & Hill, J.B. (2014). *Introduction to homeland security: Policy, organization, and Administration.* Boston, MA: Jones & Bartlett Learning.

■ *"The most marked difference in the police organization of twenty-five years ago and that of today lies in the growing tendency toward centralized effort in the suppression and prevention of crime. This trend is most in evidence . . . in the establishment of state and national bureaus of identification . . . and in the growth of state police organizations."*[1] *—August Vollmer, writing in 1933*

The largest of the 178 tribal police departments is the Navajo National Department of Law Enforcement.

CHAPTER 3

Agencies

After reading this chapter, you will be able to:

1. State the number of police departments in the United States most commonly held to exist and explain why the number may actually be much higher.
2. Explain why the United States of America has no national police force.
3. Describe the differences between countries with highly centralized police forces and America's highly decentralized police system.
4. Define what is meant by local police and detail the two main categories of these agencies.
5. Name and describe the five categories of varying special jurisdiction police agencies in the United States.
6. Explain how a county sheriff's office differs from a police department.
7. Name and describe the four models of sheriff's offices in the United States.
8. State the number of state police agencies and describe the differences among these agencies, as well as their main functions.
9. Explain the purpose and function of game wardens, constables, and marshals and their relationship with the state.
10. Name and describe the differences between federal law enforcement agencies in the Department of Homeland Security and the Department of Justice.

When August Vollmer wrote the quote that opens this chapter in 1933, he had just retired from having served 27 years as the Berkeley Police Chief and was a professor at the University of California at Berkeley. Policing had changed vastly during Vollmer's tenure as police chief (1905-1933) and what he was observing was a growth in both state police agencies and federal law enforcement. Try to imagine 1905 when Vollmer first took over the police department. The only federal law enforcement agencies in existence at that time were the U.S. Marshals, Postal Inspectors, and Secret Service.[2] The Federal Bureau of Investigation (FBI) did not exist as of yet. No state had a highway patrol because, at the time, there were only 8,000 cars in all of the United States and only 144 miles of paved roads. There were no modern state police agencies either, although Pennsylvania was about to create a State Constabulary that year. In addition, only 33 out of the 45 states had a state game warden agency.[3] The primary law enforcement agencies at the time were local and county agencies, but even those numbers were far less than they are today. With all of this growth in new police agencies, one has to wonder how many police departments there are in existence today.

The pat answer to that question is approximately 18,000. There are said to be 17,985 law enforcement agencies in the United States according to the most recent census of state and local law enforcement (see Table 3.1).[4] However that figure, 18,000, has been the same figure bandied about since the 1980s. Some have estimated that the true number of police agencies in the United States may very well be over 21,000 separate departments.[5] The reality is, because of our highly **decentralized system of policing** in America, we are not really all that sure.[6]

The problem may lie in how the agencies are actually counted. In some cases, as this author found, police departments simply disappear. When doing research in West Virginia, I discovered three police departments that existed on paper that did not exist in reality. In one case, the police chief retired, in another he died, and in yet another, no one recollected ever having had a police department. In the first two cases, the department only had one police officer—the police chief. In the last case, no one knew, but on paper, according to all documentation, that town had a police department. In other cases it may come about because of counting issues. For instance, if a state police agency has 19 state police barracks across the state, does that count as one agency or 19? Another not so clear factor is whether or not we count tribal police agencies. Native

Table 3.1 State and Local Law Enforcement by Type of Agency, 2008

Type of Agency	Agencies	Full-Time Sworn	Total
All agencies	17,985	765,246	
Local Police	12,501	461,063	593,013
Sheriff's Office	3,063	182,979	353,461
Primary State*	50	60,772	93,148
Special Jurisdiction	1,733	56,968	90,262
Constable/Marshal	638	3,464	4,031

* Note: This census includes Hawaii's investigative unit as a state police agency.
Source: Reaves, B.A. (2011). *Census of state and local law enforcement agencies, 2008.* Washington, DC: Bureau of Justice Statistics.

American tribal land is considered a free and sovereign nation, so recognized by our federal government. So, are the estimated 178 tribal police departments to be counted in the total number of police departments in the United States or not?[7] All of this leads to some confusion over the actual number count.

One reason to suspect that the number is indeed higher than 18,000 is the fact that in the 1980s, when I was a criminal justice student, I learned there were **18,000 police departments** in the United States. During the 1990s, when I became involved in the community policing movement, I witnessed the federal government implement the COPS Bill that funded the hiring of 100,000

A police officer's patch collection features some of the more than 18,000 police agencies in the United States.

cops.[8] Police departments could hire new officers, but small towns, if they did not have a police department, could actually create one and still obtain the federal funding. New police departments were created out of whole cloth in the 1990s throughout the United States. Yet, despite all of these new departments, the number of police agencies estimated to be in the United States has remained at 18,000.

The lack of clarity on the exact number, as mentioned, is derived from the highly decentralized nature of policing in the United States. Unlike most countries in the world that have only one police department, the United States from its founding did not trust government and wanted to keep the police strictly under local control.[9] This is why there is **no national police force** in the United States. To understand how highly decentralized policing is in America, it is important to understand the different types of police agencies in the United States and the extent of their jurisdiction, their legal and physical boundaries of what laws they can enforce and where they can enforce them. To do so, it is better to look at these agencies from the ground up, rather than the top down. However, if anyone ever asks, the number of police departments in the United States is 18,000 (as far as we know).

Local Police

According to one major study on American policing, "local governments exercise the greatest control over American law enforcement." [10] Yet, when it comes to thinking about the **local police**, the image most people have is that of the large, urban, metropolitan police department (see Box 3.1).[11] The reason most people immediately think this is probably because a mere 5 percent of these agencies actually employ 63 percent of all sworn

---

Box 3.1 History in Practice: What Is the Origin of the Term *Cop*?

This textbook generally refers to those men and women who are sworn to work for a police departments as **police officers**. Yet, it is very common to hear police officers referred to as **cops**, so much so, the term has become ubiquitous. We often do not even think about the term at all for we know to whom we are referring when we say the word. There are numerous books and articles that use the term, and a long running television series was called *Cops*. But where did the term come from?

The short answer is: We don't know.

The long answer is: We don't know but there are many theories as to its origins. One of the stories is that police officers were originally called constables and they walked a foot patrol, like the Peelers and Bobbies. Hence, they were referred to as Constables on Patrol

or Cops for short. Others have claimed that it is actually Citizens on Patrol because police officers are not part of the military, and are citizens with sworn powers who walk a foot patrol, so, again, Cops.

Another explanation has been that it is a variation of the Latin word *capere,* which means to grab or apprehend. So to cap someone was to put hands on them, arrest them, and take them into custody. Soon, it morphed into cop, such as to "cop someone."

Finally, another variation is that some of the early English police officers wore copper helmets and/or they wore copper badges. Seeing this, people referred to them as coppers, and eventually it was shortened to cop.

Since no one really knows which is the actual case, pick your favorite explanation.

---

personnel.[12] This creates somewhat of an oddity in policing. The typical *police officer* works for an agency employing more than 100 police officers, yet the typical *police department* in the United States only averages 15 police officers.[13] To resolve this, when talking about local police, they are typically broken into two categories: large metropolitan police and small town and rural police.[14] Since most people tend to think of large city police, let's address them first.

Large Metropolitan Police (100+ Police Officers)

According to the census bureau, a large city is any with over 50,000 population and a large police department is generally considered any employing 100 or more police officers.[15] Large cities with high population density by their very nature necessitate large **metropolitan police departments**. This is primarily because where there are high populations of people, crime tends to be much higher. Hence, police officers working for these larger agencies in large cities tend to experience far more crimes and calls-for-service than their rural counterpart (see Table 3.2).[16]

Another interesting aspect about working for a large metropolitan police department is that because the city is so large, when an urban police officer is off duty, no one knows they are a police officer and they can remain anonymous. Yet, when a police department employs more than 100 officers that can also be the case within the department itself. It becomes difficult to know

Table 3.2 Large Metropolitan Police Agencies by Population Served, 2013			
Population Served	**Agencies**	**Full-Time Sworn**	**Full-Time Total Employees**
1,000,000 or more	16	103,609	136,208
500,000–999,999	36	56,355	69,525
250,000–499,999	53	37,364	47,648
100,000–249,999	224	58,588	76,755
50,000–99,999	446	50,764	65,342

Source: Reaves, B.A. (2015). *Local Police Departments, 2013: Personnel, Policies, and Practices*. Washington, DC: Bureau of Justice Statistics.

everyone in the police department. The New York Police Department (NYPD) is the largest in the nation for it employs approximately 34,500 police officers, so it is easy to get lost in such a large agency as this.[17] New York Police Detective Edward Conlon in his book *Blue Blood* explained the anonymity of a large police department this way: "When I joined the NYPD in 1995, it was nearly four times larger than the FBI and four-fifths the size of the total staff of the United Nations. There are more cops in New York than there are people in Beverly Hills. Most people think of a cop as a uniformed officer from a precinct, or a detective in a squad, but Patrol Service and the Detective Bureau are only two of nine in the NYPD...I doubt if one cop in 10 could name each bureau at the beginning of his career, and even fewer could at the end."[18]

When it comes to what we know of large urban police departments, we tend to have better knowledge, for most studies of policing are conducted in these police agencies and from time to time a census of the approximately 1,100 police departments employing 100 or more officers has been conducted by the U.S. Department of Justice.[19] It is from this census that we know that the largest agencies are few in number (5 percent), but that they employ the majority of police officers (63 percent). We know that there are 49 police departments with over 1,000 police officers, the largest being the **New York City Police Department** with 34,454 police officers, followed by Chicago Police Department (12,042) and Los Angeles Police Department (9,920).[20] There are 775 police departments (out of 18,000) serving large cities as identified by the census bureau classification of those cities having populations of 50,000 or more. The majority of these (446 out of 775) typically serve populations of 50,000-99,999 (see Table 3.3).[21]

Members of the NYPD at Times Square. Established in 1845, the NYPD is the largest municipal police force in the United States.

Table 3.3	Top Ten Largest Police Departments, 2013	
Ranking	Agency	Full-Time Sworn
1.	NYPD (NY)	34,454
2.	Chicago Police Department (IL)	12,042
3.	Los Angeles Police Department (LAPD) (CA)	9,920
4.	Philadelphia Police Department (PA)	6,515
5.	Houston Police Department (TX)	5,295
6.	Metropolitan Police Department (Washington, D.C.)	3,865
7.	Dallas Police Department (TX)	3,478
8.	Phoenix Police Department (AZ)	2,952
9.	Baltimore Police Department (MD)	2,949
10.	Miami-Dade Police Department (FL)	2,745

Source: Reaves, B.A. (2015). *Local Police Departments, 2013: Personnel, Policies, and Practices.* Washington, DC: Bureau of Justice Statistics.

Sometimes the problem with assessing the size of the police department and the size of the city they serve is that we are really looking at two different variables. For example, with 34,454 police officers, the NYPD is the largest police department in the United States. However, it serves a population of over 8 million people. Hence, it is important to look at the ratio of the number of police officers to the population they serve. In this case, when looking at the number of officers per 100,000 population, the Washington, D.C. Metropolitan Police actually rises to the top of the list with the most police officers at 634 per 100,000 population.[22] In fact, you have to go through Chicago (472 per 100,000 population), Newark (472 per 100,000 population), and Baltimore (469 per 100,000 population), before finally arriving at New York City (432 per 100,000 population) when using this ratio to compare number of police officers to number of citizens. These ratios can also be contrasted with some of the lowest number of police officers per 100,000 population and you can see the differences that these ratios make. For instance, Montgomery County (Maryland) Police Department has only 129 police officers per 100,000 population (or 1,206 police officers for over 1 million citizens), while Fairfax County (Virginia) Police Department has 144 officers per 100,000 population, and the San Antonio (Texas) Police Department has 150 per 100,000 population.[23]

Small-Town and Rural Police (Less Than 100)

While most may think of large metropolitan police departments when they envision local police, the reality is, the majority of police departments in the United States tend to be **small-town and rural**. The United States has 19,492 municipal governments and 16,519 townships. More than 90 percent of these governments have populations under 25,000, 70 percent serve under 10,000, and more than half serve populations under 1,000.[24] Because most local governments in the United States are small, most police departments are small as well. In fact, about half (48 percent) of local police departments in the United States employ less than ten police officers.[25] And whereas the large cities employ the most police officers, small-town and rural police departments employ the least, accounting for only 4 percent of all police officers in the nation.[26]

Working in a **small-town and rural police department** is very different from the urban setting.[27] For most police officers in these departments, they grew up in the town they police and they consider it their hometown. While there may not be as much crime or calls-for-service, most of these officers are rewarded by the fact they can play such an important role in the same town they grew up in and that they can have a good career. In fact, because they grew up there, one aspect of small-town policing is the fact that everyone knows everyone and because of this there is more personal communication between the police and the public.[28] While this can be a disadvantage, (for even out of uniform, everyone knows you are a police officer) (no anonymity), it can create an advantage as well. In Tracy Kidder's book *Home Town* about a small-town police officer named Tommy, he told the story of how a metropolitan police investigator one day wanted to know about a particular male who lived in his community. Without so much as a pause, Tommy answered, "Yup, he's going out with Daisy. Hangs at the *Information Booth*. Drives a blue Mustang. You want the license number?"[29]

This is perhaps not too surprising when one thinks about how small some of these town really are. For instance, in Keystone, West Virginia, the area of the town is only 205 acres and the population in 2010 was 282 people. This is why the Keystone Police Department currently only employs one police officer, the police chief. It is the same all over America. The jurisdiction of Darby, Montana, is only 371 acres and it has 731 citizens, so the Darby Police Department employs two officers. And, another example is in Franklin, Texas, where the city is 576 acres, has a 1,562 population, and the police department consists of 4 full-time sworn police officers. And with police departments this small, there is no reason to use ratios to compare the numbers of officers to the size of the population, although if you do, the ratios are actually not much different from the large metropolitan police ratios (see Table 3.4).

The key to remember is that these examples describe the typical police department in the United

Winnetka, Illinois, police officer directing traffic. The Village of Winnetka police department employs 27 sworn officers serving a population of 12,422 citizens and is representative of a typical police department in the United States.

Table 3.4 Small-Town and Rural Police Agencies by Population Served, 2013			
Population Served	**Agencies**	**Full-Time Sworn**	**Full-Time Total Employees**
25,000–49,999	878	51,007	64,727
10,000–24,999	1,986	59,559	74,088
2,500–9,999	3,873	43,808	52,335
2,499 or fewer	4,815	16,264	18,333

Source: Reaves, B.A. (2015). *Local Police Departments, 2013: Personnel, Policies, and Practices.* Washington, DC: Bureau of Justice Statistics.

States. According to the **police census**, there are 605 police departments in the United States employing zero to one police officers. Yes, you read that correctly, zero to one, because if the one officer employed quits, retires, or dies, for a time period, the police department will have zero officers. The number of police departments employing two to four officers in the United States is 2,294, from five to nine is 2,996, and from 10 to 24 is 3,345. That just accounted for over half (51.3 percent) of all police departments in the United States and three-quarters (74.9 percent) of all local police departments.[30]

Special Jurisdiction Police Agencies

In addition to the urban and small-town police departments that serve municipalities, cities, and towns, there are also over 1,700 police departments that serve **special jurisdictions** and they employ approximately 57,000 sworn police officers.[31] These police departments have jurisdiction over a specific geographic area that is not a city or town, but generally something identifiably smaller. These may be public buildings and facilities, parks and recreation areas, or transportation systems, such as airports and mass transit commuter rails. Some of the special jurisdiction police agencies do have a broad jurisdiction geographically, such as across counties or even entire states, but they have a more narrow focus in regard to the specific violation of the law they enforce such as only investigating arsons, agricultural crimes, or enforcing gaming laws. These special jurisdiction law enforcement agencies can be divided into five types: (1) public building/facilities, (2) natural resources, (3) transportation systems/facilities, (4) criminal investigations, and (5) special enforcement (see Table 3.5).[32]

The first category of special jurisdiction police agencies, **public building/facilities**, is one that you are most likely familiar with for the most common of these are **campus police departments** (see Box 3.2).[33] There are approximately 905 campus police agencies in the United States employing over 14,500 sworn police officers.[34] While their duties are serving as police officers for the campus community, a typical college or university is usually spread beyond the main campus and campus police typically have jurisdiction when traveling from campus to other university facilities. Campus police are also

Table 3.5 Public Buildings/Facilities Special Jurisdiction Agencies, 2008		
Type of Agency	Agencies	Full-Time Sworn
All Agencies	1,126	21,418
4-Year University/College	508	10,916
Public School District	250	4,764
2-year College	253	2,648
State Government Buildings	29	1,138
Medical School/Campus	18	747
Public Hospital/Health Facility	48	715
Public Housing	13	250
Other State-Owned Facilities	7	240

Source: Reaves, B.A. (2011). *Census of state and local law enforcement agencies, 2008.* Washington, DC: Bureau of Justice Statistics.

not simply security guards, they are sworn officers who face the same perils of the job as the local town and city police departments. Campus police can find themselves in widely reported situations, for it was a campus police officer at the University of California, Davis, that created such controversy when he pepper-sprayed the Occupy movement demonstrators (he later resigned, but he received worker's compensation for the incident, while the students sprayed received a settlement from the university).[35] Another campus police officer, Sean Collier, is widely remembered for he was assassinated on the campus of Massachusetts Institute of Technology by the Tsarnaev brothers who were fleeing the authorities after perpetrating the bombings at the Boston Marathon in 2013.[36] So, while the departments tend to be smaller, the duties and tasks of the campus police officer are no different from other police officers.

In addition to the police on college campuses, many **public school districts** have their own police departments as well. For instance, the Houston Independent School District has its own police department and their jurisdiction are the school facilities in the city of Houston. There are also police

---

Box 3.2 Policing in Practice: Your Campus Police

Campus police are not simply security guards; they are sworn officers who face the same perils of the job as the local town and city police departments.

Does your college or university have a campus police department? Is it a bona fide police department or is it a private security force? Do they have full powers of arrest? What is the scope of their jurisdiction? How many officers do they have?

departments that have been created to police state government buildings, medical facilities, and public housing facilities. All told, this is the most common form of special jurisdiction police for they make up 1,126 agencies employing 21,418 sworn officers (see Table 3.5).[37]

The second type of special jurisdiction police are **natural resource agencies**.[38] Most of these agencies tend to be state-level agencies such as fish and wildlife conservation agencies, what are often referred to as game wardens. Because they typically are employed by the states in which they serve, they will be addressed later in this chapter under the section on state police agencies. There are, however, 246 of these types of agencies employing over 14,000 sworn police officers, with their jurisdiction often being defined by geography such as parks, recreation areas, waterways, or in the vicinity of New Orleans, Louisiana, the Levee District Police (see Table 3.6).[39]

The third type of special jurisdiction police are focused on **transportation systems** and their facilities. In all, there are an estimated 167 of these agencies employing over 11,500 sworn officers.[40] A good example of these police departments can be seen at certain airports in the United States such as the Minneapolis-Saint Paul Airport Police Department. Some airports are policed by a special unit of the local city's police force (such as the George H.W. Bush International Airport in Houston, Texas), but many of the nation's airports are policed by dedicated police departments patrolling and securing all of the facilities associated with the airport. Other police departments that fall under this category include harbor and port police, such as the police officers who work for the Port of Houston Authority (Texas), providing police coverage for the ports in the Houston harbor where ships from all over the world enter the United States (see Table 3.7).

Table 3.6 Natural Resources Special Jurisdiction Agencies, 2008		
Type of Agency	**Agencies**	**Full-Time Sworn**
All Agencies	246	14,571
Fish and Wildlife Conservation Laws	56	5,515
Parks and Recreational Areas	124	4,989
Multifunction Natural Resources	16	2,926
Boating Laws	10	461
Environmental Laws	7	368
Water Resources	18	185
Forest Resources	9	65
Levee District	6	62

Source: Reaves, B.A. (2011). *Census of state and local law enforcement agencies, 2008.* Washington, DC: Bureau of Justice Statistics.

Table 3.7 Transportation Systems/Facilities Special Jurisdiction Agencies, 2008		
Type of Agency	Agencies	Full-Time Sworn
All Agencies	167	11,508
Airports	103	3,555
Mass Transit Systems/Railroads	18	3,214
Transportation — Multiple Types	5	2,000
Commercial Vehicles	12	1,320
Harbor/Port Facilities	25	876
Bridges/Tunnels	4	543

Source: Reaves, B.A. (2011). *Census of state and local law enforcement agencies, 2008*. Washington, DC: Bureau of Justice Statistics.

Many urban cities also have commuter rail systems, and they often have their own transportation police departments as well.[41] One unique example of this is the Washington, D.C. Metro Transit Police, which employs nearly 500 sworn officers who police the metro rail system in the Washington, D.C. area. What is truly unique about this agency, as Chief Ron Pavlik explains, is that "Metro Transit Police Department is the only tristate police department in the United States. And what that means is our police officers have to be certified in the District of Columbia, the state of Maryland, and the commonwealth of Virginia."[42] For a person to become a metro transit police officer, that individual has to attend and pass three separate police academies, a process that typically takes 18 months.[43]

The fourth type of special jurisdiction police are **criminal investigation agencies**. There are approximately 140 such agencies employing over 7,000 sworn officers.[44] These are police departments that are dedicated to enforcing a particular set of laws, and while many are state-level agencies, not all of them are. For instance, there are 66 county/city investigation agencies and 21 fire marshal/arson investigations agencies in the United States.[45] One example of the latter is found in the state of Maine, which has its own Office of State Fire Marshal that has statewide jurisdiction over arson cases and is an independent criminal investigation agency. There are also 22 state bureau of investigations (discussed

Washington, D.C. Metro Transit K-9 police officer patrolling through the Metro station.

Table 3.8 Criminal Investigations Special Jurisdiction Agencies, 2008		
Type of Agency	**Agencies**	**Full-Time Sworn**
All Agencies	140	7,310
State Bureau of Investigation	22	3,527
County/City Investigations	66	2,006
Fraud Investigations	13	636
Fire Marshals/Arson Investigations	21	478
Tax/Revenue Enforcement	6	177
Other/Multiple Types	12	486

Source: Reaves, B.A. (2011). *Census of state and local law enforcement agencies, 2008.* Washington, DC: Bureau of Justice Statistics.

below) and six tax/revenue enforcement agencies in the United States, with the Alabama Department of Revenue having its own Revenue Enforcement Officers for the state, enforcing the licensing and registration of motor vehicles in that state (see Table 3.8).[46]

The fifth and last category of special jurisdiction police agencies are those that have a **special enforcement** responsibility, typically of a specific set of laws. There are 54 of these agencies in the United States, employing over 2,000 police officers.[47] The type of laws they enforce include alcohol, tobacco, agricultural, narcotics, gaming, and racing laws.[48] One example of this is the Nevada Gaming Control Board, which is an independent state enforcement agency employing nearly 100 investigators. The reason it is independent is because it is not a part of a larger agency such as the Louisiana Gaming Enforcement Division that is part of the Louisiana State Police, but rather it is its own police agency (see Table 3.9).[49]

Table 3.9 Special Enforcement Special Jurisdiction Agencies, 2008		
Type of Agency	**Agencies**	**Full-Time Sworn**
All Agencies	54	2,161
Alcohol/Tobacco Laws	22	1,280
Agricultural Laws	12	387
Narcotics Laws	5	233
Gaming Laws	10	231
Racing Laws	5	30

Source: Reaves, B.A. (2015). *Local Police Departments, 2013: Personnel, Policies, and Practices.* Washington, DC: Bureau of Justice Statistics.

County Sheriff's Office

County sheriffs, while still law enforcement officers, are very different from other local police.[50] The majority of counties in the United States tend to cover large geographical areas and are mostly rural. While there are some very urban county sheriff's offices, such as the Harris County Sheriff's Office, which covers much of the city of Houston and the surrounding suburbs, most are like the Greenbrier County Sheriff's Office in southern West Virginia, where there are five deputies patrolling over 1,000 square miles, while also providing courtroom security during the week.[51] Beyond just the differences in geographical jurisdiction, however, there are many differences between the police and sheriffs.

The biggest separation between police departments and sheriff's offices is the fact that in the former, the police chief is typically appointed by the mayor, while in the latter, the sheriff is elected. Being elected to the highest position in the police agency fundamentally changes the dynamic between the police agency and the population it serves. The sheriff is responsible to the people of the county the sheriff's office serves, but is dependent upon those same people to both obtain and retain the office. One retired sheriff highlights the unique aspect of having to run for the office of sheriff. He had been a deputy sheriff when the sheriff decided to step down, and as he recalled, "At the time there were four of us that wanted the position—three of us from the sheriff's office…the three of us from the sheriff's office were all good friends. We all wanted it for different reasons and all went after it."[52] This is something that police officers never consider for they typically move through the ranks to "make it to the top." In a sheriff's office, however, someone with no police experience can be elected sheriff, or, as in the case of the retired sheriff, he ran for the position as a deputy sheriff and won.

Another distinction that the political elements creates is wrapped up in the difference in names, police *department* versus **sheriff's office**. The difference in names is not just to keep them distinct from one another, rather it is a distinction of bureaucracy. A department is part of a larger organization. The police department, by way of the police chief, reports to the mayor and the city council. They are a department of city or town government. The sheriff, however, is an elected office and the office is the highest law enforcement position in the county. The sheriff reports to no higher entity, such as the county commission, because there is no higher entity. The sheriff only reports to the electorate, the people that are eligible to vote for the sheriff. That said, however, there are some sheriff's departments that do not follow this rule, such as the Los Angeles Sheriff's Department, which remains the highest law enforcement position in the county but uses the name department instead of office.

Election to the highest office in the agency is not the only difference between police and sheriffs, for what the agency actually does is very different as well.[53] Police officers typically only patrol the streets and respond to calls-for-service. Sheriff's deputies, however, often have more responsibilities than just patrolling the county; they may also perform courtroom duty, the serving of civil papers, and running the county jail. In fact, 96 percent of sheriff's offices perform traditional law enforcement functions, 98 percent serve civil paper, 96 percent provide courtroom security, and 75 percent operate at least one jail.[54]

It has been said that the majority of sheriff's offices tend to fall into one of **four models of sheriff's offices**, and they are (1) full service, (2) law enforcement, (3) civil judiciary, and (4) correctional-judiciary.[55] The **full service model**, as the name implies, means that the sheriff's office performs all of the duties mentioned. The Harris County Sheriff's Office, mentioned before, performs all of the various functions. The second model, **law enforcement**, means that these sheriff's deputies only patrol the county while other agencies serve civil papers (such as town marshals) and run the jails (especially when jails are regionally located in a state like West Virginia). The third model, **civil judiciary**, are those sheriff's offices that provide courtroom security and serve civil papers but do not patrol the streets on a routine basis or run the jails. And finally, the fourth model, **correction-judiciary**, is where the sheriffs provide courtroom security and run the jail. A good example of this is Arlington County, Virginia, which is a county with no towns or cities, as it is only 26 square miles. The county police patrol the streets, while the sheriff's office runs the jail and provides courtroom security.

There are **3,144 counties** in the United States, which includes 137 county equivalents, for some counties in the United States go by other names, such as in Louisiana where they are called **parishes**.[56] According to the National Sheriffs' Association there are 3,080 sheriff's agencies across the nation.[57] There are three states that do not have sheriff's offices and they are Alaska, which has no county governments; Connecticut, where sheriffs were replaced by a State Marshal System; and Hawaii, which has no sheriffs, but it does have deputy sheriffs that serve in the Sheriff's Division of the Hawaii Department of Public Safety. It makes sense that the states with the highest number of counties would have the highest number of sheriff's offices, so the five states with the highest number of both are Texas (254), Georgia (159), Kentucky (120), Missouri (114), and Kansas (104) (see Table 3.10).[58]

In 42 states, sheriffs are elected for four-year terms in office, while in 2 states they are elected to two-year terms (Arkansas and New Hampshire), and in 1 state, they are elected to a three-year (New Jersey) or six-year term (Massachusetts). One other state, Rhode Island, does not use an electoral system, but rather has a system whereby the governor of the state appoints the sheriff (see Table 3.11).[59]

The **3,080 sheriff's offices** in the United States employ 182,979 sworn deputy sheriffs or approximately one-fifth of all law enforcement officers in the nation.[60] The average size of a sheriff's office in the United States is 15 deputies, as most fall in the 15–24 deputies category. Like the local police, some agencies (45) employ zero to one employees—the sheriff—while 13 agencies employ over 1,000 deputies.[61] The largest of the sheriff's offices in the United States is the Los Angeles County (California) Sheriff's Department, which employs 7,614 full-time sworn deputies and serves a population of nearly

Table 3.10 County Sheriff's Offices by Size of Agency, 2013		
Size of Agency	**Agencies**	**Full-Time Sworn**
All Agencies	3,012	188,952
1,000 or More Deputies	16	37,482
500–999	34	21,785
250–499	85	29,599
100–249	235	34,790
50–99	399	26,194
25–49	700	22,786
10–24	914	12,940
5–9	452	2,854
2–4	170	516
0–1	6	6

Source: Reaves, B.A. (2016). *Sheriff's Office Personnel, 1993-2013*. Washington, DC: Bureau of Justice Statistics.

Table 3.11 The Ten Largest Sheriff's Offices, 2008		
Ranking	**County**	**Full-Time Sworn**
1.	Los Angeles County (CA)	9,461
2.	Cook County (IL)	5,655
3.	Harris County (TX)	2,558
4.	Riverside County (CA)	2,147
5.	San Bernardino (CA)	1,797
6.	Orange County (CA)	1,794
7.	Broward County (FL)	1,624
8.	Palm Beach County (FL)	1,447
9.	Sacramento County (CA)	1,409
10.	Orange County (FL)	1,398

Source: Reaves, B.A. (2011). *Census of state and local law enforcement agencies, 2008*. Washington, DC: Bureau of Justice Statistics.

Ventura County Sheriff's Office deputies in 2015.

10 million people. This is followed by the Cook County (Illinois) Sheriff's Office with 2,390 deputies, Harris County (Texas) Sheriff's Office with 2,379 deputies, and the San Diego County (California) Sheriff's Department with 2,184 deputies.[62]

Other "Local" Police

There are so many variations in American policing that it is difficult sometimes to properly categorize them. As previously mentioned, Native Americans have **tribal police departments** that police Native American reservations that are recognized as sovereign nations. This means they really are their own country, yet at the same time they are found within the United States and often these departments work alongside other law enforcement agencies, so it is important to recognize them regardless.

There are 566 recognized Native American tribes and 344 Native American Tribal reservations located in 49 states (the exception being Hawaii), of which 178 have a tribal law enforcement agency.[63] There are approximately 3,500 full-time sworn tribal officers employed by the 178 agencies, which means that the average agency employs 20 officers, but it is more likely the case that there are only ten police officers (the mode) working for the police department.[64] The largest of the tribal police departments is the Navajo Nation Department of Law Enforcement located in Arizona, which employs 321 officers covering a population of 169,617 people and covering a land area of 22,174 square miles.[65] For those tribes and reservations that do not have a dedicated police department rather than local police having jurisdiction, the US government, through the Bureau of Indian Affairs, maintains a division of law enforcement that provides law enforcement assistance to 43 of the tribes/reservations.[66]

Another variation in the United States is not really a separate police department, but the employment of what are generally referred to as either **reserve, auxiliary, special police officers, or sworn volunteers**.[67] Much of this chapter has dealt with the numbers of full-time sworn police officers, but many department employ part-time sworn police officers. In fact, in the United States there are 58,129 sworn part-time local police officers, 14,681 part-time special jurisdictional officers, and 26,052 part-time sworn deputies.[68] While all of these officers are sworn law enforcement officers, some work as volunteers for no pay, while others will work a number of hours per week, month, or year for pay. In addition, many police departments,

---

Box 3.3 Policing in Practice: Summer Police Officers Wanted

In my freshman year of college, I had the benefit of a friend who was a year older than me who had served the previous summer as a police officer on the shores of New Jersey. My friend was the ideal police officer and his father had been a career officer, and together they helped me with the process of become a summer police officer for the Wildwood Police Department.

Many of the beach towns along the eastern shore have small populations in the winter, but they balloon in the summer. Wildwood itself can go from 12,000 residents to a town with 150,000 to 250,000 people in the summer. It is not economical to have a force year-round to handle the summer numbers, so they maintain a certain sized force, but supplement it with **Summer Reserve Police Officers**.

The majority of these officers are college students working on a degree in Criminal Justice who are want the experience of working as a police officer. Many of these departments also offer the experience as an internship as well. After moving through the hiring process and an abbreviated police academy, the Summer Officers work the street, boardwalk, or beach with full police authority.

My experience in New Jersey provided me with one of the greatest experiences of my life, and it confirmed my interest in a career in the policing field.

---

especially those on the coastal areas with beaches, tend to hire seasonal police officers. In the winter, cities like Wildwood, New Jersey, or Ocean City, Maryland, may have small populations of residents, but during the summer months, when people on vacation come to the beach, populations can increase by hundreds of thousands of people, hence these agencies need summer police officers. These agencies often look for college students, majoring in criminal justice, who maintain good grades. The author of this textbook served as a summer police officer in the beach city of Wildwood, New Jersey, which ultimately led to a lifetime career in policing (see Box 3.3).

State Police

As the opening quote by August Vollmer notes, the establishment of the **state police** was one of the most marked differences in early twentieth-century policing.[69] Although state police agencies actually began developing in the century before, their focus and organization were unlike what we are familiar with today. The earliest of what could be called state police agencies was the establishment of the **Texas Rangers** in 1823, which did not become an official part of the Texas government until 1835, and, of course, it only became a state police agency when Texas became a state in 1845.[70] It would be a long time coming before another state followed suit, but there is evidence that South Carolina created a state police agency in 1868, Arizona created the

This statue honoring the Texas Rangers stands in front of the Texas Ranger Hall of Fame and Museum in Waco, Texas.

Arizona Rangers in 1901 modeled off of the Texas Rangers, and Connecticut created a state police agency in 1903.[71] Two years later in 1905 New Mexico created a mounted force and Pennsylvania created the State Constabulary.[72] According to police historian Samuel Walker, however, "The turning point was 1915," for as he notes, "over the next six years 23 states would create some form of state law enforcement agency."[73] This was why Vollmer made the observation he did.

Since Vollmer's writing in 1933, every state in the nation (with the exception of Hawaii) has a state police agency. Vollmer had advocated for the state police agencies to the point of writing a book on the topic, and many police officers prefer the idea of working for a state agency rather than a local one. One state police officer explaining why he prefers working for the state over a municipal agency, put it like this: "I like the freedom of the State Troopers, and the 24-hour squad car, and state-issued equipment, and the ability to clock in and out in my driveway. I also like the assumed higher standard of State Troopers compared to some cities. I also enjoy working traffic, but at the same time, I don't want to be limited to a section of the road, and limited to mostly traffic—I want to be able to answer some calls as well. Another advantage of being a state police, is the ability to move throughout the state, and still have jurisdiction and be under the same agency."[74] While state police do indeed have statewide jurisdiction, they still recognize that there are boundaries between the local and county police with that of the state police. The reality remains, however, that unlike local agencies, state agencies "have a less limited but still relatively small role in shaping the overall character of public law enforcement in the United States." [75] This becomes somewhat evident in the functions that the state police agencies perform.

There are **three main functions of the state police**, and they include law enforcement duties, such as responding to calls-for-service, investigations, typically of state-level fraud or crimes, and highway patrol. These duties may be reflected in the title the agency holds. Generically, we call all state-level law enforcement agencies "state police," but the reality is they actually go by different names. In some states, such as Arkansas, Maine, and New Mexico, the state police agencies are actually called the State Police and are either their own agency or work under the state Department of Public Safety conducting all three of the duties. In other states, such as Arizona, Montana, and South Carolina, they are formally titled the State Highway

Box 3.4 Policing in Practice: There Is No Five-O

Your perceptions of a state police department may have been formed by the many television programs that depict police officers, such as **Hawaii Five-O**.

For anyone over 40 years of age, the television show *Hawaii Five-O* was a police drama that aired from 1968 to 1980 and starred Jack Lord as Detective Lieutenant Steve McGarrett. The title of the show was *Hawaii Five-O* ending with the letter "O." Everyone's favorite line was when McGarrett would turn to his partner Danny Williams as say, "Book 'em Danno."

For those under 40 years of age, CBS created a reimagined *Hawaii Five-0* in 2010, this time with the title ending with a zero (although everyone still pronounces it like the letter "O").

In this new series, Steve McGarrett, played by Australian actor Alex O'Loughlin, is a lieutenant commander in the Naval Reserves who teams with Honolulu detective Danny "Danno" Williams.

The concept for the original show is believed to have been based on a special unit that a one-time governor of Hawaii had proposed, but the reality is that Hawaii Five-O, or Five-0, does not exist. Hawaii has a Department of Public Safety, which includes a law enforcement division that oversees the Sheriff Division and the Narcotics Enforcement Division. Otherwise, all policing falls under local (island) authority.

So, if you are ever in Hawaii, don't ask to visit the Five-O!

Patrol and they emphasize that specific duty. A number of states also call their state police State Patrol, such as Nebraska, Iowa, and Wisconsin, and while they primarily perform motor vehicle enforcement, they do respond to other events as well. One agency, California, titled the California Highway Patrol (and remember they don't like to be called "chips"), actually functions as a state police agency despite the name. And, finally, Hawaii is the only state that does not have a state police agency (and remember, Hawaii Five-O is a fictional organization), but rather, uses the sheriff division of the Hawaii Department of Public Safety to perform all state-level operations (Box 3.4).

The 49 state police agencies in the United States employ nearly 61,000 sworn, full-time officers.[76] Twenty of these agencies employ over 1,000 officers, with the largest of them being the California Highway Patrol, which employs 7,202 troopers.[77] California is followed by the New York State Police (4,847), the Pennsylvania State Police (4,458), and the Texas Department of Public Safety (3,529) in size.[78] The smallest of the state police agencies is the North Dakota Highway Patrol with 139 sworn personnel, followed by South Dakota Highway Patrol (152), Rhode Island State Police (201), and the Wyoming Highway Patrol (204) (see Table 3.12).

It should be mentioned here that one agency previously noted, the Texas Rangers, has always held a fascination for many Americans, but because of popular movies and television shows such as *The Lone Ranger* or *Walker: Texas Ranger,* most people do not have much of an understanding of the agency today. It was originally created in 1823, as a means of defending settlers

Table 3.12 Top Ten Largest State Police Agencies, 2008		
Ranking	**State**	**Full-Time Sworn**
1.	California Highway Patrol	7,202
2.	New York State Police	4,847
3.	Pennsylvania State Police	4,458
4.	Texas Department of Public Safety	3,539
5.	New Jersey State Police	3,053
6.	Massachusetts State Police	2,310
7.	Illinois State Police	2,105
8.	Virginia State Police	1,873
9.	Michigan State Police	1,732
10.	Florida Highway Patrol	1,606

Source: Reaves, B.A. (2011). *Census of state and local law enforcement agencies, 2008.* Washington, DC: Bureau of Justice Statistics.

coming into Texas against the Comanche Indians and soon after that, border bandits. Over the years, it went from a military unit, to a security force, to a state police agency.[79] However, with the introduction of a state police agency independent of the Texas Rangers, once again, it changed the nature of the agency. The Texas Rangers developed into a more modern state bureau of investigation, and, in 1935, it became part of the Department of Public Safety in Texas, alongside the Texas Highway Patrol.[80] Today, there are 150 sworn Texas Rangers spread across the vast state of Texas conducting state-level investigations for public corruption, officer involved shootings, and border security operations. Addressing the history of the Texas Rangers with the work they do today, one member, Captain Havra, explained, "I believe the common thread from the first days of the Rangers until today is pretty much the same. Their job 180 years ago . . . was to protect the innocent . . . citizens against the people who take advantage of the weak and defenseless. We are still doing that today. We still have that passion."[81]

In addition to the state police agencies, every state in the United States including Hawaii has a special agency dedicated to **natural resources and conservation**, generally called **game wardens** by most people. The concept of a game warden was an English invention for they were the royal keepers of the game, protecting a specific area from poachers so that the king would have a place to hunt that was always teeming with game.[82] Adopted in America, every state has maintained a variation of the game warden, but they go by many different names.[83] In 15 states, such as Alabama, Rhode Island, and West Virginia, they are called "conservation officers," while in Missouri they are "conservation agents" and in Virginia, "conservation

Table 3.13 Top Ten Largest State Natural Resource Enforcement Agencies, 2008		
Ranking	**State**	**Full-time Sworn**
1.	California Department of Parks & Recreation	645
2.	Florida Fish & Wildlife Conservation Commission	626
3.	Texas Parks & Wildlife Department	480
4.	Ohio Department of Natural Resources	394
5.	California Department of Fish and Game	330
6.	New York State Environmental Conservation	321
7.	New York State Park Police	305
8.	Tennessee Wildlife Resources Agency	275
9.	Maryland State Forest and Park Service	261
10.	Washington State Parks & Rec. Commission	250

Source: Reaves, B.A. (2015). *Local Police Departments, 2013: Personnel, Policies, and Practices*. Washington, DC: Bureau of Justice Statistics.

police officers." Other states call them environmental police officers (Massachusetts), wildlife officers (Ohio), and fish and wildlife law enforcement officers (Florida). These game wardens, depending on the agency, will perform such duties as enforcing hunting laws, fishing laws, environmental violations, and police recreational areas (for example, boating on lakes) (see Table 3.13).

In some states, in addition to the game wardens, they may have other special jurisdiction law enforcement agencies above and beyond the game wardens that enforce laws related to natural resources. Many of these are state park and recreational area police, while others specifically enforce boating laws or environmental laws, or work to protect water or forest resources. The largest of all of these natural resource police are the California Department of Parks and Recreation with 645 full-time sworn officers, followed by the Florida Fish and Wildlife Conservation Commission (626), Texas Parks and Wildlife Department (480), and the Ohio Department of Natural Resources (394).[84]

Other state-level law enforcement officials include both **constables** and **marshals**. There are 638 of these types of agencies in the United States and they employ 3,464 full-time sworn officers.[85] While some states have constables and others have marshals, Texas has both and accounts for a large portion of the 638 agencies. As in most states, the Texas Constables are a state-codified agency working at the local level who serve as the chief process server for the Justice of the Peace Court.[86] In many states, this duty is held by the sheriff's office, but in some states where it is not their function to serve papers, the constables hold that responsibility. In Texas, constables may also serve as contract law enforcement to provide police services for areas that do not have their own police department. City marshals are similar in that one of their functions is to serve warrants, a duty that oftentimes is either a duty of the local police or sheriff's office.[87]

Federal Law Enforcement

The last type of police in the United States is federal law enforcement. Again, it should be reiterated that there is no national police force in the United States, which means that federal law enforcement agencies also have a limited jurisdiction in the geographic area they cover or the type of criminal investigations they are authorized to conduct. As one major study on American policing stated, "contrary to popular belief, the federal role in shaping the character of policing is relatively small."[88] It should also be noted, as was pointed out in Chapter 2, most of the federal law enforcement agencies were created in the twentieth century.[89] Prior to that, the federal government heavily relied on local police for investigations (see Table 3.14).

There are over **70 federal law enforcement agencies** in the United States, but like counting police departments, what counts as a federal law enforcement agency can depend on the criteria used to classify them.[90] These 70-plus federal law enforcement agencies employ over 120,000 full-time sworn law enforcement officers.[91] The majority of these officers (37.3 percent) conduct criminal investigations, while others perform some form of police patrol and response (23.4 percent), and others serve as inspectors (15.3 percent).[92] Nearly half (45.5 percent) of all of these officers are under the Department of Homeland Security (DHS), while another third (33.1 percent) are under the Department of Justice.[93] The rest typically work for the legislative and judicial branches of the federal government, while some are employed by independent government agencies.

The **Department of Homeland Security,** created in 2002 as a response to the terrorist attacks on the United States on September 11, 2001, now employs the most federal law enforcement officers of any department in the federal government.[94] The largest agency within DHS is the **U.S. Customs and Border Protection (CBP)**, which enforces federal laws related to international trade, customs, and immigration. It employs nearly 46,000 federal law enforcement agents. Nearly half of these police officers (22,000) are employed by the Office of Border Patrol, who are responsible for maintaining U.S. borders with Mexico and Canada.

The second largest agency within DHS is the U.S. Immigration and Customs Enforcement (ICE). While CBP enforces customs and the Office of the Border Patrol protects America's borders, whenever a crime occurs pertaining to either customs or immigration, ICE, with its over 13,000

Table 3.14	Federal Law Enforcement Agencies				
Department of Justice	**Department of Homeland Security**	**Department of Interior**	**Department of State**	**U.S. Post Office**	**Other Agencies**
FBI	U.S. Secret Service	U.S. Park Police	Bureau of Diplomatic Security	U.S. Postal Inspectors	U.S. Supreme Court Police
Drug Enforcement Administration	Customs & Border Protection	U.S. Fish & Wildlife Service Office of Law Enforcement			U.S. Capitol Police
U.S. Marshals	Immigration Customs Enforcement	Hoover Dam Police			Amtrak Police
Bureau of Alcohol, Tobacco, & Firearms	Federal Air Marshals	Bureau of Indian Affairs			Pentagon Force Protection Agency
U.S. Marshals	Federal Protective Service				Smithsonian National Zoological Park Police
	Federal Law Enforcement Training Center				U.S. Mint Police
	Transportation Security Administration				Tennessee Valley Authority Police
	Coast Guard Investigative Service				Federal Reserve Police
					Veterans Affairs Police

Source: Marion, N.E. & Oliver, W.M. (2015). *Federal Law Enforcement Agencies in America*. Frederick, MD: Wolters Kluwer.

federal agents, is the agency that is primarily responsible for conducting the criminal investigations. Under ICE, there is also the Homeland Security Investigations (HSI), which perform many police and investigative functions for not only immigration and customs enforcement, but for homeland security in general.

Created on July 26, 1908, the FBI remains one of the top federal investigation units in the United States.

The third largest agency within DHS is the U.S. Secret Service. The Secret Service is one of the oldest federal law enforcement agencies in the United States, created in 1865 and placed under the Department of the Treasury to deal with the problems of counterfeiting U.S. currency in the aftermath of the Civil War. It was only later that it picked up the responsibility of protecting U.S. presidents, vice-presidents, and their families. In 2002, with the creation of DHS, it was moved from the Treasury and became part of DHS. While the actual number of Secret Service agents remains classified, it is estimated there are approximately 4,500 agents who continue to rotate between counterfeiting and presidential protection operations. The Secret Service has long been recognized as one of the elite of federal law enforcement agencies but also one of the most stressful. As one Secret Service agent explained, while a career with the agency "is tough on your personal and family life, it's made up for in a real sense because it *is* your family."[95]

The second department within the federal government that employs the most full-time sworn federal law enforcement officers is the **Department of Justice (DOJ)**.[96] The largest agency within DOJ, dedicated to criminal investigations, is the other elite federal law enforcement agency, the **Federal Bureau of Investigation** (see Box 3.5). As one retired agent reflected on her career with the FBI, "It was, by far, the hardest thing that I've ever done in my entire life," and she was awed by the fact she was able to "become a member of the most elite law enforcement agency in the world."[97] The FBI still fosters that tradition and today employs approximately 12,750 agents who are responsible for investigating crimes against the government, crimes that occur across state lines, and they are the lead agency for investigating acts of terrorism in the United States. In addition to the criminal investigators, the FBI maintains its own uniformed police department, employing another 230 federal law enforcement officers.

The second-largest law enforcement agency within DOJ is the **Drug Enforcement Administration (DEA)**, which employs approximately 4,300 special agents conducting investigations into drug trafficking. The third-largest DOJ agency is also considered the oldest, and that is the U.S. Marshals Service, which employs approximately 3,300 officers who are responsible for the protection of federal courts, prisoner transport, the execution of federal arrest warrants, and, as made popular in the movies, hunting down federal fugitives. And the fourth-largest DOJ agency is

Box 3.5 History in Practice: FBI Director J. Edgar Hoover

While August Vollmer was the most instrumental figure in American local policing, the **most significant figure in American federal law enforcement** was assuredly **J. Edgar Hoover**, the Director of the FBI from 1924 to 1972.

Born John Edgar Hoover on January 1, 1895, in Washington, D.C., young J. Edgar grew up around the seat of American government. After earning his law degree at George Washington University Law School he went to work for the Department of Justice as a clerk in the War Emergency Division as it was 1917, the beginning of America's involvement in World War I. He came under the wing of the U.S. Attorney General, A. Mitchell Palmer, and was part of the movement to remove radicals (e.g., communists, socialists) from the U.S.

When the Director of the Bureau, William J. Burns, resigned in scandal, President Calvin Coolidge was looking for someone who was "safe" and could take over the agency and restore its reputation. Hoover was recommended to Coolidge because Hoover was a dedicated worker and lived at home with his mother. On May 10, 1924, he was made the 6th Director of the FBI (then titled the Bureau of Investigation).

As Director, Hoover helped to restore the reputation of the FBI by going after bootleggers and the mafia during prohibition, and making sure that both he and the FBI were always at the center of attention. He helped to develop the Uniform Crime Reports, the 10 Most Wanted List, and the developed a strong network of intelligence in the United States.

It is often said that Hoover was one of the most powerful men in Washington, D.C., ever, and despite reaching the mandatory retirement age, an executive order was signed to allow him to serve indefinitely. While he often brought on controversy, he did succeed in his original charge and that was to improve the reputation of the FBI.

He died while still serving as the Director on May 2, 1972. He had served under 9 Presidential Administrations.

---

the Bureau of Alcohol, Tobacco, Firearms, and Explosives (ATF), which employs approximately 2,500 agents to conduct investigations into violations of federal law pertaining to the four areas within the agency's name (see Box 3.6).

Although the most known of the federal law enforcement agencies are found under the Departments of Homeland Security and Justice, there are many other federal law enforcement agencies that are often not well known, or many do not understand that they are federal police. For instance, the Veteran's Administration has its own police force with over 3,000 officers protecting VA Hospitals. The Pentagon, Supreme Court, U.S. Capital, and even the National Zoo have their own police forces with officers employed by the federal government. Many of the independent agencies of government also have their own police, including the U.S. Postal Inspectors (also considered to be one of the oldest law enforcement agencies in the United States) and the railroad passenger corporation Amtrak. Other departments also oversee federal law enforcement agencies such as the State Department's Bureau of

Box 3.6 **History in Practice: Match the Federal Law Enforcement Agency to the President at the Time the Agency Came into Existence**

1. U.S. Marshals

A. Andrew Johnson

2. Drug Enforcement Administration

B. Richard M. Nixon

3. Federal Air Marshal Service

C. Theodore Roosevelt

4. U.S. Secret Service

D. George Washington

5. Federal Bureau of Investigation

E. John F. Kennedy

Answers: 1D; 2B; 3E; 4A; 5C

> ### Box 3.7 Ethics in Practice: The Differences Between the Military and the Police
>
> **Police officers** and **military soldiers** wear uniforms, have similar ranks, and carry weapons. In addition, we often hear about the "militarization of the police" and we use such terms as the police fighting a "war on drugs" or a "war on crime." However, when discussing the various types of police agencies in the United States in this chapter, no mention is given to the United States Army Military Police. Nor does this chapter discuss the Air Force or Naval Security Forces, which are those service's police forces. The simple reason that these agencies are not included in this chapter is that the **military police have vastly different functions and missions,** and they are not civilian or civil law enforcement. More simply put: cops are not soldiers, and vice versa.
>
> *Ask Yourself:*
>
> **Revisit the definition of the police and discuss the similarities and differences between police officers and soldiers, as well as police departments and the military. What key characteristics define each?**
>
> **Do police officers need to understand more about the tactics and mission of military police agencies? Explain why or why not.**

Diplomatic Security, which provides Secret Service–like protection to visiting diplomatic dignitaries. The Department of the Interior has the National Park Service Park Rangers (1,400 rangers) and the U.S. Park Police (547 officers). Other federal police include the U.S. Mint Police, which guards the nation's treasury, and the National Nuclear Security Administration, which has a small police force that oversees movement of nuclear materials across the United States.

Finally, every federal department and agency employs an Office of Inspector General (OIG), an internal office dedicated to investigating claims such as fraud, waste, and abuse within an agency. Thirty-three of the 69 OIGs employ criminal investigators who are full-time sworn law enforcement officers.[98] The largest of these offices are the U.S. Postal Service, with more than 500 agents, the Department of Health and Human Services, with 389, and the Department of Defense, with 345.[99] Many OIGs, however, employ far fewer investigators, such as NASA, with 52, that National Archives and Records Administration, with six, and the Library of Congress with two (see Box 3.7).

Conclusion

Unlike most other countries in the world that have one centralized police department for the entire nation deploying the police through numerous local branches, the United States has a highly decentralized system of policing, with approximately 18,000 (if not over 20,000) police departments across the country. These agencies operate within a specified jurisdiction, enforce a specific set of criminal laws, and can be found at all levels of government, local, state, and federal. The majority of these agencies are found at the local level, with most serving municipal governments (12,000) and many more serving county jurisdictions (3,000). Others, at the local level, serve special jurisdictions that cover public buildings and facilities, such as schools, universities, and airports; natural resources, such as recreational area officers; transportation systems and their facilities, such as commuter rail and maritime ports; and criminal investigations, such as alcohol or gaming industry enforcement. There are also many Native American tribal police agencies.

At the state level, there are departments of public safety that employ state police and highway patrol officers, as well as state divisions of natural resources which employ many of the game wardens. And, finally, the level of government with the least number of sworn police officers, but sometimes the most visible, is the federal government. Taken together, all of these agencies represent what is meant by the term *policing* in America today.

Just the Facts

1. It is generally stated that there are 18,000 police agencies in the United States, but because there is no mandatory reporting requirement, nor is there any central collection agency of this information, the number may actually be higher.

2. The majority of countries in the world have one police department at the national level that works in each town and city across the country, but they work for and are beholden to the state (national government).

3. The United States has a highly decentralized police system because local, state, and (to some degree) the federal government can organize police agencies who do not report upward as they are each their own separate agencies.

4. The majority of police departments in the United States are local, which means they serve a local jurisdiction such as a town or city. These are usually divided up in the United States into large metropolitan police agencies serving over 50,000 people and small-town and rural agencies serving fewer than 50,000 people.

5. Not all local police agencies serve cities and towns as many have a special jurisdiction, laws covering a particular area that they enforce. There are five types of special jurisdiction police and they include public building/facilities, natural resources, transportation systems, criminal investigations, and special enforcement.

6. A sheriff's office is a county law enforcement office that is run by an elected sheriff, the highest law enforcement position in the county. Due to the nature of the sheriff being an elected official, he or she does not report to anyone else, other than their constituents—the people of the county.

7. There are four models of sheriff office's delivery, and they include full service,

law enforcement, civil-judiciary, and correction-judiciary.

8. There are 49 state police agencies in the United States, ranging in size from 139 officers (North Dakota) to 7,202 officers (California).

9. Game wardens, marshals, and constables are special local law enforcement officers that are empowered by the state but typically serve at the local level, whether in the county, town, or city.

10. After the terrorist attacks of September 11, 2001, the Department of Homeland Security was created and incorporated a number of existing federal law enforcement agencies dealing with the protection of the homeland, the largest of which is U.S. Customs and Border Protection. The Department of Justice, run by the U.S. Attorney General, kept the FBI, its largest agency, under its organization, responsible for investigating crimes against federal law.

Ask Yourself

1. The majority of countries in the world have only one police department for the entire country, yet America has at least 18,000. What are the pros and cons to our decentralized system of policing?

2. One of the reasons we do not know truly how many police departments there are in the United States is because there is no central authority or clearinghouse for this information. Should there be a mandatory system of accountability for reporting police information? If so, who should be in charge of that? Who should pay for it? And, more importantly, what does making this mandatory do to the relationship between federal, state, and local governments?

3. In the United States, most of the time police chiefs are appointed by the mayor and/or city council and sheriffs are elected. Which system provides a better method of holding police accountable to the people?

4. State police agencies were largely an early twentieth century creation. Are state police agencies necessary or are they a redundant government service?

5. The U.S. Constitution specifies only a few duties in which federal law enforcement would seem to be proper and necessary, such as the U.S. Marshals (security for federal courts) and the U.S. Secret Service (to address counterfeiting of U.S. currency). Most of the agencies have no specified reason for existence in the Constitution, such as the Drug Enforcement Administration, and the majority of federal law enforcement agencies were created in the late twentieth century. Should the federal government even have law enforcement agencies, especially those not specified as powers of the national government in the U.S. Constitution?

Keywords

18,000 Police departments
3,080 Sheriff offices
3,144 Counties

70 Federal law enforcement
    agencies
Campus police departments

Constables
County sheriffs

Criminal investigations agencies

Decentralized system of policing

Department of Homeland Security

Department of Justice

Federal Bureau of Investigation

Four models of sheriff's offices

Game wardens

Local police

Marshals

Metropolitan police departments

Natural resource agencies

Natural resources and conservation

New York City Police Department

No national police force

Parishes

Police census

Public school districts

Public-building facilities agencies

Reserve, auxiliary, or special police officers

Sheriff's office

Small-town and rural

Small-town and rural police departments

Special enforcement agencies

Special jurisdiction agencies

State Police

Texas Rangers

Three main functions of state police

Transportation systems/ facilities agencies

Tribal police departments

U.S. Customs and Border Protection

Endnotes

1. Vollmer, A. (1933). Police progress in the past twenty-five years. *Journal of Criminal Law and Criminology*, 24, 161-175, at p. 175.

2. Marion, N.E. & Oliver, W.M. (2015). *Federal law enforcement agencies in America*. Frederick, MD: Wolters Kluwer.

3. Marks, J. (2014). *The thin green line: A socio-historical analysis of conservation law enforcement in the United States*. Unpublished Dissertation.

4. Reaves, B.A. (2011). Census of state and local law enforcement agencies, 2008. Washington, DC: Bureau of Justice Statistics.

5. Canterbury, C. (2013). The future of law enforcement in the United States of America. *National Fraternal Order of Police*. Retrieved online at http://www.fop.net/labor/icpra/ 3 The Future of Law Enforcement in the United States of America.pdf; Roth, J., Ryan, J., & Koper, C.S. (2000). *National evaluation of the COPS program- Title I of the 1994 crime act*. Washington, DC: The Urban Institute; Skogan, W. & Frydl, K. (eds.) (2004). *Fairness and effectiveness in policing: The evidence*. Washington, DC: The National Academies Press.

6. Skogan, W. & Frydl, K. (eds.) (2004). *Fairness and effectiveness in policing: The evidence*. Washington, DC: The National Academies Press.

7. Perry, S.W. (2013). Tribal crime data collection activities, 2013. Washington, DC: Bureau of Justice Statistics.

8. Roth, J.A. & Ryan, J.F. (2000). *National evaluation of the COPS program—Title I of the 1994 crime act*. Washington, DC: U.S. Department of Justice.

9. Oliver, W.M. & Hilgenberg, J.F., Jr. (2010). *A history of crime and criminal justice in America*. 2nd ed. Durham, NC: Carolina Academic Press.

10. Skogan, W. & Frydl, K. (eds.) (2004). *Fairness and effectiveness in policing: The evidence*. Washington, DC: The National Academies Press, p. 55.

11. Alpert, G.A. & Dunham, R.G. (1996). *Policing urban America*. 3rd ed. Prospect Heights, IL: Waveland Press.

12. Reaves, B.A. (2015). *Local police departments, 2013: Personnel, policies, and practices*. Washington, DC: Bureau of Justice Statistics, p. 3.

13. Reaves, B.A. (2015). *Local Police Departments, 2013: Personnel, Policies, and Practices*. Washington, DC: Bureau of Justice Statistics, p. 3.

14. See for instance Alpert, G.A. & Dunham, R.G. (1996). *Policing urban America*. 3rd ed. Prospect Heights, IL: Waveland Press; and Weisheit, R.A., Falcone, D.N., & Wells, L.E. (2006). *Crime and policing in rural and small-town America*. 3rd ed. Long Grove, IL: Waveland Press, Inc.

15. Reaves, B.A. (2010). *Local police departments, 2007*. Washington, DC: Bureau of Justice Statistics.

16. McDonald, T.D., Wood, R.A., Pflug, M.A. (1996). *Rural criminal justice: Conditions, constraints, & challenges*. Salem, WI: Sheffield Publishing Company.

17. New York Police Department. (2014). NYPD FAQ. Retrieved online at http://www.nyc.gov/html/nypd/html/ faq/faq_police.shtml#1.

18. Conlon, E. (2004). *Blue blood*. New York, NY: Riverhead Books, p. 12.

19. To date the LEMAS studies have been conducted in 1987, 1990, 1993, 1997, 1999, 2000, 2003, 2007, and 2013. Bureau of Justice Statistics. (2015). Data collection: Law enforcement management and administrative statistics (LEMAS). Retrieved from http://www.bjs.gov/ index.cfm?ty=dcdetail&iid=248.

20. Note that the ranking is derived from the census, but current numbers are derived from the police agencies themselves with 2014 data. See Reaves, B.A. (2015). *Local police departments, 2013: Personnel, policies, and practices*. Washington, DC: Bureau of Justice Statistics.

21. Reaves, B.A. (2015). *Local police departments, 2013: Personnel, policies, and practices*. Washington, DC: Bureau of Justice Statistics.

22. Reaves, B.A. (2011). *Census of state and local law enforcement agencies, 2008*. Washington, DC: Bureau of Justice Statistics.

23. Reaves, B.A. (2011). *Census of state and local law enforcement agencies, 2008*. Washington, DC: Bureau of Justice Statistics.

24. National League of Cities. (2014). Number of Municipal Governments & Population Distribution. Retrieved from http://www.nlc.org/build-skills-and-networks/resources/cities-101/city-structures/number-of-municipal-governments-and-population-distribution.

25. Reaves, B.A. (2015). *Local police departments, 2013: Personnel, policies, and practices*. Washington, DC: Bureau of Justice Statistics.

26. Reaves, B.A. (2015). *Local police departments, 2013: Personnel, policies, and practices*. Washington, DC: Bureau of Justice Statistics.

27. Capsambelis, C. (2009). *Policing in rural America: A handbook for the rural law enforcement officer*. Durham, NC: Carolina Academic Press; Weisheit, R.A., Falcone, D.N., & Wells, L.E. (2005). *Crime and policing in rural and small-town America*. 3rd ed. Longrove, IL: Waveland Press, Inc.

28. McDonald, T.D., Wood, R.A., & Pflug, M.A. (1996). *Rural criminal justice: Conditions, constraints, & challenges*. Salem, WI: Sheffield Publishing Company.

29. Kidder, T. (1999). *Home town*. New York, NY: Washington Square Press, p. 31.

30. Reaves, B.A. (2015). *Local police departments, 2013: Personnel, policies, and practices*. Washington, DC: Bureau of Justice Statistics.

31. Reaves, B.A. (2011). *Census of state and local law enforcement agencies, 2008*. Washington, DC: Bureau of Justice Statistics.

32. Reaves, B.A. (2011). *Census of state and local law enforcement agencies, 2008*. Washington, DC: Bureau of Justice Statistics.

33. Rubenser, L. & Priddy, G. (2011). *Constables, marshals, and more: Forgotten offices in Texas law enforcement*. Denton, TX: University of North Texas Press, chapter 8.

34. Reaves, B.A. (2015). *Campus law enforcement, 2011-12*. Washington, DC: Bureau of Justice Statistics.

35. Von Baldegg, K.C.M. (2011). 4 synchronized camera angles of the UC Davis pepper spray incident. *The Atlantic Monthly*. Retrieved from http://www.theatlantic.com/video/archive/2011/11/4-synchronized-camera-angles-of-the-uc-davis-pepper-spray-incident/248863/.

36. Crimaldi, L. (2014). Fallen MIT officer Sean Collier remembered in Cambridge. *The Boston Globe*. Retrieved from http://www.bostonglobe.com/metro/2014/04/18/mit-police-officer-sean-collier-remembered-year-after-was-allegedly-slain-boston-marathon-bombing-suspects/Tj8XFFU7ipnAVNE1DJOxzH/story.html.

37. Reaves, B.A. (2011). *Census of state and local law enforcement agencies, 2008*. Washington, DC: Bureau of Justice Statistics.

38. Rubenser, L. & Priddy, G. (2011). *Constables, marshals, and more: Forgotten offices in Texas law enforcement*. Denton, TX: University of North Texas Press, chapter 13.

39. Reaves, B.A. (2011). *Census of state and local law enforcement agencies, 2008*. Washington, DC: Bureau of Justice Statistics.

40. Reaves, B.A. (2011). *Census of state and local law enforcement agencies, 2008*. Washington, DC: Bureau of Justice Statistics.

41. Rubenser, L. & Priddy, G. (2011). *Constables, marshals, and more: Forgotten offices in Texas law enforcement*. Denton, TX: University of North Texas Press, chapter 5.

42. Pavlik, Ron. (2013). Metro Transit Police Department—Policing a high-threat target. Retrieved from https://www.youtube.com/watch?v=I0NlHlBtZ7Q.

43. Washington Metropolitan Area Transit Authority. (2014). Metro transit police. Retrieved online at http://www.wmata.com/about_metro/transit_police/.

44. Reaves, B.A. (2011). *Census of state and local law enforcement agencies, 2008*. Washington, DC: Bureau of Justice Statistics.

45. Reaves, B.A. (2011). *Census of state and local law enforcement agencies, 2008*. Washington, DC: Bureau of Justice Statistics; Rubenser, L. & Priddy, G. (2011). *Constables, marshals, and more: Forgotten offices in Texas law enforcement*. Denton, TX: University of North Texas Press.

46. Reaves, B.A. (2011). *Census of state and local law enforcement agencies, 2008*. Washington, DC: Bureau of Justice Statistics.

47. Reaves, B.A. (2011). *Census of state and local law enforcement agencies, 2008*. Washington, DC: Bureau of Justice Statistics.

48. Rubenser, L. & Priddy, G. (2011). *Constables, marshals, and more: Forgotten offices in Texas law enforcement*. Denton, TX: University of North Texas Press.

49. Clinton, P. (2013). Nevada's gaming control board. *Police: The Law Enforcement Magazine*. Retrieved from http://www.policemag.com/channel/careers-training/articles/2013/01/nevada-s-gaming-control-board.aspx.

50. Kawucha, S.K. (2014). *Sheriffs—the other police*. Unpublished dissertation.

51. Harris County Sheriff's Office. (2014). Harris County Sheriff's Office. Retrieved online at http://www.harriscountyso.org; Oliver, W.M. & Meier, C.A. (2001). The siren's song: Federalism and the cops grants. *American Journal of Criminal Justice*, 25, 223-238.

52. Zamara, E.N. (2011). An oral history of retired Madison county, Ohio, Sheriff Steve Saltsman. *Ohio CJ Oral History Journal*. Retrieved from http://ohiocjoralhistoryjournal.blogspot.com/2011/11/0-0-1-12827-73115-tiffin-university-609.html.

53. Kawucha, S.K. (2014). *Sheriffs—the other police*. Unpublished dissertation.

54. Reaves, B.A. (2011). *Census of state and local law enforcement agencies, 2008*. Washington, DC: Bureau of Justice Statistics.

55. Brown, L.P. (1978). The role of the sheriff. In *The future of policing*, A.V. Cohn (Ed.), (pp. 227-247). Beverly Hills, CA: Sage Publications.

56. U.S. Census Bureau. (2014). U.S. Census. Retrieved from http://www.census.gov/.

57. National Sheriffs' Association. (2014). Frequently asked questions. Retrieved from http://www.sheriffs.org/content/faq.

58. Reaves, B.A. (2011). *Census of state and local law enforcement agencies, 2008*. Washington, DC: Bureau of Justice Statistics.

59. National Sheriffs' Association. (2014). Office of sheriff state-by-state elections information. Retrieved from http://www.sheriffs.org/sites/default/files/tb/Office_of_Sheriff_State-by-State_Election_Chart.pdf.

60. Reaves, B.A. (2011). *Census of state and local law enforcement agencies, 2008*. Washington, DC: Bureau of Justice Statistics. Note: The 2013 census, focused more on local law enforcement, states that there are 3,012 sheriff's offices, employing 188,952 deputies. Reaves, B.A. (2015). *Local police departments, 2013: Personnel, policies, and practices*. Washington, DC: Bureau of Justice Statistics.

61. Reaves, B.A. (2011). *Census of state and local law enforcement agencies, 2008*. Washington, DC: Bureau of Justice Statistics.

62. Burch, A.M. (2012). *Sheriff's offices, 2007—Statistical table*. Washington, DC: Bureau of Justice Statistics.

63. Perry, S.W. (2013). *Tribal crime data collection activities, 2013*. Washington, DC: Bureau of Justice Statistics.

64. Hickman, M.J. (2003). *Tribal law enforcement, 2000*. Washington, DC: Bureau of Justice Statistics.

65. Hickman, M.J. (2003). *Tribal law enforcement, 2000*. Washington, DC: Bureau of Justice Statistics.

66. Bureau of Indian Affairs. (2014). Division of law enforcement. Retrieved from http://bia.gov/WhoWeAre/BIA/OJS/DOLE/

67. Malega, R. & Garner, J.H. (2019). Sworn volunteers in American policing, 1999 to 2013. *Police Quarterly*, 22, 56-81; Reserve Police Officers Association. (2014). Reserve Police Officers Association. Retrieved from http://www.reservepolice.org/index.html.

68. Reaves, B.A. (2011). *Census of state and local law enforcement agencies, 2008*. Washington, DC: Bureau of Justice Statistics.

69. Vollmer, A. (1933). Police progress in the past twenty-five years. *Journal of Criminal Law and Criminology*, 24, 161-175, at p. 175.

70. Cox, M. (2008). *The Texas Rangers: Wearing the cinco peso, 1821-1900*. New York, NY: Forge; Utley, R.M. (2002). *Lone star justice: The first century of the Texas rangers*. New York, NY: Berkley Books; Webb, W.P.

(1965). *The Texas Rangers: A century of frontier defense*. Austin: University of Texas Press.

71. Bechtel, H.K. (1995). State police in the United States: A socio-historical analysis. Westport, CT: Greenwood Press.

72. Oliver, W.M. & Hilgenberg, J.F., Jr. (2010). *A history of crime and criminal justice in America*. 2nd ed. Durham, NC: Carolina Academic Press.

73. Walker, S. (1998). *Popular justice: A history of American criminal justice*. 2nd ed. New York, NY: Oxford University Press, p. 140.

74. Pack, M. (2010). State vs. city police. *Officer.com* Retrieved from www.forums.officer.com/forums/archive/index.php/t-154017.html.

75. Skogan, W. & Frydl, K. (eds.) (2004). *Fairness and effectiveness in policing: The evidence*. Washington, DC: The National Academies Press, p. 54.

76. Reaves, B.A. (2011). *Census of state and local law enforcement agencies, 2008*. Washington, DC: Bureau of Justice Statistics.

77. Reaves, B.A. (2011). *Census of state and local law enforcement agencies, 2008*. Washington, DC: Bureau of Justice Statistics.

78. Reaves, B.A. (2011). *Census of state and local law enforcement agencies, 2008*. Washington, DC: Bureau of Justice Statistics.

79. Cox, M. (2009). *Time of the rangers: Texas Rangers from 1900 to the present*. New York, NY: Forge; Utley, R.M. (2007). *Lone star lawmen: The second century of the Texas Rangers*. New York, NY: Berkley Books.

80. Texas Department of Public Safety. (2014). Texas Highway Patrol. Retrieved from http://www.txdps.state.tx.us/tle/index.htm

81. Chapman, A. & Woodson, P.D. (2002). Meet the new Texas Rangers: A breed apart. *Fort Worth Star-Telegram*, October 27; Cox, M. (2009). *Time of the Rangers: Texas Rangers from 1900 to the present*. New York, NY: Forge, p. 368.

82. Marks, J.M., Jr. (2013). *Thin green line: A socio-historical analysis of conservation law enforcement in the United States*. Unpublished dissertation.

83. Marks, J.M., Jr. (2013). *Thin green line: A socio-historical analysis of conservation law enforcement in the United States*. Unpublished dissertation.

84. Reaves, B.A. (2011). *Census of state and local law enforcement agencies, 2008*. Washington, DC: Bureau of Justice Statistics.

85. Reaves, B.A. (2011). *Census of state and local law enforcement agencies, 2008*. Washington, DC: Bureau of Justice Statistics.

86. Rubenser, L. & Priddy, G. (2011). *Constables, marshals, and more: Forgotten offices in Texas law enforcement*. Denton, TX: University of North Texas Press.

87. Rubenser, L. & Priddy, G. (2011). *Constables, marshals, and more: Forgotten offices in Texas law enforcement*. Denton, TX: University of North Texas Press.

88. Skogan, W. & Frydl, K. (eds.) (2004). *Fairness and effectiveness in policing: The evidence*. Washington, DC: National Academies Press, p. 53.

89. Marion, N.E. & Oliver, W.M. (2015). *Federal law enforcement agencies in America*. Frederick, MD: Wolters Kluwer.
90. Bumgarner, J.B. (2006). *Federal agents: The growth of federal law enforcement in America*. Westport, CT: Praeger; Marion, N.E. & Oliver, W.M. (2015). *Federal law enforcement agencies in America*. Frederick, MD: Wolters Kluwer; Reaves, B.A. (2012). *Federal law enforcement officers, 2008*. Washington, DC: Bureau of Justice Statistics.
91. Reaves, B.A. (2012). *Federal law enforcement officers, 2008*. Washington, DC: Bureau of Justice Statistics.
92. Reaves, B.A. (2012). *Federal law enforcement officers, 2008*. Washington, DC: Bureau of Justice Statistics.
93. Reaves, B.A. (2012). *Federal law enforcement officers, 2008*. Washington, DC: Bureau of Justice Statistics.
94. Marion, N.E. & Oliver, W.M. (2015). *Federal law enforcement agencies in America*. Frederick, MD: Wolters Kluwer.
95. Melanson, P.H. with Stevens, P.F. (2002). *The Secret Service: The hidden history of an enigmatic agency*. New York, NY: Carroll & Graf Publishers, p. 262.
96. Marion, N.E. & Oliver, W.M. (2015). *Federal law enforcement agencies in America*. Frederick, MD: Wolters Kluwer.
97. Mungro, S. (2014). Johnnie Mae Gibson. Retrieved from http://www.answers.com/topic/johnnie-mae-gibson.
98. Reaves, B.A. (2012). *Federal law enforcement officers, 2008*. Washington, DC: Bureau of Justice Statistics.
99. Reaves, B.A. (2012). *Federal law enforcement officers, 2008*. Washington, DC: Bureau of Justice Statistics.

■ *"Accurate studies must be made of crime, vice, and traffic conditions; charts, graphs, tables, and maps showing the "who," "what," "when," "where," "why" of these problems must be carefully prepared. Guided by such information, a solid foundation may be erected for effective police organization."*[1]
—*August Vollmer*

One Police Plaza is the headquarters of the New York Police Department, the largest police department in the Unites States.

CHAPTER 4

Organization

After reading this chapter, you will be able to:

1. Identify and explain the three types of municipal government organization and specify which is most commonly used in America today.
2. Understand the concept of a commission and differentiate between the police in a commission form of government, the historically retained title of police commissioner, and a county commission.
3. Summarize what a bureaucracy entails and how the police are inherently a government bureaucracy.
4. Differentiate between a policy, procedure, rule, and regulation.
5. Identify and explain the four ways in which police organize.
6. Identify and explain the three functions by which police organize.
7. Explain what it means when it is said that the police organize by area and time.
8. Contrast the differences between police leadership and police management.
9. Define the acronym POSDCORB and explain what it means.
10. Identify and explain the three theories of police organization.

Police departments from their very beginning have been organized along military lines.[2] They tend to have many of the trappings of the military from uniforms and weapons to a military rank structure consisting of corporals, sergeants, and lieutenants. This is what is commonly referred to as either a quasi-military or paramilitary organization.[3] When Robert Peel organized the first police department, he placed his police officers in uniforms with badges bearing a number, so as to be readily identifiable. He also brought in Charles Rowan to organize them because of his military background. Rowan was a lieutenant colonel who had served in the Peninsular War and at Waterloo.[4]

When policing began in the United States, however, very often the police did not wear uniforms, and when departments moved to their adoption, police officers protested or simply quit.[5] These early police departments did not have uniforms because it was believed they represented government authority over the people, and the American people were not fond of government control. The problems that arose, however, were twofold. On the one hand, citizens did not respect the police or even recognize nonuniformed police officers as having any authority, thus making their job difficult. On the other hand, police departments found it difficult to maintain order and control over their officers without the outward sign of a bureaucratic police force—the uniform. As a result, the adoption of the police uniform was a slow process in America. By 1860, only 15 police departments had adopted the police uniform, while another 24 would follow suit over the next decade.[6]

One other reason that police uniforms were slow to be adopted was because policing was not about control or law and order. Rather, as noted in Chapter 2, it was about serving the political machine through graft and corruption. To do this, police chiefs had to make sure that there were not too many layers between himself and the officers on the street. More layers in the police organization meant more people could skim off the top of the illegal money working its way up the chain-of-command to the police chief. Therefore, police chiefs made sure that each police district and unit reported directly to them; that way they could maintain more control over them. One example was the corrupt Chicago Police Department, which, even as late as 1930, had all 41 police districts and an additional eight specific units (for example, traffic, vice, and detective divisions) reporting directly to the police commissioner. Another 23 units reported directly to the deputy commissioner.[7] This was not a police department organized to provide police services, but one to maintain political control for purposes of graft and corruption, which were widespread and pervasive in the Chicago PD at that time.

It was during the early twentieth century that many police reformers began to criticize political influence, noting that "the incompetence, corruption, and lawlessness" were partly due to the "political interference in departmental policies."[8] August Vollmer was the most influential police reformer, who exposed the problems of graft and corruption in policing and called for change. As police historian Robert Fogelson pointed out, "This diagnosis was worked out by Vollmer in the 1920s and 1930s."[9] It was then that the legendary work of such people as Bruce Smith, who worked for the Institute of Public Administration conducting evaluations of police departments, began to expose the problems of police corruption as found in the manner in which police departments were organized and recommending change. Again, according to Fogelson, it was "not until O.W. Wilson and Vollmer's other disciples refined and popularized it after World War II did it emerge as the conventional reform wisdom of the reform movement."[10]

The conventional reform wisdom during the 1950s and 1960s was to remove politics from the police, thus allowing the police to become a profession.[11] The police professionalization movement envisioned the police as being more akin to doctors and lawyers, who had to obtain an education, specialized training, and take tests for acceptance into the profession. In addition, they had to adhere to a high level of ethical standards to remain certified to practice their profession. One way to achieve this removal of politics from police organizations, as seen by reformers such as O.W. Wilson, was to organize the police more strictly along military lines.[12]

Police scholars have asserted that the police reformers organized the police along military lines because of the similarities between the two organizations. They saw it as the best way to fight corruption "because they could not avail themselves of any other options to secure internal discipline."[13] Consider the similarities between the police and the military: both wear uniforms, use military ranks, have a hierarchical chain-of-command, maintain an authoritarian organization, and both have authorization to use force—to include deadly force—and to carry weapons.[14] Despite all of these trappings, the police are a civil force, not a military force. The police serve the citizens of the community in which they work; they are not out to destroy an opposing force. They are directed often by citizens (not solely their leaders). They are constrained by the rights of citizens and exercise discretion. And they work primarily as individuals, not as a large show of force.

In many ways, the typical police department in the United States is organized along bureaucratic lines, elements of which include a chain-of-command, division of labor, and specializations. This forms what is known as the police bureaucracy, which is derived from and directed by the local government structure, and is further organized by personnel, function, area, and time. In addition, the elements of police leadership and police management play a crucial role in the police organization. Finally, all of these factors combined have yielded a number of theories regarding how police organizations operate and change. As James Q. Wilson, the author of *Bureaucracy*, wrote, "Organizations matter, even in government agencies." This is the topic of this chapter—police (government) organization.[15]

Government Organization

To understand the political organization of the police, it is important to remember the type of government that exists in the United States (see Box 4.1). Although we talk about policing in a democracy, the United States is not a true democracy, but rather a federal republic. It is a federal government because there exists both a national government (Washington, D.C.) and state governments (all 50) with the latter overseeing local government. It is a republic because we as citizens do not vote on every issue put before the government, as in a true democracy. Rather, we vote for representatives who (ideally) represent our interests to the government in which we elected them to serve, whether federal, state, or local. This three-tiered system provides

Box 4.1 History in Practice: Grover Cleveland and Theodore Roosevelt, the Sheriff and the Police Superintendent

Although little known outside of policing circles, two of America's Presidents served in the law enforcement field before taking office. **President Grover Cleveland** served as the **sheriff** of Erie County (New York) from 1870 to 1873, and **President Theodore Roosevelt** served as the New York City **police superintendent** from 1895 to 1897.

Grover Cleveland was born in New Jersey on March 18, 1837, and grew up wanting to attend college, but had to defer in order to make ends meet. He worked as a clerk and part-time law student in Buffalo, New York, and was admitted to the bar in 1858. He served as an assistant district attorney in Erie County, and as a practicing lawyer. In 1870, he ran for election as the sheriff of Erie County and won. Cleveland discovered that one of his duties as sheriff was to serve as the local hangman in case of a death sentence, and he found himself having to execute a young Irishman who had killed his own mother. Cleveland could have delegated the responsibility to a deputy, but he did not feel that was right. He is probably the only president to have ever served as a hangman. He also became the only president to have served two non-consecutive terms, from 1885 to 1889 and then again from 1893 to 1897.

Theodore Roosevelt was born in New York City on October 27, 1858; he was home-schooled and entered Harvard College. After graduating with honors he went on to Columbia Law School, which he found frustrating, so he spent most of his time in the library writing a history of the U.S. Navy in the War of 1812. Roosevelt soon married, had a child on the way, and became a New York State Assemblyman. After he lost his wife and mother in one night, he turned his young daughter over to his sister, went west, and lived as a cowboy. He eventually came back, remarried, and became active in politics, securing a position on the U.S. Civil Service Commission. Deciding to return home to New York City, he found himself appointed to the New York City Police Commission in 1895 and, as no one wanted to serve as the president of the board, Roosevelt accepted and became the superintendent of the NYPD. The department was wholly corrupt, and Roosevelt set about cleaning up the police department by holding officers accountable, investigating cases of graft, and enforcing the laws, especially those that were unpopular such as the blue laws of no alcohol sales on Sunday. Roosevelt was successful in helping to clean up the police department, but in 1897 he was made Assistant Secretary of the Navy and the NYPD fell back into its corrupt ways. Roosevelt became the youngest president ever to serve after President McKinley was assassinated, and he went on to serve his own term in office (1905 to 1909).

Sources: Algeo, M. (2011). *The President Is a Sick Man.* Chicago, IL: Chicago Review Press; Jeffers, H. P. (1994). *Commissioner Roosevelt.* New York, NY: John Wiley & Sons, Inc.; *The New York Times,* July 7, 1912; Zacks, R. (2012). *Island of Vice.* New York, NY: Doubleday.

another form of checks and balances in our government system to prevent any particular level of government from having too much power. Although all three, in our case, exert influence over policing, because the police are typically a local government entity, overseen by city or county governments, it is important to understand how they are managed.

At the local level there are three main forms of government that exist in the United States. The most common is the **council-manager** form of government.[16] In this case, the people elect their city council members, very often in a mixed format, where some are from their precinct while others serve at-large, thus representing the entire city. The city council members are then responsible for representing the people's interest by carrying out the general administrative duties of the city, passing city ordinances, and establishing budgets. As members of the city council have their own full-time jobs, they cannot be responsible for the day-in and day-out duties of the

The majority of police departments in the United States are overseen by municipal governments which typically meet at the local city hall.

local government, so they appoint a person to serve as the city manager who will carry out these tasks. The council-manager form of government will then usually select a mayor from its members (although sometimes they are elected) to perform the ceremonial functions that are often associated with local mayors (for example, issuing proclamations and ribbon-cutting ceremonies) or the chair of the board will perform these functions. When there is a police chief vacancy, the city manager will usually conduct the search for the new police chief which then has to be approved by the city council. Some of the largest cities in the United States, including Phoenix, Arizona; San Antonio, Texas; and Charlotte, North Carolina, use this type of government.

The second most common form of local government is the **mayor-council** form of government.[17] In this case the mayor and the members of the city council are elected separately. The mayor can be either a full-time or part-time position, and generally includes some form of compensation. Depending upon the city charter, the mayor can often be a very strong position or a very weak one. In the strong mayor structure, the mayor usually chairs the city council meetings, is a voting member, has administrative authority over the hiring and firing of city employees, as well as budgetary authority. In the weak mayor structure, the mayor may chair the city council meetings, but is not a voting member, and most of the administrative and budgetary duties rest with the city council. The mayor in this case, like in the council-manager form of city governance, is relegated to ceremonial duties. In the strong mayor structure the mayor can hire and fire the police chief, whereas in the weak structure, it is the city council that has this responsibility. Many of the largest cities in the United States, including New York City, Los Angeles, Chicago, and Houston, use this form of municipal government.

Regardless of the form of municipal governance, the mayor, city manager, and city council members hold regular public meetings to conduct the city's business.

The third most common form of local municipal governance is the **commission**.[18] Although used in only less than 1 percent of all cities in the United States, it is the oldest form of local governance in the country. In commission governments, the people vote individual commissioners to a governing board and each commissioner becomes responsible for managing some aspect of the city's responsibilities, such as the police, fire, or public works. One commissioner is selected to serve as the chair of the commission (sometimes called the mayor) and that individual runs the commission meetings. While in the two forms of government the mayor or manager serves as the executive and the city council as the legislative branch, a city commission actually serves both of these functions for they are combined. Cities such as Sunrise, Florida, and Fairview, Tennessee, continue to use this form of governance today.

It should be noted here that many large cities continue to use a **police commission** to oversee the police department. For instance, Los Angeles, despite having a mayor-council form of government, retained the police commission to oversee the police department. In this form of governance, the city may still have any of the above forms of governance, but for the police department they have a police commission consisting of elected or appointed members who oversee the police department. In many ways it operates like a corporation where the police commission acts as a board of directors, while the police chief or police commissioner is the chief executive officer who actually runs the police department on a day-to-day basis.

Many police departments once used a police commission to oversee police departments, but eventually did away with them. However, many retained the title of police commissioner for the head of the police agency. The New York City Police Department is a good example of this, for while William Bratton was the police commissioner, he was appointed by the mayor and served at the mayor's will and pleasure.

The police commission should not be confused with the county form of governance which is typically called a county commission.[19] Most counties in the United States use a **county commission** form of government, which invests the legislative and executive powers in an elected commission or board of supervisors. Historically, this has been the predominant means of county governance and remains so today; however, an estimated 40 percent of counties have shifted to either a commissioner/administrator or council/executive form of government.[20] In the former, the county commission appoints an administrator who serves at their pleasure and handles the executive powers of the commission, while in the latter, the county executive is elected to serve as the chief administrative officer of the county, which means they do not serve at the will and pleasure of the commission, only of the people.

When it comes to the sheriff, the relationship with the county commission depends on whether the sheriff runs an office or a department. If the sheriff runs an office, they are the highest elected law enforcement official, and while they do not report to or serve the county commission, only the electorate, they are usually dependent upon the county commission for at least some of their budget. If the sheriff runs a true department (remember some sheriff's offices call themselves departments), then they answer to the county commission

Whether an office or a department and the type of governing structure the local government employs, all have an influence on the police agency and its form of organization. There is perhaps no better person to explain the impact of local governance on a police department than Lee P. Brown who has served as both the police chief and as a three-term mayor for the city of Houston. Because he has been on both sides, he explains, "As a police chief you have to establish a relationship with the mayor that is clear about the few things he wants to be advised on and what policies he wants to be involved in with the police department."[21] Alternatively, Brown explains "As mayor, I am the one who will ultimately be responsible for policy in all city departments."[22] Understanding the local government structure helps to inform us how the police department or sheriff's office itself will be organized. Moving down from local governance to the police organization itself and how it is organized, we must first understand bureaucracies and particularly how police bureaucracies are organized in the United States.

Police Bureaucracy

One of the most important changes in American policing that allowed reformers to get police departments under control and move their agencies from politically corrupt to professional organizations was the adoption of bureaucratic methods of organization and management. Advocated by Bruce Smith, implemented by August Vollmer, and widely disseminated by his disciple O.W. Wilson, these practices became the gold standard for the professionalization of the police in the second half of the twentieth century.[23] The ideas for police management, however, actually came from the scientific management principles of Frederick W. Taylor and the work of Max Weber on bureaucracy (see Box 4.2).

Frederick W. Taylor is known as the father of scientific management because of his research into worker productivity. Taylor observed assembly-line workers in factories and searched for ways to make their jobs easier and faster. Max Weber studied bureaucratic organizations and explained that there are certain principles evident in all of these organizations: well-defined hierarchy

> ### Box 4.2 Policing in Practice: Max Weber's Principles of a Bureaucracy
>
> An **effective bureaucracy** depends on professional methods of organization and management. Max Weber was a German sociologist who taught at numerous universities in Germany and Austria in the early twentieth century. He advocated for the removal of politics for public administration, government and business by advocating for the creation of civil service bureaucracies. He specified that all bureaucracies should have the following:
>
> 1. Division of labor (work)
> 2. Hierarchy of authority
> 3. Formal selection and promotion of employees based on technical competence
> 4. Formal written rules and regulations, policies and procedures
> 5. Impersonal work environment
> 6. Career orientation of employees
>
> These principles still hold true for today's police forces.

of authority, specialization, formalization, impersonality of management, and personnel decisions based on merit. All of these principles are most assuredly found in police departments today, but it was O.W. Wilson who played the biggest role in making that a reality as he adopted the lessons of Taylor and Weber to police administration after World War II (see Box 4.3).[24]

Orlando Winfield Wilson, or O.W. to most people, had been a police officer in the Berkeley PD under August Vollmer. With Vollmer's assistance, he quickly became the police chief in Fullerton (California) and later the police chief of Wichita (Kansas), and eventually the police commissioner in Chicago.[25] He also served as a police professor at Harvard University and University of California, Berkeley, in between his time at Wichita and Chicago. The combination of positions and experience left him well situated to write his book *Police Administration*, which was first published in 1950.[26] Wilson's book became the defining guide for policing scholars and police chiefs for the next 50 years, and his book, dubbed the "big green monster" by police officers because of its green cover, was used for police department promotional exams across America.

Wilson states that "the purpose of organization is to simplify the direction, coordination, and control of members of the force so that the objectives of the department may be gained easily, effectively, and satisfactorily."[27] To do so, police departments

The Ronald Tsukamoto Public Safety Building, named for one of the two Berkeley officers killed in the line of duty, is the headquarters of the Berkeley Police Department.

Box 4.3 History in Practice: O.W. Wilson and Police Management

If there is any name in police organization that a student of policing should know, next to August Vollmer and J. Edgar Hoover, there is **O.W. Wilson**. In some ways, when it comes to police administration, O.W. Wilson's name may need to come first for he was the author of the very influential book in **police management** in the second half of the 20th Century, *Police Administration* (McGraw-Hill), which went through three editions by Wilson and two more after his death. The book also became the primary book by which police officers across the country would study in order to prepare for promotional exams.

Wilson was born Orlando Winfield Wilson on May 15, 1900, but was always known as O.W. throughout his life. His family moved to California when he was young, and Wilson went to the University of California at Berkeley and became one of August Vollmer's college cops, working the dog shift at night and taking classes during the day. Wilson and Vollmer developed a strong relationship, and Vollmer helped Wilson obtain a position as police chief with the Fullerton (California) Police Department. The politics forced him to resign and he almost left policing, but Vollmer helped him secure a position as the chief of police in Wichita (Kansas) Police Department where he served for over ten years. He left to take the position Vollmer had vacated, professor of criminology at University of California, Berkeley. With the intervention of World War II, Wilson served as a provost marshal with the military police, with the rank of colonel, and he helped Germany reestablish a police force after the war. Wilson returned to Berkeley and was elevated to the Dean of the Berkeley School of Criminology before he was enticed to serve as the Chicago police commissioner from 1960 to 1967.

Wilson wrote the book *Police Administration* based on everything he had learned from Vollmer and having served as a police chief. The book was essentially written from scratch, as there was no other book like it in existence. Because Wilson lived near August Vollmer and they maintained a close relationship, he did have the benefit of bouncing ideas off of "the Chief." While Wilson had a storied career, his greatest contribution to American policing had to be his book and thoughts on *Police Administration,* making him, from a police organizational perspective, probably the most important pioneer.

Sources: Bopp, W.J. (1977). *O.W. Wilson and the Search for a Police Profession.* Port Washington, NY: Kennikat Press; Wilson, O.W. (1963). *Police Administration.* 2nd ed. New York, NY: McGraw-Hill, Inc.

organize using a hierarchy of authority that is commonly known as a **chain-of-command.** The concept of a chain-of-command is that the person at the top of the chain commands a limited number of people who then turn around and supervise an equally manageable number of people. This then continues down to the line officers, the police officers who patrol the streets. Looking at it from the other direction, in a chain-of-command, every police officer has one supervisor and that individual reports to one supervisor and so on, all the way to the top person in the chain—the police chief.

The chain-of-command is often typified by the pyramid organizational structure or the police organizational chart which shows where in the hierarchy each employee is situated in the organization. To further help clarify where in the hierarchy a person is located, military ranks are often used to denote the level of authority of a particular individual in the chain-of-command. So, the police officer on the street reports to a corporal, who reports to a sergeant, who reports to a lieutenant, who reports to a captain, who then reports to the police chief. Conversely, the police chief may desire some particular action of the police officers on patrol and the chief will then direct the captain, who informs the lieutenant, who directs the sergeant, and tells the corporal, who then orders the police officer on the street to implement the change.

There are many other principles of bureaucracy that elaborate further on the concept of a chain-of-command. For instance, research in public and police administration has shown that there is a finite number of people that one person can effectively manage. This is known as the **span of control.** While it is very easy to manage one or two employees, it is far more difficult to manage 20 or 120 people. Research has suggested that it is ideal for a manager to supervise between five and seven employees, and acceptable to have as many as six to ten. When looking at an organizational chart, to maintain a proper span of control, no supervisor should ever have more than ten employees underneath them.

Another principle known as the **unity of command** deals with the reverse situation. No employee should ever have to report to more than one person. Every employee in a police organization should only have one supervisor to avoid confusion and the possibility of receiving conflicting orders. So, while one supervisor should never manage more than ten police officers, each police officer should never report to more than one supervisor.

There are two other principles for having a chain-of-command and these are for purposes of delegation and the division of labor. When a police chief orders a captain to take responsibility for some new policy or to implement a program, the chief is using the power of **delegation**. It is unrealistic for a police chief to have a hand in doing everything a police department needs to accomplish unless it is a small-town police department with only one or two officers. The larger the organization, the more the police chief has to delegate responsibility down the chain-of-command and allow the midlevel managers to implement the new policies or programs. When a police chief delegates their authority, the one thing they do not delegate, however, is their responsibility. The police chief is ultimately responsible for the policies and programs implemented, so they must follow up to ensure that those to whom they delegated their authority are carrying out their orders.

The other principle involved in having a chain-of-command is the **division of labor.** Police departments do not just provide police officers to patrol the city streets and respond to 911 calls. There are also detectives who conduct investigations and maintenance crews to service police vehicles. The chain-of-command allows the police chief to supervise one captain or lieutenant who is in charge of the officers on patrol, another supervises the detectives, while yet another oversees the support functions of the police department. That allows

Berkeley Police Department

Internal Affairs Bureau

Office of The Chief
Michael Meehan, Chief of Police

Administrative & Fiscal Services Manager

Public Information Officer

Historical Foundation

Operations Division
Captain Andrew Greenwood

Investigations Division
Captain David Frankel

Professional Standards Division
Captain Cynthia Harris

Patrol

Detective
Lt. Ed Spiller

SEU
Lt. Randolph Files

Professional Standards
Lt. David Reece

Personnel and Training
Lt. Rico Rolleri

Teams 1 and 2
Lt. Jen Louis

Special Response Team

Crimes Against Persons (Homicide and Robbery)

Special Investigations Bureau

Policy &, Planning

Employee Health

Team 3 and 4
Lt. Dan Montgomery

Bomb Squad

Special Victims Unit (Youth, Domestic Violence and Sex Crimes)

Admin Narcotics

Audit, Inspection & Accreditation

Training

Teams 5 and 6a
Lt. Andrew Rateaver

Field Training Program

Property Crimes Bureau

Drug Task Force

Jail

Recruitment

Teams 6b and 7
Lt. Alyson Hart

Facility and Fleet Management

Crime Scene Investigations

Traffic Bureau
Lt. Kevin Schofield

Records Management

Firearms Training Patrol Rifles

Public Safety Computer System

Crime Analysis

Warrants Court Liaison

Chem. Agents Gas Masks

Communications Center Manager
Monique Frost

Crisis Intervention Team

Traffic Enforcement

Parking Enforcement Unit
Parking Mgr.

Property Room

Defensive Tactics

Communications Center

Community Services Bureau

Fatal Accident Investigation Team

Parking Enforcement

Backgrounds

October 2015

Reserves

Traffic Analyst

Organization Chart, Berkeley Police Department.

for multiple chains-of-command to work their way down to the individual at the bottom who performs a unique function. This allows for different types of labor to be performed, thus allowing for all of the various duties to work toward accomplishing the overall mission of the police department.

One other important aspect of any bureaucracy is the need to ensure that with so many layers of management and so much variation between jobs, there exists some uniformity throughout the organization. Police departments deal with this by issuing policies, procedures, rules, and regulations. A **policy** is a broad statement issued to every member of the department that describes in general what it wants the agency to do. For instance, a departmental policy may describe the code of conduct and appearance of its officers or deputies, off-duty conduct, and off-duty employment (see Table 4.1 for police and Table 4.2 for sheriffs). Police departments will also typically have policies on serious issues, such as use of force (see Table 4.3) and for

Table 4.1   Conduct Policies of Local Police Departments by Size of Population Served, 2007

Pop. Served	Code of Conduct and Appearance	Off-Duty Conduct	Off-Duty Employment
All sizes	96%	90%	83%
1,000,000 or more	100%	100%	100%
500,000 to 999,999	100%	97%	100%
250,000–499,999	100%	100%	100%
100,000–249,999	100%	99%	99%
50,000–99,999	100%	97%	99%
25,000–49,999	100%	99%	98%
10,000–24,999	100%	95%	98%
2,500–9,999	98%	91%	89%
Under 2,500	92%	84%	68%

Source: Reaves, B.A. (2010). *Local Police Departments, 2007.* Washington, DC: Bureau of Justice Statistics, p. 13.

Table 4.2   Conduct Policies of Sheriffs' Offices by Size of Population Served, 2007

Pop. Served	Code of Conduct and Appearance	Off-Duty Conduct	Off-Duty Employment
All sizes	97%	91%	84%
1,000,000 or more	100%	100%	100%
500,000 to 999,999	100%	98%	98%
250,000–499,999	100%	100%	93%
100,000–249,999	100%	95%	95%
50,000–99,999	100%	99%	95%
25,000–49,999	100%	97%	93%
10,000–24,999	94%	87%	79%
Under 10,000	92%	79%	64%

Source: Reaves, B.A. (2010). *Sheriffs' Offices, 2007—Statistical Tables.* Washington, DC: Bureau of Justice Statistics, p. 10.

Table 4.3 Use-of-Force Policies of Local Police Departments by Size of Population Served, 2007		
Pop. Served	**Deadly Force Policy**	**Less Than Lethal Force Policy**
All sizes	97%	96%
1,000,000 or more	100%	100%
500,000 to 999,999	100%	100%
250,000–499,999	100%	100%
100,000–249,999	100%	99%
50,000–99,999	100%	100%
25,000–49,999	100%	100%
10,000–24,999	100%	99%
2,500–9,999	99%	98%
Under 2,500	93%	91%

Source: Reaves, B.A. (2010). *Local Police Departments, 2007.* Washington, DC: Bureau of Justice Statistics, p. 18.

more mundane issues such as vehicle use (see Table 4.4). A **procedure**, on the other hand, will detail specific actions that the officers must perform. For instance, in all calls for domestic violence, officers will park one block from the address, proceed on foot to the front door only when a second officer has arrived, and they will listen at the door for at least 30 seconds before announcing their presence.

Police departments will also issue rules and regulations to maintain uniformity within the agency. While the terms "rules" and "regulations" are often used interchangeably, there are differences. A **rule** is something that specifically defines what officers can and cannot do. For instance, there may be a rule that male officers must keep the length of their hair above the collar line, and female officers with hair longer than collar length must pin it up, and no ponytails are allowed. A **regulation**, on the other hand, has the force of law behind it, such as police officers while on duty are not authorized to carry a second handgun. Regulations are often based on a body of law, such as the example of secondary weapons may be derived from statutory law.

Police Organization

While the police do organize in a quasi-military fashion using the basic principles of bureaucracy as spelled out by Max Weber, police organizations also structure their departments based on other criteria.[28] The police have to take into consideration other factors such as the role each person fills in the

Table 4.4 Vehicle Use Policies for Sworn Personnel in Sheriffs' Offices by Size of Population Served, 2007			
Pop. Served	**Driven Home**	**Used for Personal Errands**	**Operated Outside the Jurisdiction**
All sizes	93%	25%	16%
1,000,000 or more	70%	21%	42%
500,000 to 999,999	85%	30%	27%
250,000–499,999	82%	33%	28%
100,000–249,999	83%	22%	19%
50,000–99,999	87%	23%	14%
25,000–49,999	93%	29%	23%
10,000–24,999	98%	25%	13%
Under 10,000	98%	24%	12%

Source: Reaves, B.A. (2012). *Sheriffs' Offices, 2007—Statistical Tables.* Washington, DC: Bureau of Justice Statistics, p. 13.

Table 4.5 Examples of Line, Staff, and Support Positions		
Line	**Staff**	**Support**
Police Officer	Police Captain	Civilian Crime Analyst
K-9 Officer	Police Lieutenant	Dispatchers
Detective	Police Recruiting Officer	Fleet Manager
Crime Scene Investigator	Police Inspector	Civilian Planner
	Police Homeland Security Liaison	Records Manager
	Police Public Information Officer	Civilian Crime Scene Photographer
		Victim Services Liaison

organization, the various functions they perform, the geographical area they must cover, and the fact the police are available 24/7. So, the police organize by personnel, function, area, and time.

Personnel

Police departments organize based on **personnel**, and there are often divisions or separations that are delineated when talking about personnel. One that has already been mentioned is the difference between sworn personnel (police officers and detectives) and nonsworn personnel (civilians). This distinction separates those in a police organization with powers of arrest from those who have none. It should be noted, however, that they will often work side-by-side inside the police department. Civilians within a police department can be found working as secretarial support, dispatchers, crime scene evidence technicians, or crime scene photography experts.

Another simple division of personnel within a police department is the difference between management and line officers, those that supervise and those that work the streets. Often this is expanded to denote line, staff, and support personnel.[29] **Line** officers are those personnel who carry out the primary duties of the police department such as policing the streets (police officers) or conducting investigations (detectives). **Staff** personnel are those who supervise, direct, and control the line officers such as sergeants and lieutenants. **Support** personnel are those workers who are necessary to get the primary mission completed, such as vehicle and firearms maintenance or secretarial support (see Box 4.4).

Police departments also organize their personnel in the hierarchy or chain-of-command previously discussed by a separation of various layers in the organizational pyramid with command at the top, management in the middle, and officers at the bottom. **Command** consists of not only the police chief or police commissioner, but it also includes their staff and typically anyone that reports directly to the police chief. Often called the command staff, these are the people that help the police chief

Line officers, staff officers, and support staff (top to bottom).

shape policy and manage the overall agency. The police chief will then issue policies and directives to management. The middle layer of the organizational management is often referred to as **midlevel management.** These are the various ranks of supervisors often moving down the chain-of-command as captain, lieutenant, sergeant, and corporal. The captain and lieutenant ranks are management that often work within the police department itself, and they carry out the policies of the police chief. The ranks of sergeant and corporals are often called field supervisors because their more immediate concern is managing police officers or detectives working the field, but they are also responsible for carrying out the policies of the police chief as determined by the upper midlevel managers. Finally, it is, again, the line officers at the bottom of the pyramid, the police officers and detectives, who carry out the orders and perform the main functions of the police department.

When it comes to organizing a police department with only a handful of personnel, organization by personnel tends to be very easy. There are the police chief and the officers, or like in one department I visited there were four personnel: the chief, the lieutenant, the sergeant, and the officer. Yet, when looking at the extreme example of the New York City Police department, organization by personnel can get more complex. As former NYPD officer Edward Conlon explained, "in terms of hierarchy, the Job was only slightly less complex: the ranks from police officer to sergeant, to lieutenant and then captain, were determined through civil-service tests, and beyond that—deputy inspector, inspector, and four grades of chief, each gaining a star up to the four-star chief of department—the positions were appointed."[30] This highlights how the NYPD, despite employing approximately 38,000 officers, organizes using the same chain-of-command and organization by personnel.

Functions

Police departments also organize based on the functions that they perform. There are some similarities with how police organize by personnel with how they organize by function, but the concept of function takes it further down to assessing what police departments actually do. The first person to really encourage the reorganization of police departments based on their function was Bruce Smith, who conducted what were called police surveys in the early twentieth century.[31] The organization by functions allowed for Smith to reorganize the police departments so that instead of 120–140 people reporting directly to the police chief, which assuredly violates span of control, fewer people would report to the chief because individuals (usually captains) would supervise these overall functions. The three functions resemble the line/staff/support categories, and they are operations, administration, and auxiliary services.

Operations is the primary function of a police department, for these are the duties that the police perform to accomplish their mission. Operations include patrol, what is often considered to be the "backbone of the department," for these are the officers that respond to calls-for-service, one of the most visible of police functions.[32] Operations also includes criminal investigations, traffic, and other special units such as drugs, gangs, human trafficking, and anti-terror task forces (see Table 4.6).

Administration consists of all of the management personnel within a police department, so the command staff and midlevel managers, but it also includes many of the administrative functions that are necessary to accomplish the police mission. For instance, police officers need annual training, medical insurance, and they liked to be paid. Administration handles all of these issues. The functions include overseeing personnel issues, training, planning and analysis, budget and finance, secretarial support, and internal affairs.

Auxiliary services are essentially the support functions that make police departments run. Police officers and detectives often need to pull past records, secure evidence from crime scenes, obtain new uniforms, or have maintenance performed on their equipment. All of these support personnel are usually categorized under auxiliary services and include records, communications, property section, supply, and maintenance.

Many police departments in the United States separate these basic functions into more than just the three key areas discussed. In many police organizational charts, the operations functions are further separated into major commands. Often there is patrol, investigations, and specialized services, with the latter including such operational functions as juveniles, traffic, and crime prevention. Other police departments place a heavy emphasis on

Table 4.6   Percentage of Local Police Departments with Crime-Specific Operations Units by Population Served, 2007

Pop. Served	Drug Task Force	Gang Task Force	Human Trafficking Task Force	Anti-terror Task Force
All sizes	35%	12%	2%	9%
1,000,000 or more	100%	77%	54%	100%
500,000 to 999,999	94%	81%	32%	90%
250,000–499,999	98%	67%	22%	80%
100,000–249,999	83%	52%	6%	54%
50,000–99,999	82%	46%	5%	29%
25,000–49,999	73%	26%	3%	16%
10,000–24,999	54%	20%	1%	10%
2,500–9,999	36%	9%	1%	5%
Under 2,500	14%	4%	3%	4%

Source: Reaves, B.A. (2010). *Local Police Departments, 2007.* Washington, DC: Bureau of Justice Statistics, pp. 29-30.

traffic and so it will often appear as a major command unto itself. Many agencies will also separate investigations and they may appear as detectives, vice, organized crime, and narcotics. One very unique unit related to investigations is found in the Los Angeles Police Department, and it is known as Homicide Special. Miles Corwin in his book by that title described their function as consisting of "murders that involve celebrities . . . organized-crime killings, serial murders, cases that require great expertise or sophisticated technology . . . [and] any murder that is considered a priority by the chief of police is sent to Homicide Special."[33] While the circumstances of each police department are different and each police organizational chart will reflect those differences, police departments will still typically organize by operations, administration, and support.

Area

Police organizations also have to structure their police departments based on **geography** or the **area** for which they are responsible. Once again, the size of the town or city will play a major role in organizing the department. If a town is less than one square mile and there are only a few police officers working for the department, then the entire town is the area the officer on duty patrols. However, when you have the extreme example of New York City with a population of 8.337 million people, or Los Angeles, which is 502.7 square miles, police departments have to think in terms of organizing their agencies based on geography and the population density of the geographical area.

Police departments first organize based on geography by way of their jurisdictional boundaries, which are typically reflective of their geographical boundaries, but not always. In Arlington County, Virginia, although the county is 26 square miles, the police only have jurisdiction in 24 square miles—the rest are military and federal government properties and installations which are policed by various federal law enforcement agencies.

Police departments in large cities such as the NYPD will often organize their city police by establishing precincts. In New York City there are 77 police precincts, and each of these has a precinct commander who oversees what appears to be and often acts as its own police department.[34] Each of these precincts is then responsible for a specific geographical area of New York City. For instance, the 45th Precinct in New York City is located in the northeast Bronx and it is responsible for 6 miles of park area and 10.6 miles of waterfront as well as two self-contained communities: Coop City and City Island.[35]

While most police departments are not so large as to necessitate police precincts, they will often divide their jurisdiction into geographical districts or sectors. The primary means by which they do this is typically some geographic feature of the city, such as highways or rivers. Arlington County (Virginia) Police Department has Route 50 which runs east and west through the center of the county, so they refer to the "north side" and "south side," while Huntsville (Texas) Police Department has Interstate 45 running north and south and dividing it in half, so they refer to "east" and "west" sides. These sectors can then be further divided into such geographical areas as northwest and northeast. While sectors and districts are often meant to denote a specific geographic size, they are often used interchangeably or differently from agency to agency. Washington, D.C. police officer Christopher Archer explains that "Washington, D.C. is divided into police districts, which are then subdivided into sectors, with certain cars assigned to certain areas."[36] The Philadelphia Police Department, however, divides the city into districts and then within each district it maintains sectors that it calls "police service areas." So language from agency to agency is not always consistent.

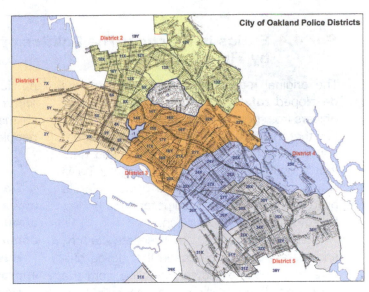

The various colors signify the various districts of the Oakland Police Department, and each district is then broken down into beats.

What is typically consistent, however, is that the lowest level of geography for most police departments in the United States is the police beat. Since the days of Robert Peel and the London Bobbies, police officers have been said to be "walking the beat." While the exact origin of the term has been lost to history, most police officers are still assigned to a beat, which is typically the smallest geographical area that a police officer is responsible for patrolling. Beats can be small or large depending on a number of circumstances. They must be small if officers are on foot, while, conversely, they may be much larger if the officers are driving. Beats can be very large if they cover areas that often have very little crime, such as warehouse districts or areas located on the outskirts of a city. In other cases they can be very small, such as one city block, due to a combination of high population density and/or high crime. In addition to changing the size of a beat based on population and crime, many police departments will also assign more than one officer to a beat based on those same characteristics.

Time

The last manner in which police are organized is **time (see** Box 4.4**)**. In many ways, this is often the most complicated of the organizational responsibilities because it can have such an impact on the officers and deputies working for the police agency. Early police in America often worked nearly around the clock with 12-hour shifts followed by 12-hour reserve shifts where the officers lived in the police barracks, similar to firefighters today, subject to answering calls for service when needed. As America began applying labor standards, the work hours and circumstances for police were

---

Box 4.4 Ethics in Practice: The Politics of Shifting Police by Time and Area

The original reason that police departments developed **rotating shifts** and moved police officers from beat to beat was to avoid political ties that might result in corruption. It was reasoned that changing both the **area** and **time** that a police works on a fairly regular basis would never allow them the opportunity to build the types of relationships for graft, bribes, and other forms of corruption.

Fast-forward to the late twentieth century, and there was the realization that police officers had become too far removed from the community that it had created a sense of hostility and distrust between the police and the public. The solution was to give officer **fixed shifts** and **fixed beats** for long periods of time so that they can develop close ties with the people in the neighborhood they work.

Ask Yourself:

Do you think police departments should maintain rotating shifts and beats to avoid corruption, at the expense of police-community relations?

How do fixed shifts and beats potentially improve police-community relations?

How can corruption be minimized while still building effective police-community relations?

---

reduced eventually to the 40-hour workweek. In addition, in the movement toward police professionalization, to avoid corrupt political ties with members of the community, police officers were moved from beat to beat, but they were also moved from shift to shift, and rotating shifts became the norm.[37]

Many police departments still use the traditional rotating shifts where police officers work eight-hour shifts on midnights, such as 10 P.M. to 6 A.M., for a week. They then rotate to the evening shift, such as a 2 P.M. to 10 P.M. shift. They then rotate to the day shift, such as a 6 A.M. to 2 P.M. shift, and then, after a certain period off, usually five to seven days, they rotate back through the process. Research into the effects of rotating shifts on officers and deputies, as well as other shift workers, has found a deleterious effect upon the physical, mental, and emotional makeup of the officer. Rotating shifts are simply bad for one's overall health.[38]

To address this problem, many police departments have moved to fixed shifts. In this case, officers do not rotate through the shifts, but remain

Police and sheriffs organize by time, either by rotating or fixed shifts, with some officers having to work the night shift.

on the same shift all the time. This is great for the health of the day shift officers and adequate for those working the evening shift, but it still has a negative impact on those working the overnight shift. To compensate, officers are often rotated to other shifts every two to three years to help deal with the negative impacts. In addition, to deal with the fact that certain officers will be forced into always working midnights, some departments offer a shift differential in pay, such as an extra 50 cents per hour for evenings and $1.00 per hour for midnights. Further, many younger officers like the evening or midnight shifts and gravitate to them because more criminal behavior occurs during those hours, while older officers, those with families, gravitate to the day shift because it allows them to lead a more "normal" life.

Police Officer William Dunn explains the differences in shift work from a new officer's perspective when he writes, "Day watch is the shift when Los Angeles is at its most manic."[39] As he describes it: "The streets are clogged with traffic, the skies are covered in smog kicked up into the atmosphere after a night resting on the city's concrete, and the ears are filled with sounds. Buses, construction, sirens from emergency vehicles; it is a time when the senses can be overloaded."[40] He also explains that day watch is called the "poke" watch within the LAPD "because officers who work during the day are generally older ones with families." Thus he explains that some of "these officers can be slow-moving 'slowpokes,' or in LAPDese, 'pokes.'"[41]

In some cities across the nation, the police organize with a fourth shift, often called a power-shift which works from around 6 P.M. to 2 A.M. in the morning. As many of the calls-for-service during this time period are criminal in nature and the traditional shift is often heavily committed to responding to calls, the power-shift allows for an overlap of officers during the busiest hours of the police department.

In the past 30 years, a majority of police departments have moved away from the traditional 8-hour rotating shifts and have experimented not only with fixed shifts, but with longer shifts as well, including 10- and 12-hour shifts. Numerous studies have been conducted on police officers and the impact that these longer shifts have on their personal well-being and safety. Recently, the Police Foundation conducted a comprehensive study and found that out of the choices of 8-hour, 10-hour, and 12-hour shifts, the best for officers was the 10-hour shift.[42] Because the 10-hour shift is a four-days-on, three-days-off schedule, these officers demonstrated better quality of work, they were better rested, and from an organizational standpoint, the 10-hour shift was cheaper because it necessitated less overtime than either the 8-hour or 12-hour shift. Interestingly, it found no difference among officers in the three shifts when it came to officer safety, work-family conflicts, or overall health.

Police Leadership and Management

When it comes to police organization, while the manner in which police agencies are organized and the adoption of bureaucratic methods are import-ant, as with any agency, good leadership and management are important for the proper function of a police agency.[43] It has been noted that the quality of police leadership has a direct impact on the quality of life of the police officers working for that agency.[44] It may sound oversimplified, but good lead-ers and good managers make for a good police department. Conversely, bad leaders and bad managers make life miserable.

There is a distinct difference between leadership and management. While we often think of **police leadership** as being the police chief or police commissioner and his or her staff, the reality is, police leaders can be found throughout the entire police department at all levels. There are certain indi-viduals in a police department that have a natural leadership ability and so people are drawn to follow them. These are the people we often call born leaders, people who have an innate quality that allow them to influence other people. For instance police field supervisors who engage in proactive stops and investigations have been found to influence the proactive activity of their patrol officers.[45] Ideally, we would like to see the leaders of the police depart-ment filling the top positions of authority, but that is not always the case (see Box 4.5).

In addition to born leaders, there are also people who have to learn to become leaders. Assuming that not all leaders have to be born that way, then it is believed that the people in the positions of authority can be taught lead-ership, that leadership can be learned. There are many theories of leader-ship, too numerous to cover here, but different police chiefs have different leadership styles, which Haberfeld described as theories in her book *Police Leadership*.[46] As a result, police chiefs have learned to be good leaders by adopting certain practices that allow them to influence their department.

New York Police Commissioner William Bratton is identified by many as the exemplar of police leadership today. The police chief of Boston, New York Transit, New York City, Los Angeles, and then New York City again, he has led a very successful career as a police chief. When asked what he believed made for a successful leader, Bratton explained that "A successful leader is first somebody that's going to set goals that even he or she is going to be measured by. Those goals have a significant amount of risk involved in them. You can't be fearful of risk; you basically have to be risk focused."[47] He then explains that good leadership then works down the chain-of-command. A good police leader must then "work with senior management and direct reports to set up strategies to meet these goals."[48] Still further, he argues that a good leader has to "create an environment where your captains and lieutenants have empowered your people with tactics that focus on strategies and focus on meeting the goals of the organization."[49] Ultimately, according to Bratton, the goal is to have as many people included in the process so that

Box 4.5 History in Practice: Chief William Parker, Hollywood Hero of the Los Angeles Police Department

William Parker, police chief of the Los Angeles Police Department from 1950 until his death from a heart attack in 1966, was a hero to many because he cleaned up the LAPD's image and made the department one of the most respected police agencies in the United States. He is also the police chief who is perhaps most often associated with television and movies.

Parker became a Los Angeles police officer in 1927 and rose through the ranks, securing the top spot in 1950. The LAPD that he took over was well known for its corruption and to clean it up, he found the blueprint offered by police pioneer August Vollmer, who had served as the police chief from 1923 to 1924, and left recommendations for how to professionalize the police department. The department was so corrupt at that time, no one wanted to even consider Vollmer's reforms. But Parker decided to try, and he at first became controversial with those in Los Angeles who were corrupt. But later, Parker came under scrutiny for his proactive methods of the LAPD, and he faced many accusations of allowing police brutality and minority discrimination.

Parker's association with the television and movie industry had much to do with Hollywood being located in Los Angeles. As the police chief in the 1950s, he served as the technical advisor for the original Jack Webb television series *Dragnet.* Gene Roddenberry, the creator of *Star Trek,* had started off as a Los Angeles Police Officer, and, because of his writing skills, he wrote speeches for Chief Parker. It has also been said that the character Spock was based on Parker. More than any other police chief, however, he has appeared as a character in multiple movies including *Mulholland Falls* (1996), *Gangster Squad* (2013), and *L.A. Confidential* (1997), although in the last film he was called Chief "Worton," despite the original book by James Ellroy identifying him as Parker. A younger Parker, this time as a captain of the LAPD, was also portrayed in the cable television series *Mob City* (2013-2014).

they feel like they have a vested interest in seeing the department succeed by meeting the goals established.

When it comes to **police management**, however, no one speaks of a natural born manager, rather, the concepts of management are all learned. Those assigned to manage officers or detectives, whether in the field or at the highest levels of the department, are part of police management. The corporal who is assigned to a shift and works the street alongside the officers he or she supervises is a manager. The police chief's chief of staff who oversees the key advisors to the police chief, as well

Former New York City Police Commissioner William Bratton.

as the various units within the police department, is part of the management staff. Even the police chief or police commissioner is part of police management.

What police managers do is the same thing managers in any organization do, and that is to ensure the overall functioning of the agency and that the desires of the command staff are implemented throughout the department. In the 1930s, Luther Gulick attempted to explain what it is managers do, and he developed what has become the commonly accepted elements of management.[50] He developed the acronym **POSDCORB**, which stands for planning, organizing, staffing, directing, coordinating, reporting, and budgeting (see Box 4.6). To best understand the elements of management that Gulick is explaining, imagine a police department developing a special response team (SRT) unit for the first time. The managers placed in charge must *plan* exactly what needs to happen for the SRT to be ready to respond to high-risk calls. The managers must determine how to *organize* the SRT team, by either having one team or one team per shift, as well as the reporting structure for the team or teams. They must *staff* the new SRT team with not only management but officers, so they must determine the type of person they want on the team and how they will select those individuals. They must then *direct* the team by issuing orders, keeping them up to date on their training requirements, and determine how they will be notified of an activation. They must *coordinate* with the department for resources, training facilities, and ranges to practice, and uniform companies for proper gear. They must *report*

Box 4.6 **Policing in Practice: Gulick and Effective Management Techniques**

Police managers do the same things as managers in any organization do. They ensure the overall functioning of the agency and that the goals of the command staff are implemented throughout the department. The management techniques of **Luther Halsey Gulick** provide a framework for achieving these goals, known by the acronym **POSDCORB**.

Gulick was born in 1892 in Osaka, Japan, as his parents were missionaries. He received a well-heeled education from Oberlin College and Columbia University, where he received his PhD in 1920. The entire focus of his career was improving public administration and did so by serving as the president of the Institute of

Public Administration from 1921 to 1962, with various additional appointments and teaching positions along the way. He is most famous for publishing a paper that looked at the key responsibilities of a chief executive, and they were encapsulated in his famous acronym:

P	Planning
O	Organizing
S	Staffing
D	Directing
CO	Coordinating
R	Reporting
B	Budgeting

their activities to the police chief, and they must always be conscious of their *budget* for running the SRT team and not exceed that which is allowed.

The elements of management that Gulick devised over 75 years ago still apply to any organization today, including the police. There can also be seen a strong relationship between police bureaucracy and management, for both of these are necessary for the ability of a police organization to function properly. Still further, there must also be a strong relationship between police leadership and management for the police organization to be successful.

Police Organizational Theories

The idea of police organizing around the concepts of Weber's bureaucracy and Gulick's POSDCORB have often been criticized as being too mechanical in describing what police organizations do. The argument is that these concepts make the people working in these organizations too much like automatons, robots doing mindless work. Since Weber and Gulick's time, there have developed three modern organizational theories in policing that argue that police organizations are not run like this, and so they provide a different explanation (theory) for how these organizations operate. They are institutional theory, contingency theory, and resource-dependency theory.

Institutional theory portrays the police organization as being embedded in an environment that is composed of traditions, mythology, symbols, and concern for legitimacy, not as an agency adapting to specific events.[51] While the police have their own internal environment (traditions, myths, etc.), it is the external environment that they must respond to and this includes external groups such as the media, community groups, politicians, other criminal justice organizations and public opinion.[52] For instance, when Bratton took over the NYPD in 2014, he noted that the people and media had a very negative view of the agency, and he stated during his inauguration that "We will work hard to identify why is it that so many in this city do not feel good about this department that has done so much to make them safe. What has it been about our activities that have made so many alienated?" Thus, Bratton was hoping to change his organization based on the external environment in which the NYPD operates, not because of an increase or crime or some external threat such as a possible terrorist attack.

Contingency theory is fairly similar to institutional theory, but rather than believing that police organizations change based on changes in the external and internal environment, the way they really change is when faced with new challenges, new threats, and/or new contingencies.[53] Again, using a NYPD example, prior to September 11, 2001 and the terrorist attacks on American soil, the NYPD had a very limited focus on issues of terrorism. The events of September 11, 2001 (the contingency) caused that to change, and today the NYPD maintains an office of the deputy commissioner for counterterrorism and a counterterrorism division.

Resource-dependency theory takes the argument even more, saying that because police organizations are so limited in their budget, they only truly change and adapt when there are resources that allow them to do so.[54] Rather than it being external or internal demands (institutional theory) or some new challenge that arises (contingency), there has to be some type of resource funding to allow them to implement organizational change. Sticking with the NYPD example, had it not been for large grants given to the NYPD from the Department of Homeland Security, it is likely that the NYPD would not have such a highly functional counterterrorism division.

Conclusion

The police have always organized as a paramilitary or quasi-military organization, but the way they organize is far beyond just a military organization. The way the government organizes has a direct influence on how its police department organizes, whether using a council-manager, mayor-council, city commission, and/or a police commission, it will affect police organization. The police are also a bureaucracy and organize along Taylor's concepts of scientific management by maintaining a chain-of-command, span of control, unity of command, delegation of authority, division of labor, and using police and procedures and rules and regulations to create a uniform organization. The police also organize by personnel, function, area, and time, further shaping how police agencies are organized. Finally, leadership plays a major role in shaping the organization, and so does management when performing their basic POSDCORB functions as described by Gulick. Furthering these basic functions, some also articulate that police organize based on institutional, contingency, or resource-dependency approaches (theories). In the end, it should be obvious that the police organization is a complicated structure, it is designed to respond to many needs to accomplish its mission, and it can vary greatly from agency to agency.

Just the Facts

1. The three types of municipal government organization in the United States today are the council-manager, the mayor-council, and the commission. The most common form today is the council-manager, while historically it was the commission.

2. The commission form of government had a commissioner to oversee each key function of city governance, for instance, a police commissioner. Although many police commissioners still exist today, it is in name only as few cities have a commission form of government. This is to be distinguished from the county commission, which invests legislative and executive powers in an elected board to oversee county governance.

3. A bureaucracy is typically an organization that adheres to certain principles such as chain-of-command, division of labor, and written policies and procedures. Police

departments and sheriffs' offices are run as bureaucracies.

4. A policy is a broad statement of what the department believes in, a procedure is a step-by-step call for specific actions to be taken in particular situations, while a rule is a statement typically of prohibition, and a regulation is a similar statement, but it is based on some body of law so it has legal backing.

5. Police organize by personnel, function, area, and time.

6. The three key police functions are operations, administration, and auxiliary services.

7. Police organize by area, usually dividing in larger units to smaller units, such as precincts, districts, sectors, and beats. Beats are almost always the smallest geographical areas that police officers are assigned to. Police also organize by time, often working rotating shifts where the hours change, or fixed shifts where the hours stay the same. Typical shifts are day, evening, and night, and sometimes there is an overlapping shift over evening and nights, often called a power-shift.

8. Police leadership are when people are drawn to follow certain individuals because they are compelling and natural leaders, whereas police management are the people that fill in certain positions within the organization to ensure that the business of the organization is accomplished.

9. POSDCORB was created by Gulick to demonstrate what chief executives do, and the acronym stands for planning, organizing, staffing, directing, coordinating, reporting, and budgeting.

10. There are three police organization theories: institutional theory posits that police organizations are adaptive organizations based on internal and external influences; contingency theory argues that police organizations change when faced with new challenges and pressures by having to develop new solutions or ways of accomplishing problems; and resource-dependency theory states that police agencies change whenever there is funding to implement the change or they cease some behavior when money is no longer available.

Ask Yourself

1. Which of the three forms of municipal governance would give the police chief the most power? Which of the three would give the police chief the least amount of power? How then does city governance affect the police organization?

2. Many argue that the police are too bureaucratic and hence they cannot get anything done. Is there a better method for organizing the police while still maintaining accountability?

3. The police are a highly centralized organization. Under community policing there were repeated calls for the police to decentralize. Studies have found that the police did not decentralize under community policing, but remained highly centralized structures. Why do you think that is the case?

4. Consider the various types of shift work in policing, 8-hour, 10-hour, and 12-hour shifts, as well as fixed shifts and rotating shifts. Which do you think is the best shift solution? Justify your reasoning. What are the drawbacks to your preferred solution?

5. Which would be better for a police department to have as a police chief, a good leader or a good manager?

6. Out of the three police organizational theories, which do you think is the most likely theory for organizational change? Now think about the theory you selected. If it is correct, how do we use that theory to improve policing today?

Keywords

Administration	Geography	POSDCORB
Area	Institutional theory	Procedure
Auxiliary services	Line	Regulation
Chain-of-command	Mayor-council	Resource-dependency theory
Command	Midlevel management	Rule
Commission	Operations	Span of control
Contingency theory	Personnel	Staff
Council-manager	Police commission	Support
County commission	Police leadership	Time
Delegation	Police management	Unity of command
Division of labor	Policy	

Endnotes

1. Vollmer, A. (1928). Police organization and management. *Public Management, 10*, 142-152, at p. 145.
2. Bittner, E. (1970). *The functions of the police in modern society.* Bethesda, MD: National Institute of Mental Health.
3. Bittner, E. (1970). *The functions of the police in modern society.* Bethesda, MD: National Institute of Mental Health.
4. Emsley, C. (2009). *The great British bobby: A history of British policing from the 18th century to the present.* London, England: Quercus; Miller, W.R. (1999). *Cops and bobbies: Police authority in New York and London, 1830-1870.* 2nd ed. Columbus, OH: Ohio State University Press; Walker, S. (1983). *The police in America: An introduction.* New York, NY: McGraw-Hill.
5. Monkkonen, E.H. (1981). *Police in urban America, 1860-1920.* New York, NY: Cambridge University Press.
6. Monkkonen, E.H. (1981). *Police in urban America, 1860-1920.* New York, NY: Cambridge University Press.
7. Haller, M. (1976). Historical roots of police behavior: Chicago, 1890-1925. *Law & Society Review, 10*, 303-323; Smith, B. (1940). *Police systems in the United States.* New York, NY: Harper & Brothers Publishers.
8. Fogelson, R.M. (1977). *Big-city police.* Cambridge, MA: Harvard University Press, p. 150.
9. Fogelson, R.M. (1977). *Big-city police.* Cambridge, MA: Harvard University Press, p. 150.
10. Fogelson, R.M. (1977). *Big-city police.* Cambridge, MA: Harvard University Press, p. 150.
11. Carte, G.E. & Carte, E.H. (1975). *Police reform in the United States: The era of August Vollmer, 1905-1932.* Berkeley: University of California Press; Fogelson, R.M. (1977). *Big-city police.* Cambridge, MA: Harvard University Press; Walker, S. (1977). *Critical history of police reform: The emergence of professionalism.* Lanham, MD: Lexington Books.

12. Wilson, O.W. (1963). *Police administration.* 2nd ed. New York, NY: McGraw-Hill Book Company.
13. Bittner, E. (1970). *The functions of the police in modern society.* Bethesda, MD: National Institute of Mental Health, p. 53.
14. Bittner, E. (1970). *The functions of the police in modern society.* Bethesda, MD: National Institute of Mental Health.
15. Wilson, J.Q. (1989). *Bureaucracy: What government agencies do and why they do it.* New York, NY: Basic Books, p. 23.
16. Fifty-five percent of cities use this form of government according to National League of Cities. (2013). *Forms of municipal government.* Washington, DC: National League of Cities; Fifty-eight percent of cities use this form of government according to International City/County Management Organization. (2007). *Council-manager form of government.* Washington, DC: ICMA. See also Bowman, A. & Kearney, R. C. (2012). *State and local government.* 9th ed. Independence, KY: Cengage.
17. Bowman, A. & Kearney, R.C. (2012). *State and local government.* 9th ed. Independence, KY: Cengage; National League of Cities. (2013). *Forms of municipal government.* Washington, DC: National League of Cities; International City/County Management Organization. (2007). *Council-manager form of government.* Washington, DC: ICMA.
18. National League of Cities. (2013). *Forms of municipal government.* Washington, DC: National League of Cities.
19. National Association of Counties. (2014). Overview of county government. *National Association of Counties.* Retrieved from www.naco.org/Counties/learn/Pages/Overview.aspx

20. National Association of Counties. (2014). Overview of county government. *National Association of Counties.* Retrieved from www.naco.org/Counties/learn/Pages/Overview.aspx.

21. Isenberg, J. (2010). *Police leadership in a democracy: Conversations with America's police chiefs.* Boca Raton, FL: CRC Press, p. 105.

22. Isenberg, J. (2010). *Police leadership in a democracy: Conversations with America's police chiefs.* Boca Raton, FL: CRC Press, p. 105.

23. Fogelson, R.M. (1977). *Big-city police.* Cambridge, MA: Harvard University Press.

24. Stojkovic, S., Kalinich, S., & Klofas, J. (2008). *Criminal justice organizations: Administration and management.* 4th ed. Belmont, CA: Thomas Wadsworth.

25. Bopp, W.J. (1977). *"O.W.": O.W. Wilson and the search for a police profession.* Port Washington, NY: Kennikat Press.

26. Wilson, O.W. (1963). *Police administration.* 2nd ed. New York, NY: McGraw-Hill Book Company.

27. Wilson, O.W. (1963). *Police administration.* 2nd ed. New York, NY: McGraw-Hill Book Company, p. 63.

28. Wilson, O.W. (1963). *Police administration.* 2nd ed. New York, NY: McGraw-Hill Book Company.

29. Geller, W.A. (Ed.). (1991). *Local government police management.* 3rd ed. Washington, D.C.: ICMA.

30. Conlon, E. (2004). *Blue blood.* New York, NY: Riverhead Books, pp. 12-13.

31. Smith, B. (1940). *Police systems in the United States.* New York, NY: Harper & Brothers Publishers.

32. Wilson, O.W. (1963). *Police administration.* 2nd ed. New York, NY: McGraw-Hill Book Company, p. 51.

33. Corwin, M. (2003). *Homicide special: A year with the LAPD's elite detective unit.* New York, NY: Henry Holt and Company, p. 3.

34. Hassell, K.D. (2007). Variations in police patrol practices: The precinct as sub-organizational level of analysis. *Policing: An International Journal of Police Strategies and Management, 30,* 257-276.

35. New York Police Department. (2014). Precincts: 45th Precinct. *NYPD.* Retrieved from www.nyc.gov/html/nypd/html/precincts/precinct_045.shtml.

36. Archer, C.M. (2006). *Miles to go before I sleep: Life, death, and hope on the streets of Washington, D.C.* Baltimore, MD: PublishAmerica, p. 35.

37. Lane, R. (1971). *Policing the city: Boston, 1822-1885.* New York, NY: Atheneum.

38. See for instance Rajaratnam, S.M.W. et al. (2011). Sleep disorders, health, and safety in police officers. *Journal of the American Medical Association, 306,* 2567-2578; Violanti, J.M. et al. (2012). Shift work and the incidence of injury among police officers. *American Journal of Industrial Medicine, 55,* 217-227.

39. Dunn, W. (1996). *Boot: An L.A.P.D. officer's rookie year.* New York, NY: William Morrow and Company, Inc., p. 124.

40. Dunn, W. (1996). *Boot: An L.A.P.D. officer's rookie year.* New York, NY: William Morrow and Company, Inc., p. 124.

41. Dunn, W. (1996). *Boot: An L.A.P.D. officer's rookie year.* New York, NY: William Morrow and Company, Inc., p. 124.

42. Amendola, K.L. et al. (2011). *The shift length experiment: What we know about 8-, 10-, and 12-hour shifts in policing.* Washington, DC: Police Foundation.

43. Wilson, O.W. (1963). *Police administration.* 2nd ed. New York, NY: McGraw-Hill Book Company.

44. Baker, T.E. (2000). *Effective police leadership: Beyond management.* New York, NY: Looseleaf Law Publications, Inc.

45. Johnson, R.R. (2015). Leading by example: Supervisor modeling and officer-initiated activities. *Police Quarterly, 18,* 223-243.

46. Haberfeld, M.R. (2006). *Police leadership.* Upper Saddle River, NJ: Prentice Hall.

47. Isenberg, J. (2010). *Police leadership in a democracy: Conversations with America's police chiefs.* Boca Raton, FL: CRC Press, p. 42.

48. Isenberg, J. (2010). *Police leadership in a democracy: Conversations with America's police chiefs.* Boca Raton, FL: CRC Press, p. 42.

49. Isenberg, J. (2010). *Police leadership in a democracy: Conversations with America's police chiefs.* Boca Raton, FL: CRC Press, p. 42.

50. Gulick, L.H. (1936). Notes on the Theory of Organization. In L. Gulick & L. Urwick (Eds.), *Papers on the science of administration* (pp. 3–35). New York, NY: Institute of Public Administration.

51. Crank, J.P. (2003). Institutional theory of police: A review of the state of the art. *Policing: An International Journal, 26,* 186-207.

52. Crank, J. P., Langworthy, R. H. (1992) An institutional perspective on policing. *The Journal of Criminal Law and Criminology, 83,* 338–363.

53. Donaldson, L. (2001). *The contingency theory of organizations.* Thousand Oaks, CA: SAGE.

54. Pfeffer, J. & Salancik, G. (1978). *The external control of organizations: A resource dependence perspective.* New York, NY: Harper & Row.

■ *"There is no higher calling than that of a policeman. I would rather be a policeman than President."*[1] —*August Vollmer*

Police officers from the San Jose Police Department receive a call-for-service while working patrol.

CHAPTER 5

Careers

After reading this chapter, you will be able to:

1. Explain the differences of nature versus nurture in terms of why certain individuals are attracted to policing and place it in the context of predisposition versus socialization.
2. List and discuss the top three reasons individuals give for wanting to become police officers.
3. Identify and explain the three most common recruitment methods for policing.
4. Describe and explain the three most common police recruit feeder programs.
5. Characterize and explain the three most commonly targeted groups for policing.
6. Detail the most common pre-employment standards for policing.
7. Define what is meant by the phrase bona fide occupational qualification.
8. Describe the screening process for policing, moving from the least expensive to the most expensive screening devices.
9. Explain the many forms of policing training that police officers receive over the course of their career.
10. Compare and discuss the differences in police academies as they relate to the educational perspective and stress.
11. Identify and explain the three most common career tracks for a police officer.
12. Examine the issues of retention and retirement when it comes to American policing.

The Chapter 5 opening quote by August Vollmer highlights how many see the profession of policing as a calling, not a job. No one ever claims to be called to serve in the fast-food industry or as a house cleaner, but people who become a doctor, a priest, or a military soldier often speak of a calling. This is very often the case with police officers. Many who enter policing feel they had a calling to the profession, while many others who entered for decent pay, good benefits, and job security find themselves awakening to the idea that policing is something greater than just a job. Vollmer also highlights the rewards of being a police officer, suggesting that the career of a police officer and the importance of their duties far outweigh even those of the president of the United States.

The career of a police officer is very different from most jobs. In fact, Chicago Officer Jay Padar says "Being a cop is not just a job or career. It is a lifestyle."[2] That lifestyle starts with police recruiting, which sets high standards for the type of person police departments want to employ as police officers. To obtain even a half-dozen new police officers, departments must often screen hundreds of individuals who apply for those positions. Once hired, the new recruit must be trained, first in the police academy and then on the street through the field training officer program. Some of the recruits may not complete the training, either deciding themselves that policing is not for them or the police department may come to the same decision for them. For those that do graduate from both forms of training, they must continue to perform satisfactorily while on probation, otherwise, again, the department may let them go. Police officers then learn mostly how to be a police officer while working the street, for experience is always the best educator.

As police officer Alley Evola explains, "The career trajectory of a police officer is more akin to a marathon, not a forty-yard dash," because it is not over quickly, but rather, "it's a hard slog."[3] After working on the street for several years, for those who decide to remain in policing, as many often move on to other jobs, an entire police career lies before them. Over the next 20 to 30 years, they will continue to receive training, move to other assignments, and possibly make it into the detective ranks or management. After reaching the proper age and number of years required to retire, the police officer will then have to determine when the appropriate time for them to officially retire has come. Leaving policing can be as difficult as entering.

The purpose of this chapter is to explore what motivates individuals to want to become a police officer in the first place and how the process to make that happen occurs. It will trace the recruitment, screening, and hiring process for the average police officer in the United States. It will then detail how these officers are trained to become police officers, as well as the continued training throughout their career. Finally, it will trace the career of a police officer all the way through retirement.

Individual

The answer to the question of what motivates an individual to become a police officer often falls into two camps, those who argue it is **nature** and those who say it is **nurture.** Some argue that certain people are born with an innate desire to become sheepdogs and that these individuals are naturally attracted to policing. In other words, they have a **predisposition**, a particular personality which leads to their desire to want to become a police officer.[4] Others argue that it is more about nurture, **socialization**, and culture.[5] As children grow up, if their parents were police officers or their role models and heroes were police officers, these people may be more inclined to go into policing themselves. In addition, television, movies, and books about police officers may also serve as a motivating factor for individuals to want to go into policing. Sergeant Landsman of the LAPD gave a colorful argument for socialization over predisposition when he explained, "Police officers are not raised on police farms where they are born and bred to be police officers. They come out of all walks of society with all the prejudices and problems of everyone else."[6] In the end, however, it is most likely a mixture of the two. The reality that a person has a natural affinity toward policing may cause those individuals to nurture that desire, ultimately leading them into the police profession.

It is very common that when the majority of police recruits are asked why they want to be a police officer, they will often give the very same answers. Chicago Police Officer Gina Gallo provides the typical response when the academy instructors asked one of her fellow recruits, "Why you wanna be the *Po*-lice, man?"[7] His answer: "I . . . I want to help people, sir."[8] This, according to research, is one of the most common answers.[9] But when pushed beyond what is often a pat answer, Gallo explains that her entire recruit class was later required to stand up and state their reasons and "some of the answers are the expected drivel: to save lives, stop the bad guys, help people, blah, blah."[10] She also points out that some are "refreshingly honest: a good way to meet women, because their other job sucked, so they'll never have to get another traffic ticket again."[11] She also explains that there were a few who faced the realities of life and cited practical reasons such as "families to support, a better way to pay the bills, get the benefits package" and, of course, "job security."[12]

Police officer William Dunn, who spent his career with the Los Angeles Police Department (LAPD), explained that at the time he applied he was a salesman and he was "looking for an employment change and steadier income than the roller-coaster earnings provided by commissioned selling."[13] Another police officer, John Baker, from nearby Compton, also voiced a similar motivation. After the birth of his daughter, he noted, "I felt . . . I had to do better than a postal worker's salary to support my new family."[14]

For some police officers, they join because it is a family tradition, for either one of their parents, or both, had careers as police officers and they grew up with the police culture. That was the case for Officer Gallo, as it was for Officer Steve Osborne of the NYPD. "When I was a kid my father was a cop," and he explains how "I loved it when his cop buddies would come by the house . . . to me these were the coolest guys in the world, real men, and I wanted to be one of them."[15] Police Sergeant Jay Padar also followed his father, Lieutenant Jim Padar, into the Chicago Police Department, and they recount this family tradition in their co-authored book *On Being a Cop: Father & Son Police Tales from the Streets of Chicago.*[16]

For most officers, the motivation to go into policing typically falls into very similar categories. In fact, these categories are echoed in the research into police motivations, which consistently finds that individuals enter policing for three reasons: altruism, job benefits, and security.[17] The **altruism** response, to help people, is the most common among police officers as voiced by Gallo and in many ways it seems to be part and parcel with being a sheepdog.[18] Many of the officers, like Dunn and Barker, also noted that they were looking for better pay, better benefits, and a decent retirement, so **job benefits** for many are a motivating factor (see Table 5.1).[19] Finally, **job security** is a key motivating factor for many of those looking for a steady job where they know that as long as they perform in a satisfactory manner, they will be able to retain their job.[20]

Table 5.1 Average Base Annual Salary for Full-Time Police Officers (2013) and Deputy Sheriffs (2007) by Population Served

Pop. Served	Police Officer		Sheriff's Deputy	
	Min.	Max.	Min.	Max.
All sizes	$38,200	$47,000	$31,100	$37,900
1,000,000 or more	45,100	75,100	45,600	60,600
500,000 to 999,999	46,800	64,400	40,000	56,000
250,000–499,999	48,600	68,800	37,600	53,300
100,000–249,999	50,700	68,500	36,100	46,700
50,000–99,999	48,600	64,100	32,500	41,600
25,000–49,999	45,700	62,000	30,300	35,700
10,000–24,999	42,600	54,600	29,100	34,500
Under 10,000	34,550	40,300	27,800	30,400

Source: Reaves, B.A. (2015). *Local Police Departments, 2013: Personnel, Policies, and Practices.* Washington, DC: Bureau of Justice Statistics; Reaves, B.A. (2012). *Sheriffs' Offices, 2007—Statistical Tables.* Washington, DC: Bureau of Justice Statistics.

For this author, it was not much different. I had always been interested in policing (nature) and had gravitated to television shows and books about the police (nurture). After watching Secret Service agent Tim McCarthy react to save President Ronald Reagan by literally taking a bullet, I knew that was what I wanted to do (protect the presidents, not get shot). Unfortunately I have bad eyesight, and, at the time, they did not allow you to correct poor vision. So instead of the Secret Service, I joined the police. But when I did join, I was newly married and just starting out on my career, so I too was concerned with job benefits and job security.

Recruitment

It is a common necessity for all police departments to recruit new police officers to keep their staffing levels at operational levels. Many of the larger police departments typically recruit for new officers on a routine basis, often annually or semi-annually. These police departments have to do this because they tend to have a steady turn-over from officers retiring, those moving on to employment with other police departments, and those leaving the police profession. Smaller agencies typically recruit for new officers only when their staffing levels drop below a certain threshold, so their recruiting practices are less routine.

Police departments then recruit for new police officers through a wide array of methods, which are always constrained by their recruitment budgets. The most common **recruitment methods** are (1) newspapers advertisements, (2) career fairs, and (3) the Internet.[21] Each of these tend to be relatively inexpensive measures for encouraging local citizens to apply to the police departments. Some agencies will reach outside of their jurisdiction and recruit from neighboring cities and counties, across state lines, and in some cases, across the United States. Most, however, tend to stay local.

More than half of the individuals recruited to be police officers come from local police department programs that serve as feeder programs for recruitment. The most common of these **police recruit feeder programs** are (1) college internships, (2) explorer programs (see Box 5.1), and (3) school resource officers. The benefit to the police department for maintaining these programs is that the participating individuals have already been screened to hold these

New York Police Department recruitment van in Midtown Manhattan.

Box 5.1 Policing in Practice: Police Explorers

Since the 1970s, many young people have had the opportunity to learn about a career in law enforcement during their high school years and many of those have transitioned into a career in law enforcement. The **Police Explorers** or **Law Enforcement Exploring program** was begun under the Boy Scouts of America as a non-scouting organization and is today run by their subsidiary Learning for Life. Police explorer posts are chartered by local law enforcement agencies with a police officer serving as the "advisor" for the group. These posts operate in a para-military, law enforcement format, and they meet on a regular basis. Some of the police agencies host an Explorer Training academy that trains the explorer cadet in policing and the explorer's program. Police Explorers then participate in ride-alongs,

perform community service, participate in tactical training, create honor guards and search and rescue teams, and learn the intricacies of crime scene investigations. Local chapters often host annual banquets for the explorers and send teams to compete at the National Law Enforcement Explorer Conference. The greatest benefit to the program is that Police Explorers learn early on about policing allowing them to obtain and transition more easily into a policing career. The greatest benefit to the police department is it creates a feeder program for future police officers for the sponsoring agency.

To explore further go to Learning for Life, click on the program, exploring tab, and look for the "Law Enforcement Exploring badge" at http://www.learningforlife.org/.

---

positions, and their participation gives the department an opportunity to come to know these individuals and to assess whether they will make good police recruits. Participation in any of these programs is an excellent means for obtaining a position within the police agency.

Police recruitment also targets certain groups for particular reasons. The three most commonly **targeted groups** in police recruitment are (1) certified police officers, (2) college graduates, and (3) women and minorities. Police departments always target currently serving police officers (in the same state) who continue to hold their Peace Officers Standards and Training certification. Current police officers are highly valued recruits because these officers not only do not need to attend the academy, saving the gaining department thousands of dollars, they can typically be working patrol inside of a month after departmental training. College graduates, or those close to graduating, are also targeted because not only do they have some of the desired skills, but most are turning 21 years of age (typically the minimum age to be hired as a police officer) and seeking employment as soon as they graduate. Finally, in support of the Equal Employment Opportunity Commission (EEOC) standards and laws, police departments actively recruit for underrepresented populations in policing.[22]

Successful police department recruitment is not always a given, for there are times when the number of applicants is small and many of those may be unqualified for the position. To have a successful hiring, police departments need to have a large applicant pool from which to choose. However, when the economy is doing very well, the number of applications to police departments tends to drop, while in economic hard times, the number of applications increases. According to Hartford County (MD) Sheriff Jeff Gahler, the current "applicant pool is not staying ahead of our needs," meaning they have more positions than they do qualified applicants.[23] It should also be pointed out that just because police departments target the college-educated, women, and minorities this does not necessarily mean they will apply, nor does it mean they will be qualified for the position.

Pre-Employment Standards

Each police department establishes its own standards for what makes for a successful police officer, and it will often make adjustments to these qualifications. These **pre-employment standards** can be quite rigid, and while individuals may apply for a position, if they do not meet these criteria, their application will be removed from the applicant pool. Although these standards may differ from agency to agency, for many reasons there is some commonality across U.S. police departments.

The majority of police departments have a minimum and maximum **age requirement**. The majority of agencies, often because of state law, have established 21 years of age as the minimum standard for policing.[24] This is typically set to ensure the applicant is mature enough for the position. A few states, including New Jersey, still allow officers to be hired at 18, but most of those agencies still wait until applicants are older. The maximum age tends to have more variation, with the average being 35, which is typically set for purposes of retirement. Retirement does not become available until after 20 to 30 years of service, so at 25 years and hired at 35, that individual would be still working as a police officer when he or she is 60 years old.

Most agencies also maintain a **height and weight requirement** that is usually based on the medically acceptable healthy proportions between the two variables.[25] While it used to be common for police departments to have height requirements, it was determined that height alone had little to do with the performance of a police officer and was widely used to discriminate against women. Like most police departments prior to the early 1970s, Chicago had a requirement that all officers had to be 5′ 10″ tall or taller. A court challenge caused this requirement to be removed, for as Officer Gallo glibly explained, "Everyone should have the right to get their asses blown to kingdom come, regardless of how short they are."[26] Today, it is more about health and that the person is not so overweight as to be unable to perform the job. As obesity rises in America, police departments have found their applicant pool getting smaller as applicant waistlines have grown larger.

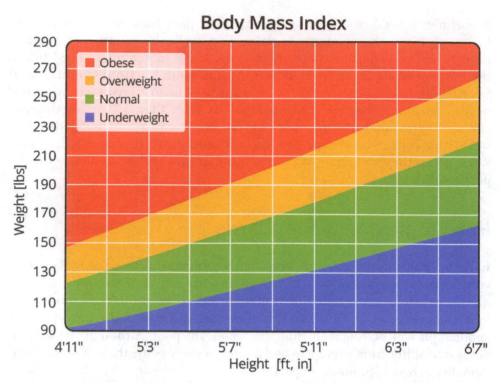

A standard height and weight chart to measure a person's body mass index is one screening method for entry into policing.

Closely associated with healthy weight is the fitness of the applicant, and nearly every police department maintains a **physical agility and strength requirement**. Many police departments today simply maintain this requirement to assess the physical fitness of the recruit by testing push-ups, sit-ups, and a run, typically one to one-and-a-half miles. These are then scored by category based on age and sex, with minimum requirements in each category. Other departments also use a physical agility test, but due to previous case law and legal suits, all of these tests must be job related, or meet what are known as **bona fide occupational qualifications** (BFOQ).[27] In the past, police departments often discriminated against women by requiring recruits to be able to scale an 8- to 10-foot wall. Due to size and upper body strength, this screened out many women. However, this is not really a job-related requirement for a police officer. When this author was a police officer, if I came to an 8- or 10-foot wall, I went around it, not over it. If I was pursuing a suspect, I had the advantage of the radio, so there was no need to try to follow precisely where the suspect went. That said, many agencies do require officers to be able to navigate an obstacle course which may include climbing up and down stairs, dragging 100 pounds of deadweight, or even changing a tire, because these all may very well be bona fide job-related requirements to perform as a police officer.

The majority of police departments also maintain a **vision requirement** which most commonly requires the candidates to have a certain natural or corrected vision.[28] The goal is usually to have the vision corrected to between 20/20 and 20/70 in both eyes. How they are corrected depends on the agency, for some allow correction with glasses, others require contacts, and some mandate that the vision must either be natural or corrected through some type of surgery (LASIK, Keratotomy, etc.).

One common part of the physical agility (fitness) test is to run 1 to 1-1/2 miles for time.

Nearly every police department (98 percent) also maintains a **minimum education requirement** (see Table 5.2).[29] Although it was said that most police departments recruit those with college education, the majority do not maintain college education as a minimum standard. The majority of those with a minimum education requirement only require a high school diploma (84 percent).[30] When it comes to higher standards, 4 percent require some college credits (usually 30–60 credit hours) and 10 percent require a two-year Associate's degree, while only 1 percent require a four-year Bachelor's degree.[31] Although the requirement for an Associate's

Table 5.2   Education Requirement for New Police Officers (2013) and Deputy Sheriffs (2007) by Population Served

Pop. Served	Police Officer (Sheriff's Deputy)			
	H.S. Dip.	Some College	2 Year	4 Year
All sizes	84 (89) %	4 (3) %	10 (7) %	1 (—) %
1,000,000 or more	64 (78)	7 (15)	29 (4)	0 (—)
500,000 to 999,999	70 (83)	19 (8)	7 (6)	4 (4)
250,000–499,999	70 (90)	15 (2)	9 (6)	7 (2)
100,000–249,999	78 (81)	8 (5)	10 (13)	3 (—)
50,000–99,999	75 (85)	8 (3)	12 (10)	4 (—)
25,000–49,999	75 (89)	4 (2)	18 (7)	2 (—)
10,000–24,999	81 (89)	6 (3)	12 (6)	— (—)
Under 10,000	86 (94)	3 (2)	9 (4)	1 (—)

Source: Reaves, B.A. (2015). *Local Police Departments, 2013: Personnel, Policies, and Practices.* Washington, DC Bureau of Justice Statistics; Reaves, B.A. (2012). *Sheriffs' Offices, 2007—Statistical Tables.* Washington, DC Bureau of Justice Statistics.

degree looks to be high, some states, like Florida, mandate a two-year college program to obtain both an Associate's degree and police officer certification—college is the academy. It should also be noted that many of the agencies that require some college education will also waive this requirement or substitute it for other experience, such as military or the ability to speak a second language. One problem with police departments making college a minimum education requirement is that their applicant pool grows smaller because there are less-qualified candidates, thus creating hiring issues.[32]

Another requirement that was common decades ago, but to which only some police departments still ascribe, is the **residency requirement**. In some cases, there is a requirement that an individual must have resided for a certain length of time in the city/county/state in which they are applying, usually one year. In other cases, the requirement was simply after accepting employment, the recruit must reside in the jurisdiction they will be policing. Today, with rapid means of transportation and the high costs of living in many cities, many agencies have removed the residency requirements. Some, however, have opted to have a residency requirement that the officer must live within so many miles of the police department so that they may be able to respond to an emergency in a reasonable amount of time.

Another, more recently established requirement in many police departments is the **no-smoking requirement**. This requirement has much to do with health as it does insurance costs, because if police officers do not smoke, they stand a greater chance of staying healthy and a healthy employee is less expensive when it comes to health insurance costs. The requirement is typically a pledge that the officer will not smoke on or off duty and that if they do so, they will immediately report such behavior to their supervisor.

Screening

Once individuals have applied to the police department by filling out the application, the applicants must go through a **screening process** that is designed to select the best applicants for the position of police officer. Individuals that are not suited for police work are typically screened out of the process, while only those officers highly suited for policing are screened into the final applicant pool from which officers are chosen. To do this, police departments use a wide array of methods to assess each individual, and these various tests are often done in a sequence, rather than all at once. The ordering of tests may differ from agency to agency, but typically they move from the least to the most expensive and time consuming. In addition to screening in and screening out candidates, for those steps in the process where candidates can be rank ordered, such as scores on a written test or the physical agility test, the candidates are often rank ordered with those scoring highest moving to the top of the list.

The majority of police departments in the United States, more than 80 percent, use a **written aptitude test** (see Table 5.3).[33] The majority of these agencies begin with this test because it is easy to deliver to a large group, the

Table 5.3 Written Aptitude Test as Screening Methods Used in Selection of New Police Officers (2007) and Deputy Sheriffs (2007) by Population Served	
	Police Officer (Sheriff's Deputy)
Pop. Served	**Written Aptitude Test**
All sizes	48 (46) %
1,000,000 or more	100 (89)
500,000 to 999,999	90 (81)
250,000–499,999	96 (75)
100,000–249,999	88 (64)
50,000–99,999	87 (59)
25,000–49,999	83 (39)
10,000–24,999	76 (42)
Under 10,000	38 (26)

Source: Reaves, B.A. (2010). *Local Police Departments, 2007.* Washington, DC: Bureau of Justice Statistics; Reaves, B.A. (2012). *Sheriffs' Offices, 2007—Statistical Tables.* Washington, DC: Bureau of Justice Statistics.

only expense being the paper and pencils, monitoring personnel, and the time it takes to grade the examination. The type of written exam used can vary, but the most common is the use of a civil service exam which tests general basic knowledge of the individual and are not police-specific. These have been found to be highly successful in determining the success of a police recruit.[34] Other exams are more police-centric in their questions by employing police scenarios and assessing how the person responds to the situations presented. Some provide a study booklet and then ask questions based on this regarding "knowledge of law enforcement language and techniques, appropriate police conduct, the criminal justice system, and city geography."[35]

The next step in the process is usually the **physical agility test**. Over 80 percent of police departments in the United States employ this as a screening method because again, the cost for the exam is primarily the expense of the monitors to the test and the purpose is to test physical health of the candidate (Table 5.4).[36] While some of these tests are to determine general physical health, both aerobic (for example, running) and strength (for example, push-ups and sit-ups), many are tailored to the job itself such as the ability to move a person in emergency situations, which can be simulated by dragging a weighted dummy. Research has demonstrated that good physical health at the time of application is a good predictor for future job performance.[37]

The next step in the process is typically a **records check** (see Table 5.5). Because every police department in the United States has access to both state and national criminal and driving records, 100 percent of police

	Police Officer (Sheriff's Deputy)
Pop. Served	**Physical Agility Test**
All sizes	60 (56) %
1,000,000 or more	100 (96)
500,000 to 999,999	97 (85)
250,000–499,999	96 (79)
100,000–249,999	86 (72)
50,000–99,999	89 (61)
25,000–49,999	90 (53)
10,000–24,999	78 (57)
Under 10,000	53 (36)

Table 5.4   Physical Agility Test Screening Used in Selection of New Police Officers (2007) and Deputy Sheriffs (2007) by Population Served

Source: Reaves, B.A. (2010). *Local Police Departments, 2007.* Washington, DC: Bureau of Justice Statistics; Reaves, B.A. (2012). *Sheriffs' Offices, 2007—Statistical Tables.* Washington, DC: Bureau of Justice Statistics.

departments conduct a **criminal records check** and a **driving records check** as a screening method for employment.[38] In doing so, the police department will know if the candidate has ever been arrested for a crime or been issued a traffic ticket. While the presence of either does not automatically remove a candidate from consideration, additional information regarding these will be conducted during the background investigation. One other records check that is becoming more common today is the use of a **credit history check**. Because the police agency must pay for this record check, the percentage of police departments employing this method drops to 83 percent, but it can reveal whether a candidate is financially stable or has problems with money that may make their employment with the agency risky.[39]

The next step in the process is generally the **medical examination**, which is used by 98.3 percent of police departments in the United States (see Table 5.6).[40] This step can be very expensive for the police agency, so only those who have been screened in will be afforded this opportunity. The exam is conducted by medical doctors and nurses who conduct a general health exam, test physical conditioning, and ensure there are no medical problems that would preclude a person from performing as a police officer. It is at this point that someone with a bad heart, diabetes, or other permanent physical conditions may be removed from consideration.

The next step can come before or after the medical exam, but is typically done alongside it, and that is **drug testing**. Nearly every police department in the United States, 95.4 percent, tests candidates for drug usage, ranging

Table 5.5 Background and Record Check Methods for New Police Officers (2007) and Deputy Sheriffs (2007) by Population Served

Pop. Served	Police Officer (Sheriff's Deputy)			
	Criminal Record	Background Investigation	Driving Record	Credit Record
All sizes	100 (99)%	99 (98)%	99 (98)%	61 (50)%
1,000,000 or more	100 (100)	100 (96)	100 (100)	85 (85)
500,000 to 999,999	100 (100)	100 (100)	100 (100)	97 (83)
250,000–499,999	100 (100)	100 (100)	100 (100)	96 (70)
100,000–249,999	100 (100)	100 (100)	100 (98)	94 (71)
50,000–99,999	100 (99)	100 (100)	100 (100)	93 (67)
25,000–49,999	100 (99)	100 (97)	100 (98)	90 (49)
10,000–24,999	100 (99)	100 (96)	100 (96)	78 (39)
Under 10,000	100 (99)	99 (98)	98 (99)	53 (35)

Source: Reaves, B.A. (2010). *Local Police Departments, 2007.* Washington, DC: Bureau of Justice Statistics; Reaves, B.A. (2012). *Sheriffs' Offices, 2007—Statistical Tables.* Washington, DC: Bureau of Justice Statistics.

from marijuana to cocaine and heroin.[41] While previous drug use does not necessarily exclude someone from employment, the presence of drugs in the system at the point of the test will, as it demonstrates bad judgment on the part of the individual. The primary method for drug testing is generally the drawing of blood, but some agencies request hair samples, which necessitate the plucking of multiple strands of hair to capture the roots (see Box 5.2).

The next step in the process is the **psychological examination**. Once again, nearly all of the police departments in the United States, 94.8 percent, use a psychological evaluation to screen candidates.[42] Because a licensed psychologist must be hired for this step and for the fact it is time consuming, this part of the screening tends to come later in the process as the applicant pool shrinks. The psychologist will most likely meet several times with the candidate, with the first meeting consisting of a battery of tests, such as the Minnesota Multiphasic Personal Personality Inventory or the California Personality Inventory (see Table 5.7).[43] These tests include hundreds of true/false questions that can detect the presence of certain psychoses such as depression, paranoia, and psychopathy, all conditions that may not be compatible with policing. Other tests that may also be employed

Table 5.6   Medical Exam and Drug Testing Screening Methods Used in Selection of New Police Officers (2007) and Deputy Sheriffs (2007) by Population Served

Pop. Served	Police Officer (Sheriff's Deputy)	
	Medical Exam	Drug Test
All sizes	89 (88)%	83 (80)%
1,000,000 or more	100 (100)	100 (81)
500,000 to 999,999	100 (98)	100 (100)
250,000–499,999	100 (94)	91 (92)
100,000–249,999	100 (90)	95 (81)
50,000–99,999	100 (93)	96 (87)
25,000–49,999	100 (88)	97 (85)
10,000–24,999	99 (88)	94 (80)
Under 10,000	86 (81)	80 (67)

Source: Reaves, B.A. (2010). *Local Police Departments, 2007.* Washington, DC: Bureau of Justice Statistics; Reaves, B.A. (2012). *Sheriffs' Offices, 2007—Statistical Tables.* Washington, DC: Bureau of Justice Statistics.

Box 5.2 Ethics in Practice: Police Employment and Marijuana

America is witnessing a dramatic change in the people's perceptions of marijuana, having moved from a "war on drugs" in the 1980s to legalizing marijuana, first for medicinal use, and more recently for recreational use. As of July 2019, 11 states have legalized marijuana for recreational purposes and 20 states for Medicinal purposes. Many more states are considering changes in their own state laws.

States passing laws to allow the use of marijuana for medicinal or recreational purposes have created a constitutional crisis, for while the states have legalized marijuana, federal laws still say marijuana is illegal. An important question to consider is which set of laws do the police enforce — state or federal.

Ask Yourself:

If marijuana is now legal in several states, can a police department in these states, as a condition of screening and employment, deny a person who smokes marijuana? Explain your answer.

Still further, should they change the policies to allow current police officers to be able to smoke marijuana while off duty? Why or why not?

Table 5.7   Psychological Screening Methods Used in Selection of New Police Officers (2007) and Deputy Sheriffs (2007) by Population Served

Pop. Served	Police Officer (Sheriff's Deputy)	
	Psychological Evaluation	Personality Inventory
All sizes	72 (62)%	46 (41)%
1,000,000 or more	100 (93)	85 (63)
500,000 to 999,999	100 (100)	68 (56)
250,000–499,999	100 (82)	67 (56)
100,000–249,999	99 (75)	64 (46)
50,000–99,999	100 (79)	66 (41)
25,000–49,999	98 (57)	64 (43)
10,000–24,999	94 (54)	57 (37)
Under 10,000	65 (47)	41 (35)

Source: Reaves, B.A. (2010). *Local Police Departments, 2007.* Washington, DC: Bureau of Justice Statistics; Reaves, B.A. (2012). *Sheriffs' Offices, 2007—Statistical Tables.* Washington, DC: Bureau of Justice Statistics.

are the Rorschach Ink blot test and the Thematic Apperception Test, a series of pictures that the individual must put in some order to tell a story. Both of these tests are normed to the general population, so that there is a common response. Anyone deviating from the norm raises questions about their psychological thought process. While all of these tests are helpful, they are never the final means for determining the candidates' status in the process, for that comes with the final interview with the psychologist who will conduct a personal interview, one-on-one, to discuss the results of the test and ask further questions. The psychologist then forwards a report to the police department giving their professional recommendation, which typically falls into one of three categories: recommended, recommended with reservations, and not recommended.[44]

Once a person makes it to this point in the selection process, only about half of the agencies will use a **polygraph examination** (see Table 5.8).[45] Integrated into policing by August Vollmer, his police officer John Larson, and his assistant Leonarde Keeler, the polygraph ("many writings") assesses the biological responses to questions to detect deception. The individual is connected to several devices to check respiration, blood pressure, pulse, and skin conductivity. They are then asked yes or no questions by the polygrapher and the biological responses are recorded on a graph for later interpretation to determine if the individual has been lying. Questions will typically include past criminal behavior and drug use. Deception on this test is commonly

Table 5.8 Polygraph and Voice Stress Analyzer Screening Methods Used in Selection of New Police Officers (2007) and Deputy Sheriffs (2007) by Population Served

Pop. Served	Police Officer (Sheriff's Deputy)	
	Polygraph Examination	**Voice Stress Analyzer**
All sizes	26 (24)%	5 (7)%
1,000,000 or more	77 (67)	0 (19)
500,000 to 999,999	74 (69)	13 (11)
250,000–499,999	83 (45)	7 (16)
100,000–249,999	77 (48)	13 (18)
50,000–99,999	63 (28)	13 (8)
25,000–49,999	51 (24)	9 (6)
10,000–24,999	42 (18)	11 (4)
Under 10,000	18 (8)	4 (2)

Source: Reaves, B.A. (2010). *Local Police Departments, 2007.* Washington, DC Bureau of Justice Statistics; Reaves, B.A. (2012). *Sheriffs' Offices, 2007—Statistical Tables.* Washington, DC Bureau of Justice Statistics.

grounds for removal from the applicant pool. A similar device, but one that is less intrusive, is the **voice stress analyzer,** which records the voice of the police candidate while being interviewed and assesses changes in the voice pattern that may indicate stress and potentially deception.

If the candidate has made it to this point in the process, the next step, and one that may have been conducted as the candidate advanced through the process, is the **background investigation.** Nearly every police department, 99.8 percent, will conduct a background investigation on the applicant.[46] This is typically assigned to a detective and it goes far beyond the previous criminal, driver, and credit checks, but may include military record checks, contacts with past employers, interviews with neighbors and friends, Internet searches, and past usage of social media. Gellman describes how an applicant who has never been married, did not change jobs or residences frequently, and had no debt, may still have "to provide 150-190 pieces of information," while "for most candidates the number will range upward from 300."[47] One of the most important aspects of the background investigation is to ensure that the candidate did not lie on the initial application form, for these always note: "any misstatement or omission of fact on the application may result in dismissal." Research suggests this is one of the most important steps in the process, for the more depth given to the background investigation, the better indicator it is for future performance.[48]

Table 5.9   Personal/Panel Interview as a Screening Methods Used in Selection of New Police Officers (2007) and Deputy Sheriffs (2007) by Population Served

Pop. Served	Police Officer (Sheriff's Deputy) Personal/Panel Interview
All sizes	99 (99)%
1,000,000 or more	100 (96)
500,000 to 999,999	97 (100)
250,000–499,999	96 (100)
100,000–249,999	98 (100)
50,000–99,999	99 (99)
25,000–49,999	100 (99)
10,000–24,999	76 (42)
Under 10,000	38 (26)

Source: Reaves, B.A. (2010). *Local Police Departments, 2007.* Washington, DC: Bureau of Justice Statistics; Reaves, B.A. (2012). *Sheriffs' Offices, 2007—Statistical Tables.* Washington, DC: Bureau of Justice Statistics.

The last step in the hiring process is generally the **personal/panel interview** (see Table 5.9). The interview is used by nearly every police department, 98.2 percent, and will often consist of a panel of individuals conducting the interview.[49] This may be as few as two or three, often the police chief and other staff, all the way to approximately a dozen individuals or more, which may consist of command staff, midlevel managers, police officers, nonsworn personnel, and citizens. Questions are often a final check on the entire screening process as well as scenario-based questions to see how the individual will react to problems, their decision-making skills, their commitment to their decisions, and their demeanor under stress. While the interview is assuredly one of the most difficult steps in the process and it can determine the candidate's final ranking, research has not found it to necessarily be the best predictor of officer success.[50]

One of the most stressful parts of the screening process is the panel interview where multiple representatives of the department and local government rapid fire questions making it a stressful environment.

For those candidates who have made it through the selection process, they are typically ranked based on certain criteria (for example, written aptitude, physical fitness, panel interview, etc.), which will vary from department to department. Then, based on the number of positions available, those individuals ranked highest are selected for employment. Police departments do, however, reserve the right to select from farther down the list, as long as the individual remained in the applicant pool, for those individuals may fill certain needs of the department, ranging from some form of special skill or training, because they speak a foreign language, or for purposes of departmental diversity.

Training

Once a person is hired by a police agency, the individual will typically work in various non-law enforcement roles for the department until they are sent to the police academy for training (see Box 5.3). This is not always the case, for "at least 30 states let some newly hired local law enforcement officers hit the streets with a gun, a badge, and little or no training."[51] These states allow for a **grace period** for officers to work the street before being trained, usually six months, but they can be as much as one year as in West Virginia or up to two years as in Mississippi and Wisconsin.[52] The grace period is set by state law.

Police Academy

Also set by state law, very often through the state's **Peace Officers Standards and Training (POST)** organization, are the training requirements required to be certified as a police officer in the state. An individual must obtain **police POST certification** to work as a police officer beyond any grace period set by law, and this is typically obtained through the police academy. There are approximately 648 state and local law enforcement training academies in the United States.[53] The majority of the police academies in the United States are aligned with local colleges and universities (45 percent), mostly community colleges, where recruits receive not only their police certification, but an Associate's Degree in Criminal Justice or Police Science, such as in the state of Florida where programs such as the Institute for Public Safety at the Florida Keys Community College help recruits obtain police certification and the Associate in Arts in Criminal Justice Studies.[54] Many of the larger police agencies, such as the New York City Police Department and the Fairfax County (Virginia) Police Department, have their own police training academies, and these account for 22 percent of all training academies.[55] The rest of the academies are then either run by a specific agency, such as the state police (7 percent), which will then train any or all law enforcement officers in the state, or they are run by a multiagency academy (8 percent), often called a regional police academy, that serves all of the police departments in a geographical area.[56]

Box 5.3 History in Practice: Police in the Movies: The Comedic Cop

Whenever someone mentions the words "police academy," many people often think of the **movie comedies** by the same name, *Police Academy*. A series of seven movies that began in 1984, continuing through to a seventh movie released in 1994, and which also generated a cartoon show and a live action television show. The story line followed a bunch of misfit police cadets attending the academy and eventually becoming police officers. The movies portrayed police officers as incompetent, bumbling fools, with low intelligence and who were mostly physically inept. It was essentially a series of movies that made fun of police officers in a slapstick comedy way.

The fact is, police officers have been portrayed in this manner ever since Hollywood began making movies. As early as 1912, a movie called *Hoffmeyer's Legacy* featured a group of police officers known as the Keystone Cops, a collection of bumbling and incompetent police officers. The movie short *Bangville Police* (1913) and *In the Clutches of the Gang* (1914) solidified the police officer as buffoon staple of Hollywood. Even by today's standards, these movies still have entertainment value (Just type in Keystone Cops into the YouTube search engine), and a number of famous comedians at the time joined in the fun including Fatty Arbuckle, Buster Keaton,

Charlie Chaplin and the comedy duo Abbott and Costello.

Over the history of Hollywood-produced movies, the incompetent police officer who bungles through the job have taken on all different kinds of forms, but they all portray police officers as incompetent. Think of such movies as *The Naked Gun, The Pink Panther, Super Troopers,* and *Reno 911*. These movies are also not a thing of the past, as more recent movies released that follow the same theme have included *Let's Be Cops, Ride Along,* and *21* or *22 Jump Street.*

Many police officers despise these types of comedies because they see it as demeaning their profession. August Vollmer was one who early on felt that movies either may the police officer totally incompetent or unrealistically competent, neither of which he felt were accurate portrayals of policing. Other police officers enjoy these types of films for in a profession that often sees the dark side of humanity, they offer a bit of comedic relief. The danger is of course citizens believing the movies portray reality, that the police are incompetent or conversely that they can solve crimes in a matter of one hour (with commercials!). Regardless of how one views these movies, Hollywood's portrayal of the bumbling and idiotic police officer are a staple of the industry and are no doubt here to stay.

When the majority of police academies began developing across the United States in the 1950s, most were modeled off of military basic training, and so they featured drill instructors creating a high-stress environment and ordering recruits around. While approximately half (53 percent) still maintain some semblance of this style of academy, many have moved away from this toward a more professional and adult learning model (47 percent).[57] The difference in academy styles is found in two differing perspectives. The first uses a **pedagogy and high stress** style of learning. The idea is that police recruits need to learn to follow orders, to be told what to do, and to do things in the same kind of high-stress environment they will find themselves in on the street. The

One part of the police academy training is the week spent on the range where the police officer qualifies with the weapon they will carry on duty.

other uses an **andragogy and low stress** style of learning. In this case, the idea is that police recruits are adults and they learn better through a collegial dialogue and low-stress learning environment, similar to college classes. While academy students are receptive to the latter style, there is no evidence that one style is better than the other.[58]

The majority of police academies in the United States are staffed by a mixture of full-time and part-time instructors, of whom 75 percent are sworn police officers.[59] The average length of a police academy is 761 hours, or 19 weeks, and recruits are trained in many facets of police operations, including report writing, investigations, basic first aid and safety, and emergency vehicle operations (see Table 5.10).[60] In addition, they are trained in self-defense tactics, they go through firearms training, and are taught state criminal law. To graduate, recruits are tested through a series of tests, including written,

	Police Officer (Sheriff's Deputy)		
Table 5.10 Number of Training Hours Required for New Police Officer (2007) and Deputy Sheriff (2007) Recruits by Population Served			
Pop. Served	**Total**	**Academy**	**Field**
All sizes	922 (894)	613 (582)	309 (312)
1,000,000 or more	1,700 (1,476)	1,033 (795)	667 (681)
500,000 to 999,999	1,783 (1,215)	1,063 (767)	720 (448)
250,000–499,999	1,542 (1,104)	906 (670)	636 (434)
100,000–249,999	1,463 (1081)	809 (637)	654 (444)
50,000–99,999	1,341 (989)	731 (626)	610 (363)
25,000–49,999	1,241 (885)	698 (561)	543 (324)
10,000–24,999	1,101 (807)	666 (545)	434 (262)
Under 10,000	835 (754)	586 (545)	249 (209)

Source: Reaves, B.A. (2010). *Local Police Departments, 2007.* Washington, DC: Bureau of Justice Statistics; Reaves, B.A. (2012). *Sheriffs' Offices, 2007 — Statistical Tables.* Washington, DC: Bureau of Justice Statistics.

skills/proficiency, physical fitness, and scenario-based tests. The graduation rates for the police academy averages 86 percent, with a mixture of recruits self-selecting out or failing out of the academy.[61]

Overall, while the quality of the police academies have improved over the past 40 years, the basics of what is taught has not. Compton (California) Police Department's Sergeant Baker went through the academy in the 1960s and described it as a program "that lasted sixteen weeks and included law and judicial procedure, weapons and tactics, physical and mental training, chain of command, criminology, basic psychology, and community relations."[62] Describing the Arizona Law Enforcement Academy in the 1980s, Gellman explains there "are classes in report writing, constitutional and criminal law, patrol and observation, laws of arrest, search and seizure, and defensive techniques."[63] And William Dunn, who attended the LAPD academy in the mid-1990s, described that "for the next six months I learned criminal law and procedures, practiced tactics to subdue suspects, fired hundreds of rounds from my 9mm Beretta handgun, and was taught the rudiments of the Spanish language as well as basics relating to the cultures of various ethnic groups."[64] While the police academies have not changed all that much overall, field training, on the other hand, has.

Field Training Officer Program

Forty years ago or more, when recruits graduated from the police academy they were usually assigned to ride with a grizzled veteran who would tell them how it was in policing. When Frank Serpico, who later single-handedly exposed systemic corruption in the NYPD in the 1970s, graduated from the police academy and reported on his first day, he was "advised that the precinct veterans would 'fill him in' on what else he had to know."[65] In fact, it was not uncommon to be told to "forget everything you learned in the academy," or "the academy is over—now you'll learn how to be a real cop."[66] Since that time, the **field training officer (FTO) program** was developed as a more formal program to fully train the officer on the street and to evaluate their performance. The ten-week program attempts to move the officer from a ride-along/observer, to equal partner, and finally to a fully responding officer who cannot lean on the FTO instructor (see Table 5.10). Because of this and the fact that the new police officer is being constantly evaluated, the FTO program can be enormously stressful.

When Officer Dunn went through the LAPD FTO program, he noted the seriousness of the program for weeding people out of policing when he explained "six of my classmates have left the LAPD so far, generally due to pressure from their training officers. One of my classmates here at Southwest has received two unsatisfactory reports. I've heard that he will have to make a big improvement if he wants to keep his job."[67] When this author went through the FTO program, the recruit class shrunk in size as several decided the pressure of the FTO program (and the street) was too much for them and they quit, while several others were "not retained" due to low performance.

The purpose of the FTO program is only, in part, to weed out those who will not be effective as police officers. And while evaluation of the police officer in training is part of the process, the primary purpose is to provide the best training and supervision of a new officer on the street. As Tucson Police Sergeant Richard Miranda added, "Field training is partly to let you make rookie mistakes."[68] The goal is to give rookies the proper training for how to perform as a police officer and then allow them to begin experiencing it by transitioning from observer, to participant, and finally to full performance. In the end, as Washington, D.C., police officer Christopher Archer explains, "Like so many other things in life, I knew this was more my chance to gain some confidence, garner some kind of working knowledge of the basic, every-day routine and prepare myself for the utter chaos that would soon serve as my career. Truly learning how to become a cop would come much later."[69]

Other Training

Once a recruit has graduated both the academy and the FTO program and begins working as a full-fledged police officer, it is not as if their training stops. Police officers also undergo roll call training, in-service training, and are often incentivized to pursue higher education. All of this is oriented on the continued career growth of the individual officer.

Roll call training dates back to the early twentieth century when police departments became more organized and held meetings with the police officers before they went on shift. As the departments implemented new policies and procedures, it became common to instruct officers in short, five-minute sessions during roll call.[70] The program became more formalized as the decades passed, the five-minute time period became the accepted time limit, and the topics included everything from policy and proper procedures to officer safety and first responder skills.

One of the earliest in-service training classes held by Police Chief August Vollmer in 1908 covered the basics of first aid and safety. Vollmer is on the far right.

In-service training traces its history back to 1907, when Police Chief August Vollmer of the Berkeley Police Department realized that police officers needed to be better trained for their job. Vollmer instituted what became known as the "crab sessions" on Friday afternoons.[71] During these sessions, Vollmer gathered every police officer not currently working the street and would allow them to openly voice any disagreements or problems within the department. In modern terms, he allowed for a weekly after-action review to judge what the department was doing well, and what it was doing poorly, and to institute a plan for corrective action. In addition, Vollmer began using these sessions to teach officers on a wide array of topics, from first aid and safety to the use of police bicycles in patrol. He also brought in guest speakers and trainers, including

Table 5.11 In-Service Training Requirements for Police Officers (2007) and Deputy Sheriffs (2007) by Population Served

Pop. Served	Police Officer (Sheriff's Deputy)	
	Percent with Requirement	Average Number of Hours Required
All sizes	92 (94)%	35 (45) hours
1,000,000 or more	100 (93)	27 (50)
500,000 to 999,999	100 (98)	31 (33)
250,000–499,999	100 (100)	31 (53)
100,000–249,999	99 (100)	39 (52)
50,000–99,999	98 (94)	42 (38)
25,000–49,999	96 (92)	41 (35)
10,000–24,999	95 (92)	39 (48)
Under 10,000	91 (91)	33 (52)

Source: Reaves, B.A. (2010). *Local Police Departments, 2007.* Washington, DC: Bureau of Justice Statistics; Reaves, B.A. (2012). *Sheriffs' Offices, 2007 — Statistical Tables.* Washington, DC: Bureau of Justice Statistics.

both current and former criminals, as well as professors from the university. Today, 92 percent of state and local police have an annual in-service training requirement, averaging 35 hours annually for police officers and 45 hours for sheriffs' offices (Table 5.11).[72]

Higher education has also become more common among today's police officers. First started by Police Chief August Vollmer at the University of California at Berkeley in 1916, the goal of requiring every police officer to have a degree from an established institution of higher education before employment with a police department became the focus of Vollmer's entire career.[73] The program he started was a summer program to allow his officers to earn a degree in what we would call police science (at the time it was called criminology). Programs began to spread across the United States and by the 1970s, with the assistance of funding from the federal government by way of the Omnibus Crime Control and Safe Streets Act of 1968, through the U.S. Department of Justice's Law Enforcement Assistance Administration, criminal justice degree programs began to flourish across the United States. While most police departments still only require a high school diploma (82 percent), and only 6 percent require some college, 9 percent a two-year degree, and 1 percent a four-year degree, more and more people are entering policing with a college degree or they are seeking one after becoming a police officer.[74] Many police departments require or encourage officers who plan to move into management to have a college degree, and many police departments offer incentive pay for those with a degree (32 percent of all departments), while offering tuition reimbursement (37 percent of all departments) for those who do not yet have one.[75]

Despite all of the training and education one can receive as a police officer, police officers primarily learn from other officers and they learn most from their **police experience**. Chicago Police Officer C.K. Rojas explains that despite all of the knowledge he learned in the academy, "I've learned more from my fellow officers than I'll ever learn in a classroom."[76] Rojas also added that "you get trained in the academy, but there's also a street way,"[77] and as his fellow Chicago Police Officer Gina Gallo explained it: "The street is the best teacher for any cop. Lessons learned are quick, harsh and, if you're smart, never forgotten."[78]

Probation

After an officer graduates the academy and field training, they are generally assigned to work patrol and, more than likely, they will still be working under a **probationary period.** Until an officer is off probation, they do not have a property interest in their job.[79] In other words, they may be let go for any or no reason and they will have no recourse to keep their job. Once they are off of their probation, then, if for any reason the police department wishes to let them go, they must show cause and the officer has the right to appeal the decision. Probationary periods can last from six months to three years, but are typically 18 months long, starting from the first day of employment. This is the case with the Chicago Police department where an entry-level officer has an 18-month probation, and only after coming off probation are they considered to be "real" cops.[80] In most police departments, a new police officer in their probationary period is generally called a "rookie," but in the Los Angeles Police Department they are called a "boot," hence the title of William Dunn's informative autobiography of his first year with the LAPD.[81]

Career Development

Once a police officer comes off probation, new opportunities will arise for them, and typically they will have to begin planning for their future career with the police department (see Box 5.4). Many officers enjoy working the street, while some wish to move into investigations and become a detective, and still others pursue a career in management. In smaller police departments, these opportunities may be limited until a senior officer moves on or retires. In larger departments, there are often opportunities to pursue any of these career directions.

Many believe that it is automatic that a police officer, after five to seven years on the street, will move into management. However, many officers

> ## Box 5.4 History in Practice: William "Bill" Parker and the Professionalization of the Los Angeles Police Department
>
> William Parker, the Los Angeles Police Department chief from 1950-1966, was assuredly a policing pioneer. Born on June 21, 1905 in Lead, South Dakota, he was raised in the famed town of Deadwood. The Parker family moved to Los Angeles in 1922 and Bill Parker decided to pursue college and eventually a law degree. In order to make ends meet, Parker joined the Los Angeles Police Department on August 8, 1927, working as a police officer by day and studying at night, graduating in 1930 with his law degree and passing the bar. He was then faced with the decision of establishing a law practice or remaining as a police officer. He decided he preferred being a cop.
>
> Parker moved rapidly through the ranks at the LAPD, but then World War II intervened and he joined the military, rising to the rank of captain. He received numerous awards during his time as a soldier, including the Purple Heart for his wounds on the beaches of Normandy. He was soon involved in assisting in prisoner detention and policing in post-World War II Germany, serving under Colonel O. W. Wilson. When the war was over, Parker returned home a war hero and rejoined the ranks of the LAPD.
>
> Once again, he rose rapidly through the ranks, going from captain, to inspector, and deputy chief. On August 9, 1950, he was appointed Police Chief of the LAPD. Parker, knowing full well the problems of politics and corruption within the LAPD, wanted to professionalize the department. He found the blueprint in a report that August Vollmer had made when he served one year as the LAPD Police Chief during 1923-1924. The report was given to the city by the departing Vollmer and was promptly ignored. Parker dusted it off and began implementing every recommendation.
>
> Parker's professionalization of the police was promoted by a number of factors, one of which was Jack Webb's radio and television show *Dragnet*. Another was when O.W. Wilson, then Dean of the School of Criminology at the University of California, edited a book titled *Parker on Police*. In addition to his publicity, Parker had instituted what was considered the premier police academy in the nation, and he had developed a police force that was proactive in its policing methods.
>
> Parker's trouble arose out of two reasons, one personal, the other a sign of the times. Parker had trouble with alcohol which often created problems for him. The other was the growing racial tensions in the 1960s and a number of comments that were seen as racist. Despite the fact that it was Parker who had desegregated the LAPD during his tenure, the LAPD was constantly being accused of racism and brutality. Despite calls for him to step down, he refused. On July 16, 1966, while receiving a commendation for his reforms of the police department, he suffered a fatal heart attack.

choose not to pursue a supervisory role, and research tells us it is for three main reasons.[82] First, officers often cite personal reasons, such as family, childcare, changes in shifts, and a potential decrease in pay. Senior officers on the street often get to select which shift they work; however, if they become a supervisor, they often end up on the midnight shift to start. And, officers working overtime often make so much money that if they become a supervisor, they are not allowed to receive overtime pay; their pay will decrease. Second, officers give professional reasons such as better shifts, they like their positions, and they wish to continue pursuing special assignments, police officer track ranks, or to move into investigations. Finally, officers often give organizational reasons such as there are not enough positions available, they have been discouraged by someone, or they do not believe they will be treated fairly in the promotional exam process. Police officers who wish to remain on patrol and working the street for their career are often considered to be on an **officer track (see** Box 5.5**)**. In larger departments, promotion positions often exist within the police officer ranks that allow the officer to remain on the street while moving up in seniority and pay. Some departments have levels of policing, such as Police Officer I, II, and III, while others have the competitive position of Master Police Officer (see Table 5.12). In addition, police officers may also seek out specialized units that allow them to remain on patrol, such as Special Weapons and Tactics, or they may move into special units that work assignments outside of patrol, but allow them to remain working in the field. These units are called by various names such as "tactical units" in Chicago, where one of the commanders explains, "We're not specialists on any one type of crime and we are not designated to do follow-up investigations. We're specially assigned to augment patrol officers in uniform and assist with preliminary investigations . . . . We normally don't respond to radio calls. We generate our own activity."[83]

Many officers, however, enjoy conducting investigations, performing the follow-up work, and they desire to be called detective. These officers

---

Box 5.5 Policing in Practice: Jack Webb's "What Is a Cop?"

Jack Webb was the actor and persona behind the original radio show and television series *Dragnet.* Whether as the producer, writer, or actor who played the lead character, Sergeant Joe Friday, throughout the 1950s and 1960s, many believed Jack Webb was a cop. Serving fictiously on the LAPD, but having the early support of Police Chief Bill Parker, Webb became for many the personification of a cop.

In one episode, called "The Big Interrogation," Sergeant Joe Friday is interviewing a man played by a very young Kent McCord, who himself would one day play a police officer in the television show *Adam-12.* In that particular episode, the young man voices interest in becoming a career police officer himself but his fiancée does not want to be married to a police officer. She thinks he can do better because he has a college degree. Sergeant Joe Friday explains that he understands how she feels and then launches into a monologue that has come to be known by those in policing circles as the famous **"What Is a Cop?" speech**. While somewhat dated in content, the basic ideas and realities behind the speech have not changed and give a good understanding of what a police officer's career will be like.

YouTube "Jack Webb — What Is a Cop?" to watch the monologue.

Table 5.12 Law Enforcement Median/Mean Salaries According to U.S. Bureau of Labor			
Type	**Number Employed**	**Mean Hourly Wage**	**Annual Mean Salary**
Police & Sheriff's Patrol	662,390	$31.00	$64,490
Detectives & Criminal Investigators	105,350	$40.06	$83,320
First Line Supervisor of Police & Detectives	104,860	$44.03	$91,590
Fish and Game Wardens	6,020	$28.16	$58,570
Transit & Railroad Police	5,520	$34.27	$71,280
Police Dispatchers	94,450	$20.26	$42,020

Source: U.S. Bureau of Labor. (2017). *National Occupational Employment and Wage Estimates United States.* Retrieved from https://www.bls.gov/oes/2017/may/oes_nat.htm#33-0000

will pursue the **detective track** for their police career. Many larger departments will have a "follow-up unit" that conducts basic investigations after receiving a police officer's report. This may entail contacting victims, witnesses, and insurance companies. They are a unit that is between police patrol and the detectives who work for the investigations command of a police organization. Those agencies that do not have a follow-up unit will often place officers moving into the detective track in a general investigations unit before allowing them to specialize in a particular area. Those on the detective track will eventually move into an area of specialization, such as robbery or burglary. They will then have to decide whether to remain in a particular specialization or move on to another area where they will once again have to master a new type of crime and the conduct of its investigation. No matter what police department one works for, however, working homicide is always the most coveted position within the detective ranks.[84]

Finally, the last form of career development for a police officer is to pursue the **management track**. First, it should be noted that this may not be mutually exclusive to the detective track, for many of those officers who become detectives will still pursue the management track to become detective supervisors. Police officers decide to pursue the management track for many reasons, but most commonly it is a personal goal, because it allows for more career opportunities, and because many within the police department saw something in themselves that would make a good manager.[85] Once the officers do decide to pursue a managerial position they are generally given some materials to review and/or provided a training session. They then take a promotional examination that tests their abilities to perform as a manager. These may include written tests, oral tests, or various exercises that simulate manager supervisory skills. In larger departments that can afford the expense, they will send officers to an assessment center, an outside company that specializes in testing individuals for their potential for management. Those testing are then rank-ordered based on these tests and the list given to the police chief to make final selection.

Once officers enter the management track, they will usually begin as field supervisors with ranks such as corporal or sergeant. From there, they can continue to advance into mid-level management with ranks such as lieutenant and captain. Working their way up toward the top echelons of policing may afford them the opportunity to be appointed as a police chief in that department or allow them to apply for positions as a police chief in other departments. Police chiefs serve at the will and pleasure of the mayor and/or city council, while sheriffs must run for election in most sheriff's offices. Once in those positions, it becomes "their" department and they are responsible for everything that happens, good or bad. While it sounds stressful, it can be quite rewarding, and recent research suggests if the size of the agency is a good fit and the chief has a strong commitment to the department, they exhibit high levels of job satisfaction.[86] Fairfield (CT) Police Chief Gary MacNamara voices this exact sentiment when he said in an interview, "When I came on as a police officer, I loved my job. I loved engaging in people, responding to calls. I don't think you can not have that same love for the job of police chief and then be successful at it because it's pretty demanding at times."[87]

Retention

Another decision every police officer must make is whether or not to remain with the department where they are employed or to remain in policing altogether. For those officers who decide to leave their current agency for another, they often seek a **lateral transfer.** If the police officer moves to another police department within the same state, their police certification will make them attractive to the other agencies because they will not have to pay to train the new employee. However, if the department the officer wishes to move to is out of state or federal, the officer's police certification will not be recognized and they will have to go through a police academy in the state where their new police department is located.

Then there are many police officers who, after a certain period of time, decide for various reasons that they wish to **leave policing** and resign from the police department. For many officers, the reason they resign is because the realities of policing did not meet their expectations about what the job entailed.[88] Reasons, however, may include inadequate recognition, dysfunctional organization, poor leadership, or they wish to pursue another career.[89] It has been found that the biggest reason police officers leave policing is because of the economy and the low salary of police officers.[90] Turnover within police agencies tends to be relatively consistent across the country, with a North Carolina study finding an annual average of 14.2 percent turnover among municipal police and a 12.7 percent among sheriff's deputies, while in Vermont a study found turnover to be an annual 8.25 percent among police, and 8.9 percent among sheriffs.[91]

Retirement

For those police officers who make policing a career, they must work for so many years and be a certain age before they are eligible to retire. While it varies from agency to agency, retirement usually comes after 25 years of service and age 50 in policing. Some departments still allow officers to retire after 20 years, and many have stretched it to 30 years, making for a long career. The decision to retire is often a difficult one for a career officer. As one Los Angeles police officer who retired explained, "I talked about it all the time, we all did, but I never thought it would happen."[92] For career police officers it is like leaving "family" behind when they retire, so it makes it a very hard decision.[93] NYPD Officer Osborne explained his decision to retire by saying, "I had some doubts about pulling the plug, everybody does, but the one thing I was sure about was that I was tired."[94] He also described what it was like by saying, "Retiring from the police department is kind of like jumping off a diving board, there's no turning back."[95] Once you retire, you are retired. Yet, at the same time, when they do decide it is time, it can be a very rewarding experience. When Chicago Police Sergeant Bill Jaconetti retired from the Chicago Police Department in 2005, at the end of his last shift, at 1 A.M., the officers from the 17th District Station lined the streets with their headlights and emergency lights flashing. It was a salute to a cop's cop, one who had given his life in service to the police department. "I never saw anything like that and I just thought it was the most fantastic thing I'd ever seen," he recounted. "It near brought me to tears. And it reminded me that everything I did—everything—was worth it."[96]

Upon retirement, most police officers are issued a retirement badge and the service weapon they carried on duty such as those featured here upon the author's retirement from the Military Police Corps.

Conclusion

The career of a police officer begins with the recruitment process, ensuring the possible candidate meets the pre-employment requirements, followed by the application. Applicants then proceed through a series of tests, generally from the least expensive to most expensive, including the written test, physical test, records check, medical exam, drug testing, psychological exam, background investigation, polygraph, and oral board. For those officers selected, they will then have to pass the police academy, the Field Training Officer program, and move through their probationary period before they are considered a fully recognized police officer. These officers will continue to receive training (roll call, in-service, etc.) and may opt to pursue a degree in higher education. Officers will then face the decision of whether to pursue an officer, detective, or management track for their career growth, all the while considering leaving policing, a lateral transfer to another agency, or remaining through retirement. Those who do end up making policing a career must then discern when the proper time is for them to retire from the police profession.

Just the Facts

1. Some people have an innate (nature) desire to become police officers, meaning they have a predisposition toward the profession, while others learn (nurture) to want to become a police officer, and are socialized into the profession.

2. Most individuals state they want to become police officers for altruistic reasons, job benefits, and job security. The first, typically described as "I want to help people," is conjectured to be either a true desire to serve the community or a pat answer when asked.

3. The three most common recruitment methods in policing are newspaper advertisements, career fairs, and the Internet.

4. The three most common methods for police recruit feeder programs are college internships, explorer programs, and school resource officers.

5. The three most commonly targeted groups for police recruitments are certified police officers, college graduates, and women and minorities.

6. The most common pre-employment standards are age, height, weight, physical agility, strength, vision, education, residency, and non-smoking, as these factors are highly associated with successful police officers on the job.

7. A bona fide occupational qualification is a requirement for someone to become a police officer because it is a necessary skill needed to perform the job.

8. The screening process to become a police officer, moving from least expensive to most, consists of written aptitude test, physical agility test, records check, medical exam, drug testing, psychological exam, polygraph exam, background investigation, and personal/panel interview.

9. Most police officers begin their training in the police academy, although some states allow a grace period where the individual can work the street gaining on-the-job training. After the academy there is the field training officer program, roll call training, in-service training, higher education, and police experience.
10. There are two predominate styles of police academies, the pedagogy/high stress style which emphasizes child education and is military oriented, or the andragogy/low stress style that emphasizes adult education and is college oriented.
11. The three most common career tracks in policing are the officer, detective, and management tracks.
12. In policing, retention of officers is difficult as many laterally transfer to other agencies or leave policing altogether. Those that do remain typically earn a retirement pension after between 20 and 30 years, depending on the department.

Ask Yourself

1. Do individuals become police officers because of a natural inclination toward policing, or is it because of various things in their life that influence them and socialize them into wanting to become a police officer?
2. When most individuals are asked why they want to become a police officer, they say because "I want to help people." Why do they almost all say this? Is this because they are altruistic? Because it sounds like the right answer and is what they think people want to hear?
3. Considering the various recruitment methods, feeder programs, and the use of targeted recruiting, explain why police recruiters often have such a difficult time finding successful applicants.
4. Think about all of the pre-employment standards that are common in policing. Should some of these be removed or should more be added to improve policing?
5. Reflect back on the various screening methods employed to ensure that only the most highly qualified people are hired as police officers, then consider why there are problems with individuals performing properly as police officers. Are there other screening measures that could be used to make sure only good people are hired as police officers?
6. Discuss the relationship between police training and career tracks as it relates to retention and retirement. Are these factors related?

Keywords

Age requirement
Altruism
Andragogy and low stress
Background investigation
Bona Fide Occupational Qualifications (BFOQ)
Credit history check
Criminal records check
Detective track
Driving records check
Drug testing
Field officer training (FTO) program
Grace period
Height and weight requirement
Higher education
In-service training
Job benefits
Job security
Lateral transfer
Leave policing
Management track
Medical examination

Minimum education requirement

Nature

No-smoking requirement

Nurture

Officer track

Peace Officer Standards and Training (POST)

Pedagogy and high stress

Personal/panel interview

Physical agility and strength requirement

Physical agility test

Police experience

Police POST certification

Police recruit feeder programs

Polygraph examination

Predisposition

Pre-employment standards

Probationary period

Psychological examination

Records check

Recruitment methods

Residency requirement

Retention

Retirement

Roll-call training

Screening process

Socialization

Targeted groups

Vision requirement

Voice stress analyzer

Written aptitude test

Endnotes

1. Reese, R. (2005). *Leadership in the LAPD: Walking the tightrope*. Durham, NC: Carolina Academic Press, p. 2.

2. Padar, J. & J. (2014). *On being a cop: Father & son police tales from the streets of Chicago*. Lake Placid, NY: Aviva Publishing, p. 71.

3. Evola, A. (2017). *So you want to be a cop: What everyone should know before entering a law enforcement career*. Lanham, MD: Rowman & Littlefield, p. 2.

4. Caldero, M. & Larose, A.P. (2003). Value consistency within the police: The lack of a gap. *Policing: An International Journal of Police Strategies and Management, 24*, 162-180; Crank, J. & Caldero, M. (1999). *Police ethics: The corruption of noble cause*. Cincinnati, OH: Anderson Publishing; Rokeach, M., Miller, M., & Snyder, J. (1971). The value gap between police and policed. *Journal of Social Issues, 27*, 155-171.

5. Van Maanen, J. (1973). Observations on the making of policemen. *Human Organization, 32*, 407—418.

6. Cannon, L. (1997). *Official negligence: How Rodney King and the riots changed Los Angeles and the LAPD*. New York, NY: Random House, p. 76.

7. Gallo, G. (2001). *Armed and dangerous: Memoirs of a Chicago policewoman*. New York, NY: Forge Book, p. 25.

8. Gallo, G. (2001). *Armed and dangerous: Memoirs of a Chicago policewoman*. New York, NY: Forge Book, p. 25.

9. Lester, D. (1983). Why do people become police officers: A study of reasons and their predictions of success. *Journal of Police Science and Administration, 11(2)*, 170-174; Harris, R.N. (1973). *The police academy: An inside view*. New York, NY: John Wiley and Sons; Westley, W.A. (1970). *Violence and the police: A sociological study of law, custom, and morality*. Cambridge, MA: MIT Press.

10. Gallo, G. (2001). *Armed and dangerous: Memoirs of a Chicago policewoman*. New York, NY: Forge Book, p. 37.

11. Gallo, G. (2001). *Armed and dangerous: Memoirs of a Chicago policewoman*. New York, NY: Forge Book, p. 37.

12. Gallo, G. (2001). *Armed and dangerous: Memoirs of a Chicago policewoman*. New York, NY: Forge Book, p. 37.

13. Dunn, W. (1996). *Boot: An L.A.P.D. officer's rookie year*. New York, NY: William Morrow and Company, Inc., p. vii.

14. Baker, J.R. with S.J. Rivele. (2011). *Vice: One cop's story of patrolling America's most dangerous city*. New York, NY: St. Martin's Griffin, p. 26.

15. Osborne, S. (2015). *The Job: True tales form the life of a New York city cop*. New York: Doubleday, p. 3.

16. Padar, J. & J. (2014). *On being a cop: Father & son police tales from the streets of Chicago*. Lake Placid, NY: Aviva Publishing.

17. Raganella, A.J. & White, M.D. (2004). Race, gender, and motivation for becoming a police officer: Implications for building a representative police department. *Journal of Criminal Justice, 32*, 501-503.

18. Cumming, E., Cumming, I., & Edell, L. (1965). Policemen as philosopher, guide and friend. *Social Problems, 12*, 266—268; Harris, R.N. (1973). *The police academy: An inside view*. New York, NY: John Wiley and Sons; Reiss, A.J., Jr. (1967). Career orientations, job satisfaction and the assessment of law enforcement problems by police officers. In the President's Commission on Law Enforcement and Administration of Justice (Ed.), *Studies in crime and law enforcement in major metropolitan areas: Field surveys III (Vol. 2)*. Washington, DC: U.S. Government Printing Office; Van Maanen, J. (1973). Observations on the making of policemen. *Human Organization, 32*, 407–418.

19. Alex, N. (1976). *New York cops talk back: A study of a beleaguered minority*. New York, NY: John Wiley and Sons; Lester, D. (1983). Why do people become police officers: A study of reasons and their predictions of success. *Journal of Police Science and Administration, 11(2)*, 170-174; Giblin, M.J. & Galli, P.M. (2017). Compensation as a police candidate attraction tool: An organizational-level analysis. *Police Quarterly, 20*, 397-419; Harris, R.N. (1973). *The police academy: An inside view*. New York, NY: John Wiley and Sons; Westley, W.A. (1970). *Violence and the police: A*

sociological study of law, custom, and morality. Cambridge, MA: MIT Press.

20. Harris, R.N. (1973). *The police academy: An inside view.* New York, NY: John Wiley and Sons; McNamara, J.H. (1967). Uncertainties in police work: The relevance of police recruits' backgrounds and training. In D.J. Bordua (Ed.), *The police: Six sociological essays.* New York, NY: John Wiley and Sons; Niederhoffer, A. (1969). *Behind the shield: The police in urban society.* Garden City, NY: Doubleday and Company; Westley, W.A. (1970). *Violence and the police: A sociological study of law, custom, and morality.* Cambridge, MA: MIT Press.

21. Taylor, B., Kubu, B., Friedell, L., Rees, C., Jordan, T., & Cheney, J. (2005). *The cops crunch: Identifying strategies for dealing with the recruiting and hiring crisis in law enforcement.* Washington, DC: Police Executive Research Forum.

22. Jordan, W.T., Fridell, L., Faggiani, D., & Kubu, B. (2009). Attracting females and racial/ethnic minorities to law enforcement. *Journal of Criminal Justice, 37,* 333-341.

23. Zumer, B. (2016). Hartford sheriff's office having 'difficult, difficult time' filling jobs, Gahler tells county council." *The Baltimore Sun,* Retrieved from https://www.baltimoresun.com/news/maryland/harford/belair/ph-ag-sheriffs-budget-review-0503-20160502-story.html.

24. Reaves, B. (2010). *Local police departments, 2007.* Washington, DC: Bureau of Justice Statistics.

25. Reaves, B. (2010). *Local police departments, 2007.* Washington, DC: Bureau of Justice Statistics.

26. Gallo, G. (2001). *Armed and dangerous: memoirs of a Chicago policewoman.* New York, NY: Forge Book, p. 46.

27. U.S. Equal Employment Opportunity Commission. (2013). Title VII/Sex/BFOQ/Caregiver. Retrieved from www.eeoc.gov/eeoc/foia/letters/2013/title_vii_sex_bfoq_11_22.html.

28. Reaves, B. (2010). *Local police departments, 2007.* Washington, DC: Bureau of Justice Statistics.

29. Reaves, B.A. (2015). *Local Police Departments, 2013: Personnel, Policies, and Practices.* Washington, DC: Bureau of Justice Statistics.

30. Reaves, B.A. (2015). *Local Police Departments, 2013: Personnel, Policies, and Practices.* Washington, DC: Bureau of Justice Statistics.

31. Reaves, B.A. (2015). *Local Police Departments, 2013: Personnel, Policies, and Practices.* Washington, DC: Bureau of Justice Statistics.

32. Taylor, B., Kubu, B., Friedell, L., Rees, C., Jordan, T., & Cheney, J. (2005). *The cops crunch: Identifying strategies for dealing with the recruiting and hiring crisis in law enforcement.* Washington, DC: Police Executive Research Forum.

33. Reaves, B. (2010). *Local police departments, 2007.* Washington, DC: Bureau of Justice Statistics.

34. White, M.D. (2008). Identifying good cops early: Predicting recruit performance in the academy. *Police Quarterly, 11,* 27-49.

35. Gellman, Stuart. (1993). *COPS: The Men and Women Behind the Badge.* Tucson, AZ: Horizon Press, pp. 18-19.

36. Reaves, B. (2010). *Local police departments, 2007.* Washington, DC: Bureau of Justice Statistics.

37. Collingwood, T.R., Hoffman, R., & Smith, J. (2004). Underlying physical fitness factors for performing police officer physical tasks. *The Police Chief, March,* 32-37.

38. Reaves, B. (2010). *Local police departments, 2007.* Washington, DC: Bureau of Justice Statistics.

39. Reaves, B. (2010). *Local police departments, 2007.* Washington, DC: Bureau of Justice Statistics.

40. Reaves, B. (2010). *Local police departments, 2007.* Washington, DC: Bureau of Justice Statistics.

41. Reaves, B. (2010). *Local police departments, 2007.* Washington, DC: Bureau of Justice Statistics.

42. Reaves, B. (2010). *Local police departments, 2007.* Washington, DC: Bureau of Justice Statistics.

43. Lee, C.B. (2006). Psychological testing for recruit screening. *Texas Law Enforcement and Administrative Statistic Program Bulletin,* March/April.

44. Gellman, S. (1993). *COPS: The men and women behind the badge.* Tucson, AZ: Horizon Press.

45. Reaves, B. (2010). *Local police departments, 2007.* Washington, DC: Bureau of Justice Statistics.

46. Reaves, B. (2010). *Local police departments, 2007.* Washington, DC: Bureau of Justice Statistics.

47. Gellman, S. (1993). *COPS: The men and women behind the badge.* Tucson, AZ: Horizon Press, p. 21.

48. Cohen, B. & Chaiken, J.M. (1972). *Police background characteristic and performance.* New York, NY: Rand Institute; Snowden, L. & Fuss, T. (2000). A costly mistake: Inadequate police background investigations. *The Justice Professional, 13,* 359-375.

49. Reaves, B. (2010). *Local police departments, 2007.* Washington, DC: Bureau of Justice Statistics.

50. Burbeck, E. & Furnham, A. (1985). Police officer selection: A critical review of the literature. *Journal of Police Science and Administration, 13,* 58-69; Doerner, W.G. (1997). The utility of the oral interview board in selecting police academy admissions. *Policing: An International Journal of Police Strategies and Management, 20,* 777-785; Falkenberg, S., Gaines, L.K., Cox, T.C. (1990). The oral interview board: What does it measure? *Journal of Police Science and Administration, 17,* 32-39; Gaines, L.K. & Kappeler, V.E. (1992). Selection and testing. In G.W Cordner and DC Hale (Eds.), *What works in policing: Operations and administration examined,* pp 107-123. Cincinnati, OH: Anderson Publishing.

51. Mohr, H. (2007). Some states put untrained cops on duty. *Associated Press.* Retrieved from www.foxnews.com/printer_friendly_wires/2007Mar06/0,4675,UntrainedPolice,00.html and http://staugustine.com/stories/030607/nation_4448707.shtml

52. Mohr, H. (2007). Some states put untrained cops on duty. *Associated Press.* Retrieved from www.foxnews.com/printer_friendly_wires/2007Mar06/0,4675,UntrainedPolice,00.html and http://staugustine.com/stories/030607/nation_4448707.shtml

53. Reaves, B.A. (Rev. 2009). State and local law enforcement training academies, 2006. *Bureau of Justice Statistics.* Washington, DC: U.S. Department of Justice.

54. Institute for Public Safety. (2014). Criminal justice/law enforcement. *Florida Keys Community College.* Retrieved from www.fkcc.edu/academics/criminal-justice.da.

55. Reaves, B.A. (Rev. 2009). State and local law enforcement training academies, 2006. *Bureau of Justice Statistics*. Washington, DC: U.S. Department of Justice.

56. Reaves, B.A. (Rev. 2009). State and local law enforcement training academies, 2006. *Bureau of Justice Statistics*. Washington, DC: U.S. Department of Justice.

57. Reaves, B.A. (Rev. 2009). State and local law enforcement training academies, 2006. *Bureau of Justice Statistics*. Washington, DC: U.S. Department of Justice.

58. For example, see Werth, E.P. (2009). Student perceptions of learning through a problem-based learning exercise: An exploratory study. *Policing: An International Journal of Police Strategies & Management, 32,* 21-37.

59. Reaves, B.A. (Rev. 2009). State and local law enforcement training academies, 2006. *Bureau of Justice Statistics*. Washington, DC: U.S. Department of Justice.

60. Reaves, B.A. (Rev. 2009). State and local law enforcement training academies, 2006. *Bureau of Justice Statistics*. Washington, DC: U.S. Department of Justice.

61. Haar, R.N. (2005). Factors affecting the decision of police recruits to "drop out" of police work. *Police Quarterly, 8,* 431-453; Reaves, B.A. (Rev. 2009). State and local law enforcement training academies, 2006. *Bureau of Justice Statistics*. Washington, DC: U.S. Department of Justice.

62. Baker, J.R. with Rivelle, S.J. (2011). *Vice: One cop's story of patrolling America's most dangerous city*. New York, NY: St. Martin's Griffin, p. 27.

63. Gellman, S. (1993). *COPS: The men and women behind the badge*. Tucson, AZ: Horizon Press, p. 32.

64. Dunn, W. (1996). *Boot: An L.A.P.D. officer's rookie year*. New York, NY: William Morrow and Company, Inc., p. vii.

65. Maas, P. (1973). *Serpico*. New York, NY: Bantam Books, p. 60.

66. Neil, R.H. Sr. (2011). *Police instructor—Deliver dynamic presentations, create engaging slides, & increase active learning*. North Charleston, SC: CreateSpace.

67. Dunn, W. (1996). *Boot: An L.A.P.D. officer's rookie year*. New York, NY: William Morrow and Company, Inc., pp. 103-104.

68. Gellman, S. (1993). *COPS: The men and women behind the badge*. Tucson, AZ: Horizon Press, p. 51.

69. Archer, C.M. (2006). *Miles to Go Before I Sleep: Life, Death, and Hope on the Streets of Washington, D.C.* Baltimore, MD: PublishAmerica, pp. 19-20.

70. Simon, R. (1950). The roll call training program of the Los Angeles Police Department. *Journal of Criminal Law and Criminology, 40,* 507-518.

71. Oliver, W.M. *(forthcoming). August Vollmer: The Father of American Policing*. Durham, NC: Carolina Academic Press.

72. Reaves, B. (2010). *Local police departments, 2007*. Washington, DC: Bureau of Justice Statistics.

73. Oliver, W.M. *(forthcoming). August Vollmer: The Father of American Policing*. Durham, NC: Carolina Academic Press.

74. Reaves, B. (2010). *Local police departments, 2007*. Washington, DC: Bureau of Justice Statistics.

75. Reaves, B. (2010). *Local police departments, 2007*. Washington, DC: Bureau of Justice Statistics.

76. Smith, D.P. (2008). *On the job: Behind the stars of the Chicago Police Department*. Chicago, IL: Lake Claremont Press, p. 40.

77. Smith, D.P. (2008). *On the job: Behind the stars of the Chicago Police Department*. Chicago, IL: Lake Claremont Press, p. 40.

78. Gallo, G. (2001). *Armed and dangerous: Memoirs of a Chicago policewoman*. New York, NY: Forge Book, p. 152.

79. Kruger, K.J. (2014). When does an employment disciplinary action violate the fourteenth amendment's protection of the liberty interest? *The Police Chief,* October. Retrieved from www.policechiefmagazine.org/magazine/index.cfm?fuseaction=display_arch&article_id=1444&issue_id=32008.

80. City of Chicago. (2010). City of Chicago personnel rules. Retrieved from www.cityofchicago.org/dam/city/depts/dhr/supp_info/Personnel_Rules_Revised11_26_2010.pdf; See also Gallo, G. (2001). *Armed and dangerous: Memoirs of a Chicago policewoman*. New York, NY: Forge Book, p. 44.

81. Dunn, W. (1996). *Boot: An L.A.P.D. officer's rookie year*. New York, NY: William Morrow and Company, Inc.

82. Haar, R.N. (2005). Factors affecting the decision of police recruits to "drop out" of police work. *Police Quarterly, 8,* 431-453.

83. Lindberg, R. (1996). Frontline warriors: A look at Chicago's 18th district tactical unit. Retrieved from www.ipsn.org/tacunit.html

84. Corwin, M. (2003). *Homicide special: A years with the LAPD's elite detective unit*. New York, NY: Henry Holt and Company; Simon, D. (1991). *Homicide: A year on the killing streets*. Boston, MA: Houghton Mifflin Company.

85. Whetstone, T.S. (2001). Copping out: Why police officers decline to participate in the Sergeants promotional process. *American Journal of Criminal Justice, 25,* 147-159; Whetstone, T.S. (2000). Getting stripes: Educational achievement and study strategy used by sergeant promotional candidates. *American Journal of Criminal Justice, 24,* 247-257.

86. Brady, P.Q. & King, W.R. (2018). Brass satisfaction: Identifying the personal and work-related factors associated with job satisfaction among police chiefs. *Police Quarterly, 21,* 250-277.

87. ValuePenguin. (2019). Being a police chief – career talk. ValuePenguin.com Retrieved from https://www.valuepenguin.com/2015/10/career-talk-being-police-chief

88. Whetstone, T.S. (2001). Copping out: Why police officers decline to participate in the Sergeants promotional process. *American Journal of Criminal Justice, 25,* 147-159.

89. Orrick, D. (2008). *Recruitment, retention and turnover in law enforcement*. Washington, DC: International Association of Chiefs of Police.

90. Orrick, D. (2008). *Recruitment, retention and turnover in law enforcement*. Washington, DC: International Association of Chiefs of Police.

91. Yearwood, D.L. (2003). *Recruitment and retention study series: Sworn police personnel*. Charlotte, NC: The North Carolina Criminal Justice Analysis Center; Litcher, C.D., Reister, D., & Mason, C. (2006). *Statewide law enforcement officer retention study — 2001–2005*. Montpelier, VT: I/O Solutions.

92. Barker, J.C. (1999). *Danger, duty, and disillusion: The worldview of Los Angeles police officers*. Prospect Heights, IL: Waveland, p. 165.

93. Barker, J.C. (1999). *Danger, duty, and disillusion: The worldview of Los Angeles police officers*. Prospect Heights, IL: Waveland.

94. Osborne, S. (2015). *The Job: True tales form the life of a New York city cop*. New York: Doubleday, p. 246.

95. Barker, J.C. (1999). *Danger, duty, and disillusion: The worldview of Los Angeles police officers*. Prospect Heights, IL: Waveland.

96. Smith, D.P. (2008). *On the Job: Behind the stars of the Chicago Police Department*. Chicago, IL: Lake Claremont Press, p. 86.

■ *"The President of the United States—you don't really know him, do you? What do your fellow citizens know of your mayor—or even your governor? But you know and they know the policeman on the beat. He represents the government. To most people he is the government."*[1]
—*August Vollmer*

New York City Police Officers throw their dress gloves in the air in celebration at the conclusion of the Police Academy graduation ceremony at Madison Square Garden, December 27, 2010.

CHAPTER 6

Authority

After reading this chapter, you will be able to:

1. Understand that the sources of police authority are not derived from any one source, but multiple sources.
2. Describe the importance of the police oath of office.
3. Explain what role crime and disorder plays in police authority.
4. Detail how administrative rulemaking influences police authority and what the standard operating procedures manual entails.
5. Explain how police unions and collective bargaining influence police authority.
6. Describe how public opinion of the police influences police authority and the important factors related to demographics.
7. Define what is meant by interest groups and describe what they are and how they influence police authority.
8. Illustrate how government, especially the relationship between the police chief and municipal government, influences police authority.
9. Recognize how the criminal law influences police authority.
10. Recognize how the civil law influences police authority.
11. Recognize how constitutional law influences police authority.
12. Explain the warrant requirement under the Fourth Amendment and under what circumstances warrantless searches may be conducted.
13. Explain the Miranda warning requirement under the Fifth Amendment and when it must be applied.
14. Analyze how administrative lawmaking influences police authority.

When police officers are hired, at some point before they begin working the street, they will be required to take an **oath of office**. At that point, they will be *sworn in*. It is this oath that will separate the individuals from the civilians that work for the police department. There will be the **sworn police officers** and the nonsworn personnel. "Taking the Oath of Office was a defining moment" for Police Officer Evola, because, as she explains, "In my mind, that made it official."[2] The swearing-in can be as simple as the police officer signing a piece of paper that they agree to adhere to the oath of office. In the case of this author, between signing up for health insurance and receiving my uniforms, I was ushered before the county clerk and was asked to raise my right hand and to repeat the oath of office; I was in and out in less than a minute. For others, such as the New Bedford (Massachusetts) Police Department, it is a formal ceremony where the director of training introduces the new officers, the mayor speaks of public safety being the number one purpose of government, the police chief recognizes the importance of the police officer's role in the community, and various members of the City Council speak prior to the city clerk issuing the oath of office. It is a short ceremony, but one that conveys the importance of the oath of office (see Box 6.1).

The oaths of office that take place in the over 18,000 police departments in the United States are similar. Generally administered by the city or county clerk, the officers either raise their right hand to affirm the oath of office or they sign what amounts to a legal document. The content of the oath typically begins with the assertion that the officers do solemnly swear to the oath itself. Many then have the officers promise to uphold both the Constitution of the United States and that of their respective state. In many cases, they also affirm that they will uphold the laws of their state and the ordinances

---

Box 6.1 **Policing in Practice: Police Officer Oath of Office**

When police officers are hired, they will be required to take an **oath of office** and be sworn in. For a good example, watch the New Bedford Police Department's formal ceremony for its new police officers which is recorded and posted on YouTube. It features police officers taking their oath of office, which for the City of New Bedford is as follows:

"I _____, do solemnly swear, that I will perform the duties as a police officer for the City of New Bedford to the best of my ability and understanding in accordance with the laws of the Commonwealth of Massachusetts, and with the ordinances of the City of New Bedford, so help me God."

Watch parts of the official ceremony to understand the importance of the police oath of office.

Source: City of New Bedford. (2012). *Police swearing in ceremony.* Retrieved from https://www.youtube.com/watch?v=F8YCEqckLD4.

of the jurisdiction for which they work. Most of the oaths conclude with a statement that the police officers will faithfully discharge their duties to the best of their abilities.

New York Police Department police officers taking the oath of office.

The oath of office and the swearing-in ceremony give officers a special charge of office. It gives them the power to enforce the law, but it also gives them a power that no other occupation has—the power to use force against citizens when necessary.[3] No other occupation has that power. While it is true the military may use force, it cannot use force against its own citizens. Police officers do have that right, including the use of deadly force to protect their lives and the lives of others, and they are authorized the use of force to enforce the law. The oath of office and the swearing-in ceremony bestow that authority upon police officers, which has been called the core element of the police role in our society.[4]

The oath of office is not, however, the sole means by which police officers are granted their authority, although the oath does suggest from whence police authority is derived. The New Bedford mayor explained at the swearing-in ceremony of new officers that "the first business of government is public safety."[5] The very reason for the office of police is because evil exists in the world and the people have charged government with the responsibility of dealing with both crime and disorder by way of the police department. The people of the community give the police their authority through their government, which is why the individual who typically issues the oath of office is the city or county clerk—a representative of the people, not of the police department. Still further, the oath of office typically invokes the Constitution, the laws of the state, and the local ordinances, which also give the police officers their authority.

The purpose of Chapter 6 is to understand more fully the sources of police authority. It first discusses the primary need for the police, resulting from the problems of crime and disorder in our society. It then addresses how the police department extends police authority upon its officers. Next, it discusses the community, detailing how the community can shape police authority, either generally, through public opinion, or more specifically by civic action, through the formation of interest groups. It then details how government, representing the people's interest, shapes police authority. Finally, it turns to the law, both criminal and constitutional.

Crime and Disorder

As one of the most important goals of government is public safety, it is the police department that is the representative of government charged with dealing with the problems of crime and disorder. While it is true that the people and the government give the police officers their authority to ensure public safety, crime assuredly drives some aspect of the authority police officers receive. Crime, however, is somewhat of an elusive concept, for while the concept is very real to those who become a victim of a crime, for the general public, it is limited to a sense of how the media, especially television and print news, convey the issue. All of this works together, allowing crime to drive the public to bestow authority upon the police, or take it away.

An example of this can be found in the New York City Police Department (NYPD). Ten years prior to September 11, 2001, there were approximately 10,000 crimes per 100,000 citizens, for which 2,489 were violent crimes. Just prior to September 11, 2001, those rates had been reduced by half, making the city far safer than it had been in decades.[6] Yet, the primary discussion on the part of the media, and to a large degree the public, was how police tactics had become too aggressive and brutal, and the police needed more oversight.[7] The call was to take away or reduce the authority of the police. Then came September 11, 2001, when 19 terrorists hijacked four planes and flew two into the World Trade Center. Many in the NYPD lost their lives that day trying to save others, and for the next several years they worked toward making New York City safe from terroristic threats.[8] Public opinion and confidence in the New York City Police rose dramatically in the wake of September 11, thus giving them more authority to do their job.[9]

New York Police Department patrol vehicle covered in ash from the fallout of the World Trade Center buildings collapsing on September 11, 2001.

Although that may be a very abstract concept of crime driving police authority, just simply looking at the number of crimes in the United States can demonstrate the need for the police in our society. Despite America reaching lows in the crime rates not seen since the beginning of the 1960s, there were still 14,827 murders, 84,376 rapes, and 354,520 robberies reported to the police in 2012.[10] Looking at the number of property crimes in the United States for the same year, the number of crimes increases greatly as there were 721,053 motor vehicle thefts, 2,103,787 burglaries, and 6,150,598 larceny-thefts.[11] That is over 2 million burglaries and 6 million larcenies. Each of these crimes necessitated some form of police response and investigation, thus driving the need for the police. As the crime problem grows and the police are needed more, the public demands them to do more, thus extending more authority to the police to address the problem.

Police Department

The police department is granted its authority from the government, while the government is granted its authority from the people (see Box 6.2). However, police officers receive much of their authority from within the police department itself. Police officers working the street typically are not concerned with the political struggles between the people (represented by the city council and mayor) and the government (represented by the municipal or county government and the police chief or sheriff). Police officers look for direction from the chain-of-command regarding what is required of them and what they are authorized to do (and conversely what they are not authorized to do).

Box 6.2 **Policing in Practice: The Police Badge**

If there is anything that is an outward symbol of police authority, it is the **police officer's badge**. The police officer's badge is an official symbol that a person is a police officer, because the officer wears it at all times on-duty on his or her uniform, over their heart. Even K-9 officers will often be seen wearing their police badge while on duty. Police officers also carry their badge with them when they are off-duty so as to identify themselves in cases of an emergency as a police officer. When police officers retire they are commonly given a retired officer's badge. And, if you think about it, we always hear the statement that when a police officer who quits the job or has failed in their job, they must "turn in their badge and their gun."

The police officer's badge is also unique to the police department for which the officers work, giving them specific pride in their police department's badge. They often give their badges special names, such as the Los Angeles Police Department's "shield" and the Chicago Police Department's "star." Sheriff's

departments often still wear a star themselves, as it reflects back to the early days of sheriffs, especially those in the Wild West.

Even within police departments and sheriff's offices, the badge may be different in that certain shaped or colored badges will signify their specific duties. Some agencies issue a special badge for detectives, while others will separate out the colors for line and command personnel, such as silver for line officers and gold for the command.

Many police officers also collect badges, either historical badges of their own police agencies or those of their state or even across the nation and the world. Others will often collect modern police badges. There are also certain badges that are highly coveted by collectors, such as FBI badges or police chief badges from the LAPD and the NYPD. Many also enjoy having pretend badges such as police badges from the *Blade Runner* Neocron Police, *Hawaii Five-O,* or one from the Gotham Police Department.

Police policy manuals are often still published in three-ring binders.

To the police officers on patrol, much of their authority is derived from the command structure.

While the police chief and command staff may issue verbal commands to the police officers on the street, the most accepted way in policing to let officers know what they are authorized to do is through **administrative rulemaking.**[12] This consists of the issuance of written policies and procedures, as well as rules and regulations, in what is collectively known as the **standard operation procedure (SOP)** manual. Police officers are typically issued an official binder in which all of these written policies are kept, and they are required to keep these SOP manuals up to date (although more and more they are being made available electronically and they automatically update). More importantly, police officers are required to know and adhere to the contents of the manual.

While the terms policies, procedures, rules, and regulations are often used interchangeably, they do have distinct meanings. **Policies** are general guidelines for police behavior, such as police officers will only use force that is reasonable and necessary in the performance of their duties. **Procedures**, on the other hand, are very specific steps that officers must take in the performance of their duties. For instance, the procedures for a domestic violence call may mandate that an officer can only respond to such a call when there is a second officer on scene, the officers must park at least one block from the address, and they must approach cautiously and listen at the door prior to announcing their presence. The procedure may also state that a report will be written for every domestic violence call.

Police departments also issue rules and regulations in their SOPs, which do not address what police are authorized to do in the performance of their duties, but rather, it oversees their behavior. **Rules** are generally set by the police department and may include: all officers will keep their patrol vehicles clean, all male officers will have hair no longer than their collar, or officers may not enter a bar on or off duty in uniform, except in the performance of their duty.[13] **Regulations** also govern police behavior, but they are generally based on a law or judicial decision. For instance, based on the Supreme Court decision in *Miranda v. Arizona* (1966), prior to interviewing a suspect, all officers will notify the suspects of their rights and secure their confirmation of waiving those rights in writing. Or, based on a state's passage of a pro-arrest policy in regard to cases of domestic violence, a regulation may require all police officers investigating a domestic violence shall make an arrest when evidence of an assault is present. Although rules and regulations are often used interchangeably, a simple way to remember the difference (when there is a difference) is that rules are what the police department demands, while regulations are what the law demands.

As stated earlier, most police officers working patrol are less concerned about the political relationship between the people and government or the government and the police department. There are, however, many officers who are concerned and they often contribute to helping shape police authority through the establishment of **police unions**. These are organizations that are authorized to represent police officers' views on the policing profession. It is estimated that 73 percent of police departments and 43 percent of sheriff's offices have police unions; however, nearly half of these are fraternal (social) organizations.[14] An example of the police fraternal organization is the *Fraternal Order of Police* (FOP), a national organization with local chapters that works to improve the working conditions of the police officers through labor advocacy, legal representation, and political action.[15]

The other half of police unions still engage in social events, but the police union is allowed to enter into collective bargaining with the police department. **Collective bargaining** is the process by which police officers can negotiate with police management to determine conditions of employment, ranging from pay and benefits, to policies, procedures, rules, and regulations. An example of this type of police union is the *International Union of Police Associations*, which is affiliated with the American Federation of Labor and Congress of Industrial Organizations (AFL-CIO).[16] Currently, in the United States, 38 percent of police departments and 28 percent of sheriff's offices allow for collective bargaining.[17] Although often controversial,[18] research has found that those police officers working in agencies that allow for collective bargaining allow officers to have more say in the extent of their authority and well-being.[19] As an example of this, the starting salaries for police officers are $6,000 (large city) to $9,000 (small-towns) higher in police departments that allow collective bargaining, and overall police salaries for all officers were 38 percent higher (or $10,900 higher on average).[20]

Community

The community is also an important factor in the authority police officers have for the performance of their job. Returning to a quote in Chapter 1, Robert F. Kennedy reminds us that "every community gets the kind of law enforcement it insists on."[21] This was evident in the research of James Q. Wilson, which found three different styles of policing, each resulting from the style of law enforcement the citizens of those communities wanted in their police.[22] And as the community authorizes its government, it thereby authorizes and gives authority to the police.

There can be difficulties with this, however, for the community's understanding of the police is, in reality, based on each individual's understanding of the police.[23] There are so many images presented to the public on television, in the newspapers, and

The community's opinion of the police goes a long way toward the successful operation of any police agency.

in popular culture ranging from comics to motion pictures. Many of these images are based on the realities of policing, but many are built on myths. Even something that appears to be real, such as the television show *COPS*, is a distortion of reality because hundreds of hours of film footage are reduced to a 20-minute episode, thus only showing the public highlights of the police experience. Still further, people often have certain expectations of the police that may not be rooted in reality. Many people call the police expecting them to solve their problems, but the police may not be authorized to deal with the situation at hand. If there is a large difference between what the public expects the police to do and what they can actually do, it can create a negative perspective on the part of the public.

It is the positive and negative perceptions that the public has of the police, which can then translate into supporting or not supporting the police thereby playing a role in shaping police authority within the community (see Box 6.3). If the public does not support the police, the police lose legitimacy in the eyes of the community, and they lose their authority with the people.[24] If the people support their police, they gain legitimacy in the community, and thereby more respect and more authority. This issue of support and the type

---

Box 6.3 Policing in Practice: Public Perspective/Police Perspective

In the summer and fall of 2014, several cases had captured all of the news media's attention — the case of Michael Brown in Ferguson, Missouri and Eric Garner in New York City. In both cases, the police had confronted individuals and these individuals, both black males, were killed.

The Washington Post carried an editorial by a 17-year LAPD officer, Sunil Dutta, which presented a police officer's view of stopping a person. In that editorial, he said:

> "Even though it might sound harsh and impolitic, here is the bottom line: if you don't want to get shot, tased, pepper-sprayed, struck with a baton or thrown to the ground, just do what I tell you. Don't argue with me, don't call me names, don't tell me that I can't stop you, don't say I'm a racist pig, don't threaten that you'll sue me and take away my badge. Don't scream at me that you pay my salary, and don't even *think* of aggressively walking towards me. Most field stops are complete in minutes. How difficult is it to cooperate for that long?"

The Washington Post carried their own editorial after the death of Eric Garner in which they noted that Garner kept telling the police, "I can't breathe" but the group of officers "paid no mind" and Mr. Garner was choked to death. They concluded:

> "It is clear — from this and other troubling cases in which black men have been killed in questionable encounters with police — that changes are in order in how police interact with communities and how these cases are investigated."

The two editorials clearly demonstrate that there is **a difference of perspective** when it comes to the police and the community.

Source: The Washington Post, August 19, 2014 and December 4, 2014.

of support the police need is voiced by one of the leading pediatric surgeons in America and 2016 presidential contender, Dr. Ben Carson. He wrote in his book *America the Beautiful,* "I have great admiration for the police, who risk their lives on a daily basis to protect *our* lives, freedom, and property. Remove all police protection for just a day, and imagine the mayhem that would ensue. Sure, corruption exists in some police departments, because police officers are human beings like the rest of us; give power to human beings and corruption naturally follows. But police provide far greater good than bad in our society."[25]

There are two primary ways in which the community can play a role in police authorization: through the general public opinion of the police and by actual involvement in what are collectively known as interest groups. The first, **public opinion** of the police, may vary from community to community, but one way of assessing public support for the police is by looking at the public perceptions of the police throughout the nation by way of public opinion polls. In a 2018 Gallup Poll that asked people to rate the honesty and ethical standards of the people working in many different professions, it found that the police rated a 54 percent favorability rating.[26] Only nurses, medical doctors, pharmacists, and high school teachers were rated higher, while accountants, bankers, and telemarketers were ranked much lower. This same question has been asked across time and the police held a favorability rating in the 40th percentile during the 1980s and 1990s, but after September 11, 2001, that rating rose to the 50th percentile, meaning slightly more than half of Americans held the police in high esteem.[27] It is also important to note how certain **demographics** respond to this question, as not all people perceive the police in the same manner (see Table 6.1).

There are also different ways of assessing the public's opinion of the police as well. The Gallup Poll typically asks respondents to report their confidence in the police once a year (see Box 6.4). For instance, the 2012 Gallup Poll found that 56 percent reported a "great deal" or "quite a lot" of confidence in the police, while 28 percent reported "some," 15 percent reported "very little," and 1 percent reported "none" (see Table 6.2).[28] Males reported a higher level of confidence in the police than females, as 59 percent of males voiced high confidence, while only 51 percent of females felt the same way. Age also makes a difference, for the young (18–29 years of age) reported a 56 percent confidence in the police, while those 60 years and older reported a 61 percent confidence. The lowest was actually among the 30–49 age group, which only voiced a 50 percent favorability rate. The greatest difference, however, appears to come from the race of the person answering the question. While whites demonstrated a high 57 percent confidence in the police, blacks only reported a 32 percent confidence in the police. Poll after poll reveals this disparity between whites and blacks over their confidence in the police, clearly revealing a different world view of the police between the races.[29] Various cases in recent history have highlighted these differences, including the cases of O.J. Simpson, Eric Garner, and events in Ferguson, Missouri. This suggests that among most whites, the police have legitimacy

Table 6.1   Citizen's Ratings of the Honesty and Ethical Standards of the Police, 2011

Demographics	Very High	High	Average	Low	Very Low
National:					
Overall	12%	42%	35%	8%	3%
Sex:					
Male	13	41	36	8	2
Female	11	43	34	8	3
Race:					
White	13	46	32	7	3
Nonwhite	9	34	43	11	4
Black	5	34	42	13	7
Age:					
18–29	13	32	41	11	3
30–49	12	44	33	10	1
50–64	12	42	37	5	4
50+	11	45	38	5	4
60+	10	50	32	4	3
Education:					
High School or less	10	36	38	12	4
Some College	14	41	38	5	3
College graduate	16	55	27	2	0
College post-graduate	9	51	31	7	2
Income:					
Under $20,000	7	30	40	14	10
$20,000–$29,999	15	31	38	11	5
$30,000–$49,999	12	38	38	11	1
$50,000–$74,999	9	51	30	7	2
$75,000+	14	47	35	6	4
Region:					
East	8	47	35	6	4
Midwest	16	40	33	10	1
South	13	42	36	5	3
West	9	39	37	12	3
Politics:					
Republican	16	51	27	4	2
Independent	11	37	39	10	2
Democrat	9	42	38	8	3
Ideology:					
Conservative	14	45	32	5	4
Moderate	12	45	34	6	2
Liberal	9	34	41	15	2

Source: *Sourcebook of Criminal Justice Statistics Online,* University at Albany, Table 2.21.2011

Box 6.4 History in Practice: Confidence in the Police

According to the Gallup Poll, despite a rash of negative publicity regarding the police, they were still ranked third in order of institutions in which Americans had the most confidence. In a June 2017 poll, the American people reported 57 percent confidence in the police, and they were ranked only behind the military and small businesses. The military was reported as having a 72 percent confidence rating, small business as 70 percent, and the police 57 percent. Behind the police were churches, the health care system, the president, and the U.S. Supreme Court. Looking historically, the police have held a more than 50 percent confidence rating since 1993 when the question first asked people about their confidence in the police. At one point, after the terrorist attacks on 9/11, America's confidence in its police went over 60 percent with 61 percent in June of 2003, 64 percent in May of 2004, and 63 percent in May of 2005. Compare these figures with the June 2017 confidence in the criminal justice system as a whole (27 percent), television news (24 percent), and the U.S. Congress (12 percent).

Source: Gallup Poll. (2017). *Confidence in Institutions.* Retrieved from https://news.gallup.com/poll/212840/americans-confidence-institutions-edges.aspx?g_source=Politics&g_medium=newsfeed&g_campaign=tiles.

and so their authority is well recognized; however, among blacks, for whom only 44 percent reported "some confidence" and 23 percent reported "very little" confidence, the police lack legitimacy and their authority is thus questioned (see Box 6.5).

Physical characteristics are not the only differences that arise among Americans in how they perceive the police, but life circumstances and ideology also apparently matter. Again, looking specifically at the 2012 Gallup Poll, it found that those who were college graduates (63 percent) or held a post-graduate degree (59 percent) were more likely to report higher confidence in the police than those with only some college (50 percent) or a high school education or less (55 percent). In addition, the income a person earns also plays a role in Americans' confidence in the police. Those with incomes over $75,000 reported a 66 percent confidence in the police, while those making less than $20,000 only reported a 36 percent confidence level. Most of the latter reported only having "some" (31 percent), "very little" (27 percent), or no (4 percent) confidence in the police. It should be noted here that all of the variables thus far discussed, race, age, education, and income are not necessarily mutually exclusive.

Political ideology and the political party that one most closely identifies with also plays an important role in how they view the police. Those with the highest level of confidence in the police were those that identified themselves as conservatives (62 percent) and Republicans (78 percent), while those with the lowest were those who reported they were either a liberal (48 percent) or a Democrat (52 percent). The confidence level in the police

Table 6.2 Citizen's Reported Confidence in the Police, 2012

Demographics	Great Deal/Quite a Lot	Some	Very Little	None
National:				
Overall	56%	28%	15%	1%
Sex:				
Male	59	24	14	2
Female	51	32	15	1
Race:				
White	57	27	14	2
Nonwhite	49	32	17	1
Black	32	44	23	<1
Hispanic	57	28	13	0
Age:				
18–29	56	28	15	1
30–49	50	29	19	3
50–64	59	27	13	<1
65+	61	28	16	2
Education:				
High school or less	55	27	16	2
Some college	50	28	20	2
College graduate	63	28	8	1
College post-graduate	59	33	7	1
Income:				
Under $20,000	36	31	27	4
$20,000–$29,999	48	27	24	2
$30,000–$49,999	55	27	17	<1
$50,000–$74,999	58	30	10	1
$75,000+	66	26	7	1
Region:				
East	60	27	12	1
Midwest	52	32	15	0
South	54	26	17	2
West	54	27	14	3
Politics:				
Republican	78	15	12	0
Independent	46	33	17	2
Democrat	52	35	13	1
Ideology:				
Conservative	62	26	12	1
Moderate	56	29	15	<1
Liberal	48	30	18	4

Source: *Sourcebook of Criminal Justice Statistics Online,* University at Albany, Table 2.12.2012.

Box 6.5 Ethics in Practice: Making Assumptions—What's Race Got to Do with It?

Police officers, like many other Americans, often **make assumptions based on race**. A well-publicized event demonstrates the pitfalls of this approach. On July 16, 2009, Sergeant James Crowley, a white police officer from the Cambridge (Massachusetts) Police Department, responded to a 911 call for a burglary in progress. Two black males were trying to break into a house as they were seen struggling with a door trying to pry it open. When he arrived on scene he found a black male in the house and he confronted him. The black male became belligerent and disrespectful toward the police officer. The Sergeant arrested the man for disorderly conduct.

The black male who was arrested was Dr. Henry Louis Gates, Jr., a professor at Harvard University. He had just come back from an all-night (and all-day) flight from China where he had been conducting research. He was tired and when he finally reached his home in a well-appointed neighborhood, he discovered he could not get into this house because the door was stuck. He asked his driver, another black male, to help him get the door unstuck. They managed to do so and then the officer showed up. Gates was in his own home, on his own property, minding his own business, and he was tired. He blew up at the presence of the cop, citing an example of racial profiling. He then found himself under arrest in his own home.

Ask Yourself:

Do you think this arrest was about race or was it about demeanor? Explain your answer.

Read accounts from July 30, 2009, of "The Beer Summit" to see how the issue was resolved at the highest levels. What could Sergeant Crowley have done differently?

were also lower for those who identified themselves as moderate (56 percent) and Independent (46 percent). This may be because over the past 20 years, more and more liberals have come to identify themselves as moderates and Independents, rather than liberals and Democrats.[30] Regardless, however, it is clear, that those with a more conservative world view are more likely to see the police as having legitimacy and are more inclined to give them more latitude when it comes to their authority.

While it may be true that everyone has an opinion, not everyone becomes actively involved in turning their ideas into action. Some individuals may take up the pen and write a letter to the editor of their local newspapers and others may pen longer commentaries, but most people join a group of like-minded people, commonly referred to as an **interest group**. The interest groups give life to people's ideas and allow them to collectively have a say in the political process, a process that gives more authority to the police or works to place limits on it.

There are many groups that form to work with the police and to support them. These organizations include *Neighborhood Watch* associations that work alongside police to address the problem of crime in their local communities.[31] Another organization is the *National Association of Police*

Organizations, which is an interest group designed to advance the interests and authority of the police through legislative advocacy, public education, and political action.[32] One more organization is *The Badge of Life*, an organization composed of people who work to assist police officers suffering from stress and to help those families who have suffered the loss of their loved one due to suicide.[33] Included in these pro-police interest groups are the police fraternal organizations and police unions mentioned earlier. Each of these groups recognizes the difficulties of the job, and their work helps to recognize the importance and legitimacy of the police and work to expand police authority so that police may better perform their role in society.

There are also many groups that form to oversee police activity and work to limit their authority. These organizations include *Copwatch*, which was first started in Berkeley, California, and advocated surveillance of the police by videotaping them.[34] Another such group is *Communities United Against Police Brutality*; located in Minneapolis-Saint Paul, Minnesota, it holds rallies, educates the public on police abuse and how to file complaints, and engages the legislature through policy actions to limit the authority of the police.[35] One other such organization is sponsored by the National Lawyers Guild, and that is the *National Police Accountability Project*, which is also focused on ending police abuse of authority by legal actions, public education, and working with other organizations combating police misconduct.[36] Each of these organizations work toward protecting the rights of the people, exposing the problems of policing, and to reign in and limit police authority.

Public opinion is a powerful force in America. Public opinion polls allow us to understand the collective will of the people, and it is one manner by which policies are shaped. Through the collective will of the people, police authority can be expanded (for example, the NYPD after September 11) or it may be contracted (for example, the Ferguson Police Department in the wake of the officer-involved shooting). More powerful than collective public opinion, however, is collective public action, where ideas are put into action. These interest groups also work to expand the authority of the police (for example, *National Association of Police Organizations*) or work to contract it (for example, *National Police Accountability Project*). It is, therefore, important to recognize that although often unclear and contradictory, the will of the people shapes police authority in America. One other means by which the will of the people shapes the authority of the police is through government, which is supposed to work on behalf of the interests and will of the people.

A good relationship between the mayor and the police chief, such as the one found in Stamford, Connecticut, makes for a successful police agency.

Government

While public opinion and interest group activity demonstrate the will of the people, the manner in which the business of the people is carried out is through the government. Individuals are elected by the will of the people through the political process, and they are then placed in charge of running the government, which includes the police. This means that first and foremost there is a relationship between the people and the government. From that relationship then develops the relationship between the government and its police force for establishing the authority of the police department to carry out its duties. Recalling the different forms of municipal governance (see Chapter 4), each form of governance can alter the relationship between the government and the police.

Regardless, however, of which form of municipal governance is used, each of these members can assert some influence over the police department, typically by influencing or directing the police chief. The mere hiring of the police chief may indicate the type of policing they want, as the person they hire may be an advocate of targeted policing or community policing. The ability to also fire the police chief (or threaten to fire) also provides another form of influence over how the police executive manages his or her department. While research has long found that all forms of governance assert their political influence over the administrative decision-making of the police department,[37] police researcher Mastrofski found three different types of relationships between the police executive and the municipal executives.[38]

The first type of relationship between the police executive and municipal executive is the **team approach** where both the municipal officers and police chief collaborate on how the police department should be managed and directed. Police Chief Darrel Stephens advocated for this type of relationship when he explained, "I think the most important thing is to establish a relationship right off the bat where you have open lines of communication."[39] The second type of relationship is the **professional autonomy approach**, where the police executive is seen as having the necessary expertise to manage the police department and is therefore left alone except for when it comes to budget requests. Former New York Police Commissioner Bratton is an advocate of this type of relationship, which he describes as "picking good people and then holding them accountable for their work."[40] The final approach Mastrofski found was the **political activist approach**, where the municipal executives all feel it is their right and duty to tell the police chief how to run the police department. In this case the police department is just one more department of the city government structure. Bratton explained that was his situation under Mayor Rudy Giuliani in the early 1990s. "Giuliani wanted to be in the police department managing day to day."[41] Despite this example from New York City, the political activist approach is most commonly found in smaller municipalities, while the professional autonomy approach is more often found in larger agencies.[42]

While the people, through the electoral process, influence the government, the government's relationship with the police influences the authority of the police. The executive branch (for example, president, governor, mayor) and the legislative branch (for example, Congress, state legislature, city council) have a profound influence over police authority and they have the ability to expand or contract that authority. One other means by which the legislative branch can influence the authority of the police is through the law, both criminal and civil. Still further, the third branch of government, the judiciary, also plays a significant role in police authority when it comes to not only the hearing of criminal and civil cases, but also through the determination of whether the actions of the police are constitutional. It is to the law and its role in establishing police authority that Chapter 6 now turns.

The Law

The authority of the police, in addition to having its source in the problems of crime, the police organization, the government, and the people, is also derived from the law. Even this, however, is a complex source of police authority. The law both gives the policy authority while at the same time it constrains their authority. The police enforce the law, but are limited by the law, and are also overseen by the law. This is because the law in America is very complex. While the original source of law in America was **common law**, the English system of judges setting precedent through customs and judicial decisions, American common law developed into two different legal concepts: criminal law and civil law. In addition, because the supreme law of the land is the U.S. Constitution, we also developed what is known as constitutional law, and because of judicial activity in this area, we have also seen court-made law come into being, which is commonly referred to as administrative law. Each of these bodies of law in America—criminal law, civil law, constitutional law, and administrative law—give the police their authority and place constraints on it as well.

Criminal Law

Chapter 6 opens with the idea that crime and disorder are one source of police authority, for it is these issues the police are tasked to address. Yet for a behavior to be considered criminal or illegal, it must be defined by a statute. A **statute** is a law passed by a legislative body that makes a particular behavior criminal, which is what we generally refer to as **criminal law**.[43] The concept behind criminal law is that these are crimes committed against the state (the government) because they disrupt the peace of our society, and therefore the government has the authority to charge for these violations of the social contract. As a body of laws, these are the criminal statutes that have been passed by the 50 state legislatures or the U.S. Congress and that define what is criminal in each state or the country. They are then published

Box 6.6 History in Policing: Eliot Ness, the Untouchables, and Police Authority

A lot of myths have been generated by **Eliot Ness** and the creation of what became known as his "**untouchables**," for going after Chicago Mob boss Al Capone in the late 1920s and early 1930s. Despite the many myths, Ness came to understand the importance of **police authority** and how it applied to bringing down the most notorious of crime bosses during Prohibition.

Born on April 19, 1903, in Chicago, Illinois, Ness went on to the University of Chicago, graduating with a degree in economics in 1925. In 1927, he joined the Bureau of Prohibition as a federal law enforcement agent working in Chicago. As he began to make a name for himself in the agency, to advance himself he returned to taking classes at the University of Chicago to earn a Master's Degree in Criminology. In 1929, he took a class from the famous police chief, August Vollmer, who,

among other things, taught him the importance of having public support.

Ness completed the course and graduated with his degree at about the time he was put in charge of a hand-picked unit to bring down Al Capone. As Ness and his men began making raids and arrests, they were not entirely successful, but the public supported their activities, and they and the media began calling them the "untouchables" because Capone was not able to corrupt them like he had so many other public officials.

Ultimately, what led to Capone's downfall was the application of another form of police authority — the law. In particular, because Capone's wealth was made through illegal operations, he was not paying taxes, and so Ness and his team managed to bring down Capone for tax evasion.

---

in the state or federal statutes and they become the body of law that the police are authorized to enforce (see Box 6.6).

Criminal law is generally written in a very specific manner so as certain behaviors must be present, an act must have occurred, and a certain mental state must be present. The first is known as the **elements of the crime** and they detail certain elements that must be present. For instance, a burglary statute may be written as "breaking and entering in the nighttime in the dwelling of another." In this case, there must be some time of forced entry, even if it means opening an unlocked door. The criminal must have actually entered the home, and it must have been at night. That does not mean breaking and entering in the daytime is legal, it just may be defined as another type of criminal behavior. Then the last element was the dwelling of another such as a home, not a storage building. When someone's home is broken into, the police must then conduct an investigation to ensure that the proper criminal statute is applied by making sure all of the elements of the crime were present.

In addition to the elements of the crime, there must have been some action on the part of the criminal. This is known in criminal law as **actus reus**. While often there is evidence that someone would like to commit a

The criminal law is the basis of the laws the police enforce and serves as an important source of police authority.

crime, until they actually exhibit the behaviors of the crime, their actions cannot be called criminal. A person may say I am going to bust into someone's house and steal all of his belongings, but until they take some action toward that end, they have committed no crime. One other factor is also typically a part of a criminal statute and that is the mental state of the individual or the **mens rea.** If a person breaks and enters in the nighttime in the dwelling of another, but this was only because they were drunk and thought it was their own home, and they did not have the intent of stealing anything, then they have not satisfied the concept of mens rea. If they broke and entered with the full intent of stealing all of the occupant's belongings, than they have met the mens rea and can be found guilty of the criminal statute. Again, the police in their investigation must show evidence for both actus reus and mens rea, otherwise they are constrained by the law and cannot apply the law by making an arrest.

The criminal law, as determined by the criminal statutes, are in large part what give the police the authority to make an arrest for a crime. The police are given the power to make an arrest when they can demonstrate before a judge or magistrate that a criminal statute has been violated. It should be noted that this power is conferred upon the police by the government, in particularly the legislature, which is elected by the people. And while it is true criminal statutes give the police much of their authority, it should be noted that absent a criminal statute, the police cannot make an arrest, and, as a result, their authority is also constrained by the criminal law as well.

Civil Law

The other branch of law that developed out of common law is **civil law.**[44] The civil law, also called tort law, is very different from the criminal law for this body of law does not deal with harms against the government or the people as a whole, but rather harm against individuals. The easiest example is if a neighbor built a fence between your property and his, but built it on your property, thus denying you the use of some of your own land, this is not a harm against the people, but rather, a harm against you. This is when most people say, "I will sue you," thus they are threatening to bring a lawsuit against the other person using civil law.

Citizens who believe they have been wronged by the police may bring a lawsuit against the police. The civil law than becomes a means by which police authority can be constrained, as civil suits may limit what police officers can and cannot do as police departments want to limit the number of lawsuits. Bringing a civil suit against a police department, however, is not like filing a complaint; it must follow an evidentiary process before a lawsuit can be won. There are also different types of torts (civil wrongs) that the police must be found to have violated, and each is very specific in the standards necessary to show proof of the wrong.

The first set of torts for which the police can be held liable are **intentional torts.** These are civil wrongs that demonstrate that the officer's actions were not within police policy or procedures and that they had the intent of causing the harm. For instance, if an officer pulled someone over and argues with the driver before shooting and killing him, this could be defined as an intentional shooting to cause harm. If, however, the driver had pulled a gun on the police officer who then shot and killed him, the officer had no malicious intent to kill in this case, and although a lawsuit can still be filed, it would most likely fail.

A second set of torts falls under the category of **negligence,** which can be defined as inadvertent behavior that causes damage, injury, or death.[45] In this case, a number of elements must be present for a civil suit to be successful. It must be demonstrated that the officer had a legal duty to act, that he or she breached that duty, and that the negligence contributed to the damage, injury, or death. An example is an officer being called to respond to a domestic dispute on Super Bowl Sunday, and instead of responding immediately, the officer decides to continue watching the game, and 30 minutes later the victim is stabbed. The officer had a legal duty to act but the duty was breached, because had the officer arrived as ordered then the stabbing may have been prevented. Police officers have been found to be negligent in their duties when they did not protect crime victims, as in the above scenario, when they failed to operate an emergency vehicle properly, failed to arrest a drunk driver and let them drive home, or failed to make an accident scene safe before investigating, causing someone else to be injured.

Another set of torts are derived from the Civil Rights Act of 1871, which was passed by the U.S. Congress during Reconstruction to protect freed slaves in the South. The act was codified under Title 42 of the U.S. Code, under Section 1983, and when lawsuits are brought against the police, these are often called **Section 1983 lawsuits.**[46] This section of the U.S. Code is primarily concerned with violations of constitutional rights. To file a civil liability lawsuit under Section 1983, the person must show that a government official, including a police officer, was "acting under the color of law" and that the official's actions deprived a person of his or her constitutional rights. The former clause refers to a government official acting in his or her official capacity. A police officer, acting under his or her official authority whether on duty or off duty, is acting under the color of law. If he or she then violates a person's constitutional rights while serving in an official capacity, the officer may be sued under this section. By way of example, say a police officer on duty and in uniform pulled over a driver who was on the way to the voting booth, and the officer detained that person for two hours because the officer didn't like the individual's political bumper stickers. Then the polls closed and the officer let the person go with a warning. The officer was acting under the color of law and deprived the person of the constitutional right to vote; thus the officer could be sued under Section 1983.

Constitutional Law

Another form of law in the United States that establishes the parameters of police authority is the body of law based upon the Constitution and is known as **constitutional law**.[47] As America is a country that operates under the rule of law, the U.S. Constitution is the supreme law of the land. That Constitution established the judiciary system in America and placed the U.S. Supreme Court as the final arbiter of all things judicial. When the Constitution was amended with the Bill of Rights, it inferred upon the people of the United States certain rights, and the Fourteenth Amendment, passed in the aftermath of the Civil War, ensured that those civil rights were granted to people not only as protections against the national government, but against state and local governments as well. By example, the people have, under the Fourth Amendment, the right against unreasonable searches and seizures. Those rights are protections against not only federal agents invading our homes, but also state and local government as well. And since the police are part of the government, these types of protections are afforded to American citizens as protections against the police.

As one can imagine, every situation is unique and determining what is a reasonable search or a reasonable seizure can become difficult. When cases arise regarding whether the action of the government (the police) is constitutional, these cases may ultimately be heard by the U.S. Supreme Court. When the Supreme Court issues its decision, these decisions carry with it the weight of the law or, more specifically, the Constitution. Hence, these court decisions become their own body of law that defines and shapes police authority.

While many of the cases involving the police do center on the freedom of speech and assembly (First Amendment) or the right of the people to keep and bear arms (Second Amendment), the amendment to the U.S. Constitution that has the most bearing upon the police is the Fourth Amendment, which protects the people from unreasonable searches and seizures by the government, most notably the police. For a police officer to search for illegal evidence (contraband) or to seize either the contraband or the person by arrest, the police must be able to show probable cause. Probable cause has been defined by the U.S. Supreme Court as more than just a hunch or suspicion, and exists when "the fact and circumstance within [the officer's] knowledge and of which they [have] reasonably trustworthy information [are] sufficient to warrant a prudent man in believing that the [suspect] had committed or was committing an offense."[48] In other words, the police must have some kind of factual information to believe a person has committed a crime to obtain an arrest warrant, or that a person is hiding contraband, something illegal, to obtain a search warrant. If they have probable cause, then, and only then, can they search us, take our property, and/or take us to jail. And while the Fourth Amendment does talk about search or arrest warrants, it does not necessarily mandate that a police officer have one to either search or arrest. So, the question arises, when can a police officer search and seize without a search warrant or arrest warrant? This is what the U.S. Supreme Court helps clarify in constitutional law.

San Francisco police officers conducting a terry stop (a pat-down).

One of the most important Supreme Court cases that defined police authority to search without a warrant arose in the case of **Terry v. Ohio (1968)**.[49] The case occurred in downtown Cleveland, Ohio, when a veteran officer by the name of McFadden saw two men standing on a street corner acting suspicious. He had never seen them. They were looking about nervously, kept retracing their steps to look into the same store window, and were talking to each other when a third man joined them. The officer walked up to them and asked them their names, which they were reluctant to provide. McFadden then grabbed the men, placed them up against the wall, and patted them down for weapons, pulling a pistol off of each of them. The lawyers in this case challenged the arrest as an illegal search and seizure because McFadden did not have probable cause—which he readily admitted. He did, however, have a suspicion, which proved to be quite accurate.

The Supreme Court decided that the police officer had a reasonable suspicion and that the reason for the stop was for the safety of both the officer and the public. In addition, because McFadden simply patted the men down for weapons, only seizing them when feeling something that felt like a gun, it was a limited intrusion and it was reasonable in scope. In the end, the Supreme Court had created what became known as the stop and frisk, which allows police officers, if they have a reasonable suspicion, for their safety and the safety of the community, to frisk or pat down individuals for weapons. This particular case, *Terry v. Ohio* (1968), has been the basis for numerous other cases, including one case, *Michigan v. Long* (1983), which essentially applied the stop and frisk to an automobile stop allowing the police to conduct a pat down of the driver and the vehicle's compartment for weapons based on a reasonable suspicion. This was more recently affirmed the unanimous Supreme Court decision of *Arizona v. Johnson* (2009). There is a long history of Supreme Court decisions, including recent decisions that have declared stop and frisks to be constitutional. This clarification of police authority, to temporarily detain a person, based on a reasonable suspicion, and to pat the person down for weapons (and only weapons) has become known in policing as a **terry stop**.

Moving beyond the reasonable suspicion and terry stops, in those cases where the police have probable cause to conduct a search, the next question that often comes before the U.S. Supreme Court is when the police have to secure a search warrant and when can they search (and seize) without one. Remember, the Fourth Amendment does not mandate a warrant in all circumstances, so constitutional law has defined when the police can search without a search warrant. Although, it should be stipulated that just because police officers do not need a search warrant, this by no means suggests that they do not need probable cause. The circumstance under which **warrant-less searches** are justified typically fall into five categories: (1) consent searches, (2) searches incident to arrest, (3) plain view searches, (4) automobile searches, and (5) searches dealing with exigent circumstances.[50]

The first exception to the warrant requirement is a **consent search**. In these cases, police officers are allowed to conduct a search without a warrant because the individual waived their Fourth Amendment rights. Essentially, the police may ask someone if they may search their house or car. If the person refuses, they have retained their Fourth Amendment rights. If someone allows the police to conduct the search, then they have given consent, effectively waiving their Fourth Amendment rights. There are two major factors that go along with consent searches. The first is that the consent cannot be "the result of duress or coercion, express or implied."[51] The police cannot surround a person's car with six other officers and their patrol cars with guns drawn and ask for consent to search someone's car. That would be duress. Coercion is more subtle and might be holding on to someone's driver's license and registration and asking if they can search the person's car. The person does not feel free to go and might, therefore, believe that they have to give consent. The second issue with consent searches is the idea that once given, a person can never restore their Fourth Amendment rights. That is not the case. If someone tells a police officer they have consent to search the car, and after searching the interior of the car, they want to search the trunk, the person has the right to say, "I no longer consent to the search." In addition, the restoration of one's Fourth Amendment rights does not provide the officer with probable cause to believe the person is hiding something in the trunk.

The next category of warrantless searches regard a **search incident to arrest**. If a police officer arrives at a call and finds someone has committed a crime, say burglarizing a home or robbing a bank, the officer is allowed to make the arrest without a search warrant and to conduct a search incident to arrest. It must, however, occur in the proper order: probable cause, arrest, and then search incident to arrest. It should be stressed that this warrant-less search is limited in scope, and according to the U.S. Supreme Court is only permitted "to remove any weapon that the person might seek to use in order to resist arrest or effect his escape" and "to seize any evidence on the arrestee's person in order to prevent its concealment or destruction."[52] Like consent searches, there are two major factors that accompany searches incident to arrest. The first derived from the Supreme Court Case of *Preston v. United States* (1964) in which the court declared that the search must be contemporaneous to the arrest. In other words, the search can be conducted only in the immediate aftermath of making the arrest. If the officer waits until the next day or after the suspect has been taken to jail, the officer will now have to secure a search warrant. The other major factor is the extent of the search. In the Supreme Court case of **Chimel v. California (1969),** the court decided that "a warrantless search 'incident to a lawful arrest' may generally extend to the area that is considered to in the 'possession' or under the 'control' of the person arrested."[53] So, whatever is within reach of the person at the time of the arrest, often called the arm-span rule, is allowed to be searched without a warrant. In other words, if you arrest a suspect in the garage, you can search most of the garage, but not the rest of the house. To do that, the officer would need a search warrant.

Another exception to the warrant requirement is known as **plain view searches.** In the Supreme Court case of *Coolidge v. New Hampshire* (1971) the Supreme Court declared the plain view doctrine that allows police to conduct a search when an illegal item (contraband) is seen by the police officer in plain view. As with the other two warrantless exceptions, there are two factors involved for the plain view search to be legal. First, the police officer has to have the legal right to be wherever the contraband is located. If the officer is on public property, then it is legal, but if he or she is on private property and has no right to be there, then it would not be an authorized search. Second, the item has to truly be in plain sight and visible. If the officer has to move something to see it, then it is not in plain view and the seizure of the item would not be in keeping with the plain view doctrine.[54] So, if the police officer sees something in plain view and that officer has the legal right to be there, then no warrant is required to seize the contraband in plain view.

The fourth warrantless search authorized by the courts is **automobile search.** Due to the rather mobile nature of a car, it is unrealistic for a police officer to tell the driver to "wait there" while going to secure a search warrant for the vehicle. The case actually came up during Prohibition, when cars were being used to transport illegal alcohol (contraband) into the cities. The Supreme Court, in the case of **Carroll v. U.S. (1925)**, stated that the warrantless search was authorized because the evidence could have been destroyed or simply driven away. This became known as the **Carroll doctrine.** The Court, however, was very explicit in that probable cause must still be present before the search can be conducted, and it had to be a vehicle that was truly mobile and easily moved (a car on blocks or an immobile mobile home does not qualify!). Numerous other cases have helped to clarify many of the nuances of an automobile search, but one of the more important was *U.S. v. Ross* (1982). In this case, the question was the scope of the search. The Supreme Court decided that the same scope applies as if the officer had secured a search warrant, noting that the size of the object the officers are

When searching a motor vehicle, there are many exceptions to the warrant requirement, but the probable cause requirement must not be diminished.

searching for matters. If searching for a bag of marijuana, the officers could search just about anywhere. If they were searching for stolen tires, it would be hard to explain why they looked inside a locked glove compartment.

The final category where warrant-less searches are allowed are those searches dealing with **exigent circumstances.** Exigent circumstances are those situations that are deemed emergencies or very unusual incidents. There are three general categories that are recognized: (1) hot pursuit, (2) escape and/or presenting a danger to others, and (3) evanescent evidence. The first of these, **hot pursuit**, arose with the case of *Warden v. Hayden* (1967). In this case the police pursued a suspect into a house without securing a warrant, but they had entered in pursuit of a robber. The Court agreed that under the circumstances it was not realistic for the police to secure a search warrant of the house, because they were in hot pursuit, the robber could escape, and he presented a danger to others. There are numerous factors that must be in place for the warrantless search to be justified: the police must be legally justified to be pursuing the suspect in the first place, a serious offense must have just occurred (no hot pursuit for someone who tore up a parking ticket!), the pursuit must truly be hot and immediately after the crime occurred, and the scope of the search is greatly limited to the suspect and where any weapon or contraband may be found (where they may have tried to get rid of it during the pursuit). Although in the *Warden v. Hayden* (1967) case, the Court stated that part of their reasoning was because the suspect could have escaped or presented a danger to others,

In another case, *Minnesota v. Olson* (1990), the Supreme Court said that a warrantless search could be made if the officers can articulate that it was necessary to prevent **escape** or if the suspect presented a **danger to others**—even absence hot pursuit. The final exigent circumstance is known as **evanescent evidence** (something that quickly fades or disappears) and this is where a warrantless search is authorized because the evidence could be easily and quickly destroyed (for example, flushing drugs down a toilet). The idea behind these exigent circumstances is that the police, acting on probable cause but under circumstances that are extreme, must have the authority to conduct the warrantless search.

It should be noted here that the police will often conduct another type of search referred to as an **administrative search** or an **inventory search,** but these are not searches in the sense of the Fourth Amendment. Rather, they are administrative in nature and conducted as part of the normal routine administrative duties of the police. For instance, if a police officer makes a DWI arrest of a lone driver with no passengers in the car, the officer must have the car towed. Because there may be items in the car that need to be accounted for, the officer is required by departmental policy to conduct an inventory of the vehicles' contents. This is not a search for contraband, but simply a search for accountability purposes. If, however, the officer comes across contraband, the officer, having the legal right to have found it, may use it as evidence for purposes of probable cause, and then secure a search warrant to search the rest of the vehicle for similar contraband.

All of these cases so far have fallen under constitutional challenges related to the Fourth Amendment, but many of the Supreme Court cases that apply to the police deal with the Fifth and Sixth Amendments, especially when it comes to confessions and interrogations. The key aspect of the Fifth Amendment is that no person "shall be compelled in any criminal case to be a witness against himself, nor be deprived of life, liberty, or property without due process of law." In this regard, people cannot be forced into confession and they have the right not to say anything to the police, for if they say something to the police, they may be acting as a witness against themselves. In addition, a person accused of a crime has a right to due process, which means they are afforded certain protections. These protections show up in the Sixth Amendment, which allows them "to be informed of the nature and cause of the accusation," meaning they have to be told why they were arrested, and they also have the right to "assistance of counsel for his defence (*sic*)." If you have ever watched a police drama on television, you can see where this is going. Most of this is encapsulated in the famous Miranda warning.

The Miranda rights are encapsulated in the U.S. Supreme Court case of **Miranda v. Arizona** (1966). In this case, Ernesto Miranda was arrested for the kidnapping and rape of a girl. Brought into the station by the police, he was questioned for two hours and after confessing, signed a statement to that effect. He was, however, never told that he had the right to remain silent under the Fifth Amendment or the right to counsel under the Sixth Amendment. Miranda was convicted and sentenced to 20–30 years in prison, but his lawyers appealed his case. The Arizona Supreme Court upheld his conviction. It was then appealed to the U.S. Supreme Court. In the famous landmark case, the Supreme Court overturned Miranda's conviction. The Court stated that Miranda's rights under the Fifth and Sixth Amendments had been violated and therefore his confession could not be used in a court of law.

Miranda addressed two key factors about police procedures in this case. First, the Miranda warning and the rights encapsulated within in it do not become necessary until a person is taken into custody. What constitutes custody can be a bit murky, but essentially it means when a person has been arrested. For instance, the police may have a suspicion that someone committed a crime, but no evidence. They then conduct a terry stop. They ask the suspect questions. At this point, the person is not in custody of the police, but then again, they are not free to go. Perhaps the suspect then says something that gives the officer probable cause to make the arrest, which

Box 6.7 History in Practice: What Happened to Ernesto Miranda?

The famous U.S. Supreme Court case of *Miranda v. Arizona* (1966), which created the famed **Miranda warning**, was titled such because of the case against Ernesto Arturo Miranda. Miranda's life consisted of multiple interactions with the law, but it was his kidnapping and raping of a 17-year-old girl for which the Phoenix Arizona Police Department arrested him. He was tried, convicted, and sentenced to 20-30 years in prison for his crimes, but the case was appealed all the way to the U.S. Supreme Court because Miranda did not know his rights under the Constitution. The case was won, but whatever happened to Ernesto?

His case was set aside and the State of Arizona retried him, this time without his confession, which was considered inadmissible now. He was still found guilty and sentenced to 20-30 years. He served 11 years in prison for his crimes and was then released in 1972. He made a meager living signing Miranda warning cards, but he was once again in and out of trouble with the law. On January 31, 1976, he ended up in a bar fight in Phoenix and was stabbed and killed. The suspect was believed to be a Mexican national named Ezequiel Moreno who, ironically, was arrested and read his Miranda warning. Moreno, however, fled the country and disappeared.

the officer does by placing handcuffs on the suspect and telling them they are under arrest. At this point, for purposes of Miranda, the suspect is in custody, and before questioning, the individual must be read their Miranda rights. This raises the second major factor in the Miranda decision and that is what constitutes interrogation. If the officer asks the suspect his name and address, without reading the Miranda warning, would that be in violation? The answer is no. Administrative questions are very different from the interrogation of a suspect for a crime. It is only when questions pertaining to the individual's involvement in the crime are asked that the Miranda warning must be read (see Box 6.7).

The Supreme Court decisions, based on the protections found in the Fourth, Fifth, and Sixth Amendments to the Constitution, not only ensure the protection of civil liberties, but they also help to define police authority. When the police can and cannot search, whether they are allowed to enter private property when in hot pursuit of a suspect, and the fact that they must read the Miranda warning prior to interrogating a suspect in a crime are all evidence of how much influence constitutional law has over the police.

Administrative Law

One final body of law that is not as well known, but equally defines police authority is **administrative law**.[55] While the legislatures make the law, they cannot plan for every eventuality and must delegate their authority to administrative officers, such as the chief of police. Administrative rules can be set by these agencies for things pertaining to employment, training, and certification.

For instance, the peace officer standards and certification (POST) organizations (detailed in Chapter 5) write the rules for what it takes to be certified as a police officer and the type of training officers must receive. The police must adhere to these administrative rules because they carry the weight of law, for it is binding upon them. In some cases, these rules are challenged in court, and when the lower courts issue their decisions, police departments must also follow these decisions because they have become essentially court-made laws and they are also binding upon the police. For instance, if the civil service test that a police department uses to screen candidates is found to be discriminatory by a court, then the police department will have to cease using that test and adopt another that meets the court's criteria.

Conclusion

It would assuredly make life easier if the police could point to one source for all of their authority, such as the police oath, but that is not possible in America, nor is it necessarily desired. By having so many sources from which the police derive their authority, if one perhaps gives the police too much latitude to perform their job, another may set stricter criteria, thus ensuring a balance between the people's freedoms and their security. The sources from which the police derive their authority as detailed in Chapter 6 include the problems of crime and disorder, the police department, the community, the government, and the law, including criminal, civil, constitutional, and administrative laws. It is a complex system, but each source is important for understanding police authority throughout the United States.

Just the Facts

1. There is no one source for police authority in America; rather it is derived from a combination of the oath of office, the need to address crime, disorder, and traffic problems, the department, the community, the government, and the law, to include criminal, civil, constitutional and administrative law.

2. The police oath of office is what gives the police officer arrest authority and is why they are considered "sworn" officers or employees of the police department.

3. As the problems of crime and disorder rise, it generates a greater need and desire on the part of citizens for the police to exist and perform their duties.

4. Police departments, through administrative rulemaking, define the authority of the police officer, typically through a written standard operating procedure manual that includes all of the policies, procedures, rules, and regulations overseeing police conduct.

5. Police unions serve as an interest group for the police, and through the use of collective bargaining powers, they can negotiate with police management to present the police officers' views on their authority, conduct, and job benefits.

6. The greater support the police have from the public, the greater legitimacy is given to the job they perform. When public opinion is high, they have full support and backing; when public opinion is low, they lose legitimacy in the eyes of the people and therefore much of their ability to perform their duties.

7. Interest groups are organizations that form as a result of like-minded people, both pro-police and antipolice, who come together to lobby politicians and government to effect some type of change.

8. The relationship between the government (typically the mayor), with the police chief, has found to enhance or constrain police authority. Three common types of relationships have been found to exist: team approach, professional autonomy approach, and political activist approach.

9. Criminal law defines what is considered behaviors that are unacceptable to the people and which present the body of law that the police enforce.

10. Civil law defines the relationship between the police and citizens when an officer may be held liable for his or her actions through either intentional torts, negligence, or by violating a person's constitutional rights as defined by Section 1983 of the U.S. Code.

11. Constitutional law establishes police authority in the relationship between the police as government agents with citizens as free individuals, protected by certain rights, specifically the Fourth and Fifth Amendments as it relates to police-citizen encounters. The Fourth Amendment to the Constitution mentions the use of search warrants by government agents, but case law specifies when officers are required to obtain one and when they may conduct a warrantless search, such as in the case of hot pursuit, searches incident to arrest, and when dealing with automobiles.

12. The Miranda warning, by way of the Supreme Court case of *Miranda v. Arizona* (1966), requires that when a suspect is in custody and is to be questioned about involvement in a crime, a police officer must inform them of their Miranda rights.

13. As the legislative branch cannot anticipate every necessity with the law, often they will delegate authority to a bureaucracy to issue administrative laws that have the binding of legislative passed law.

Ask Yourself

1. Consider some of the symbols of police authority such as the badge, uniform, gun, and oath of office. How much do these contribute to police authority from the perspective of the police? How about the citizen?

2. Police departments that recognize police unions and allow them to have collective bargaining powers typically have higher pay and benefits. What are the pros and cons and the trade-offs when police departments enter into collective bargaining? Consider this from a police authority perspective.

3. Discuss current reports in the news media about police and community relations across the nation. How would you describe the relationship? How does this impact police authority?

4. Research has found that the relationship between the police chief and the local government can impact police authority. Revisit the three types of relationships and discuss the pros and cons of each as it relates to police authority. Which provides the greatest latitude in police authority and which provides the greatest constraints?

5. Consider the various types of law—criminal, civil, constitutional, and administrative law. Which of these gives the police the widest authority and which constrains them the most? Again, what are the pros and cons to each and what are the trade offs?

Keywords

Actus reus
Administrative law
Administrative rulemaking
Administrative search
Automobile searches
Carroll doctrine
Carroll v. U.S. (1925)
Chimel v. California (1969)
Civil law
Collective bargaining
Common law
Consent searches
Constitutional law
Criminal law
Danger to others
Demographics

Elements of the crime
Escape
Evanescent evidence
Exigent circumstances
Hot pursuit
Intentional torts
Interest group
Inventory search
Mens rea
Miranda v. Arizona (1966)
Negligence
Oath of office
Plain view searches
Police unions
Policies
Political activist approach

Procedures
Professional autonomy
   approach
Public opinion
Regulations
Rules
Search incident to arrest
Section 1983 lawsuits
Standard operating
   procedures (SOP)
Statute
Sworn police officer
Team approach
Terry stop
Terry v. Ohio (1968)
Warrantless search

Endnotes

1. Collins, Frederick L. (1924). A Professor who cleaned up a city. *Collier's*, November 8, 12 & 37, at p. 12.
2. Evola, A. (2017). *So you want to be a cop: What everyone should know before entering a law enforcement career.* Lanham, MD: Rowman & Littlefield, p. 9.
3. Bittner, E. (1979). *The functions of the police in modern society.* Bethesda, MD: National Institute of Mental Health.
4. Bittner, E. (1979). *The functions of the police in modern society.* Bethesda, MD: National Institute of Mental Health.
5. City of New Bedford. (2012). *Police swearing in ceremony.* Retrieved from https://www.youtube.com/watch?v=F8YCEqckLD4
6. Zimring, F.E. (2012). *The city that became safe: New York's lessons for urban crime and its control.* New York, NY: Oxford University Press.
7. McArdle, A. & Erzen, T. (2001). *Zero tolerance: Quality of life and the new police brutality in New York city.* New York, NY: New York University Press.
8. Oliver, W.M. (2006). *Homeland security for policing.* Upper Saddle River, NJ: Prentice Hall.
9. Miller, J., Davis, R.C., Henderson, N.J., Markovic, J., & Ortiz, C.W. (2004). *Public opinions of the police: The influence of friends, family, and news media.* Washington, DC: U.S. Department of Justice.
10. Federal Bureau of Investigation. (2013). *Uniform Crime Reports—2012.* Washington, DC: U.S. Department of Justice.
11. Federal Bureau of Investigation. (2013). *Uniform Crime Reports—2012.* Washington, DC: U.S. Department of Justice.
12. American Bar Association. (1980). *Standards relating to the urban function.* 2nd ed. Boston, MA: Little, Brown, & Co.; Commission on Accreditation for Law Enforcement Agencies. (1999). *Standards for law enforcement agencies.* 4th ed. Fairfax, VA: CALEA.
13. See for instance the rules and regulations of the Chicago Police Department. Police Board City of Chicago. (2014). Rules and Regulations of the Chicago Police Department. Retrieved from: https://www.cityofchicago.org/dam/city/depts/cpb/PoliceDiscipline/RulesofConduct.pdf

14. Hickman, M.J. & Reaves, B.A. (1999). *Law enforcement management and administrative statistics, 1997.* Washington, DC: U.S. Department of Justice.

15. Fraternal Order of Police. (2014). Homepage. Retrieved from http://www.fop.net/

16. International Union of Police Associations, AFL-CIO. (2014). Homepage. Retrieved from https://iupa.org/

17. Reaves, B.A. (2010). *Local police departments, 2007.* Washington, DC: U.S. Department of Justice.

18. Isenberg, J. (2010). *Police leadership in a democracy: Conversations with America's police chiefs.* Boca Raton, FL: CRC Press.

19. Morabito, M. (2014). American police unions: A hindrance or help to innovation? *International Journal of Public Administration, 37,* 773-780; Zhao, J.S. & Lovrich, N. (1997). Collective bargaining and the police. *Policing, 20,* 508-518.

20. Reaves, B.A. (2010). *Local police departments, 2007.* Washington, DC: U.S. Department of Justice.

21. Kennedy, R.F. (1964). *The pursuit of justice.* New York, NY: Harper & Row, Publishers, p. 42.

22. Wilson, J.Q. (1978). *Varieties of police behavior: The management of law & order in eight communities.* Cambridge, MA: Harvard University Press.

23. Tooley, M., Linkenback, J., Lande, B.J., & Lande, G.M. (2014). The media, the public, and the law enforcement community: Correcting misperceptions. *The Police Chief.* Retrieved from http://www.policechiefmagazine.org/magazine/index.cfm?fuseaction=display&article_id=1828&issue_id=62009

24. Denhardt, J.V. & Crothers, A.L. (1998). *Street-level leadership: Discretion & legitimacy in front-line public service.* Washington, DC: Georgetown University Press; Walker, S. & Archbold, C.A. (2014). *The new world of police accountability.* 2nd ed. Thousand Oaks, CA: SAGE.

25. Carson, B. with Carson, C. (2012). *America the beautiful: Rediscovering what made this nation great.* Grand Rapids, MI: Zondervan, p. 167.

26. Gallup. (2013). Honesty/ethics in professions. Retrieved from http://www.gallup.com/poll/1654/honesty-ethics-professions.aspx

27. Gallup. (2013). Honesty/ethics in professions. Retrieved from http://www.gallup.com/poll/1654/honesty-ethics-professions.aspx

28. Gallup. (2013). Reported confidence in the police. *Sourcebook of Criminal Justice Statistics.* Retrieved from http://www.albany.edu/sourcebook/pdf/t2122012.pdf

29. Gallup. (2014). Gallup review: Black and White attitudes toward police. Retrieved from http://www.gallup.com/poll/175088/gallup-review-black-white-attitudes-toward-police.aspx; Gallup. (2014). Nonwhites less likely to feel police protect and serve them. Retrieved from http://www.gallup.com/poll/179468/nonwhites-less-likely-feel-police-protect-serve.aspx

30. Gallup. (2014). Record-high 42 percent of Americans identify as independents. Retrieved from http://www.gallup.com/poll/166763/record-high-americans-identify-independents.aspx; Wollner, A. (2014). Millennials grow more liberal, but identify as independents. Retrieved from http://www.nationaljournal.com/hotline-on-call/millennials-grow-more-liberal-but-identify-as-independent-20140307

31. The National Neighborhood Watch Institute. (2014). Homepage. Retrieved from http://www.nnwi.org/about_us.asp

32. National Association of Police Organizations. (2014). Homepage. Retrieved from http://www.napo.org/

33. The Badge of Life. (2014). Homepage. Retrieved from http://www.badgeoflife.com/

34. Copwatch. (2014). Homepage. Retrieved from http://copwatch.com/

35. Communities United Against Police Brutality. (2014). Homepage. Retrieved from http://www.cuapb.org/

36. National Lawyers Guild. (2014). National police accountability project. Retrieved from http://www.nlg-npap.org/

37. McClurg, V. H. (1980). *Political influence upon administrative decision-making in local law enforcement.* Unpublished dissertation, University of Nebraska, Lincoln; O'Brien, J.T. (1978). The chief and the executive: Direction or political interference? *Journal of Police Science and Administration, 6,* 394-401; Tunnell, K. & Gaines, L.K. (1996). Political pressures and influences on police executives: A descriptive analysis. In G. Cordner and D. Kenney (Eds.), *Managing police organizations.* Cincinnati, OH: Anderson Publishing.

38. Mastrofski, S. (1988). Varieties of police governance in metropolitan America. *Politics and Policy, 8,* 12-31.

39. Isenberg, J. (2010). *Police leadership in a democracy: Conversations with America's police chiefs.* Boca Raton, FL: CRC Press, p. 105; See also Haberfeld, M.R. (2006). *Police leadership.* Upper Saddle River, NJ: Prentice Hall.

40. Isenberg, J. (2010). *Police leadership in a democracy: Conversations with America's police chiefs.* Boca Raton, FL: CRC Press, p. 104; See also Haberfeld, M.R. (2006). *Police leadership.* Upper Saddle River, NJ: Prentice Hall.

41. Isenberg, J. (2010). *Police leadership in a democracy: Conversations with America's police chiefs.* Boca Raton, FL: CRC Press, p. 104; See also Haberfeld, M.R. (2006). *Police leadership.* Upper Saddle River, NJ: Prentice Hall.

42. Mastrofski, S. (1988). Varieties of police governance in metropolitan America. *Politics and Policy, 8,* 12-31.

43. Bloch, K.E. & McMunigal, K.C. (2005). *Criminal law: A contemporary approach.* Frederick, MD: Wolters Kluwer.

44. Geistfeld, M. (2008). *Tort law: The essentials.* Frederick, MD: Wolters Kluwer.

45. Kappeler, V.E. (2006). *Critical issues in police civil liability.* 4th ed. Long Grove, IL: Waveland Press, Inc.; Kappeler, V.E. (2006). *Police civil liability: Supreme courts cases and materials.* 2nd ed. Long Grove, IL: Waveland Press, Inc.

46. Kappeler, V.E. (2006). *Critical issues in police civil liability.* 4th ed. Long Grove, IL: Waveland Press, Inc.; Kappeler, V.E. (2006). *Police civil liability: Supreme courts cases and materials.* 2nd ed. Long Grove, IL: Waveland Press, Inc.

47. Massey, C.R. (2012). *American constitutional law: Powers and liberties.* 4th ed. Frederick, MD: Wolters Kluwer.

48. *Beck v. Ohio,* 379 U.S. 89 (1964), p. 91.

49. Mitchell, D.R. & Connor, G.J. (2007). *Stop and frisk: Legal perspectives, tactical procedures.* 2nd ed. Champaign, IL: Stipes Publishing L.L.C.

50. Del Carmen, R. & Walker, J.T. (2011). *Briefs of leading cases in law enforcement*, 8th ed. Cincinnati, OH: Anderson Publishing.

51. *Schneckloth v. Bustamonte,* 412 U.S. 218 (1973).

52. *Chimel v. California,* 395 U.S. 752 (1969).

53. *Chimel v. California,* 395 U.S. 752 (1969).

54. Just to note. The original *Coolidge* case added a third requirement—the discovery of the contraband had to be in advertent, but this was later struck down in a later ruling, *Horton v. California* (1990).

55. DeLeo, J.D. (2008). *Administrative law.* Clifton Park, NY: Cengage.

■ *"No opportunity was left whereby the police might sensibly dodge their duty; there was no alternative but to take action against the raffle promoters, since in enforcing the laws against vice the police man is allowed no discretion."*[1] —*August Vollmer*

The police officer in this traffic stop, using his discretion, has decided to issue the driver a written warning for speeding.

CHAPTER 7

Discretion

After reading this chapter, you will be able to:

1. Understand the meaning of discretion, how it applies to the police, and why it is so critical to police work.
2. Define what is meant by decision making and detail the decision-making process.
3. Name and briefly define the four categories of variables that research has found to influence police officer decision making.
4. Detail how, within the organizational category, organizational structure, supervision, and accountability influence police decision making.
5. Describe how, within the environmental category, community and the physical environment influence police decision making.
6. Identify how, within the situational category, police officer contacts, seriousness of the offense, location, demeanor, and attitude, as well as the presence of others, both citizens and officers, influence police officer decision making.
7. Detail how, within the individual category, officer, offender, victim, and complainant characteristics influence police officer decision making.
8. List and briefly define the five categories of limits to police officer discretion.

The issue that Police Chief August Vollmer referred to in this chapter's opening quote was a common dilemma during the late nineteenth and early twentieth century. Although games of chance, ranging from slot machines, to casino gambling, to state run lotteries are ubiquitous today, there was a time when these activities were illegal. Anyone trying to run any kind of game of chance was committing a crime. While the law was intended to primarily target the underworld groups involved in organized crime, the law applied equally to a church group holding a game of bingo or the raffling of an item to raise money for charity. If you ran a church raffle, you could go to jail. And the person tasked with taking you there was the police officer.

Vollmer's lament was that in policing, there was no discretion and police officers had little choice but to enforce the law as it stood.[2] This was one of the drawbacks of professionalizing the police. In the late 1800s, there were many laws on the books, such as saloons and bars could not be open on Sunday. Yet, all across America, somehow these establishments remained open. That was typically because the police accepted bribes and kickbacks which allowed these businesses to remain open without the police enforcing the law. For instance, in Chicago there was a price list that stated: "Saloons allowed to stay open after hours, $50 per month."[3] If the saloons paid the police the graft money, the saloon would not be shut down or the owner arrested. It was the same across America, from Los Angeles to New York City.[4] That changed, however, when cities began attempting to clean up the city and to professionalize the police. As one police historian explained, in Los Angeles the laws against games of chance were "so rigidly interpreted that LAPD officers were tracking down candy machines that occasionally returned a nickel instead of a gum ball."[5]

Imagine a world where the police would not have discretion in the law. The person speeding one mile an hour over the speed limit would be stopped and ticketed just as much as the person doing ten miles an hour over. Or, worse, the man who is rushing his wife to the hospital to give birth would be stopped and ticketed just as equally as a person flaunting the law. Vollmer lamented the problem and called for change, but it was not until the 1950s that the concept of police discretion was more fully understood and adopted in American policing. Interestingly, the change originated with the American Bar Association.[6]

The change was led by Supreme Court Justice Robert H. Jackson, a prosecutor in the Nuremberg War Crimes Trials after World War II. He called for a survey of the administration of justice looking at every aspect of the criminal justice process, not just the courts.[7] One of the findings from the survey was that many in the criminal justice system, including police officers, did use discretion, but were reluctant to admit it. They were trying to present the belief that justice was blind and applied fairly to everyone. The report and later publications demonstrated that not only was this not the case, but that for the police to be more effective, they must be able to exercise their discretion more freely.[8] Then, in 1967, with President Johnson's Commission on Law Enforcement and the Administration of Justice's report on the police, they definitively stated that police discretion was not only necessary, but an essential element for serving justice and that "the police should openly acknowledge that, quite properly, they do not arrest all, or even most, offenders they know of."[9]

This chapter explores the topic of police discretion, what it is and the importance it plays in the performance of their duty. Additionally, it details how police officers make their decisions and those factors that help them to shape their decisions and, ultimately, their use of discretion on the street. Finally, it details the limits of both police decision making and police discretion.

Police Discretion

As the calls for police to use **discretion** began to grow with both the American Bar Association and the President's Commission reports, there was much discussion over the justification in the late 1960s and early 1970s (see Box 7.1).[10] One of the common arguments for police use of discretion was that it allowed for the human element to remain in the criminal justice system, and common sense became something of great value in policing. Knowing when to stop and detain someone and when not to became part of the police culture concept of using common sense. If a police officer did detain someone, then discretion focused on how to properly intervene based on the circumstances. And, finally, if the law was to be applied, officers using discretion had to determine the most proper course of action such as issuing a summons or taking the person into custody.[11]

Associate Justice of the United States Supreme Court Robert H. Jackson 1941-1954.

As **police discretion** became a focal concern in policing during the 1970s, people soon began trying to define exactly what police discretion entailed. Some, such as Goldstein, saw police discretion as the decision not to use legal sanctions against a person when other measures may be used to affect the same or a better outcome.[12] Others, such as Wilson, explained, "The police exercise discretion *whether* to intervene and, if they do, just *how* to intervene."[13] Davis, more simply, defined it as "whenever the effective limits on [a police officer's] power leave him free to make a choice among courses of action or inaction."[14] Davis more fully observed how much discretion police officers really have when he wrote:

> The police make policy about what law to enforce, how much to enforce it, against whom, and on what occasions. Some law is always or almost always enforced, some is never or almost never enforced, and some is sometimes enforced and sometimes not. Police policy about selective enforcement is elaborate and complex.[15]

Police officers have a wide latitude of discretion and they can make the choice of whether to stop someone or not. For instance, a person driving ten miles an hour over the speed limit may be caught in police radar and the officer could pursue, stop, and issue a ticket, but the officer may decide that the fear of getting a ticket may be more than enough to get the job done, the job being to slow drivers down so that they are not exceeding the speed limit. Another

Box 7.1 History in Practice: The Police Officer as Policy Maker

The **1967 President's Commission on Law Enforcement and the Administration of Justice** assessed the status of America's policing system and offered numerous recommendations for reforms. One insightful passage from the final publication about **the police officer as policy maker** follows:

"At the very beginning of the process — or, more properly, before the process begins at all — something happens that is scarcely discussed in law books and is seldom recognized by the public: law enforcement policy is made by the policeman. For policemen cannot and do not arrest all the offenders they encounter. It is doubtful that they arrest most of them. A criminal code, in practice, is not a set of specific instructions to policemen but a more or less rough map of the territory in which policemen work. How an

individual policeman moves around that territory depends largely on his personal discretion."

Source: The President's Commission on Law Enforcement and Administration of Justice. (1967). *The Challenge of Crime in a Free Society*. Washington, DC: U.S. GPO, p. 10.

example may be stopping someone for smoking marijuana. While it may be illegal in that state, the individual may only have one small joint and it may be more effective to have the individual destroy it than to make an arrest for such

Police paddy wagon.

a small amount. Understand, the officer has the authority to make an arrest in this case, but the officer has the discretion to choose not to (see Box 7.2).

Chicago Police Officer Martin Preib, in his book *The Wagon*, highlights a police officer's use of discretion when he stopped an old pickup truck that contained a Latino driver and passenger.[16] He asked for the driver's license and registration, but the driver claimed he did not understand English. Preib then told his rookie partner that since the driver had no license and no insurance they would have to impound the car. He then asked the driver if he wanted him to

---

Box 7.2 Policing in Practice: COPS and Police Discretion

"Huh! Bad boys! Whatcha gonna do?"

No song has been more associated with policing than Inner Circle's "Bad Boys," and no television show has been more associated with American policing than *COPS*. There is no greater source for gaining some insight into **police officer discretion** than to watch the decision-making process of police officers as they decide to stop someone and then move through the process of investigating and responding to the actions and words of victims, offenders, and suspects.

From the opening "Huh!" that song has become integrally tied to the television show has brought some of the realities and vagaries of policing into America's living room for over 28 seasons. Running on Fox TV from 1989 to 2013, and now appearing on the Spike Cable TV channel, *COPS* still provides both insights into policing as well as some high entertainment value. While it must be remembered that most of what is filmed by the *COPS* crew ends up on the cutting room floor due to the uneventful and often boring aspects of police work, it is those few moments of excitement or amusement that find their way into each episode of *COPS*. Call up a past episode of *COPS* and, in light of what you have learned after reading this chapter on police discretion, consider the use of discretion of the police officers as you watch.

---

impound the car and the driver answered, "No." He then asked him if he had a license or insurance and the response was, "No." After now talking to the driver he learned that he had a job and the vehicle was the only way to get to work. Although he could have ticketed the individual and impounded the car, as Preib explained, "We cut him loose because he has a job and seems okay."[17]

Police discretion, however, often works on a sliding scale. On one end there may be minor crimes, while on the other end, major crimes. A police officer may let a person go for a minor offense, but in the event of say a murder, police officers' discretion becomes much more limited, if not nonexistent. In the case of a domestic violence, because every state has a pro-arrest policy, if there is evidence of an assault, the officer must make an arrest. Hence, their discretion is nonexistent in regard to this type of crime. In other cases, police must make a decision as to whether or not to arrest. For instance, police officers may show up on fight call at a bar, break it up, and then learn that it was two friends engaging in a fistfight over who was going to buy the beer. The police officers now have to make the decision of whether to make an arrest or just tell them to knock it off and let it go. In this case, discretion is the more narrow aspect of the larger decision. Discretion is the fact that officers have the capacity to make an arrest or let the individuals go. The decision is how they are going to use their discretion. How police officers make decisions is therefore important to understanding police discretion (see Box 7.3).

Box 7.3 History in Practice: Sheriff Buford Pusser and the Price of Enforcing the Law

There have been many policing pioneers who have entered as head of the police department and faced difficult circumstances by enforcing the law and trying to overcome political corruption. Police Commissioner Theodore Roosevelt and Police Chief August Vollmer are just two examples. While there are many sheriffs who have faced similar circumstances, perhaps no one is more tragic than **Sheriff Buford Pusser** of McNairy County, Tennessee.

Born on December 12, 1937, Pusser became a wrestler in 1957 in Chicago with the stage name, "Buford the Bull." He married his wife Pauline in 1959, and they returned home to Adamsville, Tennessee, where Pusser served as police chief and constable from 1962 to 1964. When McNairy County Sheriff James Dickey died in an auto accident, Pusser ran for sheriff and won. He became the youngest sheriff in Tennessee at the age of 27.

Pusser began enforcing the laws related to illegal gambling, moonshine, and prostitution, which he felt was his proper role as sheriff. Several groups, often referred to as the Dixie Mafia and the State Line mob, as McNairy is on the state line of Mississippi, did not like the sheriff interfering with their criminal activity,

and they began looking for ways to eliminate this new threat. In 1966, Louise Hathcock attempted to kill Pusser with a .38, but she missed, and instead was killed by Pusser. The next year, an unidentified gunman tried to assassinate Pusser and although shot three times, he survived. The most tragic of the assassination attempts came later that year, when on August 12, 1967, in an attempt to kill Buford, his wife Pauline was shot and killed. This launched the story into the national media, and Pusser vowed to not give up the fight. He continued enforcing the law until 1970, when he could no longer run for office due to term limits.

He was re-elected to serve as the constable of Adamsville in 1970, and he remained in that position until his death in a single vehicle accident in 1972. Although it has been suggested his car was tampered with, he was found to have died with a blood alcohol content over the legal limit.

While numerous books and movies have been made about his life, the most popular (and historically inaccurate) of them all was the original movie *Walking Tall*, which was released six months after his death in 1973.

Police Decision Making

Although the concept of encouraging police officers to use their discretion became well accepted in the 1960s and 1970s, as Goldstein pointed out, "these police decisions, unlike their decisions to invoke the law, are generally of extremely low visibility and consequently are seldom the subject of review."[18] In other words, while people were encouraging the police to use their discretion, there was almost no research on how police officers exercised their discretion and the **decision-making process** they used to arrive at their course of action. It, therefore, became a focus of police research beginning largely in the 1970s to come to understand how police officers make decisions.[19] To understand this concept, it is important to understand the decision-making process in general.

Making decisions is something all of us do all of the time. From the moment we awake, we begin making decisions, even starting with the decision to wake up or go back to sleep. How we make those decisions is a process that may be a long and laborious process, or it may be quick and almost instantaneous. In the former case, it may be something like purchasing a new car. In the latter, it may be something as simple as where do I go for lunch. Yet, in both instances, people typically move through a process of decision making. There are many models of decision making, sometimes with dozens of steps, but they all follow the same pattern.

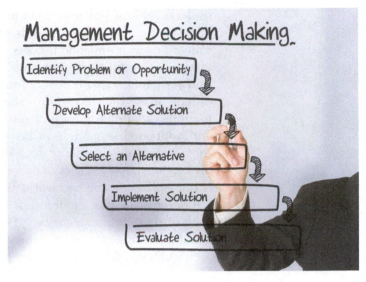

The decision-making process.

Taking the example of having to make a decision about where to go for lunch, one is faced with a problem, "I must eat." Next, the person gathers facts about the problem, such as how much money and time they have, and whether they are on a meal plan or have food at home. Next, the person must develop possible alternatives that are options and solutions to the problem. A college student may be on the meal plan and could go to the university cafeteria, they could go out to eat at a restaurant, or they could go home and eat a peanut butter and jelly sandwich. The next step in the process is to compare the pros and cons to the various courses of actions. For instance, the student may only have a dollar in her pocket and no food back at the apartment. The next step is to make a decision and implement it, which in this scenario would be to go to the cafeteria. The last step is an assessment of the decision, which may be, "the cafeteria food was horrible, I am never going there again." While the lunch decision may have been more instantaneous than say the purchase of a car, people tend to think through these steps when faced with a decision.

Now think of the police officers in the case of the two friends fighting in the bar. They have a problem: two men fighting. They break up the fight and begin their investigation by separating the two and asking each why they were fighting. The officers then get together, compare stories, and come up with solutions to the problems. They could arrest, give them a stern warning, or just tell them to knock it off. They then make a decision, such as opting to let it go, then implement it and move on to the next call. If they don't get called back for the two guys fighting, they can deem their decision a good one. If they get called back because the two guys are at it again, then they can declare they made a poor decision, reevaluate, and make an arrest.

The realities of policing, however, often require police officers to make split-second decisions, decisions that can have lasting repercussions on not only them, but people nearby or the community as a whole. This is why coming to understand how police officers make decisions has become an important area of research. The research tends to focus on those things that factor into the officers' decision-making process. Over time, researchers have tried to identify every conceivable thing that could influence police officer decision making, and they have found that there are four types of variables that influence how police officers make their decisions. The four categories are organizational, environmental, situational, and individual.[20] Each of these variables will be defined and addressed separately to better understand the many influencing factors that shape a police officer's decision-making process and use of discretion. One distinction, however, should be made here. Each of these categories of variables is not isolated in the real world and typically influence one another. Decisions are never made in a vacuum nor are they made one at a time by officers using each of these four categories.[21] The purpose of the four categories is to understand the complexity of all of the various factors that shape, influence, and form police officers' decisions and discretion on the street.

Organizational

The **organizational variables** that shape police discretion and influence their decision making has to do with the police department itself. The very core of policing is the officer on the street, responding to calls-for-service, and investigating cases of crime and disorder. The police department exists in part to support the officer on the street, while at the same time to shape and control their behavior. As previously detailed, police derive their authority from a wide array of sources, but they are also constrained by the department through the organization itself. Research tells us that everything from the professionalism of the agency, its size, how stable the department is in terms of leadership and personnel, how it deploys its officers, and the means by which it supervises them all play a role in influencing police officer discretion and decision making.

One of the organizational variables is the general **work climate** of each police department, for the overall philosophy of the department has been shown to influence police officer behavior.[22] While this may be derived from the style of policing the community desires, it may develop independently within a police department and take on a life of its own. This too can influence whether the department is service oriented or heavily into law enforcement. Either way, the department philosophy can influence what the officers do or don't do on the street.

The **organizational structure** of the police department has also been found to have a heavy influence on officer decision making. This can influence the level of bureaucracy, the professionalism of the department, how closely it adheres to the military model, as well as the type of shift work it adopts (rotating or fixed).[23] For instance, a police department that prides itself on professionalism will convey to its officers that regardless of the situation the police officers encounter they must remain in control of their tempers at all times, never curse, and always be polite. Or, a police department that operates on a very strict military model and chain-of-command may take on a military mind-set in how it enforces the law and treats its citizens.

One aspect of the organizational structure, the size of the police department itself, has also been found to influence police officer behavior.[24] Although in many ways, the size of a department is determined by a number of variables outside of police control, it has been found to influence police behavior.[25] Larger police departments tend to be more bureaucratic and are more impersonal in nature, thus police officers are lost in a shuffle of paperwork and are treated as an employee, not a person. This can dampen the spirits of any worker, not just the police, but like any worker in this situation, they may become more withdrawn and less engaged in their work. Smaller departments tend to be more personal because everyone knows each other and it is more difficult to disengage or hide, thus the chief and management can have a greater personal influence on the police officer.[26] In addition, research has also found that the relationship of small-town police with citizens also tends to be more informal and personal.[27]

Research has even demonstrated that the size of the area (beats) in which the police officer patrols can have an influence on the behavior of a police officer. Smaller beats tend to influence the police officer to focus on service, while larger beats influence them to take a more law enforcement mode.[28] However, in those areas that are small, but have a high level of crime, this no longer holds, for the introduction of the crime variable influences the officer to take a more strict enforcement approach to their work.[29] Yet even the type of assignment that officers have in these beats can also influence officer decision making, for those officers on a community policing assignment are more likely to emphasize victim's preference in their decision making than their routine patrol counterparts.[30]

While departmental philosophy is a bit abstract and the organizational structure something hard to manipulate, one primary reason for having leadership within the police department is to oversee and manage police officers in the performance of their duties. Research demonstrates that the amount of **supervision** and **accountability** affect police officer behavior.[31] The more supervision police officers have, especially field supervisors, those that are out on patrol with the officers, the more positive the impact on police officer decision making. Conversely, supervisors that are never present, are never seen by the officers, or never work the streets create a negative impact on police decision making.

Supervisors also manage their officers through rules and regulations, as well as policies and procedures (see Chapter 6). These formal rules have been found to have a mixed impact on officers, hence it may not be the best means of control, especially if it becomes a substitute for hands-on supervision.[32] One problem with a highly bureaucratic police department that manages via this method is that it can contribute to police officers developing their own informal rules and ways of doing things. And research is consistent in showing that informal norms and rules do influence police behavior (see Box 7.4).[33]

Box 7.4 Policing in Practice: Police Decision Making in Traffic Stops

One part of a police officers' job is to regulate and enforce traffic laws. This means police officers have the authority to stop a motorist for a suspected moving violation under the traffic laws. There are essentially three types of stops. The first is a "routine" stop in which a police officer observes a traffic violation and stops the motorist. The second is a "redirected" stop in which the police officer observes a violation, makes the stop, but then redirects his or her attention toward some other possible violation, such as a crime, stolen vehicle, or wanted fugitive. The third is a "pretext" stop in which the officer suspects some criminal behavior, but stops for a moving violation to initiate the investigation.

Each of these traffic stops entails a decision-making process by the officer. First, the officer has to make the decision to stop or not to stop. In some cases, even having observed a moving violation, the officer has the discretion to not stop the driver. For instance, if there were four officers working the street and three are currently on calls, if that officer initiates a traffic stop, there will be no officers readily available for calls-for-service. The officer may make the decision to let the minor traffic violation go.

Once the officer does make the stop, they have to make the decision of whether to keep the occupants of the vehicle in the car or remove them from the car, which a Supreme Court case has acknowledged their authority to do so (*Maryland v. Wilson* 1997). Often, keeping the occupants in the motor vehicle is safer for the officer as they pose less of a threat to the officer's safety while contained. Still, officers may order the occupants of a vehicle out of the car in order to ensure the safety of the driver and any occupants.

During the traffic stop, if additional information is obtained that may lead the officer to suspect a crime has been or is being committed, they must decide how to investigate. A statement from the driver, the smell of alcohol on the driver's breath, a gun in the backseat, or the return on the license's check that the driver's license is suspended, all will factor into the decision-making process of the officer.

Another decision officers must make is when to call for backup. Most traffic stops do not require a second officer, but some stops may necessitate the officer to call a backup. Sometimes it may be obvious, such as four occupants of a vehicle fitting the description from an armed bank robbery, but others may be less obvious, such as a car stopped for simply speeding, but also has four occupants.

Finally, officers have the discretion to issue a ticket for the moving violation or they may issue a warning. If giving a warning, it may be informal (verbal) or a more formal warning (written). And even in the case of a crime having been committed, the officer must make the decision to arrest or not arrest, and in cases of minor crimes (low-level misdemeanors), to issue a summons for their arrest or take them to booking.

Environmental

While the organizational variables have an influence on police officer discretion and decision making, those variables influence the officer on the street through training and repeated communication. Yet, it is important to remember that those variables are not physically present when an officer is handling a call, using their discretion, and making a decision. The next set of variables, often referred to as **environmental** or neighborhood variables, are more prevalent when officers are engaged in police work. These variables can include such things as the physical environment of the neighborhood, the level of crime within the neighborhood, the racial composition, socio-economic status, and even the political culture of the community.

Once again, the **community** has the ability to influence police behavior, and like the philosophy of the department, the philosophy of the community, or its political culture, influences officer discretion and decision making.[34] This can also be found not just in the community

The physical environment is one of the environmental variables that influences police decision making.

in general, but also in specific neighborhoods. However, there are many variables about a neighborhood that send signals to police officers which can influence their behavior.

For instance, the **physical environment** itself may send signals to the officer that a particular neighborhood may be more dangerous than others, hence making them more cautious and more aware of their surroundings. This also may influence them to be more active in enforcing the law. The presence of broken windows, abandoned cars, potholes, graffiti, trash, abandoned buildings, the homeless, and certain types of shops, such as a high number of pawn shops, tattoo parlors, and bail-bond offices, sends a signal to an officer that these neighborhoods may need more attention and more enforcement.

Where this gets complicated is the fact that research has demonstrated that the presence of these physical cues in a neighborhood are associated with the lower socio-economic communities, which are also associated with higher numbers of minorities. Research has consistently found that minority neighborhoods do see higher numbers of arrests and use of force.[35] Research has also demonstrated, however, that these arrest rates and use of force are highly correlated with criminal activity.[36] And still further, we know that high crime and violence in a community impacts police behavior and the likelihood that they will make arrests and use force.[37] Which means, we are left with a which-came-first scenario. Do lower income, minority neighborhoods have higher crime because the people living in these communities are more likely to commit crime and so the police are simply responding to the problem by making arrests? Or is it because the police feel they can be more active in low-income, minority neighborhoods and by making more arrests, they artificially drive up the crime rates in these neighborhoods? Terrill and Reisig in their study on this relationship conclude that "race is confounded by neighborhood context: Minority suspects are more likely to be recipients of higher levels of police force because they are disproportionately encountered in disadvantaged and high-crime neighborhoods."[38] Suffice it to say, all of these neighborhood variables, for whatever reason they exist, do influence police officers in their use of discretion and how they make decisions.

Situational

The third variable, **situational factors**, becomes even more focused on the specific events surrounding a police encounter with a suspect, and it is these immediate cues that shape and influence police officer discretion and decision making. These can include such things as the seriousness of the offense and whether the officer was called to the scene via police dispatch or the officer initiated the encounter by stopping and detaining a citizen.

Research has shown that how an officer engages in an encounter with a suspect can play a role in how they respond. **Police officer contacts** with citizens often fall into three categories: being dispatched because of a citizen complaint received either by the police dispatch through 911 or the nonemergency number (which makes up slightly more than half of all police contacts),[39] a citizen flagging down a police officer, or the police officer initiates the stop. It has been found that police-initiated contacts are more proactive and aggressive, and cause citizens, whether they are suspects, victims, or bystanders, to be less supportive of police behavior, while citizen-initiated contacts are more reactive and tend to be given greater support by the people.[40] This reaction on the part of the citizens to police contact based on how the contact was made becomes part of officer discretion and decision making, and how they interact with citizens.[41]

In addition to how they are called, what the officers are called for makes a significant difference in how the police officer responds. When this author worked as a police officer, I received a call for a robbery in progress. I drove to the call with lights and sirens on, arrived on scene, and jumped out with my weapon drawn. Everyone was baffled over my response, including the victim. She had set her purse down on the ground, turned away, and someone grabbed it and ran. She called the police because she had been robbed. Robbery involves some form or threat, force or intimidation, and likely the use of a weapon, which was not what she experienced. She was the victim of a larceny. Had the call gone out as a larceny, I would have driven there safely without lights and sirens and no gun would have been drawn.

Research bears this out that the **seriousness of the offense** as it initially goes out and what the offense actually is plays a role in police discretion and their decision-making process. And the more serious the crime, the less discretion officers have and the more likely they are to make an arrest.[42] While this may seem rather obvious, the more serious the crime the more likely an arrest will be made, it should be noted that arrests are based on probable cause that a law has been violated, not the perceived seriousness of the crime.[43]

The **location** in which the police initiate the contact also plays a factor in their decision making and use of discretion. Police tend to act more harshly and aggressively when they are in public places rather than private places.[44] In public places there often tend to be people standing around watching the police encounter, and this has been found to affect police behavior.[45] In fact, this could be called the "shooting the elephant" phenomenon, for George Orwell, the author of *Animal Farm* and *1984*, once wrote a short article by that title, describing the time he was a police officer in English-controlled India and felt forced to shoot an elephant because it was what the people expected him to do (see Box 7.5).

In addition to the **presence of people** in general, when those people turn hostile toward the police, this also influences the police officer's decision-making process. Not surprisingly, research has shown that police officers are more likely to take some type of formal police action when this is the case.[46] Research is also starting to look into how police officers react when suspects, victims, and bystanders begin filming police-citizen encounters, and how this

---

Box 7.5 History in Practice: Orwell Shooting an Elephant and Unexpected Situations

George Orwell, who is most famous for such books as *1984* and *Animal Farm*, was a police officer in Burma from 1922 to 1927. In this capacity, he encountered what would definitely quality as an **unexpected situation**. Burma was a province of India at the time and was under British rule, after having been conquered in 1886 after a 62-year struggle. Orwell was born in India to middle class parents, raised in England, and returned to Burma to become the Assistant Superintendent in the British Imperial Police. The local people did not take kindly to the British police, and Orwell in uniform was no exception.

One day, Orwell received a plea for assistance. An elephant was rampaging in the town square, and the police were called to handle the problem. Most elephants are normally quite tame, but they can often go into rampages as this one did that day. Orwell, armed with a .44 caliber Winchester rifle, rode into the town square on a pony.

People told him conflicting stories, and knowing the local populace, Orwell thought it was a false call, that they were baiting him. That was, at least, until Orwell saw the body of an Indian man who had been obviously trampled by the elephant and killed. He sent for an elephant rifle, and the people then all followed Orwell to where the elephant now appeared to be standing peacefully in a field.

Orwell did not want to shoot the elephant, but as he looked around, the people were all watching him, waiting for him to do something. He took the elephant rifle and shot the elephant. Unfortunately, the shot did little. So, he shot the elephant again and again. The elephant would not die, so he gave up and left. He later learned the elephant was killed and his bones stripped bare by the locals within hours. He felt bad and, talking with some other officers, questioned whether he did the right thing. They discussed this among themselves, but the one thing Orwell never told his fellow officers was that he did it solely "to avoid looking a fool."

Source: Orwell, G. (2003). *Shooting an Elephant: And Other Essays.* New York, NY: Penguin Classics.

The mannerisms of the victim, such as the woman in the picture complaining about her ex-husband violating a court order, is one of the situational variables that influences police decision making.

too becomes a variable in police officer decisions and their use of discretion.[47]

Still further, not only does the presence of other citizens play a factor in police officer decision making, so too does the presence of other officers on scene. Research has found that when police officers "**wolf-pack" stops,** where multiple officers show up on scene, police officers are more likely to be aggressive, take formal police action, and make arrests.[48]

One additional situational variable that crosses over into the individual variable but is one that can truly exacerbate a situation is the **demeanor and attitude** of both the suspect and the victim or complainant. When the suspect is disrespectful toward the officer, this increases the likelihood for formal police action and most likely arrest.[49] If there is no legal basis for formal police action, however, research suggests that this will override the challenge to an officer's legitimacy and competency through the negative attitude and demeanor.

In addition to the attitude and demeanor of the suspect, the victim or complainants' attitude and demeanor toward the police officer makes a difference as well. Typically, police will weigh the victim or complainants' wishes quite heavily in their decision-making process.[50] However, if the victim becomes disrespectful toward the police officer and has a negative attitude and hostile demeanor, this will decrease the likelihood the police will adhere to the victim's desires. Simply put, police officers, like most people, tend to listen and respond more attentively to those who show respect than those who do not.

Individual

The last set of variables is the most narrowly defined of the variables, for they consist of the characteristics and traits of the individuals in a police-citizen encounter, namely the police officer, the suspect, and the victim. When it comes to the first set of individuals, the police, numerous studies have looked at **officer characteristics** to try and see if there are certain demographics of officers that have been shown to influence police officer decision making. Countless studies have looked at age, experience, education, race, intelligence, and sex of the officers.[51] These studies occasionally find some very minor differences, such as when it comes to race and sex, yet not in the direction most people think. Several studies have found that the likelihood of

Box 7.6 Ethics in Practice: Police are Blue

The vast majority of studies find that **officer characteristics exert little to no difference on police officer decisions and discretion**. Police officers see themselves as simply **blue**, rather than a sum of their individual characteristics, such as age, gender or race. In light of the fact that police officer individual characteristics appear to play almost no role in how police officers respond and deal with calls-for-service, consider some of the following questions.

Ask Yourself:

Should race be a determination in deciding where officers are assigned?

For example, should Hispanic officers be assigned to Hispanic neighborhoods?

Likewise, should female officers be called to deal with female offenders and victims or should gay police officers be called to deal with gay offenders or victims?

What benefit do police departments gain from recruiting targeted populations, with the goal of having the police department look like the community it serves?

Why do you think police officers see themselves as blue and not by sex, gender, race, ethnicity, etc.?

arrest increases for black suspects when the race of the officer is also black.[52] And one study found that women officers are less likely to exhibit compassion toward citizens than male officers.[53] Yet, these few studies aside, time and time again the vast majority of these studies find that officer characteristics exert little to no difference in police officer decisions and discretion.[54] It gives some credence to the notion that when police officers put on the uniform and go to work they are not young or old, male or female, or black or white, instead, they are all simply blue (see Box 7.6).

Research into the **offender's characteristics** is much more mixed than that of the police officer. For instance, research has shown that women are less likely to be arrested than men, but what is not known is whether this is out of some sense of chivalry, or is it because women commit less crime than men?[55] Research shows that age matters, for the young are more likely to be arrested than those that are older, but is this out of deference to the aged or because the young tend to be more aggressive and commit crimes?[56] Race also matters, for it is clear blacks are more likely to be arrested disproportionate to their numbers, but is this because police officers are racially profiling or because blacks are more likely to display bad attitudes, resist police authority, and/or become hostile toward the police? The research on this question is very mixed.[57] Income level also has been found to matter, for those who are on the lower socio-economic status are more likely to be the subject of police action, but is this because the poor make easy police targets, or because they commit more crime?[58] Another factor in recent years has been the mental health of the offender, for officers have been called to deal with the mentally ill more often in their duties. Their response to the mentally ill is usually designed to deal with the immediate problem, not the long-term mental health of the offender, but because of the suspect's behavior they sometimes employ force to control these situations.[59] The problem with most of these demographic variables is that it is hard to tease out the true nature of suspect characteristics, their attitudes, their mental health, how they react to the police, and specifically what the police are focusing on. As Officer Dunn of the LAPD tried to explain, "It is not just the clothing that an officer takes in when trying to determine if he is dealing with a gang member. It is clothing, it is demeanor, it is verbiage, it is location, it is time of day; all of these things are taken into account. Officers try to use common sense when appraising people they contact."[60] Yet, people's behaviors toward the police often compel them to take action. As one former Los Angeles Police Officer and now professor, Sumil Datta, voiced in an editorial in *The Washington Post*: "Even though it may sound harsh and impolitic, here is the bottom line: if you don't want to get shot, tased, pepper-sprayed, struck with a baton or thrown to the ground, just do what I tell you. Don't argue with me, don't call me names, don't tell me that I can't stop you, don't say I'm a racist pig, don't threaten that you'll sue me and take away my badge. Don't scream at me that you pay my salary, and don't even *think* of aggressively walking towards me. Most field stops are complete in minutes. How difficult is it to cooperate for that long?"[61] One can sense the frustration in his words, but while there is truth that cops are not always innocent in these encounters, neither are the citizens stopped.

More recently, research has begun to focus on the individual characteristics pertaining to the mental state of the suspect. As police come into contact with the mentally ill, they are often faced with difficult decisions on how to handle them properly. Research has found that those suspects showing signs of mental illness are more likely to be arrested, but other research has found that when these individuals showed disrespect or hostile attitudes the likelihood of arrest did not increase, suggesting that officers are acutely aware the individual has a mental illness.[62]

Another factor related to individual characteristics has to do with the **victim or complainant's characteristics**. While the attitude and demeanor of the victim has already been addressed, research has also focused on the demographic characteristics of the victim or complainant. Some research has found that suspects were less likely to be arrested when the victim was black or female, but suggests that this may

The individual characteristics and behaviors of the suspect served to influence his arrest by San Francisco police officers.

Figure 7.1 Variables That Influence Police Discretion

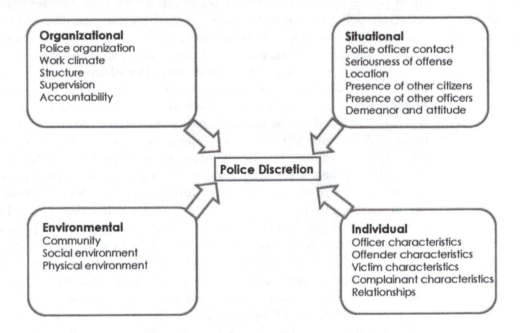

be more related to their socio-economic status than their race. Many other studies found no difference by race or many of the other characteristics. So, like the suspect characteristic studies, victim characteristic studies also are generally mixed in their findings.[63]

One other factor related to the individual variables is the **relationship** that exists between the suspect and the victim/complainant. The closer that relationship is, the less likely the police are to take formal action.[64] Conversely, when the two are strangers, the police are more likely to take formal police action and to make arrests.[65] The exception to this, of course, is when their discretion is limited, such as in the case of a domestic dispute under the pro-arrest policy, where if officers see visible signs of abuse, regardless of how close the two are, the police officer is almost always likely to make the arrest (see Figure 7.1).

Limits on Discretion and Decision Making

Just as in the case of domestic dispute cases, where there are limits placed upon the officers' discretion, there are many cases where police officers may find their discretion constrained. Previously mentioned was the seriousness of the crime itself. It is easier to issue a warning to someone violating a traffic offense than it is to someone committing a misdemeanor, such as the possession of one marijuana joint. It is also easier to issue a warning to the person with the marijuana than it is to someone who has committed an armed robbery. There are, however, many other ways that society has placed limits upon police discretion. Most of these reflect back to the previous chapter related to police authority, for not only are there many factors that give police officers their authority, many of those same factors also take away police officers' authority by limiting their discretion and decision-making abilities.

There are five categories of limits to police officer discretion, and they include the administrative, legal, social, political, and economical. The **administrative** category includes the policies and procedures and rules and regulations issued by the police department, which can place limits on the officers' discretion. The domestic violence pro-arrest police is a good example, where based on a research study conducted in the 1980s, it was found that police officers arresting whenever there are signs of physical abuse was the best course of action to keep recidivism rates low. States across America began passing pro-arrest policies which limited police discretion. The effectiveness of the policy has been mixed, but in one police department, the number of domestic violence acts decreased, but the severity of the violence increased. When a detective was asked about this he responded, "Individuals who know they are going to be arrested and convicted to the fullest extent of the law have nothing to lose by beating their partner more severely."[66]

The **legal** category of limits on police discretion do apply to the pro-arrest policy because of the fact that all 50 states made it law. Another aspect of this category includes Supreme Court decisions. A police officer in Mark Baker's book *Cops* tells a story from the 1970s, and comments, "Back then you could fire warning shots at your discretion."[67] In the 1970s and earlier, it was permissible for the police to shoot a fleeing felon. That changed with a case in 1974, when a Memphis police officer shot and killed an unarmed burglary suspect who was climbing over a fence to escape. The case made its way to the U.S. Supreme Court as *Tennessee v. Garner* (1985), and the Supreme Court ruled that it was no longer lawful to shoot a fleeing felon unless they presented an immediate threat to the lives of citizens or the officer. Since 1985, the police no longer have discretion to shoot a fleeing felon.

The **social** category has to do with the social factors related to changes in our society. One example of this comes from the early 1990s when this author worked as a police officer. Homosexuality in America was still considered taboo, but the county in which I worked had a high population of homosexuals. When the police began enforcing the solicitation laws for anonymous homosexual encounters in the libraries, malls, and local monuments, there was a backlash from the local homosexual community. They argued they were being unfairly targeted and the police were discretely told to stop enforcing those laws.

The fourth category of limits placed on police discretion is the **political** category. Two examples already used highlight this particular category. There is informal political pressure, such as that placed on the police by the homosexual community, and more formal political powers, such as the political adoption of the pro-arrest policy. And finally, the last category is the

economical category. In many cases, police discretion and decision making is limited by economic constraints. For instance, while a police department may be more efficient if every police officer wore a body camera or they might be more effective if every officer carried a Taser, the local government may not be able to fund the purchase of these items. If police officers do not have body cameras or tasers, or any other equipment for that matter, it limits their choices and constrains the options they have in making decisions (see Box 7.7).

Box 7.7 Policing in Practice: Positive Examples of Police Discretion and Good Decision-Making

When the topic of police discretion and decision-making is raised, it is often because a police officer used poor discretion and poor decision-making. When a police officer does something nice for a citizen, this is often chalked up to either the individual police officer's kind intentions, or an example of an officer just doing her job. Oddly, good uses of police discretion and good decision-making are not rewarded, but then again, negative events often have a way of sticking with people much longer than positive events. Yet, everyday there are countless unsung **examples of police officers making good decisions**. Below are just a few examples of good use of discretion and decision-making by police officers and sheriff's deputies across America:

Officer Larry DePrimo of the New York Police Department, on a cold winter night, saw a homeless man without shoes. He asked him where his shoes were and the man, Jeffrey Hillman, said he had never had shoes and for the officer not to worry about him. Officer DePrimo went into a store and bought the man a pair of boots and socks. It was only because a tourist realized what the officer was doing and took a picture that anyone ever knew.

Deputy Jorge Vargas of the Dallas County (Texas) Sheriff's Office, responded to a traffic accident where a family moving from Ohio to Texas on a shoestring budget and seeking a better life had been involved in a car wreck. They had planned to camp along the way to save money, but the accident destroyed their camping gear and they had pets. Deputy Vargas paid for the family to stay in a hotel and placed the pets in a shelter while they could get back on their feet. He then paid the shelter to later reunite the family with their pets.

Officer Ariel Soltura of the Rosenberg (Texas) Police Department was out on patrol one day and saw a black youth all by himself with a football. He looked at the officer and the officer him, and the boy made a throwing motion. Officer Soltura then got out of his patrol car and threw the football with the young boy. It was captured on his dashboard camera which his supervisors later saw, liked, and uploaded to the department's webpage.

Officer Justin Roby of the London (Kentucky) Police Department was called to a store where a black male was being held by private security officers for shoplifting. He was trying to steal baby formula. The man was a single parent trying to take care of his infant child and had simply resorted to shoplifting. The officer realized that arresting would not do the man, nor his child, any good, so he asked that charges not be pressed, and he paid for the man's baby formula.

Conclusion

While the police derive their authority from many sources, their discretion is also limited by many sources as well. In some ways, while the focus of Chapter 6 on authority tells the police what they can do, the focus of Chapter 7 on discretion tells the police what they cannot do. Police officers do need discretion in the work they do, otherwise every town would end up like the one episode of the old television show *The Andy Griffith Show* where the deputy, Barney Fife, does not use his discretion and ends up locking up the entire town, when Andy, the sheriff, goes away for a few days. However, the police must also have limits placed on their discretion and decision making, which they do, and the sources of these limitations come from administrative, legal, social, political, and economical factors. And while discretion is important in policing, it is best to remember that it remains part of the larger decision-making process that the police use when determining how to use their discretion. There are many factors that influence the police decision-making process, and they include the numerous variables coming from the four categories of organization, environmental, situational, and individual variables.

Just the Facts

1. Discretion is the freedom to decide what should be done in a particular situation, and police officer discretion entails that they have this freedom while working the street because no one can predict the various problems and situations they will encounter.

2. Decision making is the cognitive process people go through when faced with a problem, issue, or choice, by determining the various courses of actions, comparing and contrasting those choices, then selecting the best one with the goal of then taking action (or potentially, no action).

3. Research into police decision making has found there are four categories of variables that influence police officers, and they are organizational, how the police department is structured; environmental, including factors associated with the call-for-service location; situational, the particular circum-

stances of the call for the police; and individual, which includes the officer, offender, and victim/complainants' characteristics.

4. The organizational structure influences police decision making by establishing the parameters in which those decisions can be made, and are overseen by police supervisors holding officers accountable for their actions.

5. The environment influences police decision making when it comes to the cohesiveness of the community and the state of the physical environment which communicates, in essence, how much the community cares about their neighborhoods.

6. The situation influences police decision making in regard to how the police officer was summoned to the scene, the seriousness of the offense, whether the call is in a public or private place, how many other cit-

izens are present at the call, as well as how many other police officers are on scene and the demeanor and attitude of the suspect, victim, or complainant.

7. Individuals can influence police decision making in that the characteristics of the offender, victim, and complainant, as well as the relationship among them, will influence officer decisions, but rarely does the officers' characteristics have much impact.

8. Research has found there are five categories of the types of limitations that can be placed on police officers, and they are administrative, legal, social, political, and economical.

Ask Yourself

1. Consider a police department attempting to write a policy that covers when police officers may accept gratuities and when they may not. Try to craft your own policy that covers situations such as an officer being offered a free cup of coffee at a convenience store, a discount for a meal at a restaurant, and the offer to lease a car for one year for $1. Also, keep in mind, you must also craft the policy so that it also covers situations such as a police officer taking a call for a burglary from an elderly woman who offers a free cup of coffee, a local civic club inviting police officers to eat free at their pancake supper as the guests of honor, and a police officer appreciation night at the local bowling alley where officers bowl for free (they only have to pay for shoe rentals).

2. A police officer enters a convenience store and grabs an extra-large fountain soda, then stands in line to pay. The place is busy and there is a line behind the officer as well. When it is time for the officer to pay, the clerk says no, he won't take the officer's money. The officer's department has a no gratuities policy, so the officer says he has to pay. The clerk says no. The officer lays the money on the counter, but the clerk pushes it back to the officer. The people in the line are getting impatient and start grumbling, "Just take the free drink." Using the decision-making process, what are the courses of actions the officer could take?

Compare and contrast the costs and benefits of each action, then select the best one.

3. Find an episode of the television show *COPS* or other similar "reality" television show depicting police officers. After watching a particular police encounter, try to articulate how the police officer used discretion, then try to identify how many variables influenced the police officers in the decision-making process.

4. Consider a police call-for-service such as a fight in progress. The officer arrives on the scene. Does the dynamic of the scene change if there is a large crowd of people watching? Why? Does the dynamic of the scene change if all of the people have cell phones out and they are video recording? Why? Does the dynamic change if a half-dozen more officers show up on the scene? Why?

5. One of the most dangerous aspects of policing are police vehicular pursuits. If the police are not allowed to pursue people fleeing arrest, it sends a signal that all criminals have to do is flee and they can get away with their crimes. However, police pursuits are a danger to the suspect, the officers, and the public due to the often reckless nature of the fleeing suspect. Considering the five categories of limiting police discretion, discuss how police pursuits could be limited, within reason, under each of these five categories.

Keywords

Accountability

Administrative

Attitude

Community

Decision-making process

Demeanor

Discretion

Economical

Environmental variables

Legal

Location

Offender characteristics

Officer characteristics

Organizational structure

Organizational variables

Physical environment

Police discretion

Police officer contacts

Political

Presence of people

Relationships

Seriousness of the offense

Situational factors

Social

Supervision

Victim or complainant
    characteristics

Wolf-pack stops

Work climate

Endnotes

1. Vollmer, A. (1936). *The police and modern society.* Berkeley: University of California Press, p. 95.

2. Goldstein, H. (1977). *Policing a free society.* Cambridge, MA: Ballinger Publishing Company; Vollmer, A. (1936). *The police and modern society.* Berkeley: University of California Press.

3. Abbott, K. (2007). *Sin in the second city: Madams, ministers, playboys and the battle for America's soul.* New York, NY: Random House Trade Paperback, p. 53.

4. Dash, M. (2007). *Satan's circus: Murder, vice, police corruption, and New York's trial of the century.* New York, NY: Three Rivers Press; Domanick, J. (1994). *To protect and serve: The LAPD's century of war in the city of dreams.* New York, NY: Pocket Books.

5. Domanick, J. (1994). *To protect and serve: The LAPD's century of war in the city of dreams.* New York, NY: Pocket Books, p. 33.

6. Walker, S. (1998). *Popular justice: A history of American criminal justice.* New York, NY: Oxford University Press.

7. Jackson, R.H. (1954). Serving the administration of criminal justice. *Federal Probation.* Retrieved from www.roberthjackson.org/files/thecenter/files/bibliography/1950s/serving-the-administration-of-criminal-justice.pdf

8. American Bar Association. (1956). *American bar association survey of the administration of justice.* Chicago, IL: American Bar Association; LaFavre, W. (1965). *Arrest.* Boston, MA: Little, Brown; Walker, S. (1992). Origins of the contemporary criminal justice paradigm: The American Bar Foundation survey, 1953-1969. *Justice Quarterly, 9,* 47-76.

9. President's Commission on Law Enforcement and the Administration of Justice. (1967). *Task force report: The police.* Washington, DC: U.S. G.P.O.

10. American Bar Association. (1956). *American bar association survey of the administration of justice.* Chicago, IL: American Bar Association; President's Commission on Law Enforcement and the Administration of Justice.

(1967). *Task force report: The police.* Washington, DC: U.S. G.P.O.

11. Wilson, J.Q. (1968). *Varieties of police behavior.* Cambridge, MA: Harvard University Press.

12. Goldstein, J. (1960). Police discretion not to invoke the criminal process: Low-visibility decisions in the administration of justice. *The Yale Law Journal, 69,* 543-594.

13. Wilson, J.Q. (1968). *Varieties of police behavior.* Cambridge, MA: Harvard University Press, p. 7.

14. Davis, K.C. (1969). *Discretionary justice.* Baton Rouge, LA: Louisiana State University Press, p.4.

15. Davis, K.C. (1975). *Police discretion.* St. Paul, MN: West Publishing, p. 1.

16. Preib, M. (2010). *The wagon and other stories from the city.* Chicago, IL: The University of Chicago Press.

17. Preib, M. (2010). *The wagon and other stories from the city.* Chicago, IL: The University of Chicago Press, p. 108.

18. Goldstein, J. (1960). Police discretion not to invoke the criminal process: Low-visibility decisions in the administration of justice. *The Yale Law Journal, 69,* 543-594, p. 543.

19. Skogan, W.G. & Frydl, K. (2004). *Fairness and effectiveness in policing: The evidence.* Washington, DC: The National Academies Press.

20. Brooks, L.W. (1989). Police discretionary behavior: A study of style. In *Critical Issues in Policing: Contemporary Readings,* (ed.) R.G. Dunham & G.P. Alpert (pp. 121-145). Prospect Heights, IL: Waveland Press; Greene, J.R. (2007). *The encyclopedia of police science.* 3rd ed. New York, NY: Routledge; Sherman, L. (1985). Causes of police behavior: The current state of quantitative research. In *The Ambivalent Force,* (ed.) A. S. Blumberg & E. Niederhoffer (pp. 183-195). New York, NY: Holt, Rinehart and Wilson; Skogan, W.G. & Frydl, K. (2004). *Fairness and effectiveness in policing: The evidence.* Washington, DC: The National Academies Press.

21. For a similar argument, See Skogan, W.G. & Frydl, K. (2004). *Fairness and effectiveness in policing: The evidence.* Washington, DC: The National Academies Press.

22. Skolnick, J.H. (1966). *Justice without trail: Law enforcement in a democratic society.* New York, NY: Wiley; Skolnick, J.H. & Fyfe, J.J. (1993). *Above the law: Police and the excessive use of force.* New York, NY: Free Press; Wilson, J.Q. (1968). *Varieties of police behavior.* Cambridge, MA: Harvard University Press.

23. Boydstun, J.E. & Sherry, M.E. (1975). *San Diego community profile: Final report.* Washington, DC: Police Foundation; Brown, M.K. (1981). *Working the street: Police discretion and the dilemma of reform.* New York, NY: Russell Sage Foundation; Murphy, P.V. & Pate, T. (1977). *Commissioner: A view from the top of American law enforcement.* New York, NY: Simon and Schuster; Skolnick, J.H. & Fyfe, J.J. (1993). *Above the law: Police and the excessive use of force.* New York, NY: Free Press.

24. Ostrum, E., Park, R.B., & Whitaker, G. (1978). *Patterns of metropolitan policing.* Cambridge, MA: Ballinger; Mastrofski, S. (1981). Policing the beat: The impact of organizational scale on patrol officer behavior in urban residential neighborhoods. *Journal of Criminal Justice, 9,* 343-358; Brown, M.K. (1981). *Working the street: Police discretion and the dilemma of reform.* New York, NY: Russell Sage Foundation.

25. Skogan, W.G. & Frydl, K. (2004). *Fairness and effectiveness in policing: The evidence.* Washington, DC: The National Academies Press.

26. Ostrum, E. (1973). Does local community control of police make a difference?—Some preliminary findings. *American Journal of Political Science, 17,* 48-76; Ostrum, E., Park, R.B., & Whitaker, G. (1978). *Patterns of metropolitan policing.* Cambridge, MA: Ballinger.

27. Liederbach, J. & Frank, J. (2006). Policing the big beat: An observational study of county level patrol and comparisons to local small town and rural officers. *Journal of Crime and Justice, 1,* 21-44.

28. Brown, M.K. (1981). *Working the street: Police discretion and the dilemma of reform.* New York, NY: Russell Sage Foundation.

29. Brooks, L.W. (1989). Police discretionary behavior: A study of style. In *Critical Issues in Policing: Contemporary Readings,* (ed.) R. G. Dunham and G.P. Alpert (pp.121-145). Prospect Heights, IL: Waveland Press.

30. Novak, K.J., Frank, J., Smith, B., & Engle, R. (2002). Revisiting the decision to arrest: Comparing beat and community officers. *Crime & Delinquency, 48,* 70-98.

31. Reiss, A.J. Jr. (1971). *The police and the public.* New Haven, CT: Yale University Press; Walker, S. & Katz, C. (2012). *The police in America: An introduction.* New York, NY: McGraw Hill.

32. Skogan, W.G. & Frydl, K. (2004). *Fairness and effectiveness in policing: The evidence.* Washington, DC: The National Academies Press.

33. Brown, M.K. (1981). *Working the street: Police discretion and the dilemma of reform.* New York, NY: Russell Sage Foundation; Reuss-Ianni, E. (1983). *Two cultures of police.* New Brunswick, NJ: Transaction Books; Skolnick, J.H. (1966). *Justice without trail: Law enforcement in a democratic society.* New York, NY: Wiley; Skolnick, J.H. & Fyfe, J.J. (1993). *Above the law: Police and the excessive use of force.* New York, NY: Free Press.

34. Wilson, J.Q. (1968). *Varieties of police behavior.* Cambridge, MA: Harvard University Press; Rossi, P., Burke, R., & Edison, B. (1974). *The roots of urban discontent: Public policy, municipal institutions, and the ghetto.* New York, NY: Wiley; Wilson, J.Q & Boland, B. (1978). The effect of the police on crime. *Law and Society Review, 12,* 367-390.

35. Jackson, A.L. & Boyd, L.M. (2005). Minority-threat hypothesis and the workload hypothesis: A community-level examination of lenient policing in high crime communities. *Criminal Justice Studies, 18,* 29-50; Skogan, W.G. & Frydl, K. (2004). *Fairness and effectiveness in policing: The evidence.* Washington, DC: The National Academies Press; Smith, D. (1986). The neighborhood context of police behavior. In *Crime and Justice: Annual Review of Research.* Vol. 8, Ed. A. Reiss and M. Tonry. Chicago, IL: University of Chicago Press; Swanson, C. (1978). The influence of organization and environment on arrests policies in major U.S. cities. *Policy Studies Journal, 7,* 390-418; Terrill, W. & Reisig, M.D. (2003). Neighborhood context and police use of force. *Journal of Research in Crime and Delinquency, 40,* 291-323; Wilson, J.Q. (1968). *Varieties of police behavior.* Cambridge, MA: Harvard University Press.

36. Sampson, R. & Lauristen, J. (1997). Racial and ethnic disparities in crime and criminal justice in the United States. In *Ethnicity, Crime and Immigration: Comparative and Cross National Perspectives,* (ed.) M. Tonry (pp. 311-374). Chicago, IL: University of Chicago Press; Skogan, W.G. & Frydl, K. (2004). *Fairness and effectiveness in policing: The evidence.* Washington, DC: The National Academies Press.

37. Fyfe, J.J. (1980). Geographic correlates of police shooting: A microanalysis. *Journal of Research in Crime and Delinquency, 17,* 101-113; Geller, W. & Karales, K. (1981). Shootings of and by Chicago police: Uncommon crises: Part 1. Shootings by Chicago police. *Journal of Criminal Law and Criminology, 72,* 1813-1866; Kania, R.E. & Mackey, W.C. (1977). Police violence as a function of community characteristics. *Criminology, 15,* 27-48; Mastrofski, S. (1981). Policing the beat: The impact of organizational scale on patrol officer behavior in urban residential neighborhoods. *Journal of Criminal Justice, 9,* 343-358; Skogan, W.G. & Frydl, K. (2004). *Fairness and effectiveness in policing: The evidence.* Washington, DC: The National Academies Press;

38. Terrill, W. & Reisig, M.D. (2003). Neighborhood context and police use of force. *Journal of Research in Crime and Delinquency, 40,* 291-323, p. 306.

39. Reaves, B. (2010). *Local police departments, 2007.* Washington, DC: Bureau of Justice Statistics.

40. Sherman, L. (1985). Causes of police behavior: The current state of quantitative research. In *The Ambivalent Force,* (Ed.) A.S. Blumberg & E. Niederhoffer (pp. 183-195). New York, NY: Holt, Rinehart and Wilson.

41. Coupe, T. & Griffiths, M. (1999). The influence of police actions on victim satisfaction in burglary investigations? *International Journal of the Sociology of Law, 27,*413-431; Decker, S. (1981). Citizen attitudes toward the police: A review of past findings and suggestions for future policy. *Journal of Police Science and Administration, 9,* 80-87; Reisig, M.D. & Chandek, M.S. (2001). The effects of expectancy disconfirmation on outcome satisfaction in police-citizen encounters. *Policing: An International Journal of Police Strategies and Management, 21,* 88-99.

42. Black, D. (1970). The production of crime rates. *American Sociological Review, 35,* 733-748; Reiss, A.J. Jr. (1971). *The police and the public.* New Haven, CT: Yale University Press; Ricksheim, E.C. & Chrmak, S.M. (1993). Causes of police behavior revisited. *Journal of Criminal Justice, 21,* 353-382.

43. Black, D. (1980). *The manners and customs of the police.* New York, NY: Academic Press.

44. Friedrich, R.J. (1980). Police use of force: Individuals, situations, and organizations. *Annals of the American Academy of Political and Social Science, 452,* 82-97; Reiss, A.J. Jr. (1971). *The police and the public.* New Haven, CT: Yale University Press.

45. Friedrich, R.J. (1980). Police use of force: Individuals, situations, and organizations. *Annals of the American Academy of Political and Social Science, 452,* 82-97; Smith, D. & Visher, C. (1981). Street level justice: Situational determinants of police arrest decisions. *Social Problems, 29,* 167-178.

46. Black, D. & Reiss, A.J. Jr. (1967). *Studies of crime and law enforcement in major metropolitan areas.* Washington, DC: U.S. GPO; Reiss, A.J. Jr. (1971). *The police and the public.* New Haven, CT: Yale University Press; Lundman, R.J. (1974). Routine police arrest practices: A commonweal perspective. *Social Problems, 22,* 127-141; Lundman, R.J. (1996). Demeanor and arrest: Additional evidence from previously published data. *Journal of Research in Crime and Delinquency, 15,* 74-91; Westley, W.A. (1970). *Violence and the police: A sociological study of law, custom, and morality.* Cambridge, MA: The MIT Press; Worden, R.E. (1989). Situational and attitudinal explanations of police behavior: A theoretical reappraisal and empirical assessment. *Law and Society Review, 23,* 667-711.

47. Roy, A. (2014). On officer video cameras: Examining the effects of police department policy and assignment on camera use and activation. Unpublished thesis, Arizona State University. Retrieved online at http://urbanaillinois.us/sites/default/files/attachments/officer-video-cameras-roy.pdf

48. Crank, J. & Caldero, M. (1999). *Police ethics: The corruption of noble cause.* Cincinnati, OH: Anderson Publishing; Parks, R. (1982). Citizen surveys for police performance assessment: Some issues in their use. *Urban Interest, 4,* 17-26.

49. Engle, R.S. (2003). Explaining suspects' resistance and disrespect toward police. *Journal of Criminal Justice, 31,* 475-492; Herbert, S. (1997). *Policing*

50. space: Territoriality and the Los Angeles police department. Minneapolis: University of Minnesota Press.

50. Black, D. (1980). *The manners and customs of the police.* New York, NY: Academic Press; Friedrich, R.J. (1980). Police use of force: Individuals, situations, and organizations. *Annals of the American Academy of Political and Social Science, 452,* 82-97; Lundman, R.J., Sykes, R.E., & Clark, J.P. (1978). Police control of juveniles. *Journal of Research in Crime and Delinquency, 15,* 74-91; Smith, D. (1986). The neighborhood context of police behavior. In *Crime and Justice: Annual Review of Research.* Vol. 8, ed. A. Reiss and M. Tonry. Chicago, IL: University of Chicago Press; Smith, D. & Visher, C. (1981). Street level justice: Situational determinants of police arrest decisions. *Social Problems, 29,* 167-178.

51. Fyfe, J.J. (1980). Geographic correlates of police shooting: A microanalysis. *Journal of Research in Crime and Delinquency, 17,* 101-113; Geller, W. & Karales, K. (1981). Shootings of and by Chicago police: Uncommon crises: Part 1. Shootings by Chicago police. *Journal of Criminal Law and Criminology, 72,* 1813-1866; Martin, S.E. (1990). *On the move: The status of women in policing.* Washington, DC: Police Foundation; Paoline, E.A. & Terrill, W. (2005). The impact of culture on police traffic stop searches: An analysis of attitudes and behavior. *Policing: An International Journal of Police Strategies and Management, 28,* 455-472; Skogan, W.G. & Frydl, K. (2004). *Fairness and effectiveness in policing: The evidence.* Washington, DC: The National Academies Press; Worden, R.E. (1989). Situational and attitudinal explanations of police behavior: A theoretical reappraisal and empirical assessment. *Law and Society Review, 23,* 667-711.

52. Brooks, L.W. (1989). Police discretionary behavior: A study of style. In *Critical Issues in Policing: Contemporary Readings,* (Ed.) R. G. Dunham and G.P. Alpert (pp.121-145). Prospect Heights, IL: Waveland Press; Sun, I.K. & Payne, B.K. (2004). Racial differences in resolving conflicts: A comparison between black and white police officers. *Crime & Delinquency, 50,* 516-541.

53. Dejong, C. (2004). Gender differences in officer attitude and behavior: Providing comfort and support. *Women and Criminal Justice, 15,* 1-32.

54. Bloch, P.B. & Anderson, D. (1974). *Policewomen on patrol.* Washington, DC: Police Foundation; Fyfe, J.J. (1980). Geographic correlates of police shooting: A microanalysis. *Journal of Research in Crime and Delinquency, 17,* 101-113; Geller, W. & Karales, K. (1981). Shootings of and by Chicago police: Uncommon crises: Part 1. Shootings by Chicago police. *Journal of Criminal Law and Criminology, 72,* 1813-1866; Martin, S.E. (1990). *On the move: The status of women in policing.* Washington, DC: Police Foundation; Paoline, E.A. & Terrill, W. (2005). The impact of culture on police traffic stop searches: An analysis of attitudes and behavior. *Policing: An International Journal of Police Strategies and Management, 28,* 455-472; Skogan, W.G. & Frydl, K. (2004). *Fairness and effectiveness in policing: The evidence.* Washington, DC: The National Academies Press; Worden, R.E. (1989). Situational and

attitudinal explanations of police behavior: A theoretical reappraisal and empirical assessment. *Law and Society Review, 23,* 667-711.

55. Klinger, D.A. (1996). More on demeanor and arrest in Dade county. *Criminology, 34,* 61-82; Skogan, W.G. & Frydl, K. (2004). *Fairness and effectiveness in policing: The evidence.* Washington, DC: The National Academies Press; Smith, D. & Visher, C. (1981). Street level justice: Situational determinants of police arrest decisions. *Social Problems, 29,* 167-178.

56. Black, D. (1970). The production of crime rates. *American Sociological Review, 35,* 733-748; Friedrich, R.J. (1980). Police use of force: Individuals, situations, and organizations. *Annals of the American Academy of Political and Social Science, 452,* 82-97; Skogan, W.G. & Frydl, K. (2004). *Fairness and effectiveness in policing: The evidence.* Washington, DC: The National Academies Press.

57. Black, D. (1970). The production of crime rates. *American Sociological Review, 35,* 733-748; Black, D. & Reiss, A.J. Jr. (1967). *Studies of crime and law enforcement in major metropolitan areas.* Washington, DC: U.S. GPO; Eger, R.J., Fortner, C.K., & Slade, C.P. (2015). The police of enforcement: Red light cameras and racial profiling. *Police Quarterly, 18,* 397-413; Klahm, C.F. & Tillyer, R. (2015). Rethinking the measurement of officer experience and its role in traffic stop searches. *Police Quarterly, 18,* 343-367; Skogan, W.G. & Frydl, K. (2004). *Fairness and effectiveness in policing: The evidence.* Washington, DC: The National Academies Press; Smith, D. & Visher, C. (1981). Street level justice: Situational determinants of police arrest decisions. *Social Problems, 29,* 167-178; Weisburd, D. & Majmundar, K. (eds.) (2018). *Proactive policing: Effects on crime and communities.* Washington, DC: The National Academies Press.

58. Black, D. (1970). The production of crime rates. *American Sociological Review, 35,* 733-748; Black, D. & Reiss, A.J. Jr. (1967). *Studies of crime and law enforcement in major metropolitan areas.* Washington, DC: U.S. GPO; Reiss, A.J. Jr. (1971). *The police and the public.* New Haven, CT: Yale University Press; Skogan, W.G. & Frydl, K. (2004). *Fairness and effectiveness in policing: The evidence.* Washington, DC: The National Academies Press.

59. Rossier, M.T. & Terrill, W. (2017). Mental illness, police use of force, and citizen injury. *Police Quarterly, 20,* 189-212; Wood, J.D., Watson, A.C., & Fulambarker, A.J. (2017). The "gray zone" of police work during mental health encounters: Findings from an observational study. *Police Quarterly 20,* 81-105.

60. Dunn, William. (1996). *Boot: An L.A.P.D. Officer's Rookie Year.* New York, NY: William Morrow and Company, Inc., p. 123.

61. Dutta, Sunil. (2014). I'm a cop. If you don't want to get hurt, don't challenge me. *The Washington Post.* (August 19). Retrieved from: http://www.washingtonpost.com/posteverything/wp/2014/08/19/im-a-cop-if-you-dont-want-to-get-hurt-dont-challenge-me/?tid=trending_strip_2

62. Engel, R.S. & Silver, E. (2001). Policing mentally disordered suspects: A reexamination of the criminalization hypothesis. *Criminology, 39,* 225-252; Novak, K.J. & Engel, R.S. (2005). Disentangling the influence of suspects' demeanor and mental disorder on arrest. *Policing: An International Journal of Police Strategies and Management, 28,* 493-512.

63. Skogan, W.G. & Frydl, K. (2004). *Fairness and effectiveness in policing: The evidence.* Washington, DC: The National Academies Press.

64. Black, D. (1970). The production of crime rates. *American Sociological Review, 35,* 733-748; Friedrich, R.J. (1980). Police use of force: Individuals, situations, and organizations. *Annals of the American Academy of Political and Social Science, 452,* 82-97; Skogan, W.G. & Frydl, K. (2004). *Fairness and effectiveness in policing: The evidence.* Washington, DC: The National Academies Press.

65. Black, D. (1970). The production of crime rates. *American Sociological Review, 35,* 733-748; Friedrich, R.J. (1980). Police use of force: Individuals, situations, and organizations. *Annals of the American Academy of Political and Social Science, 452,* 82-97; Skogan, W.G. & Frydl, K. (2004). *Fairness and effectiveness in policing: The evidence.* Washington, DC: The National Academies Press.

66. Casella, R. (2001). *Challenging violence in urban schools.* New York, NY: Teachers College, Columbia University, p. 95; in regard to the mixed findings of the pro-arrest policy, see Egan, N. (2014). The police response to spouse abuse: An annotated bibliography. *Lloyd Sealy Library, John Jay College of Criminal Justice.* Retrieved from: www.lib.jjay.cuny.edu/research/spouse.html

67. Baker, M. (1985). *Cops: Their lives in their own words.* New York, NY: Pocket Books, p. 52.

■ *"Let the modern policeman typify the ideal American by his cheerful and kindly disposition; by his habits and industry, thoughtfulness, truthfulness, neatness, and cleanliness; by his pride in rendering public service; by his earnest efforts to improve his knowledge that he may better serve human kind; by his courteous treatment and sympathetic knowledge of human beings, regardless of their stations in life; by his simple democratic tastes, healthy interests, and strength of character; and by his patriotic devotion to our nation, serve as a model for our future generations."*[1] —*August Vollmer*

Berkeley Police Motorcycle Officers, reflecting the police culture's sense of humor, surfing on their motorcycles.

CHAPTER 8

Culture

After reading this chapter, you will be able to:

1. Understand the concepts of the "blue wall of silence" and the "blue curtain" versus the concept of unconditional loyalty.
2. Define the sociological terms of culture, subculture, and counterculture, and discuss what is meant by a police culture.
3. Explain the two theories of police culture, socialization, and predispositional theories.
4. Detail how police language serves to shape and define the police culture.
5. Describe how danger serves to shape and define the police culture.
6. Identify how authority serves to shape and define the police culture.
7. Explain how solidarity serves to shape and define the police culture.
8. Discuss how death serves to shape and define the police culture.
9. Detail how humor serves to shape and define the police culture.

The words of August Vollmer, describing the ideal police officer of his time, reads very similar to many civic organizations' oaths and laws today. For instance, the Girl Scouts' promise speaks of helping people at all times and their law invokes honesty, fairness, courtesy, and consideration for others.[2] The Boy Scouts' oath also speaks of honor, duty, and keeping physically strong, while the law invokes such values as being cheerful, trustworthy, courteous, and kind.[3] In all instances, these values are the ideal beliefs that each organization works to inculcate in each and every member of the organization. The goal of these oaths and laws, then, is for each member of the organization to realize these values and make them a part of their everyday life, and thus they become identified with the group's organizational culture. Vollmer, who was himself involved in the early years of the Boy Scouts and Girl Scouts movements, wanted these very same ideals to be a part of the police culture in America.

While these values are the ideal tenets of the police culture, like any organization striving to achieve the ideal, we do not always reach them. We are, after all, human. This does not mean that we should stop trying to achieve the ideal, only that the ideal culture and the real culture of an organization may not be in sync. Understanding the true culture of an organization, like the police, helps us to understand many of the attitudes and behaviors exhibited by members of the organization.[4]

There is, however, a caution in this. Very often we may look at an aspect of the police culture as an outsider and come to understand it solely through the outsider's perspective, which often paints the concept in a negative manner. To an insider, a police officer in this case, the concept may make total sense, and they may see it as a positive thing or something, at least, that is neutral as typified by the statement, "that's just how it is." It is important to realize that these behaviors and the values they represent may be understood differently depending upon your viewpoint. There has long been a concept in policing that is referred to as the "**blue wall of silence**" and sometimes the "**blue curtain**."[5] In an investigation into New York Police Department (NYPD) police corruption in the 1990s, a police officer was asked if any fellow officers might report on police corruption. The officer responded, "Never . . . because it was the blue wall of silence. Cops don't tell on cops."[6] All the way across the country, another commission, in the wake of the Rodney King riots, also had a police officer comment that the blue wall of silence "is basically a non-written rule that you do not roll over, tell on your partner, your companion."[7] The central value of the so-called blue wall of silence is loyalty, which begs the question: To whom does a police officer owe his or her loyalty? To the Constitution? To police management? Or to fellow officers?

Clearly, in the face of police corruption or brutality, the blue wall of silence presents a negative behavior, because police officers unwilling to speak on another police officer's criminal behavior or misconduct is very problematic. There is, however, also a neutral perspective on the value of loyalty and that is survival. As police scholar Egon Bittner once wrote, "Policing is a dangerous occupation and the availability of unquestioned support and loyalty is not something officers could readily do without."[8] Police officers patrol alone and often find themselves in situations where they need immediate backup. They need to know that they have the loyalty of the other officers to come to their aid when those times arise. The best way to ensure loyalty is to give it.

There is also a positive perspective on this, as retired police officer Michael Quinn explains. "Over a 30-year career,"

The blue wall of silence is a metaphor for the solidarity among police officers and that cops don't tell on other cops.

he writes, "many cops put their lives on the line for me. They didn't stop to ask if I was right or wrong. They just stepped in, and I wasn't always right. Like every cop, I made mistakes. Cops know that's part of the deal. Many of those willing lifesavers didn't even know me. The mere fact that I carried a badge was enough for them, men and women willing to put their lives on the line for me just because I was a cop. What kind of loyalty does that buy? Simple—it buys unconditional loyalty. That's the kind of loyalty that gives meaning to the heroic acts cops do for the good of others; even when those acts come at a tremendous cost to the officer and his family. And it gives us a reason to be proud of the cops that have made the ultimate sacrifice."[9]

Unconditional loyalty is something we all seek in our lives, but we find it difficult when the question "to whom are we more loyal" arises. Are you more loyal to your loved ones such as a girlfriend/boyfriend, fiancé, or spouse? Your friends? Or, are you more loyal to your colleagues at work? And what happens when your loyalty gets challenged and you have to pick to whom you are most loyal? Are you more loyal to your family or your job? The decision becomes difficult, and so it is with police officers. For most of us, however, it is about relationships. For police officers, it may be about their life.

This chapter discusses the concept of culture and subculture both in general and how it also applies specifically to the police culture. Then it explores many of the different themes that are commonly present when it comes to the police culture in America (see Box 8.1).

Culture and Subculture

When we speak of the word **culture**, it consists of a wide array of definitions and concepts. We often talk of popular culture, high culture, and food culture.

In all of these cases we are talking about nurture, rather than nature; we are talking about those things that a group of people share in common socially. These are the beliefs, values, customs, mores, folkways, and norms which compose the commonly acceptable behaviors of our modern-day society. The field of sociology often looks at culture and its impact upon our lives.[10] Two of the most readily identifiable representations of a culture are language and food. If you travel to another country, you will usually find both the language and the food to be the most visible and constant experiences that tell you that you are in a different culture. This strange experience is often referred to as culture shock.

Members of the New York State Police marching in a parade. Their unique dress uniform, hat, Sam Brown belt, and sidearm all convey aspects of their unique police culture.

Box 8.1 History in Practice: Wyatt Earp, Bat Masterson, and the Law in the Wild West

Whenever people think of the quintessential lawman in history, thoughts often go back to the Wild West and the frontier marshal or sheriff. The Wild West holds a special place in American history, where tough men brought law and order to the frontier. Television shows such as *Gunsmoke*, along with movies like *Tombstone* have long depicted the lawmen of the West. While we now know that many of these legends were more fiction than truth, the image of the frontier lawman still shapes perceptions of the law and order culture in America. The real lawmen of the West, such as **Wyatt Earp** and **Bat Masterson**, helped form and shape this picture of what a traditional American lawman was like. In the 1870s, Wyatt Earp and Bat Masterson both served as assistant marshals in Dodge City, Kansas (the home of Marshal Dillon from *Gunsmoke)*, and served together as deputy sheriffs in Ford County, Kansas. There is a famous picture of the two of them together, with Earp wearing a cloth pin-on badge. Masterson became sheriff, but, after losing reelection, moved to Colorado, where he worked as a marshal and a sheriff. He was also involved in the Dodge City War in 1883.

After Wyatt Earp left Dodge City, he went to Tombstone, Arizona, where he became a deputy sheriff, and his brother Virgil eventually became the town marshal. When the Clantons, who were part of a group of cattle smugglers and horse thieves known as the Cowboys, clashed with the Earp Brothers, Wyatt was deputized to help deal with the problem. This led to the famous 1881 gunfight at the O.K. Corral, a staple of Hollywood portrayals of the Old West.

While both Wyatt Earp and Bat Masterson are remembered for their days in law enforcement, the number of men they killed, and the legends they created of the Western lawman, in reality, both were also drifters, gamblers, and men who held a wide array of positions and operated businesses throughout their lives. Yet, it is for their tough lawman persona that they have become forever known as policing pioneers.

Culture is typically, although not always, equated with a society. For instance, we experience the German culture in Germany and the Italian culture in Italy. In the United States, we talk of experiencing the American culture. Within each culture, however, we also find that there are groups of people, living in that society, who do things that are a bit different, and often very odd to the majority of people. There is a name for these types of groups, depending on their circumstances, and we call them a subculture or a counterculture. A **subculture** is a group of people within the larger culture that have their own way of doing things, their own shared norms, but they still are part of and exist within the larger culture.[11] One of the best examples commonly used are Trekkies—people who share an interest and passion for the television show and movies of *Star Trek*. While Trekkies may attend *Star Trek* conferences, speak Klingon, and dress as their favorite characters, most of these people are normal in every other way because they share in the larger culture's norms, values, and beliefs.

There is another subgroup, a **counterculture**, which has its own norms, values, and beliefs, but their ways of doing things contradict and challenge the larger cultures' norms.[12] These groups, having their own self-identity, tend to live isolated from the larger society and often come into conflict over its ways of doing things. One example are groups that engage in very different marriage arrangements, such as polygamists, who come into conflict with the monogamy laws and norms of the larger society. This, then, is a counterculture.

The police are actually a subculture of the greater society, because while they identify with the norms of the larger society and its culture, they often have their own ways of speaking (for example, ten-codes), norms (for example, carrying guns), and ways of doing things. Very often, however, the terms police culture and police subculture are used interchangeably, and they are both correct. The former addresses those unique norms, values, and beliefs of police officers, while the latter discusses policing as a part of the larger culture, with its own unique ways of interacting. As both are correct, Chapter 8, for simplicity sake, refers to *police culture*.

One way of thinking about the police culture is to think about the nature of police officers. When a person meets a police officer on the East Coast or West Coast, from the North or the South, from a large metropolitan city or a small town, are there certain traits that all of these officers share in common? Very often people will answer the uniform, the badge, and the gun, and they are representative of the shared culture. But what about attitude and behavior? Do most police officers act in a similar manner? When we explore commonalities among police officers from the over 18,000 different agencies, what many researchers have found is what has come to be known as the police personality (see Box 8.2).

The **police personality** is the shared attitudes and behaviors of police officers, regardless of what police department the officer works for.[13] After James Q. Wilson identified the three styles of policing of police departments, researchers in the 1970s and 1980s became very interested in knowing if there were different styles of police officers.[14] Most of these studies resulted in the use of very different terms for different police personalities, but they still appeared to somewhat reflect the three styles of the departments (see Table 8.1).[15] Collectively, these studies all reached the conclusion that the styles of police officers are commonly derived from three sources: the organization itself, the process of police socialization (nurture), and a predisposition to policing (nature). Thus, there are two key theories about the police personality, and they are the socialization theory and the predisposition theory.

The **socialization theory** perspective of policing looks at the shared experiences of every police officer, typically focusing on the socialization process that all police officers go through, from the hiring process to training, to working the street and moving through the ranks.[16] Within the socialization process, there are really two different types of socialization studied, the formal and the informal.[17] Studies of **formal socialization** look at the formal rules and regulations, training, and the management and organization's influence over shaping the police officer's personality. Studies of **informal socialization** address the personal interactions between peers, between officers of differing ages and experience, and other interactions that are not part

> ## Box 8.2 Policing in Practice: Police Camaraderie in Police Culture
>
> Police officers, regardless of where they work, share attitudes and behaviors. This **police personality** is often portrayed in popular media.
>
> Writer, producer, and director David Ayer produced a very popular movie in 2001 titled *Training Day,* about police corruption. The movie was so far to the extreme regarding police corruption that it was an utterly implausible story with an anticop view of policing, but the movie was well received. After the success of *Training Day,* Ayer wanted to write, produce, and direct a movie that was pro-police, because he grew up in Los Angeles and had many friends who were LAPD officers. The resulting film was *End of Watch*, which was released in 2012. Like the story of *Training Day, End of Watch* also has
>
> a far-fetched plot about two officers and their encounters, but a bit more toned down.
>
> What Ayer did manage to get entirely accurate was the interplay between the two police officers and the camaraderie they shared. The constant banter, the put-downs and derogatory one-liners, and the constant insults were entirely accurate. This is how police relate with one another within the **police culture**. In addition, the true friendship of the two officers, their willingness to put their lives on the line for each other, and the fact the two officers were portrayed as honest and ethical police officers trying to survive an occupation surrounded by danger and death demonstrated many of the aspects of the policing culture, including authority, humor, but especially the element of solidarity.

Table 8.1   Styles of Policing

Author	Watchman	Legalistic	Service	Other
Wilson (1968)	Watchman	Legalistic	Service	
Coats (1972)	Community	Task officer	Service	Abusive
White (1972)	Tough cop	Rule applier/ Crime fighter	Problem solver	
O'Neill (1974)	Watchman	Crime fighter/ Law enforcer	Social agent	
Muir (1977)	Professional	Enforcer	Reciprocator	Avoider
Broderick (1977)	Realist	Enforcer	Idealist	Optimist
Brown (1981)	Professional	Crime fighter	Helper	Avoider
Hatting et al. (1983)	Blue-collar	True blue		Jaded blue
Walsh (1984)	Low-arrest	High-arrest	Medium-arrest	No arrest

of the formal police education process. Research has demonstrated that both of these factors contribute to the shaping of the police personality and police culture.

The **predispositional theory** of policing focuses on the personality traits and innate qualities of a person that makes them attracted to policing.[18] In this case, researchers argue that the police personality already exists in certain individuals, and this is why they are attracted to the police profession. The predisposition itself can be either biological or social, as well as potentially both, but that the personality is developed before the individual applies to the police department.

This raises a key question that is often debated in the literature, which is usually framed as being the socialization theory versus the predispositional theory. Many researchers appear to be arguing that it is either one or the other that explains the police personality and, hence, police culture. They treat it as a zero-sum game. In reality, however, there is plenty of evidence that certain individuals with certain personality traits are attracted to policing and upon becoming a police officer they develop the police personality more fully through the socialization process. Simply put, it is both nature and nurture. In addition, there is often a debate over whether the police personality leads to the police culture or if the police culture leads to the police personality. This unto itself is a chicken-versus-egg controversy—in reality, there is evidence that both of these clearly influence each other.

Themes of the Police Culture

To develop a better understanding of **police culture**, much of the research into this area focuses on a variety of adjectives to describe the police personality and culture.[19] The words that are often used are authoritarian, suspicious, cynical, hostility, and insecurity. As you can tell from the list, the words used to describe the police personality often have a negative connotation. Compare them to the words used by August Vollmer in the opening quote of this chapter to describe the ideal police officer, and you can see the difference. He uses words such as "cheerful," "kind," "thoughtful," "truthful," and "courteous." A very different list indeed. Equally, the words or themes used to describe the police culture can also have a negative connotation as well. The themes often include dangerousness, coercion, solidarity, and death. The rest of this chapter explores these many themes to more fully understand the police culture (see Box 8.3).

Language

There are two great ways to understand any culture in the world: learn the language and experience the food. When it comes to understanding the police there is little difference, although while I recommend learning **police language**, I would not recommend the food (for example, fast-food, doughnuts, bad coffee). John Crank, in his book *Police Culture,* notes that "language is critical to understanding the life of any group," and so it is with the police.[20] Police officers have a language all their own and learning that language often gives contextual insights into their world.[21]

Box 8.3 Policing in Practice: Firearms

One of the most important pieces of equipment police officers carry is their **firearm**. Starting with Teddy Roosevelt's adoption of the Colt New Police Revolver in a .32 caliber, American policing began standardizing the police department's weapon of choice. In 1907, the NYPD converted to the Colt Police Positive .38 caliber, while many other police departments adopted the Smith & Wesson Police Special, also a .38 caliber. For most of the twentieth century, these were the preferred sidearm of American law enforcement.

In the late twentieth century, however, policing began to move to the semi-automatic pistols as these supposedly provided more firepower and more rounds (up to 15 round magazines versus the 6 rounds carried in a revolver). The early adoptions by the police focused on the Glock 17 and the Beretta 92 which was featured in cop movies for "the look." Since then, the variety of firearms in policing has skyrocketed with many police departments authorizing multiple weapons that their officers may carry.

Source: National Gun Violence Research Center & Police Executive Research Forum. (2015). *Police Department Service Weapon Survey.* Retrieved from http://www.police-forum.org/assets/docs/Free_Online_Documents/Gun_Violence_Reduction/police%20department%20service%20weapon%20suvey%202013.pdf.

Not long ago, one of the first things a new police recruit had to learn and memorize was the ten-codes. The ten-codes were developed in 1937 by Charles "Charlie" Hopper, the communications director for the Illinois State Police, to minimize air time back when radio technology used vacuum tubes and there was a slight delay in transmitting, hence the reason for prefacing each code with "ten."[22] New police officers had to learn the ten-codes, which were usually prefaced with the number ten and followed by, in many places, one through one hundred. The problem was not every police department used the same ten-codes. For me, a 10-10 was a fight call and a 10-13 was an "officer needs assistance" call. I know in other departments a 10-10 was a police officer marking out of service and a 10-13 was a weather or road condition report. Imagine my concern when in another department a 10-13 call went out and all they really wanted was a weather report! (see Table 8.2).

In addition, learning the ten-codes was difficult for some new officers and so the reason for the ten-codes—a sort of shorthand method of communication—often ended up causing communication problems. As a result, many departments in the United States have begun moving toward the use of "plain language." So rather than saying, "2Adam80, what is your 10-20?" Officers will now say, "2Adam80, what is your location?"[23] This has become somewhat of a trend in policing for the Virginia State Police abandoned the codes in 2006 and the Maryland State Police in 2010.[24] Not all officers are happy with the change, for while they may argue it takes away their shorthand communication, it in many ways diminishes the police subculture. To show the response among some police officers to plain language, Officer Gallo told the story of a Los Angeles Police Officer visiting Chicago who

Table 8.2	Varying Police Ten-Codes in Virginia		
Ten-Code	Virginia State Police	Hampton PD	Arlington County PD
10-1	Injury to VSP personnel	Call headquarters	Poor reception
10-2	Lost/found property	Location	Good reception
10-3	Lost/found person	Report to headquarters	Stop transmission
10-4	Affirmative	Affirmative	Affirmative
10-5	Relay	Short break	Relay message
10-6	Busy	Lunch break	Change channel
10-7	Out of service	Off duty	Out of service
10-8	In service	On duty	In service
10-9	Repeat	Investigating vehicle	Repeat
10-10	Negative	Drunk driver	Fight call
10-11	On duty	Out of service–HQ	Visitor can hear
10-12	Standby	Out of service–court	Advise weather
10-13	Existing conditions	Drunk	Officer needs assist

was puzzled by the lack of a ten-code system and wanted to know how she told the dispatcher she was going to lunch. Her reply: "We say, 'We're going to lunch.'" The L.A. officer, not quite comprehending said, "Wow! That's so *weird*!"[25] (see Box 8.4).

In other cases, police often use certain slang or shorthand terms to convey information. In New York City a "perp" is short for perpetrator, "bracelets" are handcuffs, and an arrest is a "collar."[26] In many departments the police car is a "cruiser," the paddy wagon for transporting prisoners is "the wagon," and the side-handled baton is the "PR-24." In Chicago, terms are a bit different, for according to Officer Gallo, "Nobody calls the bad guy 'the perpetrator' . . . Why complicate things? The bad guy is called 'the bad guy' or for report writing, the 'offender.' The police car is a squad . . . prisoners are transported via 'squadrol' or, if you are on the South side, a 'paddy wagon.'"[27] She also notes that Chicago cops used "billy clubs," but that the Chicago Police Department, ever conscious of public relations, was trying to convince the officers to call them "nightsticks."[28] Perhaps the most interesting of Chicago's lingo is the fact that while most police officers refer to the police badge as a "badge" or sometimes, like in Los Angeles, a "shield," in Chicago, Gallo corrects this notion by stating "Chicago cops pin a star on their chest, not a badge or a shield."[29]

To understand the complicated language that has developed within the police culture, Thom Philbin wrote an interesting book titled *Cop Speak,*

Box 8.4 **Ethics in Practice: Snoozing on Duty**

Police officers **work long hours on the job**, often made even longer if they are called into court on their off days, required to work mandatory overtime, or choose to work voluntary overtime. For example, think of an officer who works a 10-hour midnight shift and then must report for court duty an hour after their shift ends. Court duty can often take a good portion of the day. The officer then returns home and has family responsibilities before going to bed. Now, on four hours of sleep, the officer must get up, go to work, and stay up all night working another 10-hour shift. About 2 A.M., when the calls all die down, police officers often pull up to each other for both safety and conversation in order to stay awake. This presents an opportunity for one of the officers to rest, or even take a nap, but that can present an ethical dilemma.

Ask Yourself:

Should an officer take a nap while the other monitors the radio, waking up the sleeping officer for a call?

Should the officer take the nap, even if the departmental policy says no sleeping on duty? Should the departmental policy be flexible, depending on the circumstances? Discuss your reasoning.

The side of a Chicago Police Department vehicle depicts the "star" that all officers of the Chicago Police Department wear.

which presents an A to Z list of the different words police officers use and their meaning.[30] Some of his examples include "airmail," which to some police officers describes when someone hurls a brick or rock from a rooftop at a passing police car, or how some departments call an arrest a collar, fall, keeper, or pinch.[31] The ten-codes, shorthand, acronyms, or slang terms that police officers use to mean certain things does not really matter. What does matter is that new police officers, if they are to be part of the policing subculture, must learn their department's specific language. By embracing the terms and using the language of their fellow officers, it helps them to identify as a police officer and with other police officers, thus becoming part of the police subculture. As a retired New York City police sergeant explained police lingo, "It is part of the lifeblood of the department because the department relies on communication."[32]

Danger

Beyond language, the one theme that appears to be most commonly discussed in the police culture and is considered to be the one at the core of shaping what has been called the "working personality of police officers" is the element of **danger** inherent within the job.[33] The element of danger generates a situation where officers must face the unknown and be prepared for the unexpected, always knowing that each call or encounter could present a threat.

While the vast majority of police calls-for-service do not, in fact, present real danger, every call presents the potential for danger. This is what Cullen and his colleagues refer to as the "paradox of danger."[34] In the scheme of things, policing is not one of the most hazardous jobs in the United States, but it has one of the greatest potentials for violence. Either way, however, the presence of danger, both real and perceived, helps to shape the police culture.

Although occupationally, policing may be a relatively low hazard job, Police officers will, in the course of their career, face real danger, and they will have to respond with the use of their authority and potentially force to gain control. Police scholar Jerome Skolnick described it in this manner: "the policeman's role contains two principal variables, danger and authority, which should be interpreted in the light of a 'constant' pressure to appear efficient. The elements of danger seem to make the policeman especially attentive to signs indicating a potential for violence and lawbreaking."[35] Police Officer Alley Evola says the same thing, but in a different way, when she explains:

> "As a police officer, you will, if you do the job long enough, have your life threatened. You will be placed in life-threatening positions, and you will step into harm's way in the defense of another. That's the gig, like it or not. You will be exposed to crimes of violence before, during, and after the fact, again, again, and again. That too, is what you signed up for." [36]

Again, police officers know there is always a potential for danger because calls that appear to be simple, such as a call for a stranded motorist, can turn into a deadly force encounter. This constant vigilance, however, toward suspecting potential violence on every call, develops a certain personality trait within all officers, and that is suspicion.

As Skolnick explains, police officers always being attentive to danger makes them naturally suspicious. "As a result, the policeman is generally a 'suspicious person,'" and the outcome of this is "the character of the policeman's work makes him less desirable as a friend since norms of friendship implicate others in his work. Accordingly the element of danger isolates the policeman socially from that segment of the citizenry whom he regards as symbolically dangerous and also from the conventional citizenry with whom he identifies."[37] In other words, the police officers becomes suspicious of everyone except other police officers, and they become more isolated. Thus, danger shapes the police culture in many ways.

One only has to look on Google for videos of police officers facing violence by searching the terms "dangers of policing" (see Box 8.5). Again, while rare, they highlight how extremely violent and dangerous policing can be, and once police officers experience these encounters or know of others who experience these encounters, a healthy fear of the unknown and suspicion become part of the everyday culture of the police officer. One LAPD officer interviewed about the dangers of policing highlighted a fellow officer and academy classmate who died, then added, "I know a lot of officers in my class who have been shot or died. I just had another classmate die a

Box 8.5 Policing in Practice: Police Danger and the Officer of the Year

Police officers never know what type of danger they will face on the street. One only has to ask Officer Mark Dallas of the Dixon, IL, Police Department, who was awarded the **2018 Officer of the Year Award** by the International Association of Chiefs of Police and Target.

On May 16, 2018, at 8 A.M., Matthew Milby, Jr., a 19-year-old, entered Dixon High School and shot at physical education teacher Andrew McKay in the hallway, outside the gym where all seniors were gathered. Hearing the gunshots, Officer Dallas was then able to respond, as President Donald Trump said when presenting him the award, "within — listen to this — seconds." Officer Dallas then exchanged fire with the suspect, striking him in the hip and right shoulder. He then chased him down, placing him in custody.

Source: IACP (2018). *Officer of the year.* Retrieved from: https://www.theiacp.org/2018-iacptarget-police-officer-of-the-year.

month ago in a traffic collision."[38] This becomes the reality of policing, and it is for this reason the police culture develops as it does. Chicago Officer Gina Gallo explains it this way, "Cops are out here, on the line, dealing with human behaviors that run the gamut from mildly eccentric to clinically certifiable. The only thing we know that's absolute is to expect the unexpected. And live with the knowledge that sometimes . . . there's going to be circumstances beyond our control, situations that we might not be able to handle . . . fear of the unknown, fear of our capabilities when it comes to the sticking point."[39]

It is also one of the attractions of the job. There is a sense of excitement in the danger, and police officers know this. For many officers, it is a personal question of whether or not they can handle the danger and can they remain cool, calm, and collected during the crisis. While the danger is often painted in dark terms, police officers in many ways relish being the one who is willing to face the danger because it sets them apart. They become the sheepdogs and not the sheep. As one officer tried to explain it, "Being a policeman is fun, it really is. You deal with danger, and tragedy, and sadness, but it is adventurous, it is interesting, it is exciting, and you spend time with other cops, whom you like."[40] These are the accepted realities of danger in the police culture.

Called to a disturbance at a hotel, Roseburg (Oregon) police officers were shot at by a man who then barricaded himself in a hotel room, creating a standoff. Multiple officers responded, and the road was shut down in front of the hotel.

Authority

As described above in the section on danger, police officers often have to rely on their authority and their ability to use force. In both cases, what police officers are relying upon is their ability to use coercion. While the terms **authority** and **coercion** often have negative connotations to them, police officers use both to gain compliance with suspects they encounter. For instance, if a person is speeding and the officer attempts to pull them over, the lights and sirens of the police-marked car are all methods for getting the citizen to show compliance by pulling over. When officers attempt to make an arrest, they use their authority to tell the person to turn around and put their hands in the air. Again, they are trying to gain compliance through their authority. If the person refuses, they may attempt to use leverage by explaining, "you can do this the hard way or the easy way, either way you are going with me." The use of leverage over someone is a form of coercion. And, if the person runs or resists arrest, the officer will have to use force, another form of coercion.

The concept of coercion is part of the culture of policing, and just wearing the uniform creates a sense of coercion on the part of the police. It should be noted, though, that for nearly every police officer, there is an early period where even that—the wearing of the uniform—is foreign. The first time you put on the uniform, pin the badge to your chest, and strap on the gun plus 30 extra pounds of equipment and look at yourself in the mirror, you don't feel very coercive. In fact, when I put on my uniform for the first time and looked in the mirror, I felt like I was dressing up for Halloween. Yet, the uniform is, in reality, only a symbol of authority, and it will only go so far in helping an officer to gain compliance.

Physical stature is helpful, for those that are tall have long had the ability to instantly gain respect and compliance from others, as well as those who are clearly all muscle. For others without the benefit of these attributes, however, to gain compliance they have to develop a way of communicating their authority to gain compliance. Police officers have to learn to coerce people through their words. This combination of the uniform, physical stature, and communication all comes to create something very important, and that is the command presence.

"Command presence is synonymous with control, and that is why it is so important for police officers," police scholar Joan Barker explains.[41] In interviewing an LAPD officer about asserting their command presence, the officer explained it was to maintain control of a situation. "When you lose control of the situation, that's when people get injured. We're supposed to win. We try to talk to them; it's easier on all of us. We always try that first, but then some people just don't want to comply. I don't know why they don't, but they don't."[42]

Another term that many often apply to command presence is attitude. Even police officers will use the term, for as Officer Gallo explains, "the most important thing about working in the projects, or any high-crime area, is attitude. In cop-speak, that means you have to walk the walk, display an equal mix of confidence and authority."[43] As she sums it up best, "When my workday starts, I become a uniform and an attitude."[44] But the reason for the attitude is not always for a negative reason. It is not to be abusive of people or to demonstrate superiority over everyone they encounter. Rather, it is a way of learning to gain compliance through a mixture of the uniform and attitude so as to not have to use force, because through the uniform and attitude, the officer has already managed to coerce most suspects into compliance.

Solidarity

Another concept that is vastly important in policing and significantly shapes the police culture is **solidarity**. As Crank describes it in his book *Police Culture,* "the loyalty of officers toward their own kind is legendary," and "there are a thousand faces for solidarity: camaraderie, cohesiveness, fealty, the brotherhood, honor, the blue curtain, spirit-de-corps, and brother and sister cops."[45] Officer Osborne of the NYPD in his book *The Job,* gave a good example of solidarity when he said, "[An] old-time instructor at the police academy told us that if you ever get shot or stabbed and need blood, instantly there will be forty thousand cops sticking out their arm and saying, 'Take mine.' It's a good feeling knowing that you belong to a family."[46] That is solidarity. And if danger sets the stage for the police officer attitude, solidarity is what brings them together and defines the importance of loyalty to each other. Danger is what makes solidarity so important in policing.

Anthony Bouza's research into *The Police Mystique* explains the importance of police solidarity. "The sense of 'us versus them' that develops between cops and the outside world forges a bond between cops whose strength is fabled," Bouza explains.[47] "It is called the *brotherhood in blue,* and it inspires a fierce and unquestioning loyalty to all cops, everywhere. It is widened by the dependence cops have on one another for safety and backup."[48] There is a reason for the solidarity and it's the number one goal of policing for police officers: to go home at the end of the shift.[49]

The dangers inherent within policing and the need to protect against these dangers is why the police culture takes officer safety and backups so seriously. Bouza explains it as "the response to a summons to help is a cop's life-line. An 'assist police officer' is every cop's first priority. The ultimate betrayal is for one cop to fail to back up another."[50] In Officer Dunn's book *Boot,* one of the officers during the orientation explained it this way: "We take backups seriously here. When your brother officers need you, you will go. Won't matter how far you are, or what you're doing. You go. If you're eating dinner and a backup comes

One of the most important aspects of the police culture is the concept of solidarity. Because of the dangers of their occupation, officers must be confident in their reliance on each other.

out, you better dump your food and get in your car. If you're sittin' on the toilet, you don't even take the time to wipe your butt. You get in your car and you go. Ain't nothing, and I mean *nothing*, more important than officer safety here."[51]

If one officer breaks that solidarity it can make things dangerous for everyone working the street, but it also make it particularly dangerous for the officer who breaks with solidarity. Officer Gallo explains that "since policing is the ultimate team effort," solidarity is important to all officers.[52] If someone runs counter to this, it is "not a healthy situation to be in, since cooperation—or lack of it—works both ways. If your watch members decide they don't like you, you're out there alone. Call for backup and nobody shows—or, if they do, take a *long* time coming. Get in a street fight, and you'll get the shit kicked out of you before anyone intervenes."[53]

Solidarity also grows over time as part of the life course of a police officer. Initially every officer tries to maintain friendships outside of policing, and nearly every officer ends up drifting away from those friendships because these friends don't understand police officers or policing, they are not part of the team. Barker, in her study of the careers of LAPD officers, explained, "As officers find it more difficult to conduct a social life with their friends from the time before they became officers, they turn more to police friends and police community friends, such as firefighters and nurses."[54] This author also once swore I would not lose my old friends, and slowly, over a period of a few years, I realized that the only people I wanted to hang around were other cops because I never had to explain myself, and I certainly never had to justify myself. That sense of solidarity became not only easy, it became comfortable.

Perhaps in the most tragic of circumstances, when an officer is killed in the line of duty, there is perhaps no greater outpouring or demonstration of police solidarity. When New York Police Officers Wenjian Liu and Rafael Ramos were assassinated in their patrol car, the thousands of police officers who arrived for the funeral, from police departments all across the country, demonstrated their solidarity. In addition to simply being present for the funeral, a symbol that all police officers wear to represent the end of watch of a fellow officer is a black band across their police badge, a sign and symbol of their solidarity with the fallen officer. Having attended the funeral of another murdered police officer, Police Chaplain Shane expresses the element of solidarity at a police funeral in this manner, "Such rituals do not alter the facts nor do they take away the oppressive grief felt by the victim's loved ones. But they do show solidarity and support and it is the right thing to do."[55] Even in death, police solidarity is an important part of the police culture (see Box 8.6).

Death

Although the loss of an officer is a rare experience in policing, dealing with **death** is not. As NYPD Officer Osborne explains, "Cops deal with death on a regular basis, it's a big part of the job, and it's something you learn to get used to."[56] Whether a person is murdered in the street or dies of natural causes at home, the police are called to the scene. In addition to investigating the

Box 8.6 Policing in Practice: Solidarity and Death on the Job

Death is part of the world of policing, and as a result, death becomes part of the police culture. The dangerous nature of the profession builds **solidarity**, an unconditional loyalty to each other. Sadly, never was there a more perfect example of the police culture regarding both death and solidarity than the events following the massacre in Newtown, Connecticut.

On December 14, 2012, at the Sandy Hook Elementary School in Newtown, in what was to have been a gun free zone, Adam Lanza shot and killed 20 children and 6 adult staff members. As the police arrived on scene, Lanza committed suicide. Police officers worked quickly to evacuate hundreds of frightened school children that day and then, even more disturbingly, they had to process a crime scene where 20 children lay dead from gunshot wounds.

Ten days later, it was Christmas. The Newtown Police Department and all of its officers, with the massacre still at the forefront of their minds, were reeling from the tragedy. Then, on Christmas Eve, police officers and deputy sheriffs from surrounding jurisdictions began reporting for duty in Newtown. They had worked together to give the Newtown Police Officers Christmas Eve and Christmas Day off so they could be with their families. Lieutenant Bob Kozlowsky of the Shelton, Connecticut, Police Department said it best, "When something like this happens . . . it's a police thing. We'll always try to help out neighboring towns. Any time there's a tragedy, we'll try our best to lend a helping hand."

Source: CNN. (2012). "It's a Police Thing." Retrieved from http://www.cnn.com/2012/12/24/us/connecticut-newtown-police-holiday/.

cause of death, police officers often have to handle the body and, in some cases, transport the body to the hospital, morgue, or funeral home. Still further, police officers have to deal with another side of death, telling the deceased's love ones of their loss. Someone has to inform the family of their loss, and it is very often that the responsibility is handed to a police officer. Another factor that has to be considered is the nature of the death, for many become routine to the officer, but some stand out for the scope of death and who has died. Dealing with one individual who has died is difficult, but it becomes compounded when there are multiple deaths, such as numerous deaths resulting from a multiple car pile-up or something, albeit rare, like the number of deaths experienced on September 11, 2001 or during Hurricane Katrina. Finally, who dies can have an impact as well. In small town and rural policing, many of the officers know the individual who has died personally, and the death of a child, especially an infant, is always hard, no matter the situation. All of these are reasons why Police Officer Evola matter-of-factly states in her book *So You Want to Be a Cop?* that "if you aren't emotionally ready to respond to these calls or to come face to face with your own issues surrounding mortality, then you don't need to be a police officer."[57]

The most common way in which police officers have to deal with death is usually the report of a DOA (dead on arrival). Each death can present a disturbing reality to the officer. In this author's experience, the female who died alone and was not found until a month later because of the "smell" presents great difficulties in dealing with the bloated body. As NYPD Officer Osborne says about responding to his first homicide, "the smell hit me like a punch in the face. Once you smell it you'll never forget it for the rest of your life."[58] In another case, a female died in her bathtub and the body had absorbed all of the standing water, bloating the body beyond all recognition. Chicago Officer Martin Preib describes these circumstances very well in his book *The Wagon*, when he wrote, "We took the...black bag and spread it next to the body, unzipping it all the way. I positioned myself as her feet and slowly tugged on the blanket, which was stuck to her decayed skin. I turned my head away from her."[59] Officers like Preib find themselves in a position where they have to deal with death, and they cannot refuse, for it is their job, but that notion does not make it any easier. "My partner and I needed more force," Preib continued, "I pulled harder and she unwrapped, her decayed skin ripping from the blanket noisily."[60] He then described the "clumps of hair stuck to the blanket, the smell billowing out of the now-exposed body and secretions on the floor," and you easily understand how difficult this task truly is.[61]

The least common way in which police officers have to deal with death is in the actual taking of a life. Until recently, the FBI tracked some data about officer shootings, but did not have a dedicated database as it does now. *The Washington Post* began tracking the data post-Ferguson, as have others, and the estimates range from 200 to about 1,000 citizens are killed by the police each year. In the majority of these cases, the suspect pulled a gun or knife on the officer and threatened their lives or the life of another. In some cases, the individual was committing what has become known as suicide-by-cop, threatening a police officer with a gun, so the police officers would kill the individual. While many have claimed that the number of police shootings of citizens is out of control, research has demonstrated that the number of police shooting citizens parallels year to year with the number of citizens killing other citizens in self-defense. Still further, while many have the notion police go into their careers to kill someone, this is nowhere close to the truth. Former police officer David Klinger, who later turned police scholar, having had to use deadly force during his police career learned, "From my own experience, discussions with numerous other officers who had also shot people, and reading law enforcement publications, I was keenly aware that police shootings can have a dramatic impact on officers who pull the trigger."[62] In Klinger's research, he specifically found that "officers who are involved in shootings can experience a variety of short- and long-term reactions, such as recurrent thoughts about the incident, a sense of

Death is something that police officers must deal with on a routine basis, thus it is one of the themes of the police culture.

numbness, nausea, sadness, crying, and trouble sleeping."[63] The taking of another's life is not easy for a police officer, and while thankfully rare, it is but another way in which some officers must deal with death.

Whether it is dealing with natural deaths, accidental deaths, murders, or suicides, death is part of the world of policing, and as a result, death becomes part of the police culture. Former police officer Michael Middleton sums it up best when he explains, "Death is a dirty part of the police business, and you hope it won't rub off on you. You become inured to its real impact and significance. By the end of your career, death doesn't mean much anymore, except you're glad it wasn't you."[64] Those very same words were once spoken to Washington, D.C., Police Officer Christopher Archer, when he explained, "I remember once asking a veteran officer how he felt about constantly being confronted with violence and death, and how he responded flatly that after a while you simply become inured to it."[65]

Humor

One aspect of becoming inured to the death that police officers must deal with on a routine basis is finding a means to cope (see Box 8.7). Dwelling on the death and violence can make anyone lose their grip on reality, so a natural way in which to deal with such tragic circumstances is through **humor**. Numerous television shows and movies have depicted this sort of macabre humor, often drawing on the absurd. Chicago Officer Preib, who described his first encounter with a dead body, also detailed later encounters where humor helped alleviate the tension. In one case, he and his partner were looking for the body parts of a newspaper delivery man in an alley. The man had been shot, robbed, and the body burned to cover up the homicide. When Preib found one of the burnt hands, he held it up to his partner and said, "Can I give you a hand?"[66] Or, on another escort of a dead body to the morgue, an irritated morgue attendant asked for the deceased's name. Preib told him to hold on, went to the corpse in the wagon, and came back, shrugging his shoulders, saying, "He won't say."[67]

While most people outside of policing may find the humor in poor taste, as one officer explained, "See, you have ghoulish policemen. I tell you,

---

Box 8.7 **Policing in Practice: Police Humor**

Go to YouTube and type in "Tony Lepore of the Providence Road Island Police Department." Officer Lepore worked as a police officer for more than 27 years, and on his beat he often directed traffic. Office Lepore had a very unique method for directing traffic in Providence, one that is all done in good **humor**.

While you're on YouTube, look for the New Orleans police officer doing The Wobble during Mardi Gras and the break-dancing officer at the Movement music festival in Detroit. These officers keep the peace and their sense of humor as they engage the public.

though. It kind of goes with the territory. See, we have a sense of humor that to somebody who doesn't know cops would seem terribly gruesome. To us, it's extremely funny."[68] By way of example, the officer uses an anecdote to describe what he means. "Back in '72, we had a plane crash," he began, "A plane caught the telephone wires, went down, took down a couple of houses, killed a bunch of people on the plane. . . . One of the victims was decapitated. And what happened was, the ambulance crew got there, they had a young female on it. . . . [the wagon man] holds the head up and says to her, 'Want to take this one?' She screamed and ran off. This brought howls, peals of laughter from the cops. This was the funniest thing they'd ever seen. Now this is sick, but that's how it is with cops."[69]

Early in her career, Officer Gallo was on the receiving end of a call where she and her veteran partner had to transport a severed head to the morgue. Wrapped in paper, she held the head in the seat next to her to prevent it from rolling on the floor. Her partner tried to impart some wisdom about dealing with death and keeping a sense of humor. She said, "You gotta have a sense of humor, girl. Otherwise you ain't gonna make it on this job. I know ain't nothing funny about that," she said, pointing to the wrapped head, "but whoever this person was can't feel it now and you gotta get through the day, so you better lighten up. Else you're gonna go crazy or quit . . . whichever happens first."[70]

One of the most interesting studies into the use of humor by police officers was conducted by Mark R. Pogrebin and Eric D. Poole.[71] In their study they found that these types of humorous exchanges first and foremost allow police officers to share stories, which in turn informs them that these experiences are shared experiences.[72] Further, they found that humor serves as a coping mechanism for police officers to deal with death and violence. Moreover, they also found that humor served as a means of building the social solidarity among police officers. In this case, officers spend much of their time in "mutual ribbing, teasing, or pulling pranks."[73] In fact, as one officer noted to this author, "the more shit they give you, the more they love you."[74]

This was the case with my career. I remember one fellow officer who was a practical joker, as well as a fisherman. He had caught several dozen fish one day, and so when he came to work, he still had eight fish left in his cooler. He hooked them all to a string, tied the string underneath his lieutenant's car, so when the lieutenant drove away, a gang of a dozen stray cats chased his police car all the way down the street. Or, when I responded to a robbery and attempted homicide call, as I was approaching the victim, I was bit on the ankle by a pit bull. I instinctively fired my gun, but missed the dog. The next day in roll call, on the announcement board was a large firing range target with a photo of the dog in the center, and written in large letters at the top was "Oliver's target."

Humor is part of the police culture, and while it may be a biting, sarcastic, and macabre humor, it is the humor of the police culture. Officer Evola explains this is so because "death is difficult and sad" and that "humor is a defense mechanism that allows us to keep going."[75] Regardless of where one serves as a police officer, humor is part of the everyday routine of the police. Perhaps Police Chaplain Shane explained it best when he noted that police "often use humor to break the tension and keep perspective. It is not a matter of ridicule or laughing at victims at all. It is finding a way to lighten the load so that one will not be crippled with the burdens of helping others in difficult times."[76]

Conclusion

John Crank, in his book on *Police Culture*, opens his prologue with a quote he read off of a police officer's t-shirt: "It's a Cop Thing: You Wouldn't Understand." The quote sent him on the path of exploring the police culture, but it also serves nicely to sum up the concept of the police culture. Whether people with the police personality gravitate to the profession (predispositional theory) or whether the police personality is made (socialization theory), police officers have their own unique culture that one has to be a police officer to fully understand and appreciate. The themes or factors that help shape and create the police culture are numerous, but some of the core ones have been detailed in this chapter: language, danger, solidarity, death, and humor. Each of these themes is not isolated from one another, for they all weave together to form the tapestry that describes the police culture; it describes what it means to be a cop.

Just the Facts

1. The "blue wall of silence" and the "blue curtain" are terms often used to describe police loyalty to one another, typically presented in a negative light. However, for police officers, due to the nature of their work, they rely upon unconditional loyalty from their fellow officers to know that those officers will be there when they are needed.

2. Culture is the shared values, behaviors, and beliefs of a group of people. A subculture is a group that lives within the larger culture and abides by their norms, but has its own set of shared values, behaviors, and beliefs. A counterculture is a group that does not share the same beliefs as the larger culture, and is its antithesis. A police culture is the shared values, behaviors, and beliefs of police officers, which can also be considered a subculture of the larger American culture.

3. The two theories of the police culture posits that individuals enter policing and are so-

cialized into the police culture, both formally and informally, while the predispositional theory posits that people who already share the same values, behaviors, and beliefs of the police culture are attracted to policing.

4. Police language is a special language, both formal (institutional language) and informal (slang), used by police that helps to identify them as a member of the police culture and serves to shape the police personality and identity.

5. The fact that danger, especially the potential for danger, is an ever present of the realities of policing, serves to shape everything from the police officers' equipment, training, personality, and behaviors, thus helping to form the police culture.

6. The police officer's authority and their ability to use coercion, help to define what it means to be a police officer, and that uniqueness which sets them apart from other occupations helps to shape and define the police culture.

7. The police officers' need for solidarity, an unconditional loyalty to each other, provides the confidence they need to work on the street, and it is that steadfast loyalty to each other that serves to define the police culture.

8. The fact that police must deal constantly with death, whether by citizens dying by violence, accidents, or natural causes, as well as the rare instance of a police officer being killed in the line of duty, is a constant reminder of the grim aspects of the job and an officer's own mortality, thus helping to define the world of the police officer and, hence, the police culture.

9. In need for finding ways of dealing with death and danger, police officers develop a gallows sense of humor, thus this form of jocularity becomes part of the police personality and shapes the police culture.

Ask Yourself

1. Consider the relationship between the sheep and the sheepdog as Lt. Col. Grossman has detailed it (revisit Chapter 1). Is there a relationship between the predispositional theory and the sheepdog? Can sheep be taught to be sheepdogs?

2. To more fully consider what is predispositional and what is socialization, consider your current status (job). For instance, if you are a college student, consider your current beliefs, values, and behaviors. Are they a product of who you were before you came to college or were they things in which you were socialized? Now, consider how the same applies to policing.

3. A police officer is engaged in a pursuit, and you are the follow-on car in the pursuit. The first officer maintains vision of the suspect and drives. Your job is to maintain eye contact on the first officer's vehicle and handle radio chatter. A supervisor comes on the radio and orders both of you to disengage from the pursuit. You turn off you lights and sirens, but the officer in pursuit continues. Do you reengage your lights and sirens to back up your fellow officer or do you do as ordered and return to your beat?

4. Go to YouTube and look for police shoot/don't shoot scenarios, sometimes referred to as use-of-force simulators. Many television crews have reported on this form of police simulation training, and many companies have loaded the actual scenarios onto YouTube for people to watch. Now, after watching one or two, preferably with others, consider the element of danger. Did you perceive a threat? How fast did you react to what you watched? Now consider how danger, or the perceived danger if the scenario was benign, may influence police behavior, the police personality, and police culture?

5. Think about the two types of police academies, those based on a pedagogy/military perspective versus those using andragogy/adult education (see Chapter 5). Now consider how the police culture is shaped from a socialization perspective, both formal and informal, by both types of police academies. Compare and contrast the two types by looking at both the positives and negatives of each style.

Keywords

Authority	Coercion	Danger
Blue curtain	Counterculture	Death
Blue wall of silence	Culture	Formal socialization

Humor

Informal socialization

Police culture

Police language

Police personality

Predispositional theory

Socialization theory

Solidarity

Subculture

Endnotes

1. Vollmer, A. (1921). A practical method for selecting a policeman. *Journal of the American Institute of Criminal Law and Criminology, 11,* 571-581, p.577.

2. Girl Scouts of America. (2015). Homepage. Retrieved from https://www.girlscouts.org/

3. Boy Scouts of America. (2015). Homepage. Retrieved from http://www.scouting.org/

4. Paoline, E.A. III. (2003). Taking stock: Toward a richer understanding of police culture. *Journal of Criminal Justice, 31,* 199-214; Paoline, E.A. III., Myers, S.M., & Worden, R.E. (2000). Police culture, individualism, and community policing: Evidence from two police departments. *Justice Quarterly, 17,* 575-605.

5. Kleinig, J. (2001). The blue wall of silence: An ethical analysis. *International Journal of Applied Philosophy, 15,* 1-23; Skolnick, J. (2002). Corruption and the blue code of silence. *Police Practice & Research: An International Journal, 3,* 7-19; Westmarland, L. (2005). Police ethics and integrity: Breaking the blue code of silence. *Policing & Society, 15,* 145-165.

6. Mollen Commission to Investigate Allegation of Police Corruption.(1994). *Commission report.* New York, NY: The Mollen Commission, p.53.

7. Christopher Commission.(1991). *Report of the independent commission to investigate the Los Angeles Police Department.* Los Angeles, CA: City of Los Angeles, p.169.

8. Bittner, E. (1980). *The functions of the police in modern society.* Cambridge, MA: Oelgeschlager, p.63.

9. Quinn, M.(2006).The cost of breaking the code of silence. *Officer.com.* Retrieved from http:// www.officer.com/article/10250500/the-cost-of-breaking-the-code-of-silence

10. Macionis, J.J. (2013). *Sociology.* 15th ed. Upper Saddle River, NJ: Pearson; Ritzer, G. (2014). *Introduction to sociology.* 2nd ed. Thousand Oaks, CA: SAGE.

11. Macionis, J.J. (2013). *Sociology.* 15th ed. Upper Saddle River, NJ: Pearson; Ritzer, G. (2014). *Introduction to sociology.* 2nd ed. Thousand Oaks, CA: SAGE.

12. Macionis, J.J. (2013). *Sociology.* 15th ed. Upper Saddle River, NJ: Pearson; Ritzer, G. (2014). *Introduction to sociology.* 2nd ed. Thousand Oaks, CA: SAGE.

13. Weiss, P.A. (2010). *Personality assessment in police psychology: A 21st century perspective.* Springfield, IL: Charles C. Thomas Publisher.

14. Wilson, J.Q. (1978). *Varieties of police behavior: The management of law and order in eight communities.* Cambridge, MA: Harvard University Press.

15. Broderick, J.J. (1987). *Police in a time of change.* 2nd ed. Prospect Heights, IL: Waveland; Worden, R.E. (1995). Police officers' belief systems: A framework for analysis. *American Journal of Police, 14,* 49-81.

16. Oberfeld, Z.W. (2013). Socialization and self-selection: How police officers develop their views about using force. *Administration & Society, 44,* 702-730; Van Maanen, J. (1973). Observations on the making of a policeman. *Human Organization, 32,* 404-418.

17. Paoline, E.A. III. (2003). Taking stock: Toward a richer understanding of police culture. *Journal of Criminal Justice, 31,* 199-214.

18. Bennett, R. & Greenstein, T. (1975). The police personality: A test of the predispositional model. *Journal of Police Science and Administration, 3,* 439-445; Caldero, M. & Larose, A.P. (2003). Value consistency within the police: The lack of a gap. *Policing: An international journal of police strategies and management, 24,* 162-180.

19. Crank, J.P. (2004). *Understanding police culture.* 2nd ed. Cincinnati, OH: Anderson Publishing.

20. Crank, J.P. (2004). *Understanding police culture.* 2nd ed. Cincinnati, OH: Anderson Publishing, p.25.

21. Crank, J.P. (2004). *Understanding police culture.* 2nd ed. Cincinnati, OH: Anderson Publishing; Cockcroft, T. (2013). *Police culture: Themes and concepts.* New York, NY: Routledge; Van Maanen, J. (1978). The asshole. In P.K. Manning and J. Van Maanen (Eds.), *Policing: A view from the streets,* pp. 221-238. New York, NY: Random House.

22. National Institute of Justice. (2010). 10-4 no more? Law enforcement agencies are phasing out old radio codes. *In Short: Towards Criminal Justice Solutions.* Washington, DC: U.S. Department of Justice.

23. National Institute of Justice. (2010). 10-4 no more? Law enforcement agencies are phasing out old radio codes. *In Short: Towards Criminal Justice Solutions.* Washington, DC: U.S. Department of Justice.

24. Weil, M. (2012). Maryland state police abandon "ten code" radio communications such as "10-4." *The Washington Post,* February 4.

25. Gallo, G. (2001). *Armed and dangerous: Memoirs of a Chicago policewoman.* New York, NY: Forge Book, p.16.

26. Lauinger, J. (2010). The hairbag's guide to NYPD lingo on 'the job.' *New York Daily News.* Retrieved online at *http://www.nydailynews.com/news/crime/hairbag-guide-nypd-lingo-job-article-1.199502*

27. Gallo, G.(2001). *Armed and dangerous: Memoirs of a Chicago policewoman.* New York, NY: Forge Book, p.15.

28. Gallo, G.(2001). *Armed and dangerous: Memoirs of a Chicago policewoman.* New York, NY: Forge Book, p.15.

29. Gallo, G.(2001). *Armed and dangerous: Memoirs of a Chicago policewoman.* New York, NY: Forge Book, p.16.

30. Philbin, T. (1996). *Cop speak: The lingo of law enforcement and crime.* New York, NY: John Wiley & Sons, Inc.

31. Philbin, T. (1996). *Cop speak: The lingo of law enforcement and crime.* New York, NY: John Wiley & Sons, Inc.

32. Lauinger, J. (2010). The hairbag's guide to NYPD lingo on "the job." *New York Daily News.* Retrieved online at *http://www.nydailynews.com/news/crime/hairbag-guide-nypd-lingo-job-article-1.199502*

33. Crank, J.P. (2004). *Understanding police culture.* 2nd ed. Cincinnati, OH: Anderson Publishing; Cockcroft, T. (2013). *Police culture: Themes and concepts.* New York, NY: Routledge; Skolnick, J. (1966). *Justice without trial: Law enforcement in a Democratic society.* New York, NY: Wiley.

34. Cullen, F., Link, B., Travis, L.T., & Lemming, T. (1983). Paradox in policing: A note on perceptions of danger. *Journal of Police Science and Administration, 11,* 457-462.

35. Skolnick, J. (1966). *Justice without trial: Law enforcement in a Democratic society.* New York, NY: Wiley, p.42.

36. Evola, A. (2017). *So you want to be a cop: What everyone should know before entering a law enforcement career.* Lanham, MD: Rowman & Littlefield, p. 109.

37. Skolnick, J. (1966). *Justice without trial: Law enforcement in a Democratic society.* New York, NY: Wiley, p.42.

38. Barker, J.C. (1999). *Danger, duty, and disillusion:The worldview of Los Angeles police officers.* Long Grove, IL: Waveland, p.75.

39. Gallo, G.(2001). *Armed and dangerous: Memoirs of a Chicago policewoman.* New York, NY: Forge Book, p.56.

40. Parker, T. (2011). True stories from a policeman's notebook. Seattle, WA; Createspace, p.61.

41. Barker, J.C. (1999). *Danger, duty, and disillusion: The worldview of Los Angeles police officers.* Long Grove, IL: Waveland, p.70.

42. Barker, J.C. (1999). *Danger, duty, and disillusion: The worldview of Los Angeles police officers.* Long Grove, IL: Waveland, p.70.

43. Gallo, G. (2001). *Armed and dangerous: Memoirs of a Chicago policewoman.* New York, NY: Forge Book, p.79.

44. Gallo, G. (2001). *Armed and dangerous: Memoirs of a Chicago policewoman.* New York, NY: Forge Book, p.83.

45. Crank, J.P. (2004). *Understanding police culture.*2nd ed. Cincinnati, OH: Anderson Publishing, p.237.

46. Osborne, S. (2015). *The Job: True tales form the life of a New York city cop.* New York: Doubleday, p. 21.

47. Bouza, A. (1990). *The police mystique: An insider's look at cops, crime, and the criminal justice system.* New York, NY: Plenum Press, p.74.

48. Bouza, A. (1990). *The police mystique: An insider's look at cops, crime, and the criminal justice system.* New York, NY: Plenum Press, p.74.

49. Gallo, G. (2001). *Armed and dangerous: Memoirs of a Chicago policewoman.* New York, NY: Forge Book.

50. Bouza, A. (1990). *The police mystique: An insider's look at cops, crime, and the criminal justice system.* New York, NY: Plenum Press, p.74.

51. Dunn, W. (1996). *Boot: An L.A.P.D. officer's rookie year.* New York, NY: William Morrow and Company, Inc., p.5.

52. Gallo, G. (2001). *Armed and dangerous: Memoirs of a Chicago policewoman.* New York, NY: Forge Book, p.69.

53. Gallo, G. (2001). *Armed and dangerous: Memoirs of a Chicago policewoman.* New York, NY: Forge Book, p.69.

54. Barker, J.C. (1999). *Danger, duty, and disillusion: The worldview of Los Angeles police officers.* Long Grove, IL: Waveland, p.70.

55. Shane, T.W. (2011) Crisis Pastoral Care: A police chaplain's perspective. Prescott, AZ: Hohm Press, p.86.

56. Osborne, S. (2015). *The Job: True tales form the life of a New York city cop.* New York: Doubleday, p. 50.

57. Evola, A. (2017). *So you want to be a cop: What everyone should know before entering a law enforcement career.* Lanham, MD: Rowman & Littlefield, p. 119.

58. Osborne, S. (2015). *The Job: True tales form the life of a New York city cop.* New York: Doubleday, p. 51.

59. Preib, M. (2010). *The wagon and other stories from the city.* Chicago, IL: The University of Chicago Press, p.4.

60. Preib, M. (2010). *The wagon and other stories from the city.* Chicago, IL: The University of Chicago Press, p.4.

61. Preib, M. (2010). *The wagon and other stories from the city.* Chicago, IL: The University of Chicago Press, p.4.

62. Klinger, D. (2004). *Into the kill zone: A cop's eye view of deadly force.* San Francisco, CA: Jossey-Bass, p.7.

63. Klinger, D. (2004). *Into the kill zone: A cop's eye view of deadly force.* San Francisco, CA: Jossey-Bass, p.7.

64. Middleton, M.L. (2000). *COP: A true story.* New York, NY: MJF Books, p.35.

65. Archer, C.M. (2006). *Miles to go before I sleep: Life, death, and hope on the streets of Washington, DC* Baltimore, MD: PublishAmerica, pp. 45-46.

66. Preib, M. (2010). *The wagon and other stories from the city.* Chicago, IL: The University of Chicago Press, p.24.

67. Preib, M. (2010). *The wagon and other stories from the city.* Chicago, IL: The University of Chicago Press, p.25.

68. Fletcher, C. (1990). *What cops know.* New York, NY: Villard Books, p.43.

69. Fletcher, C. (1990). *What cops know.* New York, NY: Villard Books, p.43.

70. Gallo, G. (2001). *Armed and dangerous: Memoirs of a Chicago policewoman.* New York, NY: Forge Book, p.167.

71. Pogrebin, M.R. & Poole, E.D. (1988). Humor in the briefing room: A study of the strategic uses of humor among police. *Journal of Contemporary Ethnography, 17,* 183-210.

72. Shearing, C.D. & Ericson, R.V. (1991). Culture as figurative action. *The British Journal of Sociology, 42,* 481-506.

73. Pogrebin, M.R. & Poole, E.D. (1988). Humor in the briefing room: A study of the strategic uses of humor among police. *Journal of Contemporary Ethnography, 17,* 183-210.

74. Interview by author with anonymous police officer, May 10, 2014.

75. Evola, A. (2017). *So you want to be a cop: What everyone should know before entering a law enforcement career.* Lanham, MD: Rowman & Littlefield, p. 131.

76. Shane, T.W. (2011). *Crisis pastoral care: A police chaplain's perspective.* Prescott, AZ: Hohm Press, p.185.

■ *"First, we must develop strategy. . . . We must focus our forces on a small area and on a particular problem, and not dissipate it over a wide area."*[1] —*August Vollmer, quoted in 1938*

Poster showing homicides and aggravated assaults hot spots in Kansas City, MO; from the Kansas City Police Department Street Narcotics Unit.

CHAPTER 9

Strategies

After reading this chapter, you will be able to:

1. Describe the three early studies of policing strategies in America and detail their findings.
2. Discuss the broken windows theory and how it applies to American policing.
3. Name and describe the early policing strategies that developed into community policing, then detail how the community policing itself has evolved.
4. List and define the four dimensions of community policing.
5. Describe the underlying concept behind problem-oriented policing, then described how police departments have implemented the concept through the SARA Model.
6. Identify the four primary methods for targeted policing and briefly describe each.
7. Describe the similarities between the policing strategies of CPTED, pulling levers, evidence-based policing, and predictive policing.
8. Summarize what the police strategy Compstat entails.
9. Tell how policing, since the terrorist attacks of September 11, 2001, has become involved in homeland security and identify the many strategies employed as a result.

Although Vollmer was quoted as saying in 1938 that the first thing the police must do is develop a strategy, he was referencing what he had learned when he served as the police chief of the Los Angeles Police Department (LAPD) from 1923 to 1924. The concept that the police should focus on a small area and on a specific problem is today known as hot spots policing, one of the police strategies that "developed" in the late twentieth century. Today in American policing there are many police strategies that are used by the police, and they are the focus of Chapter 9.

To begin, it is important to know that a **strategy** is both a broad set of ideas and a detailed set of plans for achieving a specific goal, usually over an extended period of time. **Police strategies,** then, are a broad set of ideas and a set of plans for achieving the primary goals of the police—reducing crime and disorder. It should also be noted that not all police strategies are equal, and it is certainly not the case that one strategy fits all. In fact, policing scholar Larry Hoover cautions us to also understand that each of these strategies is not a one or the other proposition, for often agencies employ many different police strategies to address the varying problems of crime and disorder in their jurisdiction.[2] Still further, it is very often the case that these police strategies overlap one another and they will sound very similar to each other or they may be implemented together at the same time. For instance, the community policing strategy and problem-oriented policing strategy may be implemented in tandem.

To gain a better understanding of all the various police crime control strategies, Chapter 9 first discusses the development of policing in the twentieth century and the strong belief that the police deter crime; at least that was until various studies were done on policing that challenged this belief. Chapter 9 then explains how policing came to find itself filled with so many different strategies, something that is largely a late twentieth-century phenomenon. Next, Chapter 9 discusses various strategies for deploying officers on the street and then it details many of the most commonly used policing strategies today including community policing, problem-oriented policing, and Compstat, as well as some of the more recently implemented strategies such as pulling levers, evidence-based policing, and intelligence-led policing.

Police Strategy Studies

As policing professionalized and reformed in the early twentieth century, policing in America developed with the intent of addressing the problems of crime through both deterrence and its ability to solve crimes. It was believed that the mere presence of the police deterred both crime and disorder. If a crime did occur, the police were the professionals and the experts and they could quickly solve the crime, first by getting to the scene faster and then by applying their training and technology to the crime. These notions built up over time to become the basic beliefs in policing: police officers deter crime through random patrols; the faster police officers arrive on scene the more likely they are to solve the crime; and given the facts of a case and all of the latest technology the police can solve crimes through their expertise. All of this turned out to be wrong.

In the 1960s with the protests against the Vietnam War, demonstrations over civil and women's rights, and because of campus unrest, many of the old police tactics were not working, nor did they look good to the American public watching them on television for the first time. When parents sent their children off to college, they did not expect to see them beaten by the local police while protesting on campus. Riots in the streets and rapidly rising crime rates caused America to demand change, and since the local and state police seemed to be inadequate, Americans began looking to the federal government. In 1964 during the presidential campaign, the Republican contender, Barry Goldwater, argued for federal intervention, while the incumbent president and Democratic nominee, Lyndon Baines Johnson, initially argued that crime and disorder were local problems. Once Johnson won the election, however, he changed his mind.

President Johnson created a crime commission to look at the problems of crime in America and asked for recommendations for change. When the **President's Commission on Law Enforcement and the Administration of Justice** issued their report, *The Challenge of Crime in a Free Society*, many of their recommendations found their way into the **Omnibus Crime Control and Safe Streets Act of 1968**.[3] This bill added or changed numerous laws and allowed for the expenditure of federal funds to improve local policing. It created criminal justice programs in colleges and universities across America and it helped to fund police officers earning those degrees through a portion of the bill known as the Law Enforcement Education Program (LEEP) funds. The bill also set aside money for police research and highlighted the need for empirical studies in the policing field. For too long, policing had operated on widely held beliefs and not on empirical evidence, and therefore, research was highly encouraged with money to support it.

In 1970, the Ford Foundation decided to create a police development fund to fund scholarly police research. The fund was soon renamed the Police Foundation, an organization that still exists today. The Police Foundation then commissioned what would become one of the first empirical studies in policing that attempted to assess the question of police deterrence. Do police officers driving around the neighborhood, through their mere presence, deter crime? George L. Kelling was the lead researcher, and the study took place between 1972 and 1973, and was published in 1974.[4] What Kelling really wanted to know was whether or not the public would notice changes in the level of police patrols, would the different levels have an impact on crime, would citizens' level of fear of crime change with the levels of police, and would citizen satisfaction change with the various levels of police?

The Kansas City Preventive Patrol Experiment

The Kansas City Preventive Patrol Experiment divided Kansas City into a number of areas and assigned each area one of three treatments. The first of the treatment areas received no routine patrol, and officers were told to stay out of the area unless they received a call from a citizen. For the second treatment areas, police deployment was left unchanged. The police conducted police patrols at the same level of staffing as they always had. The third treatment area, however, would receive two to three times as many police officers as normal. It was anticipated that the areas that received the same treatment would see no change in crime, fear of crime, or citizen satisfaction. In the areas where the police presence was all but removed, they anticipated citizens would notice, both crime and citizen fear of crime would go up, and citizen satisfaction with the police would drop. Finally, the researchers expected in the areas that received two to three times as many officers patrolling, that citizens would notice, crime and fear of crime would drop, and citizen satisfaction would go up. After running this quasi-experiment and analyzing their findings the researchers were stunned to find absolutely no changes. Citizens had not noticed the changes in police levels.[5] Crime rates remained stable in all three areas. Fear of crime and citizen satisfaction with the police did not vary. The impact of this landmark study had police professionals rethinking police deployment, and it solidified for the next 30 years the notion that police do not deter crime (another widely held belief that was not entirely accurate).

Another police study conducted in 1976 by the Kansas City Police Department wanted to assess another long-held belief in policing circles that the faster the police respond to a crime, the more likely the crime will be solved. Policing throughout the twentieth century built up around this assumption by placing police officers on bicycles, motorcycles, and automobiles with the idea of getting officers to the crime scene faster. When the police vehicle became the primary means for police deployment, the emphasis then shifted to making them faster and employing radio communication (and later computers) to allow the officers to receive calls while on routine patrol, affording them the ability to respond to the calls even faster. In addition, to make it easier to call the police for help, the Omnibus Crime Control and Safe Streets Act allocated funds to the city of Baltimore to try out a new idea: 911.

The introduction of the 911 system proved so successful, it rapidly spread to other cities all across the United States. Again, although it was popular and easy to remember, the key to 911 was really for the purposes of ensuring rapid police response. So, following in the footsteps of the Kelling study, the Kansas City Police Department evaluated how successful the rapid response of police was for solving crimes.[6]

Kansas City (Missouri) was instrumental in two of the earliest studies in policing, the Kansas City Preventive Patrol Experiment and the Kansas City Rapid Response Study.

Kansas City Rapid Response Study

What the **Kansas City Rapid Response Study** found was reminiscent of what Kelling had found in the other Kansas

City study. Other than crimes that were actually in progress, there was no increase in the resolution of a crime the faster the police responded to the call. It did not seem to matter if the police responded to a call within a few minutes or in 20 to 30 minutes. Their chances for eventually solving the crime remained the same. The researchers explored why this was the case and found it had to do with the fact that citizens, on average, delayed calling the police by 40 minutes. Meaning that if the police showed up to the crime scene 41 minutes after the crime had occurred or 60 minutes after, it would not make much difference. The issue was not to get police to the crime scene faster, it was to get citizens to call the police immediately after a crime had occurred. Once again, another long held belief in policing circles was contradicted by empirical evidence.

RAND Criminal Investigation Study

Finally, the RAND Corporation conducted a study on police detectives in 1977.[7] The researchers wanted to know how successful police detectives were when it came to solving crimes. It was believed that police detectives, through technology and skill, solved crimes. This was because throughout the twentieth century, the police had learned to adopt technology to crime scene investigations, to use crime labs, autopsy reports, fingerprints, and eventually laser technology to find trace evidence. Then, above and beyond the technology, there was the number of personnel assigned to the detective bureaus and the amount of training and education given to these personnel. In other words, detectives, like patrol officers, took up a large share of a police department's resources. What the RAND Corporation was asked to do by the National Institute of Law Enforcement and Criminal Justice (later renamed the National Institute of Justice) was to find out how successful detectives were at their job. After all, the Kansas City studies found that random patrol and rapid response, long held to be effective, were not.

Most likely you have already figured out what the **RAND Criminal Investigation Study** found. Simply put, they found that detective work was, in reality, superficial, routine, and nonproductive. More specifically, the study found that of all the cases that the detectives investigated, only 2.7 percent of them were cleared through techniques employed by the investigators. In other words, 97.3 percent of all cases handled by detectives were actually solved by the victim, witnesses, or (less frequently) by the police officers arriving on scene, NOT by the detectives. All of the personnel and technology put into enhancing criminal investigations were found to simply serve as a means for moving the case through the system or were primarily used to corroborate what the victims, witnesses, and police officers had already told the detectives. It was only very rarely (2.7 percent of the time) that a detective actually solved the crime!

Think about this. In just three years, from 1975 to 1977, three of the main pillars of policing were knocked down. Police driving around in random patrols did not deter crime (see Box 9.1). Police officers rapidly

> **Box 9.1** **Policing in Practice: Routine Policing**
>
> Despite the fact that three early studies found that the police do not deter crime while driving around in random patrols or solve more crimes through rapid response and criminal investigation personnel and technology, these remain an integral part of the **routines of policing today** for practical reasons. In the reality of routine policing, police officers assigned to beats still typically drive around in random patrols. Even if these patrols in between calls do not deter crime, police officers still detect both crime and traffic violations while doing so. In addition, many police officers visit certain locations and people as part of their routine, and despite the fact it may not deter crime, the people in those locations are usually appreciative.
>
> Police officers also continue to respond rapidly to calls-for-service based on the type of call they receive. While a study found that, on average, police do not solve more crimes by showing up on scene faster, there are still those calls that may be the exception and not the rule, such as a bank robbery in progress or a home burglary where the home owner reports the burglar is still inside the house. For the bank tellers being robbed or the homeowner being burglarized, one can rest assured that they will be happy if the police show up more rapidly.
>
> Finally, another routine of policing is to turn criminal investigations over to the detectives if the case cannot be quickly and easily handled by the patrol officer. Officers need to remain free to take other calls, so this frees officers up to continue their patrols. In addition, criminal investigators perform a valuable function by moving the investigation through the system, much in the same way a victim's advocate helps a victim navigate through the criminal justice system. It is hard to argue that neither are truly needed.

responding to calls did not increase their chance of solving crimes. And finally, throwing more personnel and technology into criminal investigations did not solve most crimes. As you can imagine, the late 1970s became a time of upheaval for the police, for if the long-held assumptions of policing did not work, what did? Criticism, challenges, and ideas are what followed, generally in that order. Policing was deemed ineffective and inefficient. The police must change. But how? And when that question was asked, that was when the ideas came—new innovations, new ways of policing: the police strategies (see Box 9.2).

Broken Windows Theory, Model, and Policing

In March 1982, George L. Kelling, already introduced from the Kansas City Preventive Patrol Experiment, and James Q. Wilson, a political scientist who was actively involved in crime policy research and had previously served on President Johnson's Commission on Crime and the Administration of Justice, co-authored a paper together.[8] The paper was published in, of all places, the *Atlantic Monthly,* a publication that focuses on bold ideas,

---

Box 9.2 Ethics in Practice: Proactive Police Strategies

The term **strategy** means the development of a plan, intended to achieve a goal, over a long period of time. A **police strategy** is then a policing plan which is intended to achieve a goal over a long period of time. Since the primary goal of the police is to focus on community safety and deal with the problems of crime, most police strategies are naturally inclined toward reducing crime, minimizing the harm caused by crimes, or, possibly, eliminating a type of crime. All strategies then are proactive measures that drive the police response.

That is very different from policing's past, when police were largely a reactive force, one that responded to calls-for-service and crimes as they occurred. Policing, then, was driven by the needs of the community through their calls-for-service. Some have argued this improves police-community relations because the police only intervene when they are asked to assist by a citizen, rather than policing by the demands of the police strategy.

Ask Yourself:

Should policing be driven by a proactive strategy or should it be driven by the needs of the people? Are these goals mutually exclusive? How can police departments effectively balance these two approaches?

Do you think community policing is an effective way to combine police-citizen relations into a strategy?

---

opinion, and commentary on a wide array of issues. The magazine article was not filled with numbers and statistical analyses, but rather with stories and examples of what the authors were trying to convey. The publication of their ideas was both widely and well received, and ultimately came to be known as both the **broken windows theory** as well as the **broken windows model**, and would contribute greatly to changes in American policing.

Wilson and Kelling talked about how Newark, New Jersey, had started a foot patrol program to reduce crime, but while citizen satisfaction with the police went up, crime did not go down. They argued that each neighborhood is different, but each neighborhood faces two problems: crime itself and fear of crime. They stated that sometimes fear of crime is not necessarily derived from actual crime, but the perceptions of crime, and that how people perceive crime can also vary. However, they articulated that very often people's fear of crime is based on the level of disorder they see in the neighborhood, so called environmental cues or social signaling. For instance, if a home has

Broken windows serves as a metaphor for the broken windows theory.

a broken window and that window does not get fixed, it sends a signal not only to the criminals that no one cares about the neighborhood, but it tells the people that live there or visit that no one cares. If no one cares and the windows do not get fixed, not only does it create a sense of fear in the community, it may also invite criminal behavior. Thus was born the broken windows theory.

To further advance their argument, Wilson and Kelling referred to a study done by Stanford psychologist Philip Zimbardo, which took place in the Bronx, New York, and Palo Alto, California. A car was abandoned in both locations and within ten minutes, the car in the Bronx was broken into and within 24 hours the car was stripped and up on blocks. In Palo Alto, the car remained untouched for a week. Zimbardo then broke a vent window on the car in Palo Alto with a sledgehammer and within hours, this car too was stripped and up on blocks. The broken windows sent a signal that no one cared about the car, and so it was free game for anyone. Which means that these environmental cues may then create fear in law abiding citizens, while telling those who do not obey the law that disorderly behavior is acceptable in this neighborhood. That invites such things as petty theft, graffiti, and destruction of property which then invites further decay from such groups as drug dealers, prostitutes, and gangs, followed by criminal activity associated with these groups including burglary, robbery, and homicide.

Recognizing how a community decays and generates both fear and crime also tells us how to reverse this downward spiral. The goal is to demonstrate that people care about their community and that they will not tolerate the crime and disorder. Those citizens that live in a neighborhood have to show they care about their community by using informal control mechanisms, such as fixing broken windows right away, covering over graffiti, or calling public works or the police when a problem first arises. It is important here to understand the difference between formal social control (the police), versus informal social control (the community). One police scholar, David Kennedy, describes the difference to large gatherings of police officers by asking them how many were afraid of the police growing up. He says he always gets a few hands that go up. He then asks how many people were afraid of their mom. He says every hand in the room goes up, including his. That, he explains, is informal social control![9]

The police role in all of this then, according to Wilson and Kelling, "is to reinforce the informal control mechanisms of the community itself."[10] They realized this could not be done by the police alone, and it would necessitate the citizens becoming involved to reassert their authority over the neighborhood. However, the police could participate first in cleaning up the criminal problem through arrest, and then assert their visible authority to deter future crimes, as long as the citizens clean up their neighborhood and reassert their own authority. This requires a police-community partnership, and thus would become one of the motivating factors for the police moving into the community era and adopting community policing.

Community Policing

The concept of **community policing** developed out of a number of factors that all merged together to create what became the predominate method of policing in the 1980s and 1990s.[11] The first factor had to do with police and community relations. In early policing there was little to no concern for developing and maintaining community relations—it just came naturally from the police on the beat. Then the police took to cars and the relationship withered. There was a realization that the public needed to be better informed, so police departments began developing **public relations** offices, usually working out of the police chief's office. This type of relationship, however, was simply a one-way communication. The police told the community what they felt was necessary for the public to know. As the Civil Rights movement developed in the 1950s, a new program developed out of Michigan State University, called **police-community relations**. Under this program, the idea was to teach police officers about various populations and to recognize that each population may perceive the police differently and may have different needs. This included educating the police on the unique perspectives of women, race, ethnicity, religion, juveniles, the elderly, the handicapped, and the mentally ill. While the information was good, too often these programs became a reverse one-way communication, the community (or at least the instructor's) telling the police what they should know and do.

In the early 1970s, **team policing** developed as a better method of improving relations with the idea of taking certain officers and assigning them to a specific neighborhood, that they may better develop police and community relationships. Unfortunately, the police officers assigned to team policing were often those who did not perform well on the street or who were close to retirement. When they were adequately staffed with those who performed well, they were typically hampered by having little authority and almost nothing in the way of additional resources. The next evolution of these concepts was to develop a program that would be a two-way communication between the police and citizens and to make team policing the norm throughout the police department so that officers were always assigned to specific neighborhoods and worked with them to address the problems of crime and disorder.

A second manner in which community policing developed was previously discussed and that was in regard to the various 1970 studies—the Kansas City Preventive Patrol, the rapid response, and the investigation study—which demonstrated that the police need the assistance of the citizenry to solve crimes and that for too long the police had distanced themselves from the citizens all in the name of professionalism. What was needed was to break down the so-called blue wall that had been built between the police and the people. Finally, a third manner in which community policing developed was via the broken windows theory, because it demonstrated that if the police and the community work together to stop the decay of a neighborhood and reestablish a sense of community, they can alleviate many of the problems of crime and disorder (see Table 9.1).

Table 9.1   Community Policing Policies and Activities of Local Police Departments, by Size of Population Served, 2013

Pop. Served	Mission Statement w/ Community Assignments Policing	Community Partnerships or Agreement	Fixed Beat for Police
All sizes	68%	32%	44%
1,000,000 or more	86	86	100
500,000–999,999	97	59	90
250,000–499,999	91	67	93
100,000–249,999	87	61	93
50,000–99,999	91	59	83
25,000–49,999	87	52	64
10,000–24,999	81	41	49
2,500–9,999	74	29	32
2,499 or fewer	50	21	40

Source: Reaves, B.A. (2015). *Local Police Departments, 2013: Personnel, Policies, and Practices.* Washington, DC: Bureau of Justice Statistics.

Community policing then developed in earnest in the early 1980s, and it became the most talked about method of policing by the late 1980s. Then in the 1990s, people were referring to that time period as the decade of community policing. Yet, one author noted that the community policing of the early 1980s and that of the mid-1990s was assuredly different. He explained what happened is that the community policing era went through **three generations of community policing.**[12] The first generation was the **innovation generation**, which ran from 1979 to about 1986. During this time period, community policing was more of a local phenomenon among innovative police departments testing out the ideas for enhancing police-community partnerships. Some of the early innovators included Madison, Wisconsin, Flint, Michigan, and Newark, New Jersey. In some cases these experiments or demonstration projects were the adoption of foot patrols to enhance police-public contacts or they consisted of police community centers established in a specific neighborhood. Regardless, the primary goal of these types of programs, which were soon being referred to as community policing programs, were to bring the police and community together to work in partnerships to improve the quality of their neighborhoods.

The second generation was the **diffusion generation**, which ran from 1987 to 1994. It was during this time period that the successful programs began to spread across the United States to other police departments. Police agencies began adopting various elements to create their own community policing programs. Many of these came with different names, such as the Community Oriented Policing and Problem Solving (COPPS) program in Hayward, California, or the Citizen Oriented Police Enforcement (COPE) program in Baltimore County, Maryland. The agencies that were adopting community policing tended to be medium- to large-sized agencies, and although community policing was believed by many to be a department-wide initiative, most of the agencies typically adopted it by way of a special unit or they designated certain neighborhoods as recipients of the community policing program.

The third generation of community policing was the **institutionalization generation**, and it ran from 1995 onward. In this generation, community policing fast became the most common method of policing that agencies were adopting or at least said they were adopting. In addition, it was supported by the passage of the *Violent Crime Control and Law Enforcement Act of 1994* that put $8.8 billion into funding 100,000 cops who were to be used for the purposes of implementing community policing in police departments across the country. As a result of this funding, even the smallest of agencies in America could receive grant dollars for the adoption of community policing, so it became a very common program across America.

Despite its wide-spread popularity, because community policing was not based on a very specific program or style of policing—there was no sole author or architect of the concept—community policing suffered from a definitional problem. No one could agree on a common definition. This became evident when police departments called their programs all kinds of variations on community policing, and what they implemented as community policing differed from agency to agency. One agency may have police-citizen neighborhood patrols, while another may adopt foot patrols for their officers, yet both were doing community policing. One agency may say it is a way of thinking about quality of life issues that is demonstrated by the agency's commitment to developing police-community partnerships, while another may explain it as a special unit, working in a specific neighborhood, to develop communal ties by officers paying house visits, conducting community meetings, and setting up a police-youth basketball program. The first is both vague and visionary, while the latter is very specific and program oriented. Both though, could have been said to have been community policing (see Table 9.2).

One leading police scholar, Gary Cordner, explained that community policing had come to mean so many things to so many different people that it was important to come to some understanding of what were at least the main themes of community policing.[13] Cordner identified the **four dimensions of community policing**: philosophical, strategic, tactical, and organizational. The first dimension, the **philosophical dimension**, is primarily focused on looking at community policing as a new philosophy or way of thinking about policing. It is oriented on the broader functions of the police, such as community service, which then bases itself on the concept of citizen input into the policing process. Whenever the police discuss things such as the values

Table 9.2 Community Policing Activities of Sheriff's Offices by Population Served, 2007			
Pop. Served	Partnered w/ Citizen Groups	Conducted a Citizens Police Academy	Conducted Citizen Surveys
All sizes	33%	11%	10%
1,000,000 or more	78	63	52
500,000–999,999	59	53	32
250,000–499,999	50	48	21
100,000–249,999	55	25	21
50,000–99,999	40	16	10
25,000–49,999	34	9	6
10,000–24,999	28	2	9
Under 10,000	15	1	4

Source: Reaves, B.A. (2012). *Sheriffs' Offices, 2007 – Statistical Tables*. Washington, DC: Bureau of Justice Statistics.

and principles of community policing, the development of partnerships, and the goal of reducing crime and disorder to improve the quality of life, this is the philosophical aspect of community policing that underlies this police initiative.

The second dimension is the **strategic dimension**. The strategic focus is an attempt to translate the philosophy into action. Cordner notes that it is often focused on geography, taking community policing to the neighborhood level, assigning police officers to those neighborhoods permanently, and having them work toward taking ownership of their community and becoming the representative of the police department to the people that live there. This action is based on the philosophy that community policing is about police-citizen partnerships at the neighborhood level. In addition, the prevention of crime and disorder is a primary focus of the community policing strategy, so this may include establishing programs that target crime problems in a neighborhood, working with citizens to have them take more responsibility for the safety of their community, and bringing in additional social services to improve the community's quality of life. Finally, focusing on the substantive issues is another strategic element of community policing in that police and members of the community work to resolve the problems in their neighborhood.

The third dimension of community policing is the **tactical dimension.** This dimension is focused on the specific programs that come to encapsulate the community policing philosophy and strategy. These include such things as foot patrols and bike patrols, police-community meetings, and problem-solving approaches to crime and disorder (see next section for problem-oriented policing). Programs aimed at implementing community policing reorient the police to focus on specific problems in the neighborhood they police; it is about solving problems and engaging the community. In short, these are the various programs that are implemented under the community policing umbrella.

The fourth dimension of community policing is the **organizational dimension**. This dimension is focused on how police departments best organize to carry out community policing. One aspect of this has already been discussed, and that is having officers permanently assigned (at least for extended periods of one to three years) to a neighborhood so that they come to know the community and the issues the neighborhood faces. The other aspect of the organizational dimension is focused on the department's ability to support the community policing officers working in these neighborhoods. By having these officers permanently assigned, they come to know what the community wants and needs; thus they are in the best position to decide what police resources are needed. However, being line officers, they are often not in a position to authorize the use of police resources, so decentralizing the police department, allowing for community policing officers to have more authority, is part of the organizational dimension.

The many dimensions and complexities of community policing that developed over the past 30 years does beg one question: how successful has community policing been?[14] To answer this we actually run into a problem. Since we don't really know what we mean by community policing because it means so many different things to so many different people, we are not sure how to judge it. If we said, does community policing reduce crime, and in one city we looked at their foot patrol program while in another we looked at a crackdown on open-air drug markets, we are really looking at two different things, despite the fact both might be labeled community policing. So, as you can see, right away we have a problem. Many have come to the realization that community policing came to mean so many different things, that it eventually came to mean nothing. What is more important is to focus on what the police are actually doing, rather than focusing on the label.

Since the police are about reducing crime, if we were to look at many of the various types of community policing programs to see if they have been successful at reducing crime we end up with mixed results.[15] A few studies claim that it has reduced crime, while others have found no supporting evidence, and yet many of those studies

Many of the programs under community policing are oriented toward enhancing the relations between the police and children.

were not necessarily looking at community policing but other policing methods still to be discussed in this chapter. In sum, there is not a strong foundation of research that has shown that community policing reduces crime. However, when the focus changes to community policing reducing the fear of crime, there is a strong consensus that it does reduce the fear.[16] As police develop stronger ties with the community, it makes citizens feel safer about their neighborhood and so, independent of crime itself, community policing reduces the fear of crime. The moral imperative here, however, is questioning whether reducing the fear of crime while at the same time not reducing actual crime creates a false sense of security amongst the community.

Problem-Oriented Policing

As part of the wave of police research in the 1970s demonstrating that long-held police assumptions had no empirical basis, one law professor, Herman Goldstein from the University of Wisconsin Law School, wrote a book in 1977 detailing many of these issues. The book was titled *Policing a Free Society*.[17] In it, Goldstein reflected on the state of American policing and set on a course to think about how policing could be improved. Two years later, he published what would become a very influential paper titled "Improving Policing: A Problem-Oriented Approach" in the journal *Crime & Delinquency*.[18] Goldstein argued that the police focused too much on the means and not on the ends, meaning that police focus on handling calls-for-service without necessarily focusing on the desired outcome or end product—solving problems. If the police could define problems with greater specificity, research the magnitude of the problem, explore alternatives such as physical changes, developing new skills, and creating new forms of authority, by implementing the process, it may have an effect on the organization. The problem, you may have figured out, was the complexity of Goldstein's ideas. Police professionals supported the concept, but they needed to know how to communicate it to line officers.

In actuality, what Goldstein was advocating was something we all do every day. He was just advocating that we apply it more formally to policing. The thing we do every day is solve problems. When your car breaks down, when you have two exams next week to study for, or when you have a friend that asks for your help—you have problems to solve. Let's take something simple: Where are you going to eat lunch? It is a problem. The problem is you are hungry and you want to eat. When faced with this problem you have to think about your options. You could eat in the cafeteria (it's already paid for), you could eat fast-food in the student center (which will cost you money), or you could go home for a peanut butter and jelly sandwich (but it is a long walk back to your dorm or apartment). You then have to think of the constraints you face, such as how much time do you have to eat lunch or how much money you have. You then have to analyze and choose the best course of action. If you only have 45 minutes and $2 in your pocket, walking back home would take too long, and you can't buy much for $2—the best course of action is probably to eat in the cafeteria. You then made a decision, implemented it, and now, after eating in the cafeteria, you decide whether or not that was a good idea—you saved time and money, but was the meal any good?

In policing, police officers respond to calls-for-service and arrive on scene to solve problems. The issue, as Goldstein saw it, however, is that often police officers treat the call as an isolated incident. The location, people, and problem have no past and no future. If the police have responded to that location for the same problem with the same people, it has been forgotten or ignored, and the police try to resolve the issue so they can leave without thinking about the future and the fact that they, or a fellow officer, will one day have to come back to the same location, for the same problem, and deal with the same people. In this case, the officer is solving the symptoms, not the underlying problem itself. Think about when you get sick on campus and you have the runny-nose, headache, and sore throat, and so you take medicine that knocks you out. In that case, you are dealing with the symptoms of the cold, but not the underlying problem causing the symptoms. Goldstein was advocating that the police solve the problem, not the symptoms, to improve policing, which would have a positive effect on the police organization as it would reduce their calls-for-service to that same address, with the same problem, caused by the same people (see Table 9.3).

Table 9.3 Police Officer Involvement in Problem-Oriented Policing Projects, by Size of Population Served, 2013		
Pop. Served	Actively Encouraged	Included in Performance Evaluations
All sizes	33%	30%
1,000,000 or more	57	36
500,000–999,999	71	54
250,000–499,999	73	64
100,000–249,999	74	57
50,000–99,999	62	49
25,000–49,999	49	42
10,000–24,999	43	38
2,500–9,999	32	30
2,499 or fewer	21	21

Source: Reaves, B.A. (2015). *Local Police Departments, 2013: Personnel, Policies, and Practices.* Washington, DC: Bureau of Justice Statistics.

It sounded good, police chiefs admitted, but what they wanted to know was how to teach their officers to do problem-solving or **problem-oriented policing (POP)**. Then along came two researchers, John Eck and William Spelman, working on a grant in Newport News, Virginia. They consulted with Herman Goldstein to develop a method of teaching police officers how to problem solve, and what they came up with was the **SARA Model**, which stands for scanning, analysis, response, and assessment (see Box 9.3). In the **scanning** phase, police officers are taught to look for problems in their beats and to make connections among the many crimes they face. They are also taught that very often much of the crime is committed by three things that

---

Box 9.3 **Policing in Practice: The SARA Model**

The SARA Model is a method of teaching police officers how to problem solve. The acronym stands for scanning, analysis, response, and assessment.

Scanning:
- Identifying recurring problems of concern to the public and the police.
- Identifying the consequences of the problem for the community and the police.
- Prioritizing those problems.
- Developing broad goals.
- Confirming that the problems exist.
- Determining how frequently the problem occurs and how long it has been taking place.
- Selecting problems for closer examination.

Analysis:
- Identifying and understanding the events and conditions that precede and accompany the problem.
- Identifying relevant data to be collected.
- Researching what is known about the problem type.
- Taking inventory of how the problem is currently addressed and the strengths and limitations of the current response.
- Narrowing the scope of the problem as specifically as possible.
- Identifying a variety of resources that may be of assistance in developing a deeper understanding of the problem.

- Developing a working hypothesis about why the problem is occurring.

Response:
- Brainstorming for new interventions.
- Searching for what other communities with similar problems have done.
- Choosing among the alternative interventions.
- Outlining a response plan and identifying responsible parties.
- Stating the specific objectives for the response plan.
- Carrying out the planned activities.

Assessment:
- Determining whether the plan was implemented (a process evaluation).
- Collecting pre- and post-response qualitative and quantitative data.
- Determining whether broad goals and specific objectives were attained.
- Identifying any new strategies needed to augment the original plan.
- Conducting ongoing assessment to ensure continued effectiveness.

Source: Center for Problem-Oriented Policing. (2015). The SARA Model. Retrieved from http://www.popcenter.org/about/?p=sara.

are most often highly connected: the offender, the location, and the target or victim. If the police can identify a problem at a specific location, often at a specific time, with the same offenders and/or the same victims, then they will have identified a problem in which the problem-solving model may work.

In the **analysis** phase, police officers begin to analyze the problem with more depth. In the problem analysis, they draw upon as much data as they can obtain, such as geographic information systems (GIS) software to see how many and what kinds of crimes occur in the location, running checks on past police calls-for-service at a location, conducting background checks on the individuals to see what kind of arrests and convictions they may have, all to get a better understanding of the true nature of the problem. Officers can also go to other government services to see if they have had problems with the same location or people, and they may also go to citizens or citizen groups to collect information. At this stage, the officer also has to determine what the desired outcome of the intervention is actually going to be. If the problem was drug-dealing and violence on a particular street corner, are the officers, after a total elimination of drug-dealing and violence (which may not be realistic), intending to substantially reduce the problem (far less violence and drug-dealing than in the past), are they wanting a reduction in harm (getting the violence to stop, but not necessarily the drug-dealing), or are they setting out to find a way of dealing with the problem more effectively (no more street corner raids, but finding a less confrontational way of dealing with the problem)?

In the **response** phase, the police officers must develop possible responses to the problem, much like developing a list of places to eat for lunch, and then weighing them against the limitations and constraints they impose. The response must address the underlying problem by dealing with the offender, victims, and locations, and ensure that the response will not cause further problems or harm. Then the officers set about implementing the best course of action from the list of possible solutions to the problem. During the response phase, the officers must also monitor the impact that the course of action has on the problem and collect data to move into the last stage of the SARA Model.

The last stage of SARA is the **assessment** phase. It is in this stage that the officers determine if the chosen course of action was successful, based on the intent of what was meant by successful (for example, reduction of harm, elimination of the problem). Once the assessment has been conducted, depending on the outcome, this will tell officers what they need to do next. If the assessment is that the course of action they selected was unsuccessful, then they should consider moving back to the response stage to select and implement another response. If the assessment was positive, then the officers must determine if they should continue the response, alter the response, or stop the response altogether.

The SARA Model has been widely used since the mid-1980s, primarily because it is a problem-solving model that can be easily taught, used to address a wide array of problems, and works so well because it concentrates police resources on a specific problem, at a specific time, in a specific location, that often involves the same people (offenders and/or victims). It also became widely used because of its natural association with community policing, and most police departments that have adopted community policing have also adopted problem-oriented policing as part of its community policing program. There are, however, many agencies that did not adopt community policing, but rather problem-oriented policing as a stand-alone program, such as one of the earliest adopters of problem-oriented policing, the San Diego Police Department. Since those early days, many advances have been made in improving police officers' problem-solving capabilities, and the SARA Model is widely used. Evidence for this can be found in the fact that there is a Center for Problem-Oriented Policing as well as an annual Problem Oriented Policing Conference. Every year at that conference the Herman Goldstein Award is given to the police department with the most innovative SARA project from the previous year (see Box 9.4).

Overall, problem-oriented policing has been considered to be an effective police strategy, though not without its own problems. One issue involves

---

Box 9.4 History in Practice: Problem-Oriented Policing and the Herman Goldstein Award

The **Herman Goldstein Award** was first introduced in 1993 in order to recognize outstanding police officers and police agencies that have developed innovative solutions through their **problem-oriented policing projects**. This international competition is named after the founder of problem–oriented policing, University of Wisconsin Emeritus Professor Herman Goldstein and was originally administered by the Police Executive Research Forum (1993-2007) and is now administered by the Center for Problem–Oriented Policing (2008 to present).

Each year there are numerous submissions and a handful of finalists, but only one winner is chosen to receive the coveted award. In 2009, the recipient was the Chula Vista (California) Police Department for their problem-oriented policing project to reduce crime and disorder at motels and hotels in their city. Chula Vista is perfectly situated to accommodate tourists visiting both the San Diego area and Baja, Mexico, but for many years, the city's overnight lodging industry consisted primarily of cheap motels that were havens for crime, drug dealing, parolees, and prostitutes. Police staff researched the problems at motels from a variety of perspectives and concluded that motel managers and owners could effectively control crime and disorder on their properties through good management practices, if they chose to do so. In collaboration with other city agencies, police staff developed an ordinance that enabled the city to hold motels accountable for meeting a "calls for service-based" public safety performance standard. As a result of the project, calls for service to motels declined 45% and crime declined 68%; in addition, motels reported taking in more revenue and catering less to a local clientele.

Source: Center for Problem-Oriented Policing. (2015). The Herman Goldstein Award 2009. Retrieved from http://www.popcenter.org/library/awards//.

the realization that police officers often find it difficult to fully implement problem-oriented policing due to numerous constraints.[19] Research has also found that most of the responses to problems by the police tend to be police-centric, meaning that most police officers do not develop or implement solutions that lie outside of police control; they nearly always default to time-honored police responses. Most of the studies regarding the impact of problem-oriented policing also tend to be short term, so the lasting effects of these projects is largely unknown.[20] Still further, there is much concern that in the assessment phase, very rarely do police officers evaluate the **displacement effect**, in which their responses simply push crime into other areas.[21] Researchers who have assessed the displacement effect in their studies, however, generally find that even when crime does displace, it tends to be at reduced levels.[22]

Targeted Policing

During the 1990s, additional programs began to spring up in police departments across the nation that went by many different names, but had commonalities in how they were implemented, and eventually specific names were given to them. All of the programs drew upon some of the aspects of the broken windows theory and the problem-oriented policing concepts. Specifically, the broken windows theory articulates that there are certain neighborhoods that have problems of crime and disorder. The problem-oriented policing literature takes it further and says there are often very specific locations that have crime and disorder problems often caused by the same offenders, and can include the same victims. Since we know that high levels of crime and disorder tend to be concentrated in specific locations and times and committed by the same offenders, the key then is for the police to target their resources toward these specific problems to deter crime. Police officers driving around the neighborhood were found not to deter crime (Kansas City Preventive Patrol Experiment), but that did not mean that police could not deter crime by concentrating their resources on specific targets.

This strategy of policing should sound familiar as it reflects the opening quote of August Vollmer and is today known as **hot spots policing**. As two leading police scholars, Anthony Braga and David Weisburd, describe it today, "hot spots policing is the application of police interventions at very small geographic units of analysis"[23] In this form of

Hot spots policing is one form of the targeted police strategies.

targeted policing, the emphasis is on geography and crime. So, here the hot spots are geographical locations that may be a city block, a building, a home, or a cluster of homes. It may also get down to the small micro locations such as a specific street corner, an alley, or the dead end of a dead end street. The concentration of crime in these locations may be very specific and may be tied to certain individuals, or maybe even one person, but the key is the concentration of police resources on the specific geographical location. The justification here is that the majority of crime in a city can often be traced back to just a handful or a dozen locations, so if police concentrate their resources in these locations, they stand a good chance of reducing the overall crime figures for the entire city. Overall, hot spots policing has been considered to be highly effective in most cases not only for reducing crime but for dealing with disorder and reducing the number of police calls-for-service.[24]

Another strategy of police targeting is **crime-specific policing**. Just as hot spots policing focuses primarily on geographical location, crime-specific policing focuses primarily on crimes. In other words, rather than looking to specific locations for crimes, the police look at specific crimes, such as rapes, burglaries, or robberies. By plotting the location of a very specific crime on a map, they can see trends within the city for the crime and concentrate their efforts on where they may be occurring. For instance, rapes may be located throughout the city, but in areas that link high traffic locations. The police then develop a specific response to that crime problem to target the offenders or protect potential victims.[25]

One targeted strategy that has a larger focus than either hot spots or crime-specific and is drawn primarily from the broken windows theory has come to be known as **zero-tolerance policing**. Again, the broken windows theory articulates that broken windows, left unfixed, send a signal to would-be criminals that no one cares about the neighborhood and thus it attracts more broken windows, disorder, and crime. People use to think that police should not focus on the little things, but rather spend their time and resources enforcing major felonious crime. Drawing upon the broken windows theory, zero-tolerance policing reverses that and says police should spend time on the minor infractions so as they do not lead to the more serious crime. Thus, the police under zero-tolerance policing focus their patrols on things that may send a signal that no one cares about the community, such as graffiti, panhandlers, and loitering. By not tolerating these types of minor nuisances, they communicate that they will assuredly not tolerate serious crime. While zero-tolerance policing has been found effective in dealing with the minor problems, it often comes across as too heavy handed and people often feel it is an abuse of police power.[26]

Another program that developed from the aggressive policing concept was the use of **stop and frisk**. In the landmark Supreme Court case of *Terry v. Ohio* (1968) it was ruled that police officers had the right to stop and frisk someone if they could articulate that they had a reasonable suspicion to believe the person had committed, was committing, or was about to commit a crime. In this case a Cleveland police detective saw several individuals he had never seen before acting suspiciously in front of a store. Suspecting it was about to be robbed, he stopped them, patted them down for weapons, and recovered several illegally concealed handguns. They appealed their convictions arguing their Fourth Amendment rights were violated, but the Supreme Court said no. Thus, officers have the right to stop and frisk a person when they have reasonable suspicion. Now, imagine training police officers how to detect when a person is carrying a weapon concealed; thus armed with that knowledge (pun intended), they could stop and frisk anyone exhibiting signs of carrying a concealed weapon to further investigate if the carrying is legal or illegal. As a result, police have learned to employ this aggressive form of policing. This particular strategy is highly controversial, and while there is some evidence to suggest that it has been effective, it also has created an enormous amount of animosity toward the police, especially in New York City, where it has been used for over 20 years.[27]

In looking at all of the strategies that are target oriented, a couple of things become clear. The first is that all of these methods learned from the Kansas City Preventive Patrol Experiment told us police officers on random patrol do not deter crime, but that concentrating police resources can, in fact, have an impact on crime. So, the conclusion reached in the Kansas City study is qualified, police do not deter crime when deploying forces in general, but when concentrating them they can deter crime. The other thing we can learn is that while each of these takes a slightly different focus, they are all inherently the same. When the police focus on a specific crime, at a specific location, at a specific time, with specific offenders, and very often specific victims, the police are very effective at dealing with crime, and they can deter it.

Data-Driven Policing

Data-driven strategies are another body of strategies that have each developed separately and are not only highly related to each other, but also share a relationship to many of the other policing strategies. These methods look at crime data to determine how best to respond to crime either through preventive measures or proactive policing methods. The first, Crime Prevention Through Environmental Design, is the older of the four and was developed based upon proven methods of manipulating the environment to reduce and prevent crime. The pulling levers strategy was associated with Operation Ceasefire, and the final two, evidence-based and predictive policing, developed out of academic applied research.

Crime Prevention Through Environmental Design

Crime Prevention Through Environmental Design (CPTED) was created by criminologist C. Ray Jeffery, and over time has been advanced through other contributions regarding urban design and what has been called defensible space.[28] In the 1980s it took on a renewed emphasis because of its close relationship to the broken windows theory and the development of community policing. CPTED is a method for analyzing how the physical environment impacts crime and criminal behavior and then altering the physical environment to deter crime. For instance, college campuses are often designed with pathways, landscaping, and lighting to attract people to follow certain pathways and to congregate in certain areas. By having commonly used areas like this with high foot traffic, it prevents the types of crime that occur down dark alleys, hidden pathways, and isolated areas. Another example is something simple like a parking lot. While we all like the hardtop parking lots, they are actually less safe than a gravel parking lot. The reason being is that it is hard for someone to approach a person getting in or out of their car silently on crunching gravel. By changing the environment, it makes people more aware. One other example is that we know from research one of the best places to live is on a cul-de-sac, because people typically will only enter such a street if they have a purpose there and because it creates a mini-community where everyone knows who belongs there and who does not. Cul-de-sacs are defendable spaces. Living in an apartment or home located on a cross-street or grid pattern is the least safe because of the open access to those locations; they are not as defendable.[29]

Pulling Levers

The **pulling-levers strategy** developed out of Operation Ceasefire in Boston in the 1990s.[30] Between 1991 and 1995, Boston experienced 44 youth homicides that were directly related to gangs. Instead of creating a program that focused on just one aspect of the problem, Operation Ceasefire was intent on creating multiple programs to deter youth violence and homicides. Some of the programs focused on the offenders, others on the victims, while others were aimed at the schools, some to the teachers, others to the problem of youth bringing guns to school, and still others were gang oriented. In addition to these types of programs, many of the "levers" that were pulled were the use of the law by police officers, school resource officers, and the prosecutor's office. By pulling every lever possible, the goal was to put pressure on those few people who were perpetrating the crimes to deter them from committing future crimes. If they committed another crime, then every possible method available to the police and community was used to target the perpetrator and to get others to think twice before committing a similar crime. While Operation Ceasefire was about telling the few gang members perpetrating most of the crime to stop the violence, as well as pulling levers, the concept of ceasefire has focused on the former, while lever-pulling has been the original program's goal of multiple methods for dealing with the problem. Regardless, the strategy has proven to be highly successful and transportable to other cities.[31]

Evidence-Based Policing

The third strategy, which developed as a part of the other strategies discussed, is **evidence-based policing**.[32] In this case, the concept was more of an evolution in police research. Starting with the use of research to test long-held assumptions in policing in the 1970s (for example, Kansas City Preventive Patrol, rapid response) to the use of evaluations as part of the assessment of the SARA Model under problem-oriented policing, research into what works in policing has developed over the past 40 years to get us to a point of using data to determine the best strategies for policing. Evidence-based policing is then about using data on offenders, victims,

Evidence-based policing draws upon analyzed data, whether through real-time crime data or geographic information systems, to help guide police deployment.

and crimes, as well as the geographic nature of all three, to help guide police intervention through the use of empirical studies. In other words, police interventions are assessed for how well they reduce crime and disorder and must be results oriented. If the intervention, based on empirical research, is found not to impact crime or disorder then it is either discontinued or modified until the intervention has been shown to work.

Predictive Policing

Recently, former New York Police Commissioner William Bratton made the statement that "Predictive policing used to be the future and now it is the present."[33] **Predictive policing** is the fourth and final strategy and is akin to taking evidence-based policing and pushing it even further. Evidence-based policing is about using empirical data to guide police toward the implementation of successful interventions and avoiding those that fail to obtain results. Predictive policing takes the use of empirical data even further by attempting to make predictions about what crimes are likely to occur, where and when. It is the "application of analytical techniques—particularly quantitative techniques—to identify promising targets for police intervention, with the goal of reducing crime risk or solving past crimes."[34] In light of the power of information technology these days, the analysis of large databases of information can often yield relationships that we were not aware of and can then be exploited for purposes of crime prevention and crime control. Still, a recent study of police strategies noted that "because the concept of predictive policing is relatively recent," this currently makes "the effectiveness of predictive policing...hard to establish."[35]

Compstat

While most of Chapter 9 has talked about the strategies of policing, one other strategy was originally developed in New York City as a management tool.[36] In the early 1990s, William C. Bratton was hired to serve as the New York City Police Commissioner, and he assembled a team that wanted to implement a way of holding the precinct commanders accountable for the crime in their jurisdictions with the idea that they should be working to implement many of the other strategies discussed above. What developed was a strategy, method, and police management mechanism that came to be known as **Compstat.** There has always been a debate over what Compstat stood for, but most have agreed it was a combination of the words computer statistics. This was because one of the innovators of the program was Jack Maple, who believed that real-time crime analysis was critical to precinct commanders reducing crime (see Box 9.5).[37]

Box 9.5 History in Practice: Jack Maple and Compstat

It is often the case that those who are in the primary positions of power are the ones who receive the most credit, while the people behind the scenes are often forgotten. When anyone talks of the implementation of **Compstat** in the New York Police Department in the early 1990s and the significant crime drop that followed, it is very often the case that Mayor Rudolph Giuliani, the Mayor at the time (1994-2001), and Police Commissioner William Bratton (1994-1996) are the ones who receive the credit. Yet, behind the scenes was **the originator of Compstat, Jack Maple**.

Jack Maple was born in 1952 in New York City and spent his entire life there. He joined the New York Metro Transit Police when it was considered one of the most dangerous jobs in the city, and he rose to the rank of lieutenant. While there, trying to get a grip on the problems of crime, Maple created a system he called, "Charts of the Future." He essentially put up maps on the walls and used colored push pins to mark where different types of crimes were concentrated on the subway system. Maple then created a rapid response team that would focus its attention on key locations. When Bratton became the Chief of the New York Transit Police in 1990, he paid attention to Maple because his system was having an impact on crime.

When Bratton was appointed as the NYPD Police Commissioner he brought Maple with him and wanted him to work his magic there. Maple renamed the system Compstat, and, through his statistical analysis, he was able to determine the key problems in each police precinct in the city. Precinct commanders were then brought in for weekly meetings to see if they understood their precinct's problems and to hold them accountable for reducing the problem. Maple, with his trademark Homburg hat, and Bill Bratton became known as the *Crime Fighting Kings*. Maple wrote a book about his experiences at the NYPD which was published in 1999. Not long after, Maple was diagnosed with cancer and died in 2001.

Source: Maple, Jack with Chris Mitchell. (1999). *The Crime Fighter: How You Can Make Your Community Crime-Free.* New York, NY: Broadway Books.

To know how to reduce crime in neighborhoods, one has to know what kind of crime problems exist there. The way Compstat worked was through command-level meetings where police commissioners and their staff met with the precinct commanders and their staff and asked about the major problems in their area of responsibility. Maple already knew the problems by conducting a crime analysis, but it was a way of making sure the commanders knew. When they did not, they were told to come back to the next meeting prepared to discuss them. When they did know, they were then asked what they were doing to reduce crime and disorder regarding those problems. Again, if they were not doing anything in particular, at the next meeting they had to let the command staff know what they were doing. Then they were told they had to reduce that problem within six months to a year. If they could not achieve a reduction in the crime or disorder, they would be fired and someone would replace them. Thus, Compstat became not only a strategy, but a managerial tool.

Compstat has long been hailed by the NYPD and many of those enthralled by its methods as having been successful. The only problem is that crime began falling in New York City two years before Compstat was implemented and continued to fall for the next 20 years, as it has all across America. So, it begs the question of whether or not Compstat contributed to the decline in crime or was just simply good timing. Compstat had been shown to be successful in other cities, but often problematic in the management side of holding the command staff accountable. In fact, what many believe is the best aspect of Compstat is the fact that it helps police focus on specific problems, very similar to many of the other strategies detailed above that are target focused (see Box 9.6).[38]

Homeland Security and Policing

On September 11, 2001, when 19 terrorists hijacked four planes and flew two into the World Trade Center, one into the Pentagon, and one crashed into a Pennsylvania field because of the courage of some of its passengers, the United States entered a new era of homeland security. This had a direct and profound impact upon policing in America, one that still reverberates today. A new strategy of policing was created out of that terrorist attack that began when the federal government created the **Department of Homeland Security (DHS)** and implemented that **National Incident Management System (NIMS)**, a template for future responses to terrorist attacks and natural disasters for all levels of responders—federal, state, and local.[39] Part of NIMS was also the implementation of the **Incident Command System** a management structure that would allow multiple agencies to handle the response to such things as terrorist bombings and hurricanes. Most of the initial focus was on ensuring that first responders were well trained, well equipped, and well prepared for similar events in the future. As the police are one of the first responders, much of the funding, training, and equipment for homeland security was directed toward them (see Table 9.4).

Box 9.6 Policing in Practice: Comparison of Various Strategies of Policing by Social Interaction and Structural Dimension

Social Interaction or Structural Dimension	Traditional Policing	Community Policing	Problem-Oriented Policing	Zero-Tolerance Policing	Homeland Security Policing
Focus of policing	Law enforcement	Community building through crime prevention	Law, order, and fear problems	Order problems	Security, anti-terrorism, counter-terrorism, law and order
Forms of intervention	Reactive, based on criminal law	Proactive, on criminal and administrative law	Mixed, on criminal and administrative law	Proactive, uses criminal, civil, and administrative law	Proactive, on criminal law and for mitigation and preparedness
Range of police activity	Narrow, crime focused	Broad crime, order, fear, and quality of life focused	Narrow to broad-problem focused	Narrow, location and behavior focused	Broad, security, terrorism, crime, fear
Levels of discretion at line level	High and unaccountable	High and accountable to the community and local commanders	High and primarily accountable to the police administration	Low, but primarily accountable to the police administration	High and primarily accountable to the police administration
Focus of police culture	Inward, rejecting community	Outward, building partnerships	Mixed depending on problem, but analysis focused	Inward focused on attacking the target problem	Mixed depending on threat, threat-analysis focused
Focus of decision making	Police directed, minimizes the involvement of others	Community-police coproduction-joint responsibility and assessment	Varied, police identify problems, but with community involvement and interaction	Police directed, some linkage to other agencies where necessary	Police directed with linkage to other agencies
Communication flow	Downward from police to community	Horizontal between police and community	Horizontal between police and community	Downward from police to community	Downward from police to community

Box 9.6 (Continued)

Social Interaction or Structural Dimension	Traditional Policing	Community Policing	Problem-Oriented Policing	Zero-Tolerance Policing	Homeland Security Policing
Range of community involvement	Low and passive	High and active	Mixed depending on problem set	Low and passive	Mixed depending on threat
Linkage with other agencies	Poor and intermittent	Participative and integrative in the overarching process	Participative and integrative depending on the problem set	Moderate and intermittent	Participative and integrative in the overarching process
Type of organization and command focus	Centralized command and control	Decentralized with community linkage	Decentralized with local command accountability to central administration	Centralized or decentralized but internal focus	Centralized decision making, decentralized execution
Implications for organizational change/development	Few, static organization fending off the environment	Many, dynamic organization focused on the environmental interactions	Varied, focused on problem resolution but with import for organization intelligence and structure	Few, limited interventions focused on target problems, using many traditional methods	Varied, focused on security and threat, but with import for intelligence and structure
Measurement of success	Arrest and crime rates, particularly serious part-one crimes	Varied, crime, calls for service, fear reduction, use of public places, community linkages and contacts, safer neighborhoods	Varied, problems solved, minimized, displaced	Arrests, field stops, activity, location-specific reductions in targeted activity	Arrests, field stops, intelligence gathering, mitigation, and preparedness

Source: Adapted by author from Greene, J.R. (2000). "Community Policing in America: Changing the nature, structure, and function of the police." In *Criminal justice 2000: Policies, processes, and decisions of the criminal justice system.* Vol. 3. Washington, DC: U.S. Department of Justice, Office of Justice Programs.

Table 9.4   Homeland Security Initiatives of Police and Sheriffs by Population Served 2007

Community Related Homeland Pop. Served	Police Officers/Sheriff's Deputies		
	Participated in Emergency Preparedness Exercise	Increased Officer Presence in Critical Areas	Held Meetings to Security
All sizes	62%/80%	36%/45%	26%/39%
1,000,000 or more	92/89	77/81	85/63
500,000–999,999	94/98	74/75	68/53
250,000–499,999	98/93	80/57	78/39
100,000–249,999	92/89	64/60	43/50
50,000–99,999	90/91	60/50	39/38
25,000–49,999	82/78	54/47	31/32
10,000–24,999	77/75	51/38	25/38
Under 10,000	55/72	29/36	25/40

Source: Reaves, B.A. (2010). *Local Police Departments, 2007*. Washington, DC: Bureau of Justice Statistics; Reaves, B.A. (2012). *Sheriffs' Offices, 2007 – Statistical tables*. Washington, DC: Bureau of Justice Statistics.

While being prepared for future threats is critical to future response, there was also the strong desire to implement methods to prevent future terrorist attacks. As a result, homeland security for policing began to develop many new programs that would assist the police in the area of prevention.[40] Once concept that had long been the focus of the military, suddenly became applied to the police, and that was **antiterrorism**, the operational methods which work to prevent or stop future terrorist attacks, and **counter terrorism**, the strategy, operations, and tactics employed to respond to terroristic threats. These include not just federal law enforcement response teams, but local response teams as well, and may include SWAT (special weapons and tactics), hostage rescue teams, and bomb squads (see Table 9.5).

In addition, the collection of intelligence as well as its analysis became necessary for the police to be able to conduct **counterterrorism** operations. Police began creating intelligence collection

A member of the FBI counter-terrorism division.

Table 9.5 Antiterrorism Task Force Participation of Police and Sheriffs by Population Served 2007		
Pop. Served	% of Police Departments with Officers Assigned	% of Sheriff's Offices with Deputies Assigned
All sizes	9%	14%
1,000,000 or more	100	93
500,000–999,999	90	63
250,000–499,999	80	49
100,000–249,999	54	21
50,000–99,999	29	15
25,000–49,999	16	9
10,000–24,999	10	6
Under 10,000	4	8

Source: Reaves, B.A. (2010). *Local Police Departments, 2007*. Washington, DC: Bureau of Justice Statistics; Reaves, B.A. (2012). *Sheriffs' Offices, 2007 – Statistical Tables*. Washington, DC: Bureau of Justice Statistics.

and analysis centers within their police departments, and this led the creation of a new police strategy, commonly referred to as **intelligence-led policing**. This model of policing is built around the collection of information, the analysis of threats, and the use of risk assessments to determine potential threats and to create actionable intelligence for police to respond to potential threats.[41] Because only the largest police agencies could afford the creation of intelligence-led policing units, the Department of Homeland Security helped to fund the creation of what became known as **fusion centers**, regional information sharing centers that would act as a focal point for information that may provide police departments the actionable intelligence they need to respond. While the concept has its merits, the execution has not been so successful. A two-year Senate investigation into their success found that "the fusion centers often produced irrelevant, useless, or inappropriate intelligence reporting to DHS, and many produced no intelligence reporting whatsoever."[42]

Conclusion

As August Vollmer noted in the Chapter 9 opening quote, the first thing in policing to develop is a strategy, and everything else will follow. It is typically described that police strategy informs police operations, and police operations informs police tactics. As American police in the late twentieth century came to realize, that old concepts of random patrol, rapid response, and investigative technology do not solve or deter crimes well. New strategies were developed including broken windows, problem-solving, community policing, targeted policing, and a whole myriad of others that singularly or in some combination have come to drive twenty-first-century policing. While these strategies continue to develop and their efficacy assessed, they stand as the current strategies that drive police deployment.

Just the Facts

1. The earliest studies in American policing were the Kansas City Preventive Patrol Experiment, the Kansas City Rapid Response Study, and the RAND Criminal Investigation Study, which found, contrary to accepted belief, police do not deter crime in random patrols, the faster police respond to crime scenes does not increase the chances crimes will be solved, and the increased use of detectives and technological resources to investigate crimes does not increase crime solvability.

2. Broken windows theory posits that neighborhood blight, such as broken windows that remain unfixed, and minor crimes, such as graffiti left unenforced, sends a signal to the criminal element that no one cares about the neighborhood, thus inviting criminal activity. Policing under this theory posits that minor crimes and issues of disorder should be addressed by the police so as to send a signal that people care about the neighborhood, creating a disincentive for criminal activity to occur.

3. Police public relations, police community relations, and team policing were all forerunners to community policing. The implementation of community policing began with numerous innovations in the 1980s that spread (diffused) across the country in the late 1980s and early 1990s,

and with assistance from the federal government became institutionalized by the mid-1990s.

4. The four dimensions of community policing are the philosophical, strategic, tactical, and organizational. The philosophical focuses on the underlying relationship between the public and the police, the strategic is how the philosophy is translated into action, the tactical are the specific skills necessary for police to carry out these actions, and the organizational are how the police department should organize to support police actions related to community policing.

5. Problem-oriented policing posits that police should engage in problem-solving when responding to calls-for-service by attempting to deal with the underlying problem rather than its symptoms. Police departments have implemented the SARA Model, a problem-solving model whose acronym stands for scanning, analysis, response, and assessment. The police scan their beats for problems, they attempt to identify the underlying problem and develop methods to address the problem, they then implement the best response and they assess the response to see if it had any effect.

6. The four primary methods for implementing targeted policing are hot spots policing,

crime-specific policing, zero-tolerance policing, and stop and frisk. Hot spots policing is geographically based that targets locations known for high crime. Crime-specific policing looks at specific problem crimes and then targets them wherever they are located. Zero-tolerance policing selects minor crimes and enforces them in a broken windows model style of policing. Stop and frisk employs terry stops for police to remain proactive against crime.

7. The methods of Crime Prevention Through Environmental Design, pulling levers, evidence-based policing, and predictive policing all draw upon crime data to understand how to deploy the police or to manipulate the environment to prevent crime or address its source.

8. Compstat is in many ways a data-driven method of policing as it draws upon computer analysis of crime statistics to determine the most pressing problems, yet it differs because it is also a means by which police management may be held accountable for the crime problems in their precincts, districts, or beats.

9. Since the terrorist attacks of September 11, 2001, the police have become an integral part of the concept and apparatus of homeland security, being part of the National Incident Management System through implementation of the Incident Command System, as first responders, they have participated in **counterterrorism** task forces, and they have developed regional fusion centers.

Ask Yourself

1. Revisit the three early studies that discovered long-held beliefs in American policing to have been without merit. Consider what police could have done differently to deter crime through patrol, solve more crimes by response, and to increase crime solvability through criminal investigations.

2. Two of the major strategies Chapter 9 are community policing and homeland security. When homeland security came into being, the predominant strategy in American policing at that time was community policing. Are these two strategies complimentary or are they at odds with one another? Revisit Chapter 2 for additional consideration of the question.

3. When it comes to policing strategies, new names are often given to strategies that bear close resemblance to other strategies already in existence. Look at the strategies of community policing, problem-oriented policing, targeted policing, and data-driven policing and consider the commonalities among them.

4. Consider the skills that police officers need under traditional policing; now consider the strategies of community policing, problem-oriented policing, targeted policing, and data-driven policing. Are there new skills that police officers will need to carry out these strategies? Should officers be hired that already have these skills or should the police department teach these skills?

5. The most recent police strategy is that of homeland security, which developed in the wake of the terrorist attacks of September 11, 2001. Due to the overwhelming nature of the emergency, police were immediately incorporated as part of the homeland security apparatus with little question. Should the local police truly be playing a role in homeland security or is this something better left to the federal government and federal law enforcement to deal with?

Keywords

Analysis
Antiterrorism
Assessment
Broken windows model
Broken windows theory
Community policing
Compstat
Counterterrorism
Crime Prevention Through
    Environmental Design
    (CPTED)
Crime-specific policing
Department of Homeland
    Security
Diffusion generation
Displacement effect
Evidence-based policing
Four dimensions of
    community policing

Fusion center
Hot spots policing
Incident command system
Innovation generation
Institutionalization generation
Intelligence-led policing
Kansas City Preventative
    Patrol Experiment
Kansas City Rapid
    Response Study
National Incident
    Management System
Omnibus Crime Control and
    Safe Streets Act of 1968
Organizational dimension
Philosophical dimension
Police strategies
Police-community relations
Predictive policing

President's Commission on
    Law Enforcement and the
    Administration of Justice
Problem-oriented policing
Public relations
Pulling levers strategy
RAND Criminal
    Investigation Study
Response
SARA Model
Scanning
Stop and frisk
Strategic dimension
Strategy
Tactical dimension
Team policing
Three generations of
    community policing
Zero-tolerance policing

Endnotes

1. Shaw, Robert (1938). "Forty Fighting Years: The Story of August Vollmer." *The Oakland Post Enquirer*, available on microfilm at the Bancroft Library, University California of Berkeley, Berkeley, California, Chapter 37.

2. Hoover, L.T. (2014). *Police crime control strategies*. Clifton Park, NY: Delmar Cengage.

3. President's Crime Commission on Law Enforcement and Administration of Justice. (1967). *The challenge of crime in a free society*. Washington, DC: U.S. GPO.

4. Kelling, G.L., Pate, T., Dieckman, D., & Brown, C.E. (1974). *The Kansas city preventive patrol experiment: A summary report*. Washington, DC: Police Foundation.

5. Kelling, G.L., Pate, T., Dieckman, D., & Brown, C.E. (1974). *The Kansas city preventive patrol experiment: A summary report*. Washington, DC: Police Foundation.

6. Kansas City Police Department. (1978). *Response time analysis: Executive summary*. Washington, DC: U.S. GPO.

7. Greenwood, P.W., Chaiken, J., & Petersilia, J. (1977). *The criminal investigation process*. Lexington, MA: D.C. Heath and Company; National Institute of Law Enforcement and Criminal Justice. (1977). *The criminal investigation process: A dialogue on research findings*. Washington, DC: U.S. GPO.

8. Kelling, G.L. & Wilson, J.Q. (1982). Broken windows: The police and neighborhood safety. *Atlantic Monthly*, March

1. Retrieved online at http://www.theatlantic.com/magazine/archive/1982/03/broken-windows/304465/

9. Kennedy, D.M. (2011). *Don't shoot: One man, a street fellowship, and the end of violence in inner-city America*. New York, NY: Bloomsbury.

10. Kelling, G.L. & Wilson, J.Q. (1982). Broken windows: The police and neighborhood safety. *Atlantic Monthly*, March 1. Retrieved online at http://www.theatlantic.com/magazine/archive/1982/03/broken-windows/304465/

11. Oliver, W.M. (2007). *Community-oriented policing: A systemic approach to policing*. Upper Saddle River, NJ: Prentice Hall.

12. Oliver, W.M. (2000). The third generation of community policing: Moving through innovation, diffusion, and institutionalization. *Police Quarterly*, 3, 367-388.

13. Cordner, G.W. (1995). Community policing: Elements and effects. *Police Forum*, 5, 1-8.

14. Braga, A.A. & Weisburd, D.L. (2011). The effects of focused deterrence strategies on crime: A systematic review and meta-analysis of the empirical evidence. *Journal of Research in Crime and Delinquency*, Retrieved online at http://jrc.sagepub.com/content/49/3/323.refs; Telep, C.W. & Weisburd, D. (2012). What is known about the effectiveness of police practices in reducing crime and disorder? *Police Quarterly*, 15, 331-357.

15. Roth, J.A. et al. (2000). *National evaluation of the COPS program – Title I of the 1994 crime act*. Washington, DC: U.S. Department of Justice.

16. Roh, S. & Oliver, W.M. (2005). Effects of community policing upon fear of crime: Understanding the causal linkage. *Policing: An International Journal of Police Strategies & Management, 28*, 670–683; Zhao, J.S., Scheider, M., & Thurman, Q.C. (2002). The effect of police presence on public fear reduction and satisfaction: A review of the literature. *The Justice Professional, 15*, 273-99.

17. Goldstein, H. (1977). *Policing a free society*. New York, NY: HarperCollins.

18. Goldstein, H. (1979). Improving policing: A problem-oriented approach. *Crime & Delinquency, 25*, 236-258.

19. Braga, A. A., and Weisburd, D. L. (2006). Problem-oriented policing: The disconnect between principles and practice. In D. L. Weisburd and A. A. Braga (eds.), *Police innovation: Contrasting perspectives* (pp. 133–154). New York: Cambridge University Press; Cordner, G. W. (1998). Community policing: Elements and effects. In G. Alpert and A. Piquero (Eds.), *Community policing: Contemporary readings* (pp. 1–8). Prospect Heights, IL: Waveland; Weisburd, D. & Majmundar, K. (eds.) (2018). *Proactive policing: Effects on crime and communities*. Washington, DC: The National Academies Press.

20. Weisburd, D. & Majmundar, K. (eds.) (2018). *Proactive policing: Effects on crime and communities*. Washington, DC: The National Academies Press.

21. Cordner, G. & Biebel, E.P. (2005). Problem-oriented policing in practice.4 *Criminology & Public Policy, 4*, 155–180; Weisburd, D., Telep, C.W., Hinkle, J.C., & Eck, J.E. (2010). Is problem-oriented policing effective in reducing crime and disorder? Findings from a Campbell systematic review. *Criminology & Public Policy, 9*, 139-172.

22. Carson, J. V. & Wellman, A.P. (2018). Problem-oriented policing in suburban low-income housing: A quasi-experiment. *Police Quarterly, 21*, 139-170; Guerette, R.T. & Bowers, K.J. (2009). Assessing the extent of crime displacement and diffusion of benefits: A review of situational crime prevention evaluations. *Criminology 47*, 1331-1368.

23. Braga, A.A. & Weisburd, D.L. (2010). *Policing problems places: Crime hot spots and effective prevention*. New York, NY: Oxford University Press; See also Haberman, C.P. (2016). A view inside the "black box" of hot spots policing from a sample of police commanders. *Police Quarterly, 19*, 488-517; Koper, C.S., Woods, D.J., & Isom, D. (2016). Evaluating a police-led community initiative to reduce gun violence in St. Louis. *Police Quarterly, 19*, 115-149.

24. Braga, A.A. & Weisburd, D.L. (2010). *Policing problems places: Crime hot spots and effective prevention*. New York, NY: Oxford University Press; Weisburd, D. & Majmundar, K. (eds.) (2018). *Proactive policing: Effects on crime and communities*. Washington, DC: The National Academies Press.

25. Hoover, L.T. (2014). *Police crime control strategies*. Clifton Park, NY: Delmar Cengage.

26. Hoover, L.T. (2014). *Police crime control strategies*. Clifton Park, NY: Delmar Cengage; McArdle, A. & Erzen, T. (2001). *Zero tolerance: Quality of life and the new police brutality in New York city*. New York, NY: New York University Press.

27. Zimring, F.E. (2012). *The city that became safe: New York's lessons for urban crime and its control*. New York, NY: Oxford University Press.

28. Jeffery, C.R. (1977). *Crime prevention through environmental design*. Thousand Oaks, CA: SAGE.

29. Peak, K. (2013). *Encyclopedia of community policing and problem solving*. Thousand Oaks, CA: SAGE.

30. Braga, A.A., Kennedy, D.M., Waring, E.J., & Piehl, A.M. (2001).Problem-oriented policing, deterrence and youth violence: An evaluation of Boston's operation cease-fire. *Journal of Research in Crime and Delinquency, 38*, 195-226; Kennedy, D.M. (1998). Pulling levers: Getting deterrence right. *National Institute of Justice Journal, 7*, 2-8; Weisburd, D. & Majmundar, K. (eds.) (2018). *Proactive policing: Effects on crime and communities*. Washington, DC: The National Academies Press.

31. Kennedy, D.M. (2011). *Don't shoot: One man, a street fellowship, and the end of violence in inner-city America*. New York, NY: Bloomsbury.

32. Sherman, L. (1998). Evidence-based policing. *Ideas in American Policing*. Retrieved online at http://www.police foundation.org/content/evidence-based-policing

33. Carson, J. V. & Wellman, A.P. (2018). Problem-oriented policing in suburban low-income housing: A quasi-experiment. *Police Quarterly, 21*, 139-170; Guerette, R.T. & Bowers, K.J. (2009). Assessing the extent of crime displacement and diffusion of benefits: A review of situational crime prevention evaluations. *Criminology 47*, 1331-1368.

34. Perry, W.L. et al. (2013). *Predictive policing: The role of crime forecasting in law enforcement operations*. Santa Monica, CA: Rand Corporation.

35. Weisburd, D. & Majmundar, K. (eds.) (2018). *Proactive policing: Effects on crime and communities*. Washington, DC: The National Academies Press, p. 51.

36. Henry, V.E. (2002). *The Compstat paradigm: Management accountability in policing, business, and the public sector*. Flushing, NY: Looseleaf Law Publications, Inc.; Silverman, E. B. (1999). *NYPD battles crime: Innovative strategies in policing*. Boston, MA: Northeastern University Press.

37. Bratton, W. & Knobles, P. (1998). *The turnaround: How America's top cop reversed the crime epidemic*. New York, NY: Random House; Henry, V. E. (2002). *The Compstat paradigm: Management accountability in policing, business, and the public sector*. Flushing, NY: Looseleaf Law Publications, Inc.; Maple, J. & Mitchell, C. (1999). *The crime fighter*. New York, NY: Doubleday.

38. Jang, H.S., Hoover, L.T., & Joo, H.J. (2010). An evaluation of Compstat's effect upon crime: The Fort Worth experience. *Police Quarterly, 13*, 387-412.

39. U.S. Department of Homeland Security. (2008). *National incident management system*. Washington, DC: U.S. Department of Homeland Security.

40. Oliver, W.M. (2007). *Homeland security for policing*. Upper Saddle River, NJ: Prentice Hall.

41. Carter, J.G. (2016). Institutional pressures and isomorphism: The impact on intelligence-led policing adoption. *Police Quarterly, 19*, 435-460.

42. United States Senate. (2012). *Federal support for and involvement in state and local fusion centers*. Washington, DC: U.S. Senate.

■ *"Patrol is the backbone of policing."*[1] *—O.W. Wilson, disciple of August Vollmer*

Patrol can be on foot, by horse, or any motor vehicle, such as this All Terrain Vehicle.

CHAPTER 10

Patrol

After reading this chapter, you will be able to:

1. Understand what O.W. Wilson meant when he called patrol the "backbone of policing."
2. List and explain the three main goals of police patrol.
3. Describe the key pieces of police equipment and their importance to police patrol.
4. Detail the wide array of patrol methods available to the police beyond automobile patrol.
5. List and describe the four primary functions of police patrol.
6. Identify and explain the three methods developed by police patrol to deal with dramatic increases in calls-for-service after the creation of the emergency number 911.
7. List and describe the four methods of targeted police patrols.
8. Explain the three methods of community policing patrols.

Police patrol is often referred to as the "**backbone of policing**."[2] As O.W. Wilson, a disciple of August Vollmer and once the Superintendent of the Chicago Police Department explained, "Patrol is an indispensable service that plays a leading role in the accomplishment of the police purpose."[3] And it is why Vollmer, in the Chapter 5 opening quote, saw it as the highest of callings, because for him it was the ultimate example of service to humanity. The police officer, riding patrol on their beat, looking for crimes and other problems to address and responding to all calls-for-service, is the primary function of the police department. In fact, according to a National Academy of Science study on American policing, "roughly 60 percent of all sworn officers in city police departments are assigned to the patrol bureau and these officers have the vast majority of police officers contacts with the general public."[4] This is what makes understanding the "backbone of policing" so important.

Most people, however, think of the police as solely crime fighters. It has been noted that, "Certainly, Hollywood plays up this image" for "they know that audiences won't be terribly interested in watching films and shows about police as service providers, traffic controllers, and conflict managers."[5] When people watch movies and television shows, they want to be entertained for "audiences want action and they want stories about the fight between good and evil."[6] It is not just Hollywood or citizens, however, who promote this myth for "police officers themselves like and perpetuate this crime-fighting self-image, even though they understand it represents but a partial truth about real policing."[7] Real policing is about a wide variety of duties and responsibilities that police patrol officers perform, and they are usually categorized into three primary goals of patrol: crime control, order maintenance, and service.

Crime control, as a focus of policing, was largely the result of the early twentieth-century police reforms. The movement to professionalize the police necessitated the adoption of a core focus of policing. As doctors save lives and lawyers represent defendants in court, the emphasis of the police profession was police control crime. Thus, crime fighting became the primary mission of the police.[8] Police strategies, tactics, and technology all worked toward emphasizing this crime fighting role. While most studies have found that police do, in fact, engage in crime control, studies consistently suggest only 15 to 30 percent of their time is spent on this role.[9]

Order maintenance is another function of the police, and this comes about when citizens come into conflict with one another or when one is creating a nuisance or disturbing the peace. James Q. Wilson argued that the police officer's role "is defined more by his responsibility for maintaining order than by his responsibilities for enforcing the law."[10] He further adds that order is defined as "the absence of disorder, and by disorder is meant behavior that either disturbs or threatens to disturb the public peace or that involves face-to-face conflict between two or more persons."[11] While order maintenance may result in crime control, more often than not a police officer can mediate the dispute and restore order without having to resort to arrest. Studies into how much time police officers spend on order maintenance also suggest that 10 to 25 percent of their time is spent in this role.[12]

Service is generally the last function of the police listed, but once everything is taken into consideration, it often becomes the one role that police officers spend most of their time performing.[13] People call the police with all manner of requests, ranging from assistance with getting into a locked car to calling the police late at night because there is a bat in the house (that was a real call for this author, who somehow managed to catch it with a heavy blanket). Research suggests that anywhere from 15 to 65 percent of an officer's time is spent on these types of calls.[14] Once you add in traffic regulation and enforcement, as well as such things as directing traffic, responding to automobile accidents, and funeral escorts, another 20 to 30 percent of an officer's time is spent on this type of service. Combined together, service can account for 35 to 55 percent of an officer's time on patrol.[15] Despite the realities of the police function emphasizing service, as police professor Larry Hoover explains, "Universal response to requests for service is often regarded as nothing but interference with the 'real' role of the police—crime control."[16]

Despite the fact the police tend to emphasize crime control, while the realities of the job suggest it is service, Hoover explains the purpose of the police, and particularly police patrol, in this manner: "One of the hallmarks of the American police service is its democratic nature—when the phone rings, we will come."[17] No one asks what income you make, have you paid your taxes, what race you are, or what sex. They simply ask what is your problem and they dispatch an officer to come provide some assistance (service), mediate a dispute (order maintenance), or, when a crime has occurred, make an arrest (crime control). Police patrol is about answering that call.

This chapter is focused on understanding all aspects of police patrol, from how officers prepare for patrol, the various patrol types used, the nature of patrol deployment, and how police officers deploy for either targeted patrols or community policing patrols.

Patrol Equipment

While generally not given much consideration, it is important to take a look at how police officers prepare for patrol service. The police officer will typically report to the police station for roll call prior to going on shift. If they have not come to work in their uniform, they will go to the locker room and put on their protective vest, uniform, and equipment belt. At roll call they are usually issued their patrol vehicle assignment, and they pick up their portable radio. When arriving at the police car, after a quick inspection, they log into the onboard computer and use the vehicle's radio to mark "in-service." The officer is now ready for police patrol. All of the equipment is a part of how police officers perform their patrol duties.

One of the most important items for police patrol is the **protective vest.** Although the concept of body armor is derived from the military, the use of a soft vest for policing dates back to the early twentieth century when a patent was filed in 1919, and the Washington, D.C. Metropolitan Police held a public demonstration on April 2, 1931.[18] It was not until the 1960s and early 1970s that improvements in the fibers allowed for maximum protection, but was of light enough weight for effective police duty. On December 23, 1975, Seattle Police Department patrol officer Raymond T. Johnson "stood in the checkout line at a local market when a robbery suspect entered the store and brandished a weapon. Johnson lunged for the suspect's gun. In the violent struggle that ensued, the suspect emptied his .38 caliber pistol, striking Johnson in the left hand and twice in the chest before fleeing."[19] Johnson survived and earned the dubious distinction of being "the first law enforcement

Police patrol—the backbone of policing. San Francisco Police Department officers on patrol.

officer saved in a field test of a new generation of soft body armor."[20]

From that time forward, police departments began fielding police body armor, and the rate of police officer deaths in the line of duty began to drop. Since Johnson's encounter, it is estimated that body armor has saved the lives of over 3,000 police officers.[21] Despite this fact, body armor can be uncomfortable to wear, especially in the summer heat, for as LAPD Officer Dunn explained it best, "My uniform shirt is soaking wet, the Kevlar vest I have on acting as a furnace in the intense midafternoon heat, cooking my heart and stomach like boiled meat."[22] Although often uncomfortable, the trade-offs are too important not to wear the protective vest.

Another piece of patrol equipment for safety, although often not thought of in that manner, is the **firearm** that officers carry.[23] Police officers are authorized to use deadly force to protect themselves, other officers, and citizens while working patrol. The firearm that the officer carries, like the protective vest, can mean the difference between life and death, so it is important that the officer is well trained in its use, practices on a regular basis, and maintains and cleans it regularly.

It was not until Police Commissioner Teddy Roosevelt made the .32-caliber Colt New Police revolver the regulation police handgun in 1896 that police departments began fielding a specific firearm for its officers.[24] What followed, according to legendary American sniper Chris Kyle, was the domination of the Colt and Smith & Wesson .38 in policing throughout the United States.[25] It was not until the end of the twentieth century that police departments began switching to semiautomatics, mostly 9mms at first, but soon a whole array of semiautomatic pistols were adopted. For instance, in Los Angeles, "Prior to 1989, officers were issued .38 revolvers. When the LAPD switched to 9mm handguns, it did not offer officers with revolvers new guns. Those officers [had] to buy their own weapons if they want[ed] a 9mm, even though the LAPD [had] decided that the 9mm is a superior weapon."[26]

A third important tool of the trade for police patrol is the **radio**. Both the patrol vehicle's radio and the portable radio that police officers carry are the primary means by which police officers are dispatched to calls and how officers communicate their situations on scene. Although this was not always the case, for police one-way radios (where dispatch could send a message to the police, but not vice-versa) did not develop until the late 1920s in both the Berkeley Police Department by Officer V. A. Leonard under Vollmer's guidance and the Detroit Police Department by Officer W. P. Rutledge.[27] Soon, however, during the 1930s, two-way radios became the norm, and police dispatching of officers by way of calls to the police was how the majority of people alerted the police to a problem or crime.

One thing that many people also do not realize, however, is the power and safety of the radio for the police officer. As Sergeant Mike Fanning of the LAPD explained it, "I've been in over 65 vehicle pursuits in my career. The most important thing I have learned is communication. That is communication not only with your partner, but with the other troops. If we don't know *where* you are, we can't get there to help you."[28] The police radio is a crucial piece of equipment for police patrol.

In addition to the vest, firearm, and radio, other equipment for police patrol is also crucial. The patrol vehicle is the primary means—although not the only means (see patrol types)—for how police officers respond to calls-for-service. In addition, another form of communication includes the onboard computers that most police patrol vehicles have today as well as GPS systems. Still further, many do not consider all of the things that police officers carry on their duty belts. While not all officers carry the same items, many of the following

Just some of the equipment police officers routinely carry on patrol.

are common among officers working patrol: extra ammunition, a baton, CS or pepper spray, a Taser (conducted electrical weapon), handcuffs, tactical flashlight, latex gloves, and knife. Finally, add in the uniform, badge, and sometimes a hat, and you have what visibly identifies a police officer working patrol. All of these items create the inventory of equipment that officers carry with them while working patrol to adhere to that old Scout motto "be prepared."

Patrol Types

The traditional method for police patrol in America from its inception, and even as far back as the watch, ward, and sheriffs, was either by foot or by horse. When policing was conducted in the towns and cities, it primarily saw officers walking a beat, while in the more rural parts of America, police patrol was on horseback. This author, when working as a summer police officer in New Jersey, walked a beat along the main drag, and I found it to be the most rewarding of my experiences as a police officer. The interaction with citizens I saw on a regular basis, including business owners, gave my police work a personal nature, and I liked the fact that they knew me and I knew them. Many people, including police officers who do not work **foot patrol**, see it

The oldest form of police patrol is the foot patrol (Table 10.1). A San Francisco police officer walks his beat along Powell Street in the financial center.

as more about public relations than policing (read "crime control"), yet that is not the case. As one police officer explained, "An aggressive, street-smart police officer, working an active post, can develop as many (or more) quality cases and arrests working foot patrol as he can working motorized patrol."[29] Foot patrols were brought back to American policing starting in the 1980s with the movement to community policing, and while there are limitations to their use, they appear to be an effective means of police patrol.[30]

Just before the twentieth century in the 1890s, there was a sudden American craze over the bicycle, and police officers from New York, to St. Louis, to Berkeley, California, began riding **bicycle patrols**. By the turn of the century, people began strapping motors to these new contraptions, and bicycles became motorcycles. While the use of **motorcycle patrols** continued to grow over the twentieth century, the police use of bicycles all but disappeared with the advent of the automobile. However, as foot patrol returned to policing in the late twentieth century because of community policing, so too did bicycle patrols. In part, the bicycle patrols were reinstituted in policing because they made police officers more approachable, thus fostering police and citizen relations, but they also allowed police officers to patrol in areas that were previously off limits, such as hike and bike trails. Once again, however, their utility is far greater than most realize, for as one police officer explained, "Officers on bike patrol have pursued and caught armed robbers, home invasion criminals, car thieves, criminals breaking into cars and criminals in possession of stolen property."[31] She also noted, "They have assisted in searches for missing children" and they have been used in open air drug markets because of their "stealth and speed."[32] Police bicycle patrols also appear to be an effective means of police patrol.[33]

The other type of patrol previously mentioned, **mounted patrol** has also seen some historical changes. Originally a mainstay of American rural police patrol, with the advent of the automobile, mounted patrol began to wane. Throughout the twentieth century, mounted patrol became limited in use, and many departments discontinued this type of patrol because of the expense of maintaining the horses (estimates have been $11,000 a year to maintain a horse, $5,000 to maintain a patrol car).[34] There was a slight return to mounted patrol with the development of community policing, but it has never been as widespread as the return of either foot or bike patrol.[35] Many departments keep them for the public relations aspect, for as a mounted police

Table 10.1 Types of Regularly Scheduled Patrols (Other Than Automobile) Used by Police Departments, by Size of Population Served, 2007

Pop. Served	Foot	Bicycle	Horse	Motorcycle	Air	Marine
All sizes	55%	32%	1%	16%	1%	4%
1,000,000 or more	92	100	77	100	100	69
500,000–999,999	81	100	61	94	71	52
250,000–499,999	78	89	50	91	57	26
100,000–249,999	59	71	17	90	17	12
50,000–99,999	56	69	5	74	5	12
25,000–49,999	52	58	2	55	2	6
10,000–24,999	50	44	1	25	1	5
2,500–9,999	58	36	--	8	--	4
Under 2,500	54	15	--	4	--	1

Source: Reaves, B.A. (2010). *Local Police Departments, 2007*. Washington, DC: Bureau of Justice Statistics.

officer explained, when a police department brings out all of its equipment, the horse is "by far the biggest attraction. Just to let people come up and talk to them, to let the kids rub them—that is a benefit for the police department. It's a bit of an icebreaker."[36] The relationship can also help to develop leads in the area of crime control, for as another mounted officer explained, "We develop a relationship with people down here. They'll tell us stuff, let us know if gangs are meeting around here."[37] In addition, horses have speed and they give the officer the advantage of height, thus allowing them a unique capability in the performance of their patrol duties.

All of this pales in comparison, however, to the impact that Henry Ford's early twentieth-century mass production of the automobile had on American policing. Very quickly, the police, like so many other Americans, adapted to the new form of transportation, and it became the primary means for police patrol. So, when O.W. Wilson said that police patrol was the

Perhaps the second oldest form of police patrol is the mounted patrol. The New York City Police Department's mounted patrol is depicted here from 1905.

"backbone of policing," he assuredly meant police **motor vehicle patrols.**[38] The advantages that the automobile gave to police officers to respond to calls-for-service were enormous, and once the two-way radio was established in the vehicles in the 1930s, there was no going back. Still further, because of American's quick adoption of the automobile, there was the growing realization that an organization needed to regulate the roads, respond to motor vehicle accidents, and enforce traffic laws, and the police were the natural agency to perform this function.

One aspect of police patrols in which O.W. Wilson played a significant role was the transition from two-officer to one-officer police patrols (Box 10.1). When police motor vehicle patrols began, most police departments had adopted the two-officer model for purposes of officer safety, based on the idea that with a back-up always available it made officers safer. In the 1950s, Wilson began researching this topic, and he argued that "one-man patrol-car operation is more efficient than two-man because the number of patrol units is thus doubled and the city is divided into twice as many patrol areas as when officers ride in pairs."[39] Of course the issue of safety was raised, but Wilson contended that when an officer worked by themselves, the officer would be far more cautious than if automatically having a backup.[40] In addition, the two-way radio allowed the officer to call for backup in situations that presented danger, something that was the exception not the rule. Interestingly, this shows how much influence Wilson had on policing at the time, for over the next 20 years, police departments began moving to one-officer patrol vehicles, and by the 1970s it had become the norm (Table 10.2).

In the latter half of the twentieth century, many additional forms of transportation have become common in policing. In addition to automobile patrols, police today often use everything from golf carts to all-terrain vehicles (ATVs) and skateboards to Segways. In addition, when police patrols extend to waterways, they will use various-sized boats such as small speed

---

Box 10.1 Ethics in Practice: One- or Two-Officer Patrols?

When police began patrolling in automobiles, the eventual norm was to staff each patrol car with two officers. The concept was to promote officer safety by always having an officer backup on each call. O.W. Wilson, after studying the issue, advocated for **one-officer patrol cars**, arguing that it was more efficient as most police contacts did not require a backup officer and were one needed, a second single-officer patrol car could arrive on scene. This study was conducted in the 1950s, and the single-officer patrol car became the norm by the 1970s. As the issues that police officers face on patrol change, the debate has reopened regarding the advantages of **one-officer versus two-officer patrol cars**.

Ask Yourself:

Should police patrol retain the one-officer method, or should American policing move back to the two-officer patrol car. Consider the pros and cons of each, decide which is preferable, and specify the arguments in favor of your decision.

Table 10.2 Types of Regularly Scheduled Patrols (Other Than Automobile) Used by Sheriffs' Offices, by Size of Population Served, 2007

Pop. Served	Foot	Bicycle	Horse	Motorcycle	Air	Marine
All sizes	25%	9%	4%	9%	7%	23%
1,000,000 or more	44	67	41	81	59	63
500,000–999,999	44	42	17	61	31	4
250,000–499,999	28	42	17	34	30	50
100,000–249,999	23	22	4	25	12	41
50,000–99,999	25	10	4	11	3	37
25,000–49,999	25	5	2	3	4	23
10,000–24,999	19	4	3	1	4	14
Under 10,000	29	1	2	--	4	9

Source: Reaves, B.A. (2012). *Sheriffs' Offices, 2007 – Statistical Tables*. Washington, DC: Bureau of Justice Statistics

boats, pontoon boats, and large-sized search and rescue watercraft. Further, larger metropolitan and state police agencies often employ various aircraft in their patrols, mostly helicopters, but some have small airplanes as well. Finally, the newest adoption of technology to police patrol, although it is still new and its proper use is still being worked out, is the deployment of police drones, sometimes call unmanned aircraft (UAs) or unmanned aerial vehicles. Police Officer Nelson of Grand Forks Police Department explains that in their department, "We only use UAs for something ongoing or that has already happened. We don't fly over an area to find a drug grow operation."[41] However, just as the proper use of drones is being worked out for all Americans, it is also still a work in progress for how it will be utilized in policing (Box 10.2).

Box 10.2 History in Practice: Paul Harvey: "What are Policemen Made of?"

For anyone who lived in the last half of the twentieth century and listened to radio, news commentator Paul Harvey was a distinct voice. He depicted the life of common Americans, including one narrative titled, "So God Made a Farmer," which was used recently in a Ram Truck Commercial during Super Bowl XLVII. One of Harvey's narratives was dedicated to the police officer and was titled, "The Policeman," although it is now often called "What are Policemen Made Of?" Look up either title on Google or YouTube and listen to the narrative in Paul Harvey's unique voice. A number of people have made videos of the narrative featuring pictures of America's police officers.

A Chicago police officer on a Segway patrolling the neighborhood.

Police Patrol Deployment

As previously described with the Kansas City Preventive Patrol Experiment (see Chapter 9), police officers in the early to mid-twentieth century were deployed based upon geography, time, and crime, and once the automobile was adopted, police officers patrolled these beats looking to deter crime, find crimes in progress, or respond to crimes that had already occurred. Research has demonstrated that there are really four primary functions of what is called routine patrol and they are (1) preventive patrol, (2) calls-for-service, (3) administrative duties, and (4) officer-initiated activities.[42] **Preventive patrol** is focused on maintaining a visible presence in the community to deter criminal behavior and disorderly conduct. Although we learned that the police driving around in random patrols do not prevent crime and that more target-specific patrols are more effective, preventive patrols still remain an element of the reason for police patrols. **Calls-for-service** are those emergency (911) and non-emergency calls that citizens place to the police, or it may simply be when a citizen flags down an officer. In these cases, it is the citizens making the request for assistance (Table 10.3). This is opposed to **officer-initiated contacts**, when officers themselves witness or discover a traffic infraction, a misdemeanor violation, or a felonious crime in progress. And the final duties that officers typically perform on routine patrol are **administrative duties**, such as filling out patrol vehicle inspections, updating policy manuals, and all of the paperwork that documents their actions and the actions of others on calls.

In the 1970s, two factors had a significant impact on police patrol. The first was the Kansas City Preventive Patrol Experiment's findings. If police officers driving around in random patrols did not deter crime, the thinking went that less police officers were actually needed to work patrol. In fact, all a police department needed was enough officers to respond to the crimes for which they were called. The fact that cities, towns, and counties across the nation were facing fiscal problems because of the poor economy in the 1970s, as officers retired many were not replaced because police officers were found not to have any deterrent effect on crime. The problem was the study did not state that police had no impact at all, only that random patrols did not appear to have any impact on crime rates. What many politicians missed was that police may very well deter crime, but not through random patrols. Still further, what they really missed was the fact that the police spend little

Table 10.3   Local Police Officers and Sheriff's Deputies Assigned to Respond to Calls for Service, by Size of Population Served, 2007

Pop. Served	Police	Sheriff's Deputies
All sizes	67%	57%
1,000,000 or more	54	44
500,000–999,999	59	50
250,000–499,999	61	52
100,000–249,999	68	59
50,000–99,999	68	59
25,000–49,999	77	70
10,000–24,999	87	83
Under 10,000	96	91

Source: Reaves, B.A. (2010). *Local Police Departments, 2007*. Washington, DC: Bureau of Justice Statistics; Reaves, B.A. (2012). *Sheriffs' Offices, 2007 – Statistical Tables*. Washington, DC: Bureau of Justice Statistics.

of their time in the crime fighting mode, and most of it is dedicated to calls-for-service, traffic problems, and other things outside of criminal violations.

The second factor that was not considered, for no one could have predicted the impact that it would have on American policing and that is the three-digit phone number: 911. Started in 1969 as a test pilot project in Baltimore, Maryland, through a grant out of the Omnibus Crime Control and Safe Streets Act of 1968, and in cooperation with AT&T, the test worked out quite well, and citizens were highly receptive and satisfied with the simple number. It was much easier to remember than the regular police phone number and the idea that when one calls 911 a police officer responds, was comforting to most Americans. In the early 1970s, the use of 911 rapidly spread across America and the number of calls-for-service rose dramatically. The problem was, calls-for-service rose at a time when the number of police officers was declining through attrition. This created a problem for police departments that has never really gone away and by the late 1980s, police departments were overwhelmed with 911 calls, and police officers going on patrol could often expect to run from one call to the next with no time left for their other duties. When combined with nonemergency calls, the whole system was becoming unmanageable.[43]

Although police departments hired heavily throughout the 1980s, still to this day, responding to calls-for-service often drives the tempo of police work and certain shifts prove to be busier than others and the busy ones can often be brutal. As one evening supervisor from the LAPD explained to his new officers, "You cannot sit on your ass here. A lot of shit goes down, and it goes down fast. On P.M. watch, you'll be chasin' the radio all night, going from one hot shot to the next. And everyone goes when there's trouble. This ain't a work environment for the fainthearted."[44]

Police patrol can very often be about going on duty and then responding from one call to the next. When a call is completed, there is still the paperwork to document what the officer did; however, if a call for an accident with injuries, a crime in progress, or an officer-needs-assistance is issued over the radio, everything must be dropped and the call responded to immediately. This then necessitates more paperwork and often, on very busy shifts, officers return to the police station at the end of their shift buried in paperwork that must be finished before they go home.

While this still remains an issue for police departments to wrestle with today, it was especially problematic in the late 1970s, and as a result, police departments began adapting police patrols to deal with the high volume of calls-for-service while still trying to perform their other crime fighting responsibilities. The answers came in the form of police departments adopting differential police response, split patrols, and/or tactical patrols.

Many departments opted to try and solve the problem of an overwhelming increase in calls-for-service by adopting what became known as the **differential police response (DPR)** system.[45] DPR was a strategy that was very similar to medical triage. When the police receive calls-for-service, many are clear emergencies where a police response is needed immediately (for example, robbery in progress, rape, carjacking), while others may not even need a police officer to respond as the problem could be handled over the phone (for example, minor traffic accident, lost valuables). Classifying the types of calls into different categories allowed for the police to respond differently to the calls they received, thus better managing one of their greatest resources: a police officer's time. The pitfall to an agency using differential police response, however, is that citizens often do not understand. When they find themselves involved in an accident or the victim of a crime, for them it is the most important problem in the world, and when the police do not respond quickly or at all, no matter how much they are educated on the reasons for the DPR system, they may still come away with a negative attitude toward the police.

Another response to the increase in calls-for-service because of 911 was the use of **split patrols**.[46] Police departments, to manage the need to perform all of the various functions of policing, would split their patrol force

Emergency 911 displayed prominently on a police car.

into two: one to respond to calls-for-service, while the other would conduct routine patrol. The two groups would rotate, each taking their turn at the calls-for-service, which usually entailed running from call to call. A study conducted in Wilmington, Delaware, found that the split-patrol (sometimes called split force) system improved both police call-handling and patrol productivity, while at the same time enhancing police professionalism and police accountability.[47] The downside to this system is that the officers who are conducting patrols or other duties are not obligated to respond to calls unless it is an officer-needs-assistance call or a felony-in-progress, while the other officers are responding to call after call and seeing the number of calls pending backing up. As one police officer responded to the use of split patrols, "The regular officers were really upset while the other guys weren't doing anything."[48]

A third response to the fact officers were becoming tied up with calls-for-service was through the use of what became known as **tactical patrol**. Often called by other names such as targeted response teams or crime response units, tactical patrols are similar to the split force concept, but in this case one group of police officers conduct routine patrols and respond to 911 calls, while the other—the tactical patrol—is freed from calls-for-service to target problem locations through multiple means. These officers may be deployed in a saturation patrol (described later in this chapter) or by targeting a specific crime problem. For instance, if there was a rash of bank robberies located at major crossroads, tactical officers may be assigned to all of the banks meeting this criteria with the idea of stopping the next bank robbery while it's in progress. It has been explained that "tactical unit officers handle the most hazardous assignments" and "their job is to be out in the community going after the worst criminals."[49] As one Chicago police officer explained, "In tac [tactical], every situation is pretty dangerous, so you treat every situation as pretty dangerous. That sort of puts you on edge."[50] Overall, however, the research on the use of tactical patrols has "tended to produce ambiguous results in terms of their crime control effectiveness."[51]

Targeted Police Patrol

Another form of police patrols that developed in the 1980s and 1990s were targeted police patrols. Once again, these were somewhat a response developed out of a reaction to the Kansas City Preventive Patrol Experiment. That study suggested that police, driving around in routine patrol, do not deter crime. What happened as a result was a strong belief that the police had no deterrent effect on crime whatsoever. For instance, Thomas Repetto in his history of the American police cites an individual who steadfastly believed this when he said, "the police do not prevent crime. Experts know it, police know it, but the police does not know it."[52] The problem was this was simply not true.

The police in random patrols did not deter crime, but what the police and police scholars soon came to learn was that the police do deter crime, but only if the focus of the police is targeted on a specific problem, often in a very specific geographical location.[53] This became known as **hot spots policing**. As two leading police scholars Braga and Weisburd explains, "Simply defined, hot spots policing is the application of police interventions at very small geographic units of analysis. It does not sound like a very radical innovation, but indeed it represents a major reform not only in how the police organize to do something about crime, but also in how scholars define and understand the crime problem."[54] The reality, however, is that as far back as 1923 in Los Angeles, then Police Chief August Vollmer already understood this, for he recalled that at the time he had learned, "The concentration of force is supremely important in military science, and it will be important to the task we have at hand. We must focus our force on a small area and on a particular problem, and not dissipate it over a wide area."[55] The reality is these practices were not new to policing, they were simply practices that had been lost or underemphasized in policing for a number of decades (see Box 10.3).

As the police developed their understanding of targeted policing and that it must be focused on a specific crime problem, at a specific location, often pertaining to a specific group of offenders, the police began developing the strategy into a means by which the police could patrol to address the problems. What soon developed became known as four different types of

---

Box 10.3 History in Practice: LAPD Police Chief Daryl Gates and Targeted Policing

Daryl Gates was the Los Angeles Police Department chief from 1978 until 1992, a time of change in the department. During his tenure, he developed a number of **targeted policing units** to address specific concerns.

Daryl Gates joined the LAPD on September 16, 1949 as a patrol officer. He was assigned to William Parker for a brief period before returning to work patrol. Gates then took the sergeant's exam and scored so high he was number one on the promotion list. He then did that for several more ranks, before rejoining Parker as a member of his command staff.

Gates is considered the father of the **Special Weapons and Tactics (SWAT)** team, the co-founder of the **Drug Abuse Resistance Education (DARE)** program, and instrumental in promoting the **Community Resource Against Street Hoodlums (CRASH)** program. He was well-loved by the line officers for his style of leadership and his pro-police officer stance as the police chief.

Daryl Gates, however, was the police chief at the time of the Rodney King beating and the subsequent riots following the jury's decision to acquit the officers. The political pressure became too great and he resigned on June 28, 1992.

There are many interesting connections between Gates and other key policing pioneers. August Vollmer served as the LAPD police chief for one year on loan from Berkeley and one of his closest disciples, O.W. Wilson, wrote a book on LAPD Police Chief William Parker. When Parker became the LAPD Police Chief-he selected Daryl Gates to serve as his driver.

patrols: (1) directed patrol, (2) aggressive patrols, (3) saturation patrols, and (4) crackdowns (see Box 10.4).

One of the earliest methods of targeted police patrols was called **directed patrol**. Police officers were often assigned to specific crime or traffic directed patrols, or they were given the option of designating their own directed patrol in their beat. Officers were then responsible for monitoring the specific location for crime and disorder by conducting patrols in the area and enforcing the law. When the author worked as a police officer, I selected a small park as my directed patrol because it had a high number of citizen complaints for criminal and disorderly activity in the park. When not on assignment, I would often check the park, and I would sit in the police car in the parking lot while writing reports from other calls. As a result of my time spent in the park, I made multiple arrests for illicit activity such as drug use, drug dealing, prostitution, as well as several arrests for felonious assault and domestic violence. I also cleaned out hypodermic needles from the sandbox and mediated disputes that arose in basketball games. While making numerous arrests and preventing some problems (children being stuck with hypodermic needles), the directed patrol also managed to result in citizen satisfaction that the police were making the park a safer place. Studies regarding these types of patrols have demonstrated that directed patrols in high crime locations can

---

Box 10.4 Policing in Practice: Trooper of the Year — Corporal Joshua Moer, 2018

On April 26, 2018, Anthony Lamar Carter kidnapped Kaylea Renee Butts in Norman, Oklahoma. He was stopped by police in Oklahoma, but the suspect fled and the pursuit was on, moving through multiple jurisdictions. The vehicle then crossed into Texas and the suspect reached speeds of approximately 150 mph. Corporal Joshua Moer was the lead pursuit unit at about the time the high-speed chase came to an end. Officers in advance of the suspect had set out spike strips and when the car crossed over them, the vehicle ended up stopping off the road. Kaylea Butts then fled the vehicle, but was chased down by Anthony Carter, who then began stabbing her with a knife. Corporal Moer fired at the suspect, who momentarily stopped; but despite commands to drop the knife, he refused. When Carter continued to stab Butts, Moer discharged his service weapon, striking Carter 11 times. No longer a threat, Moer then began performing first aid on Butts who had been stabbed 13 times and had lost a lot of blood. She was rushed to the hospital and survived. "Due to the quick and decisive actions of Corporal Moer to stop the suspect's assault on Ms. Butts and the immediate first aid provided to her, Ms. Butts survived the aggravated assault," the press release stated. "Corporal Moer displayed leadership and courageousness, which saved the life of Ms. Butts." A video of this encounter is available at the website below.

Source: IACP/Motorola Solutions Trooper of the Year Award. (2018). "Trooper of the Year Winner 2018 – Corporal Joshua Moer." Retrieved from: https://video.motorolasolutions.com/detail/videos/public-safety-%3E-law-enforcement/video/6019499852001/trooper-of-the-year-winner-2018-%7C-corporal-joshua-moer?autoStart=true.

Box 10.5 Policing in Practice: Deputy Sheriff of the Year — Deputy Terry Harper, 2018.

On Wednesday, March 8, 2017, Deputy Terry Harper of the Hamilton County Sheriff's Office, OH, started his day, as always, with a cup of coffee at a United Dairy Farmers on his way to work. Meeting some of his co-workers, he was bringing several cups of coffee to the counter when he saw a man lying on the floor. Thinking it a medical emergency, Deputy Harper started to approach the man, until he had a better view. He then saw the suspect Simeon Thomas pointing a handgun at the store's clerk while screaming for the money. Deputy Harper drew his weapon and ordered the suspect to drop his weapon. The suspect turned toward Deputy Harper and Harper fired his service weapon. Thomas, scared, fled further into the store, while Deputy Harper ordered him to drop the gun and come out with his hands up. Thomas eventually complied and was ordered on the ground, at which point he was hand-cuffed. By not pursuing him further into the store and convincing the suspect to give up, Deputy Harper, it was noted handled the situation "absolutely perfectly," and not only saved the lives of the other store occupants, but also the suspect.

Source: National Sheriffs' Association. (2018). Deputy of the Year. Retrieved from https://www.sheriffs.org/about-nsa/deputy-year.

have a significant effect on crime, disorder, and traffic issues, and raise citizen satisfaction with the police (see Box 10.5).[56]

In addition to directed patrols, another form of targeting police patrol came to be known as **aggressive patrols** or sometimes "Terry stops" after the U.S. Supreme Court case of *Terry v. Ohio* (1968). The Supreme Court decision stated that police officers, with an ability to articulate a reasonable suspicion that someone has committed, is committing, or is about to commit a crime, can stop them and temporarily detain them to conduct a field investigation and for the safety of the officer and the community, the individual may be patted down for weapons. Police officers engaging in this type of field investigation were known to be conducting Terry stops and using this to target suspicious people in specific geographic locations known for high levels of crime and subsequently became known as aggressive patrols. It should be noted here that the term *aggressive* should not be associated with illegal behavior, but rather police officers using the law to aggressively target known crime locations. For instance, a well-known house for drug dealing in a neighborhood could be dealt with through surveillance or undercover investigators as one means to close the house. Another option is to have officers aggressively monitor the one block around the house for any criminal activity or traffic infractions. With any sign of potential criminal activity, officers would conduct field investigations (Terry stops) and either make arrests or issue tickets where warranted. The idea is to aggressively target the illegal behavior so as to force the drug dealing at the house to close. Research has found this strategy to be somewhat effective, but it can create animosity between the police and citizens.[57]

Another form of targeted police patrol that developed in the 1980s and 1990s was the use of **saturation patrols**. In this case, rather than having only one officer or a few officers deal with a specific location, the police department would deploy multiple officers, sometimes as many as 40 or 50 officers, depending upon the police department's resources. Imagine if the block in which the house known to be dealing drugs all of a sudden had 15 to 20 police officers on patrol on just that one block. Officers on foot, on bicycles, and in police cars, patrolled that one block every day for weeks on end. It would not take long for the word to get out and the drug dealing establishment to close. This form of police patrol targeting, as one can imagine, is highly effective and makes an impression, but it can also create animosity between the police and the law-abiding public, and it is a major drain on police resources.

One additional method of targeted police patrols are **police crackdowns**. While these are often associated with saturation patrols, they are different

---

Box 10.6 Policing in Practice: K-9 Police Officers

Police dogs are generally referred to as **K-9s**, which is a homophone for canine. While many people think of K-9s as just another tool of policing, in policing circles, especially in regard to the K-9 handlers, these dogs are full-fledged police officers. They will often be outfitted with their own protective vest adorned with a badge, and the police dog and K-9 handler are typically seen as partners, fellow police officers. Nowhere is this more evident than when a K-9 officer is killed in the line of duty, and the same respects are given to the police dog as would be given to any other police officer.

Police dogs have been a part of policing since its earliest roots dating back to the Middle Ages. A wide variety of dogs have become police officers with the most common (and most commonly associated) dog breeds being the German Shepherds and Belgian Malinois. Other dog breeds that are commonly used include Boxers, Doberman Pinschers, Bouvier des Flandres, Giant Schnauzers, and Airedale Terriers. It is often the case that type of dog breed used for K-9 service depends on the purpose of the dog. For instance, Labrador Retrievers and Beagles are often used to locate drugs and bombs, German Shorthair Pointers and Bloodhounds are used for tracking, while German Shepherds and Belgian Malinois are used for protection.

Most police dogs spend the first year of their lives in training, often with a training instructor and later their future handler. The K-9 officer will then work for between six to nine years, depending on their breed, before being retired. In most instances, the handler will continue to keep the dog in its retirement years.

Police dogs are widely used throughout American policing in both police departments and sheriffs' offices. See Table 10.4 for more information about their widespread use.

Source: Chapman, S.G. (1990). *Police dogs in North America*. Springfield, IL: Charles C. Thomas Publisher.

Table 10.4 Use of K-9 Officers by Local Police Departments and Sheriffs' Offices, by Size of Population Served, 2007		
Pop. Served	**Police**	**Sheriffs**
All sizes	29%	57%
1,000,000 or more	100	96
500,000–999,999	100	94
250,000–499,999	100	81
100,000–249,999	95	83
50,000–99,999	87	64
25,000–49,999	66	64
10,000–24,999	51	49
Under 10,000	17	33

Source: Reaves, B.A. (2010). *Local Police Departments, 2007*. Washington, DC: Bureau of Justice Statistics; Reaves, B.A. (2012). *Sheriffs' Offices, 2007 – Statistical Tables*. Washington, DC: Bureau of Justice Statistics.

than the concentration of high levels of police officers in one location. Police scholar Michael S. Scott defines them as "sudden and dramatic increases in police officer presence, sanctions, and threats of apprehension either for specific offenses or for all offenses in specific places."[58] While police saturations are generally in a very small geographic area (for example, one house, one city block), police crackdowns can be more widely ranged, but still dealing with a specific problem in a specific area, for instance, panhandling in the downtown area or assaults taking place in an area known to have a long strip of bars. And while saturation patrols are typically a show of force by using officers in uniforms, police crackdowns may use plainclothes officers or a mixture of plainclothes and uniforms. Findings from a number of studies on police crackdowns have yielded very similar findings; while they seem to have a positive impact on crime, they can also have a negative impact on citizens' satisfaction with the police (see Box 10.6 and Table 10.4).[59]

Community Policing Patrol

As the Kansas City Preventive Patrol Experiment caused those in policing to question the proper method for deploying officers on patrol, the social climate of the 1960s caused the police to question the professional, crime-control model of policing. What resulted, beginning in the 1980s, was the development of community-oriented policing and the police entering what has been dubbed the community era. As community policing focused on developing police relationships with members of the community, this necessitated a change in the standard practices of police patrol. Most police by that time period patrolled by automobile, and when tied to 911 and calls-for-service, it diminished contacts with the community outside of those needing assistance. The focus then turned toward developing patrols that would change this.[60]

The earliest forms of community policing patrols took the police back to an earlier time when police officers conducted foot patrols. This became a central and visible style of police patrol that would come to symbolize community policing. In addition, other forms of patrol were emphasized that would put the police in closer contact with citizens and make them more approachable, such as patrols on horseback and bicycles. Other variations of these also began to develop, such as the use of Japanese-styled **kobans**. In Japan, the police occupy a small two-room building on a street corner, making the police more accessible to local residents. While one patrols, one remains in the koban waiting for any citizen coming to the koban needing assistance. Police departments throughout the United States began putting similar style police substations in shopping malls, strip malls, and in neighborhoods and communities. From these locations, police could conduct foot patrols and have greater contacts with citizens.[61]

In addition, the police began to implement the strategies of problem-oriented policing through the SARA Model (detailed in Chapter 9). While some police departments implemented SARA as a stand-alone program, many adopted it as part of their community policing programs.[62] In these departments, police officers were encouraged to work with citizens to identify problems, work toward solutions that involved police and citizens, and then carry them out. This way, citizens from the local neighborhoods could participate and take part in improving the safety of their neighborhoods and their quality of life.

An additional program that developed out of the community policing concept was known as the **weed and seed** program. This was based on a federal government grant that emphasized police officers taking back a specific crime-ridden neighborhood, making it safe for people to come out at night, and then encouraged the local residents to take a vested interest in their neighborhood, doing things that would prevent the criminal element from returning. The police activity was the weeding, while getting citizens involved

A large police presence can act as a deterrent, but it cannot be maintained for long periods of time.

One of the most famous police substations (similar to a Japanese koban) is the one on Times Square in New York City with its blue and pink neon sign.

in their neighborhood was the seeding side of the program.

These police-community partnerships also developed further in many neighborhoods and communities across the United States into **citizen patrols**.[63] In some cases, these patrols were joint ventures between the police and local citizens, and a community policing officer or two would walk patrol with local citizen volunteers, sometimes as many as 20-30. In other cases, police officers would talk to a citizens patrol group, instructing them on the limits of their authority and responsibilities, and then whenever the citizens identified a problem, they would contact the police, or very often, their specific community policing officer(s). In some locations, citizen police academies, where citizens are given instruction and insight into the police profession, were used as a method of recruiting citizens to become involved in citizen patrols.

The evidence that community policing has had any impact upon crime, however, is negligible.[64] Most of the evidence suggests that while it did not have much bearing on crime rates, it did foster positive police-community relations, and citizen satisfaction with the police increased when community policing programs were implemented with sincerity.

Conclusion

Although most citizens think of police patrol as crime fighting, and police officers do little to dispel that notion, policing is primarily about providing services, maintaining order, and then crime control, in that order. The core of police patrol is truly locked up in the phrase "when the phone rings, we will come," for police officers responding to calls-for-service is primarily what patrol is all about, and because patrol is the backbone of policing, it is primarily what policing itself is all about.[65]

Police must prepare for patrol, making sure they are ready for all of the things they will face on a given shift, and then they climb into their patrol car and mark in-service. While citizens may flag them down or the officer may initiate their own actions, most of the time patrol officers respond to the calls that dispatch sends them over the radio and/or on the computers.

In more recent times, police patrols have taken advantage of a wide array of conveyances, ranging from bicycles and motorcycles to skateboards and Segways. In addition, with the development of new police strategies, such as targeted policing and community policing, new styles of police patrol have been adopted. Yet, despite it all, patrol still mostly boils down to a well-prepared officer, tied to the radio, responding by automobile to calls-for-service.

Just the Facts

1. O.W. Wilson called police patrol the "backbone of policing" because it is the primary function of every police agency in the country and it is the means by which police deliver their services to the community.

2. The three main goals of police patrol are crime control, aimed at reducing crime and preventing crime from rising; order maintenance, maintaining a sense of community order by focusing on those things that are not inherently criminal in nature; and service, providing assistance to the people.

3. The police equipment necessary for police officers to perform their duties are the patrol vehicle, firearm, protective vest, and radio, as well as a number of additional tools to assist the officer in the many situations they will find themselves.

4. While automobile patrol is the primary means by which police officers patrol their beat, depending on geography and need, police officers may patrol by foot, bicycle, motorcycle, horse, air, boat, and even Segway.

5. The four primary functions of police patrol include preventative patrols, random police patrols through the police beat; answering calls-for-service, both emergency (911) and nonemergency; officer-initiated contacts whereby police officers take the initiative to intervene when observing violations of the law; and administrative duties as required by police department policies and procedures.

6. After the installation of the 911 emergency system, police calls-for-service increased dramatically. To deal with the high call volume, many police departments implemented a differential police response system, which instituted a triage system allowing the police to respond differently based on the nature of the call; a split patrol system, where some officers on patrol respond to calls and others conduct preventative patrol and officer-initiated actions; and others created tactical patrols aimed at addressing specific crime problems in the community.

7. The four methods of targeted police patrols include direct patrols, officer-identified problem locations; aggressive patrols, where officers focus their resources on a specific location with a strong legal presence; saturation patrols, where multiple officers are assigned to a geographic location for specific durations of time; and crackdowns, where multiple police resources are used to target a specific location and problem.

8. The three methods of community policing patrols include the use of what the Japanese call kobans, or fixed locations which they operate out of, such as police substations or satellite offices; the weed and seed program, which focuses on using targeted methods to address crime and order maintenance issues to draw out community support for policing neighborhoods; and finally, citizen patrols which consist of citizens patrol the neighborhoods, often with a police officer present.

Ask Yourself

1. Consider the three primary goals of police patrol, crime control, order maintenance, and service. Are these three goals equivalent or should they be prioritized? Regardless of your answer, how best should the police patrol function be organized to achieve that end?

2. Discuss each of the police patrol types as they relate to the three primary goals of police patrol. Which of the three goals does each of the police patrol types serve?

3. When it comes to policing research, most of the research focuses on patrol goals, patrol types, and styles of policing. Very seldom does the research focus on police patrol equipment (for example, firearms, radios). Why might this be the case?

4. Targeted policing methods are often seen by the police as being highly effective, while the public perceives them as "Gestapo-like" measures. Discuss the trade-offs between achieving the goals of police patrol with the concepts of public support for the police to determine when and if these methods are appropriate for the police.

5. Community policing and the patrols associated with it are often thought to be pro-community and citizen-friendly. Consider whether or not these types of patrols create situations where the police may be too close to the community, and question whether communities truly want this type of relationship with its police.

Keywords

Administrative duties
Aggressive patrol
Backbone of policing
Bicycle patrol
Calls-for-service
Citizen patrols
Crackdowns
Crime control
Differential police response

Directed patrol
Firearm
Foot patrol
Hot spots policing
Kobans
Motor vehicle patrol
Motorcycle patrol
Mounted patrol
Officer-initiated contacts

Order maintenance
Preventative patrols
Protective vest—patrol equipment
Radio
Saturation patrol
Service
Split patrols
Tactical patrols
Weed and seed

Endnotes

1. Wilson, O.W. (1963). *Police administration*. 2nd ed. New York, NY: McGraw-Hill Book Company, p. 231.

2. Kelling. G.L., Pate, T., Dieckman, D., & Brown, C.E. (1974). *The Kansas city preventive patrol experiment: A summary report*. Washington, DC: Police Foundation, p. 1; Wilson, O.W. (1963). *Police administration*. 2nd ed. New York, NY: McGraw-Hill Book Company, p. 231.

3. Wilson, O.W. (1963). *Police administration*. 2nd ed. New York, NY: McGraw-Hill Book Company, p. 228.

4. Skogan, W. & Frydl, K. (eds.) (2004). *Fairness and effectiveness in policing: The evidence*. Washington, DC: The National Academies Press, p. 58.

5. Plant, J.B. & Scott, M.S. (2009). Effective policing and crime prevention: A problem oriented guide for mayors, city managers, and county executives. *Center for*

Problem-Oriented Policing. Retrieved from www.popcenter.org/library/reading/pdfs/mayorsguide.pdf

6. Plant, J.B. & Scott, M.S. (2009). Effective policing and crime prevention: A problem oriented guide for mayors, city managers, and county executives. *Center for Problem-Oriented Policing*. Retrieved from www.popcenter.org/library/reading/pdfs/mayorsguide.pdf

7. Plant, J.B. & Scott, M.S. (2009). Effective policing and crime prevention: A problem oriented guide for mayors, city managers, and county executives. *Center for Problem-Oriented Policing*. Retrieved from www.popcenter.org/library/reading/pdfs/mayorsguide.pdf

8. Manning, P.K. (1997). *Police work: The social organization of policing*. 2nd ed. Long Grove, IL: Waveland Press.

9. Goldstein, J. (1960). Police discretion not to involve the criminal process: Low visibility decisions in the administration of justice. *Yale Law Journal, 69,* 453-594; Mastrofksi, S.D. (1983). The police and noncrime services. In G. Whitaker and C. Phillips (Eds.), *Evaluating the Performance of Crime and Criminal Justice Agencies* (pp. 33-61). Thousand Oaks, CA: SAGE; Reiss, A.J. Jr. (1971). *Police and the public*. New Haven, CT: Yale University Press; Scott, E. (1981). *Calls for service: Citizen demand and initial police response.* Washington, DC: U.S. GPO.; Skogan, W. & Frydl, K. (eds.) (2004). *Fairness and effectiveness in policing: The evidence.* Washington, DC: The National Academies Press.

10. Wilson, J.Q. (1968). *Varieties of police behavior: The management of law and order in eight communities.* Cambridge, MA: Harvard University Press, p. 16.

11. Wilson, J.Q. (1968). *Varieties of police behavior: The management of law and order in eight communities.* Cambridge, MA: Harvard University Press, p. 16.

12. Liederbach, J. & Frank, J. (2003). Policing Mayberry: The work routines of small-town and rural officers. *American Journal of Criminal Justice, 28,* 53-72; Mastrofksi, S.D. (1983). The police and noncrime services. In G. Whitaker and C. Phillips (Eds.), *Evaluating the Performance of Crime and Criminal Justice Agencies* (pp. 33-61). Thousand Oaks, CA: SAGE.

13. Mastrofksi, S.D. (1983). The police and noncrime services. In G. Whitaker and C. Phillips (Eds.), *Evaluating the Performance of Crime and Criminal Justice Agencies* (pp. 33-61). Thousand Oaks, CA: SAGE; Reiss, A.J. Jr. (1971). *Police and the public*. New Haven, CT: Yale University Press; Scott, E. (1981). *Calls for service: Citizen demand and initial police response.* Washington, DC: U.S. GPO.

14. Mastrofksi, S.D. (1983). The police and noncrime services. In G. Whitaker and C. Phillips (Eds.), *Evaluating the Performance of Crime and Criminal Justice Agencies* (pp. 33-61). Thousand Oaks, CA: SAGE; Reiss, A.J. Jr. (1971). *Police and the public*. New Haven, CT: Yale University Press; Scott, E. (1981). *Calls for service: Citizen demand and initial police response.* Washington, DC: U.S. GPO.; Skogan, W. & Frydl, K. (eds.) (2004). *Fairness and effectiveness in policing: The evidence.* Washington, DC: The National Academies Press.

15. Mastrofksi, S.D. (1983). The police and noncrime services. In G. Whitaker and C. Phillips (Eds.), *Evaluating the Performance of Crime and Criminal Justice Agencies* (pp. 33-61). Thousand Oaks, CA: SAGE, CT: Yale University Press; Scott, E. (1981). *Calls for service: Citizen demand and initial police response.* Washington, DC: U.S. GPO.

16. Hoover, L. (2014). *Police crime control strategies*. Clifton Park, NY: Delmar, Cengage Learning, p. 248.

17. Hoover, L. (2014). *Police crime control strategies*. Clifton Park, NY: Delmar, Cengage Learning, p. 248.

18. Bellis, M. (2015). History of body armor and bullet proof vests. Retrieved from http://inventors.about.com/od/bstartinventions/a/Body_Armor_2.htm

19. Tompkins, D. (2015). Body armor safety initiative. Retrieved from www.nij.gov/journals/254/Pages/body_armor.aspx

20. Tompkins, D. (2015). Body armor safety initiative. Retrieved from www.nij.gov/journals/254/Pages/body_armor.aspx

21. National Institute of Justice. (2015). Body armor. Retrieved from www.nij.gov/topics/technology/body-armor/pages/welcome.aspx

22. Dunn, William. (1996). *Boot: An L.A.P.D. officer's rookie year*. New York, NY: William Morrow and Company, Inc., p. 163.

23. Alpert, G.P. & Fridell, L.A. (1992). *Police vehicles and firearms*. Prospect Heights, IL: Waveland Press, Inc.

24. Kyle, C. with Doyle, W. (2013). *American gun: A history of the U.S. in ten firearms*. New York, NY: William Morrow and Company, p. 221.

25. Kyle, C. with Doyle, W. (2013). *American gun: A history of the U.S. in ten firearms*. New York, NY: William Morrow and Company; See also Rachlin, H. (1991). *The making of a cop*. New York, NY: Pocket Books.

26. Dunn, William. (1996). *Boot: An L.A.P.D. officer's rookie year*. New York, NY: William Morrow and Company, Inc., p. 109.

27. Leonard, V.A. (1938). *Police communication systems*. Berkeley, CA: University of California Press; Poli, J.A. (1942). Development and present trend of police radio communications. *Journal of Criminal Law and Criminology, 33,* 193-197.

28. Dunn, William. (1996). *Boot: An L.A.P.D. officer's rookie year*. New York, NY: William Morrow and Company, Inc., p. 175.

29. Fuller, J. (2004). Rethinking foot patrol. *Police and Security News, May-June,* 63-66, p. 63.

30. Ratcliffe, J.H., Taniguchi, T., Groff, E.R., & Wood, J.D. (2011). The Philadelphia foot patrol experiment: A randomized controlled trial of police patrol effectiveness in violent crime hot spots. *Criminology, 49,* 795-831.

31. Vonk, K.D. (2003). Bike patrol success. *Law and Order, April,* 82-86, p. 85.

32. Vonk, K.D. (2003). Bike patrol success. *Law and Order, April,* 82-86, p. 85.

33. Barclay, P. et al. (2015). Preventing auto theft in suburban Vancouver commuter lots: Effects of a bike

patrol. *Pennsylvania State University*. Retrieved from http://citeseerx.ist.psu.edu/viewdoc/download?-doi=10.1.1.375.9228&rep=rep1&type=pdf; Telemasp Bulletin. (1998). Bicycle patrols. *Telemasp Bulletin, 5*, 1-10.

34. Suarez, J. (2010). Costs and benefits for Raleigh's mounted police. *Raleigh Public Record*. Retrieved from http://raleighpublicrecord.org/news/2010/12/07/costs-and-benefits-for-raleighs-mounted-police/

35. Fine, J.C. (2001). Police on horseback: A new concept for an old idea. *FBI Law Enforcement Bulletin, July*, 6-7.

36. Suarez, J. (2010). Costs and benefits for Raleigh's mounted police. *Raleigh Public Record*. Retrieved from http://raleighpublicrecord.org/news/2010/12/07/costs-and-benefits-for-raleighs-mounted-police/

37. Suarez, J. (2010). Costs and benefits for Raleigh's mounted police. *Raleigh Public Record*. Retrieved from http://raleighpublicrecord.org/news/2010/12/07/costs-and-benefits-for-raleighs-mounted-police/

38. Wilson, O.W. & McLaren, R.C. (1977). *Police administration*, 4th ed. New York, NY: McGraw Hill.

39. Wilson, O.W. (1963). *Police administration*. 2nd ed. New York, NY: McGraw Hill, p. 246.

40. Wilson, O.W. (1963). *Police administration*. 2nd ed. New York, NY: McGraw Hill.

41. Basich, M. (2014)."Drones:" Grounded until further notice. *Police Technology*. Retrieved from www.police-mag.com/channel/technology/articles/2014/11/drones-grounded-until-further-notice.aspx

42. Cordner, G.W. (1989). The police on patrol. In *Police and policing: Contemporary issues*, Dennis J. Kenney (ed.), Westport, CT: Praeger Publishers; Gay, W.G., Schell, T.H., &Schack, S. (1977). *Routine Patrol: Improving Patrol Productivity*. Washington, DC: National Institute of Justice.

43. Sparrow, M., Moore, M.H., & Kennedy, D.M. (1992). *Beyond 911: A new era for policing*. New York, NY: Basic Books.

44. Dunn, William. (1996). *Boot: An L.A.P.D. officer's rookie year*. New York, NY: William Morrow and Company, Inc., p. 5.

45. McEwen, T., Connors, E.F., & Cohen, M.I. (1986). *Evaluation of the differential police response field test*. Washington, DC: Government Printing Office; Worden, R.E. (1993). Toward equity and efficiency in law enforcement: Differential police response. *American Journal of Police, 12*, 1-32; Skogan, W. & Frydl, K. (eds.) (2004). *Fairness and effectiveness in policing: The evidence*. Washington, DC: The National Academies Press.

46. Gaines, L.K. (1996). Specialized patrol. In *Police Operations: Analysis and Evaluation*. Edited by Gary W. Cordner, Larry K. Gaines, & Victor E. Kappeler (pp. 115-130). Cincinnati, OH: Anderson Publishing Co.; Tien, J.M., Simon, J.W., & Larson, R.C. (1977). *An evaluation report of an alternative approach to police patrol: The Wilmington split force experiment*. Cambridge, MA: Public Systems Evaluation, Inc.

47. Tien, J.M., Simon, J.W., & Larson, R.C. (1977). *An evaluation report of an alternative approach to police patrol: The Wilmington split force experiment*. Cambridge, MA: Public Systems Evaluation, Inc.

48. *Law Enforcement News*. (1991). Faced with a crime wave, Houston cops "wave back": Intensive patrols hit the streets, but union blasts directive not to field calls for service. *Law Enforcement News*, December 15, p. 3.

49. Reardon, P.T.& O'Connor, M. (1991). Police tactical teams tempt the fates daily. *Chicago Tribune*. Retrieved from http://articles.chicagotribune.com/1991-01-09/news/9101030199_1_police-officers-police-districts-tactical-unit

50. Reardon, P.T.& O'Connor, M. (1991). Police tactical teams tempt the fates daily. *Chicago Tribune*. Retrieved from http://articles.chicagotribune.com/1991-01-09/news/9101030199_1_police-officers-police-districts-tacti cal-unit

51. Skogan, W. & Frydl, K. (eds.) (2004). *Fairness and effectiveness in policing: The evidence*. Washington, DC: The National Academies Press, p. 60; See also Worden, R.E. & McLean, S.J. (2008). *Tactical patrols: A synopsis*. Albany, NY: The John F. Finn Institute for Public Safety, Inc.

52. Repetto, T.A. (2012). *American police: A history: 1945-2012*. New York, NY: Enigma Books, p. 169.

53. Braga, A.A. & Weisburd, D.L. (2010). *Policing problem places: Crime hot spots and effective prevention*. New York, NY: Oxford University Press.

54. Braga, A.A. & Weisburd, D.L. (2010). *Policing problem places: Crime hot spots and effective prevention*. New York, NY: Oxford University Press, pp. 9-10.

55. Shaw, R. (1938). Forty fighting years: The story of August Vollmer. *The Oakland Post Enquirer*. Chapter 37.

56. See for instance McGarrell, E.F., Chermak, S.,& Weiss, A. (2002). *Reducing firearms violence through directed police patrol:Final report on the evaluation of the Indianapolis police department's directed patrol project*. Washington, DC: U.S. Department of Justice; Sherman, L.W., et al. (1998). *Preventing crime: What works, what doesn't, what's promising*. Washington, DC: National Institute of Justice.

57. Hoover, L.T. (2014). *Police crime control strategies*. Clifton Park, NY: Delmar Cengage; Skogan, W. & Frydl, K. (eds.) (2004). *Fairness and effectiveness in policing: The evidence*. Washington, DC: The National Academies Press; Weisburd, D. & Majmundar, K. (eds.) (2018). *Proactive policing: Effects on crime and communities*. Washington, DC: The National Academies Press.

58. Scott, M.S. (2004). The benefits and consequences of police crackdowns. *Center for Problem-Oriented Policing*. Retrieved from www.popcenter.org/responses/police_crackdowns/

59. Scott, M.S. (2004). The benefits and consequences of police crackdowns. *Center for Problem-Oriented Policing*. Retrieved from www.popcenter.org/responses/police_crackdowns/

60. Sparrow, M., Moore, M.H., & Kennedy, D.M. (1992). *Beyond 911: A new era for policing.* New York, NY: Basic Books.

61. Oliver, W.M. (2007). *Community-oriented policing: A systemic approach to policing.* 4th ed. Upper Saddle River, NJ: Prentice Hall.

62. Oliver, W.M. (2007). *Community-oriented policing: A systemic approach to policing.* 4th ed. Upper Saddle River, NJ: Prentice Hall.

63. Oliver, W.M. (2007). *Community-oriented policing: A systemic approach to policing.* 4th ed. Upper Saddle River, NJ: Prentice Hall.

64. Oliver, W.M. (2007). *Community-oriented policing: A systemic approach to policing.* 4th ed. Upper Saddle River, NJ: Prentice Hall.

65. Hoover, L. (2014). *Police crime control strategies.* Clifton Park, NY: Delmar, Cengage Learning, p. 248.

■ *"In the attempt to establish the truth regarding a crime, investigators are everlastingly confronted with obstacles that are seemingly impossible to overcome."*[1] *—August Vollmer*

Oklahoma City Police homicide detectives survey a crime scene.

CHAPTER 11

Investigations

After reading this chapter, you will be able to:

1. Describe how the concept of detectives moved from the literary realm to the realities of policing.
2. Define the detective mystique and the impact the RAND study on criminal investigations had on the concept.
3. Detail the findings of the RAND criminal investigation study.
4. Name and explain the three goals of the detective.
5. Compare and contrast the case-oriented versus the offender-oriented type of investigation.
6. List and describe the six styles of criminal investigation.
7. Discuss how criminal investigation in police departments are organized.
8. Explain the investigative process.
9. Compare and contrast the issue of caseload and workload in regard to case management.
10. Describe some of the common issues in criminal investigations.

One of the least understood aspect of American policing is criminal investigations. While American's notion of police patrol and police traffic services is a rough approximation of what those police officers do, when it comes to criminal investigations, the general understanding is greatly skewed from reality. For instance, despite a strong belief that at least half, if not more, of an police agency's personnel are dedicated to investigations, one major study of American policing estimates that "criminal investigation units typically involve only about 10 percent of all sworn officers in an agency."[2] This disparity has much to do with American popular culture, which fills untold numbers of movies, comics, novels, and videogames that feature the American detective; not to mention the many television shows on crime scene investigations

---

Box 11.1 History in Practice: The Literary Detective

While Edgar Allan Poe's *The Murders in the Rue Morgue* was the first use of a **detective** in literature, and Charles Dickens was the first to use the word to refer to an individual, it was Sir Arthur Conan Doyle's Sherlock Holmes novels and short stories that solidified the detective as an entire genre of literature. That would soon follow with various subcategories of detectives including the private detectives made popular by Dashiell Hammett and Mickey Spillane; the amateur detectives such as Nancy Drew, the Hardy Boys, and Agatha Christie's Miss Marple; the police detectives such as Columbo, Kojack, and Inspector Clouseau; and, most recently, the crime scene and forensic scientists such as Ducky Mallard, Temperance Brennan, and every character created on the *CSI* series. Detective novels, television shows, and movies are all today a staple of the American popular culture. While *CSI*, *NCIS*, and even the modern *Sherlock* series are all quite popular and entertaining, some of the original of the genre are still the best. Consider reading some of the greatest in the genre: *The Murders in the Rue Morgue* (Poe)*, The Hound of the Baskervilles* (Doyle)*,* and *The Maltese Falcon* (Hammett).

---

and forensic science. This is, in part, understandable because in many ways, the realm of the **American detective** followed **popular culture**, rather than popular culture following the American detective (see Box 11.1).

American author Edgar Allan Poe, the creator of the literary detective.

While many claim that England's **Jonathan Wild** or France's **Eugène-Francois Vidocq** were the first detectives, they were in reality thieves turned informers, who then turned into investigators, and they were not known during their time period as detectives.[3] In fact, the earliest detective to appear in the literary world was in 1841, when **Edgar Allan Poe** published *The Murders in the Rue Morgue*, which featured the fictional French Detective **C. Auguste Dupin** (perhaps inspired by Vidocq).[4] The word "detective" was actually first used by **Charles Dickens** in his novel *Bleak House* (1852).[5] The literary invention by **Sir Arthur Conan Doyle** of the great Detective **Sherlock Holmes** in 1887 made the term a household name.[6]

Police departments began emulating the concept that had police officers serving as plainclothes detectives investigating unsolved crimes. One of the most famous (and infamous) was the head of the New York Police Department's Detectives in the late 1800s, Inspector **Thomas F. Byrnes**.[7] Byrnes is considered famous for his development of police investigation techniques such as his use of informants, his development of a rogue's gallery, a book consisting of photographs of known criminals, and his ability to solve crimes. For this he is often considered the person who created the modern American detective bureau. He was infamous, however, because he was wholly corrupt and used his position to increase his wealth and power, and he was ultimately forced to resign (see Box 11.2).

As America entered the twentieth century, police departments across the United States had developed detective bureaus or criminal investigations units within the organizational structure. As policing reformed in the early 1900s, most police departments organized into three main areas: support services, patrol, and criminal investigations.[8] The concept of police investigations had become solidified in American policing.

At the same time, however, the use of forensic science and crime labs came into existence with the first crime lab being created under Chief August Vollmer's direction in 1916, and the first dedicated crime lab being created under him in 1924 when he served as the police chief in Los Angeles.[9] This eventually developed into the field of forensic science, or more specifically criminalistics, over the next 50 years. And this development, the scientific analysis of evidence left at crime scenes, necessitated the development of

---

Box 11.2 History in Practice: Thomas F. Byrnes, the First Real Police Detective

The first real **police detective** to gain noted prominence was Thomas F. Byrnes who rose to become the head of the New York City Police Department's Detective Bureau from 1880 until he was forced to resign for graft and corruption in 1895.

Thomas F. Byrnes was born on June 15, 1842 in Dublin, Ireland, and immigrated to New York City as a child. He started out fitting gas pipes before the Civil War and then enlisted and served two years with Ellsworth's "Zouaves." He then joined the New York Fire Department for a brief period before joining the NYPD on December 10, 1863.

Byrnes rose through the ranks quickly because he was good at playing the system's game of graft and corruption, but he also was good at solving crimes by way of his many informants. He gained prominence by solving the Manhattan Savings Bank robbery in 1878 and was soon promoted to Detective Bureau Chief.

He expanded the number of police detectives and personally made more than three thousand arrests in four years. He also developed a system of photographing criminals and taking their measurements (the Bertillon system), and he published a widely popular book called *Professional Criminals of America*.

On the darker side, he was known for keeping dossiers on people, employing the third degree, and was heavily into taking bribes, graft, and paying for political power. He was so successful at this that when he was forced to retire by Police Commissioner Theodore Roosevelt, he retired the equivalent of a millionaire. Still, he is considered by many to be the first modern police detective responsible for creating the first modern police detective bureau.

Source: Conway, J. N. (2010). *The Big Policeman: The Rise and Fall of Thomas Byrnes, America's First, Most Ruthless, and Greatest Detective*. Guildford, CT: Lyons Press.

Photo of the New York Police Department's Rogue's Gallery, created by Detective Thomas F. Byrnes in the late 1800s.

another area known as criminal investigations, in which evidence is properly secured, collected, and turned over to criminalistics. Popular culture has largely blurred the lines on these three, having forensic scientists in lab coats running off to crime scenes to collect evidence and to investigate crimes. The reality, however, is that in most police departments, police officers collect evidence and investigate crimes. When a crime is not immediately solved, it is then turned over to the detectives who investigate the crime. The forensic scientists almost never leave their labs because they receive evidence, process it in the lab, and submit reports back to the detectives.

Popular culture has essentially created what Herman Goldstein once called the **detective mystique** when he wrote, "Part of the mystique of detective operations is the impression that a detective has difficult-to-come-by qualifications and skills; that investigating crime is a real science; that a detective does much more important work than other police officers; that all detective work is exciting; and that a good detective can solve any crime."[10] Writer Jay Kirk tries to explain it this way: "We have long granted detectives a lofty place in our pantheon because . . . detectives are our most reliable curators of life's waning sense of mystery. They sustain us with suspense."[11] Goldstein, however, also explains, "It borders on heresy to point out that, in fact, much of what detectives do consists of very routine and rather elementary chores, including paper process; that a good deal of their work is not only not exciting, it is downright boring; that the situations they confront are often less challenging and less demanding than those handled by patrolling police officer; that it is arguable whether special skills and knowledge are required for detective work . . . and that the capacity of detectives to solve crimes is greatly exaggerated."[12]

In his research into one of the most prestigious of detective units, homicide, in one of the busiest homicide units in the nation at the time, David Simon made similar findings. After following the work of the Baltimore (Maryland) homicide unit for one year, he noted that "Television has given us the myth of the raging pursuit, the high-speed chase, but in truth there is no such thing."[13] "This is the job," he explains in a more realistic perspective.[14] "You sit behind a government-issue metal desk on the sixth of ten floors in a gleaming, steel-frame death trap with poor ventilation, dysfunctional air conditioning."[15] He continues to describe the routine of waiting for the phone call, responding to the scene, and going through the motion of reviewing the crime scene, questioning witnesses and neighbors, and ideally, a suspect. After following the unit for a year, Simon saw no car chases, no action-packed fights, and no one solved a crime in an hour. What he saw was mostly the tedious process that Goldstein described above.

Since there is evidently a vast difference between the myths wrapped up in the detective mystique and the realities of detective work in police criminal investigation, this chapter intends to explore what police detectives really do on the job. It will begin by revisiting the landmark RAND study on criminal investigation and its findings before moving into a discussion of the goals of police investigation, its organization, its process, the issues detectives face, and then the unique impact that technology has on the criminal investigation process.

The RAND Study Revisited

To understand the research into criminal investigation and the role of the detective, one has to be familiar with the landmark **RAND study on the criminal investigation process** published in two volumes in 1975.[16] The reason for this is because whenever anyone discusses research into criminal investigations there is the pre-RAND study era and the post-RAND study era.[17] Like the Kansas City Preventive Patrol Experiment, prior to the RAND study there were no research studies into the criminal investigation process. Most of what qualified as research was simply descriptive in nature, describing how police officers on patrol received the initial complaint, filed a report, and how the actual investigation was turned over to the detectives. They were the ones that conducted the follow-up investigation; interviewed victims, witnesses, and suspects; and searched the crime scenes for evidence. They were seen as the primary entity within a police department that solved crimes.

Once the Omnibus Crime Control and Safe Streets Act of 1968 had created the National Institute of Law Enforcement and Criminal Justice (today the National Institute of Justice, or NIJ), funding was available for the conduct of research into policing.[18] As no study to date had looked at the efficacy of criminal investigations, the National Institute contracted the RAND Corporation to conduct a nationwide study into police criminal investigations. They were asked "to describe, on a national scale, current investigation organization and practice; to assess the contribution of police investigation to the achievement of criminal justice goals; to ascertain the effectiveness of technology and systems that are being adopted to enhance investigative performance; [and] to determine how investigative effectiveness is related to differences in organizational form, staffing, procedures, and so forth."[19] This was a tall order, but several leading researchers were hired by RAND and the study was conducted from 1973 to 1974.[20]

The researchers looked at a total of 153 jurisdictions, analyzing all aspects of the investigative process, from how criminal investigators are trained all the way to the effectiveness of the technology they used.[21] They also conducted on-site visits of 25 of the agencies, and they made great use of the Kansas City Police Department's Detective Case Assignment file to gain greater depth into that police department's criminal investigation process. It was clearly a comprehensive study, so when the findings were released in 1975, it was rather shocking what they concluded, and it became very controversial.

When the study assessed all of the variations in training, staffing, and the type of workload detectives were carrying, they concluded "differences in investigative training, staffing, workload, and procedures appear to have no appreciable effect on crime, arrest, or clearance rates."[22] In other words, detectives with extensive training or little training, heavy workloads or light ones, etc., had no impact on closing cases. The researchers also found that "the method by which police investigators are organized . . . cannot be related to variations in crime, arrests, and clearance rates."[23] So, it did not really matter how detective bureaus were organized.

When looking at how investigators spent their time, they concluded that "more than half of all serious reported crimes receive no more than superficial attention from investigators," that "an investigator's time is largely consumed in reviewing reports, documenting files, and attempting to locate and interview victims on cases that experience shows will not be solved."[24] They also found that for the cases solved, most detectives spent their time dealing with the post-clearance paperwork.

Then, when it came down to the most important aspect of detective work, solving cases, the researchers found that "the single most important determinant of whether or not a case will be solved is the information the victim supplies to the immediately responding patrol officer."[25] This meant that the backbone of policing, patrol officers, solved most cases, not the glorified police detective.

The study also found that police departments collect more evidence than they can typically process, that the collection of latent fingerprints is usually the best means of direct identification of a suspect, and that all of the technology going into criminal investigations had little impact on closing cases. Simply put, what closed most cases were victims providing the necessary information to police officers. Detectives didn't seem to matter much. Needless to say, this was not well received by most police departments that had spent decades building up their criminal investigation units. It also didn't sit well with the detectives themselves.

A number of people attacked the research study, arguing the study was flawed. Many researchers responded by conducting their own studies, either as a variation on the RAND study or as an outright replication.[26] The conclusion they all came to was that the

New York City police officer collecting the initial evidence at a crime scene.

RAND study was correct. Most cases are solved by victims (and sometimes witnesses) providing information to the responding patrol officers. They are rarely solved by detectives.

The detective mystique was beginning to fade.

Police Criminal Investigations

The RAND study caused police administrators to rethink criminal investigations within their police departments.[27] Despite the arguments against the study, policing had entered a post-RAND study period when it came to criminal investigations. Change was needed, so reviews of everything from the goals of criminal investigation to their proper focus to the organizational structure as it related to investigations and the nature of the cases themselves were given consideration. It is to these concerns that this chapter now turns (see Box 11.3).

The goals of criminal investigation are often oversimplified as being to solve crimes. While that may be the immediate **goal of the detectives**, the overarching goals for the police department as part of its societal role are to (1) control criminals, (2) pursue justice, and (3) to address problems.[28] While **controlling criminals** is assuredly one of the many goals of a police

---

Box 11.3 **Policing in Practice: Becoming a Police Detective**

While many people desire to become a **police detective**, most do not realize that it starts with being a police officer. One does not go straight into being a detective. In addition, becoming a police officer in order to obtain the police detective's badge is not a "bide my time" or "punch the clock until it is handed to me" job. The reality is, performance as a police officer lays the ground work for a person to become a police detective.

To become a police detective, police managers, police detectives, and police chiefs recommend several keys to success. One obvious recommendation is to work hard as a police officer, to develop good cases and write excellent reports. These are the things that will get you noticed by detectives and one way in which you will be talked about as a potential candidate for the police detective position.

Another recommendation is to take as many classes as possible related to criminal investigations as a police officer, as well as some additional courses and training outside of the workplace. Still further, become very familiar with departmental policies and procedures related to criminal investigations. This type of knowledge is necessary to become a detective as most police departments have an examination to promote to detective. The best way to score high on the examinations is to have the necessary knowledge of criminal investigation practices and procedures.

One final recommendation to get ahead in any position in policing is to stay clean. Do not become involved in anything that would tarnish your record and cause you to be overlooked when it comes to receiving the coveted detective's badge.

department, criminal investigations play an important role. Since we know that a small percentage of criminals account for a large portion of the crimes, criminal investigations help to control crime by conducting investigations into these cases. By connecting a single perpetrator to multiple crimes it allows the police department to solve numerous open cases. By making good cases against these individuals, it incapacitates them so they can no longer commit these crimes against society.

The second goal of criminal investigations is the **pursuit of justice**. Government establishes, through the law, what is deemed acceptable and unacceptable behavior. Justice is about making sure those who commit unacceptable behavior are held accountable for their actions. As the police (government) represent the local community through the process of criminal investigations and criminal proceedings, investigators uphold the virtue of justice for all of the people.

The third goal of criminal investigations is **addressing problems**. While patrol officers deal with the immediacy of many problems, criminal investigators are often able to address a problem long term by building criminal cases against someone, making the arrest, and gaining a conviction. The extreme example of this is the serial murderer or rapist who preys on victim after victim in a community. When the investigator can close a series of cases like this, it brings relief to all of the community.

To accomplish these goals, criminal investigators have generally taken two different approaches: case-oriented and offender-oriented investigations. In **case-oriented investigations**, detectives receive a case from the patrol officers and from that they begin building a case file to resolve the specific crime at hand. Research into how cases are handled have generated two very different perspectives in how cases get resolved. The first is the **effort-result hypothesis**, which states that crimes get solved when detectives put more work into the case and by putting their skills to good use. The second perspective is that cases are solved based on the **circumstances-result hypothesis**, which says if the circumstances of the case are right they will solve the case (essentially they get lucky). The former would tell us that more resources should go into case investigations to solve more crimes, while the latter would tell us that detectives should only spend their time investigating cases with good leads.

The second approach to criminal investigation is the **offender-oriented investigation** approach. The concept behind this approach is that most crimes are committed by a small number of criminals. By focusing investigations on specific offenders, detectives stand the greatest chance of solving the most crimes. This is a sort-of "biggest bang for your buck" approach. While the research into this particular method is scant, the police literature shows that there is validity to this approach when targeting those few offenders who generate the most criminal offenses.

The majority of police departments today utilize the case-oriented approach, and most have developed follow-up units to address the two hypotheses. After a patrol officer files the initial report, in many police departments the case will then go to a follow-up unit that is a unit somewhat between patrol and criminal investigations. These investigators look at the cases and do the basic follow up to see if they can quickly resolve the case and, if not, determine if there are enough circumstances present to warrant the case moving on to a specialized detective. If there is enough evidence, witnesses, and victim testimony to warrant the possibility the case will be solved, the case file then moves to an assigned detective.

In addition to the two approaches, like the styles of policing, there are also **styles of criminal investigations**. Six particular styles of investigation have been identified. The first is **reinforcing patrol**, where detectives receive cases from the first responding officers. The second is **standard reactive**, where cases like burglary or robbery are received and the amount of follow-up and investigation needed depends on the case. The third are **major cases**, such as homicides or rapes, where there are highly visible cases that gain the most attention necessitating an investigation. The fourth are **regulatory inspections**, where detectives in property theft may inspect pawn shops for stolen merchandise on a routine basis. The fifth is **passive notation**, where the type of crime is not likely to be solved due to high numbers of cases, like stolen bicycles, but the information is noted for possible future purposes. And finally, sixth is **discovery enforcement**, in which investigators go into the field and make their own cases against criminals, such as drug dealing and prostitution.

Investigative Organization

Just as the police department is organized into different units, typically patrol, investigations, and administrative services, criminal investigation is further divided and organized in most police departments. There are generally three ways in which they are divided, by function, solvability/seriousness, and crime type. The first manner in which many departments organize investigations is by the **functions of investigations**, which will often include the general "criminal investigation unit," but it will also have units such as "crime scene units" for the collection of evidence, "crime analysis units" for the examination of evidence and to handle the coordination with forensic science crime labs, and "property and evidence units" for purposes of storing and securing crime scene evidence. In the Honolulu Police Department, for example, the Investigation Bureau is divided into the following functions: criminal investigation, narcotics/vice, traffic, and scientific investigation.[29]

In many departments, criminal investigation is further divided by the **solvability and seriousness of investigations**.[30] At the lowest level, this is typically defined by a follow-up unit that looks at police officer field reports to determine if there is enough evidence, or if the case is serious enough, to warrant the case moving on to a detective. Under these circumstances, the case will then be assigned to a criminal investigator. If the seriousness of the case is very high, it may very well go to a high-profile crimes unit, which are often established in larger cities and police departments. The Honolulu Police Department, for example, has a unit called the Criminal Investigation

New York City police detective assisting in the investigation of a shooting that left two store employees dead.

Division (CID), and this unit "handles the follow-up investigations for all felonies and some misdemeanors."[31]

Finally, another way in which investigations are organized is by **crime type or crime specific investigations.**[32] In most departments, criminal investigation is divided by specific types of crimes so that detectives develop an expertise in these areas. These may include units centered around homicide, robbery, burglary, automobile thefts, or sexual assaults. In the Honolulu Police Department "felony offenses committed in the community had respective CID details that were responsible for each class of offense" which included the "burglary/theft detail . . . forgery, auto theft, and white collar crime detail."[33] Depending on the size of the agency, number of crimes, and resources available, these may be grouped together or further divided. Some agencies divide their criminal investigations into investigations and special investigations, where the latter is focused on something vastly different from the typical street-crime investigations, such as organized crime or cybercrime. Many smaller agencies group the types of street crimes together, so for instance, many departments have a "homicide/robbery" unit because of the similarities in investigations and for the fact firearms are often used in both.

In other agencies, a particular crime such as homicide may be further divided so as to provide varying levels of attention and expertise to the various types of homicides. For instance, in the Los Angeles Police Department (LAPD), because of the fact that Los Angeles experiences a high number of homicides, three levels of homicide investigators have developed in that agency.[34] The first and lowest level are the *divisional* homicide units, which consists of patrol officers and detectives who handle the more simplistic of the homicides, such as a drive-by shooting or a lover's quarrel where one spouse ends up dead. The second level is the *bureau* homicide units, which serve a number of divisions and handle the slightly more complicated homicides such as mass murders or drug hits. Finally, at the top of the LAPD hierarchy is the unit often referred to as Homicide Special, which has citywide jurisdiction and is assigned "the most brutal, most complex, most high-profile murders in Los Angeles." According to Miles Corwin who spent a year with Homicide Special, this unit is assigned "murders that involve celebrities . . . organized-crime killings, serial murders, cases that require great expertise or sophisticated technology, . . . and any murder that is considered a priority by the chief of police" such as the O.J. Simpson case.[35]

Many police departments across the nation also have **special investigation units** within criminal investigation. Some of these are mainstays and deal with continual problems such as the vice units which investigate prostitution, human trafficking, illegal pornography, as well as illegal gambling. In other departments, special investigations may arise to deal with a specific problem, and they may do so by joining with other local, state, and federal agencies. Many of these are known as joint task forces, and they have formed to conduct criminal investigations into drug dealing, human trafficking, and terrorism. The most recent of the special investigation units have come as a result of the latter, terrorism, and under the auspices of homeland security many of the large metropolitan police departments have organized special regional units known as fusion centers to conduct investigations into terrorist activity.

The police organization of investigations plays a major role in how crimes are investigated. If there is a unit that screens cases, only those that either have a high profile or a great potential for solvability will be assigned to a detective. This concept of how cases move through the investigative process is known as case management and will be discussed later. In addition, how the police department organizes its investigation unit also creates a sense of hierarchy and prestige. When Honolulu Police Officer Dias joined the CID, he recalled, "I became the low man on the proverbial pole again" because in the CID, the detective is the lowest-ranking officer on staff."[36] Yet, in the elite unit of the LAPD, "The Homicide Special detectives are proud to work in the division, proud they have been selected to work in a unit with such a storied reputation."[37] So, even within an agency, there are varying levels of prestige. Working homicides has more prestige than working auto thefts, and working in Homicide Special certainly has more prestige than working in the divisional homicide units. Hence, the more serious and high visibility the unit, the more prestige is bestowed upon the individual detective, which is driven, in part, by the way in which criminal investigations are organized.

Investigative Process

While the way in which criminal investigations units are organized affects the process, the process itself affects the outcomes of the criminal investigation. When a crime occurs, police officers are summoned to the scene of the crime. In most police departments they are the initial investigators and evidence collectors. While there are some departments that have crime scene investigation (CSI) units and many departments have specially trained police officers, in most cases in America, the police officer is the crime scene investigator for most crimes. This is why from the very beginning of an individual's police career, "One of the most elementary rules police recruits learns is to 'secure the crime scene and secure the witnesses.'"[38]

Once the scene is secured and safe, the police officer then conducts the **initial investigation**, and there are several basic steps that the police officers must perform.[39] Former Homicide Detective Dias described the key three steps when he noted, "First, we documented the crime scene by taking pictures and making a diagram. Second, we collected all the physical evidence

The initial investigation often entails the roping off of the crime scene with the iconic "police line do not cross" tape.

we could see. And third, we interviewed everyone who knew the victim."[40] In serious cases, such as a homicide or a robbery, the detectives are usually called immediately, and they will most often respond to the crime scene. In addition, if the police department has a special evidence collection unit, they may also be summoned to process the crime scene by either the police officer, the officer's supervisor, or the criminal investigators. In the more mundane and after-the-fact crimes, such as automobile thefts and burglaries, the detectives will not respond to the scene itself, but will await receipt of the police officer's report. Thus, the police officer is not only the first responding officer, but is the crime scene investigator as well. The officer's report will document all of the officer's actions on scene, detail the evidence collected, provide the names and contact information for victims and witnesses as well as potential perpetrators of the crime, and provide information derived from any interviews conducted in the field.

The next step in the process, and typically the first for criminal investigators, is **case screening**.[41] Once the police report is filed, later that day or the following day, it will end up with a criminal investigator, usually one in a follow-up unit. This initial investigator will review the police report to determine if there is evidence or leads in the case that warrant the case moving forward. If there are no evidence or leads in the case, the case will then be filed. If the police officer essentially handled most of the case, the follow-up investigator may make some phone calls to tie up any loose ends that help to close the case. If plenty of evidence or leads exist, and the case appears to have some potential for being solved, it will then be forwarded to a detective in the proper unit (for example, homicide, burglary).

If there were leads, such as suspect names, witness identification, license plate numbers of cars leaving the scene, and other such potential pieces of evidence, then a **follow-up investigation** will be conducted.[42] Again, if there is a follow-up unit and the case can be closed easily, the follow-up investigator will perform this investigation. If there is no such unit in the department, then the detective assigned the case will conduct the follow-up investigation. This will include following leads; interviewing victims, witnesses, and suspects; and often discussing the case with the initial responding officer to gather any insights or hunches the officer may have left out of the police report. This phase may also include conducting photo line-ups, where victims are shown photos of potential suspects mixed in with photos of other people, or a physical line-up where victims and/or witnesses view a potential suspect mixed in with other people.

One important aspect of the follow-up investigation is the processing of **physical evidence.**[43] The evidence collected at a crime scene is not automatically processed, but requests must be made for a forensics crime lab to conduct an analysis on the evidence. One common piece of evidence found in crime scenes are fingerprints, and detectives must decide if fingerprints will be sent through the automated fingerprint identification system (AFIS), and if they receive a "hit," they must determine if the person identified was the victim, a witness, or a potential suspect. Other evidence collected, such as shoe and tire impressions, blood samples, or items collected looking for trace evidence (for example, hair, skin, clothing fibers) must be sent to a crime lab with a request for a specific type of analysis. Once the crime lab has conducted its analysis and filed a report, the detective must retrieve the evidence and return it to the property section so as to maintain chain-of-custody of the evidence, and they must determine how the crime lab's report factors into their investigation.

Much of the investigatory process is really about **information management** with the goal of identifying, locating, and interviewing a suspect so as to build a case that warrants arresting the suspect in the crime.[44] "In developing information," however, as Sanders explains, "detectives encounter sources they take to be possibly unreliable. They meet people who intentionally lie about themselves or others."[45] The detective must sift through statements and evidence, playing each statement and piece of evidence off of one another, looking for incongruities and inconsistencies, and dealing with the many ambiguities until they "can confidently decide that one story is false and the other true."[46] This is why detectives must document everything and place it in the case file, as it is a means of having all of the information in one location, and that information can be constantly reviewed based upon any new information being added to the casefile. When it comes to homicides, because the amount of information can be so overwhelming, detectives often create "murder books," which consist of large three-ring binders, sometimes collected in multiple volumes, to manage the high volume of information pertaining to a particular case.[47]

Once an arrest is made, the detective's primary goal is to gain a confession from the suspect. This is done in many ways, but ultimately it is about convincing the suspect that the evidence demonstrates unequivocally that they were the perpetrator of the crime. If the suspect confesses, then the case can be closed. If the suspect refuses to confess, then the detective must work closely with the local prosecutor's office to demonstrate the strength of the case against the arrestee.

In the **post-arrest** phase of the investigatory process, the disposition of the case is reliant upon the close working of the detective and with the local prosecutor.[48] Simon, in his book on Baltimore homicides, describes what happens next in the process when he writes, "If the case isn't plea-bargained, dismissed, or placed on the inactive docket for an indefinite period of time, if by some perverse twist of fate it becomes a trial by jury, you will then have the opportunity of sitting on the witness stand and reciting under oath the facts

---

Box 11.4 Ethics in Practice: Eliminating Police Detectives

In the wake of the RAND Study on Criminal Investigation with the realization that police detectives have little bearing upon criminal cases being solved, there was much talk about **eliminating criminal investigation units**. Dating back as far as the 1940s, this author found a letter from an active police chief proposing that very idea to August Vollmer. The plan was to eliminate the position of detectives and return each of them to patrol. Then, every police officer would be trained in the process of criminal investigations so that whenever the police officer responded to a call that necessitated an investigation, they would handle it themselves. It was articulated by this police chief that it would increase the number of officers available on the street, and it would allow each officer to develop their own cases in the beats they patrolled, thus increasing their dedication to the citizens of the neighborhood, the taking of their initial reports, and to solving criminal cases.

Ask Yourself:

Consider the pros and cons of eliminating detectives based on what you know of the RAND Study, as well as what you know of modern-day policing and criminal investigations. Does this idea still have merit?

Do you think all police officers have the skills to conduct criminal investigations or do detectives and police officers have different strengths? Explain your answer.

---

of the case."[49] This is a difficult part of the process for detectives for their work is on display before the courts. In the preliminary hearing, a judge may determine that the detective does not have enough evidence to move the case to trial, or, if a trial does occur, a judge or jury may determine that there is not enough evidence in the case for a conviction. All of the hard work of the detective reaches this one moment where their work is put on display before others who then determine if the detective adequately did their job.

All of this, of course, assumes that a suspect was identified and enough evidence was present to warrant an arrest. If this is not the case and no suspect was arrested and there are no more leads in the case, it will be filed away until some future potential lead is discovered and the case can be returned to active investigation. Some police departments have created **cold case units** where detectives may pull out old cases and revisit them to see if any new leads, new technologies, or just simply a new perspective on the old facts, may help to solve the case (see Box 11.4).[50]

Investigations Issues

As one can probably tell by now, there are many issues revolving around criminal investigations, and **case management** is probably the number one issue. In the case of one homicide, the case file may be so big that it can cover a dozen large three-ring binders. The detective has to keep every piece of evidence and every eyewitness statement in mind as they manage a particular case, and they have to make sure that they document everything that they do because they are not the only ones who look at the case file. "Your files are looked at," explains one detective, "I mean your files have to be in good order. You have to be able to do paperwork. This job just requires you to put a good file together."[51]

In regard to most crimes, however, such as burglaries and automobile thefts, the typical case file is very thin, but there are so many cases that the sheer number can become overwhelming for a detective. Or, they might be underwhelmed. This raises a key point. There is a difference between caseload and workload. A homicide detective may have a light caseload, two homicides, but that may generate a heavy workload, causing the detective to work 12-hour days. A burglary detective may have a high caseload, 250 open cases, but a light workload, because there is scant evidence and few leads on any of the cases. **Caseload** is the number of open cases a detective has at any given time, while **workload** is the amount of time and effort a detective must put into their cases.[52] Despite all efforts by criminal investigation management to balance these two, they are almost never adequately balanced.

One must also consider that in regard to caseload, the cases never stop. They continue to keep coming in, and detectives have to decide how to manage not only their caseload, but their time (workload). Corwin found this to be the case in the LAPD when he noted that "Most cannot sustain the pace of working 24 hours, even 48 hours at a stretch, juggling dozens of old cases while attempting to keep track of an inexorable wave of new ones."[53] Unsolved cases that remain open nag at the detectives, for as one ten-year-veteran detective noted, "You always have those open cases that you go back and ask, 'Did I do everything?' And they bother you."[54] In addition, each case has the potential to go to trial, and that is where the diligence of documenting everything comes to fruition. However, since no detective knows which case will go to trial, every case has to be treated with equal diligence. One investigator explained it best when he commented that the key to being a good detective was:

> Write a good story. Document everything. Everything! Because you know when it goes to trial, everything hinges on you. . . . A lot of guys are fearful of the documentation because you know when it goes to trial everything hinges on you. The spotlight is on you. And then you know that defense attorney has a year or two years to look over through your file and figure out what I need to do to make him look incompetent. And that's one of the most stressful things when you come in you know you got one person gonna make you look good. You got that one person try his best to destroy your credibility.[55]

While it is true that detectives are scrutinized by defense attorneys on the stand, that is really the exception and not the rule. Most cases do not go to trial. The reality is where most detectives face scrutiny is by their managers and by their peers. **Clearance rates** are the primary means by which criminal investigators are judged, and a detective who has a high clearance rate is well revered, while those with low clearance rates are looked down upon (Table 11.1). Yet, only about 20 percent of all violence and property crime is actually cleared by arrest.[56] The focus on clearance rates, however, weighs

Table 11.1 Percent of Crimes Cleared by Arrest or Exceptional Means, 2010*

Crimes	Percentage Cleared
Murder and nonnegligent manslaughter	64.8%
Forcible rate	40.3%
Robbery	28.2%
Aggravated assault	56.4%
Burglary	12.4%
Larceny-theft	21.1%
Motor vehicle theft	11.8%

*Exceptional means that an offender has been identified, enough evidence exists to make an arrest, the offender's location is known, and some circumstance prevents taking the offender into custody.
Source: Federal Bureau of Investigation. (2015). Uniform Crime Reports. Retrieved from www.fbi.gov/about-us/cjis/ucr/crime-in-the-u.s/2010/crime-in-the-u.s.-2010/clearances.

upon the detective, as exemplified by one relatively new homicide investigator when he explained, "You really don't want to leave a board full of open cases. It's just not cool. It's not good for business. It's not good for the public. You just, if you're leaving them open every year it's no coincidence, there's something wrong with you."[57] What happens to a detective not performing is management comes down on them to step it up, and other detectives begin to rib the failing detective. One investigator explained that "Every once in a while you hear a guy say, 'Oh, you got a bone [easy case]. You can finally close one, huh?' So yeah, there's some of that. . . . I don't want to hear it because it's already on my mind and it bothers me."[58]

Detectives also face scrutiny from other sources as well. The **media** can often be very critical of detectives and their work, particularly in high-profile cases when they are considered to be too slow in investigating the case. As Corwin found in his time with the LAPD, "Homicide Special detectives contend that whenever they screw up, their mistakes are magnified and the criticism in the press unrelenting. But when they do their job well, they believe, reporters pay little attention."[59]

In addition, victims and their families can also be highly critical of detectives and their work. When a person has a crime committed against them, that crime has changed their world, creating a sense of distrust in other people, and they demand justice. They have become a victim. To the victim, the crime is the most important event in their life. To the detective, however, they are not handling one case at a time, but rather dozens if not hundreds of similar cases with similar victims. This difference in viewpoints can create a tension between the victim and detective, where the victim sees the detective as not caring, while the detective sees the victim as harassing. This is magnified even further when the victim is murdered and it is the victim's family that takes the place of the victim. One detective voiced the tension that develops between him and the victim's family when he explained, "They don't care about the other cases. You know, you might be having your twelfth homicide of the year. You might have had two in a month and then you get this one. But no one wants to hear [excuses]. They want to know how come six months in and my baby's case is still open. . . . You got some family that will flat just wear you out, and that's stressful."[60]

That last point is key. Detective work is highly stressful. While many believe that dealing with crimes such as rapes, robberies, and homicides, having to see the dark side of humanity, is what causes the stress, the reality is quite different. As Corwin concluded in his book *Killing Season,* about the long hours, heavy caseload, and new cases coming in all the time, "This takes its toll."[61] Research into stress and homicide detectives have made similar conclu-

A detective's badge for the New York City Police Department's crime scene unit.

sions, when researchers found that dealing with dead bodies, grieving families, and frightened communities did not generate stress among detectives, but that responsibility for high-priority cases, the uncertainty of solvability in their cases, and potential scrutiny from victims, media, lawyers, and others did.[62]

One way in which detectives deal with stress is through humor. A very dark and macabre humor. Anecdotes abound in detective work, such as the detective who discovered a murderer had transported his two victims in a van and asked, "I have one critical question, because he had the two bodies in the back of the van, did he use the carpool lane?"[63] Or when looking for the severed hand of a victim, upon finding it, the officer asked his partner, "Can I give you a hand?"[64] Or one this author recalls at a crime scene looking for a severed head, when the detective found it he held it up and said, "We really need to put our heads together on this one." Gallo gets it right when she says that Chicago cops call a burn victim a "crispy critter" which is "an apt image, but more of a 'whistling-past-the-graveyard' reference that helps to depersonalize their charred remains" which "allows you to do your job."[65] It is the same for all manner of human depravity that detectives see, often on a daily basis.

If a case goes to trial, police officers and detectives are often called upon to testify in court.

Research has found that humor among detectives serves three major purposes. First, it becomes a part of the detective subculture as it reflects the acculturation, integration, and socialization of a person into the life of a detective.[66] Second, it is a means of mitigating stress and tension. Third, it serves as a barometer on emotions. If detectives stop joking, there may be an emotional problem. As one supervisor of detectives noted, "If they are joking I don't think I would worry too much. . . . People that worry me the most is when they are quiet. . . . You have to know your people and know what is out of character. If people that normally joke aren't, there may be an issue, if people who normally don't joke are, that may also be an issue."[67] They may have psychologically been pushed too far and can no longer cope.

Another major issue of criminal investigations, which harkens back to the issues that the RAND study raised, is the use of technology in criminal investigations. While that study suggested that technology does not necessarily solve crimes, but that people do, it does serve to corroborate the testimony of witnesses and victims, so the use of technology remains an important element of criminal investigations.

Where the issues often arise is in how the technology is employed by criminal investigators. Detectives often use technology to conduct surveillance, such as video cameras, night vision goggles, and more recently drones. Still further, there are new advances in technology such as recording devices that can be placed on rooftops throughout a city that allow for gunshot detection, thus narrowing down the locations from which shots were fired. Or, license plate readers mounted in police cars that allow the agency to track the movement of vehicles throughout a city, thus providing a database that criminal investigators can tap into when trying to provide evidence of a person's movement. There are also cell phone towers that collect this same type of data that can allow the police to track the movement of the cell phone by time, date, and location, which can be ostensibly tied to the movement of the cell phone's owner.

In addition to surveillance, detectives typically use technology to assist in collecting, analyzing, and identifying perpetrators of a crime.[68] From collecting latent fingerprints and identifying the owner through AFIS to the more modern collection of bodily fluids and skin to identify an individual through their DNA, criminal investigators have an enormous amount of technology and forensic science capabilities to assist them in conducting their investigations. How these types of technologies are used often raise the issue of Fourth Amendment protections and whether or not the technology violates the "unreasonable searches and seizures" clause. In addition, as new technology comes into existence, its ability to be introduced and used in a court of law is always raised and legal challenges are common. For instance, when DNA was discovered and the potential for assisting in identification in criminal investigations, it was not a foregone conclusion that the courts would recognize or allow the findings to be used in a court of law. One of the greatest detectives I have ever had the pleasure of knowing, Joe Horgas, was the first to use DNA in a murder case in the United States, and for him it was a personally challenging move to try and obtain a conviction with new technology.[69] Thus, the use of technology in criminal investigations is always a double-edged sword, for while it can assist in a criminal investigation, it can also present multiple issues for the

Box 11.5   History in Practice: Detective Joe Horgas and the First Use of DNA

In 1988, Arlington County (Virginia) Detective Joe Horgas was the driving force behind the first murder conviction that used **DNA technology** for forensic testing.

In January of 1984, in Arlington County, Virginia, Carolyn Hamm, a 32-year-old lawyer, was found murdered. She had been strangled and raped, her nude body face down on the bed, and the house had been ransacked. The murderer left behind no fingerprints or murder weapon with which to identify him. Detectives began looking for a suspect and eventually a man named David Vasquez was identified and arrested. He confessed and was sentenced to 35 years in prison. The case was considered closed.

Then, in 1987, Susan Tucker, a 44-year-old writer who lived near Carolyn Hamm's home, was found dead under similar circumstances. Yet, Vasquez was still in prison. Then, later that year, several similar murders turned up in Richmond, Virginia. Despite having a confession from Vasquez, some were wondering if the real murderer was still at large.

Arlington County Detective Joe Horgas, then with 16 years on the force, believed that Vasquez was innocent and someone else was responsible. That did not make him very popular. He pursued the Arlington murders, including Hamm's, as if the real murderer had not been caught. He interviewed Vasquez to no avail, and he ran up against departmental rivalries with the Richmond detectives who did not think the two city's murders were connected. Detective Horgas eventually came to believe a convicted burglar, Timothy W. Spencer, out on parole, had committed the murders, despite the fact that it is not typical for burglars to become rapists and especially murderers.

Lacking any evidence to tie Spencer to the murderers, other than blood and semen found at several crime scenes, Horgas turned to a private laboratory in New York, Lifecodes, which was using DNA technology. Horgas pressed for them to help him determine if the known DNA of Spencer matched that found at the crime scenes. Eventually, it was discovered that they did indeed match.

Spencer was the first person convicted with the use of DNA and he was executed in 1994. Had it not been for the relentless pursuit of justice by Detective Horgas, Spencer may not have been held accountable for his crimes, and Vasquez would never have been freed and exonerated.

Source: Mones, P. (1995). *Stalking Justice: The Dramatic True Story of the Detective Who First Used DNA Testing to Catch a Serial Killer.* New York, NY: Pocket Books.

investigator and it can never replace the more crucial means for solving crimes—people (see Box 11.5).

Conclusion

In addition to patrol and administration, the other main component of American policing is criminal investigations. Although the RAND study found that many of the long-held assumptions in criminal investigations did not hold, the importance of detectives and their work has not disappeared, but the realities of what it can achieve have become more realistic, exposing the realities of the detective mystique. The way in which criminal investigations are organized in a department makes a significant contribution to its success, particularly in how the criminal investigation process itself is organized. Still, there are many issues that detectives face on the job such as dealing with the darker side of humanity, enduring the stress of high-profile cases, feeling intense scrutiny from so many outside of policing, and finding a means of coping. The work of the detective is often grueling, tedious, and exhausting, but it is coveted by those who earn the title of detective.

Just the Facts

1. Literary giants such as Edgar Allen Poe, Charles Dickens, and Sir Arthur Conan Doyle made popular the concept of the detective, which then began to develop into the realities of policing in the 1800s with such notables as NYPD Inspector Thomas F. Byrnes the Chief of Detectives.

2. The detective mystique, as defined by Herman Goldstein, resulted in part from the part-science, part-art style of criminal investigations, combined with the literary popularity of the detective novel, and elevated the status of the police detective. The RAND study on criminal investigations revealed the realities of criminal investigation, namely that their literary counterparts were far more successful than the real detectives, thus diminishing their status and mystique.

3. The RAND Criminal Investigation study found that detectives and the vast resources contributed little to solving crimes, and that citizens coming forward with statements and evidence was by far more successful.

4. The three goals of detectives are to control criminals by knowing that certain criminals commit the most crime; to pursue justice by enforcing the laws; and to address problems that come to the forefront of public concern.

5. Case-oriented investigations are driven by police reports of crimes and attempt to solve each case while offender-oriented investigations focus on specific offenders who commit the majority of crimes. Although case-oriented investigations are the predominate method, the argument for offender-oriented investigations provides the department with the potential solvability of many crimes all at once.

6. The six styles of criminal investigation are reinforcing patrol (taking over the cases of first responding officers); standard reactive (responding when called); major cases (focusing on cases with high visibility); regulatory inspections (police routinely canvas certain locations for criminal activity); passive notation (taking reports for future connections to a known criminal); and discovery enforcement (detectives developing their own cases).

7. Police criminal investigation units are generally organized by the functions of the investigations that cover different stages of the investigation; by the solvability and seriousness of investigation potential, as in how likely the cases will be resolved; by crime type, such as burglary or homicide; and, in some cases, by special investigation units for special circumstances.

8. The investigative process moves from the initial investigation, case screening, follow-up investigation, handling and processing of physical evidence, information management, and arrest/post-arrest process. In some departments, cold case units are also employed to review old cases.

9. Caseload is the number of open cases a detective has at any given time, which may not correspond to the actual workload a detective has, for someone with only a handful of cases may work twice as hard as someone with 100 open cases without any leads or chance of solvability.

10. Criminal investigators are often judged by their clearance rates, which are often something out of their hands, the media can often create difficulties for detectives, working with victims and their families can cause issues because of expectations versus realities, and detectives often operate under high levels of stress.

Ask Yourself

1. Why is the entire genre of detective novels, movies, and television so popular with the American public, and how does this create difficulties for the real detective?

2. Recognizing the findings of the RAND criminal investigation units, what are some ways to resolve the inefficiency and ineffectiveness of police detectives?

3. Considering the goals of criminal investigations, do the approaches to criminal investigation support these goals? Does the actual process of criminal investigation also support these goals?

4. Compare and contrast the styles of criminal investigations. Are each of these styles equivalent to each other or are they dependent upon certain circumstances? If the latter, what are those circumstances?

5. From a case management perspective, do you think police criminal investigations should be case-oriented or offender-oriented? Then consider if criminal investigation should focus on caseload or workload.

Keywords

Addressing problems
American detectives
C. Auguste Dupin
Case management
Case screening
Caseload
Case-oriented investigations
Charles Dickens
Circumstances-result
  hypothesis
Clearance rates
Cold-case units
Controlling criminals
Crime type/crime specific
  investigations
Detective mystique

Discovery enforcement
Edgar Allan Poe
Effort-result hypothesis
Eugène-Francois Vidocq
Follow-up investigation
Functions of investigation
Goal of the detectives
Information management
Initial investigation
Jonathan Wild
Major cases
Offender-oriented
  investigation
Passive notation
Physical evidence
Popular culture

Post-arrest
Pursuit of justice
RAND study on the criminal
  investigation process
Regulatory inspections
Reinforcing patrol
Seriousness of investigations
Sherlock Holmes
Sir Arthur Conan Doyle
Solvability of investigations
Special investigation units
Standard reactive
Styles of criminal
  investigation
Thomas F. Byrnes
Workload

Endnotes

1. Vollmer, A. (1942). Criminal investigation. In *Elements of Police Science* by R. Perkins (Ed.), pp. 37-60. Chicago, IL: The Foundation Press, Inc., p. 37.

2. Skogan, W. & Frydl, K. (eds.) (2004). *Fairness and effectiveness in policing: The evidence.* Washington, DC: The National Academies Press, p. 73.

3. Eck, J.E. (1996). Rethinking detective management: Or, why investigative reforms are seldom permanent or effective. In *Quantifying Quality in Policing,* Larry T. Hoover (Ed.), pp. 167-184. Washington, DC: Police Executive Research Forum; Fielding, H. (1743/2008). Jonathan Wild. New York, NY: Oxford University Press; Morton, J. (2004). *The first detective: The life and revolutionary times of Eugene-Francois Vidocq, criminal spy and private eye.* London, England: Ebury Press.

4. Poe, E.A. (2006). *The Murders in the rue morgue: The Dupin stories.* New York, NY: Modern Library.

5. Dickens, C. (2003). *Bleak house.* New York, NY: Penguin Books; Note: Dickens had also written several short stories before *Bleak House* in which he used the word detective.

6. Doyle, Sir A.C. (1986). *The complete Sherlock Holmes (2 volumes).* New York, NY: Bantam Classics.

7. Conway, J.N. (2011). *The big policeman: The rise and fall of Thomas Byrnes, America's first, most ruthless, and greatest detective.* Guilford, CT: Lyons Press.

8. Smith, B. (1940). *Police systems in the United States.* New York, NY: Harper & Brothers Publishers.

9. Tilstone, W.J. (2006). *Forensic science: An encyclopedia of history, methods, and techniques.* Santa Barbara, CA: ABC-CLIO.

10. Goldstein, H. (1977). *Policing a free society.* Cambridge, MA: Ballinger Publishing Co., p. 55.

11. Kirk, J. (2004). Watching the detectives. In *Best American Crime Writing, 2004 edition,* Otto Penzler and Thomas H. Cook (Eds.), pp. 125-156. New York, NY: Vintage Books, p. 128.

12. Goldstein, H. (1977). *Policing a free society.* Cambridge, MA: Ballinger Publishing Co., pp. 55-56.

13. Simon, D. (1991). *Homicide: A year on the killing streets.* Boston, MA: Houghton Mifflin Company, p. 15.

14. Simon, D. (1991). *Homicide: A year on the killing streets.* Boston, MA: Houghton Mifflin Company, p. 13.

15. Simon, D. (1991). *Homicide: A year on the killing streets.* Boston, MA: Houghton Mifflin Company, p. 13.

16. Chaiken, J.M. (1975). *The criminal investigation process, volume II: Survey of municipal and county police departments.* Santa Monica, CA: RAND; Greenwood, P.W. & Petersilia, J. (1975). *The criminal investigation process, volume I: Summary and policy implications.* Santa Monica, CA: RAND.

17. Eck, J.E. (1996). Rethinking detective management: Or, why investigative reforms are seldom permanent or effective. In *Quantifying Quality in Policing,* Larry T. Hoover (ed.), pp. 167-184. Washington, DC: Police Executive Research Forum.

18. Greenwood, P.W. & Petersilia, J. (1975). *The criminal investigation process, volume I: Summary and policy implications.* Santa Monica, CA: RAND.

19. Greenwood, P.W. & Petersilia, J. (1975). *The criminal investigation process, volume I: Summary and policy implications.* Santa Monica, CA: RAND, p. iii.

20. Greenwood, P.W. & Petersilia, J. (1975). *The criminal investigation process, volume I: Summary and policy implications.* Santa Monica, CA: RAND.

21. Greenwood, P.W. & Petersilia, J. (1975). *The criminal investigation process, volume I: Summary and policy implications.* Santa Monica, CA: RAND.

22. Greenwood, P.W. & Petersilia, J. (1975). *The criminal investigation process, volume I: Summary and policy implications.* Santa Monica, CA: RAND, p. vi.

23. Greenwood, P.W. & Petersilia, J. (1975). *The criminal investigation process, volume I: Summary and policy implications.* Santa Monica, CA: RAND, p. vi.

24. Greenwood, P.W. & Petersilia, J. (1975). *The criminal investigation process, volume I: Summary and policy implications.* Santa Monica, CA: RAND, p. vii.

25. Greenwood, P.W. & Petersilia, J. (1975). *The criminal investigation process, volume I: Summary and policy implications.* Santa Monica, CA: RAND, p. vii.

26. Eck, J.E. (1996). Rethinking detective management: Or, why investigative reform are seldom permanent or effective. In *Quantifying Quality in Policing,* by Larry T. Hoover (Ed), pp. 167-184. Washington, DC: Police Executive Research Forum; Spelman, W. & Brown, D.K. (1981). *Calling the police: Citizen reporting on serious crime.* Washington, DC: Police Executive Research Forum; Willman, M. & Snortum, J. (1984). Detective work: The criminal investigation process in a medium-size police department. *Criminal Justice Review, 9,* 33-39.

27. Eck, J.E. (1996). Rethinking detective management: Or, why investigative reforms are seldom permanent or effective. In *Quantifying Quality in Policing,* Larry T. Hoover (Ed.), pp. 167-184. Washington, DC: Police Executive Research Forum.

28. Geller, W.A. (1991). *Local government police management.* 3rd ed. Washington, DC: ICMA.

29. Honolulu Police Department.(2014). Honolulu Police Department. Retrieved from www.honolulupd.org/department/index.php?tab=tabs-5

30. Eck, J.E. (1983). *Solving crimes: The investigations of burglary and robbery.* Washington, DC: Police Executive Research Forum; Skogan, W. & Frydl, K. (eds.) (2004). *Fairness and effectiveness in policing: The evidence.* Washington, DC: The National Academies Press.

31. Dias, G.A. (2002). *Honolulu cop: Reflections on a career with HPD.* Honolulu, HI: The Bess Press, p. 150.

32. Sanders, W.B. (1977). *Detective work: A study of criminal investigations.* New York, NY: Free Press.

33. Dias, G.A. (2002). *Honolulu cop: Reflections on a career with HPD.* Honolulu, HI: The Bess Press, p. 150.

34. Corwin, M. (2003). *Homicide special: A year with the LAPD's elite detective unit*. New York, NY: Henry Holt and Company; Dunn, W. (1996). *Boot: An L.A.P.D. officer's rookie year*. New York, NY: William Morrow and Company, Inc.

35. Corwin, M. (2003). *Homicide special: A year with the LAPD's elite detective unit*. New York, NY: Henry Holt and Company, p. 3.

36. Dias, G.A. (2002). *Honolulu cop: Reflections on a career with HPD*. Honolulu, HI: The Bess Press, p. 150.

37. Corwin, M. (2003). *Homicide special: A year with the LAPD's elite detective unit*. New York, NY: Henry Holt and Company, p. 41.

38. Corwin, M. (2003). *Homicide special: A year with the LAPD's elite detective unit*. New York, NY: Henry Holt and Company, p. 219.

39. Geller, W.A. (1991). *Local government police management*. 3rd ed. Washington, DC: ICMA; Osterburg, J.W. & Ward, R.H. (2014). *Criminal investigation: A method for reconstructing the past*. 7th ed. Waltham, MA: Anderson Publishing.

40. Dias, G.A. (2002). *Honolulu cop: Reflections on a career with HPD*. Honolulu, HI: The Bess Press, p. 191.

41. Geller, W.A. (1991). *Local government police management*. 3rd ed. Washington, DC: ICMA; Sanders, W.B. (1977). *Detective work: A study of criminal investigations*. New York, NY: Free Press.

42. Geller, W.A. (1991). *Local government police management*. 3rd ed. Washington, DC: ICMA.

43. Geller, W.A. (1991). *Local government police management*. 3rd ed. Washington, DC: ICMA; Osterburg, J.W. & Ward, R.H. (2014). *Criminal investigation: A method for reconstructing the past*. 7th ed. Waltham, MA: Anderson Publishing.

44. Erickson, R.V. & Haggerty, K.D. (1997). *Policing the risk society*. Toronto, Canada: University of Toronto Press; Osterburg, J.W. & Ward, R.H. (2014). *Criminal investigation: A method for reconstructing the past*. 7th ed. Waltham, MA: Anderson Publishing; Skogan, W. & Frydl, K. (eds.) (2004). *Fairness and effectiveness in policing: The evidence*. Washington, DC: The National Academies Press.

45. Sanders, W.B. (1977). *Detective work: A study of criminal investigations*. New York, NY: Free Press, p. 13.

46. Sanders, W.B. (1977). *Detective work: A study of criminal investigations*. New York, NY: Free Press, p. 15.

47. Corwin, M. (2003). *Homicide special: A year with the LAPD's elite detective unit*. New York, NY: Henry Holt and Company; Simon, D. (1991). *Homicide: A year on the killing streets*. Boston, MA: Houghton Mifflin Company.

48. Geller, W.A. (1991). *Local government police management*. 3rd ed. Washington, DC: ICMA.

49. Simon, D. (1991). *Homicide: A year on the killing streets*. Boston, MA: Houghton Mifflin Company, p. 16.

50. Walton, R. (2006). *Cold case homicides: Practical investigative techniques*. Boca Raton, FL: CRC Press.

51. Dabney, D.A., Copes, H., Tewksbury, R. & Hawk-Tourtelot, S.R. (2013). A qualitative assessment of stress perceptions among members of a homicide unit. *Justice Quarterly, 30*, 811-836, at p. 823.

52. Geller, W.A. (1991). *Local government police management*. 3rd ed. Washington, DC: ICMA.

53. Corwin, M. (2003). *Homicide special: A year with the LAPD's elite detective unit*. New York, NY: Henry Holt and Company, p. 22.

54. Dabney, D.A., Copes, H., Tewksbury, R. & Hawk-Tourtelot, S.R. (2013). A qualitative assessment of stress perceptions among members of a homicide unit. *Justice Quarterly, 30*, 811-836, at p. 823.

55. Dabney, D.A., Copes, H., Tewksbury, R. & Hawk-Tourtelot, S.R. (2013). A qualitative assessment of stress perceptions among members of a homicide unit. *Justice Quarterly, 30*, 811-836, at p. 824.

56. Skogan, W. & Frydl, K. (eds.) (2004). *Fairness and effectiveness in policing: The evidence*. Washington, DC: The National Academies Press.

57. Dabney, D.A., Copes, H., Tewksbury, R. & Hawk-Tourtelot, S.R. (2013). A qualitative assessment of stress perceptions among members of a homicide unit. *Justice Quarterly, 30*, 811-836, at p. 827.

58. Dabney, D.A., Copes, H., Tewksbury, R. & Hawk-Tourtelot, S.R. (2013). A qualitative assessment of stress perceptions among members of a homicide unit. *Justice Quarterly, 30*, 811-836, at p. 826.

59. Corwin, M. (2003). *Homicide special: A year with the LAPD's elite detective unit*. New York, NY: Henry Holt and Company, p. 119.

60. Dabney, D.A., Copes, H., Tewksbury, R. & Hawk-Tourtelot, S.R. (2013). A qualitative assessment of stress perceptions among members of a homicide unit. *Justice Quarterly, 30*, 811-836, at p. 829.

61. Corwin, M. (1997). *The killing season: A summer inside an LAPD homicide division*. New York, NY: Simon & Schuster, p. 22.

62. Dabney, D.A., Copes, H., Tewksbury, R. & Hawk-Tourtelot, S.R. (2013). A qualitative assessment of stress perceptions among members of a homicide unit. *Justice Quarterly, 30*, 811-836.

63. Corwin, M. (2003). *Homicide special: A year with the LAPD's elite detective unit*. New York, NY: Henry Holt and Company, p. 111.

64. Preib, M. (2010). *The wagon and other stories from the city*. Chicago, IL: University of Chicago Press, p. 24.

65. Gallo, G. (2000). *Crime scenes*. Portland, OR: Blue Murder Press, p. 51.

66. Vivona, B.D. (2014). Humor functions within crime scene investigations: Group dynamics, stress, and the negotiation of emotions. *Police Quarterly, 17*, 127-149.

67. Vivona, B.D. (2014). Humor functions within crime scene investigations: Group dynamics, stress, and the negotiation of emotions. *Police Quarterly, 17*, 127-149, at p. 140.

68. National Institute of Justice. (2007). *Investigative uses of technology: Devices, tools, and techniques*. Washington, DC: U.S. Department of Justice.

69. Mones, P. (1995). *Stalking justice: The dramatic true story of the detective who first used DNA testing to catch a serial killer*. New York, NY: Pocket Books.

■ *"True courage is required in many situations and [the police officer] must be always ready in an emergency to risk health and life."*[1] —*August Vollmer, 1921*

Bust of Sergeant Jimmie Rutledge, one of two Berkeley Police officers killed in the line of duty. Summoned to a disturbance call, Rutledge confronted the suspect and was shot and killed. End of watch: June 6, 1973.

CHAPTER 12

Force

After reading this chapter, you will be able to:

1. Comprehend the relative dangers of the occupation of police officer.
2. Define police use of force and its parameters, especially in light of the two related Supreme Court decisions.
3. Explain the use-of-force continuum and the progression of steps/stages.
4. Compare and contrast the reason many agencies are adopting a force options model.
5. Detail the number of deadly force encounters that occur on an annual basis and explain the varied causes of these deaths.
6. Identify the number of annual assaults on police officers and detail the circumstances related to these unlawful attacks.
7. Identify the number of police officers annually injured in the line of duty and what is known about the circumstances of these injuries.
8. Identify the number of police officers annually killed in the line of duty and what is known about these deaths.

The Realities of Force

One thing that should be very clear by now is that the use of force is one of the primary factors that define American policing. From Chapter 1, we learned that Carl Klockars believed the best way to define the police had to do with their "general right to use force by the state within the state's domestic territory."[2] Force is also a topic of consideration under the history of the police, police careers (training), authority, discretion, and it is described as playing a central role in shaping the police culture. Force and coercion are, simply put, part of the job of being a police officer.

Police officers are tasked with the responsibility of enforcing the law. They are authorized the ability to use coercion and force to apply the law. Yet one must understand that the use of force comes in many different forms. Out of all of the police-citizen encounters annually in the United States, the majority of them (80–90 percent) are simply the police officer talking to the citizen. These have been defined as definitional encounters where the police officers asks questions ("Do you know how fast you were going?") or makes accusation ("You were speeding, sir.").[3] In most cases, citizens simply comply with the officer. There are some cases where police officers must issue such commands. These are referred to as imperatives, where an officer gives a command and demands compliance ("Put your hands where I can see them."). Out of the millions of police-citizen encounters (recently estimated to be 40–45 million a year),[4] only a small percentage (8–12 percent) require the police to issue commands.[5] And finally, the use of force, which includes either the threat to use force ("Put the gun down or I will shoot.") or its actual use, accounts for less than 1 to 3 percent of all police encounters.[6] And even in these rare cases, it has been found that in most of these incidents, the vast majority of them consist of minor forms of force.[7] Despite all of this, it remains that in those statistically rare cases, when officers use major forms of force, including deadly force, they are the focus of much attention and are the most controversial. Former Minneapolis Police Chief Robert K. Olsen said it best when he called the use of force "the single most volatile issue facing police departments" and that "just one use-of-force incident can dramatically alter the stability of a police department and its relationship with a community."[8] And it probably goes without saying that they are the most dangerous situations for police officers.

How dangerous is an important question and one that requires some perspective. Policing is not *the* most dangerous job in America, but it *is* dangerous. To compare with other occupations, policing does not fall in the top ten jobs with the most fatal injuries. According to the federal government's Bureau of Labor statistics, the most dangerous job in 2012 was logger, with 127.8 deaths per 100,000 workers.[9] This was followed by fishers (117 per 100,000 workers), flight engineers (53.4 per 100,000 workers), and roofers (40.5 per 100,000 workers). Number ten was construction laborer at 17.4 deaths per 100,000 workers. The police were farther down the line with 16 deaths per 100,000 workers in 2012. Policing can be a very dangerous job, but in perspective, it is not *the* most dangerous job. Still, over 100 police officers are killed in the line of duty on an annual basis, and many of these are by violent acts.[10]

All of the focus on violence against police officers and officers killed in the line of duty also tends to mask another issue centered on the need to use force, and that is the number of injuries sustained in the line of duty. The routine occupation of being a police officer often places the officer in situations that have the high potential for injuries, including the amount of time they spend driving in traffic and the dangerous situations they find themselves responding to, such as automobile accidents or when they have to place handcuffs on an individual who is resisting arrest. The police occupation has a high number of line-of-duty injuries, something that is seldom discussed outside of policing circles.

One of the most dangerous aspects of policing is not use of force but driving in and working traffic.

The purpose of this chapter is to understand the police use of force from both the legal perspective and the training that police officers receive. It explores when and how officers are authorized the use of force to gain a better understanding of one of the most important, serious, and often controversial aspects of American policing. In addition, the chapter looks at what happens when force is used against police officers, to gain a better understanding of police officer line of duty injuries and the more tragic, line-of-duty deaths (see Box 12.1).

Box 12.1 **History in Practice: Morgan Earp, Killed in the Line of Duty**

One of the most famous lawmen to have been **killed in the line of duty** was **Morgan Earp**, brother of Wyatt Earp, who was serving as a marshal in Tombstone, Arizona. Born on April 24, 1851, in Pella, Iowa, he and Wyatt were the two youngest in the family. They were left behind to tend the farm when their older brothers went off to fight in the Civil War. After the war, Morgan went West with his brother James and later became a marshal in Dodge City, Kansas. Eventually he moved to Tombstone, Arizona, with his brothers, and he became a Deputy U.S. Marshal under his brother Wyatt. Morgan was there at the O.K. Corral when the confrontation with the Clantons and the so-called Cowboys came to a head on October 26, 1881. Morgan was shot across the back in the gunfight, but, like all the other Earps, he survived. Then, two months later, there was an assassination attempt on Virgil Earp, who was serving as Tombstone's marshal. He was badly wounded, and Morgan stepped up to essentially take his place. Worried about the Clantons, Morgan sent his wife to California, and the following month, while shooting pool, Morgan was assassinated. Morgan's death was investigated and arrests were made, but the Clantons were freed for a lack of evidence, which ultimately led to Wyatt Earp's famous vendetta ride.

Use of Force

Government is ostensibly created for the greater good of a society. The people form governments to help regulate the behaviors of people and define, through the law, what is acceptable and unacceptable behavior. Whenever a law is passed, there must be some means of enforcing the law, otherwise the law becomes meaningless. This is where the role of the police in our society comes into play. As agents of the government, they are tasked with the responsibility of enforcing the law, and when people choose to ignore or violate the law, the police are tasked with bringing these violators to justice by bringing them before the courts to be judged. When an individual resists, police officers are authorized to use force. According to the International Association of Chiefs of Police (IACP), the **use of force** is defined as "the amount of effort required by police to compel compliance by an unwilling subject."[11]

As noted above, the amount of effort may consist of talking to a suspect, issuing commands, or having to use some type of physical force to gain compliance. The authorization for police to use such force is generally found in state law. For instance, in Florida, there is a statute that authorizes law enforcement officers the right to use force when making an arrest. In part, the statute reads, "A law enforcement officer . . . need not retreat or desist from efforts to make a lawful arrest because of resistance or threatened resistance to the arrest. The officer is justified in the use of any force: (1) which he or she reasonably believes to be necessary to defend himself or herself or another from bodily harm while making an arrest, (2) when necessarily committed in retaking felons who have escaped, or (3) when necessarily committed in arresting felons fleeing from justice."[12] This statute includes the use of deadly force, which is then further defined in a following statute. This type of state law is generally what authorizes police use of force.

When police officers attempt to make an arrest, sometimes suspects do not comply with the officer's commands, necessitating the use of force, as in the case of an Occupy Wall Street protestor refusing to comply with the NYPD officer's commands.

In addition to state laws, the U.S. Supreme Court has heard many cases centered on police use of force, in particularly the use of deadly force. Two specific cases have come to define the legal parameters of when police officers may use deadly force. The first was the case of ***Tennessee v. Garner*** **(1985)** in which two Memphis Police Officers, responding to a burglary call (which is a felony), shot and killed the suspect as he tried to escape by climbing a chain-link fence (see Box 12.2). The state statute authorized police the use of deadly force to shoot a fleeing suspect, but the U.S. Supreme Court in its decision stated that law enforcement officers pursuing an unarmed suspect may use deadly force to prevent escape only if the officer has probable cause to believe that the suspect poses a significant threat of death or serious physical injury to the officer or others.[13]

Box 12.2 Policing in Practice: Use of Deadly Force, Tennessee v. Garner (1985)

The first U.S. Supreme Court case that has come to define the legal parameters of when police officers may use **deadly force** is *Tennessee v. Garner*. The Court's reasoning is below:

The use of deadly force to prevent the escape of all felony suspects, whatever the circumstances, is constitutionally unreasonable. It is not better that all felony suspects die than that they escape. Where the suspect poses no immediate threat to the officer and no threat to others, the harm resulting from failing to apprehend him does not justify the use of deadly force to do so. It is no doubt unfortunate when a suspect who is in sight escapes, but the fact that the police arrive a little late or are a little slower afoot does not always justify killing the suspect. A police officer may not seize an unarmed, nondangerous suspect by shooting him dead. The Tennessee statute is unconstitutional insofar as it authorizes the use of deadly force against such fleeing suspects.

It is not, however, unconstitutional on its face. Where the officer has probable cause to believe that the suspect poses a threat of serious physical harm, either to the officer or to others, it is not constitutionally unreasonable to prevent escape by using deadly force. Thus, if the suspect threatens the officer with a weapon or there is probable cause to believe that he has committed a crime involving the infliction or threatened infliction of serious physical harm, deadly force may be used if necessary to prevent escape, and if, where feasible, some warning has been given. As applied in such circumstances, the Tennessee statute would pass constitutional muster.

Source: U.S. Supreme Court Decision, *Tennessee v. Garner* (1985).

The other U.S. Supreme Court case that has come to define police use of force was ***Graham v. Connor*** (1989) (see Box 12.3).[14] In this case, Graham, a diabetic, was having an insulin reaction and ran into a convenience store to purchase some orange juice to raise his blood sugar. There was a long line, so Graham went and asked a friend to drive him to another friend's house to get something to eat. Connor, the police officer, witnessed Graham's erratic behavior and suspecting a crime, made an investigative stop. Graham tried to explain but the officer did not believe his story. Connor was trying to gain compliance over the agitated Graham and a struggle ensued as the officer attempted to place handcuffs on Graham. In the process, Graham sustained several injuries. The case was filed as an excessive-force case in violation of Graham's Fourteenth Amendment rights. The U.S. Supreme Court ruled that an objective reasonableness standard should apply to a free citizen's claim that law enforcement officers used excessive force in the course of making an arrest, investigatory stop, or other seizure. The reasonableness standard is used to say that under the facts and circumstances confronting the police officer, a reasonable person would believe that the amount of force used was necessary and proper for the situation at hand.

> ## Box 12.3 Policing in Practice: Use of Deadly Force, Graham v. Connor (1989)
>
> The second U.S. Supreme Court case that has come to define the legal parameters of when police officers may use **deadly force** is *Graham v. Connor*. The Court's reasoning is below:
>
> The "reasonableness" of a particular use of force must be judged from the perspective of a reasonable officer on the scene, rather than with the 20/20 vision of hindsight (See *Terry v. Ohio*). The Fourth Amendment is not violated by an arrest based on probable cause, even though the wrong person is arrested (See *Hill v. California*), nor by the mistaken execution of a valid search warrant on the wrong premises (See *Maryland v. Garrison*). With respect to a claim of excessive force, the same standard of reasonableness at the moment applies: "Not every push or shove, even if it may later seem unnecessary in the peace of a judge's chambers" (See *Johnson v. Glick*), violates the Fourth Amendment. The calculus of reasonableness must embody allowance for the fact that police officers are often forced to make split-second judgments—in circumstances that are tense, uncertain, and rapidly evolving—about the amount of force that is necessary in a particular situation.
>
> As in other Fourth Amendment contexts, however, the "reasonableness" inquiry in an excessive force case is an objective one: the question is whether the officers' actions are "objectively reasonable" in light of the facts and circumstances confronting them, without regard to their underlying intent or motivation. An officer's evil intentions will not make a Fourth Amendment violation out of an objectively reasonable use of force; nor will an officer's good intentions make an objectively unreasonable use of force constitutional.
>
> *Source:* United States Supreme Court Decision, *Graham v. Connor* (1989).

In light of the U.S. Supreme Court decisions, in the 1980s, many police departments began looking for a method of teaching police officers what is reasonable for a given situation, and the result was the **use-of-force continuum model**.[15] This model informs police of the escalating levels of force, typically moving from physical to chemical, electronic, impact, and finally firearms.[16] The model generally teaches police officers that they can use one level higher than what is being used against them, so if a suspect is trying to kick them, they may use pepper spray. Or if a suspect comes at them with a knife, they are authorized to use their firearm. The concept was to promote officers considering what was reasonable for a given situation. Over time, the use-of-force continuums have become more detailed, and because of advancing technology and equipment, the police have many more options than they did in the 1980s. It is, therefore, important to take a closer look at the continuum as a means of understanding how police officers may use force.

The first step, or stage, in the use of force is merely **officer presence**.[17] In this case no force is actually used, but "the mere presence of a law enforcement officer works to deter crime or diffuse a situation."[18] Returning to the figures given in the introduction to this chapter, this accounts for the majority (approximately 90 percent) of the over 40 million contacts the police have with citizens in a given year.[19] The police officer being present with a uniform, badge, and a gun, which conveys a sense of authority, is usually enough to prevent any need for force.

The second step/stage in the use-of-force continuum is **verbalization.**[20] In this case the force is not physical as officers "issue calm, nonthreatening commands," or, if the situation escalates they "may increase their volume and shorten commands in an attempt to gain compliance."[21] Again, returning to the figures presented in the introduction, the use of these directive commands in police-citizen encounters accounts for approximately 8–12 percent of the 40 million contacts per year.[22]

The third step/stage of the use-of-force continuum is the first in which true force is actually employed and that is generally referred to as **empty-hand control.** In this stage, "officers use bodily force to gain control of a situation."[23] Simply put, they lay hands on the suspect to gain compliance. This may include what are referred to as soft techniques where "officers use grabs, holds, and joint locks to restrain an individual," or hard techniques where "officers use punches and kicks to restrain an individual."[24] It should be considered that within this stage, officers moving from soft to hard techniques are escalating the use of force on the continuum.

The fourth step/stage of the use-of-force continuum is **less-than-lethal methods** (see Table 12.1). In this stage, "officers use less-lethal technologies to gain control of a situation."[25] The number of technologies available to the police have increased over the past several decades, and there is some

Table 12.1 Less-Than-Lethal Weapons Authorized for Use by Police Officers and Sheriffs' Deputies, by Size of Population Served, 2007			
	Police Officers (Sheriffs' Deputies)		
Pop. Served	**Pepper Spray**	**Baton**	**CED**
All sizes	97(96)%	93(90)%	60(66)%
1,000,000 or more	92(96)	100(100)	100(78)
500,000–999,999	100(100)	100(96)	77(81)
250,000–499,999	100(100)	100(97)	93(77)
100,000–249,999	100(99)	99(94)	76(80)
50,000–99,999	99(98)	99(88)	78(71)
25,000–49,999	99(98)	98(89)	70(70)
10,000–24,999	99(98)	96(89)	67(67)
Under 10,000	96(89)	92(90)	57(49)

Source: Reaves, B.A. (2010). *Local Police Departments, 2007*. Washington, DC: Bureau of Justice Statistics; Reaves, B.A. (2012). *Sheriffs' Offices, 2007 – Statistical Tables*. Washington, DC: Bureau of Justice Statistics.

dispute over whether one form of less-than-lethal instrument is a greater use of force than other forms.[26] Generally, the less-than-lethal instruments can be divided into three categories. The first is **blunt instruments**, which include the so-called billy club or night stick, which was traditionally made of wood; the PR-24, which is a polycarbonate side-handled baton; or the more modern ASP, which is a telescoping baton. In the United States, 93 percent of all police departments authorize their officers to carry a baton, with 88 percent authorizing the telescoping baton, 45 percent authorizing the traditional night stick, and 36 percent authorizing the PR-24.[27] The over 3,000 Sheriffs' Offices in the United States are very similar in their authorization in that 90 percent authorize the carrying of a baton with 85 percent allowing the telescoping baton, 39 percent the traditional night stick, and 27 percent the PR-24.[28] In the past, when powerful flashlights required five D batteries and flashlights such as a Mag-Light were the size of a police baton, these were often included in the blunt instrument category.[29] With today's tactical flashlights, they are typically no longer included. Regardless, police officers are taught to use all of these blunt instruments primarily to strike large meaty areas of the body to gain compliance. This includes the arms and legs. They are generally taught to try and avoid striking joints, such as knees and elbows, as blows to these locations may cause more lasting trauma, but that they are an optional target area. Finally, officers are taught to never strike the head, neck, spine, or groin, as these could prove fatal, *unless* the situation has escalated to the use of deadly force (see Table 12.2).

Table 12.2   Types of Batons Authorized for Use by Police Officers and Sheriffs' Deputies, by Size of Population Served, 2007

Pop. Served	Police Officers (Sheriffs' Deputies)			
	Any Type	Collapsible	Traditional	PR-24
All sizes	39(90)%	88(85)%	45(39)%	36(27)%
1,000,000 or more	100(100)	92(96)	69(67)	54(30)
500,000–999,999	100(96)	94(94)	55(45)	62(29)
250,000–499,999	100(97)	87(96)	50(35)	30(23)
100,000–249,999	99(94)	98(92)	56(39)	35(24)
50,000–99,999	99(88)	96(83)	48(47)	32(26)
25,000–49,999	98(89)	94(79)	34(32)	28(27)
10,000–24,999	96(89)	90(84)	40(40)	32(28)
Under 10,000	92(90)	87(88)	46(36)	36(26)

In the less-than-lethal step/stage of the use-of-force continuum, the second category of instruments are **chemical** weapons. This includes the more traditional tear-gas sprays CS and CN or the more modern pepper sprays, for which 97 percent of all police departments and 96 percent of all sheriffs' offices in the United States authorize officers to carry.[30] The former are a synthesized chemical compound, while the latter is a naturally occurring chemical, oleoresin capsicum, which is derived from hot chili peppers. It is the chemical that makes hot peppers hot. In both cases, they are delivered through an aerosol spray, for which the canister can be carried on a police officer's duty belt. Both of these chemical weapons compel an almost immediate reaction causing a person's eyes to close and tear, their breathing to constrict, and their nose to run. They may also develop a cough. They are incapacitating agents designed to allow the police officer the opportunity to gain compliance over a suspect. There have been some deaths of suspects when pepper spray was used against them, but most of these were due to a pre-existing medical conditions, including asthma, various diseases, drug use, or a combination of these.[31] In addition, another study found that when departments employed the use of pepper sprays, the number of annual injuries to police officers declined, as did injuries to suspects.[32]

In the less-than-lethal step/stage of the use-of-force continuum, the third category of instruments are **conducted energy devices (CED)**. A census of law enforcement agencies in the United States found that 60 percent of police departments authorize the use of CEDs by their officers, while 66 percent of sheriffs' offices allow their deputies to carry them.[33] These weapons are often referred to as Tasers because of the popularity of the CEDs sold by the company Taser International, which is akin to calling a tissue a Kleenex even if it is not made by that company. The name Taser is actually derived by the inventor's childhood fascination for the action hero genius, Tom Swift, who had an electric rifle, hence **T**homas **A**. **S**wift's **E**lectric **R**ifle is how Jack Cover generated the most common name for the device. The device fires small dart-like electrodes which allow for an electrical current to run between the two, generating up to 50,000 volts of electricity, that lasts anywhere from 5 to 30 seconds, depending on the brand and version. The use of these devices have resulted in some deaths typically due to a medical condition on the part of the individual being struck; however, a Police Executive Research Forum study in 2009 found after analyzing the use of CEDs by police departments, there was a 70 percent decrease in officer injuries and a 40 percent decrease in suspect injuries after the agencies began using these devices.[34]

The police Taser — an acronym for Thomas A. Swift's Electric Rifle.

The fifth step/stage of the use-of-force continuum is **lethal force,** more commonly referred to as **deadly force.**[35] The primary means of deadly force tends to be when officers use their firearm "to gain control of a situation"[36] (see Table 12.3). Police officers are trained to use deadly force when their life, the lives of their fellow officers, or the lives of citizens are in immediate danger. Police officers are then taught to shoot to stop the suspect by shooting center mass. The reason for this is because on a human being, center mass (chest) is the largest target. If an officer is off by six inches left or right, they still have a good chance of hitting the suspect. If they shoot for anything else, there is a good chance they will miss. Due to the stress of a deadly force encounter, officers often lose almost all of their auditory ability, and they develop tunnel vision. The ability to simply pull the trigger, aiming at a moving target, can be difficult. Police officers are thus trained to shoot at the largest target with the hopes of stopping the deadly force being used by the suspect. It should also be noted here that when police officers are authorized to employ the use of deadly force, they are not limited to only the use of their firearm. If an officer is in a situation where their life or the lives of citizens are in grave danger, they can use any means necessary to stop the threat, such as the Tucson (AZ) police officer who, when faced with a man walking down a neighborhood street firing off a rifle, used his patrol vehicle to strike the suspect, thus stopping the threat.[37] Although the number of

Table 12.3 Types of Sidearms Authorized for Use by Police Officers and Sheriffs' Deputies, by Size of Population Served, 2007

| | Police Officers (Sheriffs' Deputies) | | | |
| | Semiautomatic | | Revolver | |
Pop. Served	Primary	Backup	Primary	Backup
All sizes	100(100)%	77(80)%	22(22)%	51(52)%
1,000,000 or more	100(100)	100(89)	62(33)	69(48)
500,000–999,999	100(100)	100(87)	23(19)	55(27)
250,000–499,999	100(100)	100(74)	17(26)	52(51)
100,000–249,999	100(100)	100(83)	19(13)	55(58)
50,000–99,999	100(100)	95(78)	11(14)	53(55)
25,000–49,999	100(100)	73(86)	7(19)	47(59)
10,000–24,999	100(100)	70(80)	10(23)	50(50)
Under 10,000	100(100)	77(77)	26(31)	51(47)

Source: Reaves, B.A. (2010). *Local Police Departments, 2007.* Washington, DC: Bureau of Justice Statistics; Reaves, B.A. (2012). *Sheriffs' Offices, 2007 – Statistical Tables.* Washington, DC: Bureau of Justice Statistics.

cases of police officers using deadly force tends to be small, they receive the most attention, so because of this, police use of deadly force will be treated more fully later in this chapter.

The concept behind the use-of-force continuum was to teach police officers the escalation of force. They were taught that as a suspect increased his use of force, they were authorized to use one level above the suspect. So, if the suspect punched the officer, the police officer could use nonlethal force. Or, if a suspect pulled a lead pipe on them (a blunt force instrument), they were authorized to use deadly force. Teaching the continuum was, in part, to teach officers to use only the force which is necessary, when they were authorized to use force and what kind of force, but it was also used to teach officer safety. For instance, Marion, in her participant observational study of a police academy class, found, "The force continuum is stressed in self-defense training, where cadets are taught to use no more force than necessary to subdue a subject. But once again, officer safety is the primary concern of all the training."[38]

The continuum models were created in the 1980s as a means of teaching police officers about the use of force, but over the years, they have come under much criticism.[39] It has been noted that the continuum was not based directly on the law, nor did the model effectively convey the reasonable standard as described in the Graham case.[40] In most continuum models, like the one described above, officer presence and verbal commands are placed in the continuum, but the reality is, there is no force being used, not as that term is commonly applied. Officers also developed the wrong perception that they had to move through the various steps/stages before using deadly force, but that was not the case. If someone pulled a gun on them, they did not have to move through the other steps to respond with deadly force. It also suggested that officers had to use lesser alternatives and work their way up the ladder, and much debate ensued over whether one weapon (the PR-24) was further up or down the use-of-force continuum than other weapons (say a CED). This was a specious argument and took the focus off of the more important elements of use-of-force encounters. Finally, the continuum suggests that there was always a proper level of force, because the model said so. The problem is, the model did not always convey every situation a police officer encountered. Imagine a police officer confronting a person on the street who breaks a wine bottle and threatens the police officer with the jagged edge. Consider where that falls on the use-of-force continuum.

Today, many police departments have abandoned the use-of-force continuum for many of the above reasons. The San Jose Police Department moved to a **force options model**, while others have moved to a wheel variant of the continuum model, such as the one made popular by the Ontario Police Department. What each of these variations are attempting to do is to move away from the step-ladder approach and teach a **reasonableness standard model** that is based on the reality that the situation will often dictate how a police officer responds.[41] What force option may be reasonable in one situation may not be reasonable in another. One example is the reasonable use of pepper spray against violent protestors such as those in New York City engaged in the Occupy Wall Street movement, versus the unreasonable use of pepper spray against Occupy movement college students at the University of California, Davis, who were peacefully protesting by sitting and blocking a sidewalk.

Deadly Force

The topic of deadly force stands as one of the most talked about and important topics of concern when it comes to the police in America (see Box 12.4). As James Q. Wilson once noted, "No aspect of policing elicits more passionate concern or more divided opinions than the use of deadly force."[42] Yet, we know that of all of the police-citizen contacts each year, only less than 1 to 3 percent involve any type of force and less than one-one hundredth of 1 percent of these are deadly force encounters. And, of those, most are declared justifiable homicides as the police are engaging people committing violent criminals who are most typically armed with a gun. Yet, it is these very few incidents that receive the most attention when it comes to policing.

Box 12.4 History in Practice: National Law Enforcement Officers Memorial Police Week Ceremony

It is not how these officers died that made them heroes, it is how they lived.
— Vivian Eney Cross, Survivor

In valor there is hope.

— Tacitus

The wicked flee when no man pursueth: but the righteous are as bold as a lion.
— Proverbs 28:1

In 1962, President John F. Kennedy proclaimed that May 15 would be known as National Peace Officers Memorial Day and that the calendar week in which that date falls would be **National Police Week**. When the National Law Enforcement Memorial was dedicated on October 15, 1991, the memorial became the national focus of both the day and the week. Since then, every year, there is a week-long ceremony to honor the police officers who were killed in the line-of-duty over the previous year. Surviving members of the officers' family and fellow police officers are encouraged to attend the week-long services, which end with a candlelight vigil held at the site of the two curving 304-long blue-gray marble walls which depict the names of the more than 20,000 police officers who, since 1791, have been killed in the line of duty. The striking symbols of the memorial are the statues of the lions, derived from the passage from Proverbs, and the quotes listed above, which are etched into the stone beneath them.

To gain some perspective on police use of deadly force, it is important to look at the research that has been done in this area. In the early 1990s, at a time when homicides in America were at an all-time high (peaking in 1993 with 24,530 murders), an in-depth study of police-involved shootings was undertaken by the Police Executive Research Forum.[43] The study found that of the approximately annual 45 million police encounters with citizens, there were 3,600 cases of police officers firing their weapons in a deadly force encounter. Of these, 1,800 suspects were shot at and missed; 1,200 were shot at, wounded, and recovered; and 600 were killed by the police on average each year.[44] The

Although police shootings are rare, police officers must be prepared for the eventuality that they may have to use deadly force.

last figure, 600 suspects killed by police officers, also tracked very consistently with not only the annual number of citizens killed by other citizens in self-defense (See Box 12.6), but also with the number of homicides in a given year as well. Nearly all of the 600 police shootings were also found to be justifiable homicides.

In more recent times, since the mid-1990s, the annual number of police cases of use of deadly force have dropped and now appear to hover just below 400 annual cases. The one problem that should be noted here is the fact there is no one definitive source for this data. There are three official agencies that have data which can track these numbers in various forms: the Federal Bureau of Investigation (FBI), the National Victimization Survey, and the Bureau of Justice Statistics. More recently, since 2009, websites such as Wikipedia have also started tracking police deadly force encounters when a citizen is killed by a police officer by recording the date, location, and providing a description of the circumstances surrounding the incident.[45] All of these sources, however, appear to be largely in agreement and consistent across time.

One major study, published in 2001, reported that from 1976 to 1998, an average of 373 people were killed justifiably each year by the police.[46] In another report, covering 2003 to 2005, the average number of justifiable homicides was reported as 365 per year.[47] In both studies, the majority of times officers used deadly force was when they were attacked. It should also be pointed out that the average annual number remained relatively stable, despite the fact that the population continued to increase between 1976 and 2005. As the earlier study has cited 600 and the current studies cite just under 400, the data is somewhat reflective of the fact that overall homicides dropped in America, beginning in the early 1990s, from the high of over 20,000 to just over 14,000 annually. More importantly, perhaps, is the fact that the

Box 12.5 Policing in Practice: The Black Band

In keeping with the strong solidarity among police, the death of an officer in the line of duty is honored respectfully with the tradition of the **black band**. As this book was being written, I paid a visit to the San Francisco area. Everywhere I went, every police officer or police chief I came across were wearing a black band across his or her badge. Some of the police cars that drove by me even had a piece of black electrical tape across the police badge depicted on the side of the police cruiser. The police officers in the area were in mourning for one of their own, Sergeant Scott Lunger, had been killed in the line of duty.

Sergeant Lunger was a 48-year-old police officer with the Hayward Police Department in California who had 15 years on the force. On July 22, 2015, he observed a vehicle driving erratically and conducted a traffic stop. As Sergeant Lunger approached the vehicle, the occupant of the vehicle opened fire, killing Sergeant Lunger. The other officer on scene returned fire, wounding the suspect, who was later taken into custody. Sergeant Lunger is survived by two daughters. The mourning bands worn by the police were in his honor.

The mourning band tradition has been around for a long time, but grew to be more common in the late twentieth century. Today, it is a standard method for police officers to honor their own, and protocols have been developed more recently in order to preserve the ritual's meaning. Commonly a one-half-inch solid black band is worn over the badge, centered to cross over the state or city seal. In the case of a star badge, it is recommended that the band be worn at the 11 to 5 o'clock position. Many agencies authorize the wearing of the band until the day after the funeral of the fallen officer, while others authorize a set period such as two weeks or one month after the officer was killed.

If you ever see a police officer wearing a black band across the badge, you will now know the reason. A sad reality of the occupation but an honorable gesture to those who gave so much.

Source: Officer Down Memorial Page. (2015). ODMP Remembers Sgt. Scott Lunger. Retrieved from https://www.odmp.org/officer/22547-sergeant-scott-lunger; and Mourning Band Protocol. Retrieved from https://www.odmp.org/info/mourning-band-protocol.

---

number of civilian justifiable homicides from 1980 to 2008 have been found to track very consistently with the number of police justifiable homicides.[48] While there are less citizen encounters annually than police encounters, this is primarily because of the fact that when someone is committing violence, the police are called and they respond. Because of this, the police simply find themselves in more deadly force encounter situations (see Box 12.5).

In the wake of the Ferguson shooting, however, more attention has been paid to officers' use of deadly force. *The Washington Post* began collecting data on officer use of deadly force by drawing not only on official data, but news reports, public records, internet databases, and other sources and found that there are more deaths than previously reported. They reported there were "995 people shot dead by police in 2015," 963 in 2016, 987 in 2017, and 998 in 2018.[49] The difference in numbers is most likely due to the differences in how the data is collected.[50] Still, in light of this increase in the number of police officers using deadly force, researchers have questioned whether there has been an increase in these deadly force encounters and whether they are the result of racial disparity.

One study that used *The Washington Post* data for its analysis found that the number of incidents were not increasing, but rather were remaining stable, and that "the patterns are not consistent with the national rhetoric that the police are killing Black people because of their race and that officer-involved shooting fatalities are increasing."[51] Another study looked to other databases, including the FBI's Summary Report System and their National-Incident Based Reporting System, the Bureau of Justice's National Crime Victimization Survey, and the Center for Disease Control's death database called WONDER. While they do find black people are shot and killed at a number disproportionate to their population, "when adjusting for crime" they found "no systematic evidence of anti-Black disparities in fatal shootings, fatal shootings of unarmed citizens, or fatal shootings involving misidentification of harmless objects."[52] One other study used not only *The Washington Post's* database, but one kept by *The Guardian*, and two databases maintained by citizens online, and also concluded that there was "no evidence that the number of fatal police shootings either increased *or* decreased post-Ferguson."[53]

There are many reasons the police find themselves in deadly force encounters. The majority of the encounters are typically what we think of when we hear of police officers using deadly force.[54] A police officer is responding to a call for someone committing a disturbance or violent crime, they encounter a suspect who threatens their life, and they use deadly force. Just a review of the cases on the Wikipedia website demonstrates this. On January 29, 2015, Fort Worth police shot and killed a suspect when they "responded to a domestic disturbance and Wendell King was shot and killed after he fired a weapon and hit a police officer."[55] Or on March 21, 2015, at the New Orleans Airport, when a man "sprayed several TSA agents with insecticide and attempted to attack them with a machete. He was shot by a deputy and died one day later."[56]

There are other circumstances, however, that may not be as evident. Recent research into police use of deadly force is finding that many of those who are killed had a **mental illness**, such as the man who attacked the TSA agents with a machete.[57] Although, once again, no agency tracks the number of mentally ill involved in police justifiable homicides, according to a recent report attempting to assess this very phenomenon, they stated, "Multiple informal studies and accounts support the conclusion that 'at least half of the people shot and killed by police each year in this country have mental health problems.'"[58] Still further, this study found that many of these cases are what is known as suicide by cop.[59]

The term **suicide by cop** is used to describe those cases where an individual wants to commit suicide, but they cannot bring themselves to do it, so they pull a knife or gun on a police officer with the intent that the police officer will fire upon them. One example was in San Francisco, when a man entered a restricted police lot and pulled what looked like a gun on an officer. It later turned out to be an air gun. When the officers investigated the man's home they found a letter that read, in part, "Dear Officers, . . . Please, don't blame yourself. I used you. I took advantage of you [to] end the life of a man who was too much of a coward to do it himself."[60]

The report on police encounters with the mentally ill concluded that these "studies suggest that approximately one-third of the shootings by law enforcement officers results from the victim attempting to commit suicide-by-cop."[61] While this does not negate the justifiableness of the homicide on the part of the police, it does raise an awareness that if the mentally ill were more effectively treated, potentially up to half of the 400 annual police cases of deadly force might be prevented. More importantly, research has also found that these types of deadly force encounters are not simply dismissed by the police, but that "suicide by cop incidents are painful and damaging experiences for the surviving families, the communities, and all law enforcement professionals."[62]

At this point, it should be very clear that despite much attention to police use of deadly force, these cases are actually very rare, and when they do occur, nearly all are declared **justifiable homicides** (see Box 12.6). It is the few cases where deadly force is considered to be excessive that generate the most attention (see Chapter 13 on accountability), or when there are multiple incidents in a short time period. Mayor John Street from Philadelphia made some remarks to this second case after his police force had three deadly force encounters in one week. Frustrated, he stated, "When we ask people to put on a uniform and to go out and fight crime and to go out into some of the most difficult and the most troubling areas of our community, under circumstances that most of us really wouldn't want to even think about, it is unfair for people to second-guess everything they do, every time they do it."[63] It is also unfair to assume that every time police use deadly force, it was excessive. As New York Police Department Police Commissioner William Bratton once wrote, "Cops do not want to kill anyone."[64] People do not go into policing to kill. They also do not go into policing to die (see Box 12.7).

A recent study (and one that is a great read) was conducted by Professor David Klinger, a former police officer who himself had been in a deadly force encounter. His book, entitled *Into the Kill Zone,* interviewed police officers who had used deadly force, to gain some insights into their past, their experience, and the aftermath of the shooting.[65] Klinger first explores why these officers went into policing—it was never to kill, but almost always to serve, and often because of a family tradition or to have a good steady job to support their families (see Chapter 5).

Klinger then wanted to know when these officers first considered they might have to use deadly force in the course of their career. He found that for many of the officers, the use of deadly force was far from their minds when they applied and entered the academy. It was only when they began to learn about the weapon they will carry, practice on the firing range, and perform combat scenarios that the realities of what it means to carry a firearm began

Box 12.6 Ethics in Practice: Justifiable Homicide

One of the purposes of a police department is to respond to emergency situations when people are in trouble or need. Police officers are often called to investigate suspicious persons, armed robberies, and shootings. They are summoned to specific locations where individuals pose a threat to the community. In some of those cases, the individual involved is engaged in violence and threaten the lives of officers and citizens. Citizens call the police to respond to these dangerous situations in order to restore peace. The figure below, created by the U.S. Department of Justice, shows the number of **justifiable homicides** annually across time (1980-2008), by both the police and citizens.

Ask Yourself:

Is it conceivable that no other alternative exists than to use deadly force to stop violence? Give an example of a situation that you think justifies the use of a firearm with possibly deadly results.

Having considered the realities of police use of deadly force and justifiable homicides, consider whether or not it is possible that an individual citizen may have to use deadly force against an attacker. Is it possible that, like the police, citizens may also commit justifiable homicides in order to save their lives and the lives of their loved ones?

Referring to the data in the figure below, consider why the police engage in more justifiable homicides than citizens. Why do you think the two trend lines, the yearly numbers of justifiable homicides by both the police and citizens, parallel each other so well? Can you draw any conclusions from this data about the police use of deadly force?

Number of justifiable homicides, by police and citizens, 1980-2008

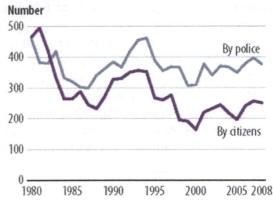

Note: Justifiable homicides are defined as the killing of a felon by a law enforcement officer in the line of duty or the killing of a felon during the commission of a felony by a private citizen. Numbers are based on only justifiable homicides reported to the FBI's Supplementary Homicide Reports Program from 1980 through 2008.

Source: Cooper, A. & Smith, E.L. (2011). *Homicide Trends in the United States, 1980–2008*. Washington, DC: U.S. Department of Justice, p. 32.

to sink in. Klinger's findings are echoed by veteran Chicago Officer Gallo who noted that after carrying and training with the firearm, "You realize that someday, the only thing standing between you and the grave will be your own instincts and Smith & Wesson."[66]

The next insightful question Klinger posed was whether these officers who had used deadly force had ever, prior to that encounter, been in a situation where they could have used deadly force but they held their fire. Klinger asked this because as an officer he had many such incidents as a police officer, as had this author when he served as a police officer. Overwhelmingly the answer was yes, and these officers shared many stories where they faced

---

Box 12.7 Policing in Practice: K-9 Line of Duty Deaths

*Near this spot are deposited the Remains of one who possessed
Beauty without Vanity, Strength without Insolence, Courage without
Ferocity, and all the virtues of Man without his Vices*

— Lord Byron, *Epitaph to a Dog*

K-9 officers are considered police officers, and their death in the line of duty is treated with similar honors. These officers are put in harm's way no differently than their handlers or fellow officers, and they too often pay the ultimate sacrifice. Below is just one story of **heroism involving a K-9 officer**.

On January 25, 2019, Bexar County (Texas) Sheriff's Office K-9 Officer Chucky was shot and killed in the line of duty. Karnes City Police attempted to pull over a vehicle, but the male driver fled the police. Throughout the pursuit, the male fired shots at the officers, and he eventually abandoned the car in San Antonio. K-9

Officer Chucky and his handler arrived on the scene, and Chucky was deployed to apprehend the fleeing felon. Chucky managed to chase down and bite the suspect, but the suspect shot and killed Officer Chucky. When police officers and deputy sheriffs arrived on scene, there was a brief exchange of gunfire and the suspect was wounded, and taken into custody.

Chucky was a Belgian Malinois, aged five years, and served as an officer for over two years. He was trained in narcotics detection and patrol. He was credited with saving the lives of his fellow officers and honored with a memorial service.

---

suspects with knives and guns, many pointed right at them, and for some reason they did not shoot. One officer had a suspect pointing a gun right at him before he dropped it, and the officer tried to explain, "I think the only reason I didn't shoot him was his age."[67] When I was a police officer, I also had a similar deadly force encounter where I held my fire. In my case, it was a shooting at a restaurant across the street from where I was located, and a man had been shot. When my partner and I entered the restaurant, a man brought up a gun and started to point it at us, then dropped it. I was starting to pull the trigger but stopped. It was a good thing. It turned out he was an off-duty police officer who had been eating in the restaurant.

Klinger then interviewed countless officers who had been in deadly force encounters, and they described the situation, how they perceived their life was in danger, and how they reacted by using deadly force. They then explain the aftermath of having their weapon taken from them, how they were reassigned to desk duty while the case was investigated, and how almost all of them felt they were being treated as if they had done something wrong. Many of the officers felt remorse for the shooting because they had taken a human life and then had to deal with the nightmares, depression, and their nerves, fear, and anxiety. Some of the officers, he found, actually felt no remorse. Officer Gallo, after her deadly force encounter said, "And [I] am surprised when I feel nothing."[68] Lt. Col. Dave Grossman in his book *On Killing: The*

Psychological Cost of Learning to Kill in War and Society, however, explains that this is a very common reaction because "they feel bad that they don't feel bad!" but that there is actually nothing wrong with them.[69] It is a normal reaction to many police officers, military soldiers, and civilians who have taken a life in a justifiable shooting.

Officer Safety

So far in this chapter, it has been noted that policing is not the most dangerous job in America. That ranking is based on fatalities of employees in various occupations. It should also be clear that most of the 40-45 million police encounters do not involve police use of force. Only less than 1 to 3 percent of police-citizen contacts involve police use of force. And in most of these cases, it is merely police officers placing hands on a citizen to get them to comply. Very rarely do police officers have to resort to the use of deadly force. This is offered as a means of gaining perspective on police use of force. Simply put, the vast majority of police-citizen contacts do not require the police to use force and most police-citizen encounters are safe for the police. There is, however, always the potential for danger, and line-of-duty injuries and line-of-duty deaths are an unfortunate reality of American policing.

One must consider that in many cases, citizens will use **unlawful force** against the police. Citizens do not always comply with the police and many will outright assault police officers. In more extreme cases, each year, some citizens attempt to kill or do in fact kill police officers. Police officers are often injured on the job though both assaults and accidents, so much so that in policing it is never *if* an officer is going to be injured, but *when*. In addition, although officer safety awareness, training, and technology have contributed to fewer officers being killed annually in the line of duty in recent decades, many police officers often make the ultimate sacrifice in service to their community. The rest of this discussion serves to gain some perspective on the use of force, including deadly force, against police officers in a given year.

Line-of-Duty Injuries

The FBI, in addition to tracking the number of crimes occurring each year in the United States, also tracks the number of **assaults on police officers**.[70] In 2013, the FBI recorded that there were 49,851 assaults on police officers while they were performing their duties. That number was actually down from 2004 when 59,692 police officers were assaulted, and the peak year of 2007 when 61,257 police officers were assaulted. The majority of these officers were assaulted when responding to a disturbance call (31.2 percent) and attempting to arrest a suspect (16.3 percent). Of the total number of police officers who were assaulted, the weapon used tended to be what the FBI defines as "personal weapons," being punched or kicked (79.8 percent), while 4.5 percent were assaulted with firearms and 1.8 percent with knives.

It is not uncommon for officers to be injured when confronting suspects, such as when these NYPD officers confronted protestors attempting to disrupt the annual Thanksgiving Day parade.

In addition to tracking the number of police officers assaulted, the FBI also recorded how many of these police officers were injured. Of the 49,851 assaults in 2013, 14,565 police officers were injured that year, which means that 29.2 percent of all assaults ended in the officers being injured. Of the total number of police who were assaulted and were injured in the attack, most were injured by personal weapons (31 percent), followed by "other dangerous weapons" (27 percent), knives (14.6 percent), and firearms (10.9 percent).

The latter two categories are often a focus of officer safety training, and the FBI focuses much of its attention on the circumstances surrounding these particular cases. The majority of these cases, where an officer was stabbed or shot, occurred in a large city or metropolitan county, between the hours of midnight and 2 A.M., and involved a disturbance or suspicious person call. Of the firearms cases, the majority involved a handgun, with a 9mm being the most common. Most of these officers were working patrol, were of typical police patrol age (25-40), and were operating one-officer patrol vehicles.

The potential for a police officer to be assaulted while on patrol (10 percent) and injured in that assault (2 percent) is high, because these focus on citizen assaults on the police, it hides the many other ways in which police officers are injured in the line of duty.[71] As one police officer explained, "Everyone assumes that the only way an officer gets injured is being shot, stabbed, or beaten. The truth is far from that. Some of us do get injured or killed by an offender actively attacking, but police officers are far more likely to be injured in a much more mundane way."[72]

To gain a better understanding of how many police officers are **injured in the line of duty** each year, the International Association of Chiefs of Police and the Bureau of Justice Assistance conducted a study in 2010 by looking at 18 police departments over a one-year period to see how many injuries police officers sustained that year.[73] Assessing agencies from across the country, both large and small, the lead researcher, Brian Lawton, found there were 1,295 reported injuries in the one-year time-frame.[74] The majority of these cases (610) were for sprains and soft tissue tears, followed by contusions (189) and lacerations (179). On average, the number of work days lost for these injuries was 4.5 days, as it took typically 3.5 days to rehabilitate; however, 3 percent of these cases required surgery and 2 percent required hospitalization.[75] The report also assessed the circumstances under which these officers were injured. They found that the majority of the officers were working patrol (66.1 percent). Out of the total number of injuries, 154 were from motor vehicle crashes, for which most officers were the ones operating the vehicle at the time (126). In 453 of the total 1,295 injury cases there was a suspect involved. In 151 of those injuries the suspect had prior convictions, 125 were under the influence at the time they contributed to the injury, 41 possessed a weapon, and 38 were mentally impaired.

Another study by the National Institute for Occupation Safety and Health (NIOSH), conducted in 2018, supported these findings.[76] Their data of non-fatal injuries among law enforcement officers showed that they were three times more likely to sustain a nonfatal injury at work than all other U.S. workers. The study covered the years 2003 through 2014, finding that 669,100 officers were treated in an emergency room for their injury during this study, and that the numbers of injuries increased across the 12 years of the study (all other U.S. workers saw declines in their number of injuries over the 12 years). The leading cause of these injuries were assaults and violent acts (36 percent), over exertion (e.g., chasing a suspect) (15 percent), and transportation incidents (14 percent). It also found no differences between male and female officers.

In light of the high number of police injuries on duty, some research has also attempted to look at ways of reducing it. The IACP study offers a suggestion that those officers who were underweight or of a healthy weight were less likely to receive injuries when compared with those officers who were overweight, obese, or morbidly obese.[77] Staying healthy and in good shape can be a protection against injuries, just like wearing protective gloves and masks can help prevent the transmission of infectious diseases. Some research has also suggested that the greater availability of nonlethal weapons, such as CEDs, may also assist in lowering the number of injuries to police officers.[78]

Line-of-Duty Deaths

While policing may not be the *most* dangerous job in America, that fact that over 100 police officers lose their lives each year highlights the fact that it is still a **dangerous occupation** (see Box 12.8). Since the first recorded police officer death in 1791, when Sheriff Cornelius Hogeboom of Hudson, New York, was killed serving a writ of ejectment, there have been at least 20,538 police officers who have died in the line of duty.[79] The deadliest decade ever recorded was the 1920s during Prohibition and the rise of the Mafia, when 2,390 police officers lost their lives, an average of 239 per year.[80] The deadliest year on record was 1930, as Prohibition reached its breaking point and America was plunged into the Great Depression and 297 officers were killed.[81] The deadliest day in law enforcement history finds itself in our modern times, and it was September 11, 2001, when 72 officers were killed in New York City due to the terrorist attack on American soil.[82] Since the founding of America, the New York City Police Department has lost more officers than any other police department in the nation, with 697 officers killed, while the state with the most line-of-duty deaths is Texas, which has lost 1,675 police officers.[83]

Box 12.8 Policing in Practice: News Reporting of Line-of-Duty Deaths

Which of the following set of names stands out more readily to you?

Wenjian Wu	Michael Brown
Rafael Ramos	Eric Garner
James Bennet, Jr.	Freddie Gray
Scott Lunger	Tamir Rice
Sean Bolton	Walter Scott

Most likely it is the second set, while the first may be entirely unknown. The first group is made up of police officers who were killed because they were police officers. The second group is comprised of individuals killed by the police. The news media has a strong influence on our understanding of the world, including our understanding of the police. Often, when a citizen is killed by a police officer, it makes the news on a national level, whereas if a citizen kills a police officer, it makes the news within a local area. Consider the differences in how the media handles these cases and how this influences people in their views of the police.

To gain some perspective on recent years, it helps to review changes over the last half of the twentieth century and now in the twenty-first century. In the 1950s, the number of officer **line-of-duty deaths** in a given year was a little over 100.[84] As crime began to rise in the 1960s, so too did the number of police officers killed, peaking in 1974 with 280. As crime leveled out in the 1970s, so too did police officer deaths, generally averaging just under 200 a year. Then, starting in the 1990s, the numbers began to drop. While some argue that protective vests, which began seeing wide-spread deployment beginning in the 1970s, and improved emergency medical response has contributed to less officers being killed in the line of duty, the fact that crime began to drop in the 1990s has shown a close correspondence with officer deaths. Since 2000 (except of course for 2001), police officers deaths have averaged 150 a year with 2013 and 2014 showing some of the lowest years in decades with 107 and 117, respectively.

Once again, it is important to note that there is also no definitive database when it comes to recording the number of officers killed in the line of duty. The oldest of the sources is the FBIs Uniform Crime Reports, which, for instance, records that there were

Police deal with death on a routine basis, but it is most difficult when it is the loss of one of their own. Members of the NYPD bear the casket of one of their own, Police Officer Wenjian Liu who was assassinated alongside Officer Rafael Ramos on December 20, 2014.

46 officers feloniously killed in 2017, and another 47 died from accidents, for a total of 93 officers.[85] Another source is the Officer Down Memorial Page (ODMP), a website dedicated to officers killed in the line of duty started by Chris Cosgriff as a way to honor fallen police officers, because he once said, "When a police officer is killed, it's not an agency that loses an officer, it's an entire nation."[86] The ODMP, for example, recorded that in 2017, 152 officers were killed in the line of duty. The way that ODMP versus FBI records police officer deaths is different, and ODMP also includes correctional officer deaths as well. The most recent database was created by the National Law Enforcement Officers Memorial Fund, which is associated with the National Law Enforcement Officers Memorial in Washington, D.C. and soon-to-be museum.[87] In 2017, they recorded that 129 police officers lost their lives. Despite the fact that each uses different criteria, it is important to understand how these officers died to better understand police officer line-of-duty deaths.

Drawing on the ODMP data for 2017, it shows that of the 152 police officers who were killed in the line of duty, 28 died in automobile accidents, 4 died in motorcycle accidents, 4 were struck by vehicles, 5 died in a vehicle pursuit, and 6 died in a vehicular assault.[88] These numbers highlight the fact that the majority of police officer line-of-duty deaths in any given year are due to traffic-related deaths. Because police officers on patrol spend most of their time driving in traffic, it is not surprising that this is the most common cause of officer deaths. Similar to other occupations that spend much of their time behind the wheel, policing is no different because of the many hours spent driving.

Typically, however, when we think of police officer deaths in the line of duty, we generally associate them with violence. These deaths are, unfortunately, the second most frequent. According to the ODMP, in 2017, there were 45 officers killed by gunfire, 6 officers were killed by assaults, and 1 officer was stabbed to death.[89] Looking at the FBI data, they record that 46 officers were feloniously killed that year, detailing that 4 were killed in arrest situations, 6 were investigating suspicious persons, 5 were ambushed, 6 were involved in tactical situations, 1 was answering a disturbance call, 2 were conducting a traffic pursuit, and 2 were conducting an investigation.[90]

The third and fourth most frequent cause of deaths tend to vary year to year between two factors: accidents and health-related deaths.[91] For instance, the accident-related deaths in 2017 included two officers who were killed in an aircraft accident, two in a boating accident, five that drowned, one died from exposure to toxins, and one was animal related. Police officers often find themselves in perilous situations trying to assist other people, and sometimes tragedies strike and they become a victim of circumstance. The other factor is health-related deaths. Each year, many police officers suffer heart attacks while on duty and die. In 2017, 17 such deaths occurred. In addition, 21 police officers lost their lives in 2017 due to complications of their health that resulted from their responding to Ground Zero on September 11, 2001. The dust they were breathing included all manner of toxic chemicals and biological matter that had affected their respiratory system, which finally took its toll on their bodies.

The annual data also tracks many of the demographics of the line-of-duty deaths. In 2017, the most deaths were in the months of January and September (17), followed by February (15) and August (14).[92] The states with the highest number of deaths were some of the larger states New York (24), Texas (14), and Florida (11). In addition to the state and local police officers killed in the line of duty, the number of federal agents killed in the line of duty in 2017 was zero. The majority of the officers killed were male (140), with 12 female officers killed in the line of duty. The average age of the officers was 44 and the average length of their tour of duty was 13 years and 7 months.

More recently, data has begun to be kept of K-9 officers killed in the line of duty.[93] To most police officers and especially the K-9 handlers, a police dog is a police officer, and their line of duty death is seen as the death of a fellow officer. In many cases, the K-9's death helped to avoid the handler or other police officers from being killed or injured. In 2017, 24 K-9 officers lost their lives, with 7 by gunfire, 2 stabbed, and 2 struck by vehicles. Other K-9 officers died from falls, heat exhaustion, and duty-related illnesses.

One problem with all of these facts and figures is that they tend to hide the trauma and impact that an officer injured or killed in the line of duty has. As one career police officer explained, "It's frightening to see an officer who's been shot. You know it could have been you. I saw many officers shot, and the impact never lessened over the years. It makes you realize how deadly serious police business can be."[94] Another officer adds, "Line of duty deaths, suicides, and catastrophic injuries inflicting permanent disabilities—those are the worst of times."[95] Philadelphia Police Commissioner Charles Ramsey tried to put the impact into words when he explained, "Any time you lose someone, you know it's going to take an emotional toll. We've had a lot of police officers that have died tragically . . . but we're not able to shut our doors of mourning. We all have to keep pushing forward."[96] When it comes to mourning, it is not just the police department that is impacted either. As a retired LAPD officer explains, "Sometimes the death of an officer reaches far beyond the original incident. A life has been lost, and families are changed forever. The news media effectively portrays the grieving widow and her children as the flag is presented by the chief of police. Their sorrow is very real. In a different sense, sometimes others die as well."[97] Wives and husbands, children, and parents are all impacted . . . forever.

Conclusion

The use of force is part of the role of police officers in our society, and one that shapes, defines, and sets policing apart from most occupations. Police officers are authorized to use force in the performance of their duties to gain compliance with suspects. And in those cases where the officer's life or the lives of other officers and citizens are placed in jeopardy, police officers are authorized the ultimate use of force: they are authorized to use deadly force. Despite the inability to predict every circumstance, to try and give police officers a sense of when they can use force and what type of force they are authorized, police use-of-force continuums are generally taught to most police officers in the United States.

One reality of policing, however, is that force may be used against the police officer, and this can result in injuries for police officers, a topic not often discussed but widely recognized as something that, unfortunately, comes with the job. In rare cases, police officers are also killed in the line of duty, predominately from traffic accidents, followed by felonious killings, and other accidents and health-related problems. The impact that an officer's death has on police officers and the police department is great, but the impact reaches farther, extending to family and friends who must bear the loss.

Just the Facts

1. Policing is a dangerous job, but according to the Bureau of Labor statistics, it is not the most dangerous job, and, in fact, generally ranks just outside of the top ten most dangerous occupations on an annual basis.

2. Police officers are authorized the use of force when they are attempting to make an arrest, pursuing an escaped felon, or protecting their lives and the lives of citizens. The Supreme Court case of *Tennessee v. Garner* (1985) states that police officers may not shoot fleeing felons unless they pose an immediate threat to citizens, while *Graham v. Connor* (1989) adopted a reasonableness standard for how much force was necessary related to the circumstances surrounding the situation.

3. The use-of-force continuum teaches police officers that there is a progression of force and that they are authorized to use a level of force one-step over the force being used on them. The stages include officer presence, verbalization, empty-hand control, less-than-lethal methods, and lethal force.

4. The force options model has been adopted to avoid the notion that many officers believe they must go through each step in the continuum model, and is more in line with the reasonableness standards established by the U.S. Supreme Court in *Graham v. Connor* (1989).

5. There are approximately 400 encounters each year where police officers use deadly force against a citizen. While many of these cases are justifiable homicides due to deadly force or threats of deadly force being used against the police officer or citizens in the officers' presence, many are also attributed to mental illness and suicide by cop.

6. The annual number of assaults on police officers demonstrates that there are between 50,000 and 60,000 assaults by citizens on police officers, and that most occur on disturbance calls and when trying to arrest a suspect, and the majority of officers are either punched or kicked in the process.

7. According to government data, of the 50,000 assaults, approximately 15,000 officers on injured. In addition, there is evidence that many of the line-of-duty injuries that occur are more mundane such as sprains and contusions from accidents, especially motor vehicle accidents.

8. Since 2000, the average number of police officers killed in the line of duty has been between 100 and 150 officers, with a majority typically being killed by way of motor vehicle accidents, followed by deadly violence, then other accidents and health-related deaths.

Ask Yourself

1. Consider the fact that governments are created to establish laws that allow societies to better function. Now consider what happens when people violate those laws. How does government get people to comply? Are there any other means available beyond coercion and, when that fails, violence?

2. Although widely taught in police academies in the United States, the use-of-force continuum has come under scrutiny. Is the model the best way to teach police officers when to use force or is the force options model a better alternative? Compare and contrast these two methods.

3. Read closely the Supreme Court decision of *Graham v. Connor* (1989). Which model, use-of-force continuum or force options model is more in keeping with that decision?

4. Recently, there has been much discussion in the news about police shootings of citizens. After reviewing the data on police shootings of citizens, does this comport with the media reporting? Discuss the ramifications of media reporting on police shootings.

5. After reviewing the number of officers assaulted, injured, and killed in the line of duty, what does this tell us about the dangers of the occupation of policing?

Keywords

Assaults on police officers
Blunt instruments
Chemical
Conducted energy
    devices (CED)
Dangerous occupation
Deadly force
Empty hand control
Force options model
Graham v. Connor (1989)

Injuries in the line of duty
Justifiable homicides
Less-than-lethal methods
Lethal force
Line-of-duty deaths
Mental illness
Officer presence
Reasonableness
    standard model
Suicide by cop

Tennessee v. Garner (1985)
Thomas A. Swift's Electric
    Rifle (TASER)
Unlawful force
Use of force
Use-of-force continuum
Use-of-force
    continuum model
Verbalization

Endnotes

1. Vollmer, A. (1921). A practical method for selecting policemen. *Journal of the American Institute of Criminal Law and Criminology, 11*, 571-581, at p. 574.
2. Klockars, C.B. (1985). *The idea of police.* Beverly Hills, CA: SAGE, p. 12.
3. Bayley, D.H. (1986). The tactical choices of police patrol officers. *Journal of Criminal Justice, 14*, 329-348; Bayley, D.H. & Garofalo, J. (1989). The management of violence by police patrol officers. *Criminology, 27*, 1-12; Eith, C. & Durose, M.R. (2011). *Special report: Contacts between police and the public,* 2008. Washington, DC: U.S. Department of Justice; Sykes, R.E. & Brent, E.E. (1983). *Policing: A social behaviorist perspective.* New Brunswick,

NJ: Rutgers University Press; Terrill, W. (2001). *Police coercion: Application of the force continuum.* New York, NY: LFB Scholarly Publishing; Terrill, W. (2003). Police use of force and suspect resistance: The micro-process of the police-suspect encounter. *Police Quarterly, 6*, 51-83.
4. Bureau of Justice Statistics. (1999). *Use of force by police: Overview of national and local data.* Washington, DC: National Institute of Justice; Community Oriented Policing Services. (2012). *Emerging use of force issues: Balancing public and officer safety.* Washington, DC: COPS/IACP; Eith, C. & Durose, M.R. (2011). *Special report: Contacts between police and the public,* 2008. Washington, DC: U.S. Department of Justice;

Skogan, W. & Frydl, K. (eds.) (2004). *Fairness and effectiveness in policing: The evidence*. Washington, DC: The National Academies Press.

5. Eith, C. & Durose, M.R. (2011). *Special report: Contacts between police and the public*, 2008. Washington, DC: U.S. Department of Justice; Sykes, R.E. & Brent, E.E. (1983). *Policing: A social behaviorist perspective*. New Brunswick, NJ: Rutgers University Press.

6. Eith, C. & Durose, M.R. (2011). *Special report: Contacts between police and the public*, 2008. Washington, DC: U.S. Department of Justice; Skogan, W. & Frydl, K. (eds.) (2004). *Fairness and effectiveness in policing: The evidence*. Washington, DC: The National Academies Press; Sykes, R.E. & Brent, E.E. (1983). *Policing: A social behaviorist perspective*. New Brunswick, NJ: Rutgers University Press.

7. Garner, J., Buchanan, J., Schade, T., & Hepburn, J. (1996). Understanding the use of force by and against the police. Washington, DC: National Institute of Justice; Klinger, D.A. (1995). Policing spousal assault. *Journal of Research in Crime and Delinquency*, 32, 308-324; McLaughlin, V. (1992). *Police and the use of force: The Savannah study*. Westport, CT: Praeger Publishers; Skogan, W. & Frydl, K. (eds.) (2004). *Fairness and effectiveness in policing: The evidence*. Washington, DC: The National Academies Press.

8. Community Oriented Policing Services. (2015). COPS Office: Use of Force. Retrieved from http://www.cops.usdoj.gov/default.asp?Item=1374

9. United States Department of Labor. (2013). *Census of Fatal Occupational Injuries*. Washington, DC: U.S. Department of Labor; See also Smith, J. (2013). America's 10 deadliest jobs. *Forbes*. Retrieved from http://www.forbes.com/sites/jacquelynsmith/2013/08/22/americas-10-deadliest-jobs-2/

10. National Law Enforcement Officers Memorial Fund. (2015). Officer deaths by year. Retrieved from http://www.nleomf.org/facts/officer-fatalities-data/year.html

11. International Association of Chiefs of Police. (2001). *Police use of force in America, 2001*. Washington, DC: IACP, p. 66.

12. 2014 Florida Statutes. Chapter 776: Justifiable Use of Force. Specifically see 776.05.

13. *Tennessee v. Garner, et al.* (1985).

14. *Dethorne Graham v. Connor, et al.* (1989).

15. Skolnick, J. & Fyfe, J. (1993). *Above the law: Police and the excessive use of force*. New York, NY: Free Press; Stetser, M. (2001). *The use of force in police control of violence: Incidents resulting in assaults on officers*. New York, NY: LFB Scholarly Publishing.

16. International Association of Chiefs of Police. (2001). *Police use of force in America, 2001*. Washington, DC: IACP.

17. National Institute of Justice. (2009). *The use-of-force continuum*. Washington, DC: National Institute of Justice.

18. National Institute of Justice. (2009). *The use-of-force continuum*. Washington, DC: National Institute of Justice.

19. Eith, C. & Durose, M.R. (2011). *Special report: Contacts between police and the public*, 2008. Washington, DC: U.S. Department of Justice; Sykes, R.E. & Brent, E.E. (1983). *Policing: A social behaviorist perspective*. New Brunswick, NJ: Rutgers University Press.

20. National Institute of Justice. (2009). *The use-of-force continuum*. Washington, DC: National Institute of Justice.

21. National Institute of Justice. (2009). *The use-of-force continuum*. Washington, DC: National Institute of Justice.

22. Eith, C. & Durose, M. R. (2011). *Special report: Contacts between police and the public*, 2008. Washington, DC: U.S. Department of Justice; Sykes, R.E. & Brent, E.E. (1983). *Policing: A social behaviorist perspective*. New Brunswick, NJ: Rutgers University Press.

23. National Institute of Justice. (2009). *The use-of-force continuum*. Washington, DC: National Institute of Justice.

24. National Institute of Justice. (2009). *The use-of-force continuum*. Washington, DC: National Institute of Justice.

25. National Institute of Justice. (2009). *The use-of-force continuum*. Washington, DC: National Institute of Justice.

26. Terrill, W. & Paoline, E.A. III. (2012). Examining less lethal force policy and the force continuum: Results from a national use-of-force study. *Police Quarterly*, 16, 38-65.

27. Reaves, B.A. (2010). *Local police departments, 2007*. Washington, DC: Bureau of Justice Statistics.

28. Burch, A.M. (2012). *Sheriffs' offices, 2007 – Statistical tables*. Washington, DC: Bureau of Justice Statistics.

29. McEwen, T. (1997).Policies on less-than-lethal force in law enforcement agencies. *Policing*, 20, 39-59.

30. Burch, A.M. (2012). *Sheriffs' offices, 2007 – Statistical tables*. Washington, DC: Bureau of Justice Statistics; Reaves, B.A. (2010). *Local police departments, 2007*. Washington, DC: Bureau of Justice Statistics.

31. Kaminski, R.J, Edwards, S.M., & Johnson, J.W. (1999). Assessing the incapacitative effects of pepper spray during resistive encounters with police. *Policing*, 22, 7-29; National Institute of Justice. (2003). *The effectiveness and safety of pepper spray*. Washington, DC: National Institute of Justice.

32. National Institute of Justice. (2003). *The effectiveness and safety of pepper spray*. Washington, DC: National Institute of Justice.

33. Burch, A.M. (2012). *Sheriffs' offices, 2007 – Statistical tables*. Washington, DC: Bureau of Justice Statistics; Reaves, B.A. (2010). *Local police departments, 2007*. Washington, DC: Bureau of Justice Statistics.

34. Taylor, B. et al. (2009). *Comparing safety outcomes in police use-of-force cases for law enforcement agencies that have deployed conducted energy devices and a matched comparison group that have not: A quasi-experimental evaluation*. Washington, DC: Police Executive Research Forum; See also Williams, H.E. (2015). *Tasers and arrest-related deaths*. El Paso, TX: LFB Scholarly Pub. LLC.

35. Geller, W.A. & Scott, M.S. (1992). *Deadly force: What we know.* Washington, DC: Police Executive Research Forum; National Institute of Justice. (2009). *The use-of-force continuum.* Washington, DC: National Institute of Justice.

36. National Institute of Justice. (2009). *The use-of-force continuum.* Washington, DC: National Institute of Justice.

37. Bonvillian, C. (2015). Arizona cop hailed as hero after running over rifle-toting suspect with patrol car. *Alabama.com.* Retrieved online at https://www.al.com/news/2015/04/arizona_cop_hailed_as_hero_aft.html

38. Marion, N. (1998). Police academy training: Are we teaching recruits what they need to know? *Policing, 21,* 54-79.

39. Fridell, L., Ljames, S., & Berkow, M. (2015). Taking the straw man to the ground: Arguments in support of the linear use-of-force continuum. *The Police Chief.* Retrieved from http://www.policechiefmagazine.org/magazine/index.cfm?fuseaction=display_arch&article_id=2548 &issue_id=122011;Skolnick, J. & Fyfe, J. (1993). *Above the law: Police and the excessive use of force.* New York, NY: Free Press.

40. *Dethorne Graham v. Connor, et al.* (1989).

41. Fridell, L., Ljames, S., & Berkow, M. (2015). Taking the straw man to the ground: Arguments in support of the linear use-of-force continuum. *The Police Chief.* Retrieved from http://www.policechiefmagazine.org/magazine/index.cfm?fuseaction=display_arch&article_id=2548 & issue_id=122011

42. Wilson, J.Q. (1980). Police use of deadly force: Research and reform. *FBI Law Enforcement Bulletin, August,* p. 16.

43. Geller, W.A. & Scott, M.S. (1992). *Deadly force: What we know.* Washington, DC: Police Executive Research Forum.

44. Geller, W.A. & Scott, M.S. (1992). *Deadly force: What we know.* Washington, DC: Police Executive Research Forum.

45. Wikipedia. (2015). List of killings by law enforcement officers in the United States.Wikipedia.Retrieved from http://en.wikipedia.org/wiki/List_of_killings_by_law_enforcement_officers_in_the_United_States

46. Brown, J.M. & Langan, P.A. (2001). *Policing and homicide, 1976-1998: Justifiable homicide by police, police officers murdered by felons.* Washington, DC: National Institute of Justice.

47. Mumola, C.J. (2007). *Arrest-related deaths in the United States, 2003-2005.* Washington, DC: Bureau of Justice Statistics.

48. Cooper, A. & Smith, E.L. (2011). Homicide trends in the United States, 1980-2008. Washington DC: U.S. Department of Justice.

49. *The Washington Post.* (2019). Number of people shot dead by police by year 2015-2018. Retrieved from https://www.washingtonpost.com/graphics/national/police-shootings/

50. C.f. Loftin, C., Wieserman, B., McDowall, D., & Dobrin, A. (2003). Underreporting of justifiable homicides committed by police officers in the United States, 1976-1998." *American Journal of Public Health, 93,* 1117-1121.

51. Shane, J.M., Lawton, B., & Swenson, Z. (2017). The prevalence of fatal police shootings by U.S. police, 2015-2016: Patterns and answers from a new data set. *Journal of Criminal Justice, 52,* 101-11, p. 101.

52. Cesario, J., Johnson, D.J., & Terrill, W. (2018). Is there evidence of racial disparity in police use of deadly force? Analyses of officer-involved fatal shootings in 2015-2016." Social Psychological and Personality Science, Online First, 1-10

53. Campbell, B.A., Nix, J., & Maguire, E.R. (2018). Is the number of citizens fatally shot by police increasing in the post-Ferguson era? *Crime & Delinquency, 64,* 398-420, p. 398.

54. Pinchevsky, G.M. & Nix, J. (2018). Domestic disturbances and fatal police shootings: An analysis of the Washington post's data. *Police Quarterly, 21,* 53-76.

55. Wikipedia. (2015). List of killings by law enforcement officers in the United States. Wikipedia. Retrieved from http://en.wikipedia.org/wiki/List_of_killings_by_law_enforcement_officers_in_the_United_States

56. Wikipedia. (2015). List of killings by law enforcement officers in the United States. Wikipedia. Retrieved from http://en.wikipedia.org/wiki/List_of_killings_by_law_enforcement_officers_in_the_United_States

57. Torrey, E.F., Kennard, A.D., Eslinger, D.F., Biasotti, M.C., & Fuller, D.A. (2013). *Justifiable homicides by law enforcement officers: What is the role of mental illness?* Washington, DC: Treatment Advocacy Center & National Sheriffs' Association.

58. Torrey, E.F., Kennard, A.D., Eslinger, D.F., Biasotti, M.C., & Fuller, D.A. (2013). *Justifiable homicides by law enforcement officers: What is the role of mental illness?* Washington, DC: Treatment Advocacy Center & National Sheriffs' Association; For an example of an informal study see Portland Press Herald. (2011). *Deadly force: Police & the mentally ill.* Retrieved from http://www.pressherald.com/interactive/maine_police_deadly_force_series_day_1/

59. Torrey, E.F., Kennard, A.D., Eslinger, D.F., Biasotti, M.C., & Fuller, D.A. (2013). *Justifiable homicides by law enforcement officers: What is the role of mental illness?* Washington, DC: Treatment Advocacy Center & National Sheriffs' Association; See also Lord, V. B. (2004). *Suicide-by-cop: Inducing officers to shoot: Practical directions for recognition, resolution, and recovery.* Flushing, NY: Looseleaf Law Publications, Inc.

60. Bender, K.J. (2015). Man shot by SF officers left suicide note. *Policeone.com.* Retrieved from http://www.policeone.com/suicide-by-cop/articles/8085061-Man-shot-by-SF-officers-left-suicide-notes/

61. Torrey, E.F., Kennard, A.D., Eslinger, D.F., Biasotti, M.C., & Fuller, D.A. (2013). *Justifiable homicides by law enforcement officers: What is the role of mental illness?* Washington, DC: Treatment Advocacy Center & National Sheriffs' Association.

62. Pinizzotto, A.J., Davis, E.F., & Miller, C.E. III. (2005). Suicide by cop: Defining a devastating dilemma. *FBI Law Enforcement Bulletin, 74,* 8-20, p. 15.

63. Moran, R. (2006). At ceremony, Street says police critics are 'unfair' amid a string of killings by police, the mayor defended officers. *Philly.com*. Retrieved from http://articles.philly.com/2006-05-04/news/25401081_1_police-shootings-fatal-shootings-lives-of-police-officers

64. Bratton, W. (1998). *Turnaround: How America's top cop reversed the crime epidemic*. New York, NY: Random House, p. 247.

65. Klinger, D. (2004). *Into the kill zone: A cop's eye view of deadly force*. San Francisco, CA: Jossey-Bass.

66. Gallo, G. (2001). *Armed and Dangerous: Memoirs of a Chicago Policewoman*. New York, NY: Forge Book, p. 34.

67. Klinger, D. (2004). *Into the kill zone: A cop's eye view of deadly force*. San Francisco, CA: Jossey-Bass, p. 61.

68. Gallo, G. (2001). *Armed and Dangerous: Memoirs of a Chicago Policewoman*. New York, NY: Forge Book, p. 74.

69. Grossman, D. (2009). *On killing: The psychological cost of learning to kill in war and society*. New York, NY: Back Bay Books, p. 245.

70. Federal Bureau of Investigation. 2014. *2013 Law enforcement officers killed & assaulted*. Retrieved from http://www.fbi.gov/about-us/cjis/ucr/leoka/2013/officers-assaulted/assaults_topic_page_-2013

71. Brandl, S.G. & Stroshine, M.S. (2003). Toward and understanding of the physical hazards of police work. *Police Quarterly, 6*, 172-191.

72. Weisskopf, R. (2012). Injured on duty. *Law Enforcement Today*. Retrieved from http://www.lawenforcementtoday.com/2012/03/17/injured-on-duty/

73. International Association of Chiefs of Police & The Bureau of Justice Assistance. (2010). *Reducing officer injuries: Final report*. Washington, DC: IACP.

74. Hi Brian!

75. International Association of Chiefs of Police & The Bureau of Justice Assistance. (2010). *Reducing officer injuries: Final report*. Washington, DC: IACP.

76. Tiesman, H.M., Gwilliam, M., Konda, S., Rojek, J., & Marsh, S. (2018). Nonfatal injuries to law enforcement officers: A rise in assaults. *American Journal of Preventive Medicine, 54*, 503-509.

77. International Association of Chiefs of Police & The Bureau of Justice Assistance. (2010). *Reducing officer injuries: Final report*. Washington, DC: IACP.

78. Brandl, S.G. & Stroshine, M.S. (2012). The physical hazards of police work revisited. *Police Quarterly, 15*, 262-282; Paoline, E.A. III, Terrill, W. & Ingram, J.R. (2012). Police use of force and officer injuries: Comparing conducted energy devices (CEDs) to hands- and weapon-based tactics. *Police Quarterly, 15*, 115-136; Taylor, B. & Woods, D.J. (2010). Injuries to officers and suspects in police use-of-force cases: A quasi-experimental evaluation. *Police Quarterly, 16*, 260-289; Womack, V.G., Morris, R.G., & Bishopp, S.A. (2016). Do changes in taser use policy affect police officer injury rates? *Police Quarterly, 19*, 410-434..

79. National Law Enforcement Officers Memorial Fund. (2015). Important Dates in Law Enforcement History. Retrieved from http://www.nleomf.org/facts/enforcement/impdates.html; National Law Enforcement Officers Memorial Fund. (2015). Law enforcement facts. Retrieved from http://www.nleomf.org/facts/enforcement/

80. National Law Enforcement Officers Memorial Fund. (2015). Law enforcement facts. Retrieved from http://www.nleomf.org/facts/enforcement/

81. National Law Enforcement Officers Memorial Fund. (2015). Law enforcement facts. Retrieved from http://www.nleomf.org/facts/enforcement/

82. Oliver, W.M. (2007). *Homeland security for policing*. Upper Saddle River, NJ: Prentice Hall.

83. National Law Enforcement Officers Memorial Fund. (2015). Law enforcement facts. Retrieved from http://www.nleomf.org/facts/enforcement/

84. National Law Enforcement Memorial Fund. (2014). Latest memorial fund fatalities report. Retrieved from http://www.nleomf.org/facts/research-bulletins/

85. Federal Bureau of Investigation. (2018). 2017 Law Enforcement Officers Killed & Assaulted. Federal Bureau of Investigation: UCR. Retrieved from https://ucr.fbi.gov/leoka/2017

86. Officer Down Memorial Page. (2015). Homepage. Retrieved from https://www.odmp.org/

87. National Law Enforcement Officers Memorial Fund. (2015). Homepage. Retrieved from http://www.nleomf.org/

88. Office Down Memorial Page. (2019). Honoring Officers Killed in 2018. Retrieved from https://www.odmp.org/search/year?year=2018

89. Office Down Memorial Page. (2019). Honoring Officers Killed in 2017. Retrieved from https://www.odmp.org/search/year?year=2017

90. Federal Bureau of Investigation. (2018). 2017 Law Enforcement Officers Killed & Assaulted. Federal Bureau of Investigation: UCR. Retrieved from https://ucr.fbi.gov/leoka/2017

91. Office Down Memorial Page. (2019). Honoring Officers Killed in 2017. Retrieved from https://www.odmp.org/search/year?year=2017

92. Office Down Memorial Page. (2019). Honoring Officers Killed in 2017. Retrieved from https://www.odmp.org/search/year?year=2017

93. Office Down Memorial Page. (2019). Honoring Officers Killed in 2017. Retrieved from https://www.odmp.org/search/year?year=2017

94. Middleton, M.L. (2000). *Cop: A true story*. New York, NY: MJF Books, p. 205.

95. Padar, J. & J. (2014). On being a cop: Father & son police tales from the streets of Chicago. Lake Placid, NY: Aviva Publishing, p. 81.

96. Brune, K.L. (2012). Officer down: How police deaths affect us all. PoliceOne.com Retrieved from http://www.policeone.com/police-heroes/articles/5952921-Officer-down-How-police-deaths-affect-us-all/

97. Middleton, M.L. (2000). *Cop: A true story*. New York, NY: MJF Books, p. 212.

■ *"The [officer's] fidelity and loyalty to the department must be great enough to resist whatever temptation beset him, and truthfulness, honesty, and definiteness of purpose are demanded in all of his dealings with the public. No matter how tantalizing or abusive the individual or the crowd may be, the policeman under all circumstances must have self-control and never lose his temper. Experience has taught us that the cheerful, sympathetic, kind-hearted, gentle but firm police-man . . . is much more valuable to the department than the grouchy, sullen or brutal one."[1]*
—*August Vollmer, 1921*

May 13, 2019, East Haven Police Department receives national accreditation from CALEA Standards Group.

CHAPTER 13

Accountability

After reading this chapter, you will be able to:

1. Understand the impact that the Lexow Committee and the Knapp Commission's findings on policy corruption had on American policing.
2. Recognize the many terms and categories used when talking about police misconduct and demonstrate a general understanding of the different types.
3. Present a realistic perspective on the type and level of police misconduct in America, drawing upon both the Cato Institute's research and the Stinson data.
4. Identify the many terms and categories used when talking about police corruption and demonstrate a general understanding of the different types.
5. Name and define the three main theories of police corruption.
6. Explain the difference between excessive force and police brutality.
7. Describe and discuss the various means of internal controls that hold police accountable.
8. Describe and discuss the various means of external controls that hold police accountable.

When Police Chief August Vollmer wrote the lines of the opening quote to this chapter, he had been the Berkeley police chief for 16 years and was beginning to be recognized as a reform-minded chief on the national stage. Policing in America had been highly connected to American local politics in the nineteenth century, and as local machine politics were highly corrupt, so too were the police. One of the earliest exposures of the high level of police corruption was the **Lexow Committee** and its investigation into the New York City Police Department (NYPD). The investigation, which took place between 1894 and 1895, found that the police department was

Police Commissioner Theodore Roosevelt did not institute the Lexow Committee, but he proved instrumental in helping to hold those who were exposed for corruption accountable during his tenure (1894–1896).

being used by the local political machine to funnel graft money from illegal establishments (for example, gambling casinos, houses of ill repute), while making many of the police officers and most of the command staff rich beyond a policeman's salary. In addition, the police were also being used as a means of strong-arming people who threatened the power of the sitting political party (Tammany Hall at the time). Although reform-minded **Theodore Roosevelt** had become the police commissioner in 1896 in the wake of the Lexow Committee's finding and had managed to implement some changes, he was politically stifled and ultimately left the NYPD to serve as the Assistant Secretary of the Navy. Sadly, this type of political and police corruption continued into the next century.

The beginning of the twentieth century is commonly referred to as the **Progressive Era** in America, a time period in which many reform-minded individuals began working to remove the corrupt politics of the day. Vollmer became the police chief synonymous with police reform during this time period. He believed that the police needed to be separated from politics, and he advocated for civil service protections for police departments, including the police chief. He also fought police corruption and all forms of police brutality, referred to as the "**third degree**" during his time period. National reforms and the Vollmer method of policing slowly began to take hold, and American policing moved toward a **professional model** of policing.

While the police professionalization model and the reform era brought about many changes, various investigations revealed ongoing problems of police corruption well into the twentieth century. When **Frank Serpico** joined the NYPD in the 1960s, he discovered that corrupt practices were systemic throughout the department, and after numerous attempts at trying to report the problems internally, he became what is commonly known today as a whistleblower. This resulted in the creation of the **Knapp Commission** in 1970, which exposed the problems of police corruption in the NYPD (see Box 13.1).

The investigation even revealed specific language for the type of corrupt cops. A small number of police officers were known as **meat-eaters.** These were the police officers who actively sought out bribes to the police and extorted both legal and illegal businesses for graft. The majority of the officers, however, were known as **grass-eaters**, those who when offered a bribe took it, but they did not actively seek them out. Often, meat-eaters funneled money to grass-eaters to ensure their loyalty. When Serpico testified before the Knapp Commission, the true extent of police corruption was revealed. Although his testimony made him a traitor in the eyes of many officers, he

---

Box 13.1 History in Practice: Frank Serpico and Reporting of Corruption

Frank Serpico went into policing because he wanted to be a good cop. What he found was that good policing in New York City in the 1960s entailed taking gratuities, accepting kickbacks, extorting businesses, and rolling drug dealers. Frank Serpico realized he did not want to be "good cop" in that sense; he wanted to be a moral cop. So, he decided to do something about it.

Serpico decided to do the right thing and went to his supervisors to report the high level of graft going on. He was told to keep quiet. Serpico went higher up the chain-of-command and was told the same thing. Then Serpico attempted to notify the command staff and, again, he was rebuked. Finally, without any other recourse, he went to the *New York Times* and exposed the corruption.

That **reporting** (**whistle-blowing** in today's parlance) was the catalyst for the creation of the Knapp Commission, which began investigating the systemic police corruption in the NYPD. That exposure, however, made Serpico a bad name among the NYPD, and when conducting a drug arrest, he discovered he had been set up. As he attempted to enter the door of the drug suspect, he was shot in the face. He called for backup and none came.

Serpico survived, testified before the Knapp Commission, and received the NYPD's Medal of Honor, before retiring and moving to Europe. Peter Maas authored a best-selling book titled, *Serpico,* and a movie by the same name, starring Al Pacino, was also highly successful.

---

stated, "Through my appearance here today I hope that police officers in the future will not experience the same frustration and anxiety that I was subjected to for the past five years at the hands of my superiors because of my attempts to report corruption."[2]

When people consider the presence of police corruption and brutality today, many have the belief and attitude that all police officers are corrupt. There are indeed bad cops in policing, just as there are bad teachers, bad doctors, and bad priests. But the vast majority of the men and women working in law enforcement, and in the other professions listed, are good people working to perform an admirable job. Yet, it is no wonder that so many have the belief that all cops are bad, for as retired Police Officer Gina Gallo has so succinctly stated, "Bad cops make good press."[3] The news media is always quick to jump on any case that might possibly be an example of police corruption or brutality because of the sensation it can cause. Magazine articles and books are routinely published on the topic, and movies, either based on real events (for example, *Serpico, Rampart*) or entirely fictitious (for example, *Brooklyn's Finest, Training Day*), are a common staple of Hollywood motion pictures. This perception of police misconduct is, however, often not rooted in reality. That does not mean that police misconduct, corruption, and brutality do not exist. It does. And when and where it exists, these officers must be held accountable.

To better understand the scope of the problem, this chapter focuses on the nature and reality of police misconduct, corruption, and brutality, and it discusses how the system holds officers accountable for their transgressions, both internally and externally to the police department.

Misconduct

When discussing the topic of police misconduct, there are often numerous words used to describe police officers and their wrongdoing. Some speak of **police deviance**, which refers to officers doing things outside of the norms of police behavior, while others use the term **police misconduct** to mean the very same thing. Still others will address the problem of **police corruption**, which has been defined as "acts involving the misuse of authority by a police officer in a manner designed to produce personal gain for himself or others."[4] Still, one more common term that is used is **police brutality**, which is when police officers go beyond their authorized use of force, known as **excessive force**, or to simply engage in a physical attack on someone without any provocation or justification at all.

Over time, many researchers had tried to categorize all of these behaviors. Barker tried to give an overview of police behavior in general by extending the Knapp Commission's findings, so he saw those honest and upstanding officers as white knights, the officers that do the right thing but turn their heads to others' transgressions as straight shooters, then the grass-eaters and meat-eaters, and finally the rogues, those totally out of control and criminal.[5] Others have focused specifically on the misconduct, and they address police corruption and abuse of authority.[6] The former is when officers use their police powers and position of authority for personal gain, while the latter consists of officers going beyond what was authorized, which could include excessive force, psychologically abusing people (for example, screaming at people, harassing them, demeaning them), or violating a person's Constitutional or other legal rights.

Police researchers Kappeler, Sluder, and Alpert attempted to define four categories of police deviance, which include **police crime**, when officers used their position to commit criminal activity; **occupational deviance**, when officers use their position for personal gain; police corruption, where officers misuse their authority to gain material rewards; and **abuse of authority**, a catchall category for inappropriate contact.[7] While helpful, the occupational deviance and police corruption categories appear similar, and the last category is rather vague.

Protests against police brutality are not a modern phenomenon, as demonstrated by protestors in Selma, Alabama, during the Civil Rights Movement in 1965 attest.

Two other researchers attempted to classify misconduct in more specific categories by looking at profit motivation, on or off duty status of the officers, and the specific nature of the misconduct.[8] Their categories included: profit-motivated crimes, off-duty crimes against persons, off-duty public order crimes, drugs, on-duty abuse, obstruction of justice, administrative/failure to perform, and conduct-related probationary failures.

While all of these categories contribute to our understanding of police misconduct, the fact that they are trying to classify human behavior is what makes things so difficult. Despite the fact that these are all somewhat overlapping categories, for simplicity sake, this chapter refers to police misconduct as the general term of police officers violating norms, policies, or the law while functioning in their capacity as a police officer. It discusses police corruption as being the use of power and authority for personal gain, and it uses police brutality as any use of excessive or illegal use of force.

Police misconduct can include a wide range of behaviors. For instance, if police officers violate a departmental policy, such as not keeping their hair a proper length, smoking in a patrol car when not authorized, or taking a free cup of coffee when the department does not allow such behavior, these could all be considered examples of police misconduct. More serious behaviors of this sort may include sleeping, having sex, or drinking while on duty. Still further, overzealous enforcement, racial and sexual harassment of citizens, or being overly rude and callous in their interactions with citizens are additional examples of police misconduct. At the extreme end are sexual quid pro quos, for example not writing a traffic ticket in exchange for a sexual favor, taking illicit drugs, committing perjury in a court of law by lying on the stand, arresting a person falsely, or conducting a raid falsely to intimidate a person. More modern examples of police misconduct have included making inappropriate statements using social media and an abuse of technology such as drones.

Attempting to gain some understanding about the extent of police misconduct in America is hampered by a typical problem that there is not a definitive clearinghouse for national statistics on police misconduct.[9] In an attempt to address this issue, the Cato Institute began collecting data in 2009 and again in 2010 under their national police misconduct reporting project.[10] This at least provided an indicator of the level of misconduct among police officers across the United States. In 2009, covering the months April to December they found there were 3,445 reports of police misconduct against 4,012 police officers. In 2010, for which they covered the entire year, they found 4,861 reports of police misconduct against 6,613 police officers. That would translate into approximately .008 percent of all police officers in 2010 having a report of police misconduct made against them. Overall, that is a very small percentage of all police officers in the United States.

It is also important to point out that the Cato Institute's statistics were for citizen allegations of police misconduct, not cases that were sustained through investigations. So, while there were 4,861 reports of police misconduct in 2010, that does not mean that all of those cases were verified as being

Dashboard cameras (alongside GPS devices) became commonplace in patrol vehicles in the 2000s.

legitimate allegations. A study conducted in 2002 that looked at all allegations of complaints over police use of force found that 34 percent of the allegations were not sustained (evidence did not support the allegation), 25 percent were unfounded (no evidence either way), 23 percent were exonerated (force was used, but it was not considered excessive), and 8 percent were sustained.[11] In other words, out of all the allegations, only 8 percent were found to be legitimate claims upheld by evidence. Another U.S. Department of Justice and International Association of Chiefs of Police study on the outcome of police misconduct allegations when there was dashboard camera (dashcam) evidence available, found that 93 percent of the officers were exonerated of the misconduct complaint and only 5 percent of the complaints were sustained.[12] That means that there is the potential that well over half, if not nearly all, of the reported allegations of police misconduct reported by the Cato Institute were not sustained.

Turning back to the Cato Institute allegations of police misconduct, they found that overwhelmingly, the majority of complaints of police misconduct had to do with excessive force accounting for 23.8 percent of the complaints.[13] The second most frequently cited was sexual misconduct at 9.3 percent, and the third most frequent was fraud/theft accounting for 7.3 percent of the complaints. Additional complaints included false arrest (6.8 percent), drugs (5 percent), DUI (4.2 percent), bias (1.5 percent), and animal cruelty (1.1 percent).

Another means by which to assess police misconduct is by the number of police officers arrested each year and the types of crimes for which they are arrested. This line of research was developed by former police officer and now professor Philip Stinson at Bowling Green State University.[14] Prior to Stinson's research, there was no data recorded detailing how many police officers are arrested on an annual basis. Using news media sources through Google News, Stinson was able to track the number in his research because of the fact that a police officer being arrested almost always makes the news. While a police officer being arrested for a crime does not mean they were guilty of the crime, it does mean that the offense for which they were accused has reached the most serious level.

In looking at the number of police officers arrested for violence-related crime from 2005 to 2011, Stinson and his colleagues found that 3,328 police officers had been arrested in that time frame.[15] While that number does seem exceptionally high, keeping a perspective, that is approximately 500 police officers being arrested on an annual basis. And while that number too seems high, knowing that there are 800,000 police officers, that amounts to .0006 percent of all police officers each year.

The majority of the police officer arrestees from this time frame were male (96 percent), between the ages of 28 and 39 (46.4 percent), and had three to eight years of experience (25.9 percent). In most of the cases, the crime was committed when the officers were off duty (64.8 percent), and they were arrested by another police agency other than their own (63.1 percent). Most of the officers worked for a municipal police department (75.2 percent), they held the rank of police officer (79.8 percent), and they were assigned to patrol (84 percent).

Stinson's research has also looked at specific categories of police officers. One study looked at the arrests of police officers who were at the late stages of their career.[16] While it found that most of the crimes committed by police officers were in the fourth and fifth year of police service, and then steadily declined after that across a career, they still found that one in five police officers arrested had 18 or more years of police service. These were police officers who were fast approaching retirement (20-25 years for most police departments). The majority of the crimes were usually motivated by profit, seeking to make some extra money before retiring. In most instances, the officers arrested were allowed to resign from the department.

Another study focused on the police officers being arrested off duty. This study looked at the 2,119 criminal cases committed by 1,746 off-duty police officers over a three-year period (2005-2007).[17] The researchers found that the most common offenses were driving under the influence (226 officers), simple assaults (207 officers), and aggravated assaults (149 officers). In the majority of these cases, alcohol was a contributing factor, while in some it was drug-related. In the DUI cases, most of the officers were arrested when they were intoxicated and involved in a traffic accident (53.2 percent) or a traffic accident with injuries (24.4 percent). Interestingly, many of the officers actually refused to take the blood alcohol content test (19.6 percent).[18] Specifically focusing on the arrests of police officers for drugs, most were for drug-only offenses (unlike most criminal offenders where drug arrests are associated with other crimes) (44.3 percent), with stimulants being the most common drug class (58.7 percent) and cocaine the most common drug (49 percent), while the next most

One of the most common forms of police misconduct for off-duty officers involves alcohol-related violations, including simple assaults and driving under the influence.

common cause of arrest was officers committing a drug-related robbery (19 percent), typically of a street-level dealer or known user.[19]

In regard to the 324 arrests for domestic violence, they found that the majority were committed by a male officer against their non-police officer's spouse, and that the majority of the offenses charged were for simple assault (40.7 percent), aggravated assault (20.1 percent), and forcible rape (9.9 percent).[20] And, in regard to sexual assaults, of the 548 cases, they found that most of the victims were female (83.2 percent), between the ages of 14 and 17 (28.3 percent), and were unrelated and not previously known to the officer.[21] Many of these are what Gallo calls "cop groupies," but when an officer has sexual relations with someone who is between the ages of 14 and 17, regardless of the circumstances, it is still a sexual assault.[22]

One additional study looked at the unique circumstances of female police officers who were arrested for a crime.[23] Of the 105 cases, most were similar to their male counterparts, in that they were off duty (61.9 percent), assigned to street patrol (92.4 percent), were between 28 and 43 years of age (55.3 percent), and had 1-11 years of service (54.3 percent). Of the policewomen arrested, most were arrested for driving under the influence (16.2 percent), aggravated assault (12.4 percent), and simple assault (9.5 percent). The most common of the crimes were not at all different from the most common crimes among male police officers who were arrested. However, when looking at all of the crimes overall, the one difference found between male and female police officer arrests was the fact that more female officers were arrested for profit-motivated crimes including shoplifting, embezzlement, bribery, counterfeiting, and thefts.

Corruption

As is perhaps made clear from the misconduct detailed above, police misconduct comes in many forms. Researchers often try to categorize the forms of misconduct into types of corruption, but as can be seen by the definitional problems at the beginning of this chapter, there are no consistent categories.[24] There are, however, groupings of consisting behaviors. Police crimes are one consistent category and were highlighted by the research of Philip Stinson and his colleagues. Another category is when police officers lie under oath in a court of law and commit **perjury** in their testimony or they **obstruct justice** such as a criminal investigation, typically as a means of deception to conceal some illicit behavior on their part. In other cases, the motivation, as we have seen, is for **profit-making**, and this often falls under the category of **extortion**, where police officers can gain something, usually money, through the power of their position and authority, by using force or threats. While extortion is commonly used to make money, it can also be used to gain things such as sexual favors. A related category is **bribery**, where officers may solicit or receive something of value to influence someone's behavior, such as suggesting that someone give the officer money and they won't write them a ticket. Another category is the abuse of authority, where officers think they can get away with certain behaviors because they are police officers, such as we have seen in the examples of driving under the influence or engaging in fights off duty (see Box 13.2).

One other category, often debated as to whether or not it is corruption, is **gratuities.** A gratuity is the acceptance of something of value, such as a cup of coffee, a soda, or a free meal. In many police departments, this is a violation of departmental policy because there is a realization that the vendors are seeking a quid pro quo, extra protection for their business establishment in return for the free coffee, soda, or meal. Yet, as Detective Petrocelli once wrote, "on the surface this may seem like a reasonable safeguard against corruption, but in practice it means I can't accept a brownie from a nun after I change her flat tire on a rainy night."[25] Petrocelli goes on to note that the most common reason for the no gratuities policy is the slippery slope argument, that a free cup of coffee will lead to free meals, which may lead to free vacations and cars, then other forms of corruption. Despite the argument, however, no study has demonstrated this to be the case.[26] Regardless of the lack of evidence for the assertion, most police scholars and leadership suggest that the taking of gratuities should be frowned upon.[27] Police officers, on the other hand, do not see the taking of gratuities as a form of corruption, for most simply view it as normal behavior.[28]

Recognizing the many types of police misconduct and categories of police corruption, the question typically turns to why the problem exists.

Box 13.2 **Policing in Practice: *Training Day* and the Police in the Media**

From the same writer and director of *End of Watch,* an ostensibly pro-police officer movie, came his earlier movie, *Training Day,* about police corruption. The film stars Denzel Washington as the corrupt LAPD detective Alonzo Harris who is a veteran narcotics officer. He receives a rookie, Jake Hoyt (played by Ethan Hawke), whom he is responsible for training. The film then follows the training of Hoyt over a 24-hour period, hence the title, *Training Day.*

As the movie unfolds, we learn that Harris has a unique way of performing as a top narcotics officer and Hoyt (and the audience) are taken aback by his style, which is justified at every move. As the film progresses, Hoyt finds himself in ethical dilemma after ethical dilemma, questioning the morality of Harris.

Hoyt, however, is not entirely innocent, for he is motivated by his ambition to succeed as a detective that he compromises his principles. Eventually Harris' antics become so sensational, corrupt, and brutal, that no one, Hoyt or the audience can have any doubts and how dangerous this rogue cop — who has learned to manipulate the system to his own advantage — has become.

The film proved to be very popular, was a box office success, and earned Washington the Academy Award for Best Actor. However, the portrayal of not only the Harris character as being corrupt, but the entire police department, was not received favorably by police officers across the country, especially those in the LAPD.

The old saying that it takes "one rotten apple to spoil the barrel" is the basis of the rotten-apple theory in policing.

There are several key explanations, or theories of corruption. The first is known as the **"rotten-apple" theory**. There is an old saying that it takes "one bad apple to spoil the barrel," which alludes to a time when apples were sold out of a barrel and one rotten apple could cause the entire barrel of apples to spoil. That saying is actually based on reality, because a rotten apple puts off ethylene, which acts as a ripening agent on the other apples. The analogy then is that one bad police officer spoils the police department, or, at least, makes the entire police department look bad.

Why the individual officer becomes corrupt can be for many reasons. It could be because they lack the necessary moral foundation, or when faced with enticements, they do not have the ability to control themselves. It could be out of strong sexual desires that they commit the sexual assaults previously detailed, or their out-of-control spending habits motivate them to commit profit-related crimes. It should be noted, however, that the entire reason for selection criteria for the position of police officer, such as educational requirements or no DUI or drug-related arrests, is for this very reason.[29] And the screening measures taken during the hiring process such as the psychological evaluation or lie detector are conducted for the very purpose of preventing potential problem individuals from becoming police officers in the first place. However, no screening device is foolproof, and the rotten-apple theory argues that some bad individuals get through or that some individuals turn corrupt while serving as a police officer.

A second theory of police corruption is the **systemic theory.** In this case it is not the individual who becomes corrupt on their own, but rather they are influenced by their peers, their unit, their shift, or their department. The case of Frank Serpico in the late 1960s revealed systemic corruption in the NYPD because so many officers and detectives were in on the corruption, as well as so many layers of the NYPD's organization.[30] Serpico tried to transfer to a noncorrupt part of the department, but he found that impossible to do, and when he tried reporting the problem up the chain-of-command, he found most were involved in the corruption as well.

The systemic theory of corruption has also been divided into two types, the organized and the unorganized. In the former, it is a process that is somewhat planned out and intentional. The NYPD's collection of graft money was well organized. However, sometimes police corruption, while systemic, extending to a unit or shift of officers, may not be planned. It develops out of police practices on the street, poor supervision, or actions of a few officers that are then imitated by others.

In regard to both of these theories, rotten apple and systemic, the individual is corrupt to gain a personal advantage, whether it is free merchandise, money, or sex. One more theory of police corruption has suggested that some forms of corruption may not, in fact, be self-motivated, but may be a misguided focus on the greater good. This form of corruption has been called **noble-cause corruption.**[31] In this case, the police officer or officers find that the system does not adequately deliver justice to every criminal and so they take the law into their own hands by either physically punishing the individual or taking something they feel will hurt the individual, such as a drug-dealer's profits and merchandise. These officers, under this theory, are not committing the corrupt acts for their own benefit, but for the greater good of society. In reality, this is nothing more than an ends justifies the means argument, suggesting corruption or brutality is acceptable if it is seen as being for a greater cause.

Brutality

One other category of police misconduct that is often separated out as its own distinct category and problem is police brutality. There is, again, both a definitional issue and one of perspective.[32] Police officers are agents of government, and to gain compliance with the laws, government uses both force and coercion. Police officers are authorized the use of force in the conduct of their duties, and as long as they follow departmental policy, state law, and federal case law, the use of force is legal (see Chapter 12). There are times when police officers use excessive force, more force than is necessary. If a police officer attempts to arrest someone and they resist, the officer will use force to gain compliance. If, say, after a struggle, the officer finally subdues the suspect and, out of anger slaps the handcuffs on the individual, causing swelling or a fracture, this would be excessive force. The officer used more force than was necessary to effect the arrest. However, if a police officer targets a person, corners them, and proceeds to unleash on them with the baton, beating them senseless for no discernible reason, this would be an example of police brutality. When the use of force is grossly unwarranted, it is usually defined as police brutality.

Police use-of-force encounters can often turn from a proper use of force to policy brutality within seconds. A good example is the Los Angeles Police Department's (LAPD) arrest of Rodney King, which turned into police brutality.

Allegations of police brutality dramatically increased in late 2014 with a number of cases sparking widespread protests and demonstrations.

On March 3, 1991, King and two friends were out drinking and watching a ball game on television. They left their friend's house, and King proceeded driving on the Los Angeles freeway at high rates of speed. Two California Highway Patrol officers initiated a stop, but King fled and a pursuit ensued. The LAPD joined the pursuit, and after traveling between 55 and 80 miles per hour through residential neighborhoods, the car was finally stopped. The LAPD ordered the men out of the car and to lie face down on the ground. The two passengers complied, were handcuffed, and taken into custody. King refused to leave the car, was behaving erratically, and acted as if he was reaching for a gun. When it was revealed that he had no gun, the officers were ordered to holster their weapons and employ the Taser. Although hit twice with the Taser, King continued to resist arrest and batons were then used to gain compliance. As the officers hit King with the batons, trying to get him to lie face down on the ground so they could handcuff him, they were still within compliance of use-of-force law. Several of the blows glanced off of King's arms and struck him in the head, while others struck his shoulder, but this was most likely not excessive force because King was moving. While the use of the batons looks horrendous to the common person, it was still within the law. However, when one officer stomped his foot on King's head and King's knees, ankles, and head became intended targets of the baton blows, the situation moved from legal use of force to police brutality almost instantly. The only way in which the stomp or baton blows to the head could have been justified was if the officers truly believed and could articulate they felt they were about to die, thus authorizing deadly force. That was clearly not the case.

One difficulty in talking about police officers using excessive force and police brutality is that the policies and laws for what amounts to both of these charges varies by jurisdiction and state. The most commonly shared understanding of when force is authorized and when it is not comes from two U.S. Supreme Court cases that arose in the 1980s, both of which were discussed under use of force in Chapter 12. In this case, it helps to reexamine the two cases from a different perspective. In the previous chapter these two cases were discussed from the perspective of when force is authorized, whereas here, it helps to look at it from the perspective of when police use of force is excessive and brutal. The first case, *Tennessee v. Garner* (1985), established the fleeing felon rule that police officers may not shoot a fleeing felon unless they can articulate that they believed their lives or the lives of others were in immediate threat of danger and loss of life. To do otherwise, after the Garner case, would be considered excessive, brutal, and illegal. The second case, *Graham v. Connor* (1989), established the objective reasonable person standard, which states that police are authorized the use of force, but if the force they use goes beyond what a reasonable person would believe is necessary to gain compliance then it would be excessive or police brutality. The problem with this decision is that there are no well-defined and accepted definitions of "reasonable" and "necessary." This led William Terrill, a former military police officer and now criminal justice professor, to state, "Excess is in the eye of the beholder."[33] He explains that "to one officer 'objectively reasonable' means that if you don't give me your license, I get to use soft hands, and in another town, the same resistance means I can pull you through the car window, I can Tase you."[34]

Accountability

In keeping a healthy perspective on police misconduct, two things should be very clear. The first is that the majority of police officers in the United States are doing a good and honest job serving the people in their community. The second is that police officers, like the rest of us, suffer from that affliction of human failings and that many make mistakes, engage in misconduct, and commit crimes. Recognizing this last point, it is important that we have a system that takes police officer **accountability** into consideration. New York Police Commissioner William Bratton perhaps said it best when he told his police officers, "Very simply we are saying, look, I trust you to go out and police this city. But I'm going to hold you accountable. If you're corrupt, brutal, or racist, I'm going to find out about it. I'm going to fire you and I'm going to jail you if it's corruption. Other than that, I'm going to empower you."[35] As he most succinctly stated, "We have to hold officers accountable for their power."[36] Police departments do indeed hold their officers accountable in many ways, and there are also many ways in which the police are held accountable outside of the agency itself.[37] It is to these internal and external means of control that this chapter now turns.

Internal Control

One method of internal control of the police is somewhat related to the topic of the police subculture (see Chapter 8), and that is **organizational culture**. Police departments often have their own culture about them, and they can be very different from agency to agency. If the agency's culture is one of professionalism, and like William Bratton's, it communicates to its officers that they are to be held accountable for their actions, it makes accountability a part of the organizational culture and that can serve as a means of controlling officers and their behavior. One LAPD officer gave an interesting example when he told the story of being a young rookie who, after bringing in a group of 15 arrestees, found a wad of cash in the paddy wagon. He told his field trainer, who said to turn it into the desk sergeant. His trainer later told him that the people they arrested didn't have that kind of cash and that it was internal affairs planting the cash to see how he would react. The officer explained, "Suddenly, I realized I'd been tested. I knew my organization's cultural values taught in the academy were important to an officer's behavior and actions on the job."[38]

While the concept of organizational culture suggests that police departments take on a life of their own, much of the influence comes from **leadership and management**, from the police chief down to the field supervisors who demand their police officers perform honestly and justly.[39] They essentially set the stage and establish the precedents for what is acceptable behavior within the organization. For Serpico, leadership, management, and supervision were seen as the answers to police corruption. "Police corruption cannot exist unless it is at least tolerated at higher levels in the department. Therefore, the most important result that can come from these hearings is a conviction by police officers, even more than the public, that the department will change."[40]

Since police departments are also bureaucratic organizations, one of the means by which it is organized is through the chain-of-command, which allows for oversight of all of its employees. Through the chain-of-command, the department can issue both oral and written directives. Most police agencies require their officers to maintain a **police manual** of the written directions which details the dos and don'ts of their job.[41] In these police manuals are the rules and regulations as well as the policies and procedures that the police officers must follow in the performance of their duties. Despite the impersonality of the police manual, research has demonstrated they are quite effective in controlling police behavior.[42] As the rules, regulations, policies, and procedures are each a distinct type of written directive, they will be explained separately.

A **rule** is a specific statement that identifies something the police officer must do or, more likely, something they are prohibited from doing in the course of their duties. Rules tend to be very straightforward and succinct. Examples of rules include, "no smoking in a police vehicle," "male hair must be no longer than collar length," or "police officers working patrol may have no visible tattoos." Rules are typically determined by the police chief and his or her administration, and they are designed to set specific standards of professionalization.

The second category, **regulation**, is often used interchangeably with a rule, but there is actually a difference. A regulation is like a rule in that it states what a police officer can and cannot do, but it is based on some form of case law that establishes the rule. For instance, earlier the U.S. Supreme Court case of *Tennessee v. Garner* (1985) was mentioned, which established the fleeing felon rule. In the wake of this decision, police departments across the nation instituted a new regulation that said police officers could not shoot a fleeing felon unless they could justify that the individual posed an immediate threat to life. Another regulation would be the police requirement to read a suspect their Miranda rights prior to interviewing them, as this is based on the Supreme Court case of *Miranda v. Arizona* (1966).

A **policy** is a much broader statement about what the police department believes in and the stance that it will take in regard to certain behaviors. For instance, a police department may have an overarching policy that states it takes a zero-tolerance stance on police officers using any type of illicit drug or abusing legal drugs. Or, it may take a strong stance on a particular type of crime, such as a department with a domestic violence policy which states that the department will take seriously all allegations of domestic violence calls-for-service, that each incident will be documented with a report regardless of case disposition, and that whenever signs of abuse are present, the suspect will be arrested. Police policies are designed to communicate to officers the things the department feels are most important for the agency and the performance of their role in society.

Procedures are much more specific than are policies in that they very often describe specific actions that police officers should take under certain circumstances. For instance, a procedure related to a domestic violence call may read as follows:

Policies and procedures have demonstrated to be one successful method for internal accountability of police officers.

> Officers responding to a domestic violence call must always wait for a backup officer to arrive. The officers will park one to one-and-a-half blocks from the residence and proceed on foot. They will approach the front door in a circuitous route and pause to listen at the door for approximately 30 seconds prior to announcing their presence. When entering the establishment, they will separate the two individuals so that their backs are turned to each other so as the two officers may maintain eye contact.

While officers have discretion in the performance of their duties, the goal behind police procedures is to provide guidelines of best practices based upon lessons learned from previous calls of a similar nature. Very often, the purpose of a police procedure is to ensure officer safety and that in a complex case they do not overlook any details.

Supervisors also have a number of methods for overseeing the officers they police. Many police departments employ **field supervisors**, often with the rank of corporal or sergeant, who work patrol alongside the police officers and serve as a street-level supervisor monitoring the activities of their patrol team, squad, or shift.[43] In addition, many police departments require **daily activity reports** from their officers to monitor their actions in the field or to determine if they have met their **quotas** (see Box 13.3). Many police departments do have specific quotas (although rarely will they acknowledge that fact), while others assign point values to various police activities and then they assess the police officers' performance based upon the number of points they "earn" each day. In either regard, whether quotas or daily activity reports, while these may serve as a means for monitoring police officer activity, they can also be abused and lead to poor management. As one New York police officer explained, "The culture is, you're not working unless you are writing summonses or arresting people."[44] He gives the example that "I can

---

Box 13.3 Policing in Practice: Police Quotas

If you ever want to ask a fully-loaded question to a police officer, ask if the police have **quotas** for arrests and other activities. Some police officers will deny it, others will avoid the question, some will explain they have daily activity reports, while others will tell you that quotas are unlawful. While citizens assuredly do not like the idea that the police have quotas, police officers often don't like the idea either and have sued their departments, and in many cases they have won.

The issue boils down to a conflict between **police discretion** versus a method of **internal control** (and often revenue generation). Police discretion allows the officer the wide latitude of choosing to stop, warn, or ticket a citizen depending upon the circumstances of each individual case. Requiring quotas allows the police department to track the performance of a police officer while on duty, but it also limits their discretion. So, one debate over quotas is whether or not there should be more or less police discretion.

---

tell my supervisors that I took three people to the hospital and I saved their lives. That the child that I helped deliver is healthy. I can tell them that. But that's not going to cut it."[45] It does not cut it because it does not fall into either the required quotas or an assigned category of daily police activity, and management fails to recognize behaviors that fall outside of these categories because many departments have become numbers-driven.

Another police officer monitoring tool that many police departments have employed is the **early warning system**.[46] Research has demonstrated that problem officers often exhibit certain behaviors that may be associated with police misconduct. For instance, an excessive number of citizen complaints, an unusual number of supervisor write-ups, or taking more sick days than other officers. While each of these may be easily explained away, the early warning system alerts police supervisors to a potential problem, thus allowing for early problem identification to determine if the officer is facing problems, and, if so, to engage in early intervention. "It's not a guarantee that you will catch all of those officers that are struggling," explained Police Foundation President Jim Bueermann. "These systems are designed to give you a fore-warning of problems—and then you have to do something."[47] The effectiveness of the system is debated, but that is in part due to the reality that if the system is successful, no misconduct occurs, and thus we do not know if the absence of misconduct was because of the system or other factors.

One of the most common interventions of the early warning system, as well as another mechanism of internal control of police officers is through **training**. Every officer is required to perform a certain number of hours of training each year to maintain their police certification, and these training sessions can also serve as a means of conveying to officers the proper procedures and behaviors for conducting themselves on the street. In nearly every state, a portion of the training also includes a certain number of hours set aside for legal training, which provides police officers instructions on new state laws, local ordinances, and Supreme Court decisions that may affect how they perform their duties.

When a complaint over an officer is received by a police department, there are internal mechanisms for investigating the allegations. Supervisors are usually made aware of the complaint or problem, and they will conduct a preliminary investigation. In those cases that are deemed serious enough, the matter will be turned over to the **internal affairs** unit, a special investigatory unit of the police department that reports directly to the police chief on matters of police officer misconduct.[48] Most of the larger police departments have internal affairs units, while smaller agencies often rely upon a specific supervisor, the police chief, or another agency, often the state police agency, to conduct the investigation. At the end of the investigation, the internal affairs unit will deliver a report to the police chief detailing their findings. It is then up to the police chief to determine if and how the officer will be punished. While police officers often fear internal affairs investigations and citizens distrust them, the evidence suggests that they deal fairly with cases of police conduct.[49]

One other mechanism of internal control is the teaching of **police ethics and integrity** to police officers. Establishing and maintaining an ethical culture and teaching officers the importance of adhering to the core values embraced by the agency is one more method of preventing police misconduct (see Box 13.4).[50] As New Orleans Police Chief Richard Pennington explains, "I think integrity is number one. People have to view you as being of the highest integrity and that comes from the community and also from your own police personnel."[51] The concept of a police code of ethics is not new, and in fact dates back to August Vollmer. Vollmer had established certain principles by which a police officer should live, and it was his disciple, O.W. Wilson, who helped to promulgate the Law Enforcement Code of Ethics, a code that many officers are still required to sign as a personal pledge that they will live by when becoming a police officer.

External Control

In addition to the internal mechanisms of control that exist to prevent police misconduct, there are many external control mechanisms of police accountability as well. These are methods that come from outside of the police department itself. Many of these have been discussed in some form or fashion so far in this chapter and book. One of the primary external controls is **citizen complaints** of the police.[52] Police departments establish a wide array of methods for citizens to file a complaint with the police department. Police departments will often have methods for citizens to file anonymous complaints, as well as more formal complaints where the individual is identified. A police supervisor is usually made available to listen to citizen complaints and forms exist both in hardcopy and online for citizens to file their grievance. Each complaint is handled seriously by the police department, and serious allegations will be handed over to the internal affairs unit. While

Box 13.4 **Policing in Practice: Police Code of Ethics**

Establishing and maintaining an ethical culture helps prevent police misconduct. Below is the **Police Code of Conduct**, originally developed by O.W. Wilson in the 1950s, and updated and adopted by the International Association of Chiefs of Police in 1989.

AS A LAW ENFORCEMENT OFFICER . . .

My fundamental duty is to serve mankind; to safeguard lives and property; to protect the innocent against deception, the weak against oppression or intimidation, and the peaceful against violence or disorder; and to respect the Constitutional rights of all men to liberty, equality and justice.

I WILL . . .

Keep my private life unsullied as an example to all; maintain courageous calm in the face of danger, scorn, or ridicule; develop self-restraint; and be constantly mindful of the welfare of others. Honest in thought and deed in both my personal and official life, I will be exemplary in obeying the laws of the land and the regulations of my department. Whatever I see or hear of a confidential nature or that is confided to me in my official capacity will be kept ever secret unless revelation is necessary in the performance of my duty.

I WILL . . .

Never act officiously or permit personal feelings, prejudice, animosities or friendships to influence my decisions. With no compromise for crime and with relentless prosecution of criminals, I will enforce the law courteously and appropriately without fear or favor, malice or ill will, never employing unnecessary force or violence and never accepting gratuities.

I WILL RECOGNIZE . . .

The badge of my office as a symbol of public faith, and I accept it as a public trust to be held so long as I am true to the ethics of the law enforcement service. I will constantly strive to achieve these objectives and ideals, dedicating myself before God to my chosen profession . . . Law Enforcement.

Source: Kleinig, J. & Zhang, Y. (1993). *Professional Law Enforcement Codes: A Documentary Collection.* Westport, CT: Greenwood Publishing.

citizen complaints may be investigated internally, the filing of them comes from outside of the department, hence they are seen as an external method of police accountability.

Another method of external control comes from the **media**. Whether television, Internet, or print mediums, local news may identify a problem with the police department or a police officer and their reporting may bring the problem to the attention of the police department. In addition, citizens authoring letters to the editor serve as another method of notifying the police department of a potential problem. Citizens may also contact their local elected officials about a problem or present before the local town or city council about a problem, and these testimonies are often reported on by the local news media.

In addition to citizens filing complaints through a variety of means, in more recent times, citizen involvement in the investigation of allegations of police misconduct has become more widespread. **Citizen review boards** have developed in many of the larger jurisdictions as a means of dealing with police misconduct.[53] Not all citizen review boards are the same, however, and what sets them apart is the scope of their authority and how far their investigation extends (Table 13.1). It has been found that there are essentially four models of citizen review.[54] The first type of citizen review is the independent **citizen-review model**, which is the most powerful because a body of citizens can investigate allegations of police misconduct and make recommendations to the police chief or sheriff. Even if the internal affairs unit is conducting its own investigation, this type of citizens review board can still

Media interviews of the police have traditionally been one successful method for external accountability of police officers.

Table 13.1 Citizen Review Boards: Four Model Types		
Type	**Process**	**Cost**
1. Citizen-review model	Citizen investigate allegations of police misconduct and recommend findings to the chief or sheriff.	These are the most expensive because professional investigators must be hired to conduct the investigations — lay citizens do not have the expertise or the time.
2. Citizen-input model	Police officers investigate allegations and develop findings; citizens review and recommend that the chief or sheriff approve or reject the findings.	These tend to be inexpensive because volunteers typically conduct the reviews.
3. Citizen-monitor model	Complainants may appeal findings established by the police or sheriff's department to citizens, who review them and then recommend their own findings to the chief or sheriff.	These can also be inexpensive because of the use of volunteers.
4. Citizen auditor	An auditor investigates the process by which the police or sheriff's department accepts and investigates complaints and reports on the thoroughness and fairness of the process to the department and the public.	These fall in the midlevel price range. On the one hand, like type 1 systems, only a professional has the expertise and time to conduct a proper audit. On the other hand, typically only one person needs to be hired because the auditing process is much less time consuming than conducting investigations of citizen complaints.

Source: Finn, P. (2001). *Citizen review of police: Approaches and Implementation.* Washington, DC: National Institute of Justice.

proceed with its own investigation as it is independent of the police investigation. The second type is a **citizen-input model**, where the police internal affairs unit investigates the allegations and the citizen review board reviews the investigation and makes recommendations based on their interpretations of the facts of the case. The third type is a **citizen-monitor model**, where the police conduct the investigation and make a recommendation for the case disposition, and only if the citizen is dissatisfied with the findings and/or the recommendation of the police may they appeal to the citizen review board. The board then reviews the police investigation and makes their own recommendation to the police chief or sheriff. The fourth and final method is the appointment of an external **citizen auditor** to investigate the process by which the police conducted their investigation and reached their recommendation. The auditor is independent of the police department and is ostensibly a citizen, but they are hired for the express purpose of conducting the audit (Table 13.2).

The success of citizen review boards is largely mixed, but that may be in part due to the fact they are not all the same.[55] The real key appears to be how much power they have to conduct their own investigation and make their own recommendations versus being simply an additional check on the process to ensure that the manner in which the police conducted an internal review was fair.[56] While those with independent investigatory abilities wield the most power, they are the most seldom adopted model. Most

Table 13.2   Use of Force Citizen Review Policies of Local Police Departments and Sheriffs' Offices, by Size of Population Served, 2007

Pop. Served	Police Departments (Sheriffs' Offices)		
	Outside Review Required for Complaints	Citizen Complaint Review Board (CCRB)	Independent CCRB with Subpoena Power
All sizes	31 (33)%	8 (3)%	4 (1)%
1,000,000 or more	77 (44)	77 (15)	31 (--)
500,000–999,999	74 (51)	52 (2)	26 (--)
250,000–499,999	54 (31)	37 (7)	17 (--)
100,000–249,999	43 (39)	18 (3)	3 (--)
50,000–99,999	43 (32)	8 (--)	-- (--)
25,000–49,999	33 (29)	3 (4)	1 (1)
10,000–24,999	35 (30)	5 (5)	2 (2)
Under 10,000	29 (38)	9 (2)	4 (1)

Source: Reaves, B.A. (2010). *Local Police Departments, 2007*. Washington, DC: Bureau of Justice Statistics; Reaves, B.A. (2012). *Sheriffs' Offices, 2007 – Statistical Tables*. Washington, DC: Bureau of Justice Statistics.

serve as another layer of bureaucracy. Tulsa (Oklahoma) Police Chief Drew Diamond echoes this problem and expands upon it when he bluntly states, "I find almost none of them . . . have any great value or any real potential to enhance departments. One of two things happens during the civilian-review process of the police department, no matter how they got started or no matter what their history. What happens is they either become 'cop groupies,' another layer of bureaucracy, or they basically slow down the internal processes."[57] He goes on to say, "Cops resist them, and I don't blame them," because "it never works to change the norms or the culture that got them in there in the first place," and that communities "reach for them because they don't know what else to reach for."[58]

In some cases, people who feel that they have been wronged by the police or that their rights have been violated will turn to civil litigation. Police **civil liability** is where police officers may be sued in a civil court for improper behavior based on various aspects of civil law concepts. Civil liability generally falls under state tort law for which the term **tort** is used to describe a wrongful act or an infringement on a right which leads to civil liability. The two most common types of civil litigation are for negligence torts and intentional torts. In the case of **negligence torts**, an officer could be sued because they failed to do something or did something that caused harm. In civil court, to prove negligence, it must be shown that the officer had a legal duty to act, that he or she failed to perform this duty, that this breach in duty caused some kind of harm, and that actual damage or injury occurred. There was a situation that took place in the 1970s, when Tracey Thurman was facing repeated attacks by her estranged husband, and when she called the police, they said it was a family matter. This case was the catalyst for much of the domestic violence awareness campaign in the 1980s. When Thurman called the police for help, the officer took his time responding, and Thurman ended up in the hospital nearly dying. The officers, the department, and the city were held liable because the officers did not do their duty.

The other form of civil liability is **intentional torts**, and these are when an officer specifically intended to cause some type of injury or harm. In this case, the act is not through a failing but one that is intended. If an officer, in the course of arresting someone, injures the suspect, as long as the officer was following proper procedures and did not intend the harm, there is no liability. However, if the officer was arresting a person and the person resisted, then the officer intentionally beat the person to cause harm, then it would be an excessive use of force, and the officer could be held liable. The key is what the officer intended in his or her actions. What was the officer's "culpable state of mind"? If the officer intended to arrest, the officer is not liable; if he or she intended to do harm, the officer is liable.

In addition to the fact that if the officer was neither negligent nor intending harm, the officer cannot be held liable, there are a number of common defenses in state tort liability. There is a **public-duty defense**, which makes the valid argument that the police protect the general public and not specific individuals. There is a **contributory negligence** defense, which argues that if the plaintiff was also negligent, than the officer cannot be held liable, and one referred to as **assumption of risk**, which states that if the plaintiff engaged in dangerous activities which brought the officer to the scene, then the officer cannot be held liable. There is also a **comparative negligence** defense which argues that if both the plaintiff and the officer were negligent, then both should have liability equitably split between them. Finally, many officers have defended themselves under what is known as a **sudden peril defense**, which argues that the officer was required to make a split second decision and they did the best they could under the circumstances.

An officer can also be held civilly liable in federal court as well, but this is generally focused on what are known as **Section 1983 lawsuits** because they are based on Title 42 of the United States Code at, naturally, Section 1983 (Box 13.5). In these cases, the officer had to be acting **under the color of law**, which is an archaic way of saying they were acting in their role as a police officer regardless of whether they were on duty or not. So, even if they were off duty, but announced they were a police officer, they can be held liable under this section. The key to the 1983 lawsuit is that they violated someone's Constitutional rights. If an officer prevented someone from going to the polls to vote or denied an individual the right to free speech, they can be held civilly liable in federal court under Section 1983. There is one common defense for these cases, and that is qualified immunity, where officers can demonstrate that they either had a lapse in good judgment or that they made an honest mistake.

In addition to civil proceedings, if an officer has been found to have committed a crime, **criminal proceedings** can be brought against the

---

Box 13.5 Policing in Practice: 42 U.S. Code, Section 1983

An officer can be held civilly liable in federal court, typically in what are known as **Section 1983 lawsuits**. A lawsuit based on Section 1983 asserts that an officer violated someone's Constitutional rights. Below is the text of the statute:

"Every person who, under color of any statute, ordinance, regulation, custom, or usage, of any State or Territory or the District of Columbia, subjects, or causes to be subjected, any citizen of the United States or other person within the jurisdiction thereof to the deprivation of any rights, privileges, or immunities secured by the Constitution and laws, shall be liable to the party injured in an action at law, suit in equity, or other proper proceeding for redress, except that in any action brought against a judicial officer for an act or omission taken in such officer's judicial capacity, injunctive relief shall not be granted unless a declaratory decree was violated or declaratory relief was unavailable."

individual police officer. Examples of these are derived from the work of Stinson and his colleagues, who have studied the extreme cases where police officers were arrested for criminal charges. Still further, as previously noted in Chapter 7 on discretion, the U.S. Supreme Court has the means of external control over police behavior in the decisions they render.

The federal government also has, in recent years, begun using its federal powers to launch Department of Justice **Civil Rights Division** investigations into police departments that may be violating individual civil rights. Many police departments have come under investigation for such violations as racial profiling and differential treatment of certain populations, thus alleged to be violating the **equal protection clause** of the **Fourteenth Amendment**. In many cases, the agencies either face federal lawsuits or the possibility of a **consent decree**, where the federal government can take over partial or complete control of a department, and mandating that the agency make certain changes. Examples include the Seattle (Washington) Police Department which, after a Department of Justice (DOJ) investigation, entered into negotiations to avoid a consent decree, and the Cleveland (Ohio) Police Department, which was placed under a DOJ consent decree because of findings of excessive force violations. While DOJ investigations and consent decrees may be an effective external control measure for holding police accountable, it has also been found it generates its own problems for "The fact . . . federal oversight itself . . . can erode morale in a police department, sapping the confidence and spirit that effective policing requires."[59] It has also been found the consent decrees are only a short-term solution for they are not sustainable for any length of time.[60]

One additional mechanism of external control is police department **accreditation**. Like most colleges and universities are accredited by certain accrediting organizations, police departments can go through the process to become an accredited police agency. The primary organization for police accreditation is the Commission on Accreditation for Law Enforcement Agencies (CALEA) (Box 13.6).[61] A department can request and pay to have CALEA come to their agency and conduct a review of their organization, policies, and procedures, and if in compliance with all of CALEA's standards, they can be awarded the honor of being accredited. The concept is that an accredited police agency operates at a higher standard of professionalism, bestowing upon it honors and offering protection against lawsuits. However, the cost may outweigh the benefits, for in addition to paying CALEA, the agency must come into compliance with all of CALEA's policies, and that can cost an enormous amount of money that may be better spent elsewhere, especially for budget-strapped smaller agencies.[62]

Box 13.6 Ethics in Practice: Commission on Accreditation for Law Enforcement Agencies (CALEA)

The cost of **CALEA accreditation** can be tens of thousands of dollars for the initial review and then continuation fees can range in the several-thousands of dollars for years to come. The argument for accreditation is it makes the agency more professional, it gives them a distinct honor of being accredited, it expedites their ability to apply for grants, and it places the department on the cutting edge of police policies and procedures in the United States. The argument against accreditation is that it really makes no difference in day-to-day operations, it is a waste of very limited resources (namely taxpayer dollars), and it only benefits the accrediting agency.

Ask Yourself:

Should police departments go through the accreditation process? What do you think is the main advantage? Disadvantage?

As a citizen, would you have more confidence in a police department with CALEA accreditation? Why or why not?

Conclusion

If one were to assess the level of police misconduct from the news media or from our popular culture (for example, movies and books), one might think that the entire police profession was corrupt. Yet when looking at the actual studies into police misconduct, it appears that it is relegated to a very small population of police officers, averaging around .008 percent of all police officers in America. That means that over 99 percent of police officers are good, honest people, trying to make a living by performing a very difficult job.

Another issue with talking about police misconduct is that it can range from poor choices on the part of the officer such as drinking, driving, and fighting off duty, to more serious crimes motivated by profit or addictions. The problem lies in the fact that police officers are—and should be—held to a higher standard, so that any incident of police misconduct reflects poorly upon all police. Therefore, it is critical that police agencies do all they can to ensure that no person is hired that may present problems for the agency and there must be internal mechanisms of control in place to prevent misconduct and immediately deal with it when it occurs. Police agencies employ a wide range of measures from field supervisors, to internal affairs investigations, and early warning systems. There are also a variety of external mechanisms of control to ensure that the police are held accountable. There are, in fact, many methods, ranging from citizen complaints, the media, and civil suits, to citizen review boards, and accreditation.

Just the Facts

1. The Lexow Committee (1895) and the Knapp Commission (1970) both exposed high levels of police corruption in the New York Police Department, specifically the use of the third degree in the former, and the meat-eaters/grass-eaters analogy in the latter, which influenced reforms not just in the NYPD, but throughout American policing.

2. There are many terms describing police misconduct including police deviance, police misconduct, police corruption, police brutality, and excessive force. These terms, describing negative police behaviors, have often been categorized, but essentially police misconduct is violations of the norms and policies of policing, police corruption is the use of power and authority for personal gain, and police brutality is used to describe police use of force not authorized.

3. Drawing upon both the Cato Institute's research and the Stinson data to describe police misconduct in American policing, it is noted that .008 percent of all police officers have allegations of police misconduct annually filed against them, and that only a small percentage of those allegations are sustained. Most of the complaints allege excessive force. In the case of the Stinson data, less than .0006 percent of all police officers are arrested for crimes, and many of these crimes are for poor behavior off duty ranging from DUI, to domestic violence, to simple assaults.

4. There are many terms used to describe police corruption including police crimes, perjury, obstruction of justice, extortion, and bribery, but most are abuses of police authority to gain some personal benefit, both tangible and intangible.

5. The three theories of police corruption are the rotten-apple theory, which argues they are individual police officers committing bad behavior; systemic theory, which argues the corruption runs through the unit, shift, or the entire department; and noble-cause corruption, which argues that the officers do not commit the bad behaviors for personal gain, but rather to right a wrong when the criminal justice system fails.

6. Excessive force is the authorized use of force that, for various reasons, is slightly more than was authorized in the situation. Police brutality is the use of force that goes beyond all policies and procedures covering police use of force or is done for no identifiable reason.

7. Policing and police departments employ multiple internal controls to hold police officers accountable for their actions, including influencing the organizational culture, leadership, and management, policy manuals detailing the rules, regulations, policies, and procedures of the department, field supervisors, daily activity reports (quotas), early warning systems, training, internal affairs, and police codes of ethics and integrity.

8. Government and the people have multiple methods of external oversight over the police available to them to hold police officers accountable for their actions, including citizen review boards, media, civil liability, Section 1983 law suits, US DOJ Civil Rights Division investigations including Fourteenth Amendment charges and consent decrees, as well as accreditation of police departments.

Ask Yourself

1. Read about the early twentieth-century police use of the third degree to gain confessions from suspects, and consider modern day allegations of police brutality. Are these two morally equivalent?

2. Consider all of the terms used to describe police misconduct, police corruption, and police brutality. Is there a better way of trying to categorizing these bad behaviors of the police to better understand the terms often employed and the meaning behind them?

3. Based on your understanding of the media's news reports about the police today, what are the major problems in America with police misconduct? Now, reviewing the various studies by the Cato Institute and Stinson, do the types of complaints/arrests comport with your understanding of the media's? How are they similar? How do they differ? Why do you think this is the case?

4. After looking at the types of allegations of police misconduct, as well as the Stinson data on police officers being arrested, which of the three theories of police misconduct appears to explain the majority of police misconduct in America?

5. In light of the many internal and external controls regarding police accountability, and recalling the numerous screening methods police departments use to hire future police officers, are there any additional methods the police should be using to hold police officers accountable? Consider in your answer the rights of the individual police officer as well as the expense to the government to implement these alternative measures.

Keywords

Abuse of authority
Accountability
Accreditation
Assumption of risk
Bribery
Citizen auditor
Citizen complaints
Citizen-input model
Citizen-monitor model
Citizen review boards
Citizen-review model
Civil liability
Civil Rights Division
Comparative negligence
Contributory negligence
Criminal proceeding
Daily activity reports
Early warning system
Equal protection clause

Excessive force
Extortion
Field supervisors
Fourteenth Amendment
    consent decree
Frank Serpico
Grass-eaters
Gratuities
Intentional tort
Internal affairs
Knapp Commission
Leadership and management
Lexow Committee
Meat-eaters
Media
Negligence tort
Noble-cause corruption
Obstruct justice
Occupational deviance

Organizational culture
Perjury
Police brutality
Police corruption
Police crime
Police deviance
Police ethics and integrity
Police manual
Police misconduct
Policy
Procedure
Professional model
Profit-making
Progressive Era
Public-duty defense
Quotas
Regulation
Rotten-apple theory
Rule

Section 1983 lawsuit   Theodore Roosevelt   Training
Sudden peril defense   Third degree   Under the color of law
Systemic theory   Tort

Endnotes

1. Vollmer, A. (1921). A practical method for selecting policemen. *Journal of the American Institute of Criminal Law and Criminology, 11,* 571-581, at p. 575.
2. Maas, P. (1973). *Serpico.* New York, NY: Bantam Books, p. 303.
3. Gallo, G. (2001). *Armed and dangerous: Memoirs of a Chicago policewoman.* New York, NY: Forge Book, p. 303.
4. Goldstein, H. (1975). *Police corruption: A perspective on its nature and control.* Washington, DC: Police Foundation, p. 3
5. Barker, T. (1996). *Police ethics: Crisis in law enforcement.* Springfield, IL: Charles C. Thomas Publishers.
6. Goldstein, H. (1977). *Police a free society.* Cambridge, MA: Ballinger Books; Sherman, L.W. (1978). *Scandal and reform: Controlling police corruption.* Berkeley University of California Press.
7. Kappeler, V.E., Sluder, R.D., & Alpert, G.P. (1998). *Forces of deviance: Understanding the dark side of policing.* 2nd ed. Prospect Heights, IL: Waveland Press.
8. Kane, R.J. & White, M.D. (2009). Bad cops: A study of career-ending misconduct among New York City police officers. *Criminology and Public Policy, 8,* 737-769.
9. Chappell, A.T. & Piquero, A.R. (2004). Applying social learning theory to police misconduct. *Deviant Behavior, 2,* 89-108; Ivkovic, S.K. (2003). To serve and collect: Measuring police corruption. *The Journal of Criminal Law & Criminology, 93,* 593-649; Skogan, W. & Frydl, K. (2004). *Fairness and effectiveness in policing: The evidence.* Washington, DC: National Academies press.
10. The Cato Institute. (2010). *National police misconduct reporting project.* Washington, DC: The Cato Institute.
11. Hickman, M.J. (2006). Citizen complaints about police use of force. *Bureau of Justice Statistics Special Report.* Washington, DC: U.S. Department of Justice.
12. International Association of Chiefs of Police & U.S. Office of Community Oriented Policing Services. (2010). *The impact of video evidence on modern policing.* Washington, DC: U.S Department of Justice.
13. The Cato Institute. (2010). *National police misconduct reporting project.* Washington, DC: The Cato Institute.
14. Stinson, P.M., Sr. (2009). *Police crime: A newsmaking criminology study of sworn law enforcement officers arrested, 2005-2007.* Unpublished dissertation, Indiana State University of Pennsylvania. Retrieved from https://dspace.iup.edu/bitstream/handle/2069/207/Philip per-cent20Stinson.pdf?sequence=1
15. Stinson, P., Brewer, S.L., & Bridges, J. (2015). Violence-related police crime arrests in the United States,

2005-2011. Unpublished paper presented at the Annual Conference of the Academy of Criminal Justice Sciences, Orlando, Florida. Retrieved online at http://works.bepress.com/cgi/viewcontent.cgi?article=1041&context=philip_stinson
16. Stinson, P.M., Sr., Liderbach, J., & Freiburger, T.L. (2010). Exit strategy: An exploration of late-stage police crime. *Police Quarterly, 13,* 413-435.
17. Stinson, P.M., Sr., Liederbach, J., & Frieburger, T.L. (2011). Off-duty and under arrests; A study of crimes perpetrated by off-duty police. *Criminal Justice Policy Review, 23,* 139-163.
18. Stinson, P.M., Liederbach, J., Brewer, S.L., & Todak, N.E. (2014). Drink, drive, go to jail? A study of police officers arrested for drunk driving. *Journal of Crime & Justice, 37,* 356-376.
19. Stinson, P.M., Sr., Liederbach, J., Brewer, S.L., Jr., Schmalzried, H.D., Mathna, B.E., & Long, K.L. (2012). A study of drug-related police corruption arrests. *Policing: An International Journal of Police Strategies & Management, 36,* 491-511.
20. Stinson, P.M., Sr. & Liederbach, J. (2012). Fox in the henhouse: A study of police officers arrested for crimes associated with domestic and/or family violence. *Criminal Justice Policy Review, 24,* 601-625.
21. Stinson, P.M., Sr., Liederbach, J., Brewer, S.L., Jr., & Mathna, B.E. (2014). Police sexual misconduct: A national scale study of arrested officers. *Criminal Justice Policy Review.* Retrieved from http://cjp.sagepub.com/content/early/2014/04/21/0887403414526231.full.pdf
22. Gallo, G. (2001). *Armed and dangerous: Memoirs of a Chicago policewoman.* New York, NY: Forge Book, p. 239.
23. Stinson, P.M., Todak, N.E., & Dodge, M. (2015). An exploration of crime by policewomen. *Police Practice and Research, 16,* 79-93.
24. Ivkovic, S.K. (2014). Police misconduct. In *The Oxford Handbook of Police and Policing,* Michael D. Reisig and Robert J. Kane, (Eds.), pp. 302-336. New York, NY: Oxford University Press.
25. Petrocelli, J. (2006). Free cup of coffee? *Officer.com.* Retrieved from www.officer.com/article/10250436/free-cup-of-coffee
26. See Newburn, T. (1999). Understanding and preventing police corruption: Lessons from the literature. *Police Research Papers.* Retrieved from www.popcenter.org/problems/street_prostitution/PDFs/Newburn_1999.pdf
27. Coleman, S. (2004). When police should say "no!" to gratuities. *Police Ethics,* winter-spring, 33-44; Ruiz,

J. & Bono, C. (2004). At what price a "freebie"? The real cost of police gratuities. *Criminal Justice Ethics*, January, 44-53.

28. Chappell, A.T. & Piquero, A.R. (2004). Applying social learning theory to police misconduct. *Deviant Behavior*, 2, 89-108.

29. Shjarback, J.A. & White, M.D. (2016). Departmental professionalism and its impact on indicators of violence in police-citizen encounters. *Police Quarterly*, *19*, 32-62.

30. Maas, P. (1973). *Serpico*. New York, NY: Bantam Books.

31. Crank, J. & Caldero, M. (1999). *Police ethics: The corruption of noble cause*. Cincinnati, OH: Anderson Publishing.

32. Carter, D.L. (1985). Police brutality: A model for definition, perspective, and control. In *The Ambivalent Force: Perspectives on the Police*, A.S. Blumberg & E. Niederhoffer (Eds.). New York, NY: Holt, Rinehart, & Winston; Kania, R.R.E. & Mackey, W.C. (1977). Police violence as a function of community characteristics. *Criminology*, *15*, 27-48; Reiss, A. (1971). *The police and the public*. New Haven, CT: Yale University Press.

33. Dokoupl, T. (2014). What is police brutality? Depends on where you live. NBC News. Retrieved from http://usnews.nbcnews.com/_news/2014/01/14/22293714-what-is-police-brutality-depends-on-where-you-live

34. Dokoupl, T. (2014). What is police brutality? Depends on where you live. NBC News. Retrieved from http://usnews.nbcnews.com/_news/2014/01/14/22293714-what-is-police-brutality-depends-on-where-you-live

35. Isenberg, J. (2010). *Police leadership in a democracy: Conversations with America's Police Chiefs*. Boca Raton, FL: CRC Press, p. 125.

36. Isenberg, J. (2010). *Police leadership in a democracy: Conversations with America's Police Chiefs*. Boca Raton, FL: CRC Press, p. 125.

37. Ivkovic, S.K. (2014). Police misconduct. In *The Oxford Handbook of Police and Policing*, Michael D. Reisig and Robert J. Kane, (Eds.), pp. 302-336. New York, NY: Oxford University Press

38. Vernon, B. (2008). Organizational culture. *Law Officer*. Retrieved from www.lawofficer.com/articles/print/volume-4/issue-8/leadership/organizational-culture.html

39. Weisburd, D. & Greenspan, R. (2000). *Police attitudes toward abuse of authority: Findings from a national survey*. Washington, DC: National Institute of Justice.

40. Knapp Commission. (1972). *The Knapp commission report on police corruption*. New York, NY: George Braziller.

41. Reaves, B. (2010). *Local police departments*. Washington, DC: U.S. Bureau of Justice Statistics.

42. Alpert, G.P. (1997). *Pursuit policies and training*. Washington, DC: National Institute of Justice; Fyfe, J. (1979). Administrative interventions on police shooting discretion: An empirical examination. *Journal of Criminal Justice*, 7, 303-323; Geller, W.A. & Scott, M.S. (1992). *Deadly force: What we know: A practitioner's desk reference on police-involve shootings*. Washington, DC: Police Executive Research Forum.

43. Weisburd, D. & Greenspan, R. (2000). *Police attitudes toward abuse of authority: Findings from a national survey*. Washington, DC: National Institute of Justice.

44. Rose, J. (2015). Despite laws and lawsuits, quota-based policing lingers. *NPR*. Retrieved from www.npr.org/2015/04/04/395061810/despite-laws-and-lawsuits-quota-based-policing-lingers

45. Rose, J. (2015). Despite laws and lawsuits, quota-based policing lingers. *NPR*. Retrieved from www.npr.org/2015/04/04/395061810/despite-laws-and-lawsuits-quota-based-policing-lingers

46. Walker, S., Alpert, G., & Kenney, D. (2000). *Responding to the problem officer: A national evaluation of early warning systems*. Washington, DC: National Institute of Justice; Vera Institute of Justice. (1999). *Respectful and effective policing: Two examples in the South Bronx*. New York, NY: Vera Institute of Justice.

47. Abdollah, T. (2014). "Early warning systems" aim to ID troubled police officers. *Los Angeles Daily News*. Retrieved from www.dailynews.com/government-and-politics/20140907/early-warning-systems-aim-to-id-troubled-police-officers

48. Noble, J.J. & Alpert, G.P. (2009). *Managing accountability systems for police conduct: Internal affairs and external oversight*. Long Grove, IL: Waveland Press Inc.

49. Liderbach, J., Body, L.M., Taylor, R.W., & Kawucha, S.K. (2007). Is it an inside job? An examination of internal affairs complaint investigation files and the production of nonsustained findings. *Criminal Justice Police Review*, *18*, 353-377; Office of Community Oriented Police Services. (2009). *Building trust between the police and the citizens they service*. Washington, DC: Office of Community Oriented Policing Services.

50. See for instance Office of Community Oriented Police Services. (2009). *Building trust between the police and the citizens they service*. Washington, DC: Office of Community Oriented Policing Services.

51. Isenberg, J. (2010). *Police leadership in a democracy: Conversations with America's Police Chiefs*. Boca Raton, FL: CRC Press, p. 40.

52. Rojek, J., Decker, S.H., & Wagner, A.E. (2005). Addressing police misconduct: The role of citizen complaints. In *Critical Issues in Police: Contemporary Readings*, 5th ed., edited by Roger G. Dunham and Geoffrey P. Alpert, pp. 258-279. Long Grove, IL: Waveland Press Inc.; Terrill, W. & Ingram, J.R. (2016). Citizen complaints against the police: An eight city examination. *Police Quarterly*, *19*, 150-179; Worden, R.E., Bonner, H.S., & McLean, S.J. (2018). Procedural justice and citizen review of complaints against the police: Structure, outcomes, and complainants' subjective experience. *Police Quarterly*, *21*, 77-108.

53. Finn, P. (2001). *Citizen review of police: Approaches and implementation*. Washington, DC: National Institute of Justice; Sen, S. (2010). *Enforcing police accountability through civilian oversight*. Thousand Oaks, CA: SAGE; Walker, S. (2005). *The new world of police accountability*. Newbury Park, CA: SAGE Publications; Walker, S. (2001). *Police accountability: The role of citizen oversight*. Belmont, CA: Wadsworth.

54. Finn, P. (2001). *Citizen review of police: Approaches and implementation*. Washington, DC: National Institute of Justice.

55. Ivkovic, S.K. (2014). Police misconduct. In *The Oxford Handbook of Police and Policing,* Michael D. Reisig and Robert J. Kane, (Eds.) pp. 302-336. New York, NY: Oxford University Press.

56. Terrill, W. & Ingram, J.R. (2016). Citizen complaints against the police: An eight city examination. *Police Quarterly, 19*, 150-179.

57. Isenberg, J. (2010). *Police leadership in a democracy: Conversations with America's Police Chiefs.* Boca Raton, FL: CRC Press, p. 111.

58. Isenberg, J. (2010). *Police leadership in a democracy: Conversations with America's Police Chiefs.* Boca Raton, FL: CRC Press, p. 111.

59. Stone, C., Fogleson, T., & Cole, C.M. (2009). *Policing Los Angeles under a consent decree: The dynamics of change at the LAPD.* Cambridge, MA: Harvard Kennedy School, p. 19.

60. Alpter, G.P., McLean, K., & Wolfe, S. (2017). Consent decrees: An approach to police accountability and reform. *Police Quarterly, 20*, 239-249.

61. CALEA. (2015). *CALEA.* Retrieved from www.calea.org/

62. Dees, T. (2015). Is accreditation a crock? *Lawofficer Connect.* Retrieved from http://connect.lawofficer.com/profiles/blogs/is-accreditation-a-crock

■ *"The citizen expects police officers to have the wisdom of Solomon, the courage of David, the strength of Samson, the patience of Job, the leadership of Moses, the kindness of the Good Samaritan, the strategical training of Alexander, the faith of Daniel, the diplomacy of Lincoln, the tolerance of the Carpenter of Nazareth, and, finally, an intimate knowledge of every branch of the natural, biological, and social sciences. If he had all of these, he might be a good policeman."*[1] —*August Vollmer*

Policing is one of the most stressful jobs there is, so it never hurts to smile and laugh on the job.

CHAPTER 14

Stress

After reading this chapter, you will be able to:

1. Name and define the different types of stress and how they can affect a person.
2. Understand the relationship between chronic/acute stress with burnout/posttraumatic stress disorder (PTSD).
3. List and describe the four types of stressors in policing in their ascending order from least stressful to most stressful.
4. Identify the consequences of stress on police officers with special attention paid to the realities, not the myths.
5. Explain the impact that stress has on police officers and how it manifests in four different types of problems.
6. Identify the most common methods for stress reduction.

The opening quote by August Vollmer highlights the often unrealistic expectations that citizens have about the police. Police officers find themselves in situations where the image of police officers and the beliefs of what they can do differ greatly from what they actually can do in any given situation. These false expectations versus the realities of the job can generate many problems for the police officer. One of those problems is centered on stress.

Police officers are called to a scene to provide help to troubled people. They often deal with people criticizing them and filming them with their cell phones. They hear people hurl expletives their way, and these are sometimes followed by rocks. They often find themselves having to use force because people resist arrest, but then they receive complaints because they were "mean" or used excessive force, a common complaint as seen in Chapter 13. These officers often have to respond to crime scenes where a victim is seriously injured, raped, or found dead. They respond to automobile accidents where people have lost limbs or have died a horrible death, and then they must go and notify the next of kin. And in some cases, the brutally injured, raped, or deceased is a child. And through all of this, officers are required to remain calm and not let what they see affect them or their judgment. As NYPD Officer Osborne explains, "I'm not heartless or uncaring, it's just that I see a lot of misery on my line of work, and you have to be a survivor. Normal people don't live like this, but cops do."[2] What is so often missed in all of this is that police officers are human, and seeing human tragedy and the dark side of humanity on a daily basis, does, in fact, take its toll.

This, once again, returns us to the difference between popular beliefs and realities. Just like with police officer misconduct, we hear how corrupt and brutal police officers are, but discover that the majority of police officers are honest employees. It is the same when it comes to police stress. We often hear how much of an emotional wreck police officers are, suffering burnout, **posttraumatic stress disorder (PTSD)**, getting divorced, becoming alcoholics and drug abusers, all of which results in suicides or early deaths. None of these are the realities for most police officers. All police officers have stress, but the vast majority manage and cope with it. Trying to understand the realities of police stress in and amongst all of the false narratives is the focus of this chapter.

Stress

Stress is defined as something that can exert a force or strain on a person.[3] It can impact them **physically** in that the person experiences a biological reaction to the stressor, which is the body's way of dealing with or reacting to that which is causing them stress. Psychologists often refer to the body's reaction to stress as the "**fight-or-flight response**," the body's way to either flee the stress or be prepared to fight back.[4] There is also **psychological** stress in that the stressors cause us to react mentally or emotionally over the adversity. So, it is important to remember that stress is both a physical and a psychological response to some form of stressor.

Another aspect of stress is that it is not always bad. There is good stress and bad stress, typically referred to as eustress or distress.[5] The former, **eustress,** is your body's reaction to stress, but it is helpful to the body. If you lift weights or run races, these are both forms of stressors on your body, but they have an advantageous effect on both your physical and psychological well-being. On the other hand, **distress** is when one

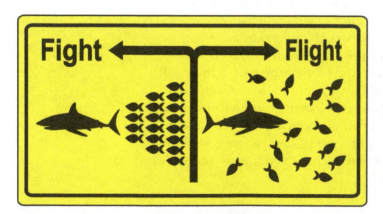

A simple depiction of the "fight-or-flight" response.

experiences pain or trauma, and the demands placed on our bodies can affect us negatively, again both physically and psychologically. It should be noted that the "eu" and the "dis" in eustress and distress come from the source of the stress, the stressor, not the effect of the stressor itself. Yet, that too breaks down into two categories (see Box 14.1).

The way the body reacts to stress is often dependent upon the type of stress experienced, resulting in either chronic stress or acute stress.[6] **Chronic stress** is the type of stress that builds over time from the day-in and day-out stressors that are placed on our body. For police officers, this can be such things as the constant demand of management, the stress of racing from

---

Box 14.1 Policing in Practice: Reacting Under Stress, Officer Amador Gonzalez, Corpus Christi (TX) PD

The account below demonstrates of how Officer Amador Gonzalez, winner of the TOP COPs Award in 2015, reacted under **acute stress**.

On March 20, 2014, Officer Gonzalez heard a call for a suspicious person suspected of breaking and entering into a house. Officers arrived on scene and cleared with no sign of the suspect. Officer Scott Goodman, on patrol in his beat, approximately one mile from the call, spotted a man fitting the description. He marked out and Officer Gonzalez responded as back up.

As Gonzalez arrived on scene, he heard Goodman ask the suspect if he had any weapons as he approached him to conduct a Terry-pat down. As he was starting to pat the suspect down, the man pulled a gun from his waistband. Gonzalez yelled, "Gun!" and drew his weapon. Goodman grabbed the suspect, pulling him down, but the suspect managed to turn and fire two rounds into Goodman. One entered his neck, the other his left leg. Gonzalez then rushed the suspect while firing, and the suspect fired back, striking Gonzalez in the left thigh.

The suspect then moved behind a tree while still firing and Gonzalez retreated behind his Tahoe. Gunfire continued to be exchanged, and at one point the suspect made a sound as if he was hit and he began to run away from the tree. Then he did something totally unexpected, he charged toward the Tahoe in the hopes of driving away. Gonzalez fired round after round into the suspect, wondering how he could be hit so many times and still be able to drive away. Somehow, he did.

Gonzalez then radioed for assistance and grabbed his go-bag and ran to Goodman's side. He placed a tourniquet on his partner's leg, then one on his own to stop the loss of blood. That action saved both their lives that day.

The suspect was soon captured, having crashed the Tahoe into a utility pole, most likely losing consciousness from the two gunshot wounds to his chest and leg. He was later charged with two counts of attempted capital murder.

Gonzalez attributed his SWAT medical training with saving the lives of his partner and himself and he advocates all officers should receive the training on how to apply a tourniquet and to carry one (or two) with them at all times.

Source: Burger, L. (2014). RISE Award Nominee. *Police One.com* Retrieved from http://www.policeone.com/police-heroes/articles/7296547-RISE-Award-Nominee-How-a-Texas-cop-saved-partner-and-self-with-tourniquets-and-SWAT-training/; National Association of Police Organizations. (2015). NAPO Salutes the 2015 Top Cop Winners. *NAPO.org* Retrieved from http://www.napo.org/top-cops/winners-2015/.

one call to another, and the toll that rotating shifts takes on the body. This is chronic stress, and chronic stress is typically cumulative over time, which can then lead to police **burnout**.[7]

The other type of stress is **acute stress**, and this is a sudden instance of trauma that becomes so overwhelming that the body, both physically and mentally, cannot effectively deal with it. A good example is the bombing at the Boston Marathon in 2013. One second, runners were experiencing eustress, the next second, they were experiencing distress. The distress in particular was not chronic, because it did not build up over time, but rather happened all at once. Think of the police officers who responded on September 11, 2001, when the Islamic terrorists flew the planes into the World Trade Center buildings and the two towers collapsed.[8] Dealing with a human tragedy on that scale is acute stress, which can bring about PTSD, a physical and psychological reaction to a major trauma that the individual finds difficult to deal with.[9]

In police work, officers and deputies find themselves working in jobs where they experience constant stressors. Whether this is because of the nature of the job, being called to assist and deal with the darker side of humanity, or the job's demands on their personal lives, police officers face a multitude of stressors. To understand the different types of stressors, researchers have attempted to categorize the stressors police face in their jobs, and it is to these four types of stressors that this chapter now turns.

Types of Stressors

There is a very large body of research that has looked into the causes and levels of police stress over the past 50 years. In addition to those who study policing and criminal justice, psychologists, psychiatrists, social workers, and those in the medical profession have assessed police stress. The general conclusion for many of these studies is that police officers are no more stressed than most other occupations, despite the nature of their job. Yet, like all professions, there are particular things that cause them stress. These stressors have generally been categorized into four types: external, personal, operational, and organizational stress.[10] These also are presented in the order of the impact these stressors have been found to have on police officers, so external stress is considered the least stressful, while organizational stress is considered the highest stressor for police officers.

External Stress

The first category, **external stress**, is concerned with the inherent dangers of being a police officer.[11] As discussed in Chapter 12, policing is a dangerous occupation, but it is not *the most* dangerous job, as many often believe.[12] In fact, for many police officers, it is not the actual danger that generates stress, but rather the occupation's inherent **potential for danger** that creates most of the external stress.[13] This is highlighted by the Los Angeles Police

Department's (LAPD) heavy emphasis from the academy to roll call training that police officers must remain aware of the dangers they face on the street. As one training officer explained to new boots (rookies), "Basically, you better be prepared mentally and physically. You better tell yourself right now that sometime over the next year some asshole is gonna try to kick your butt."[14] While police officers can go to hundreds of calls safely, eventually they will encounter a call where their lives will be put in danger, whether it is something to the extreme such as a deadly force encounter or a high-speed pursuit, to something as simple as a person refusing to be arrested and handcuffed.

Police officers face the potential of danger, whether it is a potential threat from a suspect or the hazards of working daily in traffic.

While there is always the potential for fear, police officers typically do not dwell much on this reality. As one Los Angeles police officer explains, "I don't think about the danger every day when I go out because I think that if you get that paranoid about it, you can't be free enough to work . . . but you know it's there."[15] Officer Dunn, who also worked for the LAPD, offered how one training officer explained it when he noted that although everyone has fears, even police officers, "You can't give in to the fear. Because if you do, if you give into the fear on this one thing, you'll give in to the fear on others. And you'll go crazy."[16] The very fact that officers understand this and know there is always a potential for danger is most likely what makes the external stressors the least stressful of the four categories. Police officers know that danger is part of the job, and they accept that for what it is.

Another example is injuries on the job. The Chicago Police had a saying for the realities of injuries and that is, "Some days you eat the bear, some days the bear eats you."[17] As detailed in Chapter 12, one of the realities of policing is injuries sustained on the job. It is not a matter of *if* an officer is going to get injured, but rather *when* are they going to get injured. Gallo explains how police officers accept this fact when she wrote, "Injury is part of a cop's life, accepted without question. When it happens, you simply deal with it and go forward."[18] In fact she drives home this point when she describes the reaction of police officers to another officer's injuries: "Injured on duty? What else is new? You're the police—get over it! Broken arm? So what? A steel plate in your shattered ankle? How long before you bring your malingering ass back to work? You learn to live with pain and injury. To *laugh* about it with other cops. There's nothing else you can do. It's part of the deal."[19] The very fact that injuries are part of the job highlights that most police officers, like Gallo, understand and accept it, hence their expectations and their realities are not far apart, thus the fear of an injury is not a high level stressor.

Another important example of this is the use of deadly force. Many police officers will go their entire career without ever having to pull their firearm from its holster, and most officers that do, rarely ever discharge the weapon. Police use of deadly force, despite media depictions to the contrary, are a rare event in policing. Yet, once again, there is always the potential for the use of deadly force both on and off the job. Most police officers do not dwell upon this potential use of deadly force, and many do not consider they will ever have to kill someone in the line of duty until the police academy or even later.[20] In addition, despite many alarming allegations about how a deadly force encounter will cause untold amounts of stress on the police officers and that it will destroy their career, there is no evidence that this is the case. The reality is, every police officer reacts differently. As one police officer explained to former officer and current professor David Klinger in his book *Into the Kill Zone,* "I've gone through some really tough times after my shootings, and I've talked to a lot of other officers who've been in shootings about how they handled it. Some have had some tough times like me, and some it hasn't really bothered much at all. I teach shootings up at the academy, and one of the biggest things I tell those recruits is that everybody handles things different."[21] So, while most police officers recognize the potential for deadly force, most do not dwell on it, and for those that have been in those situations, each reacts differently.

Personal Stress

The second category of stressors is **personal stress**.[22] In this regard, police officers start with stress that is not much different from any other occupation. Every person that is employed faces difficulties of managing their careers with their personal life. Whether a person runs a pet-grooming business or a Fortune 500 company, they are always trying to balance their work life with their family life. Police officers are no different in this regard. There are many aspects about policing, however, that set it apart from other occupations, and these differences begin to add to the levels of personal stress police officers often face (Box 14.2).

The life of a police officer is typically one that is very hectic. Because police officers must be available 24/7, their atypical work schedules can lead to complications at home. If officers work the nightshift or if they are on rotating shifts, these generate difficulties in families having time together. If Mommy is sleeping because she worked night shift, everyone in the house has to be quiet while she sleeps. When she awakes, she is most likely still tired, and then has to get ready to go back to work. In addition, because of the hours and duty requirements, it is common for police officers to miss birthdays, anniversaries, piano recitals, and most holidays, including Christmas and Easter, because they are working. As one police officer told a new recruit, "I'm not going to lie to you, it's tough . . . sometimes you're not there to see your kids grow up. It's going to be difficult balancing out life and priorities."[23] The life of a police officer leaves very little time for marital interaction or time spent with the children.

Box 14.2 Policing in Practice: Police Stress and *Courageous*

A 2011 movie that was very popular with movie goers but not so much with the critics was the film *Courageous.* It depicts a group of small town police officers who, in dealing with the demands of their jobs, often forget the needs of their own families. After tragedy strikes one of the families, the officers pledge to be better parents, better husbands, and better men. What they discover is that by living their pledge, not only do they enhance the lives of their families, but they also become better adept at dealing with the stress of policing. While not intended as a movie about police stress, the film depicts many of the realities of police stress, its consequences, and the means to effectively cope with the policing occupation.

Source: Courageous (2011). Sherwood Pictures.

It is not just the odd hours, but often the odd jobs as well.[24] Many officers work all evening or all night and then have to appear the next morning for court duty. Or police officers may engage in undercover work, in which case they are gone for long periods of time. Whenever there is a major incident, police officers off duty will be called back on duty to assist. When the officer is involved in a critical incident, it may impact them physically and emotionally, necessitating time to recover, whether in the hospital or in some type of therapy, all of which can pull time away from the family. Still further, because the police culture is very insular and officers rely on their time with other officers to deal with the job, this type of interaction also pulls the police officer away from his or her family. All of this can then lead to miscommunication or a lack of communication, something that is at the core of marital relations and family health.[25]

Most of the factors of personal stress, so far, are presented from the perspective of the police officer. It is, however, important to understand that very often the family's perceptions generate the personal stress that the officer feels. This is not out of any fault of their own, but simply how they perceive their spouse or parent as a police officer. For some it is the fact that shift work, overtime, court duty, and spending time with fellow officers leave them little time to spend time with their spouse/parent, and they resent this. It can also be the family's fear that their loved one may be killed in the line of duty or injured on the job. A good example of the disconnect between officer and family is relayed in an anecdote by Steve Osborne, a career officer with the NYPD:

> Whey my wife would call me at work and ask how things were going, I would always tell her I was having a nice quiet night. Even if I was sitting on some dark street, armed with two guns strapped to my hip, waiting for some perp wanted on a homicide to show up so we could jump him. My answer was always the same. I'm having a nice quiet night.[26]

Still further, some family members may feel that the police officer spouse/parent cannot leave his or her role as a law enforcer and that he or she treats them like they are a cop and not like they are a spouse/parent by being overly paranoid, excessively vigilant, and overprotective. Furthermore, for some family members it may be hard for them to develop friendships because their spouse/parent is a police officer. If the family members have any of these problems and they are not effectively dealt with, it is natural that this will add more personal stress to the police officer who feels this strain.

Operational Stress

Operational stress is, as the name implies, derived from the daily operations of a police department. These are the stressors that are derived from the so-called "routine" encounters that police officers have on a daily basis, whether in an urban or rural setting. While each may pose its own unique stressors, such as gangs in an urban setting or livestock blocking roads in a rural setting, many of these stressors are shared by both, such as routinely dealing with death, the psychological impact that calls involving children have on officers, or simply the fact that many people do not like it when the police show up.[27] One officer describes it this way: "It is very rare for people to call the police when everything is going well. Instead, the police arrive when dad hits mom, when mom burns her child with a cigarette, when a brother or friend has been found dead with heroin needles in his or her arms, when a rollover accident has taken the life of a young family . . . seeing these things day in and day out will take a toll on any officer."[28] Many of these encounters are shocking to rookie officers, but as the officers grow in experience they are supposed to learn to deal with them. Over time, however, they wear the officer down and stress takes its toll. For instance, one study suggests that for patrol officers over the course of their career, after their first year, their productivity starts to decline and grows progressively worse as the years pass.[29]

One example of police operational stress already mentioned is death. For a police officer, dealing with death, as noted in Chapter 8, is part of the police culture. Yet, this routine encounter with death can create stress in a police officer. As Henry and Lifton note in their book on *Death Work,* "Police death encounters . . . differ from more 'ordinary' human encounters with death because police work is permeated with an overarching perception of danger—to a far greater extent than in other occupations, contemporary urban police officers perceive in their work the realistic and continual potential for meeting their own demise in the course of their professional duties."[30] Think of the many different ways in which police officers deal with death: responding to those who have died at home of natural causes, those who have died in automobile accidents, and those who have been murdered or committed suicide. In addition, police officers must notify the living next of kin about their loved ones dying, for as Richard Weinblatt, a former police chief, now professor, has explained it, "handling death notifications is a necessary part of the job that few law enforcement officers enjoy [but] it can be traumatic for the officer, as well as for the family members."[31]

When police officers deal with death, it highlights their own mortality, and it can also highlight the mortality of their loved ones, especially on calls where there is a connection such as the victim being the same age or having the same features as their spouse or child. This is driven home even further when a fellow police officer is killed in the line of duty, as it once again makes them think of how it could have just as easily been them that was killed.

In addition to responding to calls for death, another type of operational response that generates stress in police officers are calls dealing with children. As Charlotte Hopkins explains, police officers deal with a wide variety of calls, but "Its calls involving children that have always been particularly difficult for police officers because of the heart wrenching circumstances that the young impressionable children are forced into."[32] Officer Gallo echoes this sentiment when she states definitively, "Ask any cop, anywhere, what the most dreaded part of the job is, and the answer will be unanimous. It's crimes against children."[33] She recalled the difficulties she and her partner faced when responding to one call where they discovered a chicken box in which had been placed leftover food and a dead newborn baby. Even her stalwart partner had difficulties maintaining his composure. In addition to the death of a child, officers often come across malnourished children, abandoned children, and both physically and sexually abused children, some as young as two or three months old. It would wear on anyone to see that once, much less on a more frequent basis.

Another aspect of operational stress is the fact that all too often, people are not happy to see the police. Even when police officers try to help a person, they often find themselves a target. Sergeant Woods of the Chicago Police Department explains the realities of policing to new academy recruits when he says, "one thing you need to understand now, and for the rest of the time you on this job, is that you the *Man*. And as long as you the Man, you a target. People gonna call you for help, but they gonna resent you while you helpin' 'em. Most folks don't like us; lot of 'em hate us. Get used to it. This job ain't no popularity contest. If you wanted that, you shoulda joined the fire department."[34] His statements remind me of one incident I had as a police officer. I was walking a foot beat, and coming around a van I saw a man haul off and slug a woman, knocking her to the sidewalk. I grabbed him, spun him around, and pushed him up against the wall. As I was putting handcuffs on him, someone jumped on my back and starting hitting me. It was the woman, his wife, beating me. She did not want her husband arrested. I thought I was helping her, but she apparently did not want my help.

Organizational Stress

Ask a police officer pretty much anywhere, anytime, what causes them the most stress in their job and their answer will be "management." One career police officer noted that while "I love this job," he explained, "It's just the department takes away so much of the joy."[35] Research on police stress generally supports their assertions as well, for study after study finds that police officers rate the organization and management as one of the highest causative factors of stress.[36] The complaints range from petty rules enforcement, to role ambiguity, to a lack of support for the officers.[37] Police management is accused of becoming overzealous in enforcing small rules that the police do not find to be critical to the job, such as making sure they meet proper grooming standards or surprise inspections of the cleanliness of the interior of their patrol car. To the lack of support, officers often feel that as soon as someone complains about them, management abandons them and does not support them, regardless of whether the compliant is false, unfounded, a simple miscommunication, or a mistake. However, research into this particular area of stress has found that the one factor that causes the most stress is when police officers believe that they are being disciplined for something unfairly or that the punishment is excessive.[38]

There are other aspects of **organizational stress**, including how police agencies organize by time.[39] Police departments often organize with fixed shifts, where the officers work the same days on and have the same days off, but many still use rotating shifts, where the officers will move through midnight shifts, evening shifts, and day shifts, and their days off will vary. While police officers will often debate the best shift to work, universally they seem to recognize the problems of shift work, for as one officer explained, "Shift work just plain sucks. It's bad for your body, it's bad for your family life, and it's just plain bad period."[40] As for the preference of the best shift, it can vary. LAPD Officer Dunn explains, "All officers are duty-bound at one time or another to work at night and sleep during the day. But the human body does not understand duty."[41] Yet, many officers like night shift for the fact there is a time period early in the morning when the number of calls drop, because some departments pay a shift differential, and because the beginning of the shift is usually filled with interesting calls for service. Some officers hate the night shift and prefer to work days, for as one officer explains it, "You can lead more of a normal life. I mean as normal as life gets when you're on the job."[42] The benefit is it allows these officers to have more normal routines (for example, waking, sleeping) that are the same as most other people. Yet, research has shown that regardless of all of the individual preferences, we know that night shifts are bad for the body and that the absolute worst and most stressful are rotating shifts (see Box 14.3).[43]

Consequences

The stress of policing accumulates over time, and the job has consequences on every aspect of a police officer's life. It changes them and makes them different, and it is not just the major incidents such as a deadly force encounters, but the day-in and day-out routine of the job as well. Sergeant Woods explained to the new Chicago Police Department recruits, "In case you had any doubts, this

Box 14.3 Policing in Practice: Match the Scenario with the Category of Stress

1. An officer responds to assist processing an accident where an entire family died, including a 2-year-old. She then does to a call where an elderly man has been abandoned by his children and uncared for for over a month, and he is lying is his own feces and has bed sores that have turned gangrenous. She then responds to a child abuse case. On her way to the station, she pulls over an erratic driver who says, "Don't you have anything better to do?" She cusses out the driver.

A. External

2. A police officer goes on duty and just marks in operation when his field supervisor asks to meet with him. During the meeting, the supervisor notes the uncleanliness of the patrol car and writes up the officer for not maintaining a clean car in accordance with policy and procedure 16.a paragraph 3.

B. Personal

3. A police officer pulls over a vehicle for expired tags when the occupant exits the vehicle, charges the officer, and she finds herself fighting with the individual. She manages to subdue him and get the handcuffs on him, but in the process she breaks her wrist.

C. Operational

4. A police officer ends up with a DUI arrest at the end of his shift and goes over his shift by two hours. He now has no time to stop at the store to pick up items his wife asked him to pick up for dinner, he has missed dinner, and he is about to miss his daughter's piano recital at 6 p.m., all because of a drunk who thought he could drive even though he blew a .19 on the breathalyzer.

D. Organizational

Answers : 1:C; 2:D; 3:A; 4:B

---

job can be a mother. It's dangerous, it's stressful, and it ain't like what you see on TV. Yeah, sometimes there's car chases and shoot-outs and chasing the bad guys, but there's also long stretches where it's boring as hell."[44] He then hits on ways in which the job changes the police officer over time. "A lot of nights you go home and don't want to see another human being cuz you think they *all* full of shit. This job's going to change the way you walk, the way you talk and think, even something as simple as sittin' in a restaurant. Your family and friends'll notice it first, but when they tell you about it, you won't believe it. Cuz you can't see it. It's what the job does, and you don't even notice."[45]

Every cop, like every person, is different in how they react to stress and how much stress they can deal with throughout their career.[46] Some police officers find they cannot handle the stress and they leave policing. Others find they cannot tolerate the stress and it causes them to take drastic measures, to the extreme of committing suicide. For most police officers, however, they find a way to cope with their stress. Many officers spend their off-duty hours with other police officers so that they are not judged by nonpolice officers and can share police stories and unwind. Others, however, gravitate away from other police officers off-duty and try to associate with people who are not in policing as a way of forgetting about the troubles of the job.

Police officers face all manner of stress while on the job, and ultimately that stress can take its toll.

One mean of coping that is not seldom discussed is the police officer's desire for an **adrenaline rush**. Officer Gallo, in her book *Armed and Dangerous,* devoted an entire chapter to the topic of the adrenaline junkie.[47] In policing, the **adrenaline junkie** is the officer always looking for the next high-speed pursuit, the next fight, the next deadly encounter, because the high of the adrenaline rush becomes both physically and mentally addicting. One police officer explains that the reason he went into policing was because, "I love the adrenaline rush."[48] And for many, the seeking out of the calls-for-service that are the most dangerous is simply "another way of dealing with the job, an outlet for the stress that might otherwise build to dangerous levels."[49] In many ways, it is also a method for dealing with the boredom and tedious nature of policing, but regardless, one can imagine that it can become dangerous. As the police officer who loved the adrenaline rush acknowledges, "Adrenaline, much like fear, needs to be controlled."[50]

One method that people have long used as a means of dealing with stress is alcohol. It is generally believed that police officers work in a job where there is a strong potential for **alcoholism** because the police culture embraces social drinking, because it is a male-dominated occupation, and because alcohol is commonly used as a coping mechanism for most officers. While it is true that many police officers drink, some become alcoholics, and some find themselves being arrested for driving under the influence, the policing occupation as a whole, despite widely held beliefs, is not associated with high levels of alcoholism.[51] In fact, they are very far down the list of occupations that are most highly associated with alcoholism. The number one occupation, which should not be surprising, is bartenders. This is followed by such occupations as roofers, painters, cooks, sailors, and musicians.[52] Although policing has a strong potential for alcoholism, most police officers are not alcoholics (see Box 14.4).

The same can also be somewhat said for drug abuse. While the police culture does not embrace **illicit drug use**, police officers have access to illegal drugs, and many people resort to drugs as a means of coping with stress. While some have suggested that police officers have the potential for abuse, this does not comport with occupational research.[53] In fact, one nationwide study of worker substance abuse by occupation found, "Illicit drug use was lowest among public safety occupations, including, police, teachers, child care workers, and data clerks."[54]

Box 14.4 Policing in Practice: The Cop Bar

One aspect of American policing that is little known or discussed outside of policing circles is the **cop bar**. One of the few to recognize this was Gallo in her book *Armed and Dangerous,* where she devotes a whole chapter to the subject. While not every police force has one, there are many cities and towns that either have a bar run by cops (usually retired) for cops, a private club such as a Fraternal Order of Police bar, or a public bar that cops are known to frequent. Regardless of how organized, the cop's bar becomes a focal point for police officers to gather after shifts or on weekends.

The cop bar is, however, a double-edged sword. There is a strong benefit to the cop bar in that it can be a place where cops can talk about their work without being judged or questioned for amongst fellow cops, no explanations are needed. It is a place where cops can talk to other cops, learn from other cops, and laugh with other cops; all of the things that help reduce stress. However, because alcohol is the primary focus of a bar there is an inherent danger. While most cops, like most people, drink responsibly, there are some that may come to rely more upon the alcohol than the camaraderie to help alleviate stress, and there is also the possibility that the officer may make the mistake of driving home with the same feeling of invisibility that all intoxicated drivers have that they won't get caught. After all, DWIs were one of the most common forms of police arrests/misconduct off-duty.

Police bars and the time spent there and the friendships made are often a part of many career officers' fondest memories. Shakespeare captured it best when he wrote the line, "We few, we happy few, we band of brothers."

Another commonly held belief within the policing profession is that one of the greatest consequences of police stress is the high rate of **divorce** among police officers. If you are going to get married as a police officer, the belief goes, you are going to get divorced. As an example, one police forum notes that "the police divorce rate is high," elaborating that "on average, the large departments are about 70–80 percent."[55] On another forum, a sheriff asks, "Why does law enforcement have the highest divorce rates of all professions?"[56] Neither of these assertions are true, and it is Police Officer Jeff Shannon who gets it right when he states, "The popularly-held belief that cops get divorced more than others is not supported by research."[57] The notion that most police officers' marriages will end in divorce is simply not true. It is a myth.[58]

Two researchers, Shawn P. McCoy and Michael G. Aamodt (the latter being one of my former professors), addressed this commonly held belief.[59] They found untold citations without empirical evidence that stated police divorce rates were astronomically high, and they attributed this to the high levels of stress of the police profession, as well as the police personality, which was believed to be more prone to divorce.[60] The researchers looked at the divorce rate for various occupations in America based on the 2000 census. They found that the top three professions with high divorce rates were dancers (43 percent), bartenders (38.4 percent) (evidently a troubled profession), and massage therapists (38.2 percent). It should be noted that not even the top three highest divorce rate occupations came close to the 70–80 percent level people often believe or say the police have. In fact, to find the police in the ranking of highest divorce rates, one has to go down well over 300 occupations on the list to finally come to "police and sheriff's patrol officers."[61] And then the rate is even lower than anticipated because the national average was 16.35 percent and police officer and sheriff deputies working patrol was a 15.01 percent divorce rate. As the author's concluded, "The idea that divorce rates are unusually high for law enforcement workers is unfounded."[62]

The reality that police officers divorcing is not a consequence of the high levels of stress police officers face in their occupation highlights a problem that is often generated by the myth. The problem is the notion that police officers who get married will get divorced leads many to conclude that the marriage is either the problem or at least part of the problem of police stress and, therefore, leads some to believe that marriage is not a good thing for a police officer. What this misses is the fact that marriage is very likely to be one factor that helps police officers deal with and mitigate their high levels of stress.[63] The idea that there is someone to come home to, who can listen to the officer's problems, and can help bear some of life's other burdens may very well contribute to the well-being of the police officer, rather than being someone who will just merely add more stress to life.

Another consequence of stress that is often discussed as being problematic in policing circles is police officer **suicide**. While it is true that police officers are susceptible to suicide, this author knows this all too well, having lost a colleague and friend to suicide, the realities of police suicide are also filled with many myths or very limited studies.[64] There are some police studies that have looked at one or only several departments and found elevated levels of suicide among the police that are above the general population. However, when looking at studies that include data from across the nation, they tend to find little difference between police officer suicide and that of the general population.[65] One organization, *The Badge of Life*, which deals with the issue of police suicide, has conducted their own national studies and they find that the suicide rate ranges from 14 to 17 per 100,000 police officers, whereas for the public it is around 11-12 per 100,000, while for the military it was 20 per 100,000.[66] That means there are 125-150 police suicides in the United States each year. It should be noted this is almost always consistently three times the number of police officers who are killed by felonious assault each year (but not killed in the line of duty—see Chapter 12). So, while one extreme consequence of police stress is suicide, it is by no means a commonplace outcome.

There is another consequence of police stress that should be mentioned here because while it is also widely believed, it is nothing more than an urban myth, and that is the belief most police officers die within two to five years of retirement.[67] The **early death myth** is derived from the belief that officers experience so much stress in their careers that when they retire and no longer have the high stress, it acts as a shock to the body.[68] It is believed to have come from someone looking at the pension records of one police department and drawing a false conclusion. Those that have looked at the actuarial tables on police officers in retirement have found, "The results show very little difference at age 60 in the life expectancy of police and fire as compared with other public employees."[69]

The most common and real reactions to stress in policing are what is described as burnout. One police officer described burnout as, "the occupational plague that numbs your soul, armors your heart, and leaves whatever remains to carry you through the rest of your career."[70] Police officers begin to feel alienated in their job and they become very cynical. As NYPD Officer Steve Osborne explains, "Being a cop for twenty years makes you very cynical, and skeptical. Every day when you're on patrol people lie to you, or at least tell you what you want to hear."[71] The stress of seeing the worst side of humanity on a daily basis begins to accumulate. Burnout is typically the result of this chronic stress that has accumulated over time. One police officer described this perfectly when he said, "There was no one thing that set me off. Just over a period of time it built up. I got burned out."[72] Or another who stated, "This wasn't caused through any one thing. It was a cumulative amount of stress, of handling shit over a period of time."[73] The real problem is that this type of stress can manifest in so many different ways, including affecting an officer's physical and emotional health, as well as causing both cognitive and behavioral problems.

Stress can generate all manner of **physical problems** in police officers.[74] One police officer described how, "I was a sick boy," for he had "Heavy stress. Colitis. Insomnia. Memory loss. Migraines. Bleeding gums."[75] Another officer explained that every time he went on duty he would throw up. And still another officer came to the realization that "I'd chosen this, I was doing what I wanted to do and I couldn't get it that it was making me sick."[76] Police officers will often develop stress headaches, muscle aches, and high blood pressure. They may have a drop in appetite, sexual desire, and the inability to sleep. And so many police officers have developed ulcers that it is common to find them on duty chewing on such things as Rolaids. Stress can take a physical toll.

Stress can also create **emotional problems** in police officers. One police officer described the problem well after a deadly force encounter when he had to see a psychologist. He told the doctor he was fine because as he described, "I was afraid that if I'd sat there and told him all my emotions, all my fears, all of what I was going through, that he would say 'You're not fit to go back to duty,' and I'd lose my job. So I didn't tell him I was still having an emotional time dealing with it, that I was afraid to go on calls. That fear lasted for a very long time."[77] Fear, anxiety, guilt, anger, and irritability are all the types of emotional reactions police officers may face, either from a major incident or simply from burnout. Stress can take an emotional toll.

The causes of stress are many and varied, but so too are the effects of stress on a police officer.

Box 14.5 Ethics in Practice: The McKinney Police Officer and the Emotional Toll of Police Stress

On June 5, 2015, Cpl. David Eric Casebolt of the McKinney (Texas) police department, responded to a disturbance at a pool party. A bystander took a cell phone video that soon went viral on the Internet. It showed the officer pulling a gun on a gathering of teenagers and putting a young bikini-clad girl down on the ground in handcuffs. The officer was placed on administrative leave, was sued, and soon resigned.

The officer offered a public apology, and his lawyer explained there were circumstances of which most people were not aware. Prior to responding to the pool disturbance, Cpl. Casebolt had responded to a call where he helped console a grieving widow. Her husband had just shot himself in the head in front of his own children. Cpl. Casebolt assisted in photographing the body and what was left of the bloodied head. He then was called to another suicide call, this time an attempt, in which a girl had threatened to jump off her parent's roof. He calmed her down and avoided having to photograph another dead body. He was then called to the pool party.

Mr. Bishkin, Cpl. Casebolt's lawyer stated, "The nature of these two suicide calls took an emotional toll on Eric Casebolt. With all that had happened that day, he allowed his emotions to get the better of him."

Ask Yourself:

After reviewing the circumstances of the case — a summary of the case and the video are both available online — do you think stress explains Cpl. Casebolt's behavior? Does it justify it? Does it excuse it? Explain your answer.

What type of stress do you think the officer experienced and how was it manifested in his actions?

Do you think the McKinney police department should have been aware of the stress Cpl. Casebolt was experiencing? What could the department have done to avoid the incident that occurred?

Stress can also cause problems with the officers' **cognitive abilities**, their ability to essentially function. One police officer described how he was having difficulties remembering anything by saying, "I'd leave the house and I'd forget my keys, gun, wallet. It was like a crippling disease. I was doing such brainless stuff then—and that scared me."[78] Other police officers find they are often disoriented, slow thinking, and have serious memory lapses. Many others will experience flashbacks and often have nightmares. Stress can take a toll on the cognitive abilities of the officer.

Finally, many police officers experience **behavioral problems**, typically in the ability to cope on the job. One LAPD officer experienced this inability to cope when he described what he was feeling. "I can't imagine doing this for one more day. It's like there is only today. Do the watch. Keep it all together. Keep everything in line. Nothing out of the ordinary. Just keep it from pulling apart. Now I just do that today, today is all I'm thinking and it will be alright."[79] Police officers will find that because of the high levels of stress, they will no longer be motivated by the job and, hence, they become dissatisfied with their chosen occupation. As a result of their inability to cope, they will often stop being involved in the job, withdraw, and call in sick more frequently. The real danger of no longer being able to cope is finding some other means, such as alcohol, drugs, or suicide. Policing can truly take a toll on an officers' ability to cope (see Box 14.5).

While most of this discussion has centered on the accumulation of stress that results in burnout, many officers in their career will also experience acute stress. For most, it is a major catastrophic event, such as a mass murder or the terrorist attacks on September 11, 2001. For many, however, it can be something not on such a grand scale, but that affects them in a sudden and impactful manner, such as the death of a child. In a sense, the officer becomes overloaded or overwhelmed by the event, and it affects them severely. The consequences of this type of event are

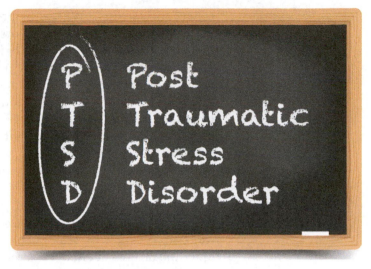

The acronym PTSD defined.

commonly referred to as PTSD.[80] Research has found that certain experiences can overload an officer, but that it may not happen right away; rather, it can come to impact them up to three days after the incident.[81] The police officer then becomes preoccupied with the event, reliving it over and over, and they often report having fits of anger that it happened at all or that it happened to them. In addition, officers can experience many of the problems previously detailed, including physical and emotional issues, as well as cognitive and behavioral problems.

Stress Reduction

Stress reduction is not necessarily just about finding ways to deal with the accumulated stress officers will endure working on the street, but it is also a means for survival, a way to prevent injury, and a method for preparing for the next stressful encounter. Officer Horten from the LAPD explained it this way to his new boots: "Fight's gonna happen. So you better get your mind in line. You better think you're a bad muthafucka. So keep your body in shape. Run your ass off and lift weights. And if you ain't good with that Beretta on your belt, you may want to think seriously about putting in some extra time."[82] Being mentally prepared for future encounters is a means of reducing stress because it gives the officer a plan for how to act when presented with various scenarios. Running and lifting weights are both great stress relievers, as well as keeping the mind mentally prepared to perform on duty. And ask any gun owner who spends time on the firing range and they will tell you that "putting rounds on target" is also a great stress reliever.

The key to stress relief is to find ways to deal with the stress. The research in this area is very consistent in its findings, and we know what helps people relieve their stress.[83] Where the problem truly lies is in people actually adapting themselves to these behaviors. To relieve stress, we must often change our circumstances and/or our behaviors. Research has shown that officers who change their assignments, especially taking on a specialized position with the department such as school resource officer, have reduced levels of stress and greater job satisfaction.[84] However, sometimes we find ourselves in circumstances where we cannot change assignments, so it may necessitate a change in behaviors. That can be difficult, but even more so when the situation is compounded by the fact that people enduring a lot of stress often show the signs and symptoms previously discussed, thus making it even harder for them to change their behaviors.

One example is diet and exercise. Whenever there is a health problem, the preventive measure or solution to that health problem is better diet and more exercise. We know these are beneficial for us; however, people often have poor diets and do not get enough exercise, if any. Just talking about one's diet, everyone should know that less processed food, more fruits and vegetables, and less oils, fats, and sweets are good for the body. Yet, police officers work erratic schedules and they often resort to fast-food because it's fast. Yet, if police officers took the time to pack their meals for their shift and to do so with foods that are better for them, this would improve their diet, most likely help control their weight, and assist them in relieving stress. Yet, to change from the fast-food mentality to packing one's lunch requires a behavioral change.

One of the best stories about diet and cops comes from an LAPD training officer dealing with the issue of cops and doughnuts. When he received a new boot, he took him to the doughnut shop and bought himself and his recruit doughnuts. The boot ate his and the field training officer (FTO) placed his on the dashboard of the patrol car and left it there. Later, the boot asked his FTO if he was going to eat the doughnut and he said, no, he hates doughnuts. He just takes the new recruits to the doughnut shop because all new recruits think cops eat doughnuts.[85] Police should follow the FTO's example and cease eating doughnuts, not because of the "cops and doughnut" jokes, but because doughnuts are really bad for the body.

Another example of what we know alleviates stress versus what we actually do is exercise. To prevent disease, control your weight, and live a healthy life, we all know that we should exercise.[86] The government minimums say about three to five hours a week, but those are minimums. Really, the amount of time each week we should spend working out is at least 8 to 12 hours a week. Whether it is lifting weights, swimming, running, yoga, Pilates, or good old-fashion walking, we need to exercise. However, finding the time and making it part of our daily routine takes a behavioral change. We know from ample research that making that lifestyle change will reap us many benefits. Police officers keep long hours, rotate shifts, or work enormous amounts of overtime, all of which makes the officers too tired to exercise or prevents them from finding the time, yet we know that it is to the determent of their health.

There are two other ways to alleviate stress, and these fall under the category of not abusing the body. We know from plenty of research that those who smoke and those who binge drink (more than five drinks in a sitting) are harming their body, not improving their health.[87] If police officers smoke, they should quit. If they drink excessively, they should cut back. As soon as a person stops smoking, despite the withdrawals, the body starts to improve, so it is a matter of finding a way to overcome the effects of withdrawal. As research tells us, no more than two to three drinks for a male, and one to two for a female, keeps a person in the healthy category. Drinking in moderation can be part of a healthy lifestyle, and it can help to reduce stress, but when it is needed to reduce stress it becomes problematic.

There are many ways to manage stress, but they all require behavioral changes in ourselves.

There are other things police officers can do to help alleviate stress. Research demonstrates that having a number of good friends and associating with them frequently is part of a healthy lifestyle. Going to church once a week also has been found to be associated with a healthy lifestyle and one that experiences less stress.[88] Engaging in healthy sexual relations is also associated with lower stress among people, police officers included.[89] Also one police officer said, "Sex as a stress reducer is as common for some cops as sex to relieve boredom, sex to dispel anger, sex because it's there."[90] Still further, taking vacation time and getting away from the job is also a stress reliever. Unfortunately, too many police officers refuse to take the time off or they use it up for things other than taking a vacation. Studies have shown that the best trips are well planned, far enough away so you cannot easily be recalled (no stay-at-home vacations), and are not too hectic. In addition, those vacations that are less connected (no electronics!) and are out of doors are the best.[91] Trips such as hiking, camping, and backpacking in the wilderness without electronic devices have been found to be one of the best ways to reduce stress, and it has been found to be successful in resetting our natural biological clocks (see Box 14.6).[92]

There is also another method for dealing with stress that is specific to policing, and that is talking with other police. Because it has often been said that, "The only ones who understand [cops] are other cops,"[93] when police officers spend time talking with other cops, it can help alleviate stress. This is primarily for the fact they understand what their fellow officers are going through because they have experienced similar issues, and because they will not judge them for thoughts, feelings, or actions like those outside of the police profession would. This is why, when it comes to major traumatic events, many police departments have establish **critical incident stress debriefing (CISD)** or, more recently called, **critical incident stress management** programs in their department.[94] These programs are created so that whenever there is a major incident, such as a mass shooting, multiple fatality accident, or the loss of a

---

Box 14.6 **History of Policing: The First African-American Police Officer, Horatio Julius Homer**

Although it is truly unknown who the **first black police officer** in America was, the earliest so far uncovered appears to have been **Sergeant Horatio Julius Homer** of the Boston (Massachusetts) Police Department.

Born in Farmington, Connecticut, sometime in 1848, Homer worked during his teenage years as both a waiter and a railroad porter. He was hired by Henry Sturgis Russell, chairman of the board of police commissioners, on Christmas Eve 1878, when Homer was 30 years old. Homer then worked for the next 41 years as a member of the BPD, rising to the rank of sergeant and serving through 12 different police commissioners.

"Can you imagine in 1878, you were the only black officer on the force?" reflected Boston Police Officer Robert Anthony in an article in The Boston Globe. "Imagine how he persevered; imagine the trials and tribulations he had to endure." Imagine the stress he faced throughout his career.

Source: Nicas, J. (2010). Boston's First Black Officer Receives His Long Overdue Honors. *Boston.com* Retrieved from http ://www.boston.com/news/local/massachusetts/articles/2010/06/27/bostons_first_black_officer_receives_his_ long_overdue_honors/.

---

fellow officer—the types of events that are most likely to trigger PTSD—it has police officers come together for a counseling session to discuss their reactions to the situation. And, rather than having an outsider come into the department to lead these counseling sessions, police officers are trained how to conduct these therapy sessions so that it remains police officers talking to police officers. While there is much support for CISD within policing circles,[95] research outside of policing has found that CISD has no impact upon the recipients of this type of counseling, and, in some cases, it has been found to make their problem worse.[96] More research is clearly needed.

Conclusion

Every person in every occupation experiences stress on the job, and policing is the type of career that can be laden with all manner of stress. While stress can be good (eustress) and bad (distress), most of the research is on the latter. Stress can also accumulate in police officers throughout their career, which is known as chronic stress, and can lead to burnout. Stress can also be sudden, known as acute stress, and can lead to posttraumatic stress disorder. Research has demonstrated consistently that there are certain factors that cause police officers stress, and they are external stressors, personal stressors, operational stressors, and management, with the latter typically being cited as causing the most stress in police officers.

There are consequences to the high levels of stress that police officers experience, but it is not to the extreme that is often falsely stated in policing and popular culture circles. Police officers do suffer from divorce, alcoholism, drug abuse, and some commit suicide, but these are not to the extremes that many people believe. Most of the outcomes revolve around the physical and emotional troubles that officers experience, as well as behavioral and cognitive problems. While research is replete with methods for reducing stress, including proper diet, exercise, stopping smoking, consume alcohol in moderation, attend church regularly, take vacations to get away from the job, and to surround oneself with good friends, turning these ideas into behaviors is often the challenge for most police officers due to the long, odd, and rotating hours, as well as the nature of the job itself.

Just the Facts

1. Eustress is good stress, while distress is bad stress, and distress can build up over time, causing chronic stress, or it can come all at once as acute stress. Both of these types of stress can affect a person both physically and psychologically.

2. Chronic stress that builds up over time can lead to burnout, while acute stress, the sudden high level of stress that a person finds difficult to cope with, can lead to post-traumatic stress disorder.

3. There are four identifiable categories of police stress, and moving from the least to most they are external stress, the inherent dangers of being a police officer; personal stress, the nature of the job and how it conflicts with family life; operational stress, the day-in and day-out routines and encounters police officers have; and organizational stress, the direction of police management and its focus on bureaucracy can generate frustration and stress.

4. The consequences of stress on police officers are many and varied and often consist of poor methods of adapting to the stress, which can include officers becoming adrenaline junkies, alcoholism, the use of illicit drugs, suicide, and burnout. Two long-held beliefs regarding the consequences of police stress, high levels of divorce, and early deaths after retirement have both been demonstrated to be myths.

5. The most common way in which stress manifests in police officers is through accumulated stress that leads to burnout, which can manifest as physical stress, emotional stress, a loss of cognitive abilities, and behavioral problems.

6. The most common methods for stress reduction, both in and out of policing, include eating a healthy diet, exercising, smoking cessation, and leading a generally healthy lifestyle, which helps provide the body both the physical and mental ability to cope with stress.

Ask Yourself

1. Revisit the opening quote by August Vollmer. It is one of his more famous quotes. The quote has to do with the expectations that citizens have of the police versus what the police can actually do. How does the difference between expectations and reality cause stress?

2. Studies on police stress almost always find that police officers better handle the stress of the dangers of policing than they do the organizational stressors. In other words, cops can deal more effectively with people fighting them and shooting at them than they can deal with supervisors and management. Why is this consistently the case in these research studies?

3. Compare and contrast the differences between chronic stress and acute stress. Which

do you think takes more of a toll on a police officer? Which do you think is easier to identify? Which do you think police departments direct more resources toward dealing with?

4. Reflecting on the four ways in which stress can manifest as problems for police officers (for example, physical, emotional, cognitive, and behavioral), how do you believe these consequences impact police performance on the job? Returning to the issues and findings from Chapter 13 on police accountability, are there any types of police misconduct that might be associated with these four problems?

5. The means by which police officers can reduce their stress are not limited to just policing, but apply to everyone, for dealing with stress is a daily occurrence for most people. The problem, however, is found to be between knowing what helps reduce stress and actually changing our behaviors to reflect that knowledge. Consider your own levels of stress and how you deal with stress. Do you incorporate any poor coping mechanisms? Do you incorporate all of the good coping mechanisms? And if you know what is good for you (for example, eating healthier, quitting smoking), will you change your behaviors?

Keywords

Acute stress
Adrenaline junkie
Adrenaline rush
Alcoholism
Behavioral problems
Burnout
Chronic stress
Cognitive abilities
Critical incident stress debriefing

Critical incident stress management
Distress
Divorce
Early death myth
Emotional problems
Eustress
External stress
Fight-or-flight response
Illicit drug use
Operational stress

Organizational stress
Personal stress
Physical problems
Physically
Posttraumatic stress disorder
Potential for danger
Psychological
Stress
Stress reduction
Suicide

Endnotes

1. Vollmer, August. (1936). *The Police and Modern Society.* Berkeley: University of California Press, p. 222.
2. Osborne, S. (2015). *The Job: True tales form the life of a New York city cop.* New York, NY: Doubleday, p. 147.
3. Blum, L.N. (2000). *Force under pressure: How cops live and why they die.* New York, NY: Lantern Books; Ellison, K.W. (2004). *Stress and the police officer.* Springfield, IL: Charles C. Thomas Publisher, LTD.; Stevens, D.J. (2008). *Police officer stress: Sources and solutions.* Upper Saddle River, NJ: Prentice Hall.
4. Blum, L.N. (2000). *Force under pressure: How cops live and why they die.* New York, NY: Lantern Books; Ellison, K.W. (2004). *Stress and the police officer.* Springfield, IL: Charles C. Thomas Publisher, LTD.; Stevens, D.J. (2008). *Police officer stress: Sources and solutions.* Upper Saddle River, NJ: Prentice Hall.
5. Stevens, D.J. (2008). *Police officer stress: Sources and solutions.* Upper Saddle River, NJ: Prentice Hall.
6. Stevens, D.J. (2008). *Police officer stress: Sources and solutions.* Upper Saddle River, NJ: Prentice Hall.
7. Schaible, L.M. & Six, M. (2016). Emotional strategies of police and their varying consequences for burnout. *Police Quarterly, 19,* 3-31.
8. See especially the epilogue in Henry, V.E. (2004). *Death work: Police, trauma, and the psychology of survival.* New York, NY: Oxford University Press.
9. Schiraldi, G. (2009). *The post-traumatic stress disorder sourcebook: A guide to healing, recovery, and growth.* 2nd ed. New York, NY: McGraw Hill; For a personal police account of having PTSD see Mahoney, T.J. (2014). *Police blues: Police post-traumatic stress disorder.* Charleston, SC: Createspace.

10. McGuire, R.J. (1979). The human dimension in urban policing: Dealing with stress in the 1980s. *Police Chief, November,* 27; Victor, J. (1986). Police stress: Is anybody out there listening? *New York Law Enforcement Journal, June,* 19-20.

11. Volanti & Aron (1995). Police stressors: Variations in perception among police personnel.*Journal of Criminal Justice,* 23, 287-294; Zhao, J.S., He, N., & Lovrich, N. (2002). Predicting five dimensions of police officer stress: Looking more deeply into organizational settings for sources of police stress. *Police Quarterly,* 5, 43-62.

12. Remsberg, C. (2013). 7 LEO myths that stress you out and scare your family. Policeone.com Retrieved from http://www.policeone.com/off-duty/articles/6283418-7-LEO-myths-that-stress-you-out-and-scare-your-family/ . United States Department of Labor. (2013). *Census of Fatal Occupational Injuries.* Washington, DC: U.S. Department of Labor; See also Smith, J. (2013). America's 10 deadliest jobs.*Forbes.* Retrieved from www.forbes.com/sites/jacquelynsmith/2013/08/22/americas-10-deadliest-jobs-2/

13. Cockcroft, T. (2013). *Police culture: Themes and concepts.* New York, NY: Routledge: Crank, J.P. (2004). *Understanding police culture.* 2nd ed. Cincinnati, OH: Anderson Publishing; Henry, V. E. (2004). *Death work: Police, trauma, and the psychology of survival.* New York, NY: Oxford University Press.

14. Dunn, W. (1996). *Boot: An L.A.P.D. officer's rookie year.* New York, NY: William Morrow and Company, Inc., p. 7

15. Barker, J.C. (1999). *Danger, duty, and disillusion: The worldview of Los Angeles police officers.* Long Grove, IL: Waveland Press, Inc., p. 71.

16. Dunn, W. (1996). *Boot: An L.A.P.D. officer's rookie year.* New York, NY: William Morrow and Company, Inc., p. 84.

17. Gallo, G. (2001). *Armed and dangerous: Memoirs of a Chicago policewoman.* New York, NY: Forge Book, p. 296.

18. Gallo, G. (2001). *Armed and dangerous: Memoirs of a Chicago policewoman.* New York, NY: Forge Book, p. 296.

19. Gallo, G. (2001). *Armed and dangerous: Memoirs of a Chicago policewoman.* New York, NY: Forge Book, p. 325.

20. Klinger, D. (2004). *Into the kill zone: A cop's eye view of deadly force.* San Francisco, CA: Jossey-Bass.

21. Klinger, D. (2004). *Into the kill zone: A cop's eye view of deadly force.* San Francisco, CA: Jossey-Bass, p. 270.

22. Borum, R. & Philpot, C. (1993). Therapy with law enforcement couples: Clinical management of the high risk lifestyle. *American Journal of Family Therapy,* 21, 122-135; Miller, L. (2007). Police families: Stresses, syndromes, and solutions. *American Journal of Family Therapy,* 35, 21-40; Roberts, N. & Levenson, R. (2001). The remains of the workday: Impact of job stress and exhaustion on marital interaction in police couples. *Journal of Marriage & Family,* 63, 1052-1111.

23. Officer.com. (2008). Being a COP and maintaining family life . . . difficult? *Officer.com* Retrieved from http://forums.officer.com/t87940/

24. Borum, R. & Philpot, C. (1993). Therapy with law enforcement couples: Clinical management of the high risk lifestyle. *American Journal of Family Therapy,* 21, 122-135; Torres, S., Maggard, D.L., Jr., & To, C. (2003). Preparing families for the hazards of police work.*The Police Chief.* Retrieved from www.policechiefmagazine.org/magazine/index.cfm?fuseaction=display_arch&article_id=120&issue_id=102003

25. Borum, R. & Philpot, C. (1993). Therapy with law enforcement couples: Clinical management of the high risk lifestyle. *American Journal of Family Therapy,* 21, 122-135; Miller, L. (2007). Police families: Stresses, syndromes, and solutions. *American Journal of Family Therapy,* 35, 21-40; Roberts, N. & Levenson, R. (2001). The remains of the workday: Impact of job stress and exhaustion on marital interaction in police couples. *Journal of Marriage & Family,* 63, 1052-1111.

26. Osborne, S. (2015). *The Job: True tales form the life of a New York city cop.* New York, NY: Doubleday, p. 1.

27. Scott, Y.M. (2004). Stress among rural and small-town patrol officers: A survey of Pennsylvania municipalities. *Police Quarterly,* 7, 237-261.

28. Anonymous. (2014). 4 stresses cops deal with that non-cops should know about. *Copslife.net.* Retrieved from www.coplife.net/4-stresses-cops-deal-with-that-non-cops-should-know-about/

29. Bonkiewicz, L. (2017). Shooting stars: Estimating the career productivity trajectories of patrol officers. *Police Quarterly,* 20, 164-188.

30. Henry, V.E. (2004). *Death work: Police, trauma, and the psychology of survival.* New York, NY: Oxford University Press, p. 3.

31. Weinblatt.R. (2005). Death notifications: A tough police assignment. *Policelink.* Retrieved from http://policelink.monster.com/training/articles/1927-death-notifications-a-tough-police-assignment

32. Hopkins, C. (2012). *Everything you wanted to know about the heroes in blue.* Raleigh, NC: Lulu, p. 118.

33. Gallo, G. (2001). *Armed and dangerous: Memoirs of a Chicago policewoman.* New York, NY: Forge Book, p. 115.

34. Gallo, G. (2001). *Armed and dangerous: Memoirs of a Chicago policewoman.* New York, NY: Forge Book, p. 22.

35. Gellman, S. (1993). *Cops: The mean and women behind the badge.* Tucson, AZ: Horizon Press, p. 285.

36. Brown, J.A. & Campbell, E.A. (1990). Sources of occupational stress in the police. *Work and Stress,* 4, 305-318; Crank, J.P. & Caldero, M. (1991). The production of occupational stress in medium-sized police agencies: A survey of line officers in eight municipal departments. *Journal of Criminal Justice,* 19, 339-349; Violanti, J.M. & Aron, F. (1993). Sources of police stressors, job attitudes and psychological distress. *Psychological Reports,* 72, 899-904.

37. Rhodes, T.N. (2015). Officers and school settings: Examining the influence of the school environment on officer roles and job satisfaction. *Police Quarterly,* 18, 134-162.

38. Ingram, J.R. & Lee, S.U. (2015). The effect of first-line supervision on patrol officer job satisfaction. *Police Quarterly,* 18, 193-219; Van Craen, M., & Skogan, W.G. (2016). Achieving fairness in policing: The link

between internal and external procedural justice. *Police Quarterly, 20,* 3-23; Reynolds, P.D., Fitzgerald, B.A., & Hicks, J. (2018). The expendables: A qualitative study of police officers' responses to organizational injustice. *Police Quarterly, 21,* 3-29; Violanti, J.M. (2011). Police organizational stress: The impact of negative discipline. *International Journal of Emergency Mental Health, 13,* 31-36; Wolfe, S., Piquero, A. (2011) Organizational justice and police misconduct. *Criminal Justice and Behavior,* 38(4): 332–353.

39. Bell, L.B., Virden, T.B., Lewis, D.J., & Cassidy, B.A. (2015). Effects of 13-hour 20 minute work shifts on law enforcement officers' sleep, cognitive abilities, health, quality of life, and work performance: The phoenix study. *Police Quarterly, 18,* 293-337.

40. Anonymous. (2000). Shift work (love it or hate it?). *Officer.com* Retrieved from http://forums.officer.com/t6013/

41. Dunn, W. (1996). *Boot: An L.A.P.D. officer's rookie year.* New York, NY: William Morrow and Company, Inc., p. 219.

42. Barker, J.C. (1999). *Danger, duty, and disillusion: The worldview of Los Angeles police officers.* Long Grove, IL: Waveland Press, Inc., p. 56.

43. Violanti, J.M. (2006). *Shifts, extended work hours, and fatigue: An assessment of health and personal risks for police officers.* Washington, DC: U.S. Department of Justice.

44. Gallo, G. (2001). *Armed and dangerous: Memoirs of a Chicago policewoman.* New York, NY: Forge Book, p. 24.

45. Gallo, G. (2001). *Armed and dangerous: Memoirs of a Chicago policewoman.* New York, NY: Forge Book, p. 24.

46. Mumford, E.A., Taylor, B.G., & Kubu, B. (2015). Law enforcement officer safety and wellness. *Police Quarterly, 18,* 111-133.

47. Gallo, G. (2001). *Armed and dangerous: Memoirs of a Chicago policewoman.* New York, NY: Forge Book, p. 213.

48. Motorcop. (2014). Confessions of an adrenaline junkie. Motorcopblog.com. Retrieved from http://motorcopblog.com/confessions-adrenaline-junkie/

49. Gallo, G. (2001). *Armed and dangerous: Memoirs of a Chicago policewoman.* New York, NY: Forge Book, pp. 213-214.

50. Motorcop. (2014). Confessions of an adrenaline junkie. *Motorcopblog.com.* Retrieved from http://motorcopblog.com/confessions-adrenaline-junkie/

51. Ballenger, J.F. et al. (2010). Patterns and predictors of alcohol use in male and female urban police officers. *American Journal on Addictions, 20,* 21-29; Swatt, M.L., Gibson, C.L., & Piquero, N.L. (2007). Exploring the utility of general strain theory in explaining problematic alcohol consumption by police officers. *Journal of Criminal Justice, 35,* 596-611.

52. Larson, S.L, Eyerman, J., Foster, M.S., & Gfroerer, J.C. (2007). Worker substance use and workplace policies and programs. Washington, DC: U.S. Department of Health and Human Services; National Institute for Occupational Safety and Health. (2011). *National occupations mortality surveillance.* Atlanta, GA: Centers for Disease Control; See also Gang, V. & Lubin, G. (2011). The 17 jobs where you're most likely to become an alcoholic. *Business Insider.* Retrieved from www.businessinsider.com/most-alcoholic-jobs-2011-10

53. See for instance Carter, D.L. & Stephens, D.W. (1994). An overview of issues concerning police officer drug use. In *Police Deviance,* 3rd ed. Edited by Thomas Barker and David L. Carter (pp. 101-122). Cincinnati, OH: Anderson Publishing.

54. Larson, S.L., Eyerman, J., Foster, M.S., & Gfroerer, J.C. (2007). Worker substance use and workplace policies and programs. Washington, DC: U.S. Department of Health and Human Services.

55. Police-Officer-Pages.com. (2015). Police divorce rates. Retrieved from www.police-officer-pages.com/policedivorcerate.html#axzz3cfSIl86e; See also McCoy, S.P. & Aamodt, M.G. (2010). A comparison of law enforcement divorce rates with those of other occupations. *Journal of Police and Criminal Psychology, 25,* 1-16.

56. Nash, R. (2010). Divorce rate. Officer.com. Retrieved from http://forums.officer.com/t141738/

57. Shannon, J. (2010). The myths and realities of cops and divorce. *Policeone.com* Retrieved from www.policeone.com/off-duty/articles/2140036-P1-First-Person-The-myths-and-realities-of-cops-and-divorce/

58. Remsberg, C. (2013). 7 LEO myths that stress you out and scare your family. *Policeone.com* Retrieved from www.policeone.com/off-duty/articles/6283418-7-LEO-myths-that-stress-you-out-and-scare-your-family/

59. McCoy, S.P. & Aamodt, M.G. (2010). A comparison of law enforcement divorce rates with those of other occupations. *Journal of Police and Criminal Psychology, 25,* 1-16.

60. McCoy, S.P. & Aamodt, M.G. (2010). A comparison of law enforcement divorce rates with those of other occupations. *Journal of Police and Criminal Psychology, 25,* 1-16.

61. McCoy, S.P. & Aamodt, M.G. (2010). A comparison of law enforcement divorce rates with those of other occupations. *Journal of Police and Criminal Psychology, 25,* 1-16, p. 13.

62. McCoy, S.P. & Aamodt, M.G. (2010). A comparison of law enforcement divorce rates with those of other occupations. *Journal of Police and Criminal Psychology, 25,* 1-16, p. 5.

63. Kirschmna, E. (2007). *I love a cop: What police families need to know. Revised edition.* New York, NY: The Guilford Press.

64. See for instance Violanti, J.M., Vena, J.E., & Marshall, J.R. (1986). Disease risk and mortality among police officers. *Journal of Police Science and Administration, 14,* 17-23; Violanti, J.M. & Vena, J.E. (1995). Epidemiology of police suicide. *Research in Progress.* Washington, DC: National Institute of Mental Health.

65. Stack, S. & Kelley, T. (1999). Police suicide. In *Police and Policing: Contemporary Issues,* 2nd ed., edited by D.J. Kenney and R.P. McNamara (pp. 94-107). Westport, CT: Prager.

66. The Badge of Life. (2015). The Badge of Life: Psychological Survival for Police Officers. Retrieved from http://www.badgeoflife.com/

67. Greenhut, S. (2014). Police and fire continue to promote "early death" fiction. *Public Sector Inc.* Retrieved from www.publicsectorinc.org/2014/08/police-and-fire-continue-to-promote-their-early-death-untruth/; Greenhut, S. (2009). Police pensions and voodoo actuarials. *Newgeography.* Retrieved from www.newgeography.

com/content/001145-police-pensions-and-voodoo-actuarials; Remsberg, C. (2013). 7 LEO myths that stress you out and scare your family. *Policeone.com* Retrieved from www.policeone.com/off-duty/articles/6283418-7-LEO-myths-that-stress-you-out-and-scare-your-family/

68. Greenhut, S. (2009). Police pensions and voodoo actuarials. *Newgeography.* Retrieved from www.newgeography.com/content/001145-police-pensions-and-voodoo-actuarials

69. Greenhut, S. (2014). Police and fire continue to promote 'early death' fiction. *Public Sector Inc.* Retrieved from www.publicsectorinc.org/2014/08/police-and-fire-continue-to-promote-their-early-death-untruth/

70. Gallo, G. (2001). *Armed and Dangerous: Memoirs of a Chicago policewoman.* New York, NY: Forge Book, p. 322.

71. Osborne, S. (2015). *The Job: True tales form the life of a New York city cop.* New York, NY: Doubleday, p. 4.

72. Baker, M. (1985). Cops: Their lives in their own words. New York, NY: Pocket Books, p. 349.

73. Baker, M. (1985). Cops: Their lives in their own words. New York, NY: Pocket Books, p. 357.

74. Copes, H. (2004). *Policing and stress.* Upper Saddle River, NJ: Prentice Hall; Toch, H. (2002). *Stress in policing.* Washington, DC: American Psychological Association.

75. Barker, J.C. (1999). *Danger, duty, and disillusion: The worldview of Los Angeles police officers.* Long Grove, IL: Waveland Press, Inc., p. 118.

76. Barker, J.C. (1999). *Danger, duty, and disillusion: The worldview of Los Angeles police officers.* Long Grove, IL: Waveland Press, Inc., p. 118.

77. Klinger, D. (2004). *Into the kill zone: A cop's eye view of deadly force.* San Francisco, CA: Jossey-Bass, pp. 231-232.

78. Barker, J.C. (1999). *Danger, duty, and disillusion: The worldview of Los Angeles police officers.* Long Grove, IL: Waveland Press, Inc., pp. 118-119.

79. Barker, J.C. (1999). *Danger, duty, and disillusion: The worldview of Los Angeles police officers.* Long Grove, IL: Waveland Press, Inc., p. 118.

80. Copes, H. (2004). *Policing and stress.* Upper Saddle River, NJ: Prentice Hall; Toch, H. (2002). *Stress in policing.* Washington, DC: American Psychological Association; Loo, R. (1986). Suicide among police in a federal force. *Suicide and Life-Threatening Behavior, 16,* 379-388; Schiraldi, G. (2009). *The post-traumatic stress disorder sourcebook: A guide to healing, recovery, and growth.* 2nd ed. New York, NY: McGraw Hill.

81. Loo, R. (1986). Suicide among police in a federal force. *Suicide and Life-Threatening Behavior, 16,* 379-388.

82. Dunn, William. (1996). *Boot: An L.A.P.D. officer's rookie year.* New York, NY: William Morrow and Company, Inc., p. 7.

83. Centers for Disease Control. (2015). Managing Stress. Retrieved from www.cdc.gov/features/handlingstress/

84. Rhodes, T.N. (2015). Officers and school settings: Examining the influence of the school environment on officer roles and job satisfaction. *Police Quarterly, 18,* 134-162.

85. Dunn, William. (1996). *Boot: An L.A.P.D. officer's rookie year.* New York, NY: William Morrow and Company, Inc.

86. Centers for Disease Control and Prevention. (2015). Physical Activity. Retrieved from www.cdc.gov/physicalactivity/index.html; Quigley, A. (2008). Fit for duty? The need for physical fitness programs for law enforcement officers. *The Police Chief.* Retrieve from www.police-chiefmagazine.org/magazine/index.cfm?fuseaction=display_arch&article_id=1516&issue_id=62008; Ruiz, J. & Hummer, D. (2008). *Handbook of police administration.* Boca Raton, FL: CRC Press.

87. Centers for Disease Control and Prevention. (2015). Alcohol and public health. Retrieved from www.cdc.gov/alcohol/index.htm

88. Cooperman, A., et. al (2016). *Religion in everday life.* Washington, DC: Pre Research Center; Ellison, C.G. & Levin, J.S. (1998). The religion-health connection: Evidence, theory, and future directions. *Health Education & Behavior, 25,* 700-720.

89. Watson, R. (2012). Activity, sex, laughter and meditation are stress relief secrets. *Psychology Today.* Retrieved from www.psychologytoday.com/blog/love-and-gratitude/201207/activity-sex-laughter-and-meditation-are-stress-relief-secrets

90. Gallo, G. (2001). *Armed and dangerous: Memoirs of a Chicago policewoman.* New York, NY: Forge Book, p. 242.

91. Nawijn, J., Marchand, M.A., Veenhoven, R., & Vingerhoets, A.J. (2010). Vacationers happier, but most not happier after a holiday. *Applied Research in Quality of Life, 5,* 35-47; Vindum, T. (2011). Reduce stress in the great outdoors. Retrieved from www.athleta.net/2011/02/23/reduce-stress-in-the-great-outdoors/

92. Rosen, M. (2012). Camping resets internal clock. *Science News.* Retrieved from www.sciencenews.org/article/camping-resets-internal-clock

93. Gallo, G. (2001). *Armed and dangerous: Memoirs of a Chicago policewoman.* New York, NY: Forge Book, p. 98.

94. Mitchell, J.T. & Everly, G.S., Jr. (2001). *Critical incident stress debriefing: An operations manual for CISD, Defusing and other group crisis intervention services.* Columbia, MD: Chevron Publishing Corporation.

95. Clark, D.W. & Haley, M. (2007). Crisis response tools for law enforcement. *The Police Chief.* Retrieved from www.policechiefmagazine.org/magazine/index.cfm?fuseaction=display_arch&article_id=1245&issue_id=82007; Madonna, J.M., Jr., & Kelly, R.E. (2002). *Treating police stress: The work and the words of peer counselors.* Springfield, IL: Charles C. Thomas Publisher, LTD.

96. Blesdsoe, B.E. (2003). Critical incident stress management (CISM): Benefit or risk for emergency services? *Prehospital Emergency Care, 7,* 272-279; Emmerik, V., Kamphuis, J.H., Hulsbosch, A.M., & Emelkamp, P.M.G (2002). Single-session debriefing after psychological trauma: A meta-analysis. *Lancet, 360,* 766–771; Kagee, A. (2002). Concerns about the effectiveness of critical incident stress debriefing in ameliorating stress reactions. *Critical Care, 6,* 88-96; Rose R., Bisson J., & Wessley S. (2002). Psychological debriefing for preventing post-traumatic stress disorder (PTSD). *Cochrane Review, 2,* The Cochrane Library.

■ *"There are . . . policemen who take their jobs seriously. They are found both in executive positions and in the ranks. They are honest men and they are willing to die for their country. They have the same feeling of doing their duty as policemen as the soldier on the firing line. Policemen with that kind of attitude are a real bulwark against criminals. They are doing a good job of policing, but the public forgets their achievements too soon."*[1] —August Vollmer

One of the current issues in policing is the adoption of body-worn cameras.

CHAPTER 15

Issues

After reading this chapter, you will be able to:

1. Identify the four components of PEST and define each.
2. Explain the modern political concept that the police should reflect the community they serve and discuss the pros and cons.
3. Describe the modern economic constraints faced by police departments and how that relates to the militarization of the police.
4. Discuss what is meant by the term "the Ferguson effect" and how that relates to the concept of depolicing.
5. Describe and discuss the modern calls for the police to adopt body cameras and their pros and cons.

August Vollmer often lamented how the police were treated by the media and the public. He lived at a time when movies depicted the police as idiots and buffoons (for example, the *Keystone Cops*), and public attitude toward the police was very negative, perceiving all officers as brutal and corrupt. Vollmer saw another side of many police officers, that they were people who wanted to do good, and they worked hard to do their duty for the benefit of their communities. As discussed throughout this book, not much has changed. The media, whether it is television, motion pictures, or the news, often portrays police as corrupt and brutal, and public opinion of the police is often mixed.

Vollmer argued that one of the most difficult aspects of policing was that there were so many external influences on the police and that it was these types of issues that put the most strain on the police. He commonly railed against politicians interfering with police chiefs and using police departments for political purposes. Yet, politics is not the only type of external influence on the police, there are actually four significant categories of external influences and they go by the acronym PEST.

PEST stands for **political, economic, social, and technological.**[2] It is an acronym that is used as a means of looking at the larger external influences on any public policy or organization, and they have just as much bearing on the police. Political issues include government influences over the police, such as laws and court decisions that tell the police what they can and cannot do, as well as public opinion and media perspectives of the police. Economic issues include the influences that money can have on the police, whether through budget increases or, more likely, budget cuts, as well as grant-funding opportunities. Social influences include our changing American culture and how it prompts the police to change how they carry out their mission, or how changes in culture may change the police mission itself. Finally, technology, which is a neutral entity, but can be used for good or bad by different parties, usually raises issues centered on freedom versus security in America. These four external influences over the police are often the source of many of the issues facing America's police today.

While there are many issues in policing, the purpose of this chapter is not to raise every possible issue in American policing today (that would generate a whole other book), but to only raise one in each of the four PEST categories. By doing that, it will allow for the issues to be explored more deeply than just the sort of "drive by" news media soundbites that we often hear on the news or read on the Internet. Each of the issues was selected because it was currently in the news at the time of the writing of this book, and they are issues that will no doubt continue to be raised for many years to come.

The political issue will center on the public calls, often by the news media and social commenters, arguing that the police departments should reflect the communities they police, especially in terms of sex, gender, race, and ethnicity. The economic issue will look at the problem of agency budget cuts over the past 20 years and how that has led police departments down the path of actively participating in the military equipment program, which many have argued has contributed to the militarization of the police. The social issue is one that has most recently (2015) been dubbed "the Ferguson effect" and that is the relationship between the police and the community, especially in minority communities. And, finally, the technological issue is one that has been raised as a possible solution to the social issue, and that is the deployment of police officer body cameras.

PEST defined.

Political—The Police Should Reflect the Community They Serve

There has been a continued call in recent years for the police in America to reflect the community that they serve.[3] Even U.S. Attorney General Eric Holder has weighed in on this topic by publicly stating, "Police forces should reflect the diversity of the communities they serve."[4] The public seems to agree. In one survey, it was found that 70 percent of respondents believed that the racial composition of the police department should be the same as or similar to their communities.[5] As one of the authors of the study, Ronald Weitzer, explained, "Ethnic minorities favor reforming police departments so that they reflect the composition of the local population."[6]

In many police departments in America, there is an imbalance in the number of minority officers to minority population (not to mention an overwhelming imbalance in the number of female officers to the female population). For instance, in Baltimore, Maryland, the population is 28 percent white, while the police department is 50 percent white.[7] In Philadelphia, the population is 37 percent white, but the police department is composed of 58 percent white. In fact, out of the 50 most populous cities in the United States, 49 of them have more white police officers than citizens on a percentage basis. The only exception is the Atlanta Police Department.

Some of the most racially imbalanced police include Jersey City, New Jersey, where the department is 44 percent more white than its citizens. Other highly disparate police departments include Sacramento, California; Buffalo, New York; and Cleveland, Ohio.[8] Some of the most representative police departments have been found to be Brownsville, Texas; Los Angeles, California and Colorado Springs, Colorado.[9]

While in most cases, the disparities assessed are for black officers to black citizens, one recent analysis has found a much larger disparity when it comes to Hispanic officers.[10] For instance, in Waco, Texas, where the community is more than 30 percent Hispanic, only 27 of the 231 police officers are Hispanic, or less than 12 percent.[11] Sheriff Adrian Garcia of the Harris County Sheriff's Office in Texas explained, "It is one of the challenges that I inherited," when he was elected sheriff.[12] Although he qualified his statement by saying "I do not think a police department that does not look like the community it protects is more prone to discrimination than more racially diverse departments." He

NYPD Community Affairs unit officer meeting with citizens at a community event.

did articulate that, "It leaves that perception. As long as the community can point and say, 'There's no one that looks like me, and as a result, I feel I was treated unjustly,' it opens up the argument that maybe the policies are short-sighted in how you work with a diverse community."[13]

Sheriff Garcia's comment is also echoed by Police Chief Edward Flynn of the Milwaukee Police Department, for he explains, "When it comes to role models or empathy, it would certainly be extraordinarily valuable if the police force could reflect our communities. We all want community acceptance. We all recognize that makes us more effective."[14] Or, as Police Chief Thomas Wydra of the Hamden Police Department in Connecticut explained, when a police department looks like the community it serves, "That gives the department legitimacy."[15] That is one of the fundamental reasons for police departments to look like the community it serves; it gives the department legitimacy in the eyes of the community in order to better perform their job (see Box 15.1).

Box 15.1 History in Practice: Joseph D. McNamara, Father of Community Policing

A New York City Police officer who walked a beat, eventually earned a doctorate from Harvard University, and became a police chief for two major police departments in the nation, **Joseph D. McNamara** is often considered to have been policing's **Father of Community Policing.**

McNamara was born and raised in New York City and became a NYPD beat cop patrolling the streets of Harlem. He rose through the ranks while furthering his education, and at one point, he was given a criminal justice fellowship to study at Harvard University's law school. He eventually attended the Kennedy School of Government at Harvard, earning his Ph.D. in public administration. In 1973, McNamara became the police chief of Kansas City (Missouri) Police Department, the department instrumental in both the Kansas City Preventive Patrol Experiment and the Kansas City Rapid Response study. In 1976, he was appointed the police chief of the San Jose (California) Police Department where he served until his retirement in 1991.

During his time at Kansas City and San Jose, McNamara experimented with various aspects of **police and community relations**, **neighborhood watch**, and **police-community partnerships**. He also explored the concepts of Herman Goldstein's **problem-oriented policing**. His ideas were far ahead of his time and were often ridiculed, but he persevered and with the **community policing** movement taking hold in the late 1980s and 1990s, he was somewhat vindicated. When policing moved toward focusing on officer safety, homeland security, and the militarization of the police, he was an ardent opponent.

Never one to sit still long, in retirement McNamara lectured across the country, wrote a crime prevention textbook, and several detective novels that still make for good reads.

McNamara passed away from pancreatic cancer on September 19, 2014.

Source: McNamara, J.D (2015). Joseph D. McNamara website. Retrieved from http://www.josephdmcnamaracopnoir.com/.

There are many other reasons given for why police departments should reflect the communities they serve. As Weitzer explains, "This can pay dividends in terms of increasing public trust and confidence in a police department. What the public is critical of are departments that are lopsided."[16] Another reason is as Catherine Sanz, the president of Women in Federal Law Enforcement Foundation, said, "When you talk to somebody from your community, there's a lot of things you don't have to say to each other. There's this connectivity."[17] A further reason is given by retired New York Police Sergeant Joseph Giacalone when he said, "We have to have a jury of our peers, so we like to have a police department of our peers. I'm a strong proponent of diversified police departments. I mean you have to have them. It's crazy not to have them in 2015."[18] And, as the Executive Director of the National Organization of Black Law Enforcement Executives explained, "It is important that diversity be reflected within the faces of the organizations. You need to make sure you are marketing your product in a way that it can attract those that are interested in buying your product."[19]

While citizens appear to overwhelmingly voice their support that police officers should reflect the community they serve, it has been pointed out that there is never a similar call for other public service occupations.[20] In other words, no one ever states that in order to improve our public schools, garbage collection, or social services that school teachers, garbage collectors, or social workers should reflect the community they serve. It appears that only the police are subject to this reform.

Another factor that has been noted in regard to the attempt at trying to make police departments more reflective of their communities is that it may not necessarily improve police-community relations. Some of the police departments that are most reflective of their local populations are not well known for having good police-community relations, such as the Los Angeles Police Department (LAPD) or the New Orleans Police Department.[21] As one citizen commented about the LAPD becoming more diverse, "They just cleaned up their act a little. Before it was white against blacks. Now it's just blue against blacks."[22]

It should also be considered that often the policies of trying to make people feel more comfortable by having officers that are similar to them respond to their calls has itself created discriminatory practices. For instance, when a female suspect is taken into custody, very often female police officers are called out of their patrol areas to handle the call so that a female officer is with a female suspect (or victim). This discriminates against the female officer for she is not allowed to patrol like her male counterparts, because she is beholden to responding to other officers' need for a female officer. Put another way, no department known pulls a male police officer out of his beat because a female officer arrested a male suspect. The same type of discrimination can occur when black officers are only assigned to black neighborhoods, while white officers are rotated through various neighborhoods assignments.

One aspect of the relationship between black citizens and police officers should be noted here. If you recall from Chapter 6, there was a distinct difference between how blacks and whites viewed the police with blacks consistently more likely than whites to hold unfavorable views of the police.[23] Additionally, many black citizens not only do not like white police officers, they often have even more negative views of black police officers. As one 25-year veteran of the Birmingham (Alabama) Police Department, Dexter Cunningham, a black officer, has explained when he has shown up on calls with black citizens, "I've been called an Uncle Tom and a sellout."[24] This then raises the question of whether black citizens even want more black officers patrolling their communities.

The evidence would suggest that the percentage of blacks wanting exclusively black police officers to patrol in their communities has never been overwhelmingly high. For instance, one study found that only 12 percent of blacks in Detroit wanted all-black officers.[25] Another in Milwaukee found it was 33 percent, whereas in Denver it was only 8 percent.[26] Another study, looking at three neighborhoods in Washington, D.C., found that those wanting all-black officers were 13 percent, 5 percent, and 0 percent, based on the community. The last study used in-depth interviews and one reason given for not wanting all-black officers in an all-black neighborhood was put in this manner: "It's amazing but white officers are far more courteous to black people than black officers are . . . . White officer, when he comes to you [he says] 'I'm sorry, sir, but you ran that red light,' or 'Sir, you're doing this, that, and the other thing.' But the black officer, he's in charge, you see . . . the arrogance that black officers have about being in authority."[27] Another female interviewed described it in a similar fashion when she said, "If the police force in [Washington] D.C. was white, I would say that was racial, but with the police force being black here in [Washington] D.C., I feel that they feel they have to be harder on Blacks to show White people that, 'Hey, we're not showing any favoritism.'"[28]

Despite the overwhelming call for police departments to accurately reflect their community, when people are asked about whether they would like all-black officers or all-white officers in a black neighborhood, the people generally conclude, "I think [mixed] teams create the necessary interaction with the residents. If you have an all-white team you could probably have a racial situation . . . if you have all blacks, you have a situation where there's complacency in the sense that they can conduct themselves any way that they choose because they're not being governed. If you have the balance, then perhaps you'd have a good relationship."[29] In fact, that was the overall conclusion of Weitzer's study, that while "the conventional wisdom and prevailing public policy in the United States presumes" that the police should racially reflect the community, "there was little support for assigning mostly same-race officers to the neighborhoods."[30]

After interviewing Washington, D.C., residents about their desires, Weitzer further concluded, "With respect to the behavior of white and black officers, many respondents subscribed to the 'blue cops' principle that occupation outweighs racial identity."[31] Another scholar that has looked into the research has found, "There are studies finding that black officers shoot just as often as white officers; that black officers arrest just as often as white officers; that black officers are often prejudiced against black citizens; that black officers get less cooperation than white officers from black citizens."[32] Indeed, there is ample evidence to show that race usually does not play a role in officer decision making. One 2004 study by the National Research Council found that there is no strong statistical correlation between the race of the officer and how officers treat citizens.[33] Another study found that while the racial makeup of a community had an impact on police violence, the proportion of minority police officers to white police officers in a department "had no significant influence on levels of police violence."[34] As Brad Smith, the author of the study explained, "Regardless of who is carrying out the police function, police will always be seen as representatives of the larger establishment. As such, tensions between police and citizens may be a function of the police role."[35]

Also, drawing from the discussion regarding police decision making from Chapter 7, recall that most of the studies have found that whether a police officer is white or black, male or female, they all respond in a similar manner. There are some studies that have suggested there is a difference, but they tend to demonstrate that black officers are more likely to arrest black suspects and female officers are more likely to arrest female suspects, but the vast majority of studies have found no differences between police officers.[36] As one author concluded, "The color of the uniform may be more significant than the color of the skin."[37] Simply put: A cop is a cop is a cop. They are not black or white, male or female, but rather, they are occupation oriented; they are all blue.

The outcome of this, then, should be made clear. Even if a police department accurately reflected a community by race, ethnicity, sex, and gender, there is no evidence that it would make any difference in the way police officers police. In fact, one individual who works with gangs and the police in Southern California has explained the reality of calling in a minority officer when she explained: "When brown or black people are being apprehended or responding to white officers, a Latino officer will always be brought in to negotiate, and seem to speak from a place of empathy, when they're really just conveying the same thing."[38] In other words, rather than the Latino police officer acting with empathy for the Latino suspect as envisioned by those desiring to have the police reflect the community, in reality, they have just another police officer treating the suspect in the same manner as a white, black, or female officer would have because there is little difference among police officers.

This raises a number of concerns. Police Officer Kong Lee, an officer with a Hmong background hired to police a Hmong community, voiced one of his concerns when he said, "I hope we don't get to the point where we're hiring based on race. You just want the best person for the job, regardless if they speak Hmong, Arabic, or Spanish."[39] This is a legitimate concern for already a number of police departments have been found to have lowered their standards in order to higher more minority candidates, and more recently Attorney General Eric Holder has ordered the Dayton Police Department to lower its standards for that very purpose.[40] When a department lowers its standards for who may be hired as a police officer, this benefits neither the police department nor the citizens.

The bottom line with this political issue is that despite the seemingly high demand that police departments should reflect the communities they serve, when people are interviewed about the proper race of the police in their neighborhoods, they seemingly call for a mixed race response, not an all or the other. And, even if we can achieve the most difficult goal of hiring a racially representative or even ethnic, sex, and gender representative police department, because research has consistently demonstrated there is little difference among police officers, there is a strong likelihood that it may do nothing to change police-community relations, and some suggest that it may actually harm this relationship. Clearly, this is a very debatable issue.

Economic—The Unintended Consequences of Fiscal Constraints

There is ample evidence to suggest that over the past 20 years, police departments in America have been facing an economic crisis.[41] The more recent economic recession in America, which began in 2007 and resulted from the housing bubble bursting, has placed even more undue pressure on police department budgets. These agencies have resorted to a number of budgetary changes from simple things such as limiting overtime, hiring freezes, and disbanding special units, to more radical large-scale changes such as contracting, consolidation, multi-tasking, cross-training, civilianization of police duties, officers taking over civilian duties, sharing resources, and external grants, all as a means for dealing with the budgetary problems.[42]

It should be noted that while police department budgets have increased, rising from $55 billion in 2008 to $62 billion in 2013, the costs of everything from salaries, health care, and equipment have also risen.[43] In fact, it is estimated that there are slightly fewer police officers in 2013 than there were in 2008 due to lay-offs and hiring freezes. For a long time period, 1995-2007, police budgets were propped up by federal government grants for community policing under the COPS bill of 1994, but after September 11, 2001, many of those grants shifted to homeland security. Although police departments were still eligible for some of those grants, it required a refocus of police services (see Box 15.2).

Listening to many of the police executives, one can come to understand the problems that the police face. "We are preparing to lay off 167 police officers," explained Newark, New Jersey, Police Director Garry McCarthy.[44] "It wasn't fat that we had to cut; it was effective crime reduction strategies."[45]

Box 15.2 Ethics in Practice: Government Budgets and the Police

A large portion of a government's budget is dedicated the police. In some instances, the proportion of tax revenue that is dedicated to the police department can be from 15 percent to as much as 65 percent, depending upon the government and the agency. It is often said that one of the most important functions of government is to provide security. How far should governments go to provide funding for its police force?

Every agency, including every police agency, is cash strapped. Police departments can help the government raise revenues by issuing more tickets, but they do not necessarily get more budgetary funds if they write more tickets. There are some ways in which police departments can obtain external funding—funding that comes outside of tax revenue—such as donations, asset forfeiture programs, military equipment programs, and grant funding from other governments and foundations.

Ask Yourself:

Should police departments receive additional funding from the budget if they write more tickets? Explain your reasoning.

Should police departments be authorized and encouraged to receive external funding or should they be relegated to only receiving budgetary allowances from tax revenues? Explain your answer.

Police Chief Charles Ramsey of the Philadelphia Police Department described his problems in that, "Basically, we have a freeze on civilian employees," and "My last two academy classes have been cancelled."[46] And, Police Director Jonathan Monken of the Illinois State Police detailed his budgetary problems when he said, "Out of a $450 million budget, we've been cut about $40 million over the last two years."[47] Police departments all over are facing fiscal exigencies.

While there are many issues that could be raised regarding the economic issues facing police departments, the particular issue to be dealt with here is an unintended consequence of state, municipal, and county budgetary crises on state, local, and county police agencies. In particular, the one issue that is constantly in the news these days is in part due to these fiscal constraints and that is the **militarization of the police**.[48]

While it would not seem that budgetary issues would have much to do with the militarization of the police, the reality is when police departments face internal budgetary problems, they can only do so much internally before they

The difference between military equipment and police equipment has become less defined in recent decades.

begin looking externally for other sources of "external funding" or "alternative revenue streams."[49] In many cases, police departments will apply for state and federal grants in order to obtain additional funding or equipment. One such grant program arose at the same time as an identified need among police departments in the United States. This would ultimately contribute to the militarization of the police.[50] And it all began in a small town called Columbine.

On April 20, 1999, two senior students at Columbine High School in Columbine, Colorado, murdered 12 fellow students and a teacher and wounded an additional 21 people.[51] The police response was to secure the perimeter and wait for the SWAT team to assemble before entering the school. There was a 45-minute delay in assembling the regional SWAT team, which was cobbled together from multiple agencies, and by the time they entered the school, the two students, Eric Harris and Dylan Klebold, had shot and killed their victims and themselves. Policing changed because of this tragedy, moving to an active shooter policy in which all officers arriving on scene of an active shooting in progress should move toward the shooter—a policy that fit with the police officer sheepdog mentality.[52]

Another result of Columbine was the growth of departments, no matter how small, having their own SWAT teams so as not to have to wait for a regional SWAT team to assemble. SWAT teams were already growing in America because of the war on drugs, but they began to proliferate.[53] Still further, after September 11, 2001, there was even more of an incentive to continue growing these special units. Along the way, however, police departments, often in the name of rising violent crime, the war on drugs, or homeland security, began moving toward a SWAT mentality for all of its officers, what has been dubbed the militarization of the police.

One of the major issues revolving around the creation and maintenance of SWAT teams, or the movement of an entire police department toward a more prepared role for extreme violence, was a lack of funding. One temporary source of funding was created after Operation Desert Storm, in which excess military equipment was authorized to be given to state and local police departments and was known as the 1208 program.[54] The program proved so successful and popular with police departments that took advantage of the opportunity that a more permanent program was created in 1997 and became known as the 1033 program, which still exists today.

This programs "permits the Secretary of Defense to transfer, without charge, excess U.S. Department of Defense personal property (supplies and equipment) to state and local law enforcement agencies."[55] Since its commencement in 1997, it is estimated that the federal government has transferred more than $4.3 billion in equipment and that in 2013 alone it moved "half a billion dollars" of military equipment.[56] Just in the Obama Administration alone, "According to Pentagon data, police departments have received tens of thousands of machine guns; nearly 200,000 ammunition magazines; thousands of pieces of camouflage and night-vision equipment; and hundreds of silencers, armored cars, and aircraft."[57]

There have been many who have praised the 1033 program, seeing it as a solution to the budgetary constraints of many police departments across the country, as well as assisting them in preparing for major incidents like Columbine. While Kevin E. Wilkins, the police chief of a small town department in Neenah, Wisconsin, lamented "I don't like it. I wish it were the way it was when I was a kid," he goes on to say, "We're not going to go out there as Officer Friendly with no body armor and just a handgun and say 'Good enough.'"[58] In fact, the primary justification for taking on the military equipment is for officer safety. Sheriff Doug Cox of the Johnson County Sheriff's Office in Indiana, when explaining the Mine Resistant Ambush Protected (MRAP), which is "a bulletproof, 55,000-pound, six-wheeled behemoth with heavy armor, a gunner's turret, and the word 'SHERIFF' emblazoned on its flank," that his department obtained, he first acquiesced, "We don't have a lot of mines in Johnson County," but he went on to say, "My job is to make sure my employees go home safe."[59] Still, another police executive, Deputy Chief David Lutz of the Edinburgh Police Department, explains it with even more advocacy when he said, "Oh, yeah, anything for the safety of the officers. SWAT is after the worst of the worst. It's what they do."[60] He went on to describe in one SWAT call out that, "Pretty soon, here comes this massive, intimidating truck. I'm thinking, that's almost a tank. I could not imagine what the guy inside the house would think. Can you imagine seeing that, how intimidating that would be? Everybody was in awe."[61]

Many police executives, like Pulaski County Sheriff Michael Gayer, have also articulated the need for the equipment in terms of a changing situation in America. "The United States of America has become a war zone," he said.[62] "There's violence in the workplace, there's violence in schools, and there's violence in the streets. You are seeing police departments going to a semi-military format because of the threats we have to counteract. If driving a military vehicle is going to protect officers, then that's what I'm going to do."[63] While Captain Chris Cowan of the Richland County Sheriff's Department in South Carolina argued that by obtaining one of the large military vehicles it "allows the department to stay in step with the criminals who are arming themselves more heavily every day," and he noted that there was also a community benefit as well, because when displayed at schools and community events it becomes a conversation starter, "All of a sudden, we start relationships with people."[64] Captain Tiger Parsons of the Buchanan County Sheriff's Department explains that even when some people are a bit hesitant about the use of the military equipment, "When you explain that you're preparing for something that may never happen, they get it."[65] This falls under the old adage of "prepare for the worst, hope for the best." In this case, prepare for the worst case terrorist scenario, but hope you never have it occur.

Others, such as Andy Skoogman of the Minnesota Chiefs of Police Association has presented it more pragmatically by explaining, "The equipment comes from the military, but it is not being used in Minnesota in most cases in that type of traditional military fashion."[66] For instance, he explains,

"It provides officers with equipment, guns, and night-vision goggles to help solve crimes as well as keep citizens safe. It provides office equipment that many departments and cities cannot afford. It provides fitness equipment that keeps officers in shape and in good health."[67] Assistant Chief of Police Jim Rhodes of the Anderson Police Department has argued in a similar fashion, when he stated, "All of it is a legitimate tool for legitimate law enforcement functions. It makes us safer. Ironically, it makes the suspects safer."[68] He also made the argument that "All of this stuff is just sitting there in storage. Our taxpayers paid for that. Why can't we give some of that back to the local communities?"[69]

Another Police Chief, Phil Johanson from the Anoka Police Department, tries to explain that there really is a lot of misconceptions about the equipment police departments are obtaining. For instance, in one case his department is listed as having a grenade launcher, but "It's actually not a grenade launcher; it's a 37mm gas launcher for tear gas . . . it's a single shot that could be used to deploy tear gas to hopefully get (a suspect) to come out if we had a hostage or barricaded subject, maybe an active shooter situation."[70]

Some, however, have perhaps taken the argument a bit far when it comes to articulating the safety of the police officers argument, when Sgt. Dan Downing of the Morgan County Sheriff's Department stated, "You have a lot of people who are coming out of the military that have the ability and knowledge to build [improvised explosive devices] and to defeat law enforcement techniques."[71] Despite articulating that every military soldier may be mentally unstable and has the ability to blow things up, the point is that any argument in the name of officer safety is a justifiable argument for securing any and all of the military equipment.

There are many people, however, including officers, who do not see the military equipment as acceptable for the police. A citizen from the small Wisconsin town of Neenah perhaps described the argument against his small town agency's militarization when he noted, "It just seems like ramping up a police department for a problem we don't have."[72] He further explained, "This is not what I was looking for when I moved here, that my children would view their local police officer as an M-16 toting, SWAT-apparel-wearing officer."[73]

Not all police executives support the militarization of the police either. Chief Chris Burbank of the Salt Lake City Police Department has said, "We're not the military, nor should we look like an invading force coming in."[74] Keeping the police and the military separate is typically one of the greatest arguments against the militarization of the police. While there are indeed similarities, the reality is the end goals of the two organizations are vastly different (see Chapter 1).

Another argument against the militarization of the police, by the police, is actually the same argument made *for* the militarization and that is officer safety. One former LAPD officer explained, "Captains like to attack even the smallest problem, like a domestic dispute, with overwhelming force. Swamping makes them feel safer but it also increases the chances of stuff going bad."[75] In other words, when too much force is brought to bear on a problem, there is an increased chance that that force will be used in a situation that could have been prevented. Instead of deescalating problems, police, in their military gear and tactics, end up escalating the situation. A retired police detective, John Baeza, from the NYPD, describes the issue in this manner: "A profession that I was once proud to serve in has become a militarized police state. Officers are quicker to draw their guns and use their tanks than to communicate with people to diffuse a situation. They love to use their toys and when they do, people die. The days of the peace officer are long gone, replaced by the militarized police warrior wearing uniforms making them indistinguishable from military personnel."[76] He succinctly concludes, "Once something is defined as a 'war' everyone becomes a 'warrior.'"[77]

In addition, while many who argue for the militarization argue that America has changed for the worst or become a war zone, crime statistics do not bear this statement out. In fact, America has seen some of the lowest crime rates since the FBI began collecting the data, with current crime rates equaling 1960 rates. Still further, while many argue that the military equipment is a conversation starter, it is not a justification for the equipment. And responding to the fact that militarized equipment is often popular with the children of today and creates a conversation when they go to the schools, the Police Chief of South Bend, Indiana, Ronald E. Teachman, put it this way: "I go to schools, but I bring *Green Eggs and Ham*."[78]

The issue of the militarization of the police has caught the attention of many law makers across the country as well. One state senator in Minnesota, Branden Petersen, has spoken out against the militarization of the police in his state saying, "You get these pictures that just shock the conscience."[79] He has proposed a bill that would prevent the state local police agencies from receiving 1033 equipment. Similar bills have been introduced in California, Connecticut, Montana, Tennessee, and Vermont. And United States Senator Rand Paul has also spoken out against the 1033 program arguing that it "has incentivized the militarization of local police precincts and helped municipal governments build what are essentially small armies."[80]

In the wake of Ferguson (see the next section), with the visible evidence of the 1033 program equipment obtained by the Ferguson Police Department on display, there was an outspoken cry for change. President Obama addressed the issue by explaining, "We've seen how militarized gear can sometimes give people a feeling like they're an occupying force as opposed to a force that's part of the community that's protecting them and serving them," and that it can "alienate and intimidate local residents and may send the wrong message."[81] He then explained to the American people, "So, we're going to prohibit some equipment made for the battlefield that is not appropriate for local police departments."[82] Despite the move to ban some equipment by way of executive order, it has been noted that what was banned, "Tracked armored vehicles, firearms and ammunition of .50 caliber or higher, grenade launchers . . . bayonets, and camouflage uniforms," were mostly items that were not obtained by police departments to begin with and will have little impact on the 1033 program.[83] It has also been noted that the executive order does not prevent the police departments from obtaining those items through other external sources, some of them federal, or by paying for them out of their own budget. Yet, as Sheriff Amerson of Calhoun County (AL) stated when he found out he had to return the M-113 armored vehicle he was given, "Now, if we have an active-shooter situation with an armed person, we don't have any piece of equipment to move in safely for my deputies or the people I'm sworn to protect."[84] Sheriff Bouchard of Oakland County (MI), also lamented the fact his agency had to return its bayonets, which were often used by deputies to cut through seatbelts after car crashes, "There's no police department in America that fixes bayonets to rifles and charges into a crowd. I mean, if you can trust our folks with a semiautomatic handgun, you can't trust them with a knife?"

The bottom line with this economic issue is that when there is an opportunity for cash-strapped agencies to obtain either funding or equipment through external sources, they are going to take it. The question becomes whether or not the securing of military equipment is acceptable for police departments in the United States. And, of course, once securing the equipment does it truly make the police officers safer, is it good for community relations, and does it cause the agency to change its tactics and style of policing, one that has seemingly become more militarized?

Social—The Ferguson Effect

On August 9, 2014, Officer Darren Wilson of the Ferguson Police Department in Missouri had just left a medical call and was driving down the street when he saw a group of young men, black males, walking down the middle of the street. He asked them to walk on the sidewalk, and when they ignored him, he pulled over to conduct a stop. During that stop, an altercation broke out, and it is at that point that accounts of what happened began to vary.

Some said that the officer attacked one of the males, Michael Brown, and a struggle ensued. Michael Brown tried to escape from the violent police officer, and when the officer drew his weapons, he put up his hands as if to say "don't shoot." Brown was then shot and killed in cold blood, dying on the streets of Ferguson.

Others, including Officer Wilson, said that Brown attacked him before he even exited his vehicle, by pinning him inside his vehicle and reaching through the window for his gun. A struggle

The police shooting of Michael Brown in Ferguson, Missouri, sparked widespread protests against the police, which some have argued as created "the Ferguson effect" in policing.

ensued over the weapon, and it was discharged from inside the vehicle. Brown then turned to run, and Wilson exited the vehicle to give chase. Brown then stopped, turned, and charged Officer Wilson, who then shot and killed him in self-defense.

Protests over the police shooting developed into violent demonstrations and rioting over the next several days. Sympathetic protests then began to spread across America. A grand jury was convened to look at the evidence and no less than three autopsies were performed on Michael Brown. Indirectly, the officer pleaded his case, but ultimately resigned from the police department because of the public outcry over the shooting. The grand jury, after meeting for 45 days over several months, released their findings.[85] The evidence and testimony in the case supported Officer Wilson's version of events, and there was to be no indictment of the former police officer. Once again, riots broke out, which lasted for several days and sympathetic demonstrations, protests, and violence occurred across the United States.

In addition to the grand jury investigation, U.S. Attorney General Eric Holder had ordered a Department of Justice investigation into the Ferguson Police Department and the actions of Officer Wilson. While that investigation took longer than the grand jury investigation, when it was released on March 4, 2015, the report acknowledged that they found nothing different from the grand jury's findings regarding Officer Wilson's conduct, but the report concluded that because the department did not racially represent the community they police and because of past allegations of racism, the department had a "pattern or practice of unlawful conduct."[86]

The resulting effect of this incident generated a highly tenuous relationship between the police and communities across the country. What many have argued is that what resulted from Ferguson was an antipolice mentality that spread across the country, developing into many cases a disrespect of officers and often outright violent attacks, which has caused the police to cease being proactive out of frustration, fear of law suits, and from a desire to avoid situations that may make them a target of the media. As police disengage, criminals become emboldened, and violent crime has risen in those cities experiencing a public backlash. This is what led St. Louis Police Chief Sam Dotson to call this phenomenon **"the Ferguson effect."**[87]

The exact nature and meaning of the term *Ferguson effect* has been somewhat in dispute, but it has been associated with a number of incidents and their outcomes. This had developed from "a handful of highly publicized deaths of unarmed black men, often following a resisted arrest—including Eric Garner in Staten Island, New York, in July 2014, Michael Brown in Ferguson, Missouri, in August 2014 and Freddie Gray in Baltimore, Maryland [in April 2015]—have led to riots [and] violent protests."[88] Each of these cases have had an impact not just on the cities involved, but they have influenced the police and community relationship across America, which has portrayed all police as being violent, aggressive, and racist (see Box 15.3).

Public dissatisfaction with the police is one thing, but the other effect that has been noticed has real consequences, and that is the number of

> ## Box 15.3 Ethics in Practice: Ferguson, Depolicing, and the Influence of the Media
>
> From the first media news reports on Officer Darren Wilson's shooting of Michael Brown to the reporting on the one-year anniversary riots, consider the **role of the media** in shaping the event.
>
> In general, the media's early portrayal of the shooting was that Michael Brown was innocent and the victim of police brutality, yet later it was found that Officer Wilson's version of the events was supported by the evidence. As people began to riot the first time, many media sources accused the police of being heavy handed and over-reactive in their response. Then, during the riots after the grand jury decision was released, the media accused the police of not being proactive enough in their response to the riots.
>
> The media also argued that the police, in general, were too aggressive and continued to highlight that fact with numerous other incidents from McKinney to Baltimore, yet, when police began to engage in depolicing because of the Ferguson effect, news reporting on this phenomenon criticized the police for not doing their job.
>
> *Ask Yourself:*
>
> **How complicit is the media in shaping Americans' perceptions of the Ferguson incident and generating a negative attitude toward the police?**

attacks on police officers have increased. Specifically, "murders of officers jumped 89 percent in 2014, to 51 from 27."[89] More specifically, there have been attacks on police officers for the mere fact they were police officers. In March of 2015, two police officers from the Ferguson Police Department were ambushed, shot, and seriously injured. "These police officers were standing there and they were shot," explained Chief of Police Jon Belmar of the St. Louis County Police, "Just because they were police officers."[90] A week before that, a Georgia police officer, Terence Green, was killed in an ambush, and in December, two New York Police officers, Wenjian Liu and Rafael Ramos, were sitting in their police vehicle when they were shot and killed by a suspect who vowed to put "wings on pigs."[91] As Police Commissioner Bratton stated, "No warning, no provocation—they were quite simply assassinated, targeted for their uniform."[92] Milwaukee County Sheriff David Clarke took it even farther when he stated unabashedly, "War has been declared on the American police officer."[93]

In addition, to the attacks on officers, more subtly, one of the Ferguson effects has been the loss of police legitimacy. A law enforcement officer explained the impact by the telling of an incident in which the parents of a 16-year-old called the police to control their violent son who was wielding a knife.[94] When the officer and his partners arrived, the son began cussing them and became combative. The officers managed to calm him down and handcuff him. His parents were amazed, for they had never seen their son act this way. When asked why he was so combative, the officer explained, "His response? Ferguson. The cops couldn't be trusted because of what happened in Ferguson, Missouri. He told us that he wanted to kill all white cops because of what 'they' had done to Michael Brown."[95] The officer went on explain, "I live and work more than 1,900 miles west of Ferguson, but the effects of that case are still being felt here," and "'Ferguson' has become the latest defense for committing crime, often invoked by people we arrest and their loved ones."[96]

The impact this has on the police officers themselves should also be recognized, for as Milwaukee Police Chief Edward Flynn laments, "I've never seen anything like it. I'm guessing it will take five years to recover."[97] It also should not be assumed that in the wake of the attacks on the police, that police behavior will remain the same. A New York Police Officer explained, "Any cop who uses his gun now has to worry about being indicted and losing his job and family. Everything has the potential to be recorded. A lot of cops feel that the climate for the next couple of years is going to be nonstop protests."[98] In fact, what the officer is articulating often leads to a phenomenon that has been noted in the past and it is called **depolicing**.[99] In the aftermath of riots, civil suits, or other negative public or media complaints of the police, officers become frustrated and no longer see any reason to be proactive in their police work, meaning that they answer calls but do little else while on duty. A recent survey of nearly 8,000 police officers in the United States by the Pew Research Center found evidence that, since Ferguson, 93 percent of these officers reported more concern for their safety, 76 percent of the officers have been more reluctant to use force when it is appropriate, and 72 percent reported that officers had become less willing to stop and question people who seem suspicious, supporting the reality of depolicing.[100] One officer described depolicing as "No contact, no problems," but while this may keep the officer free of public scrutiny and safe, it may not be the same for the community. As the president of the Police Foundation, Jim Bueermann, explained "there's a belief that when de-policing occurs, crimes go up. But we don't know that's the case."[101]

In a number of cities across the United States since the Ferguson incident, there have been reported spikes in violent crime. For instance, "Gun violence is up more than 60 percent compared with this time last year, according to Baltimore police."[102] It has been reported that the number of homicides in Milwaukee were up 180 percent, and in St. Louis, near Ferguson, shootings were up 39 percent, homicides up 25 percent, and robberies were up 43 percent.[103] A citizen in Baltimore, where arrests are down and violent crime is up, explained the change in this manner: "Before it was over-policing. Now there's no police."[104] He went on to say, "People feel as though they can do things and get away with it. I see people walking with guns almost every single day, because they know the police aren't pulling them up like they used to."[105] The argument is, if police play it safe and de-police, criminals become emboldened to commit more crime and, hence, violent crime rises. This is not a new phenomenon, for instance, after the Cincinnati, Ohio, riots in 2001, police arrests dropped 50 percent and traffic stops dropped 55 percent, while violent crime rose 39 percent.[106]

Many criminologists have, however, been quick to dismiss the sudden rise in crime as being a result of Ferguson. Many will refer to it as the "so-called 'Ferguson effect,'" and then state, "It is simply too early to know whether there is any long-term violent crime trend at work."[107] While it is true that given the limited data and time period, it is hard to know scientifically the cause of crime rates suddenly spiking, but it is also interesting to note that after saying that it is too early to tell, many then proceed to argue why the Ferguson effect is not a valid argument.[108] One professor noted, "If we're talking about a Ferguson effect where it means more people challenging police, more people filing suits against the police, and more people confronting police publicly, I think you are seeing that."[109] Yet, he also states that, "The other dynamic of this so-called Ferguson effect is the notion that when people know their rights, they become dangerous criminals" is "utterly absurd."[110] One recent study of depolicing among Missouri police departments in the aftermath of Ferguson, suggests that depolicing may be a very real phenomenon for the researchers found that at least in the case of traffic stops, the number of stops did decrease significantly.[111] Yet, what they also found was that when officers did stop and search the vehicle, they were more likely to find contraband, meaning the officers were making better stops and searches.

Table 15.1   Percentage of Agencies That Had Acquired Body-Worn Cameras by Agency and Size (2016)

	Police Departments (Sheriff's Office)	
Size of Agency	**Number of Agencies**	**Acquired BWCs**
Total	12,267 (3,012)	47.7% (46.4%)
1,000+	45 (18)	80.5 (66.7)
500-999	53 (28)	79.6 (52.2)
250-499	97 (95)	62.9 (55.9)
100-249	470 (223)	55.7 (46.4)
50-99	845 (356)	42.4 (47.8)
25-49	1,614 (624)	41.6 (48.6)
10-24	2,920 (911)	47.6 (44.5)
5-9	2,435 (554)	51.3 (44.6)
1-4	3,530 (203)	30.7 (44.1)

Source: Hyland, S.S. (2018). *Body-Worn Cameras in Law Enforcement Agencies, 2016.* Washington, DC: Bureau of Justice Statistics.

Evidently, the concept of the Ferguson effect is quite controversial, and pinning down exactly what the concept means can vary. But it would also seem that people, depending on their perspective, have distinct differences in whether it exists at all and how much of an impact it will have on the police, community, and crime. It is clear, however, that the issue will remain a source of debate for years to come.

Technology—Body Cameras

The final issue to be addressed in this chapter is one with which police departments will be wrestling with for years to come, and that is the adoption of body camera technology for all police officers. Technology has always presented issues for the police, and these new innovations often transform how policing is conducted.[112] When the automobile become commonplace, police officers moved from walking a beat to permanently patrolling in police cars, and this fundamentally shaped how policing was conducted in America. Additionally, such innovations as fingerprinting, polygraphs, and DNA (see Chapter 11) have also changed policing, so there is little doubt that the newest of the technologies, body cameras, will as well. This does, however, present many challenges for the police. As Police Chief Charles Ramsey has said, "Because technology is advancing faster than policy, it's important that we keep having discussions about what these new tools mean for us. We have to ask ourselves the hard questions. What do these technologies mean for constitutional policing? We have to keep debating the advantages and disadvantages. If we embrace this new technology, we have to make sure that we are using it to help us do our jobs betters."[113] That statement assuredly applies to the adoption of police body cameras today.[114]

In the wake of Ferguson, one of the solutions for restoring public confidence in the police has been the call for all police officers to wear body cameras. Even President Obama made the call for this solution noting that, "This time will be different because the president of the United States is deeply vested in making it different. In the two years I have remaining as president I am going to make sure we follow through."[115] President Obama then pledged to spend $75 million on body cameras for law enforcement officers nationwide, and his hope was that all police officers would soon be required to wear them as simply another part of their routine equipment. The White House justified this by explaining that

While the idea of the police wearing body cameras may sound simple, it creates a number of issues that must be dealt with for proper implementation.

"Evidence shows that body worn cameras help strengthen accountability and transparency, and that officers and civilians both act in a more positive manner when they're aware that a camera is present."[116] Despite this assertion, most likely born out of the hopes that body cameras might be the panacea to police-community relations, the evidence is not as straight-forward as they paint it, for there are many problems associated with the body camera technology, as well as many unintended consequences.

One factor for any new technology is always going to be the cost, especially in light of the fact police departments are often facing budget shortages. It has been estimated that the price tag for the cameras can range "around $800-$1,000 each" and that there is the added cost of the systems to store the video and to allow the police to sift through the data they collect and maintain.[117] In fact, videos take up a large amount of space on a computer, so the systems will have to be able to handle the large amount of data. Even a dozen officers on each shift, bringing in their video recordings and uploading them to the system, can generate more than 250 hours of video a day. In addition, police officers or technicians will need to be hired to sift through the video whenever it is needed for an allegation against the police, a civil suit, or a court case. Then, the video cannot just be handed over as raw footage, but rather, every frame of the video must be scrutinized to ensure that when released it does not violate a person's rights if someone was captured on the video that had nothing to do with the case. Still further, as police departments are public institutions they are subject to Freedom of Information Act requests, and any citizen can request to see specific video footage, which can require countless hours of an officer or technician's time to locate. There is also the issue of what to keep and what not to keep. As Austin (Texas) Police Chief Art Acevedo explained when they adopted the body cameras, "We didn't have a policy about retaining video footage from body cameras, so we're working with lawyers to draft a policy. We're going to say that officers are utilizing this equipment while on duty as part of their employment, so anything they record with evidentiary value will have to be kept with the department. Otherwise we can't let them use the body cameras" (see Box 15.4).[118]

Another issue that is continually raised about body cameras is privacy.[119] The natural thought is that police officers hook on their body camera, turn it on, and go on duty. At the end of the shift, they upload the video footage for future need. The reality, however, is not so simple. Police officers often come across people during their shift that have done nothing wrong and have no desire to be recorded, so the officer may need to turn off the camera, especially if they request it. Additionally, police officers do not just deal with criminals and citizens, but often victims. Many victims, especially those of a sexual assault, already have difficulties talking with an officer, so one can only imagine their response to being recorded. LAPD Police Chief Charlie Beck explains, "In a sensitive investigation, such as a rape or child abuse case, if you have a victim who doesn't want to be recorded, I think you have to take that into account. I think that you cannot just arbitrarily film every encounter. There are times when you've got to give your officers some

---

Box 15.4 Policing in Practice: Technology and Equipment

Police officers have always been a resourceful lot and have adapted **modern technology and equipment** to the needs of their job. It is often the case that they have employed modern technology before it was ever fielded to the departments. Many police officers, out of concern for their own protection, have worn **body cameras** long before they ever became mandatory. Most adopted the use of **cellphones** for purposes of work long before departments ever issued phones (and most still don't). Many police officers adopted **tactical flashlights** or the large mag-lights long before the department authorized it. Still further, many police officers in the 1960s and 1970s wore **protective vests** long before departments fielded them or made them mandatory to wear. Police officers find themselves in difficult situations, and they often innovate to find ways to solve problems — for in many ways, that is what the police truly are, problem solvers. Do not be surprised if you see police officers today employing the use of **drones** to solve a problem long before their police departments ever purchase order their first drone, or employ a throwable, wirelessly controlled **robotic camera** to scout out a location before the department ever considers the adoption of such technology to policing. Police officers are innovative thinkers. They have to be to stay alive.

---

discretion to turn the camera off. Of course, the officers should be required to articulate why they're not recording or why they're shutting it off, but we have to give them that discretion."[120]

The cases do not necessarily have to be as serious to raise the same issue, for more mundane police calls may create the same problem. Police Chief Don Lanpher of the Aberdeen (South Dakota) Police Department provided an anecdote that reflects this kind of situation when he explained, "We had an incident when officers were called to assist a female on a landing in an apartment building who was partially undressed. All of the officers had cameras, but they did not record her until she was covered. Officers are encouraged to use discretion in those cases."[121] It should be clear that not all encounters with citizens need to be or should be recorded. However, knowing which encounters to record and which ones not to because they violate the privacy of the citizens is left up to the discretion of the officer. Yet this in itself can raise other issues. Imagine in the case above if the female had later filed allegations of a sexual assault by the responding officers prior to her being clothed. Would the fact that the video not being turned on be used against the officers to raise a reasonable doubt as to their conduct? Yet, conversely, as Police Chief Ken Miller of the Greensboro (North Carolina) Police Department has argued, "If people think that they are going to be recorded every time they talk to an officer, regardless of the context, it is going to damage openness and create barriers to important relationships."[122]

Another concern with the issue of privacy is that of the police officers themselves. In a recent poll of police officers, their privacy was, in fact, their number one concern when it came to body cameras.[123] In some cases, police officers may make a personal phone call or meet a loved one for a lunch break while on duty, raising the question of whether or not the officer should turn off the camera. While one may say that this makes total sense, this can raise some issues. For one, if officers suddenly find themselves in a situation, for instance while having lunch, someone decides to rob the restaurant, the officers may forget—or not have the luxury—to turn their camera back on. More importantly, however, is the danger that too much missing footage on a shift may raise a doubt as to the evidentiary value of the video. In other words, if officers turn off the camera, people may want to know why they did so or it may raise the thought that they were trying to hide something, even if it was simply because they were having lunch with their spouse or did not want to further alienate a rape victim.

There is an extension to this last issue with body cameras. While interviewing a police officer about the wearing of body cameras, I was told they were running into the problem of prosecuting attorneys constantly asking for video footage, otherwise they would drop the case. The officer thought the body cameras were supposed to corroborate and be an enhancement to his testimony, not a replacement for it. As one officer explained, "Courts will expect video footage of incidents. When no footage is available the officer's integrity and the case will be put into question."[124] One researcher found the same thing when he noted, "The credibility of police testimony against defendants could be discounted in the absence of footage to corroborate the officer's version of events. It's the legal equivalent of 'pics or it didn't happen.'"[125] This may explain why cases of domestic violence with body-worn camera evidence are more likely to result in arrest, have charges filed, and have cases resolved with a guilty plea or verdict.[126] So there is the potential that the video footage which is being adopted to provide proof of an officer's testimony could lead to second guessing them or total dismissal of the officer's word.

There are a number of other issues with body cameras that many often do not consider either. The video is first and foremost from the officer's perspective because of its location. If the officer does not see it, is not facing the right way, or the camera gets blocked for some reason, the video footage may not present a visual representation of the officer's testimony. There have been many instances where police dashboard cameras filming the same encounter show widely different versions of events. Cameras simply do not see in the same manner as the human eye.[127]

Still further, there is yet another issue with the storage of the video footage. As Police Chief Kenton Rainey of the Bay Area Rapid Transit Police Department has explained, "Once you put cameras in the field, you're going to amass a lot of data that needs to be stored. Chiefs need to go into this with their eyes wide open. They need to understand what storage is going to cost, what their storage capacities are, and the amount of time it takes to review videos for public release. It is a major challenge."[128] Storage is a serious issue, but so too is review, for Lieutenant Rankin explains, "Responding to public disclosure requests is one of the biggest challenges that my department faces. When a request for a video comes in, an officer has to sit for at least two hours and review the video to find the footage and identify which portions must by law be redacted. And the actual redactions can take over ten hours to complete."[129] This then raises questions about the validity of the video footage as well. Chief Ken Miller of the Greensboro Police Department addresses these issues when he explains to police departments considering the adoption of body-camera, "Whether you store video internally or externally, protecting the data and preserving the chain of custody should always be a concern. Either way, you need something built into the system so that you know that video has not been altered."[130]

Police officer views of the wearing of body cameras also seemed to be widely mixed, with one study showing one-third oppose them and two-thirds support them.[131] One officer interviewed who was initially against wearing them, became an advocate after video footage vindicated him against a citizen complaint for brutality, while another officer interviewed who was initially for the adoption of body cameras, turned against them when the local prosecuting attorney stopped talking to the officer and only wanted to see what the video had to say about his cases.[132] This seems to raise a more

Table 15.2 Percentage Response for Reasons Why Police and Sheriff's Offices Acquired Body-Worn Cameras	
Reason	**% Response***
Improve officer safety	81.6%
Reduce/resolve civilian complaints	80.7
Improve evidence quality	78.6
Reduce agency liability	77.6
Improve officer/agency accountability	73.5
Make cases more prosecutable	69.6
Improve officer professionalism	60.1
Improve community perceptions	56.7
Simplify incident review	50.3
Improve training	48.8
Reduce use of force	33.8
Strengthen police leadership	24.5
Pilot testing only	17.3
Other	15.5

*Note: Percentages will not add to 100% as agencies could report multiple reasons.
Source: Hyland, S.S. (2018). *Body-Worn Cameras in Law Enforcement Agencies, 2016*. Washington, DC: Bureau of Justice Statistics.

nuanced acceptance of the body-worn cameras. Lieutenant Harold Rankin of the Mesa (Arizona) Police Department has noted that, "In the beginning, some officers were opposed to the cameras. But as they began wearing them, they saw that there were more benefits than drawbacks. Some officers say that they would not go out on the street without a ballistic vest; now they say they will not go out without a camera."[133] Yet, Baltimore Police Detective Bob Cherry offers another perspective when he explains, "I have heard officers say that while they are not opposed to using body-worn cameras, they do have some concerns. Some of these concerns are more practical, like whether adding new equipment will be overly burdensome. But the larger philosophical concern is whether these cameras send the wrong message about the trust we place in officers. What does it say about officer professionalism and credibility if the department has to arm every officer with a camera?"[134] In the end, the statement of one police officer may be the most accurate: "Video footage is much more likely to get a cop out of trouble than in trouble. Officers get false accusations thrown at them all the time. Video is a great equalizer."[135] Or, as Chief of Police Sean Whent of the Oakland (California) Police Department has noted, "We have about 450 body-worn cameras actively deployed, and in the overwhelming majority of cases, the footage demonstrates that the officer's actions were appropriate."[136]

Just as the police officers are mixed over the adoption of body cameras, the research into the use of body cameras by officers is also mixed. In an attempt to understand the research into police officer body-worn cameras, Professor Michael D. White reviewed all of the research studies conducted in order to reach some conclusions about what we currently know of this new technology.[137] He found that while many claim the cameras increase police legitimacy among citizens, since no study has studied citizen views of the technology, there is no evidence for this assertion. He did find that many of the studies show a reduction in citizen complaints of police officers as well as use-of-force cases by the police, yet what is not known is whether this is because police officers act differently wearing the cameras, that citizens act differently when being filmed, or it is a combination of the two. One study since White's does suggests that citizens might be more willing to report crimes to the police wearing body cameras, but only in low-crime neighborhoods, while another study in Washington, D.C. found no effect on police use of force, citizen complaints, policing activity, or judicial outcomes.[138] Still, as for many of the other claims and concerns, the research is even less clear. White appropriately concludes that "agencies interested in adopting body-worn camera technology should proceed cautiously and consider the issues."[139] And it would appear that there are many issues to consider when police departments adopt body-worn cameras.

Conclusion

There are many issues to consider when it comes to policing in America. The four issues in this chapter are just a few of the many challenges that police officers and police departments face. The use of the acronym PEST, which explores the political, economic, social, and technology perspectives of policies and institutions, is a good framework from which to explore some of these issues. Whether the political perspective of trying to make police departments reflect the communities they serve; the economic constraints police departments face causing them to adopt the 1033 program that many believe is leading to the militarization of the police; the social concerns of the Ferguson effect for police losing legitimacy in the eyes of the community leading to depolicing and rising crime rates; or the technological issues associated with the adoption of police body-worn cameras; each of these highlights many of the unresolved and highly complex issues that our modern police officers face today. Each of these issues is in need of some serious debate among both police and the community alike.

Just the Facts

1. The four components of PEST are political, economic, social, and technological, all factors that influence various policies, to include police policies.

2. A modern political call has been for police to reflect the population they serve by race. It is believed that this would have a positive influence on improving police-community relations in America, primarily because people would feel that the police force better represents them. The arguments against this is that identity politics are being brought into policing without any evidence a police department that looks like the community would perform better and due to the numerous issues related to hiring and the fact that population demographics change, it is unlikely or difficult at best to achieve this end.

3. The modern police departments have been facing economic constraints, especially during America's recessions. Police departments have looked outside of local funding for alternative sources and the federal government, having created a program to give excess military equipment to police departments took full advantage. Many have argued that the resulting effect has been to militarize the police and that with the military equipment has come a military focus.

4. In the aftermath of the justified shooting of Michael Brown by Officer Darren Wilson in Ferguson, Missouri, and the subsequent riots, many police officers are seeing citizens and the media turn against them, thus they have becoming disinclined to engage in proactive policing, and have begun to withdraw to only doing that which is demanded and necessary, a concept known as depolicing.

5. In light of the Ferguson incident and many other police encounters, there has been a call to have every police officer wear a body camera. The benefits to this is it provides video footage and audio sound of police-citizen encounters, thus providing evidence to verify citizen complaints or officer statements. The drawbacks to the body cameras are that cameras view things differently than humans, they do not provide context, they may violate the officer and citizen's privacy, and too much reliance on them by prosecutors may damage the justice process.

Ask Yourself

1. Select an issue currently facing the police or one that is associated with the police in some manner. Consider each of the PEST perspectives to see how politics, economics, social, and technological factors impact the issue.
2. Hold an honest debate over whether or not police departments should look like the communities they serve.
3. Hold an honest debate over whether or not the police should take excess military equip-

ment and whether or not the militarization of the police is real and, if so, does it have a positive or negative impact on American policing?
4. Have an honest debate over the actual Ferguson incident, the investigation, the riots, and the fall out it has caused to relations between American citizens and their police.
5. Have an honest debate over whether or not it should be mandatory that the police wear body cameras.

Keywords

Depolicing
Militarization of the police

PEST: political, economic,
    social, and technological

The Ferguson effect

Endnotes

1. Vollmer, A. & Parker, A.E. (1937). *Crime, crooks, & cops.* New York, NY: Funk & Wagnalls Company, p. 253.
2. PEST is sometimes associated with PEST Analysis in the business world. For more information see http://www.businessballs.com/pestanalysisfreetemplate.htm
3. Badger, E. (2014). When police departments don't look like the cities they're meant to protect. *The Washington Post.* Retrieved from http://www.washingtonpost.com/blogs/wonkblog/wp/2014/08/12/when-police-departments-dont-look-like-the-cities-theyre-meant-to-protect/; DeCamp, J.D. (2014). A police force should reasonably reflect the racial makeup of the community it serves. *The Columbus Dispatch.* Retrieved from http://www.cleveland.com/opinion/index.ssf/2014/09/a_police_force_should_reasonab.html; Harris, D.A. (2015). What does good policing look like? *Pittsburgh Post-Gazette.* Retrieved from http://www.post-gazette.com/opinion/Op-Ed/2015/05/10/What-does-good-policing-look-like-Here-are-10-policies-that-every-police-department-should-adopt/stories/201505100056
4. Associated Press. (2014). AP analysis: Police across country short on Hispanic officers. *PBS Newshour.* Retrieved from http://www.pbs.org/newshour/rundown/ap-analysis-disparity-seen-number-hispanic-officers-police-departments/
5. Weitzer, R. & Tuch, S.A. (2006). *Race and policing in America: Conflict and reform.* New York, NY: Cambridge University Press.
6. Fountain, M. (2015). How important is racial diversity in community policing? *SanLuisObispo.com* Retrieved from http://www.sanluisobispo.com/2015/04/18/3593337/how-important-is-racial-diversity.html
7. Schatz, B. & Vicens, A.J. (2015). The thin white line: Most cops don't look like the residents they serve. *Mother Jones.* Retrieved from http://www.motherjones.com/politics/2015/05/police-are-whiter-communities-they-serve
8. Ungar-Sargon, B. (2015). Lessons for Ferguson in creating a diverse police department. *FiveThirtyEightPolitics.* Retrieved from http://fivethirtyeight.com/features/lessons-for-ferguson-in-creating-a-diverse-police-department/
9. Ungar-Sargon, B. (2015). Lessons for Ferguson in creating a diverse police department. *FiveThirtyEightPolitics.* Retrieved from http://fivethirtyeight.com/features/lessons-for-ferguson-in-creating-a-diverse-police-department/
10. Associated Press. (2014). AP analysis: Police across country short on Hispanic officers. *PBS Newshour.* Retrieved from http://www.pbs.org/newshour/rundown/ap-analysis-disparity-seen-number-hispanic-officers-police-departments/
11. Associated Press. (2014). AP analysis: Police across country short on Hispanic officers. *PBS Newshour.* Retrieved from http://www.pbs.org/newshour/rundown/ap-analysis-disparity-seen-number-hispanic-officers-police-departments/
12. Associated Press. (2014). AP analysis: Police across country short on Hispanic officers. *PBS Newshour.*

Retrieved from http://www.pbs.org/newshour/rundown/ap-analysis-disparity-seen-number-hispanic-officers-police-departments/

13. Associated Press. (2014). AP analysis: Police across country short on Hispanic officers. *PBS Newshour.* Retrieved from http://www.pbs.org/newshour/rundown/ap-analysis-disparity-seen-number-hispanic-officers-police-departments/

14. Ungar-Sargon, B. (2015). Lessons for Ferguson in creating a diverse police department.*FiveThirtyEightPolitics.* Retrieved from http://fivethirtyeight.com/features/lessons-for-ferguson-in-creating-a-diverse-police-department/

15. Kirchner, L. (2014). Making police departments more diverse isn't enough. *Pacific Standard.* Retrieved from http://www.psmag.com/politics-and-law/ferguson-missouri-protest-increasing-diversity-among-police-officers-isnt-enough-88671

16. Fountain, M. (2015). How important is racial diversity in community policing? *SanLuisObispo.com* Retrieved from http://www.sanluisobispo.com/2015/04/18/3593337/how-important-is-racial-diversity.html

17. Alcindor, V. & Penzenstadler, N. (2015). Police redouble efforts to recruit diverse officers. *USA Today.* Retrieved from http://www.usatoday.com percent2Fstory percent2Fnews percent2F2015 percent2F01 percent2F21 percent2Fpolice-redoubling-efforts-to-recruit-diverse-officers percent2F21574081 percent2F&ei=nXOJVeKvO 8H9yQSkoYHQDw&usg=AFQjCNEAhMBkKlIJOjQL-lDjpqHEnr1aJQ&bvm=bv.96339352,d.aWw

18. Alcindor, V. & Penzenstadler, N. (2015). Police redouble efforts to recruit diverse officers. *USA Today.* Retrieved from http://www.usatoday.com percent2Fstory percent2Fnews percent2F2015 percent2F01 percent2F21 percent2Fpolice-redoubling-efforts-to-recruit-diverse-officers percent2F21574081 percent2F&ei= nXOJVeKvO8 H9yQSkoYHQDw&usg=AFQjCNEAhMB kKlIJOjQL-lDjpqHEnr1aJQ&bvm=bv.96339352,d.aWw

19. Alcindor, V. & Penzenstadler, N. (2015). Police redouble efforts to recruit diverse officers. *USA Today.* Retrieved from http://www.usatoday.com percent2Fstory percent2Fnews percent2F2015 percent2F01 percent2F21 percent2Fpolice-redoubling-efforts-to-recruit-diverse-officers percent2F21574081 percent2F&ei=nXOJVeKv O8H9yQSkoYHQDw&usg=AFQjCNEAhMBkKlI JOjQL-lDjpqHEnr1aJQ&bvm=bv.96339352,d.aWw

20. The following three observations have been made by multiple police officers in interviews with this author.

21. Grimm, A. (2015). NOPD gets low marks from citizens in survey by federal monitors. *The Times-Picayne.* Retrieved from http://www.nola.com/crime/index.ssf/2015/04/nopd_community_survey_consent.html; Jennings, A., Mather, K., Mozingo, J., Vives, R. & Winton, R. (2015). LAPD is more diverse, but distrust in the community remains. *The Los Angeles Times.* Retrieved from http://www.latimes.com/local/california/la-me-lapd-race-20150329-story.html#page=1

22. Jennings, A., Mather, K., Mozingo, J., Vives, R., & Winton, R. (2015). LAPD is more diverse, but distrust in the community remains. *The Los Angeles Times.* Retrieved from http://www.latimes.com/local/california/la-me-lapd-race-20150329-story.html#page=1

23. See also Decker, S. (1981). Citizen attitudes toward the police: A review of past findings and suggestions for future policy. *Journal of Police Science & Administration, 9,* 80-87; Flanagan, T. & Vaughn, M. (1996). Public opinion about police abuse of force. In W. Geler& H. Toch (Eds.), *Police Violence* (pp. 113-128). New Haven, CT: Yale University Press; Tuch, S. & Weitzer, R. (1997). Trends: Racial differences in attitudes toward the police. *Public Opinion Quarterly, 61,* 642-663; Weitzer, R. (2000). White, black, or blue cops?Race and citizens assessments of police officers. *Journal of Criminal Justice, 28,* 313-324.

24. Alcindor, V. & Penzenstadler, N. (2015). Police redouble efforts to recruit diverse officers. *USA Today.* Retrieved from http://www.usatoday.com percent2Fstory percent2Fnews percent2F2015 percent2F01 percent2F21 percent2Fpolice-redoubling-efforts-to-recruit-diverse-officers percent2F21574081 percent2F&ei=nXOJVe KvO8H9yQSkoYHQDw&usg=AFQjCNEAhMBkKlIJO jQL-lDjpqHEnr1aJQ&bvm= bv.96339352,d.aWw

25. Aberbach, J. & Walker, J. (1970). The attitudes of blacks and whites toward city services. In J. Crecine (ed.), *Financing the Metropolis* 9pp. (519-538). Beverly Hills, CA: SAGE.

26. Dresener et al. (1981). *The state of police-community relations.* Milwaukee, WI: Milwaukee Fire and Police Commission; Bayley, D. & Mendelsohn, H. (1969). *Minorities and the police: Confrontation in America.* New York, NY: Free Press.

27. Weitzer, R. (2000). White, black, or blue cops? Race and citizens assessments of police officers. *Journal of Criminal Justice, 28,* 313-324, at p. 318.

28. Weitzer, R. (2000). White, black, or blue cops? Race and citizens assessments of police officers. *Journal of Criminal Justice, 28,* 313-324, at p. 318.

29. Weitzer, R. (2000). White, black, or blue cops? Race and citizens assessments of police officers. *Journal of Criminal Justice, 28,* 313-324, at p. 320.

30. Weitzer, R. (2000). White, black, or blue cops? Race and citizens assessments of police officers. *Journal of Criminal Justice, 28,* 313-324, at p. 322.

31. Weitzer, R. (2000). White, black, or blue cops? Race and citizens assessments of police officers. *Journal of Criminal Justice, 28,* 313-324, at p. 322.

32. Ungar-Sargon, B. (2015). Lessons for Ferguson in creating a diverse police department. *FiveThirtyEightPolitics.* Retrievedfromhttp://fivethirtyeight.com/features/lessons-for-ferguson-in-creating-a-diverse-police-department/

33. National Research Council. (2004). *Fairness and effectiveness in policing: The evidence.* Committee to review research on police policy and practices. W. Skogan & K. Frydl (Eds.). Committed on Law and Justice, Division

of Behavioral and Social Sciences and Education. Washington, DC: National Academies Press.

34. Smith, B.W. (2003). The impact of police officer diversity on police-caused homicides. *Policy Studies Journal, 31,* 147-162.

35. Kirchner, L. (2014). Making police departments more diverse isn't enough. *Pacific Standard.* Retrieved from http://www.psmag.com/politics-and-law/ferguson-missouri-protest-increasing-diversity-among-police-officers-isnt-enough-88671

36. See for instance, Brown, R.A. & Frank, J. (2006). Race and officer decision making: Examining differences in arrest outcomes between black and white officers. *Justice Quarterly, 23,* 96-126.

37. Kirchner, L. (2014). Making police departments more diverse isn't enough. *Pacific Standard.* Retrieved from http://www.psmag.com/politics-and-law/ferguson-missouri-protest-increasing-diversity-among-police-officers-isnt-enough-88671

38. DePillis, L. (2014). Do diverse police forces treat their communities more fairly than almost-all-white ones like Ferguson's? *The Washington Post.* Retrieved from http://www.washingtonpost.com/news/storyline/wp/2014/08/22/do-diverse-police-forces-treat-their-communities-more-fairly-than-all-white-ones-like-fergusons/

39. Alcindor, V. & Penzenstadler, N. (2015). Police redouble efforts to recruit diverse officers. *USA Today.* Retrieved from http://www.usatoday.com percent2F-story percent2Fnews percent2F2015 percent2F01 percent2F21 percent2Fpolice-redoubling-efforts-to-recruit-diverse-officers percent2F21574081 percent2F&ei=nXOJVeKvO 8H9yQSkoYHQDw&usg=AFQjCNEAhMB kKlIJOjQL-lDjpqHEnr1aJQ&bvm=bv.96339352,d.aWw

40. McDaniel, M. (2011). Diversity of safety? Justice Department orders lower standards for police exam. *PJ Media.* Retrieved from http://pjmedia.com/blog/diversity-or-safety-justice-dept-orders-lower-standards-for-police-exam/

41. COPS office. (2015). *The impact of the economic downturn on American police agencies.* Washington, DC: Office of Community Oriented Policing Services; PERF. (2010). *Critical issues in policing series: Is the economic downturn fundamentally changing how we police?* Washington, DC: Police Executive Research Forum.

42. PERF. (2010). *Critical issues in policing series: Is the economic downturn fundamentally changing how we police?* Washington, DC: Police Executive Research Forum.

43. Reaves, B.A. (2011). *Census of state and local law enforcement agencies, 2008.* Washington, DC: Bureau of Justice Statistics; Reaves, B.A. (2015). *Local police departments, 2013: Personnel, policies, and practices.* Washington, DC: Bureau of Justice Statistics.

44. PERF. (2010). *Critical issues in policing series: Is the economic downturn fundamentally changing how we police?* Washington, DC: Police Executive Research Forum, p. 5.

45. PERF. (2010). *Critical issues in policing series: Is the economic downturn fundamentally changing how we police?* Washington, DC: Police Executive Research Forum, p. 5.

46. PERF. (2010). *Critical issues in policing series: Is the economic downturn fundamentally changing how we police?* Washington, DC: Police Executive Research Forum, p. 6.

47. PERF. (2010). *Critical issues in policing series: Is the economic downturn fundamentally changing how we police?* Washington, DC: Police Executive Research Forum, p. 7.

48. Balko, R. (2013). *Rise of the warrior cop: The militarization of America's police forces.* New York, NY: PublicAffairs.

49. LaCommare, P. (2010). Generating new revenue streams. *The Police Chief.* Retrieved from http://www.police-chiefmagazine.org/magazine/index.cfm?fuseaction=display_arch& article_id=2108&issue_id=62010; Maguire, E.R. (2003). *Organizational structures in American police agencies: Context, complexity, and control.* Albany, NY: State University of New York Press.

50. Balko, R. (2013). *Rise of the warrior cop: The militarization of America's police forces.* New York, NY: PublicAffairs.

51. Cullen, D. (2010). *Columbine.* New York, NY: Twelve.

52. PERF. (2014). *Critical issues in policing series: The police response to active shooter incidents.* Washington, DC: Police Executive Research Forum.

53. Balko, R. (2013). *Rise of the warrior cop: The militarization of America's police forces.* New York, NY: PublicAffairs; Kraska, P.B. (2001). *Militarizing the American criminal justice system: The changing roles of the armed forces and the police.* Boston, MA: Northeastern.

54. Wofford, T. (2014). How American's police became an army: The 1033 program. *Newsweek.* Retrieved from http://www.newsweek.com/how-americas-police-became-army-1033-program-264537

55. Ingraham, C. (2014). The Pentagon gave nearly half a billion dollars of military gear to local law enforcement last year. *The Washington Post.* Retrieved from http://www.washingtonpost.com/blogs/wonkblog/wp/2014/08/14/the-pentagon-gave-nearly-half-a-billion-dollars-of-military-gear-to-local-law-enforcement-last-year/

56. Ingraham, C. (2014). The Pentagon gave nearly half a billion dollars of military gear to local law enforcement last year. *The Washington Post.* Retrieved from http://www.washingtonpost.com/blogs/wonkblog/wp/2014/08/14/the-pentagon-gave-nearly-half-a-billion-dollars-of-military-gear-to-local-law-enforcement-last-year/

57. Apuzzo, M. (2014). War gear flows to police departments. *The New York Times.* Retrieved from http://www.nytimes.com/2014/06/09/us/war-gear-flows-to-police-departments.html?_r=0

58. Apuzzo, M. (2014). War gear flows to police departments. *The New York Times.* Retrieved from http://www.nytimes.com/2014/06/09/us/war-gear-flows-to-police-departments.html?_r=0

59. Alesia, M. (2014). Police officer safety or surplus zeal: Military equipment spurs debate. *Indy Star.* Retrieved from http://www.indystar.com/story/news/2014/06/07/police-officer-safety-surplus-zeal-military-equipment-spurs-debate-mrap-military-vehicle/10170225/

60. Alesia, M. (2014). Police officer safety or surplus zeal: Military equipment spurs debate. *Indy Star.* Retrieved

from http://www.indystar.com/story/news/2014/06/07/police-officer-safety-surplus-zeal-military-equipment-spurs-debate-mrap-military-vehicle/10170225/

61. Alesia, M. (2014). Police officer safety or surplus zeal: Military equipment spurs debate. *Indy Star*. Retrieved from http://www.indystar.com/story/news/2014/06/07/police-officer-safety-surplus-zeal-military-equipment-spurs-debate-mrap-military-vehicle/10170225/

62. Alesia, M. (2014). Police officer safety or surplus zeal: Military equipment spurs debate. *Indy Star*. Retrieved from http://www.indystar.com/story/news/2014/06/07/police-officer-safety-surplus-zeal-military-equipment-spurs-debate-mrap-military-vehicle/10170225/

63. Alesia, M. (2014). Police officer safety or surplus zeal: Military equipment spurs debate. *Indy Star*. Retrieved from http://www.indystar.com/story/news/2014/06/07/police-officer-safety-surplus-zeal-military-equipment-spurs-debate-mrap-military-vehicle/10170225/

64. Apuzzo, M. (2014). War gear flows to police departments. *The New York Times*. Retrieved from http://www.nytimes.com/2014/06/09/us/war-gear-flows-to-police-departments.html?_r=0

65. Apuzzo, M. (2014). War gear flows to police departments. *The New York Times*. Retrieved from http://www.nytimes.com/2014/06/09/us/war-gear-flows-to-police-departments.html?_r=0

66. Gootfried, M.H. & Sinner, C.J. (2014). Police benefit from military gear; critics fear it could alter tactics. *Twincities.com* Retrieved from http://www.twincities.com/localnews/ci_26394731/police-see-benefits-from-military-gear-critics-fear

67. Gootfried, M.H. & Sinner, C.J. (2014). Police benefit from military gear; critics fear it could alter tactics. *Twincities.com* Retrieved from http://www.twincities.com/localnews/ci_26394731/police-see-benefits-from-military-gear-critics-fear

68. Bibbs, R.B. (2015). Local law enforcement agencies benefit from military surplus. *Herald Bulletin*. Retrieved from http://www.heraldbulletin.com/news/local_news/local-law-enforcement-agencies-benefit-from-military-surplus/article_08e43c61-4385-57ff-a9c4-afd13c0afadf.html

69. Bibbs, R.B. (2015). Local law enforcement agencies benefit from military surplus. *Herald Bulletin*. Retrieved from http://www.heraldbulletin.com/news/local_news/local-law-enforcement-agencies-benefit-from-military-surplus/article_08e43c61-4385-57ff-a9c4-afd13c0afadf.html

70. Gootfried, M.H. & Sinner, C.J. (2014). Police benefit from military gear; critics fear it could alter tactics. *Twincities.com* Retrieved from http://www.twincities.com/localnews/ci_26394731/police-see-benefits-from-military-gear-critics-fear

71. Apuzzo, M. (2014). War gear flows to police departments. *The New York Times*. Retrieved from http://www.nytimes.com/2014/06/09/us/war-gear-flows-to-police-departments.html?_r=0

72. Apuzzo, M. (2014). War gear flows to police departments. *The New York Times*. Retrieved from http://www.nytimes.com/2014/06/09/us/war-gear-flows-to-police-departments.html?_r=0

73. Apuzzo, M. (2014). War gear flows to police departments. *The New York Times*. Retrieved from http://www.nytimes.com/2014/06/09/us/war-gear-flows-to-police-departments.html?_r=0

74. Apuzzo, M. (2014). War gear flows to police departments. *The New York Times*. Retrieved from http://www.nytimes.com/2014/06/09/us/war-gear-flows-to-police-departments.html?_r=0

75. Balko, R. (2013). Former cops speak out about police militarization. *Huffington Post*. Retrieved from http://www.huffingtonpost.com/2013/08/01/cops-speak-out-on-police-_n_3688999.html

76. Beck, D. (2013). Rise of the warrior cop by Radley Balko. *Law Enforcement Against Prohibition*. Retrieved from http://copssaylegalize.blogspot.com/2013/07/rise-of-warrior-cop-by-radley-balko.html

77. Beck, D. (2013). Rise of the warrior cop by Radley Balko. *Law Enforcement Against Prohibition*. Retrieved from http://copssaylegalize.blogspot.com/2013/07/rise-of-warrior-cop-by-radley-balko.html

78. Apuzzo, M. (2014). War gear flows to police departments. *The New York Times*. Retrieved from http://www.nytimes.com/2014/06/09/us/war-gear-flows-to-police-departments.html?_r=0

79. Grovum, J. (2015). Can states slow the flow of military equipment to police? *The Pew Charitable Trusts*. Retrieved from http://www.pewtrusts.org/en/research-and-analysis/blogs/stateline/2015/3/24/can-states-slow-the-flow-of-military-equipment-to-police

80. Walker, R. (2014). US police go military with 1033 program. *DeutcheWelle*. Retrieved from http://www.dw.com/en/us-police-go-military-with-1033-program/a-17857709

81. Korte, G. (2015). Obama bans some military equipment sales to police. *USA Today*. Retrieved from http://www.google.com/url?sa=t&rct=j&q=&esrc=s&source=web&cd=1&ved=0CB4QFjAA&url=http percent3A percent2F percent2Fwww.usatoday.com percent2Fstory percent2Fnews percent2Fpolitics percent2F2015 percent2F05 percent2F18 percent 2Fobama-police-military-equipment-sales-new-jersey percent2F27521793 percent2F&ei=c8aKVdGKO8LF sAWU2IGwCQ&usg=AFQjCNHZ3PKscZFuQ-BCxdet JxyHo4Ucsw&bvm=bv.96339352,d.b2w

82. Korte, G. (2015). Obama bans some military equipment sales to police. *USA Today*. Retrieved from http://www.google.com/url?sa=t&rct=j&q=&esrc=s&source=web&cd=1&ved=0CB4QFjAA&url=http percent 3A percent2F percent2Fwww.usatoday.com percent2Fstory percent2Fnews percent2Fpolitics percent2F2015 percent2F05 percent2F18 percent2Fobama-police-military-equipment-sales-new-jersey percent2F27521793 percent2F&ei= c8aKVdGKO8LFsAWU2IGwCQ& usg=AFQjCNHZ3PKsc ZFuQ-BCxdetJxyHo4Ucsw&bvm=bv.96339352,d.b2w

83. Giraldi, P. (2015). Obama won't demilitarize police. *The American Conservative*. Retrieved from http://www.theamericanconservative.com/articles/obama-wont-demilitarize-police/

84. Williams, T. (2016). Some officers bristle at recall of military equipment. *The New York Times*. Jan. 26. Retrieved from https://www.nytimes.com/2016/01/27/us/some-sheriffs-bristle-at-recall-of-military-equipment.html

85. As there are numerous documents from the grand jury, the following is a good source for the many reports: CNN. (2014). Documents from the Ferguson grand jury. Retrieved from http://www.cnn.com/interactive/2014/11/us/ferguson-grand-jury-docs/

86. U.S. Department of Justice. (2015). *Department of Justice report regarding the criminal investigation into the shooting death of Michael Brown by Ferguson, Missouri, Police Officer Darren Wilson*. Washington, DC: U.S. Department of Justice.

87. Mac Donald, H. (2015). The new nationwide crime wave. *The Wall Street Journal*. Retrieved from http://www.wsj.com/articles/the-new-nationwide-crime-wave-1432938425; Shjarback, J.S., Pyrooz, D.C., Wolfe, S.E., & Decker, S.H. (2017). De-policing and crime in the wake of Ferguson: Racialized changes in the quantity and quality of policing among Missouri police departments. *Journal of Criminal Justice, 50*, 42-52.

88. Mac Donald, H. (2015). The new nationwide crime wave. *The Wall Street Journal*. Retrieved from http://www.wsj.com/articles/the-new-nationwide-crime-wave-1432938425

89. Banker, A. (2015). Worries about "Ferguson effect" after police killed on duty jumps 90 percent. *Fox News*. Retrieved from http://fox2now.com/2015/05/12/danger-in-the-line-of-duty/; Mac Donald, H. (2015). The new nationwide crime wave. *The Wall Street Journal*. Retrieved from http://www.wsj.com/articles/the-new-nationwide-crime-wave-1432938425

90. Berman, M. (2015). Two police officers shot, seriously injured in Ferguson "ambush." *The Washington Post*. Retrieved from http://www.washingtonpost.com/news/post-nation/wp/2015/03/12/two-police-officers-shot-seriously-injured-in-ferguson/

91. Celana, L., Cohen, S., Schram, J., Jamieson, A., & Italiano, L. (2014). Gunman executes 2 NYPD cops in Garner 'revenge.' *The New York Post*. Retrieved from http://nypost.com/2014/12/20/2-nypd-cops-shot-execution-style-in-brooklyn/; USA Today. (2015). Officer's fatal shooting by suspect called "ambush." *USA Today*. Retrieved from http://www.usatoday.com/story/news/nation/2015/03/04/police-officer-killed-shooting/24359961/

92. Celana, L., Cohen, S., Schram, J., Jamieson, A., & Italiano, L. (2014). Gunman executes 2 NYPD cops in Garner "revenge." *The New York Post*. Retrieved from http://nypost.com/2014/12/20/2-nypd-cops-shot-execution-style-in-brooklyn/

93. Sanchez, R., Fantz, A., & Darlington, S. (2015). Police advocates: We're worried about recent spate of ambushes. *CNN*. Retrieved from http://www.cnn.com/2015/03/12/justice/ferguson-police-shot-ambush-tactics/

94. Deputy Matt. (2015). The Ferguson effect: A cop's-eye view. *The New York Post*. Retrieved from http://nypost.com/2014/10/14/the-ferguson-effect-a-cops-eye-view/

95. Deputy Matt. (2015). The Ferguson effect: A cop's-eye view. *The New York Post*. Retrieved from http://nypost.com/2014/10/14/the-ferguson-effect-a-cops-eye-view/

96. Deputy Matt. (2015). The Ferguson effect: A cop's-eye view. *The New York Post*. Retrieved from http://nypost.com/2014/10/14/the-ferguson-effect-a-cops-eye-view/

97. Mac Donald, H. (2015). The new nationwide crime wave. *The Wall Street Journal*. Retrieved from http://www.wsj.com/articles/the-new-nationwide-crime-wave-1432938425

98. Mac Donald, H. (2015). The new nationwide crime wave. *The Wall Street Journal*. Retrieved from http://www.wsj.com/articles/the-new-nationwide-crime-wave-1432938425

99. Oliver, W.M. (2015). Depolicing: Rhetoric or reality? Criminal Justice Police Review. Retrieved from http://cjp.sagepub.com/content/early/2015/05/15/0887403415586790.full.pdf+html; Oliver, W.M. (2019). *Depolicing: When Police Officers Disengage*. Boulder, CO: Lynne Rienner Publishers, Inc.

100. Morin, R., Parker, K., Stepler, R., & Mercer, A. (2017). *Behind the Badge*. Washington, DC: PewResearchCenter.

101. NBC News. (2015). As violence spikes in some cities, Is "Ferguson" effect to blame? *NBC News*. Retrieved from http://www.nbcnews.com/news/us-news/violence-spikes-some-cities-ferguson-effect-blame-n368526

102. Mac Donald, H. (2015). The new nationwide crime wave. *The Wall Street Journal*. Retrieved from http://www.wsj.com/articles/the-new-nationwide-crime-wave-1432938425

103. Mac Donald, H. (2015). The new nationwide crime wave. *The Wall Street Journal*. Retrieved from http://www.wsj.com/articles/the-new-nationwide-crime-wave-1432938425

104. Ross, K. (2015). Rise in crime thanks to "Ferguson effect." *Redstate*. Retrieved from http://www.redstate.com/2015/06/01/rise-crime-thanks-ferguson-effect/

105. Ross, K. (2015). Rise in crime thanks to "Ferguson effect." *Redstate*. Retrieved from http://www.redstate.com/2015/06/01/rise-crime-thanks-ferguson-effect/

106. Prendergast, J. (2002). Cincinnati's riots, one year later, violence up, arrests down. *Cincinnati Enquirer*. Retrieved from http://www.enquirer.com/oneyearlater/

107. Rocque, M., Posick, C., & Barkan, S.E. (2015).4 reasons to doubt the "Ferguson effect" and claims of a national crime wave. *Bangor Daily News*. Retrieved from http://bangordailynews.com/2015/06/10/the-point/4-reasons-to-doubt-the-ferguson-effect-and-claims-of-a-national-crime-wave/

108. Jonsson, P. (2015). Just what is the "Ferguson effect"? It depends on how you view the police. *The Christian Science Monitor*. Retrieved from http://www.csmonitor.com/USA/Justice/2015/0612/Just-what-is-the-Ferguson-effect-It-depends-on-how-you-view-police; Rocque, M., Posick, C., & Barkan, S.E. (2015). 4 reasons to doubt the "Ferguson effect" and claims of a national crime wave. *Bangor Daily News*. Retrieved from http://bangordailynews.com/2015/06/10/the-point/4-reasons-to-doubt-the-ferguson-effect-and-claims-of-a-national-crime-wave/; Rosenfeld, R. (2015). Was there a "Ferguson Effect" on crime in St. Louis? *Sentencing Project*. Retrieved from http://www.sentencingproject.org/doc/publications/inc_Ferguson_Effect.pdf; Townes, C. (2015). The myth of the "Ferguson effect." *Thinkprogress*. Retrieved from

http://thinkprogress.org/justice/2015/06/17/3670203/ferguson-effect-isnt-real-in-st-louis/

109. Jonsson, P. (2015). Just what is the "Ferguson effect"? It depends on how you view the police. *The Christian Science Monitor*. Retrieved from http://www.csmonitor.com/USA/Justice/2015/0612/Just-what-is-the-Ferguson-effect-It-depends-on-how-you-view-police

110. Jonsson, P. (2015). Just what is the "Ferguson effect"? It depends on how you view the police. *The Christian Science Monitor*. Retrieved from http://www.csmonitor.com/USA/Justice/2015/0612/Just-what-is-the-Ferguson-effect-It-depends-on-how-you-view-police

111. Shjarback, J.S., Pyrooz, D.C., Wolfe, S.E., & Decker, S.H. (2017). De-policing and crime in the wake of Ferguson: Racialized changes in the quantity and quality of policing among Missouri police departments. *Journal of Criminal Justice, 50*, 42-52.

112. Lum, C., Koper, C.S., & Willis, J. (2017). Understanding the limits of technology's impact on police effectiveness. *Police Quarterly, 20*, 135-163; Police Executive Research Forum. (2012). How are innovations in technology transforming police? *Critical Issues in Policing Series*. Washington, DC: Police Executive Research Forum.

113. Miller, L., Toliver, J., & Police Executive Research Forum. (2014). *Implementing a body-worn camera program: Recommendations and Lessons*. Washington, DC: Office of Community Oriented Policing Services, p. 1.

114. Lum, C., Koper, C.S., & Willis, J. (2017). Understanding the limits of technology's impact on police effectiveness. *Police Quarterly, 20*, 135-163.

115. Lee, T., Roth, Z, & Timm, J.C. (2015). Obama to announce $75 million for body cameras. *MSNBC*. Retrieved from http://www.msnbc.com/msnbc/obama-announce-75-million-body-cameras

116. Friedman, U. (2015). Do police body cameras actually work? *The Atlantic*. Retrieved from http://www.theatlantic.com/international/archive/2014/12/do-police-body-cameras-work-ferguson/383323/

117. Friedman, U. (2015). Do police body cameras actually work? *The Atlantic*. Retrieved from http://www.theatlantic.com/international/archive/2014/12/do-police-body-cameras-work-ferguson/383323/

118. Police Executive Research Forum. (2012). How are innovations in technology transforming police? *Critical Issues in Policing Series*. Washington, DC: Police Executive Research Forum, p. 21.

119. Gaub, J.E., Choate, D.E., Todak, N., Katz, C.M. & White, M.D. (2016). Officer perceptions of body-worn cameras before and after deployment: A study of three departments. *Police Quarterly*, 19, 275-302; Feeney, M. (2015). Police body cameras raise privacy issues for cops and the public. *Cato at Liberty*. Retrieved from http://www.cato.org/blog/police-body-cameras-raise-privacy-issues-cops-public

120. Miller, L., Toliver, J., & Police Executive Research Forum. (2014). *Implementing a body-worn camera program: Recommendations and Lessons*. Washington, DC: Office of Community Oriented Policing Services, p. 14.

121. Miller, L., Toliver, J., & Police Executive Research Forum. (2014). *Implementing a body-worn camera program: Recommendations and Lessons*. Washington, DC: Office of Community Oriented Policing Services, p. 1.

122. Miller, L., Toliver, J., & Police Executive Research Forum. (2014). *Implementing a body-worn camera program: Recommendations and Lessons*. Washington, DC: Office of Community Oriented Policing Services, p. 13.

123. PoliceOne Staff. (2014). Poll results: Cops speak out about body cameras. *Policeone.com* Retrieved from http://www.policeone.com/police-products/body-cameras/articles/7790682-Poll-Results-Cops-speak-out-about-body-cameras/; See also Gaub, J.E., Choate, D.E., Todak, N., Katz, C.M. & White, M.D. (2016). Officer perceptions of body-worn cameras before and after deployment: A study of three departments. *Police Quarterly*, 19, 275-302

124. PoliceOne Staff. (2014). Poll results: Cops speak out about body cameras. *Policeone.com* Retrieved from http://www.policeone.com/police-products/body-cameras/articles/7790682-Poll-Results-Cops-speak-out-about-body-cameras/

125. Friedman, U. (2015). Do police body cameras actually work? *The Atlantic*. Retrieved from http://www.theatlantic.com/international/archive/2014/12/do-police-body-cameras-work-ferguson/383323/

126. Morrow, W.J., Katz, C.M., & Choate, D.E. (2016). Assessing the impact of policy body-worn cameras on arresting, prosecuting, and convicting suspects of intimate partner violence. *Police Quarterly, 19*, 303-325.

127. Force Science Institute. (2014). 10 limitations of body cams you need to know for you protection. *Force Science Institute*. Retrieved from http://www.policeone.com/police-products/body-cameras/articles/7580663-10-limitations-of-body-cams-you-need-to-know-for-your-protection/

128. Miller, L., Toliver, J., & Police Executive Research Forum. (2014). *Implementing a body-worn camera program: Recommendations and Lessons*. Washington, DC: Office of Community Oriented Policing Services, p. 32.

129. Miller, L., Toliver, J., & Police Executive Research Forum. (2014). *Implementing a body-worn camera program: Recommendations and Lessons*. Washington, DC: Office of Community Oriented Policing Services, p. 33.

130. Miller, L., Toliver, J., & Police Executive Research Forum. (2014). *Implementing a body-worn camera program: Recommendations and Lessons*. Washington, DC: Office of Community Oriented Policing Services, p. 16.

131. Gaub, J.E., Choate, D.E., Todak, N., Katz, C.M. & White, M.D. (2016). Officer perceptions of body-worn cameras before and after deployment: A study of three departments. *Police Quarterly*, 19, 275-302; Morin, R., Parker, K., Stepler, R., & Mercer, A. (2017). *Behind the Badge*. Washington, DC: PewResearchCenter; PoliceOne Staff. (2014). Poll results: Cops speak out about body cameras. *Policeone.com* Retrieved from http://www.policeone.com/police-products/body-cameras/articles/7790682-Poll-Results-Cops-speak-out-about-body-cameras/

132. Personal Interviews by the author with anonymous members of the Texas Department of Public Safety.

133. Miller, L., Toliver, J., & Police Executive Research Forum. (2014). *Implementing a body-worn camera program: Recommendations and Lessons.* Washington, DC: Office of Community Oriented Policing Services, p. 28.

134. Miller, L., Toliver, J., & Police Executive Research Forum. (2014). *Implementing a body-worn camera program: Recommendations and Lessons.* Washington, DC: Office of Community Oriented Policing Services, p. 25.

135. PoliceOne Staff. (2014). Poll results: Cops speak out about body cameras. *Policeone.com* Retrieved from http://www.policeone.com/police-products/body-cameras/articles/7790682-Poll-Results-Cops-speak-out-about-body-cameras/

136. Miller, L., Toliver, J., & Police Executive Research Forum. (2014). *Implementing a body-worn camera program: Recommendations and Lessons.* Washington, DC: Office of Community Oriented Policing Services, p. 6.

137. White, M.D. (2014). *Police officer body-worn cameras: Assessing the evidence.* Washington, DC: Office of Community Oriented Policing Services.

138. Ariel, B. (2016). Increasing cooperation with the police using body worn cameras. *Police Quarterly, 19,* 326-362; Yokum, D., Ravishankar, A., & Coppock, A. (2017). *Evaluating the effects of police body-worn cameras: A randomized controlled trial.* Washington, DC: The LAB@ DC.

139. White, M.D. (2014). *Police officer body-worn cameras: Assessing the evidence.* Washington, DC: Office of Community Oriented Policing Services, p. 10.

70 federal law enforcement agencies the estimated number of police agencies that serve the national U.S. government. (Chapter 3)

3,080 sheriff offices the estimated number of active sheriff's offices in the United States. (Chapter 3)

3,144 counties the number of counties or county-like governments in the United States. (Chapter 3)

18,000 police departments the commonly held estimate of the number of police agencies in the United States. (Chapter 3)

Accountability the nature of being responsible for one's actions or the actions of others. (Chapter 7)

Actus reus the physical elements of a crime, the actual acts. (Chapter 6)

Addressing problems the third goal of detectives, which is aimed at dealing with major crime issues that surface in the community. (Chapter 11)

Administration consists of all management personnel that oversee, supervise, and direct the organization. (Chapter 4)

Administrative of or pertaining to the police organization and how it conducts itself. (Chapter 7)

Administrative duties a necessary function of police patrol that is focused on taking care of a variety of tasks and departmental requirements during police patrol time. (Chapter 10)

Administrative law the body of law that governs the activities of administrative agencies of government. (Chapter 6)

Administrative rulemaking rules issued by the agency, typically by the command staff, in order to oversee the conduct of the police employees. (Chapter 6)

Administrative search a search that is done for purposes of an administrative policy, such as conducting an inventory. (Chapter 6)

Age requirement typically a minimum age, most often 21, to become a police officer, and often a maximum age, which varies by agency. (Chapter 5)

Aggressive patrol officers using aggressive legal measures, such as checkpoints, in order to address specific problems in a specific geographic location. (Chapter 10)

Altruism the belief or practice that a person acts for the well-being of others and never out of personal selfishness or gain. (Chapter 5)

American detectives the entire genre of police detectives that grew up largely in American literature. (Chapter 11)

Analysis the second step in the SARA Model, which focuses on understanding the underlying reason for the problem identified in the first step, not its symptoms. (Chapter 9)

Andragogy and low stress the use of adult education measures, often in a college-like environment with low levels of pressure on the police recruits in the academy, to ensure that they understand the information and knowledge they will need to draw upon when they find themselves in stressful situations when they become police officers. (Chapter 5)

Antiterrorism often used interchangeably with counterterrorism, the term more specifically defines those measures employed to prevent terrorism. (Chapter 9)

Area the specific geographical locations of police officers usually divided into one or more of the following: precincts, districts, sectors, and beats. (Chapter 4)

Arrest the act of depriving a person of his or her liberty through legal authority and taking the person into custody. (Chapter 1)

Assessment the fourth step in the SARA Model, which is aimed at assessing how effective the response to the problem was in solving the problem. (Chapter 9)

Attitude an outward expression of the body that reflects the mental state of the individual. (Chapter 7)

Authority the police officers' authority, from the nature of being sworn officers wearing a badge and a gun, that gives them the power to make arrests and use force, which contributes to the development of the police culture. (Chapter 8)

Automobile searches the warrantless requirement to search an automobile because of the nature of the vehicle's ability to be rapidly moved. (Chapter 6)

Auxiliary services those support functions that assist operations to be able to perform their duties. (Chapter 4)

Backbone of policing the term first used by O.W. Wilson to describe police patrol, meaning that it is the primary means and function of policing. (Chapter 10)

Background investigation a police investigation, usually by a detective, into the police candidate's past to determine if there is any reason the individual should not serve as a police officer and to judge the truthfulness of answers on their application. (Chapter 5)

Band a small group consisting of dozens of people, who are related, are typically nomadic, and are egalitarian, who use informal means for resolving conflict. (Chapter 2)

Bicycle patrol a method of police patrol made popular under the community policing movement. (Chapter 10)

Blue curtain another descriptor for the blue wall of silence. (Chapter 8)

Blue wall of silence a phrase used to describe an unwritten code that police officers do not inform on each other to supervisors. (Chapter 8)

Bona Fide Occupational Qualifications (BFOQ) tests that are considered to be legitimate skills or requirements necessary in order to fulfill the job of police officer and not designed so as to be discriminatory. (Chapter 5)

Bow Street Runners an early quasi-police force created by Henry Fielding in his Bow Street magistrate's office to investigate crimes, make arrests, and bring cases before the magistrate. (Chapter 2)

Broken windows model a policing method based on the theory that addresses social disorder and minor crimes in order to restore order to a community. (Chapter 9)

Broken windows theory the theory developed by James Q. Wilson and George L. Kelling that posits that when minor signs of disorder are not repaired (e.g., potholes, graffiti, abandoned cars, broken windows), it communicates that no one cares about the neighborhood, ultimately allowing a criminal element a location to engage in criminal behavior. (Chapters 2 and 9)

Byrnes, Thomas F. the first modern police detective who worked for the New York City Police Department, served as the Chief of the Detectives Bureau, and developed the Rogue's Gallery. (Chapter 11)

Calls-for-service a primary function of police patrols is to answer calls to the police either through the 911 emergency system or the nonemergency system. (Chapter 10)

Campus police departments bona fide police departments enforcing laws whose jurisdiction is university and college campuses in the United States. (Chapter 3)

Carroll doctrine the common name for the ability to search an automobile without a search warrant and based on the U.S. Supreme Court case of *Carroll v. U.S.* (1925). (Chapter 6)

Carroll v. U.S. (1925) the U.S. Supreme Court case that established the right of the police to search an automobile with probable cause without a search warrant. (Chapter 6)

Case-oriented investigations the criminal investigation approach that is based on the cases presented to detectives by police officers on patrol. (Chapter 11)

Case screening the process by which cases are assigned based on seriousness, solvability, etc. (Chapter 11)

Chain-of-command hierarchy of authority that runs in a police department from the police chief at the top to the police officers at the bottom. (Chapter 4)

Checks and balances limits imposed on all branches of government by giving each the right to amend acts of the other branches. (Chapter 1)

Chiefdom a collection of thousands of people separated by class and residence who typically live fixed in one or more villages and are centralized with an emphasis on heredity and use the powers of the chief to resolve conflicts. (Chapter 2)

Chimel v. California (1969) the U.S. Supreme Court case that defined the warrantless search in a search incident to arrest. (Chapter 6)

Circumstances-result hypothesis the hypothesis that cases typically resolve themselves and detectives merely handle the inevitability of the case. (Chapter 11)

Citizen patrols neighborhood residents who patrol together with or without the police and notify the police of any problems in the neighborhood. (Chapter 10)

Civil law the body of law that regulates wrongs committed by one person against another. (Chapter 6)

Civil rights those rights afforded to American citizens for the protection of their freedoms according to the U.S. Constitution. (Chapter 1)

Coercion the ability of police officers to use force, whether words or deadly force, in accordance with the laws, rules, and regulations of their police agency in the course of their duties that contributes to the development of the police culture. (Chapter 8)

Collective bargaining a process of negotiations between a group of employees, the police union, and the representatives of the police agency, the command staff, to negotiate agreements related to working conditions. (Chapter 6)

Command the upper echelons who have command authority to run the organization. (Chapter 4)

Commission oldest form of municipal governance seldom used today, consists of elected commissioners who oversee a segment of government business such as policing. (Chapter 4)

Common law law derived from custom and judicial precedent rather than statutes. (Chapter 6)

Community a group of people living in a specific location together, as well as the degree of fellowship that they share amongst each other. (Chapter 7)

Community organization a purpose of the police to bring the community together for purposes of communal security. (Chapter 1)

Community policing the philosophy, strategy, and tactics of bringing police and citizens together at the neighborhood level to work together in partnership toward the goal of reducing crime and disorder and improving the quality of life. (Chapters 2 and 9)

Compstat often called computer statistics, it is the use of data to assess problems in specific beats, neighborhoods, districts, or precincts and is then used as a management accountability tool to make sure those responsible for those jurisdictions are working to reduce the problem. (Chapter 9)

Consent searches a person waiving his or her Fourth Amendment rights and allowing the police to conduct a search. (Chapter 6)

Constables peace officers who have a very limited police authority typically in small-town and rural locations, similar to marshals. (Chapter 3)

Constitutional law the body of law that defines the relationship of different entities within a state (country) and defines the protections of the people against their government. (Chapter 6)

Contingency theory a theory that an organization is shaped based on the internal and external problems it faces by finding methods for overcoming these problems. (Chapter 4)

Controlling criminals the first goal of detectives that is aimed at focusing investigatory resources on the few criminals who cause the most crime. (Chapter 11)

COPS Bill formally the Violent Crime Control and Law Enforcement Act of 1994, it spent $8.8 billion on hiring 100,000 police officers for community policing. (Chapter 2)

Council manager city council members are elected and a city manager is appointed to handle the daily business of government. (Chapter 4)

Counterculture a group that does not share the same beliefs as the larger culture but is the larger council's antithesis. (Chapter 8)

Counterterrorism often used interchangeably with antiterrorism, the term more specifically defines those measures employed in response to a terrorist attack or threat. (Chapter 9)

Counterterrorism units the use of police strategy and tactics to counter the threat of terrorism. (Chapter 2)

County commission an elected county government board of elected members with both executive and legislative responsibilities. (Chapter 4)

County sheriffs law enforcement agencies at the county level in the United States that often have responsibilities for patrolling, serving civil papers, operating jails, and providing courtroom security. (Chapter 3)

Credit history check a check with one or more of the three major credit reporting agencies to assess if a police candidate is responsible with his or her finances and has no outstanding debts. (Chapter 5)

Crime control one of the many goals of police patrol, which, in this case, is focused on crime reduction. (Chapter 10)

Crime control model one of two models describing the criminal justice system's purpose, this one focused on enforcing the law and removing criminals from the streets in order to make America safe. (Chapter 1)

Crime control/reduction a purpose of the police to reduce or control the amount of crime present through the enforcement of the laws. (Chapter 1)

Crime prevention a purpose of the police focused on preventing crimes before they happen rather than the traditional response to crimes after they have occurred. (Chapter 1)

Crime prevention through environmental design (CPTED) the police strategy that is focused on environmental manipulation as a means of crime reduction. (Chapter 9)

Crime specific policing a crime-focused form of police targeting strategy that is aimed at determining the specific location where certain crimes occur and directing police resources to the most frequent location. (Chapter 9)

Crime type/crime specific investigations one of the ways in which criminal investigation is organized focused on type of crime such as homicide, or groupings of crime such as homicide/robbery. (Chapter 11)

Criminal investigations agencies police agencies responsible for enforcing a specific set of laws such as arson cases or state tax revenue violations. (Chapter 3)

Criminal justice system a system of justice that includes the three key components police, courts, and corrections. (Chapter 1)

Criminal law laws passed by a legislative body that define illegal behaviors and the punishment for committing those behaviors. (Chapter 6)

Criminal records check an investigation into existing criminal records to ensure a candidate for police officer has no felony or misdemeanor arrests or convictions that were not indicated on the police application. (Chapter 5)

Culture the shared values, behaviors, and beliefs of a group of people. (Chapter 8)

Danger the threats and dangers, both perceived and real, that police officers face on the street, which help shape the police culture. (Chapter 8)

Danger to others the exigent circumstance for a warrantless search when the suspect presents an immediate threat to the life of a person or may cause bodily harm. (Chapter 6)

Death the reality that police officers often deal with death on a routine basis, whether through violence, accidents, or natural causes, to include the death of fellow police officers, which contributes to the formation of a police culture. (Chapter 8)

Decentralized system of policing the American system of policing where each government is entitled to the authority to create its own law enforcement agency to enforce local ordinances and state or federal law. (Chapter 3)

Decision-making process the cognitive process when faced with a problem, issue, or choice, to develop multiple courses of action, determine the costs and benefits of each, and then select the best option for purposes of action (or potentially no action). (Chapter 7)

Delegation when authority is given to a lower member of the hierarchy of authority, but the person delegating does not lose responsibility for the task so delegated. (Chapter 4)

Demeanor a person's outward behavior or bearing. (Chapter 7)

Democracy a system of government in which power is vested in the people that also inherently means that each citizen has a rightful vote on every issue. (Chapter 1)

Demographics the various quantifiable characteristics of a population. (Chapter 6)

Department of Homeland Security the cabinet level department of the U.S. government responsible for providing security against all hazard threats, especially acts of terrorism in America. (Chapters 3 and 9)

Department of Justice the cabinet level department responsible for enforcing federal laws whose head is the only person not named a Secretary but is, rather, the U.S. Attorney General. (Chapter 3)

Depolicing when police officers disengage from proactive policing in the aftermath of such things as riots, civil suits, or other negative public or media complaints of the police. (Chapter 15)

Detection one of the three functions of the police in the criminal justice system, which is to discover criminal/illegal activity. (Chapter 1)

Detective mystique the myths of real detectives built up by the literary detectives. (Chapter 11)

Detective track a career track in which a police officer chooses to leave patrolling the street and to begin conducting investigations. (Chapter 5)

Dickens, Charles the first author to use the term "detective" to describe an individual. (Chapter 11)

Differential police response the police patrol method that uses a form of triage to determine which calls are most important to the least important when dispatching officers to the calls. (Chapter 10)

Diffusion generation the second generation of community policing lasting from 1987-1994, which consisted of the sharing of innovative community policing programs among police departments causing the strategy to spread across the country. (Chapter 9)

Directed patrol officer selected locations in their beats that are known for criminal and order maintenance problems that are then monitored by the officers. (Chapter 10)

Discovery enforcement the style of criminal investigation where detectives go into the field and create their own cases. (Chapter 11)

Discretion the freedom to decide what should be done in a particular situation. (Chapter 7)

Disorder control/reduction a purpose of the police focused on reducing or controlling those things that bring instability to a neighborhood that may or may not be illegal. (Chapter 1)

Displacement effect the concept that eliminating crime in one location will cause it to simply move to another location. (Chapter 9)

Division of labor having specialized assignments rather than having everyone in an organization be a generalist. (Chapter 4)

Doyle, Sir Arthur Conan the author of four novels and 56 short stories depicting the most famous literary detective Sherlock Holmes. (Chapter 11)

Driving records check an investigation into existing division of motor vehicle records to determine the number, if any, of moving violations or accidents the police candidate may have. (Chapter 5)

Drug testing an examination, usually by blood, urine, or both, to determine if the police candidate has recently taken illicit drugs that may discriminate them out of the position of police officer. (Chapter 5)

Due process model one of two models describing the criminal justice system's purpose, this one focused on ensuring that those who have been arrested and charged with a crime are afforded their civil rights and given an opportunity to defend themselves against the allegations. (Chapter 1)

Dupin, C. Auguste the first literary detective by author Edgar Allen Poe in the story *The Murders in the Rue Morgue*. (Chapter 11)

Economical the production, distribution, and consumption of goods and services. (Chapter 7)

Effort-result hypothesis the hypothesis that more crimes are solved when detectives put more work into the case. (Chapter 11)

Elements of the crime aspects of a crime, typically combining *actus reus* and *mens rea*. (Chapter 6)

Environmental variables factors associated with physical environment at the location in which a police officer is responding to a call-for-service. (Chapter 7)

Escape the exigent circumstance for a warrantless search when the person has effected in escape from custody. (Chapter 6)

Evanescent evidence evidence that can easily be destroyed. (Chapter 6)

Evidence-based policing the police strategy that uses data to assess how police resources would most effectively be deployed. (Chapter 9)

Exigent circumstances exceptions to the general requirement of a warrant under the Fourth Amendment. (Chapter 6)

Fear reduction a purpose of the police focused on reducing the amount of fear that citizens have regarding crime in their neighborhoods. (Chapter 1)

Federal Bureau of Investigation the largest federal law enforcement agency under the U.S. Department of Justice, which is the lead agency in federal crimes investigations and is also the lead in terrorist investigations. (Chapter 3)

Federalism a system of government that recognizes separate government entities that share powers, in the United States this includes state governments and the national government (often referred to as the federal government). (Chapter 1)

Field officer training (FTO) program a formal program, often ten weeks in duration, that moves the new police officer from ride along, to equal partners, to solo with an observer as a gradual means of releasing the officer on his or her own to work as a police officer. (Chapter 5)

Firearm one of the most important pieces of police patrol equipment that serves the purpose of protecting the officer and the community in the event of deadly force. (Chapter 10)

Follow-up investigation the stage in the criminal investigation process when detectives follow up with victims, witnesses, and re-examine physical evidence to begin building a case. (Chapter 11)

Foot patrol the standard form of police patrol before the advent of the automobile, and a renewed style of police patrol under community policing. (Chapter 10)

Formal socialization the aspect of the socialization theory that posits the formal police setting, such as the training academy and field training officer program, are the mechanisms by which individuals are socialized into policing. (Chapter 8)

Four dimensions of community policing the recognition that the community policing strategy was multidimensional consisting of the philosophical, strategic, tactical, and organizational. (Chapter 9)

Four models of sheriff's offices the four different types of sheriffs by their functions, which include full service, law enforcement, civil judiciary, and correctional-judiciary. (Chapter 3)

Frankpledge system English system of kin policing for resolving conflicts through the grouping of ten families (a tithing) with a chief (tithing-head), and overseen by the larger collection of ten tithings (the hundred) and its chief (hundred-head). (Chapter 2)

Functions of investigation one of the ways criminal investigation is organized based on the overall functions such as crime scene evidence collection, criminal investigation, and crime analysis. (Chapter 11)

Fusion centers regional and state centers that share resources in order to collectively perform the data-gathering and analysis aspects of intelligence-led policing. (Chapters 2 and 9)

Game wardens the commonly used name for most state-level natural resource and conservation police officers. (Chapter 3)

Geography physical area in which a city, town, or county is divided into manageable segments. (Chapter 4)

Goal of the detectives the list of three major goals of detectives: controlling crime, the pursuit of justice, and addressing problems. (Chapter 11)

Grace period in some states, the time period between an individual being hired to serve as a police officer who can work patrol, and prior to their having to report to the police academy for training. (Chapter 5)

Height and weight requirement typically a proportion between height and weight that is accepted as being healthy for successful application as a police officer. (Chapter 5)

Higher education programs at colleges and universities where police officers can earn degrees either in their field (e.g., policing, criminal justice) or outside of their field. (Chapter 5)

Holmes, Sherlock the creation of Sir Arthur Conan Doyle who became the most famous of the literary detectives. (Chapter 11)

Homeland Security both the strategy for protecting America against natural and man-made threats, especially terrorism, as well as the name of the cabinet-level department in the federal government's bureaucracy. (Chapter 2)

Hoover, J. Edgar the Director of the Federal Bureau of Investigation from 1924 until his death in 1972. (Chapter 2)

Hot pursuit the exigent circumstance for a warrantless search when immediately in the process of pursuing a suspect. (Chapter 6)

Hot spots policing a geographic-based form of police targeting strategy that is aimed at locating specific locations that have high crime and problems of disorder and concentrating police resources at those locations. (Chapters 9 and 10)

Hue and cry the shout for assistance that the night watch and ward were required to raise in the face of criminal activity, fires, or enemy attacks. (Chapter 2)

Humor a common strategy used by police officers to either effectively deal with the vagaries of police work or used as a means of engaging in deprecating humor that contributes to the formation of a police culture. (Chapter 8)

Incident Command System (ICS) a nationally standardized system of emergency management response. (Chapters 2 and 9)

Informal socialization the aspect of the socialization theory that posits the informal police setting, police officers hanging out with each other off-duty discussing how to handle calls with other cops, are the mechanisms by which individuals are socialized into policing. (Chapter 8)

Information management the system for dealing with large amounts of information, statements, evidence, etc., in order to effectively deal with it as a means of solving cases. (Chapter 11)

Initial investigation the first step in the investigatory process, typically conducted by the first responding officer who conducts an immediate investigation and writes a report, that then goes to the criminal investigators. (Chapter 11)

Innovation generation the first generation of community policing, which consisted of various innovative programs that were relatively isolated experiments and demonstration projects lasting from 1979 to 1986. (Chapter 9)

In-service training the annual number of training hours/days required where officers attend training sessions in lieu of working the streets, which is also conducted to keep up the police officers POST certification. (Chapter 5)

Institutionalization generation the third generation of community policing, which consisted of federal funding for community policing that helped to institutionalize community policing as a primary strategy for policing, lasting from 1995 to the 2000s. (Chapter 9)

Intelligence-led policing the use of data-gathering and analysis to create actionable intelligence for the law enforcement community. (Chapters 2 and 9)

Intentional torts civil wrongs that were intended to cause harm. (Chapter 6)

Interest group a collection of like-minded people who join together in a group to advocate for a particular position. (Chapter 6)

Inventory search a search conducted to document items present in order to protect the property and to return it to the rightful owner at a later date. (Chapter 6)

Investigation one of the three functions of the police in the criminal justice system that is conducted to gather facts and evidence that a crime has been committed. (Chapter 1)

Job benefits the ideas that the position of police officer offers a steady pay, good health insurance, and a retirement pension. (Chapter 5)

Job security that the position of a police officer offers a steady and mostly guaranteed civil service job, which a police officer does not lose because of politics whenever there is a regime change. (Chapter 5)

Joint Terrorism Task Force (JTTF) the shared resources of federal, state, and local government police resources to address the problems of terrorism in a specific city or region. (Chapter 2)

Justice the process by which the law is applied to everyone, regardless of their individual characteristics or their station in life, in order to punish crimes and criminals. (Chapter 1)

Kansas City Preventative Patrol Experiment the first study to assess the efficacy of police practices. In this case, police routine patrol was found to have no deterrent effect on crime. (Chapter 9)

Kansas City Rapid Response Study another early study in the 1970s that assessed the police practice of ensuring officers responded to calls faster, which was found to have no discernible influence on the solvability of crimes. (Chapter 9)

Kin policing the use of family relations, typically in bands, tribes, and chiefdoms, to resolve conflicts and administer justice. (Chapter 2)

Kobans the Japanese term used for police substations or mini-satellite offices that one or two police officers staff and operate out of in order to be more accessible to a specific neighborhood. (Chapter 10)

Lateral transfer when a police officer working for one agency applies and transfers to work for another agency. (Chapter 5)

Leave policing when a police officer decides, for whatever reason, that policing is not a career choice for them and they leave the profession altogether. (Chapter 5)

Legal matters connected to the law and the way in which it is practiced. (Chapter 7)

Legalistic a style of policing focused on enforcing the law. (Chapter 1)

Line those personnel who carry out the prime mission of the organization. (Chapter 4)

Local police the majority of police agencies in the United States are local police agencies at the municipal level. (Chapter 3)

Location the physical place where the police respond to calls-for-service. (Chapter 7)

Major cases the style of criminal investigation where the focus is on highly visible cases that gain the attention of the public. (Chapter 11)

Management track a career track in which a police officer seeks to move into supervisory roles. (Chapter 5)

Marshals peace officers who have a very limited police authority typically in small-town and rural locations, similar to constables. (Chapter 3)

Mayor-Council the mayor and the city council are elected separately and then interact within a strong mayor structure where the mayor runs city council meetings and votes, versus a weak system in which the mayor is a figurehead. (Chapter 4)

Medical examination an examination by a licensed physician to determine if the police candidate is medically healthy enough to perform as a police officer. (Chapter 5)

Mens rea the crime's mental elements of the criminal intent; the intent. (Chapter 6)

Metropolitan Police Act of 1829 the act that created the first modern police department in the world. (Chapter 2)

Metropolitan police departments police departments serving cities with populations over 50,000 citizens. (Chapter 3)

Midlevel Management those senior officers who carry out the command orders and supervise the line officers. (Chapter 4)

Minimum education requirement the necessary level of education necessary to become a successful applicant to a police department, which is most typically a high school diploma. (Chapter 5)

Miranda v. Arizona (1966) the U.S. Supreme Court case that established the need to inform a suspect of his or her constitutional rights prior to questioning them as a suspect in a crime. (Chapter 6)

Motorcycle patrol a method of police patrol common since the late 1800s, typically used for traffic control. (Chapter 10)

Mounted patrol perhaps the second most common method of police patrol prior to the automobile, and having seen a decline in use ever since. (Chapter 10)

National Incident Management System (NIMS) a systems approach for government agencies at all levels and nongovernment agencies to respond to a natural or man-made disaster. (Chapters 2 and 9)

National Response Framework (NRF) the most current iteration of a national process for dealing with natural and man-made disasters from preparedness and prevention to the mitigation of the impact and on through response and recovery. (Chapter 2)

Natural resource agencies police agencies, typically at the state level, that enforce laws related to protecting natural resources. (Chapter 3)

Natural resources and conservation natural resources are those things occurring in nature that can be used for the benefit of all the people, such as lakes, rivers, and forests, and conservation is the protection of these resources. (Chapter 3)

Nature the concept that our personalities and desires, such as wanting to become a police officer, are innate and hereditary. (Chapter 5)

Negligence civil wrongs that unintentionally caused a harm. (Chapter 6)

New York City Police Department the largest police department in the United States with well over 30,000 police officers. (Chapter 3)

Night watch a group of men in early England (in the 1100s and earlier) who were responsible for watching for criminal activity, fires, and enemy attacks. (Chapter 2)

No national police force the realization that despite the many federal law enforcement agencies, each of those has a very limited set of laws that it enforces, and hence there is no national police force in the United States. (Chapter 3)

No-smoking requirement a preapplication requirement that, as a condition of employment, the individual attests that he or she does not smoke and will not start. (Chapter 5)

Nurture the concept that our personalities and desires, such as wanting to become a police officer, are a result of our environment and socialization. (Chapter 5)

Oath of office an oath or affirmation that a police officer takes prior to undertaking duties as a police officer, given typically by the city/county clerk, and bestowing arrest powers upon the individual. (Chapter 6)

Offender characteristics the demographic characteristics of the suspect including sex, ethnicity, and race. (Chapter 7)

Offender-oriented investigation the criminal investigation approach that is based on detectives focusing on a small number of criminals who commit the most crime. (Chapter 11)

Officer characteristics the demographic characteristics of the police officer including, sex, ethnicity, and race. (Chapter 7)

Officer-initiated contacts a function of police patrol when officers who are not engaged in calls-for-service look for criminal activity and/or traffic violations. (Chapter 10)

Officer track a career track in which a police officer chooses to remain working on the street. (Chapter 5)

Omnibus Crime Control and Safe Streets Act of 1968 the federal bill passed that implemented many of the recommendations from the President's Crime Commission on Law Enforcement and the Administration of Justice. (Chapter 9)

Operations the primary function of the organization, which is focused on police officers performing their duties. (Chapter 4)

Order maintenance a purpose of the police focused on maintaining civil order through legal methods of intervention and suppression of behaviors that create disorder and threatens public peace. (Chapters 1 and 10)

Organizational dimension the fourth of the four dimensions of community policing focusing on how best for police departments to organize in order to carry out community policing. (Chapter 9)

Organizational structure the quasi-military rank structure combined with the hierarchy of policing. (Chapter 7)

Organizational variables factors associated with the police department itself that influence police officer decision making. (Chapter 7)

Parishes the alternate name for counties in Louisiana. (Chapter 3)

Parliamentary reward system (thief-taker) the system of paying thieves rewards to turn in other thieves. (Chapter 2)

Passive notation the style of criminal investigation where the likelihood of solvability is low, so information is recorded for future purposes. (Chapter 11)

Patronage system the specific hiring of people who supported the winning candidate, typically friends and family (see *spoils system*). (Chapter 2)

Peace Officer Standards and Training (POST) the state level organizations that set the standards for the length of police academy training as well as what subjects are taught. (Chapter 5)

Pedagogy and high stress the use of child education measures, often military style environments with high levels of pressure on the police recruits in the academy, to teach them how to think and deal with stressful situations when they become police officers. (Chapter 5)

Peel, Robert considered the father of policing for his creation of the London Metropolitan Police. (Chapter 2)

Personal/panel interview an interview by an individual or group of individuals to question the police officer candidates' ability to respond to questions and scenarios in order to determine if they are fit to serve. (Chapter 5)

Personnel employees of the organization. (Chapter 4)

Philosophical dimension the first of the four dimensions of community policing primarily focused on looking at community policing as a new philosophy or way of thinking about policing. (Chapter 9)

Physical agility and strength requirement physical tests and requirements that measure both strength and dexterity of an individual that are typically minimum standards for becoming a police officer. (Chapter 5)

Physical agility test a physical fitness test that assesses the strength, endurance, and dexterity of an individual to perform as a police officer. (Chapter 5)

Physical environment the area in which humans live; including such things as the air, water, land, buildings, roads, and so forth. (Chapter 7)

Physical evidence the physical items processed at the crime scene and taken into police custody as potential evidence to assist in solving the case. (Chapter 11)

Plain view searches the ability for police to search without a warrant for contraband that is in plain view and where they are legally authorized to be. (Chapter 6)

Poe, Edgar Allan the author of the first story to feature a detective, Dupin, in *The Murders in the Rue Morgue*. (Chapter 11)

Police a civil force of a specific government responsible for the prevention and detection of crime. (Chapter 1)

Police brutality the police use of extra-legal physical punishment to gain compliance for retribution or for other political purposes. (Chapter 2)

Police census a survey of American police departments conducted from time to time by the U.S. Department of Justice. (Chapter 3)

Police commission traditionally an elected body that oversees policies of the police department and the police commissioner or chief of police acted as the CEO. (Chapter 4)

Police-community relations an educational and awareness program for police officers to be educated on how to work with the various populations they police. (Chapters 2 and 9)

Police culture the shared values, behaviors, and beliefs of police officers in America. (Chapter 8)

Police discretion when police officers have the freedom to decide what should be done in a particular situation. (Chapter 7)

Police experience the real-world encounters that police officers have that give them the knowledge and know-how to deal with similar future calls-for-service. (Chapter 5)

Police jurisdiction the legal and geographical boundaries of police authority. (Chapter 1)

Police language words and symbols, both formal (e.g., ten codes) and informal (e.g., slang), that help to shape the police culture. (Chapter 8)

Police leadership those individuals in a police department that officers follow, ideally they are the command staff and managers. (Chapter 4)

Police management those individuals assigned into administrative positions who are responsible for the daily performance of the agency. (Chapter 4)

Police officer contacts the manner in which police officers come into contact with citizens. (Chapter 7)

Police personality the shared attitudes and behaviors of police officers regardless of what police department the officer works for. (Chapter 8)

Police POST certification the official certification by the state POST agency that authorizes an individual to be able to serve as a police officer signifying that they have been trained by state standards. (Chapter 5)

Police recruit feeder programs methods that police departments can routinely recruit from, knowing that these programs often produce good employees, such as college internships or police explorers. (Chapter 5)

Police roles the various functions and duties the police are required to do in the performance of their duties. (Chapter 1)

Police strategies police department plans of action or policy designed to achieve an overall long-term goal, most typically crime reduction. (Chapter 9)

Police tasks the specific piece of work a police officer performs in order to carry out his or her duties. (Chapter 1)

Police unions unions, typically backed by a larger union organization, that represent the interests before the police departments command staff and often having the power of collective bargaining. (Chapter 6)

Policing paradox the recognition that the police serve to protect the people's freedom, but is the same entity that can take away those freedoms. (Chapter 1)

Policy a broad statement that describes what the agency believes in and supports. (Chapters 4 and 6)

Politeuein Greek root of the term police that means a citizen engaged in politics. (Chapter 1)

Political the methods by which a people influence each other through governance. (Chapter 7)

Political activist approach one of three relationships between the police chief and government that has the government attempting to influence the police department. (Chapter 6)

Political Machine nineteenth-century political organizations that were commanded by a political boss, using money and rewards to buy votes in order to stay in power. (Chapter 2)

Polygraph examination a machine often referred to as a lie detector machine, which measures the physiological response to questions to test for deception and answering questions about the police candidate's past. (Chapter 5)

Popular culture the aspects of our culture that are popularly shared, typically via books, magazines, television, and movies, for which the American detective is a large part of our popular culture. (Chapter 11)

POSDCORB acronym describing the responsibilities of chief executives: planning, organizing, staffing, directing, coordinating, reporting, and budgeting. (Chapter 4)

Post-arrest the stage of the criminal investigation process when investigators prepare for their testimony in court if needed. (Chapter 11)

Pre-employment standards conditions that must be met prior to an individual being able to successfully apply to become a police officer. (Chapter 5)

Predictive policing the police strategy of analyzing past criminal and social disorder data to predict where future crimes and disorder are likely to occur in order to deploy police resources. (Chapter 9)

Predisposition that people have an innate or hereditary nature to become police officers. (Chapter 5)

Predispositional theory the theory that individuals enter into policing with traits and characteristics that already exist that are complementary to the police personality and police culture. (Chapter 8)

Presence of people the number of citizens at a police calls-for-service who are not involved in the situation directly. (Chapter 7)

President's Commission on Law Enforcement and the Administration of Justice President Johnson's Commission to assess the issues facing the criminal justice system, in particular the police, and to make recommendations for reform. (Chapter 9)

Preventive patrol the concept that police officers conducting routine motor vehicle patrol will prevent crime from occurring. (Chapters 2 and 10)

Probationary period a set time period between hiring and when the probation period ends in which an individual does not have a property interest in his or her job and can be terminated with no explanation. (Chapter 5)

Problem-oriented policing created by Herman Goldstein in the 1970s, it applies problem-solving methods to police situations in order to more effectively deal with repetitive problems of crime and disorder. (Chapters 2 and 9)

Procedure a step-by-step statement of tasks officers should perform in specific situations. (Chapters 4 and 6)

Professional autonomy approach one of three relationships between the police chief and government that lets the police chief run the department. (Chapter 6)

Professional model of policing based on other professions such as doctors, lawyers, and dentists where a novice attends a school to be licensed, must pass an examination, and is bound by the ethics of the organization. (Chapter 2)

Protective vest a standard piece of patrol equipment since the 1970s aimed at reducing fatalities from firearms being used against the police. (Chapter 10)

Psychological examination an examination by a licensed psychologist or psychiatrist to determine if the police candidate is mentally healthy enough to perform as a police officer. (Chapter 5)

Public-building facilities agencies police agencies that enforce laws related to public property such as colleges, universities, schools, and hospitals. (Chapter 3)

Public opinion the collective attitudes of citizens. (Chapter 6)

Public Relations an early twentieth-century movement for police departments to communicate to the public as to their strategies, methods, and daily operations. (Chapter 9)

Public school districts bona fide police departments enforcing laws and whose jurisdiction are public schools in the United States. (Chapter 3)

Pulling levers strategy the police strategy that is focused on a multiple response method to address crime and disorder problems. (Chapter 9)

Pursuit of justice the second goal of detectives which is aimed at enforcing the law and holding offenders accountable. (Chapter 11)

Quality of life a purpose of the police that is focused on serving the community so that the benefits of living in the neighborhood policed improve. (Chapter 1)

Radio one of the most important pieces of police patrol equipment that allows the police to communicate with central headquarters as well as with each other. (Chapter 10)

RAND Criminal Investigation Study the RAND corporation study into the use of criminal investigators and technology to enhance crime solvability, which found that detectives had no discernible influence on the solvability of crimes. (Chapters 9 and 11)

Rapid response the concept that the faster police officers respond to a call-for-service, the more likely they will solve the crime. (Chapter 2)

Records check an investigation into various existing documents to ensure the candidate is acceptable to serve as a police officer. (Chapter 5)

Recruitment methods how police departments make citizens aware and want to apply for the position of police officer. (Chapter 5)

Regulation a statement, usually a prohibition, which has the backing a law or judicial case law. (Chapters 4 and 6)

Regulatory inspections the style of criminal investigations that inspects certain locations for evidence of criminal activity. (Chapter 11)

Reinforcing patrol the style of criminal investigation that receives cases from patrol officers. (Chapter 11)

Relationships the way in which two or more people are connected. (Chapter 7)

Republic a system of government where power is vested in the people by allowing them to vote for those who will represent their interests in government. (Chapter 1)

Reserve, auxiliary, or special police officers various names for part-time police officers who either work part-time hours throughout the year or full-time for specific seasons. (Chapter 3)

Residency requirement the requirement that a person applying to or once becoming a police officer must live in the jurisdiction in which they work. (Chapter 5)

Resource-dependency theory a theory that an organization is shaped solely based upon the available resources to carry out functions that are desired. (Chapter 4)

Response the third step in the SARA Model which focuses on developing multiple responses to the problem and implementing the most viable option. (Chapter 9)

Retention the ability of a police department to keep police officers for an entire career to retirement. (Chapter 5)

Retirement when a police officer has served the requisite number of years and decides to retire from the police department at which point they begin drawing their retirement pension. (Chapter 5)

Role ambiguity when the role a person plays is not well defined and expectations, behaviors, and consequences are uncertain. (Chapter 1)

Role conflict when two or more roles that a person plays come into opposition with one another. (Chapter 1)

Role expectation the role that people believe a person should be performing, which may or may not resemble the role the person actually plays in society. (Chapter 1)

Roll-call training short training sessions delivered to all officers prior to going on duty. (Chapter 5)

Rowan, Charles and Richard Mayne the two men placed in charge of the London Metropolitan Police by Robert Peel in 1829. (Chapter 2)

Royal forester/games-keeper the early English game warden responsible for protecting the king's personal forest or preserve against poachers. (Chapter 2)

Rule a statement, usually of prohibition, established by the department's leadership. (Chapters 4 and 6)

SARA Model the practical implementation model of problem-oriented policing, which stands for scanning, analysis, response, and assessment. (Chapter 9)

Saturation patrol the use of multiple officers in a small geographic area to create a deterrent police presence in order to address a crime or order maintenance problem for certain prolonged periods of time. (Chapter 10)

Scanning the first step in the SARA Model, which focuses on police officers looking for problems in their beat and making connections between actors, times, location, and situations. (Chapter 9)

Screening process the methods by which a police departments tests individuals to ensure that they will be successful police officers. (Chapter 5)

Search incident to arrest the ability of the police to search a person and their immediate surroundings after effecting an arrest without a search warrant. (Chapter 6)

Section 1983 lawsuits the U.S. code section that prohibits a person, acting under the color of law, from violating a person's constitutional rights. (Chapter 6)

Separation of powers the system of dividing the powers and duties of a government into different branches. (Chapter 1)

Seriousness of investigations the consideration for how serious the case is as to the level of time spent investigating. (Chapter 11)

Seriousness of the offense a sliding scale that ranges from felonies, to misdemeanors, to minor infractions of the law. (Chapter 7)

Service a style of policing focused on providing services to the citizens of a community. (Chapters 1 and 10)

Service delivery a purpose of the police that is focused on providing various services to the citizens of a community. (Chapter 1)

Sheepdog the analogy that certain people, such as the police, feel responsible for watching over the citizens of a society (sheep) in order to protect them against the criminals of a society (wolves). (Chapter 1)

Sheriff the early Englishman who served the king's interest at the lowest levels by maintaining order and collecting taxes. (Chapter 2)

Sheriff's Office the formal title of the office run by an elected sheriff who is the highest law enforcement official in a county. (Chapter 3)

Shire-reeve the early English term for the Americanized sheriff. (Chapter 2)

Situational factors elements outside of the officer that are particular to the calls-for-service the officer is responding to. (Chapter 7)

Small-town and rural municipalities and counties with populations under 50,000 citizens. (Chapter 3)

Small-town and rural police departments police agencies serving municipalities and counties with populations under 50,000 citizens. (Chapter 3)

Social having to do with the nature of humans and how they develop and relate to one another in groups. (Chapter 7)

Socialization that people learn from their environment and as a result of this nurturing desire to become police officers. (Chapter 5)

Socialization theory the theory that the police culture is derived from a socializing process where current police officers instruct new officers how to act and behave. (Chapter 8)

Solidarity the concept that police officers stick together and give each other unconditional loyalty, which helps to shape the police culture. (Chapter 8)

Solvability of investigations the consideration for whether or not a case is likely to be solved in the future. (Chapter 11)

Span of control the number of employees any one supervisor can effectively handle, which is generally between five and seven employees. (Chapter 4)

Special enforcement agencies police agencies responsible for enforcing a very specific set of laws such as gaming laws or race-track laws. (Chapter 3)

Special investigation units specific units formed to deal with special problems such as terrorism cases, high profile murders, or perhaps serial/ mass murders. (Chapter 11)

Special jurisdiction agencies police agencies that have a very defined set of laws that it enforces. (Chapter 3)

Split patrols the police patrol method that divides the patrol shift in half, with one half answering calls-for-service and the other half engaging in administrative duties and officer-initiated contacts. (Chapter 10)

Spoils system based on the notion that "to the victors go the spoils," those winning elective office could hire friends and relatives and lavish money on the winning party members (see *patronage system*). (Chapter 2)

Staff those personnel who supervise the line personnel. (Chapter 4)

Standard operating procedures (SOP) a manual that collects the policies, procedures, rules, and regulations overseeing the behavior of its police officers. (Chapter 6)

Standard reactive the style of criminal investigation that reacts to the type of crimes and where they are located and then investigates as needed. (Chapter 11)

State a group number over 50,000 people separated by class and residence who reside in multiple villages, towns, and cities who are centrally organized and use the police, laws, and judges to resolve conflict. (Chapter 2)

State police law enforcement agencies at the state level in the United States for which there are 49. (Chapter 3)

Statute laws that are passed by a legislative body. (Chapter 6)

Stop and frisk the use of Terry stops via the Supreme Court case *Terry v. Ohio* (1968) that allows officers to temporarily stop and detain citizens who they believe may be engaging or are about to engage in some type of criminal behavior and allows them to pat them down for weapons for their safety and the safety of the community. (Chapter 9)

Strategic dimension the second of the four dimensions of community policing focused on translating the philosophy into action. (Chapter 9)

Strategy a plan of action or policy designed to achieve an overall long-term goal. (Chapter 9)

Styles of criminal investigation the six styles of criminal investigation, which include reinforcing patrol, standard reactive, major cases, regulatory inspections, passive notation, and discovery enforcement. (Chapter 11)

Styles of policing the three styles of policing that are a reflection of what a community wants out of their police. (Chapter 1)

Subculture a group that lives within the larger culture and abides by their norms but has its own set of shared values, behaviors, and beliefs. (Chapter 8)

Supervision the act of overseeing the work of someone else. (Chapter 7)

Support those personnel who provide assistance to the line and staff personnel so that they can carry out their prime duties. (Chapter 4)

Sworn police officers those police officers who have taken an oath of office and are granted authority to make arrests and use coercion in the performance of their duties. (Chapters 1 and 6)

Systems theory a theory that an organization is a living entity that adapts to its environment from both internal and external stimuli. (Chapter 4)

Tactical dimension the third of the four dimensions of community policing is focused on the specific programs that come to encapsulate the community policing philosophy and strategy. (Chapter 9)

Tactical patrols a separate unit of police patrol officers dedicated to addressing specific crime problems, often through plainclothes and surveillance assignments. (Chapter 10)

Targeted groups specific groups from which police departments wish to recruit so their advertising is directed toward that population for example, women, minorities, and military veterans. (Chapter 5)

Team approach one of three relationships between the police chief and government that takes a shared powers approach to managing police matters. (Chapter 6)

Team policing an early 1970s attempt at assigning a team of police officers to a neighborhood in order to develop police-community relations. (Chapters 2 and 9)

Terry v. Ohio (1968) U.S. Supreme Court case that gave the police the authority to temporarily detain someone to conduct an investigation and to conduct a pat-down for weapons. (Chapter 6)

Terry stop the police use of the Supreme Court case *Terry v. Ohio* (1968). (Chapter 6)

Texas Rangers one of the oldest state level organizations that began before Texas became its own country providing security for settlers, then becoming a state militia, and eventually a bona fide law enforcement agency. (Chapter 3)

Thin blue line an analogy that all that stands between peace and anarchy is the police officers of our society. (Chapter 1)

Third degree the use of police brutality in order to gain a confession (origin of the term is unknown). (Chapter 2)

Three generations the community policing era's three generations, innovation (1979-1986), diffusion (1987-1993), and institutionalization of community policing (1994-2001), which recognize that the implementation of community policing was not static over time, but moved through three different generations. (Chapters 2 and 9)

Three main functions of state police include law enforcement duties, such as responding to calls-for-service, investigations, typically of state-level fraud or crimes, and highway patrol. (Chapter 3)

Time the separation of policing into shifts of time that are either fixed or rotate. (Chapter 4)

Transportation systems/facilities agencies police agencies responsible for enforcing the laws and whose jurisdiction covers transportation systems such as airports, ports, and railways. (Chapter 3)

Tribal police departments police departments run by Native American tribes that exist as sovereign nations. (Chapter 3)

Tribe a group of hundreds of people who are kin-based, typically living fixed in a village, and are egalitarian with a tribal head, and use informal means of resolving conflicts. (Chapter 2)

United States Constitution the document that establishes the system of government for the American government. (Chapter 1)

Unity of command states that no employee should ever report to more than one supervisor. (Chapter 4)

U.S. Customs and Border Protection the largest federal law enforcement agency under the Department of Homeland Security responsible for securing the borders against illegal immigrants and terrorists entering the United States. (Chapter 3)

Victim or complainant characteristics the demographic characteristics of the victim or person calling the police including sex, ethnicity, and race. (Chapter 7)

Vidocq, Eugène-Francois often considered to be the first detective, although he was a French criminal turned detective. (Chapter 11)

Vision requirement the minimum uncorrected and/or corrected vision necessary for a successful application to be a police officer. (Chapter 5)

Voice stress analyzer a device that measures the psychophysiological stress response to questions by assessing changes in the voice when answering questions regarding the police candidate's past. (Chapter 5)

Vollmer, August considered the father of American policing, he was the police chief in Berkeley, California (1905-1932), and the first police professor at the University of Chicago (1929-1931). (Chapter 2)

Ward the day version of the night watch in early England. (Chapter 2)

Warrantless search police searches where no search warrant is required; however, the standard of needing probable cause to search remains. (Chapter 6)

Watchman a style of policing focused on limited intervention and only when necessary will a limited response be made to restore order. (Chapter 1)

Weed and seed a federal program based on the broken windows theory, which advocates cleaning up a neighborhood both physically and criminally (weed), so residents feel safe to come out of their homes and reassert their communal interest in protecting the community (seed). (Chapters 2 and 10)

Wickersham Commission officially known as the National Commission on Law Observance and Enforcement, headed by former Attorney General

George Wickersham, it was created by President Herbert Hoover to study the problems of crime and criminal justice in America. (Chapter 2)

Wild, Jonathan one of the earliest English thief takers who was paid to turn in other thieves. (Chapter 11)

Wilson, O.W. a disciple of August Vollmer, having served under him as a police officer, he was the police chief in Wichita, Kansas, and later the Police Commissioner of the Chicago Police Department, and in between was the chair of the Criminology program the University of California, Berkeley. He authored *Police Administration*, the definitive police administration book for most of the twentieth century. (Chapter 2)

Wolf-pack stops a term used to denote multiple officers arriving on a scene and their influence on each other to take action. (Chapter 7)

Work climate social and physical environment of a work place. (Chapter 7)

Written aptitude test a general knowledge or sometimes police-specific test that assesses the individuals' intellectual capabilities to perform as a police officer. (Chapter 5)

Zero-tolerance policing a form of policing that takes a total enforcement strategy for crimes or forms of social disorder that are believed to contribute to the overall crime and social disorder of a specific location. (Chapter 9)

Chapter 1

Chapter opener, Dallas Police Department automobile.
Source: Pixabay.com, photo by skeeze.
p. 2, The Thin Blue Line.
Source: Wikimedia Commons, photo by WClarke.
p. 3, Sheepdog watching over the sheep.
Source: Shutterstock.com, photo by Volodymyr Burdiak.
p. 6, New recruits for the BART police in San Francisco.
Source: Bay Area Rapid Transit Police Department.
p. 8, Los Angeles Police Officers.
Source: Shutterstock.com, photo by shalunts.
p. 13, Three Branches of Government.
Source: Wikimedia Commons, graphic by 111Alleskönner.
p. 14, The Three Branches of Government.
Source: Shutterstock.com, photos by J. Main, Andrea Izzotti, & Steve Heap.

Chapter 2

Chapter opener, August Vollmer.
Source: Michael Holland of the Berkeley Police Department Historical Preservation Society.
p. 29, Guns, Germs, and Steel.
Source: Shutterstock.com, photos by Burlingham, 3Dalia, & Dabarti CGI.
p. 31, Charlie Rouse.
Source: Library of Congress.
p. 34, Henry Fielding.
Source: Library of Congress.
p. 38, Robert Peel.
Source: University of Texas Portrait Gallery.
p. 35, London Metropolitan Police Officer, or "Peeler."
Source: Library of Congress.
p. 41, Theodore Roosevelt.
Source: Library of Congress.
p. 44, J. Edgar Hoover.
Source: Federal Bureau of Investigation.
p 47, Border Patrol.
Source: Pixabay.com, photo by Hetsumani.

Chapter 3

Chapter opener, Navajo Police Chevy Tahoe.
Source: Wikimedia Commons, photo by Syellowhorse.
p. 57, Police officer's patch collection.
Source: Shutterstock.com, photo by loan nicolae.
p. 59, Members of the New York City Police Department at Times Square.
Source: Shutterstock.com, photo by pio3.
p. 61, Winnetka, Illinois, police officer directing traffic.
Source: Shutterstock.com, photo by Francis L. Fruit.
p. 65, Washington, D.C. Metro Transit K-9 police officer.
Source: Washington, D.C. Metropolitan Area Transit Authority, photo by Larry Levine.
p. 70, Three deputies.
Source: Wikimedia Commons, photo by Ventura County Sheriff's Office.
p. 72, Statue honoring the Texas Rangers.
Source: Shutterstock.com, photo by Ricardo Garza.
p. 78, Federal Bureau of Investigation.
Source: Federal Bureau of Investigation.

Chapter 4

Chapter opener, One Police Plaza.
Source: Shutterstock.com, photo by Northfoto.
p. 93, Local police department.
Source: Shutterstock.com, photo by dustin77a.
p. 94, Public meeting.
Source: Shutterstock.com, photo by Nagel Photography.
p. 96, Ronald Tsukamoto Public Safety Building.
Source: Berkeley Police Department.
p. 99, Organization chart of Berkeley Police Department.
Source: Berkeley Police Department.
p. 103, Line officers.
Source: Shutterstock.com, photo by Joseph Sohm.
p. 103, Staff officers.
Source: Shutterstock.com, photo by a katz.
p. 103, Support staff.
Source: Shutterstock.com, photo by auremar.
p. 107, Police beat.
Source: Shutterstock.com, photo by Joe Belanger.
p. 109, Police nightshift.
Source: Shutterstock.com, photo by Mike Focus.
p. 111, New York City Police Commissioner William Bratton.
Source: Shutterstock.com, photo by a katz.

Chapter 5

Chapter opener, San Jose Police Department Officers.
Source: San Jose Police Department.
p. 123, New York Police Department recruiting van.
Source: Shuttertock.com, photo by Leonard Zhukovsky.
p. 126, Height and weight measurement chart.
Source: Shutterstock.com, photo by Zerbor.

p. 127, Physical agility test.
Source: Shutterstock.com, photo by Gabi Moisa.
p. 135, Panel interview.
Source: Shutterstock.com, photo by AVAVA.
p. 138, Range where the police officer qualifies to carry a weapon.
Source: Shutterstock.com, photo by bikerriderlondon.
p. 140, Early in-service training class with August Vollmer.
Source: Michael Holland of the Berkeley Police Department Historical Preservation Society.
p. 147, Police officer retirement badge and service weapon.
Source: Willard M. Oliver.

Chapter 6

Chapter opener, Graduation Ceremony.
Source: New York Police Department.
p. 157, NYPD police officers taking the oath of office.
Source: Shutterstock.com, photo by a katz.
p. 158, NYPD patrol vehicle covered in ash from fallout of World Trade Center on 9/11.
Source: Shutterstock.com, photo by Anthony Correia.
p. 160, Police policy manuals.
Source: Shutterstock.com, photo by dockstockmedia.
p. 161, Police at community meeting.
Source: Mission Local, photo by Lola M. Chavez.
p. 168, Mayor and police chief of Stamford, Connecticut.
Source: Shutterstock.com, photo by Barbs image.
p. 172, Representations of the law.
Source: Shutterstock.com, photo by Sebastian Duda.
p. 175, San Francisco police officers conducting a Terry stop.
Source: Shutterstock.com, photo by Chameleon's eye.
p. 178, Car Search.
Source: Wikimedia Commons, photo by Josh Denmark/US Customs and Border Protection.

Chapter 7

Chapter opener, Police Officer in Traffic Stop.
Source: Wikimedia Commons, photo by Jeff Dean.
p. 189, Robert H. Jackson.
Source: Library of Congress.
p. 190, Chicago Police van.
Source: Wikimedia Commons, photo by nathanmac87.
p. 193, The decision-making process.
Source: Shutterstock.com, photo by Shawn Hempel.
p. 197, Physical environment with graffiti.
Source: Shutterstock.com, photo by stockelements.
p. 200, Woman complaining about her ex-husband violating a court order.
Source: Shutterstock.com, photo by a katz.
p. 202, Suspect under arrest by the San Francisco police.
Source: Shutterstock.com, photo by Michael Warwick.

Chapter 8

Chapter opener, Berkeley Police Motorcycle Officers, reflecting the police culture's sense of humor, surfing on their motorcycles.
Source: Photo courtesy of the Berkeley Police Department, photo by Officer Jennifer Coats.
p. 214, The blue wall of silence.
Source: Shutterstock.com, photo by Bokic Bojan.
p. 215, Members of the New York State Police marching in parade.
Source: Shutterstock.com, photo by Stuart Monk.
p. 222, Chicago police department vehicle.
Source: Shutterstock.com, photo by Keith Levit.
p. 224, Roseburg, Oregon, police officers at a disturbance at a hotel.
Source: Shutterstock.com, photo by Keith Levit.
p. 226, Police solidarity.
Source: Shutterstock.com, photo by Leonard Zhukovsky.
p. 229, Death scene.
Source: Shutterstock.com, photo by LukaTBD.

Chapter 9

Chapter opener, Hot Spots.
Source: Alamy, photo by Mikael Karlsson.
p. 240, Kansas City, Missouri.
Source: Shutterstock.com, photo by Marco Scisetti.
p. 243, Broken windows.
Source: Shutterstock.com, photo by Roy Pedersen.
p. 249, Police officer with children.
Source: Shutterstock.com, photo by a katz.
p. 255, Crime hot spot.
Source: Shutterstock.com, photo by Duard van der Westhuizen.
p. 259, Police officers analyzing data.
Source: Shutterstock.com, photo by Scott Prokop.
p. 264, A member of the FBI counter-terrorism division.
Source: Federal Bureau of Investigation.

Chapter 10

Chapter opener, Portland Police quad cycle.
Source: Wikimedia Commons, photo by pdxjeff.
p. 274, Police patrol in San Francisco.
Source: Shutterstock.com, photo by Eric Broder Van Dyke.
p. 275, Police officer equipment.
Source: Wikimedia Commons, photo by US Army.
p. 276, Foot patrol in San Francisco.
Source: Shutterstock.com, photo by Chameleon's eye.
p. 277, Mounted patrol in New York City (1905).
Source: Library of Congress.
p. 280, Chicago police officer on a Segway.
Source: Wikimedia Commons, photo by Brett Gustafson.
p. 282, Emergency 911 on a police car.
Source: Shutterstock.com, photo by Erasmus Wolff.

p. 289, Large police presence.
Source: Shutterstock.com, photo by Scott Cornell.
p. 290, Police substation in Times Square.
Source: Shutterstock.com, photo by Sean Pavone.

Chapter 11

Chapter opener, Detectives survey a crime scene.
Source: Oklahoma City Police Department.
p. 298, Edgar Allan Poe.
Source: Library of Congress.
p. 300, New York Police Department's Rogue's Gallery.
Source: Library of Congress.
p. 302, New York City police officer collecting evidence at a crime scene.
Source: Shutterstock.com, photo by a katz.
p. 306, New York City police detective assisting at an investigation.
Source: Shutterstock.com, photo by a katz.
p. 308, Police line.
Source: Shutterstock.com, photo by carl ballou.
p. 313, New York City detective's badge.
Source: Shutterstock.com, photo by Stephen Mulcahey.
p. 313, Police detective on the witness stand.
Source: Alamy, photo by ZUMA Press, Inc.

Chapter 12

Chapter opener, Bust of Sergeant Jimmie Rutledge, one of two Berkeley Police Officers killed in the line of duty. Summoned to a disturbance call, Rutledge confronted the suspect and was shot and killed. End of Watch: June 6, 1973.
Source: Berkeley Police Department, photo by Community Service Officer Patricia Subia.
p. 323, Police officer working in traffic.
Source: Shutterstock.com, photo by Anne Kitzman.
p. 324, NYPD police officers using force during an Occupy Wall Street protest.
Source: Shutterstock.com, photo by Daryl Lang.
p. 329, Police Taser.
Source: Shutterstock.com, photo by Khiros.
p. 333, Police officer preparing to use deadly force.
Source: Shutterstock.com, photo by guruXOX.
p. 340, NYPD police officers confronting protestors.
Source: Shutterstock.com, photo by a katz.
P 342, Funeral of New York Police Officer Wenjian Liu.
Source: Shutterstock.com, photo by lev radin.

Chapter 13

Chapter opener, East Haven Police Department receives accreditation.
Source: New Hampshire Register, photo by Marc Zaretsky.
p. 352, Police Commissioner Theodore Roosevelt.
Source: Library of Congress.
p. 354, Protestors in Selma, Alabama, during the Civil Rights Movement.
Source: Library of Congress.

p. 356, Dashboard camera.
Source: Shutterstock.com, photo by Supirak Jaisan.
p. 357, Alcohol and driving.
Source: Shutterstock.com, photo by Chimpinski.
p. 360, Rotten apple.
Source: Shutterstock.com, photo by Ariene Studio.
p. 361, A protest against police brutality.
Source: Shutterstock.com, photo by a katz.
p. 365, Policies and procedures.
Source: Shutterstock.com, photo by dockstockmedia.
p. 369, Police officer at a media interview.
Source: Shutterstock.com, photo by Dan Holm.

Chapter 14

Chapter opener, Officer at The Circle City Classic Parade, Indianapolis.
Source: Alamy, photo by roberto galan.
p. 382, "Fight-or-flight" response.
Source: Shutterstock.om, photo by Sangoiri.
p. 385, Police officer stopping a driver.
Source: Shutterstock.com, photo by bikeriderlondon.
p. 392, Officer at funeral.
Source: Adobe Stock Images, photo by Carlo Allegri/Reuters.
p. 395, Effects of stress.
Source: Shutterstock.com, photo by Jomar Aplaon.
p. 397, PTSD defined.
Source: Shutterstock.com, photo by Phoelix.
p. 399, Managing stress.
Source: Shutterstock.com, photo by Dizain.

Chapter 15

Chapter opener, Metropolitan Police Officers.
Source: Metropolitan Police Department (Washington, DC), photo by Lateef Magnum.
p. 408, PEST defined.
Source: Shutterstock.com, photo by Dizain.
p. 409, NYPD Community Affairs unit officer greeting the community.
Source: Shutterstock.com, photo by lev radin.
p. 415, Militarized equipment.
Source: Shutterstock.com, photo by Jose Gil.
p. 420, Protests in Ferguson, Missouri.
Source: Shutterstock.com, photo by Rena Schild.
p. 425, Police body camera.
Source: AP Images, photo by Bebeto Matthews.